SAMS Teach Yourself

Office® Productivity

All in One

Greg Perry
Rogers Cadenhead
Alexandria Haddad
Heidi Steele
Herb Tyson
Trudi Reisner

SAMS *201 West 103rd St., Indianapolis, Indiana, 46290 USA*

Sams Teach Yourself Office Productivity All in One

Copyright © 2003 by Sams Publishing

International Standard Book Number: 0-672-32534-9

Library of Congress Catalog Card Number: 2003102939

Printed in the United States of America

First Printing: May 2003

06   05   04   03   4   3   2   1

Trademarks

Warning and Disclaimer

Sams Publishing offers excellent discounts on this book when ordered in quantity for bulk purchases or special sales. For more information, please contact

U.S. Corporate and Government Sales
    1-800-382-3419   corpsales@pearsontechgroup.com
For sales outside of the U.S., please contact International Sales
    1-317-581-3793   international@pearsontechgroup.com

ACQUISITIONS EDITOR
Betsy Brown

DEVELOPMENT EDITOR
Damon Jordan

MANAGING EDITOR
Charlotte Clapp

PROJECT EDITOR
George E. Nedeff

INDEXER
Rebecca Salerno

TEAM COORDINATOR
Vanessa Evans

DESIGNER
Gary Adair

Contents at a Glance

Contents

Lead Author

Greg Perry is a speaker and a writer on both the programming and the application sides of computing. He is known for skillfully presenting advanced computer topics to the novice level. Perry has been a programmer and a trainer since the early 1980s, teaching at computer conferences and colleges. He received his first degree in computer science and a master's degree in corporate finance. Perry has sold more than two million computer books, including such titles as *Sams Teach Yourself Windows XP in 24 Hours*, *Sams Teach Yourself Visual Basic 6 in 21 Days*, and *Sams Teach Yourself Microsoft Office XP in 24 Hours*. He also writes about rental property management and loves to travel. His favorite place when away from home is either New York's Patsy's or Italy, because he enjoys only the best pasta!

Contributing Authors

Rogers Cadenhead is the author of several books on the Internet, Java, and Web publishing, including *Sams Teach Yourself Microsoft FrontPage 2000 in 24 Hours*. He also writes a trivia column for the Fort Worth Star-Telegram and Knight-Ridder News Service.

Alexandria Haddad (`alex@cobia.net`) has been using computer software applications to improve business communications and operations for almost 15 years. She currently co-manages Cobia Communications, a full-service computer consulting firm that operates in a virtual office environment. Her role also includes creating Web sites and writing technical books and manuals for various software products. In addition, Alexandria is a part-time instructor at local colleges. Her specialties include presentation software, desktop publishing, word processing, and spreadsheet design. Alexandria is the author of *Sams Teach Yourself Microsoft PowerPoint 2000 in 24 Hours*.

Heidi Steele is an experienced Microsoft Word consultant, trainer and author. She has taught beginner and expert users for numerous companies and organizations and trained hundreds of people to effectively use the software—from teachers and administrators to corporate executive assistants to online editors for publishing companies. Her clients have included the University of California at San Francisco and several Bay area classroom training facilities. She is the author of *Sams Teach Yourself Microsoft Word 2000 in 24 Hours*.

Herb Tyson is a consultant and writer based in the greater Washington D.C. area. Known for his clear, conversational writing style, he has written several books on Microsoft Word and OS/2, and he's a Microsoft MVP (Most Valuable Professional), awarded for technical contributions in supporting Microsoft applications. Herb is the author of *Sams Teach Yourself Microsoft Outlook 2000 in 24 Hours*.

Trudi Reisner is a computer technical writer specializing in software technical writing and courseware development. As both a Microsoft Office Proficient Specialist and a Microsoft Office Expert Specialist in Microsoft Excel, Trudi is the author of numerous books including *Sams Teach Yourself Microsoft Excel 2000 in 24 Hours*.

Dedication

My lovely and gracious bride stands by my side night and day. Thank you once again. You, precious Jayne, are everything that matters to me on earth. The best parents in the world, Glen and Bettye Perry, continue to encourage and support me in every way. I am who I am because of both of them.

—Greg Perry

Acknowledgments

I want to send special thanks to Betsy Brown and Damon Jordan for putting up with me on this project. They were the driving force behind the work. They kept me on schedule, and what a schedule it was! Fortunately, with Sams Publishing, the people behind the books keep things flowing smoothly even when the authors don't.

This book is a compendium of information from so many sources. I had the able help of numerous other authors who helped with the fundamental material within this book. My fiercely sincere gratitude goes to the following masters of writing: Rogers Cadenhead, Alexandria Haddad, Trudi Reisner, Heidi Steele, and Herb Tyson.

In addition, the other staff and editors on this project, namely Damon Jordan, George Nedeff, and Charlotte Clapp, made this book better than it otherwise could be.

We Want to Hear from You!

As the reader of this book, *you* are our most important critic and commentator. We value your opinion and want to know what we're doing right, what we could do better, what areas you'd like to see us publish in, and any other words of wisdom you're willing to pass our way.

You can email or write me directly to let me know what you did or didn't like about this book—as well as what we can do to make our books stronger.

Please note that I cannot help you with technical problems related to the topic of this book, and that due to the high volume of mail I receive, I might not be able to reply to every message.

When you write, please be sure to include this book's title and author as well as your name and phone or email address. I will carefully review your comments and share them with the author and editors who worked on the book.

Email: consumer@samspublishing.com

Mail: Mark Taber
Associate Publisher
Sams Publishing
201 West 103rd Street
Indianapolis, IN 46290 USA

Reader Services

For more information about this book or others from Sams Publishing, visit our Web site at www.samspublishing.com. Type the ISBN (excluding hyphens) or the title of the book in the Search box to find the book you're looking for.

Introduction

Microsoft Office is not one program, but one gigantic *suite* of programs. For many folks, their entire computer-based work finds its roots in Microsoft Office. Have you ever wished you had just one book, a truly complete reference that tells you what you need to know about Microsoft Office? Have you wanted one that's written in plain talk, one that tells you what you need to know to get started, and one that takes you to the next level without being too techie? Have you wanted a book that could talk to your level without talking down to you?

You are holding such a book. *Sams Teach Yourself Office Productivity All in One* is one massive title out of the team of tomes in the *All in One* series.

The goal of this book is to provide you with all the information you need, and no more, to understand these topics:

- Word letters and documents
- Excel worksheets
- PowerPoint presentations
- Outlook email
- FrontPage Web sites

The expert teachers, trainers, and technical writers who put this book together all understand precisely what computer problems you face, and they know how to provide the solutions. For example, if you've just started using a computer and have no idea how to start a program, let alone make sense out of the huge Microsoft Office suite of programs, the answer is here. If you want to create an organized and integrated personal information system that tracks your appointments, email, documents, and even presentations you might make at work, this book provides all that and more.

This text takes you from the beginning to a mastery of Office. If you're already an Office user, you will also gain more insights here than anywhere else because when a topic requires depth, you get it, and only then.

Who Should Read This Book?

This book is for everyday computer users who want a single book that helps make them better Office users. In addition, this text takes most users to a higher level of mastery.

Don't buy five or more books when this one takes you to where you want to go.

What This Book Does for You

Although this book is not a complicated reference book, you learn something about almost every aspect of Microsoft Office from a typical user's point of view. As you progress through the book, your skills will increase.

Those of you who are tired of the plethora of quick-fix computer titles cluttering today's shelves will find a welcome reprieve here. This book presents both the background and descriptions that a Microsoft Office user needs. In addition to the background, this book is practical, and provides hundreds of step-by-step walkthroughs that you can work through to gain practical hands-on experience. These tasks guide you through all the common actions you need to make your computer work for you.

Conventions Used in This Book

This book uses several common conventions to help teach its topics most effectively. Here is a summary of those typographical conventions:

- Commands, computer output, and words you type appear in a special monospaced computer font.
- To type a shortcut key, such as Alt+F, press and hold the first key, and then press the second key before releasing both keys.
- If a task requires you to select from a menu, the book separates menu commands with a comma. For example, File, Save As is used to select the Save As option from the File menu.

In addition to typographical conventions, the following special elements are included to set off different types of information to make them easily recognizable:

Special notes augment the material you read in each chapter. These notes clarify concepts and procedures.

You find numerous tips that offer shortcuts and solutions to common problems.

 The cautions are about pitfalls. Reading them saves you time and trouble.

Sidebars

Take some time out of your training to sit back and enjoy a more in-depth look at a particular feature. The sidebars are useful for exploring unusual features and show you additional ways to utilize the chapter material.

PART I
Looking at Office from a Bird's-eye View

Chapter

CHAPTER 1

Office: Seeing the Big Picture

Microsoft Office offers tools you typically need to manage a busy day, both at work and at home. Whether you work in an office environment where you must share corporate-wide information with others or if you spend time at home writing letters and managing household tasks, the Office suite of products provides exactly the right amount of power you need to get your job done.

In this introductory chapter, you'll see what Microsoft Office can do. If you are familiar with one or more of the Office programs but have not looked at others, this chapter's overview is general enough to tell you what you're missing. Then, you can decide if you need to add to your computer toolkit by learning another Office program. If you decide you want to, you'll find all the necessary help right here throughout the rest of these chapters.

Welcome to the Microsoft Office Suite of Products

Microsoft has released many versions of Office over the past several years. Today, the majority of users use Office 2000. Those who have upgraded to later releases such as Office XP find that the upgrade process from Office 2000 is relatively simple because of the foundational power that Microsoft put in the Microsoft Office 2000 product.

Sams Teach Yourself Office Productivity All in One will focus on the Office 2000 version for its features, but if you use a later version, you'll be pleased to note that most of the features discussed throughout this book also work virtually identically in Office XP and versions that will be released later. One reason for this is because Microsoft put so much power in Office 2000 that the subsequent Office XP was more of a facelift than anything else. And the version released after Office XP is an even more minor upgrade from Office XP.

Throughout this text, when the latest version of Office has a new feature related to the current topic, you'll know about it through the use of sidebars and notes such as these. This approach keeps you on the cutting edge while still bringing in the large readership that needs Office 2000 training.

Office automates many of your computing chores and provides products that work in unison by sharing data among them. Office combines Microsoft's most powerful applications, such as Word and Excel, in a single package. The programs work well together and the final overall product, Microsoft Office, is called a *suite of programs*. You can still purchase the Office programs individually, building your own suite of products, but the Microsoft Office packages offer you the best deal.

Microsoft sells its Office suite in several versions. The three most common are

- *Microsoft Office Academic Edition*: Also called *Microsoft Office Standard for Students and Teachers*, this suite includes Word, Excel, Outlook, and PowerPoint, which are considered the core Office products. Microsoft sells this edition of Office for a significant discount for qualified buyers. Buyers will be unable to take advantage of upgrade discounts when they are ready to upgrade to the next version, whereas owners of the other Office suites can take a substantial discount when upgrading to the next version.

- *Microsoft Office Standard Edition*: Contains the core products: Word, Excel, Outlook, and PowerPoint. You can upgrade to a subsequent Office release at discounted prices.

- *Office Professional Edition*: In addition to Word, Excel, Outlook, and PowerPoint, the Professional Edition contains Microsoft Access, a database product that enables you to manage large amounts of information.

If any or all of Microsoft Office's component programs, such as PowerPoint or Excel, are unfamiliar to you, the rest of this chapter describes each one so that you'll have the big picture. The rest of this book explores each of the Office products in more detail.

> In addition to Word, Outlook, PowerPoint, and Excel, *Sams Teach Yourself Office Productivity All in One* teaches FrontPage, a Web page creation program that only comes with a special version of Office called the *Developer Edition*. FrontPage is also sold as a product you can purchase separately. *Sams Teach Yourself Office Productivity All in One* does not cover Access due to the more limited audience for Access compared to the other Office products.

You'll notice that *office* is used throughout this book to refer to general work and home office environments as well as Microsoft Office when *Office* is capitalized.

What's in Microsoft Office and Quicken?

The following is a quick overview of the major Microsoft Office programs:

- Word is a *word processor* with which you can create notes, memos, letters, school papers, business documents, books, newsletters, and even Internet Web pages.

- Outlook is a *personal information manager* (*PIM*) that organizes your contact addresses, phone numbers, and other information in an address-book format. Use Outlook to track your appointments, schedule meetings, generate to-do lists, keep notes, manage all your Internet email, and keep a journal of your activities.

- PowerPoint is a presentation program with which you can create presentations for seminars, schools, churches, Web pages, and business meetings. Not only can PowerPoint create the presentation overheads, it can also create the speaker's presentation notes.

- FrontPage enables you to create your own Web pages without having to learn tricky coding languages. With FrontPage, you'll combine documents from the other Office products into a series of Web pages you can be proud of.

- Excel is an *electronic worksheet* program with which you can create charts, graphs, and numerical worksheets for financial and other numeric data. After you enter your financial data, you can analyze it for forecasts, generate numerous what-if scenarios, and publish worksheets on the Web.

> The products taught here, especially Word, Excel, PowerPoint, and FrontPage, share many common features and menu options. The advantage is that once you learn one program, you already will be familiar with many features of the others.

In addition to sharing common interface elements, you can almost always transfer data from one program to another, often by dragging data and filenames with your mouse. You can move an Excel worksheet to FrontPage so your table appears on a Web site you maintain that displays your portfolio for an investment group you attend. Take that same table and embed it in a PowerPoint presentation for training sessions at your financial group's meetings.

> One of the most helpful features of Office is its ability to adjust menus and toolbars to work the way you do. For example, Word does not display all menu commands on the File menu when you display the File menu. Instead, Word displays only those commands you use most often. The less often you use a menu option, the more likely Word will remove that option from the initial menu that first appears. All the commands are there, however, so when you click the arrows at the bottom of a menu, the menu expands to show all its commands. The Office products, thus, attempt to keep your screen as free from clutter as possible. As you use menus and toolbars, Office analyzes the menu options and buttons you use most; those options and buttons you use infrequently will begin to go away so that only your common choices remain. You can always access these hidden menu options and toolbar buttons, but Office puts them out of the way until you need them.

This book always displays all menu options although your Office installation may show the shortened *personalized menus* that reflect the options you use most. You can show the full set of menu commands by selecting Tools, Customize, Options and unchecking the option labeled Menus Show Recently Used Commands First.

Introducing Word

When you need to write any text-based document, look no further than Word. Word is a word processor that supports many features, including the following:

- Integrated grammar, spelling, and hyphenation tools
- Wizards and templates that create and format documents for you
- Automatic corrections for common mistakes as you type using special automatic-correcting tools that watch the way you work and adapt to your needs
- Advanced formatting capabilities
- Numbering, bulleting, and shading tools
- Multiple document views so that you can see a rough draft of your document or the look of a final printed page as you write
- Drawing, border, and shading tools that enable you to emphasize headers, draw lines and shapes around your text, and work with imported art files
- Simple Web-page development for Internet users so that they can turn their documents into Web pages

Figure 1.1 shows a Word editing session. The user is editing a business letter to send to a client.

Introducing Outlook

Outlook is a simple-to-use tool that manages your business and personal meetings, email, to-do lists, contacts, and appointments. Outlook provides many features, including the following:

- The capability to track your contact information, including multiple phone numbers and computerized email addresses
- The capability to track your computer activities in a journal
- Management of your email, phone calls, and to-do lists
- The capability to schedule appointments

FIGURE **1.1**
Word helps you create, edit, and format letters.

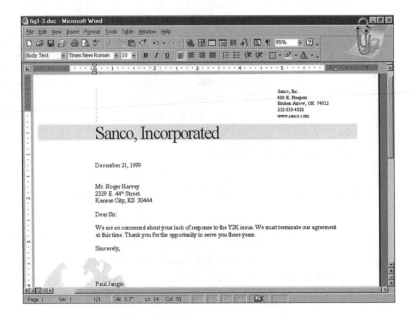

- The capability to plan people and resources you need for meetings
- The capability to sound an alarm before an important event

Figure 1.2 shows an Outlook calendar screen. The user is getting ready to schedule a meeting on a particular day. As with all the Office programs, you can modify screen elements in Outlook so that they appear in the format most helpful to your needs.

Introducing PowerPoint

Before PowerPoint's original version, users had no way to generate presentations without making a tedious effort to design each color slide using some kind of graphics drawing program. Although presentation products similar to PowerPoint exist, PowerPoint is recognized as a leader. PowerPoint supports many features, including the following:

- The capability to turn your Word document outlines into presentation notes
- Automatic proofing tools such as spelling and hyphenation
- Sample slide and slide collection templates that provide you with a fill-in-the-blank presentation
- A slide projector that displays your presentation on your screen
- Complete color and font control of your presentation slides
- A collection of clip art files, icons, sounds, and animations that you can embed to make presentations come alive

Figure 1.2

Outlook tracks appointments and events.

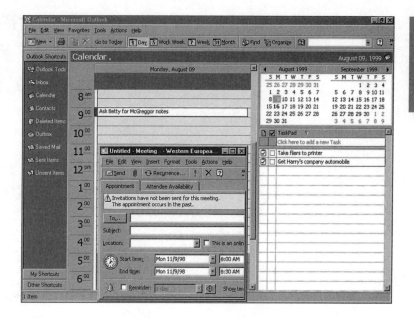

- Numerous transitions and fades between presentation slides to keep your audience's attention
- The capability to save presentations as Web pages that you can then present on the Internet

Figure 1.3 shows a PowerPoint editing session. The user is getting ready for a presentation and has only a few minutes to prepare 10 color slides for the meeting. With PowerPoint, a few minutes are more than enough time!

Introducing FrontPage

FrontPage is a Web page creation tool that helps you design Web pages by clicking and dragging objects and text and other Web page elements to their final location. Before tools such as FrontPage, you would have to master advanced programming commands to create Web pages. With the visual tools available in FrontPage, you can create Web pages as easily as you create documents in Word. In addition, you can combine documents from the other Office products into your Web pages and manage your complete site's Web pages. FrontPage includes features such as the following:

- The ability to send your Web pages directly to the Internet or a company intranet
- Menus and toolbars that closely match those of the other Office products so that you can more quickly begin creating Web pages
- Numerous samples of Web pages from which you can add your own elements
- A collection of predesigned themes from which you can select that gives your Web pages design consistency

Figure 1.3

PowerPoint helps you create, edit, and format presentations.

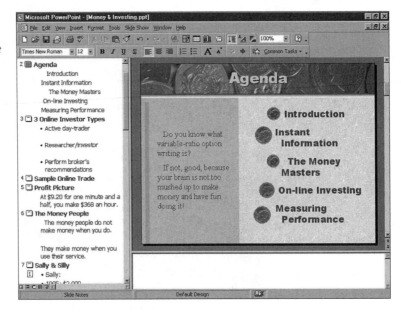

Figure 1.4 shows a Web page being edited inside FrontPage. Without learning tedious commands, you, too, can create such effective pages.

Figure 1.4

Create your own effective Web pages with FrontPage.

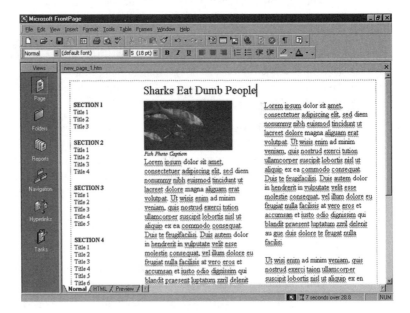

Introducing Excel

Although Excel can be used for non-numeric worksheets, the primary goal for Excel is to help you organize and manage financial information such as income statements, balance sheets, and forecasts. Excel is an electronic worksheet program that displays financial information in a series of rows and columns whose intersections form *cells*. Excel supports many features, including the following:

- Automatic cell formatting
- Worksheet proofing tools, such as spell checking
- Automatic row and column completion of value ranges with AutoFill
- Automatic worksheet formatting to turn your worksheets into professionally produced reports
- Built-in functions, such as financial formulas, that automate common tasks
- Powerful maps, charts, and graphs that can analyze your numbers and turn them into simple trends
- Automatic worksheet computations that enable you to generate multiple what-if scenarios and decide between different courses of action

Figure 1.5 shows an Excel editing session. The user is getting ready to enter invoice information for a sale. As you can see, Excel can start with a predesigned form. If you have worked with other worksheet programs, you might be surprised at how fancy Excel can get. The wizards make creating advanced worksheets easy.

FIGURE 1.5

Excel helps you create, edit, and format numeric worksheets.

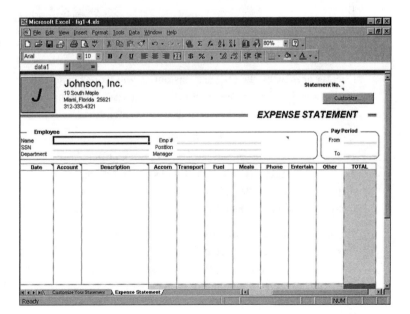

The Office Assistant

When you start any Microsoft Office program, the first feature you might notice is the *Office Assistant*, an online cartoon character that hangs around as you work. Figure 1.6 shows the default Office Assistant (named *Clippit*) that appears when you start any Office program.

FIGURE 1.6

Clippit, the helpful Assistant, remains faithful as you use Office.

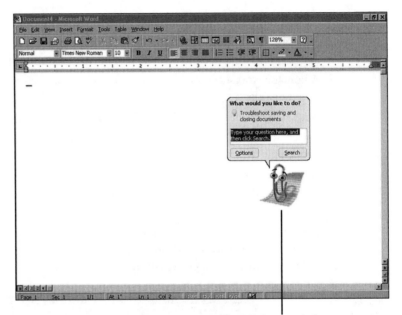

Clippit is here to help you

Keep your eyes on the Office Assistant as you work because you will be amused at the contortions it goes through as it provides advice. If you have your speakers turned on, the Office Assistant makes noises to draw your attention.

Suppose that you want help italicizing Word text. You can search through the online help system (via the Help menu), or you can click Office Assistant and type a question, such as How do I italicize text?, and press Enter. Office Assistant analyzes your question and displays a list of related topics (as shown in Figure 1.7). Click the topic that best fits your needs, and Office Assistant locates that help topic and displays the Help dialog box.

If you do something and Office Assistant can provide a better way, a yellow light bulb that you can click for shortcut information displays. If you begin to create a numbered list using menus, for example, Office Assistant displays the light bulb to let you know that you can create a numbered list by clicking a button on the toolbar.

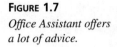

Figure 1.7

Office Assistant offers a lot of advice.

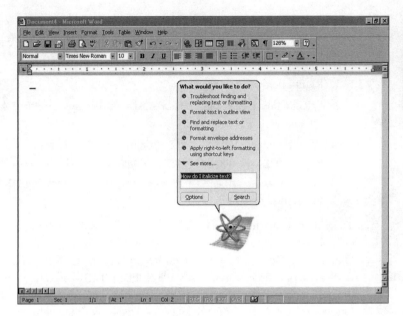

Customizing Office Assistant

If you work on a slow computer, you might want to disable Office Assistant to keep things moving a little faster. When you right-click Office Assistant, a pop-up menu appears with these options:

- *Hide*—Gets rid of Office Assistant. Display Office Assistant again by clicking the toolbar's Office Assistant button.

- *Options*—Displays an Office Assistant dialog box from which you can control the behavior of the Office Assistant (such as Office Assistant's response to pressing the F1 key).

- *Choose Assistant*—Enables you to change to a different animated Office Assistant character. As you work with Office, check out all the Office Assistants (they are fun to see). You will learn how to change the Office Assistant character in the steps that follow.

- *Animate!*—Causes Office Assistant to dance around its window; Office Assistant likes to show off! Select Animate a few times to see Office Assistant's contortions. As Office Assistant offers advice, it also moves through these animations. If you attempt to exit a program without saving your work, for example, Office Assistant gets your attention. (You will even hear Rocky, the canine assistant, barking!)

Office includes several Office Assistants to help you do your job. They differ in animation, but not in their advice. Suppose you get tired of Clippit and decide that you want to see a different Office Assistant. Try this:

1. Right-click Office Assistant.

2. Select Choose Assistant. Office Assistant displays an Office Assistant Gallery screen.

3. Click Back and Next to cycle through the Office Assistants. Each Office Assistant goes through a song and dance to convince you that it is the best.

4. When you come to an Office Assistant you like, click the OK button to begin using that Office Assistant.

The Office Assistant appears when you press F1, although you can return to the normal content-based help system if you prefer by right-clicking over Assistant and selecting Options and click the option labeled Respond to the F1 Key to disconnect the Assistant from the F1 keypress. Office uses a Web-like HTML-based help so that you can navigate the online help as you navigate Web pages. As Figure 1.8 shows, when you display non-Office Assistant help, Office displays two panes with the help text in the left pane and a condensed Office program screen in the right pane. (You can drag the center bar left and right to adjust the width of the panes.) With the help shown in a second pane, you can keep working in the right pane while referring to helpful instructions in the left pane.

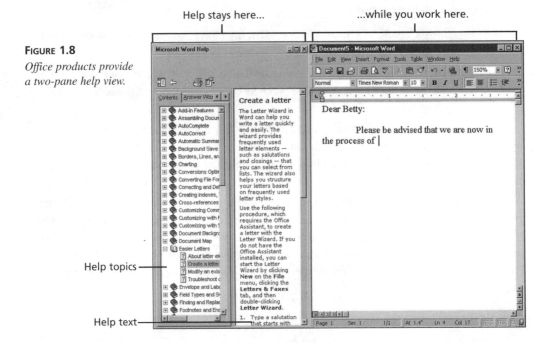

FIGURE 1.8
Office products provide a two-pane help view.

Making Office Easier to Use

Several accessibility features make Office easier to use. You will become familiar with many of these features as you work with Office. Following is a sample of some of these features:

- The Change document option magnifies documents for easier viewing. Even the toolbar buttons are larger to make them easier to find.

- The Office programs contain many *AutoComplete* features with which you can begin typing items such as dates, times, days of the week or month, names, and any other AutoText entries you set up. Office completes the entry for you. If you begin typing a month name such as Nov, for example, Word displays a small box with November above your month abbreviation. If you press Enter, Word completes the month name for you! If you type a full month name, such as July, Word offers to complete your entry with the current date, such as July 7, 2003. You can accept the complete date by pressing Enter or ignore it by typing the rest of the sentence as you want it to appear.

- You can rearrange toolbar buttons and customize toolbars so that they contain only the buttons you use most frequently. As you learned in the previous lesson, Office analyzes how you use the menus and toolbars and begins to hide those options and buttons you use less frequently to reduce screen clutter. You can always see all menu options and toolbars when you want by displaying a menu for a couple of seconds until the hidden options appear. In addition, you can drag a toolbar left or right to see hidden options.

- PowerPoint presentations provide a special high-contrast viewing mode in which you can more easily see the details of a presentation in virtually any light.

- You can assign shortcut keys to just about any task in any Office product. Suppose that you often need to color and boldface an Excel value. Create a shortcut keystroke and press it whenever you want to apply the special formatting.

Clip Art

Not only can Office work with text, numbers, and even Web hyperlinks, but it can also work with sound, pictures, and moving video.

Office includes a huge collection of royalty-free *clip art* files for personal use that you can use when you want to embed a special data item—such as a picture or video—into a document, spreadsheet, or Web page. When you need a graphic to spice things up, or when you want to include an attention-getting sound file in an Outlook email message, select Insert, Picture, Clip Art to access the Office clip art collection (sometimes called the *Microsoft Clip Art Gallery*). The gallery includes several hundred sounds, pictures, and drawings arranged by category, as Figure 1.9 shows.

FIGURE 1.9

You will have no short-age of clip art to use with Office.

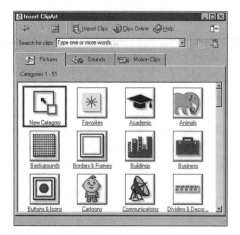

Perhaps one of the most impressive features from the Office clip art is that you can click the Clips Online button to link to Microsoft's clip art Web site and search for even more files to use in your documents.

Templates

A *template* is nothing more than a formatted outline of a document. Suppose that you follow a monthly budget, and you prepare monthly statements to follow. You like to include your savings account interest calculations, so you determine that Excel will function well as the creation tool for your statements.

When you create your monthly statements, you have three options:

- Create each monthly budget from scratch.
- Modify a saved monthly budget to change the details for each subsequent statement.
- Create a monthly budget template and fill in the details for each statement.

Obviously, the first option requires the most work. Why create a new statement for each budget, adding the titles, date, time, details, summaries, creditors, and new investment information if many of those details remain the same from statement to statement?

The second option is not a bad idea if the statements are fairly uniform in design and require only slight formatting and detail changes. Some people feel more comfortable changing an existing statement's details than creating statements from scratch or using a template. New Office users might prefer to change an existing statement until they get accustomed to Office's programs.

> Although templates are great for Office newcomers, you do not always want to start with them. Sometimes, it's easier to understand an Office program if you create your first few data files (documents, databases, electronic worksheets, and so on) from scratch.

When you get used to Office, however, you discover that the template method makes the most sense for repetitive statement creation. The template literally provides a fill-in-the-blank statement. You don't have to format the same information from statement to statement, and you're guaranteed a uniform appearance.

Using Existing Templates

Office supplies several common templates, and each Office product contains templates of its own. For example, when you want to create a new Excel electronic worksheet, you can select from a blank worksheet or you can click the Spreadsheet Solutions tab to see four icons that represent templates. When you click a template icon, Office shows you a preview of that template (as shown in Figure 1.10).

FIGURE 1.10

Office provides several templates that you can preview.

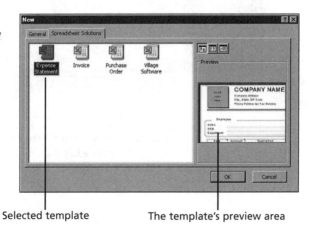

Selected template   The template's preview area

After you select a template, the Office program opens it and presents the file. Edit the template and save the details in a new file. The new file becomes your template file that you use for subsequent documents.

Wizards

One reason so many users have switched to Microsoft-based Office products is Microsoft's wizard technology. *Wizards* are step-by-step guides that walk you through the development of a document or through a complicated process such as creating an Internet Web page from scratch. (You learn more about Office's Internet integration throughout this book.)

Although each wizard differs in its goal, all follow a similar pattern. Wizards display a series of dialog boxes, and each dialog box asks for a set of values. As you fill in the dialog boxes, you answer questions to help the program perform a specific job.

Generally, each dialog box within a wizard contains Next and Back buttons, which you can click to move back and forth through the wizard. If you change your mind after leaving one dialog box, you can back up to that dialog box and change its values.

Microsoft supplies you with several wizards you can use to create Office documents. For example, if you use Word to create a résumé, you can select the Résumé Wizard. Figure 1.11 shows the Résumé Wizard's opening dialog box.

FIGURE 1.11

The opening Résumé Wizard box.

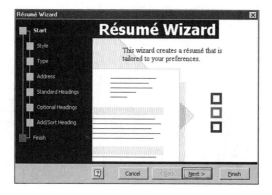

When you select File, New, each Office product offers a list of template and wizard icons. You'll know the difference between them because the wizard icons include a magic wand waving across the icon.

1

Many wizards contain opening dialog boxes that display information about the wizard. Figure 1.12 informs you that you selected the Résumé Wizard. If you click the Next button, the wizard asks which of the following kinds of résumés you want to create:

- Entry-level résumé
- Chronological résumé
- Functional résumé
- Professional résumé

Clicking Next again displays a dialog box that requests your name and address information for the top of the résumé. Office is smart enough to automatically pull your name from the Office registration information, but you can change the name if you create résumés for other people. Often, wizard dialog boxes present you with a selection of styles, formats, graphic elements, and colors.

Every wizard's final dialog box includes a Finish button that you will click to complete the wizard and generate the document based on the wizard. Generally, wizards create shells of documents, such as Word template documents or Excel worksheets that contain no data. It's your job to enter the details.

After a wizard designs a document, you are free to make whatever additional edits you need.

Summary

This chapter introduced the Office programs to you by showing you a little of what each program can accomplish. Before learning specifics, you need to get the big picture. This hour provided that big picture and now you're ready to launch into each program and learn the nuances of each.

Part II
Getting Started with Word

Chapter

CHAPTER 2

Welcoming You to Word

You are beginning a long-term relationship with Word, so it makes sense to spend a bit of time getting to know your surroundings. This chapter introduces you to key terms and techniques that enable you to maximize your use of Word.

You will see that Word has an intuitive interface that lets you access commonly used commands, yet it is full of powerful features that enable you to create a wide assortment of specialized documents. This chapter concludes by giving you an overview of some of Word's more powerful features.

What Is Word Designed to Do?

Word's fundamental mission is simple: to help you type, revise, and format text. To this end, it offers a complete set of tools that enables you to create just about any type of document imaginable. You can produce anything from basic letters and memos to complex documents such as reports, papers, newsletters, brochures, résumés, mass mailings, envelopes, and mailing labels. You can even compose email messages and design Web pages in Word.

Each person who uses Word needs a slightly different combination of features. Learn the areas of Word that you need, and don't feel compelled to explore every nook and cranny.

Elements of the Word Window

Once you master Word's interface, you'll better understand all the screen features of the other Office programs. Understanding your interface is essential for understanding the instructions throughout the rest of this book. Figure 2.1 labels the most important parts of the Word window.

FIGURE 2.1

It's a good idea to learn the names of the different parts of the Word window.

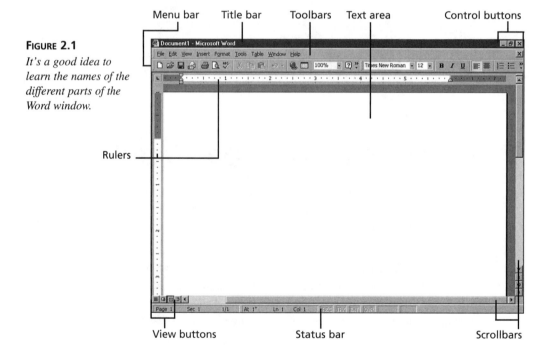

Here is a description of these elements:

- *Title bar*—The title bar of any Windows application lists the name of the application—in this case, Microsoft Word. Word's title bar also contains the name of the open document. As you'll see in the section "Controlling the Word Window," you can use the title bar to move the Word window around the desktop, or to minimize or maximize the window. When the Word window is active, the title bar is colored. When another window is active, the title bar is gray.

- *Menu bar*—The menu bar contains a set of pull-down menus that you use to issue commands.

- *Toolbars*—The toolbars contain buttons that you can click to issue commands.

- *Rulers*—The vertical and horizontal rulers show you where your text is on the page. The gray sections at the ends of the rulers indicate the margin areas. You can use the rulers to change some formatting, including tabs, indents, and margins (see Chapter 6, "Formatting Characters, Paragraphs, and Pages"). Depending on which *view* you're using, you may see only a horizontal ruler. (You'll learn about views in Chapter 5, "Viewing and Printing Your Documents.") To hide the rulers, choose View, Ruler. To display them, choose View, Ruler again.

- *Text area*—This is the area in which you can type text.

- *View buttons*—You can use these buttons to switch views (see Chapter 5).

- *Status bar*—The status bar tells you about the current status of your document. The left section tells you the current page number and the total number of pages. The middle section tells you the location of the insertion point (the cursor), and the right section tells you whether some special features are turned on.

- *Scrollbars*—The horizontal and vertical scrollbars let you bring different parts of a document into view. You'll learn how to use them in Chapter 3, "Entering Text and Moving Around."

- *Control buttons*—These buttons let you control the Word window.

Issuing Commands

Word enables you to "talk" to it in a variety of ways. The exact methods that you use are a matter of personal preference. If you like reading text instead of deciphering tiny pictures on toolbar buttons, you probably prefer using the menus. If, on the other hand, you are visually oriented and like using a mouse, you may find yourself using toolbar buttons most of the time. Perhaps you're a fast typist and hate to take your hands away from the keyboard to reach for the mouse. If this is the case, you may come to rely almost completely on keyboard shortcuts. Experiment with all of the methods described here and see which ones you like best.

Working with Menus

The menu bar at the top of the Word window contains nine pull-down menus—File, Edit, View, and so on. You can issue all of the commands in Word via these menus. Chances are, you use toolbar buttons or keyboard shortcuts for many commands, but you can always fall back on the menus if you forget the alternate methods.

Menu Basics

To display a menu, click its name in the menu bar. For example, to display the Format menu, click *Format* in the menu bar, as shown in Figure 2.2. Then click a command in the menu to instruct Word to carry it out. If you want to close a menu without issuing a command, click anywhere outside the menu in the text area.

Figure 2.2

Click a menu name to display the menu.

Some menu commands, such as those shown in the Format menu in Figure 2.2, are followed by three dots (...). These commands lead to dialog boxes, which you use to give Word more information before it carries out a command. If a menu command is not followed by three dots, Word performs the command as soon as you click it.

If a menu command has a small triangle at its right, it leads to a submenu. To display the submenu, just point to the command. In Figure 2.3, the Insert, Picture submenu is displayed.

Figure 2.3

Menu commands with triangles lead to submenus.

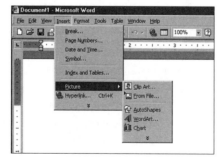

When a menu command is dim, it is not currently available. In Figure 2.4, the first four commands in the Edit menu are dim.

Many menu commands list keyboard shortcuts to their right. For example, in Figure 2.4, the keyboard shortcut Ctrl+A is listed to the right of the Select All command. You can use these keyboard shortcuts as an alternative to clicking the commands in the menus. See "Using Keyboard Shortcuts" later in this chapter for more information.

FIGURE 2.4
Dimmed commands are not currently available.

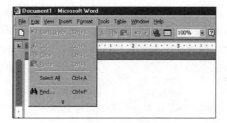

2

Using the Keyboard to Issue Menu Commands

You can use the keyboard instead of the mouse to display menus and issue commands in them. To display a menu, press the Alt key, and then press the underlined letter in the menu name. For example, to display the Format menu, you press Alt+O. (It doesn't matter whether you type an upper- or lowercase letter.) After the menu is displayed, press the underlined letter in the command that you want to issue. For example, to issue the Paragraph command in the Format menu, press P. To close a menu without issuing any command, press the Alt key.

> You can also use the keyboard to interact with dialog boxes. See "Working with Dialog Boxes" later in this chapter for more information.

Right-Clicking to Display Menus On-the-Fly

You learned in the previous chapter that Office uses personalized menus (if you elect to use them) to display only those menu options you use most. In addition to using the menus at the top of the Word window, you can also use *context menus* (sometimes called *shortcut menus*). These are small menus that you display by clicking the right mouse button. The commands in a context menu vary depending on where you right-click. For example, if you right-click text, you get commands for editing and formatting text (see Figure 2.5), and if you right-click a toolbar, you get a list of available toolbars (see Figure 2.6).

To choose a command in a context menu, use a left-click. To close a context menu without choosing a command, click anywhere outside it.

Working with Toolbars

For many people, the fastest way to issue commands in Word is via the toolbars. Word comes with 16 toolbars in all. By default, it displays two of them—the Standard and Formatting toolbars, as shown in Figure 2.7. The Standard toolbar contains buttons for performing file-management tasks, such as starting, saving, opening, and printing documents. The Formatting toolbar contains buttons for common formatting tasks, including changing the font and font size, and adding boldface, italic, and underline to your text.

FIGURE 2.5

Right-clicking text displays a context menu with commands for working with text.

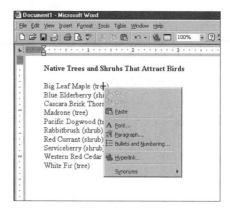

FIGURE 2.6

Right-clicking a toolbar displays a context menu that lists available toolbars.

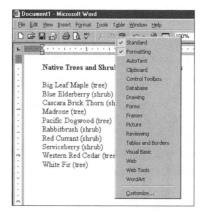

FIGURE 2.7

The Standard and Formatting toolbars are displayed by default.

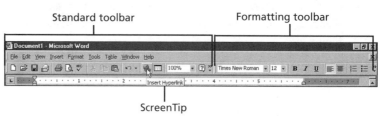

To see what a toolbar button does, rest your mouse pointer on it for a moment. A ScreenTip appears with the button's name, as shown in Figure 2.7.

Displaying and Hiding Toolbars

The 14 toolbars that aren't displayed by default can help you with all kinds of tasks. For example, the Tables and Borders toolbar has buttons for creating and formatting tables, and the Reviewing toolbar contains buttons that are useful if you're editing someone else's document. Some of these toolbars appear automatically when needed, but you can also display any of them manually whenever you like. You may also want to hide toolbars that you never use to create more space in the Word window.

To display or hide a toolbar, choose View, Toolbars (see Figure 2.8). The toolbars that are currently displayed have check marks next to them. The ones that are currently hidden do not. Click the toolbar that you want to display or hide.

FIGURE 2.8

Use the Toolbars submenu to display or hide toolbars.

 You can also display or hide a toolbar by right-clicking any toolbar that's currently displayed, and then clicking the desired toolbar in the context menu that appears (refer to Figure 2.6).

Accessing Hidden Toolbar Buttons

Depending on the size of your Word window, the number of toolbars that are sharing the same row, and so on, Word may not have room to display all of a toolbar's buttons. If you want to use a toolbar button that's currently hidden from view, click the More Buttons arrow at the right (or bottom) end of the toolbar. Word displays a list of all the hidden buttons (see Figure 2.9).

More Buttons arrow

FIGURE 2.9

Word puts any toolbar buttons that are currently hidden in the More Buttons list.

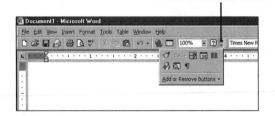

Click the button that you want to use. As soon as you click it, Word removes it from the More Buttons list and places it in a visible spot on the toolbar. (See "Moving Buttons Around a Toolbar" later in this chapter if you want to adjust the button's position in the toolbar.)

If you want to restore the default set of visible buttons in your toolbars, choose Tools, Customize, click the Options tab, click the Reset My Usage Data button, click Yes, and click Close.

Adding and Removing Toolbar Buttons

In addition to accessing hidden toolbar buttons, you can also use the More Buttons list to add new buttons to a toolbar, or to remove buttons that you never use. Click the More Buttons arrow at the right (or bottom) end of the toolbar, and then click Add or Remove Buttons (see Figure 2.10). Buttons that don't have check marks are not currently included in the toolbar; those that do have check marks are included. Click the button that you want to add or remove.

If you've made a mess of a toolbar and want to reset it to the state it was in when you installed Word, click the More Buttons arrow, click Add or Remove Buttons, and then click Reset Toolbar.

Moving Toolbars Around the Word Window

You can position your toolbars anywhere you like in the Word window. One reason to move a toolbar is to make it easier to see. If you have several toolbars displayed at the top of the Word window, they may seem to merge into one jumbled clump of buttons. You can visually separate the toolbars by spreading them out in different parts of the Word window.

FIGURE 2.10

Click a button in the Add or Remove Buttons list that you want to add to or remove from the tool-bar.

Another reason to move a toolbar is to bring all of its buttons into view. If a toolbar is sharing a row with other toolbars, some of its buttons are probably hidden. If you want to access all of the buttons without using the More Buttons list (see "Accessing Hidden Toolbar Buttons" earlier in this chapter), you can move the toolbar onto its own row.

> A quick way to put the Standard and Formatting toolbars on separate rows is to choose Tools, Customize, click the Options tab, clear the Standard and Formatting Toolbars Share One Row check box, and click the Close button.
>
> The remaining chapters on Word assume that the Formatting toolbar is positioned on its own row, directly beneath the Standard toolbar.

Word lets you *dock* toolbars on the top, left, right, and bottom edges of the window, or "float" them over the screen (see Figure 2.11).

To move a docked toolbar, point to the line at the left end (or top) of the toolbar. The mouse pointer becomes a four-headed arrow. If you want the toolbar to float, drag it into the text area of the window, and release the mouse button. (To *drag* something, you point to it and then press and hold down the left mouse button as you move the mouse.) To move the toolbar after you've released the mouse button, drag its title bar. (You can also change the shape of a floating toolbar by dragging one of its borders.)

Floating toolbar

FIGURE 2.11

*You can dock toolbars
or let them float.*

Docked toolbars

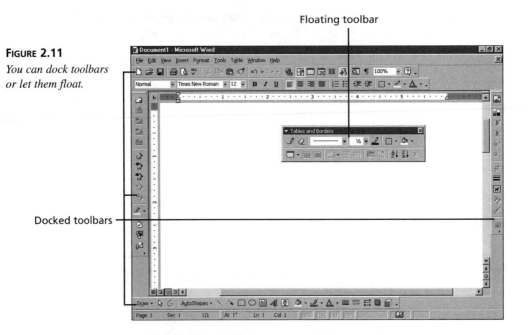

If you want to dock a toolbar on an edge of the Word window, drag it toward that edge
until its title bar disappears and it "flattens out," and then release the mouse button.

> If a toolbar is floating, you can quickly dock it on the edge of the window
> where it was most recently docked by double-clicking its title bar.

Moving Buttons Around a Toolbar

You can rearrange the order of the buttons on a toolbar if you like. To move a button,
point to it and hold down your Alt key as you drag it to the desired position. As you
drag, a black I-beam with a button icon attached to it shows where the toolbar button
will end up. When the I-beam is in the right place, release the Alt key and your mouse
button.

Working with Dialog Boxes

Dialog boxes let you specify exactly what you want Word to do before it carries out your
command. There are a few standard elements in dialog boxes that you use to set options.
The Print dialog box (choose File, Print), shown in Figure 2.12, contains most of these.

Drop-down list

FIGURE 2.12

The Print dialog box contains common dialog box elements.

Option button

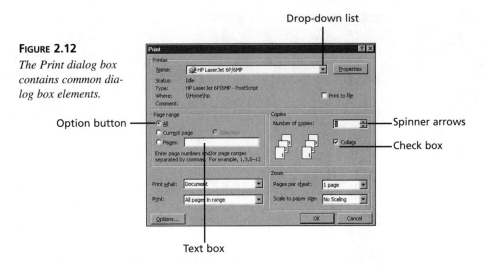

Spinner arrows

Check box

Text box

Here is a description of these elements:

- *Drop-down list*—Click the down arrow at the right end of a drop-down list to display a set of choices, and then click an item in the list. As soon as you click an item, the list closes. If you display a drop-down list and then decide not to change its current setting, click the down arrow again to close the list (or click anywhere else in the dialog box).

- *Option button*—To mark an option button, click it. A black dot appears in its center. To clear an option button, you have to click another option button in the same group. Only one option button in a group can be marked. (Option buttons are sometimes called *radio buttons*.)

- *Check box*—To mark a check box, click it. A check mark appears in the box. To clear the check mark, click the check box again. If you see a group of check boxes, you can mark as many of them as you like.

- *Text box*—A text box is a box in which you can type text. Click in a text box to place the insertion point in it, and then start typing. If there is already text in the box, you can replace it by dragging over it with the mouse to select it before you start typing.

- *Spinner arrows*—Some text boxes have spinner arrows. You can click the up and down arrows to increment the number in the text box up or down. Alternatively, you can just type the number in the box.

Some dialog boxes also contain *tabs* across the top of the dialog box. Each tab contains a separate set of options. Figure 2.13 shows the Options dialog box (Tools, Options), which contains 10 tabs. To bring a tab to the front, just click it.

FIGURE 2.13

In many dialog boxes, related sets of options are organized in tabs.

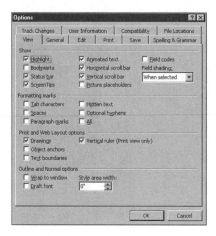

After you've made your selections in a dialog box, click the OK button to tell Word to carry out the command. (If a dialog box doesn't have an OK button, look for another likely candidate, such as a button labeled *Close* or *Insert*.) If you decide not to go ahead with a command, you can back out of the dialog box by clicking the Cancel button. Clicking the Close button (the X) in the upper-right corner of a dialog box is the same as clicking the Cancel button.

If you want, you can use the keyboard to make selections in a dialog box. To do so, first press the Tab key to move the *focus* to the option that you want to change. (To move in the reverse direction, press Shift+Tab.) When the option has the focus, it will be high-lighted or have a dotted box around it. Then make your selection by using one of these methods:

- To choose an item in a drop-down list, bring the focus to the list, press the down-arrow key to display the list, use the up- and down-arrow keys to select the desired item, and then press Enter.

- To mark an option button, focus on the group of option buttons and then use the up- and down-arrow keys to mark the button.

- To mark or clear a check box, focus on it and press the Spacebar.

- To type in a text box, bring the focus to the text box (if the text box is currently empty, an insertion point appears in the box; if it contains text, the text will be selected) and then type your text.

- To choose a button in a dialog box, bring the focus to the button and then press Enter. If the button name has an underlined letter (or *hot key*), you can press the Alt key plus that letter to choose the button. For example, to choose the Properties button in the Print dialog box (refer to Figure 2.13), you can press Alt+P.

After you've made your selections, press Enter to choose the OK button. (If the OK button doesn't have a dark border around it, press the Tab key until it does, and then press Enter.) If you decide to back out of the dialog box without making any changes, press the Escape key. This is the equivalent of clicking the Cancel button.

Using Keyboard Shortcuts

Many common commands have keyboard shortcuts that you can use instead of the menus or toolbars. Some of these keyboard shortcuts are listed to the right of the commands in the menus. For example, the keyboard shortcut Ctrl+O appears to the right of the Open command in the File menu.

> Make sure that you hold down the first key in a keyboard shortcut as you press the second key. For example, to issue the File, Open command with the keyboard, you press and hold down the Ctrl key as you press the letter O. If there are three keys in a keyboard shortcut, such as Shift+Ctrl+End, keep the first two held down as you press the third.

For a complete listing of keyboard shortcuts in Word's help system, ask the Office Assistant to search for *shortcut keys*. If you like, you can print the shortcuts and keep them next to your computer for reference. (See "Getting Help" later in this chapter.)

Controlling the Word Window

You can change the appearance of the Word window in a variety of ways. You can make it disappear temporarily so that you can see what's behind it on the Windows desktop, or make it fill up the screen to give you more room to work. You can also move the Word window around on your desktop, or adjust its size.

Using the Control Buttons

The Control buttons appear in the upper-right corner of the Word window. The function of these buttons is the same for all Windows applications.

Click the Minimize button to temporarily hide the Word window, leaving only its taskbar button. To redisplay the Word window, click its taskbar button. If you want to make the Word window cover the entire desktop, click the Maximize button (see Figure 2.14).

As soon as the Word window is maximized, the Maximize button becomes a Restore button (see Figure 2.15). Click the Restore button to return (*restore*) the window to the size it was before you maximized it.

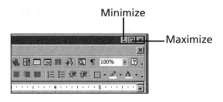

FIGURE 2.14

The Minimize button shrinks the Word window to a taskbar button; the Maximize button enlarges it to cover the desktop.

FIGURE 2.15

Click the Restore button to return the window to the size it was before it was maximized.

Use the Close button (the X) to the right of the Maximize/Restore button closes the Word window. If you have only one Word window open, a second Close button appears beneath the first one. Clicking this lower button closes only the document, leaving the Word window open.

Moving and Resizing the Window

If the Word window isn't maximized, you can move it around the Windows desktop or change its size.

To move the Word window, point to its title bar, drag the window to a different location, and release the mouse button.

To resize the Word window, point to the lower-right corner of the window. The mouse pointer becomes a diagonal black arrow, as shown in Figure 2.16. Drag in the desired direction to enlarge or shrink the window. (You can actually drag any edge or corner of the Word window to resize the window—the lower-right corner is just the most convenient spot.)

FIGURE 2.16

Drag a border or corner of the Word window to resize the window.

Getting Help

If you putter around in Word trying to figure things out on your own (which you are strongly encouraged to do!), you are bound to have some questions once in a while. Maybe a feature isn't working as you think it should, or you know that a particular task must be possible, but you don't know how to approach it. At these times, a solid familiarity with Word's help system can be of tremendous assistance. Not only can you often find the exact information you need, you can do it without pestering your co-workers or family members.

Using Word's Help System

In the previous chapter, you learned about the Office Assistant, the animated character that offers you help with Word and the other Microsoft Office programs.

 Starting in the next chapter, the Office Assistant will be hidden in the examples shown in this book. If you keep yours visible, certain messages from Word may be delivered to you by the Office Assistant instead of the standard message boxes you see in this book.

In addition to the Office Assistant, Word and the other programs taught here contain additional help features with which you can get help on a feature or problem. Whether the Office Assistant leads you to the Microsoft Word Help window or you get there on your own by turning off your Office Assistant, you need to know how to sift through the various resources Help offers.

The Word Help window is divided into two panes. When you access it through the Office Assistant, the window is collapsed to show only the right pane. To display the left pane, which lets you navigate through the help system, click the Show button in the upper-left corner of the right pane (refer to Figure 2.17). As soon as the window expands, the Show button becomes a Hide button. Click this button if you want to collapse the window to show only the right pane again.

The Microsoft Word Help window opens to the right of the Word window so that you can refer to it as you're working on your document. When you've finished reading the topic, click the Close button (the X) in the upper-right corner of the window. If you want to explore other topics in the help system, see "Using the Microsoft Word Help Window" later in this hour.

Tabs at the top of the left pane let you access the Contents, Answer Wizard, and Index portions of the help system (see the next three sections). If you don't see these tabs, click the Options button at the top of the Microsoft Word Help window, and choose Show Tabs. As you explore topics in the help system, you can move back and forth among them by clicking the Back and Forward buttons at the top of the help window.

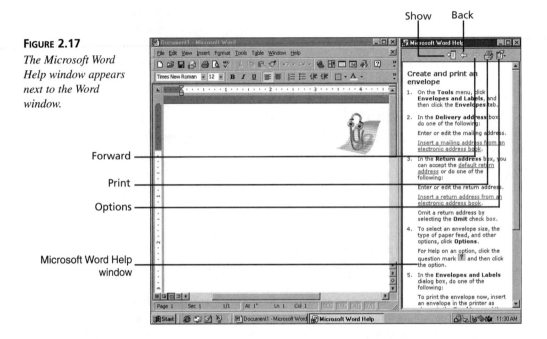

FIGURE 2.17

The Microsoft Word Help window appears next to the Word window.

To print a help topic, click the Print button at the top of the window. In the Print dialog box that appears, click OK. (If you print from the Contents tab, described in the next section, you see two Print dialog boxes. Click OK in both of them.)

Using the Contents Tab

The Contents tab of the Microsoft Help Window organizes help topics into books. Click the plus sign next to a book to display the topics, and possibly other books, that it contains. (The topics have icons that look like pages with question marks on them.) As soon as you expand a book, the plus sign changes to a minus sign, which you can click to collapse the view again. When you find a topic that you want to read, click it to display its contents in the right pane.

Some help topics, such as the one about customizing toolbars, contain links (colored words) that you can click to jump to other help topics or Show Me buttons that you can click to have Word demonstrate the task at hand.

Using the Answer Wizard Tab

The Answer Wizard tab of the Microsoft Help Window works much like the Office Assistant. You can type a word or two describing your question in the What Would You Like to Do? box, and then click the Search button. In the topics that appear in the Select Topic to Display list, double-click the topic that you want to read about. Its contents appear in the right pane.

Using the Index Tab

The Index tab of the Microsoft Help Window provides a searchable index of keywords in the help system. To use it, type a word describing your question in the Type Keywords text box. As you type, the Or Choose Keywords list scrolls to keywords matching the letters you've typed. You can double-click any of these keywords to display a list of related topics in the Choose a Topic list. To display topics related to the exact word you've typed in the Type Keywords text box, click the Search button. Double-click any topic in the Choose a Topic list to display it in the right pane of the help window.

Summary

Getting familiar with the Word environment is the first step toward learning to use the program effectively. You now have a vocabulary to describe the Word window, you know how to issue commands, and you know how to find help. In the next chapter, you go right to the heart of using Word: entering text and producing documents.

CHAPTER 3

Entering Text and Moving Around

Typing text is what word processing is all about. You can, in fact, create a perfectly respectable document by typing alone. Everything else—all of the formatting that you can apply—is icing on the cake. In this chapter, you first learn the basic principles of typing in a word processing program. After you know how to get text onto the page, you then practice moving around the document so that you can edit the text and apply formatting.

Typing Text

When you start Word, it gives you a blank document to let you start typing right away. Word makes some assumptions about how the document will look, so you don't need to worry about formatting at all unless you want to change the default settings. Here are the most important ones:

- 8 ½- by 11-inch paper
- 1-inch margins on the top and bottom of the page, and 1 ¼-inch margins on the left and right sides of the page

- Single spacing
- Times New Roman, 12-point font

Throughout the remaining chapters about Word, you learn how to change these formatting options. For now, you can just focus on typing.

Typing Paragraphs and Creating Blank Lines

The key to having a happy typing experience is knowing when to press Enter. Follow these two rules for typing paragraphs of text:

- When your text reaches the right margin, just continue typing. When Word can't fit any more text on the line, it automatically wraps the text to the next line for you. You should not press Enter at the ends of the lines within a paragraph.
- When you reach the end of the paragraph, you do need to press Enter. This brings the insertion point (the cursor) down to the next line.

Figure 3.1 illustrates these two rules.

FIGURE 3.1

Do not press Enter within a paragraph. Do press Enter at the end of the paragraph.

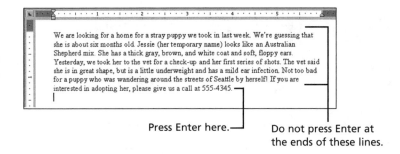

We are looking for a home for a stray puppy we took in last week. We're guessing that she is about six months old. Jessie (her temporary name) looks like an Australian Shepherd mix. She has a thick gray, brown, and white coat and soft, floppy ears. Yesterday, we took her to the vet for a check-up and her first series of shots. The vet said she is in great shape, but is a little underweight and has a mild ear infection. Not too bad for a puppy who was wandering around the streets of Seattle by herself! If you are interested in adopting her, please give us a call at 555-4345.

Press Enter here.

Do not press Enter at the ends of these lines.

If you do accidentally press Enter at the end of lines within a paragraph, your line breaks go haywire as soon as you add or delete any text. If your paragraph has some lines that are much shorter than they should be (a tell-tale sign that you pressed Enter within the paragraph), follow the instructions in "Seeing Your Paragraph, Tab, and Space Marks" later in this chapter to hunt down the offending paragraph marks and delete them.

When you press Enter, you actually insert a hidden character called a *paragraph mark*, which tells Word to end the paragraph. Word's definition of a paragraph may be a little broader than yours. It considers a *paragraph* to be

> any amount of text that ends with a paragraph mark. So as far as Word is concerned, blank lines and short lines of text—such as headings or the lines in an address block—are separate paragraphs.

To create blank lines between your paragraphs, press Enter twice between each paragraph, once to end the paragraph you just typed and once to create the blank line. If you need several blank lines, just continue pressing Enter. If you press Enter too many times and need to delete a blank line, press the Backspace key. You'll learn much more about deleting in Chapter 4, "Managing Documents and Revising Text."

Figure 3.2 illustrates when to press Enter to create short lines of text and blank lines.

FIGURE 3.2

Press Enter to end short paragraphs and create blank lines.

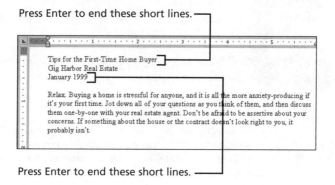

Press Enter to end these short lines.

Press Enter to end these short lines.

> In Chapter 6's "Paragraph Spacing" section, you'll learn how to automatically add a blank line after each paragraph without pressing Enter a second time.

As you type, you may see an occasional red or green wavy line under your text. These lines indicate possible spelling or grammatical errors. You'll learn how to use them (and hide them if they bother you) in Chapter 8, "Correcting Documents and Using Columns and Tables."

Inserting Tabs

Word gives you default tab stops every one-half inch across the horizontal ruler. (If you don't see your rulers, choose View, Ruler.) Each time you press the Tab key, the insertion point jumps out to the next tab stop. Any text to the right of the insertion point moves along with it. Figure 3.3 shows the beginning of a memo in which the Tab key was pressed after the labels To:, From:, Date: and Re: to line up the text at the half-inch mark on the horizontal ruler.

Default tab stops

FIGURE 3.3

Press the Tab key to push text out to the next tab stop.

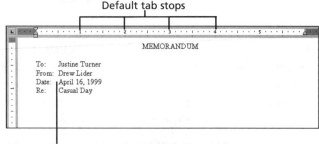

MEMORANDUM

To: Justine Turner
From: Drew Lider
Date: April 16, 1999
Re: Casual Day

The text lines up at the half-inch mark on the ruler.

If you press the Tab key too many times, press the Backspace key to delete the extra tabs.

You can also press the Tab key at the beginning of a paragraph to indent the first line by one-half inch. Figure 3.4 shows a document whose paragraphs are indented in this way.

> By default, when you press Tab at the beginning of a paragraph, Word sets a *first-line indent* for the paragraph. You'll learn much more about indentation in Chapter 6. What's important to understand now is that if Word applies this formatting, then when you press Enter at the end of the paragraph, Word automatically indents the next paragraph for you. If this default behavior has been turned off, just press Tab at the beginning of each paragraph.

Seeing Your Paragraph, Tab, and Space Marks

As you're typing your document, you may occasionally want to check whether you accidentally pressed Enter at the end of a line within a paragraph, or pressed Enter too many times between paragraphs. Or, maybe you think you may have pressed the Tab key one time too many, or typed an extra space between two words. You can use Word's Show/Hide feature to solve these mysteries. To turn it on, click the Show/Hide button on the Formatting toolbar (or press Ctrl+Shift+*). This is a *toggle* button, meaning that you click it once to turn it on, and again when you want to turn it off (see Figure 3.5).

The Show/Hide feature uses the paragraph mark symbol to indicate you where you pressed Enter, a right arrow to show where you pressed the Tab key, and a dot to mark where you pressed the Spacebar.

FIGURE 3.4

Press the Tab key at the beginning of each paragraph to indent the first line.

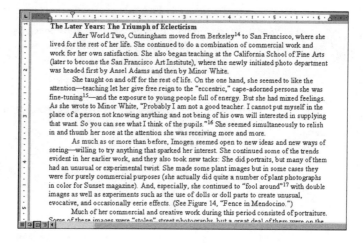

FIGURE 3.5

The Show/Hide feature lets you see your paragraph, tab, and space marks.

Extra tab   Extra space   Show/Hide

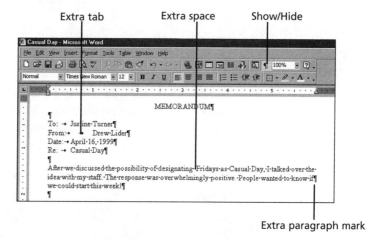

Extra paragraph mark

Figure 3.5 shows a document that has an errant paragraph, tab, and space mark. The user accidentally pressed the Tab key a second time on the From: line, typed an extra space between the words *designating* and *Fridays,* and pressed Enter at the end of a line within a paragraph.

To delete any of these hidden characters, click immediately to the left of the character and press the Delete key. Figure 3.6 shows the same document after these three problems were fixed.

Your document looks cluttered when Show/Hide is enabled, so you may want to turn it on just long enough to investigate and fix a mistake relating to hidden characters, and then turn it off.

FIGURE 3.6

The extra paragraph, tab, and space marks have been deleted.

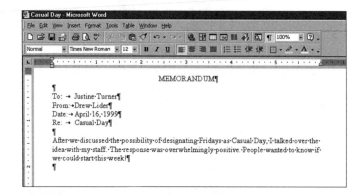

Typing onto the Next Page

As you're typing, Word calculates how many lines fit on a page. When the page you're on is full, Word automatically inserts a page break and starts another page. Figure 3.7 shows the break between two pages of text, as it appears in Print Layout view. (You'll learn about views in Chapter 5, "Viewing and Printing Your Documents.")

FIGURE 3.7

Word breaks pages for you.

Page break

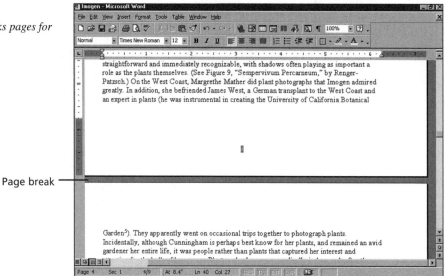

As you add or delete text, Word adjusts the page break so that it is always in the right place. This type of "adjustable" page break is called a *soft page break* (or *automatic page break*). There may be times when you need to break a page even though it is not yet full. For example, you might want to start the next section of a report on a new page, or create a title page. To do this, you have to insert a *hard page break* (or *manual page break*). You'll learn how to do this in Chapter 6.

Navigating Through Text

As you're typing a document, you will surely want to revise what you've written. Maybe you want to add a paragraph earlier in the document, change some wording, or delete a sentence or two. Before you can edit your text, however, you have to move the insertion point (*navigate*) to the location where you want to make the change. Word enables you to navigate with both the keyboard and the mouse. In the remainder of this chapter, you practice both types of navigation techniques.

3

It's important to differentiate between the *insertion point* and the *I-beam* (see Figure 3.8). The insertion point is the flashing vertical bar that shows where text will be inserted or deleted. When you navigate with the keyboard, the insertion point moves as you press the navigation keys. The I-beam is the mouse pointer that appears when you move the mouse over text. It does not show you where text will be inserted or deleted. In fact, its sole mission in life is to move the insertion point when you click. (If you're using the click-and-type feature, you need to double-click. This is discussed in Chapter 4's "Inserting Text" section.)

FIGURE 3.8

The insertion point shows you where text will be inserted or deleted; the I-beam lets you move the insertion point.

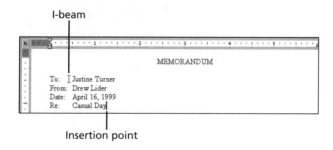

I-beam

Insertion point

Navigating with the Mouse

To navigate with the mouse, simply point to the location where you want to place the insertion point and click. If the location is currently offscreen, you need to use the scrollbars or the Browse buttons to scroll the location into view, as described in the next two sections.

Using the Scrollbars

Word provides a vertical scrollbar on the right side of the Word window and a horizontal scrollbar across the bottom of the window. You will frequently use the vertical scrollbar to scroll up and down through your document. By default, the entire width of your document is visible in the Word window, so you rarely need to use the horizontal scrollbar.

> When you use the scrollbar to scroll a document, the insertion point doesn't move to the portion of the document that you've scrolled onscreen until you click.

You can click the up and down arrows at either end of the vertical scrollbar to scroll approximately one line at a time. To scroll more quickly, point to the up or down arrow and hold down the mouse button. To move longer distances, it's faster to drag the scroll box along the scrollbar. As you drag, a ScreenTip tells you what page you are on, and, if your document has headings, what section of the document you're in (see Figure 3.9).

FIGURE 3.9

Page 8 of this nine-page document is scrolled into view.

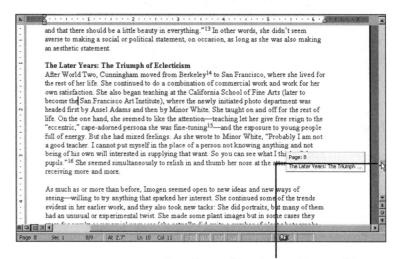

Drag the scroll box to travel longer distances.

To scroll up one screen at a time, click directly on the scrollbar above the scroll box; to scroll down one screen at a time, click the scrollbar below the scroll box.

Using the Browse Buttons

Browsing is a fast way to move sequentially through your document. You can use several types of objects as the focus point for browsing—including pages headings, graphics, and footnotes—and you can change the browse object at any time. To browse, you use the three Browse buttons in the lower-right corner of the Word window (see Figure 3.10).

FIGURE 3.10

The Browse buttons let you move sequentially through your document.

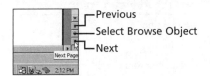

The default option is to browse by page, so the ScreenTips for the Next and Previous buttons are *Next Page* and *Previous Page*. Click the Next Page button to travel directly to the top of the next page; click the Previous Page button to go to the top of the previous page.

If you want to browse by a different type of object, click the Select Browse Object button. Word displays a grid containing various browse objects (see Figure 3.11). Point to each square to see its description in the gray area at the bottom of the grid. Some objects, such as Field and Comment, are useful only if you have used certain features in your document. The two squares on the left end of the lower row, Go To and Find, display the Find and Replace dialog box. (Go To is described in "Jumping to a Specific Page" later in this chapter, and Find is described in Chapter 8's "Editing Shortcuts" section.) Select the object that you want to use, and click OK.

FIGURE 3.11

Click the Select Browse Object and choose an object to browse by in the grid.

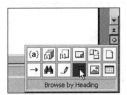

As soon as you choose a browse object other than Page, the Next and Previous buttons turn blue, and their ScreenTips change to reflect the currently selected object (*Next*

Heading and *Previous Heading*, for example). Clicking these buttons now takes you to the next or previous instance of the browse object you selected.

Navigating with the Keyboard

You can, if you like, move the insertion point through an entire document by using only the four arrow keys (see the first four items in Table 3.1), but you won't get anywhere fast. To navigate more efficiently, use the keyboard shortcuts listed after the arrow keys in Table 3.1. Learning these shortcuts will save you huge amounts of time later as you're editing your documents.

TABLE 3.1. Keyboard Techniques for Moving the Insertion Point

Keyboard Technique	Moves the Insertion Point
↓	Down one line
↑	Up one line
→	One character to the right
←	One character to the left
Ctrl+→	One word to the right
Ctrl+←	One word to the left
Ctrl+↓	Down one paragraph
Ctrl+↑	Up one paragraph
End	To the end of the line
Home	To the beginning of the line
Page Down	Down one screen
Page Up	Up one screen
Ctrl+Page Down	To the top of the next page
Ctrl+Page Up	To the top of the previous page
Ctrl+End	End of document
Ctrl+Home	Beginning of document

Jumping to a Specific Page

When you're typing a long document, you often need to get to a particular page to make a change. You can, of course, navigate to that page by using the standard mouse and keyboard techniques described in this chapter. However, it's often faster to use Word's Go To feature, which enables you to jump directly to any page in your document.

Jump to a Specific Page

To use the Go To command to jump to a specific page, follow these steps:

1. Choose Edit, Go To to display the Go To tab of the Find and Replace dialog box.
2. Type the number of the page in the Enter Page Number text box (see Figure 3.12).

FIGURE 3.12

Type the desired page number in the Enter Page Number text box.

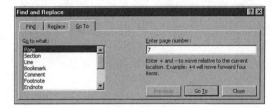

3. Click the Go To button (or press Enter). Word jumps to the page you specified. (You can check the page number in the status bar to confirm this.)
4. Repeat steps 2 and 3 if you want to go to other pages. Otherwise, click the Close button.

One unusual aspect of the Find and Replace dialog box (and a few other dialog boxes as well), is that you can click outside of the dialog box and edit your text while the dialog box is open. Most dialog boxes close as soon as you click the OK button, and you can't edit your document while the dialog box is displayed.

Word leaves the Find and Replace dialog box open after you click the Go To button so that you can continue using the dialog box to jump to other pages in the document. If you need to edit text on the current page, click outside of the dialog box to deactivate it and activate the document. The dialog box's title bar turns gray to let you know that it no longer has the focus. Revise your text, and then click the title bar of the dialog box to activate it again. You can then use the Go To command to travel to another page. When you're finished using Go To, click the Close button in the dialog box.

As you can see in Figure 3.12, the Go to What list in the Go To tab of the Find and Replace dialog box lets you go to other items besides pages. When you click a different item in this list—Line or Footnote, for example—the options on the right side of the dialog box change to enable you to tell Word which specific instance of the item you want to go to.

Summary

Typing in a word processing program is easy and straightforward. You now know how to type simple documents and navigate within them. Don't worry about editing your text and correcting mistakes yet. You will learn many ways to revise your documents throughout the rest of this book. The most pressing task at the moment is learning how to save your documents so that you can come back to them later. You'll learn this and other document-management and text-editing techniques in the next chapter.

CHAPTER 4

Managing Documents and Revising Text

You're now ready to learn how to manage your Word documents and enter and edit text. You can type and format all of your documents from scratch, but you don't have to. Word's templates can help you create a variety of documents, from memos and letters to fax cover sheets, résumés, and reports. You should also explore the wizards that ask you a series of questions and then create "made-to-order" documents based on your answers.

In Word, you spend the bulk of your time with editing text. Here, you learn the skills required to polish your documents. You will learn to insert new text, delete unwanted text, and move and copy text from one spot to another within your documents.

Saving Documents

As you are typing a new document, it exists only in your computer's memory. When soon as you turn off your computer, memory is wiped clean and everything in it is lost. For this reason, you need to save your documents to a permanent storage medium, such as your hard disk, a removable disk such as a floppy disk or a Zip disk, or a network drive (if you're on a network).

Saving a Document for the First Time

Before you save a document for the first time, Word assigns it a temporary name, such as *Document1*, and if you create another document before closing the first one, Word names the second one *Document2* and so on.

As soon as you decide that the document you're typing is worth saving, follow these steps:

1. Click the Save button on the Standard toolbar (or choose File, Save). Because this is the first time you are saving the document, Word displays the Save As dialog box to ask what you want to name the file and where you want to store it (see Figure 4.1).

Places Bar   Save In box   Up One Level

FIGURE 4.1

Use the Save As dialog box to choose a name and location for your file.

2. Look at the location in the Save In box. If you want to save the file in this location, skip to step 5. Otherwise, continue with the next step.

3. Click the down arrow to the right of the Save In list, and click the drive on which you want to save the file. (The main area of the dialog box then lists the drives and folders to which you have access if you run on your network.)

4. Double-click folders in the main area of the dialog box until the desired folder appears in the Save In box. If you want to move back to a parent folder (the folder that contains the folder in the Save In box), click the Up One Level button.

5. Type the filename that you want to use in the File Name text box. Word automatically adds the extension .doc to the name. (Depending on your Windows settings, your file extensions may not be visible.)

6. Click the Save button.

Word saves your document. If it finds an existing document in the same folder with the same name, Word tells you and gives you a chance to type a new name or replace the existing file.

Saving As You Work

After you've saved your document for the first time, you need to continue to save it every few minutes as you work on it. Each time you save, Word updates the copy of the file on your hard disk with the copy on your screen (in memory). If you save religiously, then in the event of a crash or power outage, you lose, at most, a few minutes' worth of work.

To save your document periodically, click the Save button on the Standard toolbar (or choose File, Save or press Ctrl+S). It looks like nothing is happening when you issue the Save command because Word assumes that you want to keep the same filename and location, so it automatically overwrites the original file on disk without asking you any questions.

Saving a Document with a New Name or Location

If you want to create a document that's very similar to one you have already saved, you don't need to type the new document from scratch. Rather, you can open the first document, make changes to it, and then save the new document under a different name or in a different location. Because you're giving the document a new name, it won't overwrite the original file. For example, you can create monthly invoices for a particular company by opening the previous month's invoice, changing the invoice number and other details, and then saving the revised invoice under a new name.

Recovering Documents After Crashes or Power Outages

As you're typing a document, you may have noticed that at periodic intervals the Save icon (the icon that appears on the Save toolbar button) flashes briefly at the right end of the status bar. When this happens, Word's AutoRecover features is taking a "snapshot" of your document (saving a copy of the file in its current state). By default, the AutoRecover feature updates this snapshot every ten minutes when the document is open. If you close the document normally, it deletes the AutoRecover information.

However, if a computer crash or power outage prevents you from saving your document before Word closes, Word keeps the most recent snapshot for you. If you did not save for a long period of time before the crash or outage, the snapshot can contain a much more current version of your document than the one you most recently saved.

The next time you turn the computer on and start Word, Word displays the AutoRecover snapshot with the word *Recovered* in the title bar. If you want Word to replace the copy you most recently saved with this AutoRecover version, choose File, Save As, click the filename in the Save As dialog box, and click Save. When Word asks whether you want to replace the original file, click the Yes button.

> You can adjust the time between autosaves by displaying the Options dialog box and clicking the Save tab. Make sure the Save AutoRecover Info Every X Minutes check box is marked, change the number of minutes, and click OK.

Opening Documents

When you want to work on a file that you previously saved to disk, you have to tell Word to open it. Click the Open button or choose File, Open to display the Open dialog box. You can open a document from a location that is not shown by selecting from the Look In box. Once you see the document filename you want to open, select the file and Word loads the document.

Switching Among Open Documents

You can open as many Word documents at a time as you like. In general, however, it's best to use a little restraint. The more documents you have open, the slower your computer runs. When you have more than one Word document open, you can easily switch among them.

Each document that you open appears in its own Word window, with its own taskbar button. The simplest way to switch from one to another is to click their taskbar buttons. In Figure 4.2, six Word windows are open. The active Word window is maximized, so the other Word windows are hidden behind it.

You can also switch among open documents by using the Window menu in any Word window. All of your open documents are listed at the bottom of the Window menu (see Figure 4.3), and a check mark appears next to the one that's currently active. Click the desired document to switch to it.

FIGURE 4.2

Click the taskbar button of an open document to switch to it.

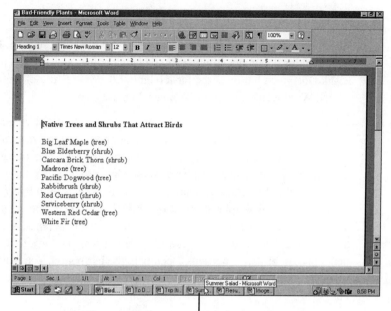

When you point to a taskbar button, the entire document name appears in a ScreenTip.

4

FIGURE 4.3

Click the document that you want to switch to at the bottom of the Window menu.

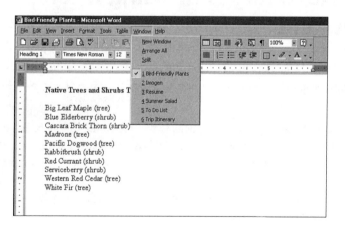

You can switch among all of your open windows, including the Word windows, by using the Alt+Tab keyboard combination. Press and hold down the Alt key as you press the Tab key to display a small window containing icons for each open window.

Starting New Documents

Word presents a new blank document when you start the program. If, after you've started typing in this document, you decide to begin another new document, click the New Blank Document button at the far-left end of the Standard toolbar (or press Ctrl+N). A second Word window opens with a new blank document.

When you use the New Blank Document toolbar button to start a document, Word assumes that you want to base the document on the *Normal template*. All Word documents are based on a template, which is like a blueprint for a document that includes formatting and possibly text. The Normal template produces a plain-vanilla blank document with all of Word's default formatting. Word also comes with many other templates (including special templates called *wizards*) that can help you create a wide variety of documents, including letters, memos, fax cover sheets, reports, and so on. If you want to base your new document on one of these templates, you have to use the File, New command instead of the New Blank Document toolbar button. You learn how to use other templates in the next section, and in Chapter 7 you'll learn how to create your own templates.

The Advantages of Using a Template or Wizard

The most obvious advantage of using a template (or wizard) is that either is quicker than creating documents from scratch. If you use a template that includes the standard text that doesn't change from one document to the next, you can avoid the tedium of typing this text yourself.

Another benefit of using templates is that the formatting is handled for you. Professionals who know how to use Word's formatting features to their best advantage designed the templates that come with Word. With the help of templates, you can produce documents with sophisticated formatting that you haven't yet learned how to apply yourself (although by the end of this book, you will know how to apply most of the formatting included in Word templates).

Templates also enable you to create a consistent look for all your documents. This is especially helpful in an office, where you can use templates to standardize the letters, memos, reports, and so on that you and your co-workers generate.

Finally, templates can be used repeatedly without ever being overwritten. If you have to type the same basic document over and over, each time making only minor changes to it, a template can contain all the standard text and formatting and you simply make changes as needed and save those changes in a separate document.

Wizards are step-by-step questions that Word asks you as Word creates a new document template that suits your needs.

Selecting a Template or Wizard

When you click the New Blank Document button in the Standard toolbar to start a new document, Word assumes that you want to base the document on the Normal template. If you want to use a different template or wizard, you have to use the File, New command.

Follow these steps to start a document based on a template or wizard other than the Normal template:

1. Choose File, New to display the New dialog box (see Figure 4.4).

FIGURE 4.4

Use the New dialog box to choose a template other than the Normal template.

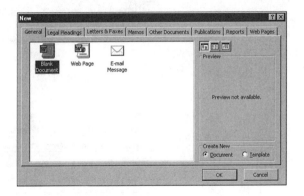

2. Click the tab that contains the template or wizard that you want to use.

3. Click the icon for the template or wizard, and check the Preview area on the right side of the dialog box. If you see the message "Template not installed yet. Click OK to install it now." dig out your Office or Word CD and insert it into your CD-ROM drive. (As soon as you click OK, Word will copy the necessary files from the CD to your hard drive.)

4. If the template is already installed, you'll see a picture of it in the Preview area of the New dialog box. The Preview area enables you to see what your finished document might look like.

5. Click OK (or double-click the template or wizard).

In a moment, you'll see a new document based on the template or wizard. You need to complete the document by adding your personalized text.

Creating a Document with a Template

Each template is unique, but there are a few characteristics that crop up in most of them. The Contemporary Fax and template is one common example.

To create a fax cover sheet from the Contemporary Fax template, follow these steps:

1. Choose File, New to display the New dialog box.

2. Click the Letters & Faxes tab, and double-click Contemporary Fax.

3. If the template isn't already installed, Word installs it now (make sure to have your Office CD handy). A document based on the Contemporary Fax template then appears onscreen (see Figure 4.5).

FIGURE 4.5

A document based on the Contemporary Fax template, before it's been filled in.

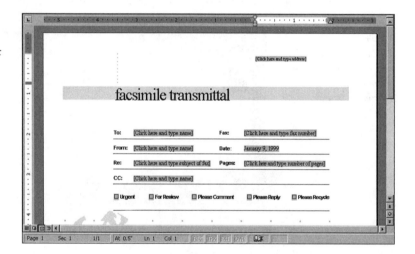

4. In the upper-right corner, click the gray [Click Here and Type Address] text. (The prompts are gray to indicate that you need to replace them with your own text. The gray color won't print.) Type your address, pressing Enter after each line. The text you type replaces the dummy text.

5. Continue to replace the other [Click Here and Type] prompts with the text that you want to include in the fax coversheet. If you want to leave an area blank (for example, you don't want to type a name after cc:), click the prompt text and press Delete.

6. Double-click any of the check boxes (Urgent, For Review, Please Comment, and so on) in which you want to mark to place a check mark. (You can double-click when your I-beam mouse pointer is over the check box.)

7. In the body of the memo, drag over the text following the word Notes: to select it. (To drag, press and hold down your mouse button as you move the mouse pointer

across the text. The text becomes selected as you drag.) Type over it with the text that you want in the body of the memo. Your new memo should now be completely filled in.

8. Click the Save button in the Standard toolbar. In the Save As dialog box, notice that Word Document is selected in the Save As Type drop-down list. Doing so tells you that Word saved the file as a Word document, and not as a template, so it won't overwrite the template itself. Choose a name and location for the file, and click the Save button.

9. Click the Close button in upper-right corner of the Word window to close the document.

Creating a Document with a Wizard

Wizards give you as much hand-holding as possible, short of sending you the final document in the mail. Here, you practice using two kinds of wizards. The first one, the Memo Wizard, is an example of the standard type that you find in the New dialog box. You progress through a series of dialog boxes, answering a different set of questions in each one. Clicking Finish at the end generates the document. The second one, the Letter Wizard, is a bit atypical. You access it through the Tools menu, not the New dialog box, and instead of presenting a series of dialog boxes, it gives you only one dialog box, with all of the questions arranged in different tabs. After you've made your selections in each tab, you click OK to generate the document.

4

The Memo Wizard

When you need to dash off a quick memo, the Memo Wizard can be a great help. It fills in most of the details so you need to do little more than type the memo text.

Use the Memo Wizard to Create a Memo

To create a memo by using the Memo Wizard, follow these steps:

1. Choose File, New to display the New dialog box.

2. Click the Memos tab, and double-click Memo Wizard.

3. If the wizard isn't already installed, Word installs it now (insert your Office CD if necessary).

4. The first of the Wizard dialog boxes appears onscreen (see Figure 4.6). Along the left side of the dialog box is a "progress line" that shows you all of the steps you'll go through to get from start to finish. This progress line appears in all of the wizard dialog boxes. As you move through the wizard, the box next to the current step turns green so that you know where you are.

FIGURE 4.6

The first dialog box of the Memo Wizard.

The progress line lets you keep track of where you are in the wizard.

5. Click Next to move to the next dialog box, and choose the style for your memo. Continue clicking Next to move from one dialog box to the next, answering the wizard's questions about the memo title, heading fields, recipient, and so on. If you change your mind about the options you chose in a previous dialog box, click the Back button to move back to it and change your settings, and then click Next to get back to where you were.

6. When you get to the last step, click the Finish button. A memo that incorporates all of your instructions appears onscreen. Replace the [Click Here and Type Your Memo Text] prompt with the text you want in the memo (see Figure 4.7).

FIGURE 4.7

Type the body of the memo; the wizard has done everything else for you.

7. Save and close the document.

The Letter Wizard

The Letter Wizard, although different in its appearance, performs the same role as the Memo Wizard. If you don't have much time to compose a letter, you should find it helpful.

To create a letter by using the Letter Wizard, follow these steps:

1. Choose Tools, Letter Wizard to display the Letter Wizard dialog box, as shown in Figure 4.8.

FIGURE 4.8

Design your letter in the Letter Wizard dialog box.

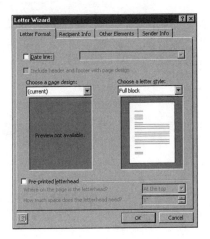

4

2. In the Letter Format tab, mark the Date Line check box if you want a date at the top of the letter, and choose the format for the date in the drop-down list to the right of the check box. Choose a page design and a letter style in the two drop-down lists in the middle of the dialog box. If you have preprinted letterhead, mark the Pre-Printed Letterhead check box, and specify where the letterhead is on the page and how much space it needs.

3. Click the Recipient Info tab and fill in the recipient's name and address and the salutation.

4. Click the Other Elements tab. If you want to include a reference line, mailing instructions, an attention line, or a subject line, mark the appropriate check boxes. For each check box you mark, choose the exact text from the associated drop-down list, or type your own text in the box at the top of the list. At the bottom of the dialog box, type the names of any people who you want to receive courtesy copies.

5. Click the Sender Info tab, and fill in the sender's name and address. Mark the Omit check box if you are using letterhead that includes the return address. Under Closing at the bottom of the dialog box, choose standard text from the drop-down

lists for the complimentary closing, your job title, and so on, or type your own text in the text boxes at the top of each list. The Preview area shows what your closing will look like.

6. After you've made your selections, click OK.

7. The letter appears onscreen. Type the body of the letter (see Figure 4.9) and then save and close it.

FIGURE 4.9

A letter written with the help of the Letter Wizard.

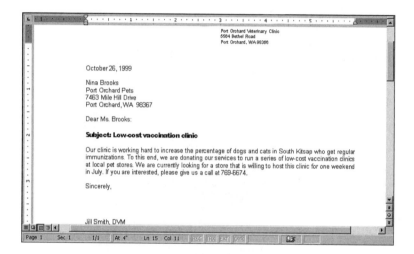

Inserting Text

When you want to insert text in the middle of text that you've already typed, Word assumes that you want the existing text to move out of the way to make room for the new text. Word calls this default behavior *insert mode*. To insert text, then, you simply move the insertion point to the place where you want the text to go and start typing. Any text to the right of the insertion point shifts over as you type. Note that when you insert text, you usually need to add a space either at the beginning or the end of the insertion.

Typing over Existing Text

Once in a while, you might want the text that you insert to replace existing text. To do this, press the Insert key to switch to *Overtype mode*. When you're using Overtype mode, every character you press replaces the character immediately to the right of the insertion point. The Insert key is a toggle, so you press it again when you want to return to Insert mode.

Watch your screen carefully when you're using Overtype mode. If you forget that you're in Overtype mode and merrily type away, you'll likely replace not only the text you wanted to delete but a sizable chunk of text that you wanted to keep as well.

Double-Clicking to Move the Insertion Point Anywhere on the Page

Word introduces *click-and-type,* a feature that enables you to start typing in a blank area of your document by simply double-clicking at the desired location. For example, you can double-click in the middle of the page to center your text, double-click on the right margin to make the text flush right, or double-click several lines below your last line of text to create a large block of white space above the text. You don't have to first change your alignment, insert custom tabs, or press Enter repeatedly to create white space at the end of the document. (You learn about alignment and custom tabs in Chapter 6, "Formatting Characters, Paragraphs, and Pages.") Word makes these changes for you when you double-click.

Click-and-type works only in Print Layout view and Web Layout view. To make sure you're using Print Layout view (Web Layout view is useful only if you're using Word to design Web pages), choose View, Print Layout. You learn more about views in the next chapter.

4

To practice using click-and-type, start a new document, and move your I-beam to the right margin of the page. After a moment, an icon appears next to the I-beam indicating your text is right-aligned (see Figure 4.10). Double-click to move the insertion point to this spot. If you start typing, your text is flush against the right margin.

Figure 4.10

This click-and-type I-beam indicates right alignment.

If double-clicking doesn't move the insertion point, choose View, Print Layout if you haven't already. Choose Tools, Options, click the Edit tab, make sure the Enable Click and Type check box is marked, and click OK.

Now position the I-beam about halfway across the page. The I-beam icon changes to indicate center alignment. Double-click to move the insertion point. Any text you type now is centered horizontally on the page.

Next, point to a location approximately midway between the horizontal center of the page and the left margin. The I-beam icon indicates left alignment. Double-click to move the insertion point. If you start typing now, your text is left-aligned at the location you double-clicked.

Finally, move the I-beam several inches down from the top margin of the page, and double-click. Word moves the insertion point down to the line you double-clicked on. If you start typing now, you have several blank lines above your text.

Combining and Splitting Paragraphs

As you're typing, you may at times want to combine two paragraphs into one, or split a longer paragraph into two or more shorter ones. While there is nothing mysterious about doing this, it can be a little puzzling to beginners.

To join two paragraphs, click at the very end of the first paragraph, just past the period, and press the Delete key one or more times until the second paragraph moves up to join the first. (Alternatively, you can click at the very beginning of the second paragraph and press the Backspace key one or more times.) You may need to add a space where the two paragraphs came together.

When you press the Delete or Backspace key to join paragraphs, you're actually removing the hidden paragraph marks separating the paragraphs. (See "Deleting Text" later in this chapter for more about deleting hidden characters.) Remember that you can click the Show/Hide button in the Standard toolbar to make paragraph marks and other hidden characters visible.

To split a paragraph into two separate ones, click just before the first letter of the sentence that begins the second paragraph, and press Enter. If you want a blank line between the two paragraphs, press Enter again.

Selecting Text

Selecting (highlighting) text is an essential word processing skill. In many situations, you have to select text before issuing a command so that Word knows what text you want the command to affect. For example, you have to select text before cutting and pasting it or applying many kinds of formatting.

The most basic way of selecting text is to drag across it with the mouse. To do this, you position the I-beam at the beginning of the text you want to select, press and hold down the mouse button, drag across the text, and then release the mouse button. When text is selected, it becomes white against a black background, as shown in Figure 4.11. If you want to deselect text (remove the highlighting) without doing anything to it, click anywhere in the text area of the Word window, or press a navigation key such as one of the arrow keys, Home, or End.

FIGURE 4.11

Selected text is white against a black background.

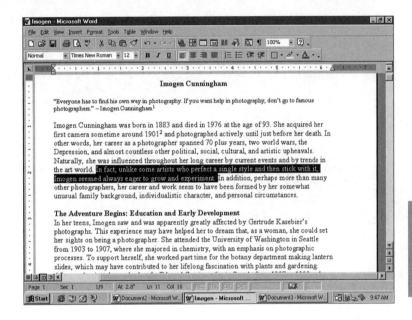

If you accidentally drag over too much text, you can remove the extra text from the selection by keeping the mouse button held down as you drag back up and/or to the left.

Although dragging always works to select text, it is often not the most efficient method. Table 4.1 lists some shortcuts for selecting different amounts of text.

Three of the shortcuts involve clicking in the *selection bar,* the white area in the left margin of the page. When the mouse pointer is in this area, it becomes a white arrow angled toward your text. Some of the shortcuts also require you to Ctrl+click or Shift+click—in other words, hold down the Ctrl key or Shift key as you click.

TABLE 4.1   Selection Shortcuts

Amount of Text Selected	Shortcut
One word	Double-click the word.
One sentence	Ctrl+click the sentence.
One line	Click in the selection bar to the left of the line.
One paragraph	Double-click in the selection bar to the left of the paragraph. (You can also triple-click directly on the paragraph.)
Entire document	Triple-click or Ctrl+click anywhere in the selection bar.
Any amount of text	Click at the beginning of the text you want to select, and then Shift+click at the end of the text.

If you like using the keyboard, you may prefer to select text by using only the keyboard. All of the keyboard selection techniques involve adding the Shift key to a navigation keyboard shortcut (whichever one travels the distance that you want to select). Table 4.2 lists some of the most common keyboard selection techniques.

TABLE 4.2   Keyboard Selection Techniques

Keyboard Technique	Amount Selected
Shift+→	One character to the right
Shift+←	One character to the left
Shift+↓	One line down
Shift+↑	One line up
Shift+Ctrl+→	One word to the right
Shift+Ctrl+←	One word to the left
Shift+Ctrl+↓	One paragraph down
Shift+Ctrl+↑	One paragraph up
Shift+End	From the insertion point to the end of the line
Shift+Home	From the insertion point to the beginning of the line
Shift+Ctrl+End	From the insertion point to the end of the document
Shift+Ctrl+Home	From the insertion point to the beginning of the document
Ctrl+A	The entire document (same as choosing Edit, Select All)

With the keyboard techniques involving pressing an arrow key, you can add to the selection by keeping the other keys in the combination held down as you repeatedly press the arrow key. For example, to select six words to the right, you would hold down the Shift and Ctrl keys as you pressed the right-arrow key six times.

Deleting Text

Knowing how to delete text is almost as important as knowing how to type it in the first place. Although you can delete any amount of text if you bang on the Delete or Backspace key enough times, it's much more efficient to use other methods when you want to select more than a few characters. Table 4.3 lists techniques for deleting different amounts of text.

TABLE 4.3 Techniques for Deleting Text

Technique	Result
Delete key	Deletes character to the right of the insertion point
Backspace key	Deletes character to the left of the insertion point
Ctrl+Delete	Deletes word to the right of the insertion point
Ctrl+Backspace	Deletes word to the left of the insertion point
Select text and press the Delete key	Deletes selected text (can be any amount)
Select text and start typing	Deletes selected text (can be any amount) and replaces it with the text you type

To delete several words, hold down the Ctrl key as you press Delete or Backspace several times. If you want to delete only the end of a word—for example, you want to change the word *functionality* to *function*—click in front of the part you want to delete (before the letter *a* in this example) and press Ctrl+Delete. If you want to delete the beginning of a word—to change the word *ultraconservative* to *conservative,* for instance—click just after the part you want to delete (just past the letter *a* in this example) and press Ctrl+Backspace.

Word treats paragraph marks, tabs, and spaces just like other characters, so you can delete them with the Delete and Backspace keys, just as you delete other characters. In most cases, it's obvious where they are even though they are hidden. At times, however, you may find it helpful to display these hidden characters onscreen so that you can see exactly where they are. To do this, click the Show/Hide button in the Standard toolbar. (You learned about the Show/Hide feature in the section "Seeing Your Paragraph, Tab, and Space Marks" in the previous chapter.)

Undoing Mistakes

If you know how to delete text, you surely want to know how to restore it when you delete it accidentally. Word's Undo feature enables you to bring back deleted text as well as undo many other actions. You are not limited to undoing the most recent action you performed; Undo enables you to undo multiple actions. For example, if you delete a paragraph by mistake and then go on to issue a few more commands before realizing that the paragraph was gone, you can undo all of your actions back to, and including, the deletion.

Word cannot undo saving or printing commands.

To undo the most recent action, click the Undo button on the Standard toolbar or press Ctrl+Z. To continue undoing previous actions one by one, keep clicking the Undo button or pressing Ctrl+Z.

If you know that you want to undo something you did a few minutes ago and don't want to click the Undo button several times, click the down arrow to the right of the Undo button. This displays a list of all of your actions, with the most recent action at the top (see Figure 4.12). Scroll down the list and click the action that you want to undo. Word undoes all of your actions back to and including the one you click.

FIGURE 4.12

Click an action in the Undo drop-down list to undo everything back to that point.

If you undo an action and then decide that you want to perform it after all, click the Redo button on the Standard toolbar or press Ctrl+Y or F4. As with Undo, you can redo multiple actions by clicking the button repeatedly, or by choosing an action in the Redo drop-down list.

Cutting and Pasting

The capability to move and copy text from one place to another is one of the most appreciated features of word processing programs. The term *cutting and pasting* actually refers to both moving and copying text. When you *move* text, you remove (*cut*) it from one location in your document and paste it in another. When you *copy* text, you leave the text in its original location and paste a duplicate of it somewhere else.

The location that contains the text you want to move or copy is called the *source*, and the place you want to paste it is called the *destination*. The destination can be in the same document, another Word document, another Office document (such as an Excel spreadsheet or a PowerPoint presentation), or a document created in another Windows application.

When you cut or copy text, it is placed on the Windows Clipboard, a temporary storage area available to all Windows applications. Issuing the Paste command copies the text from the Windows Clipboard into your document. (It actually stays on the Windows Clipboard until you perform the next cut or copy, so you can paste the same text multiple times if you like.)

Moving Text

As you're typing a document, you'll probably want to restructure it a bit. You may need to move a word or phrase within a sentence, reorganize the flow of sentences within a paragraph, or change the order of some paragraphs.

Follow these steps to move text:

1. Select the text that you want to move.
2. Click the Cut button on the Standard toolbar or press Ctrl+X. The text disappears from its current location.
3. Navigate to the destination, and place the insertion point exactly where you want the text to appear.

   If the destination is in a different document, copy the data to your Clipboard. Then, open the second document and click the document's taskbar button to switch to it, and then navigate to the place where you want to insert the text.
4. Click the Paste button in the Standard toolbar or press Ctrl+V. The text is pasted into the destination, and existing text to the right of the insertion point moves over to make room for the inserted text.

Copying Text

If you want to insert a block of text that you've already typed somewhere else, it's much faster to copy it than to type it from scratch.

Follow these steps to copy text:

1. Select the text that you want to copy.
2. Click the Copy button on the Standard toolbar or press Ctrl+C. The original text remains in its current location.

4

3. Navigate to the destination, and make sure that the insertion point is exactly where you want the text to appear. (See the note in the steps for moving text in the preceding section if the destination is not in the current document.)

4. Click the Paste button in the Standard toolbar or press Ctrl+V. The text is pasted into the destination, and existing text to the right of the insertion point moves over to make room for the inserted text.

> If you want to copy an entire file into the current document, click at the location where you want to insert the file, choose Insert, File, select the file in the Insert File dialog box, and click the Insert button.

Moving and Copying with Drag-and-Drop

If you are handy with the mouse, you may find it easiest to move and copy text with *drag-and-drop*. This feature enables you to select text and then drag it to its destination. Drag-and-drop is best suited for moving or copying small amounts of text a short distance.

To move text with drag-and-drop, select the text that you want to move or copy and release the mouse button. Point to the selected text. The mouse pointer becomes a white arrow. Drag the selection to the destination. As you drag, the mouse pointer indicates that you're performing a drag-and-drop. Drag until the dashed insertion point attached to the mouse pointer is in the right place, and then release the mouse button.

To copy the text instead of dragging it, Ctrl+drag it to the destination (hold down the Ctrl key as you drag). The drag-and-drop mouse pointer gains a plus sign to indicate that you're performing a copy, not a move. When the dashed insertion point is in the right place, release the mouse button and then the Ctrl key. (If you release the Ctrl key before the mouse button, Word performs a cut instead of a copy.)

Once you drag or copy the text, click in the document anywhere to deselect the text.

If you accidentally drop the selected text in the wrong place, click the Undo button on the Standard toolbar.

Moving and Copying Multiple Items

With the traditional cut-and-paste procedure, you can cut or copy only one selection at a time. The Office Clipboard, enables you to "collect" up to 12 (24 with Office XP and later) selections of cut or copied data and then paste them in any order into any Office document. The Office Clipboard can handle all of the standard data types, including text, numbers, graphic images, and so on.

To practice using the Office Clipboard, follow these steps:

1. Choose View, Toolbars, Clipboard to display the Clipboard toolbar and the Office Clipboard.

2. Select a block of text in a Word document, and click the Cut or Copy button on the Standard toolbar, and then cut or copy another block of text in the document. Two Word icons appear on the Office Clipboard to represent the two items that you've cut or copied (see Figure 4.13).

FIGURE 4.13

Each item you cut or copy appears as an icon on the Office Clipboard.

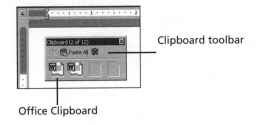

Clipboard toolbar

Office Clipboard

 Office XP and later uses a Clipboard Task Pane instead of the floating tool-bar to show you which items you've sent to the Office Clipboard. The Task Pane normally appears on the right of your screen. If you don't see the Task Pane, select View, Task Pane.

3. Cut or copy a couple more items to the Office Clipboard, and then point to one of them. A ScreenTip appears with the beginning of the text in that item so that you can identify it.

4. Click in a location where you want to insert one of the items on the Office Clipboard, and then click the item to paste it into that spot.

5. Paste some of the other items in the Office Clipboard if you like, and then click the Close button in the Clipboard toolbar to close it and the Office Clipboard.

 If the Clipboard toolbar is visible, you can click its Copy button instead of the Copy button in the Standard toolbar to copy text. If you want to paste all of the items in the Office Clipboard at once, click the Paste All button in the Clipboard toolbar. To remove all the items from the Office Clipboard, click the Clear Clipboard button (the button to the right of the Paste All button).

When the Clipboard toolbar is visible, you can cut or copy items from any Windows application to the Office Clipboard. (When it isn't visible, you can still use it to cut or copy items in an Office application.) Items that you've cut or copied from applications other than Word show as icons that match those applications.

Summary

If you need to dash off a letter, memo, or fax and don't have the time or inclination to fiddle with formatting, use a template or wizard. They can help you produce professional documents with a minimum of hassle.

Revising text is at the heart of word processing. As soon as the techniques described here become second nature, you'll be able to place your attention squarely on the content of your document, where it belongs, rather than the commands required to edit text. Word's editing features are so easy to master that you should feel comfortable tinkering with the text of your document in no time. In the next chapter, you learn different ways of viewing and printing your documents.

CHAPTER 5

Viewing and Printing Your Documents

Word offers a wide assortment of options for changing the appearance of your document onscreen. If you type only simple letters and memos, you may never need to change these settings. However, if you create documents with sophisticated formatting, have trouble reading small print, or want to view different parts of a document or more than one document at the same time, you can tailor the view options to suit your preferences. And when you've finished typing your documents and like their appearance onscreen, you'll most likely want to print them out.

Viewing Your Document

Word's view options are so plentiful that you can surely find one or two that work well for you. You can use any of these six views to work with your documents:

- Print Layout (View menu)
- Normal (View menu)

- Full Screen (View menu)
- Print Preview (File menu)
- Web Layout (View menu)
- Outline (View menu)

You'll learn about Print Layout, Normal, and Full Screen views in the next three sections. Print Preview is discussed in "Previewing a Document Before Printing." Web Layout view is covered in Chapter 13, "Using Word with the Web," and Outline view is explained in Chapter 8, "Correcting Documents and Using Columns and Tables."

You can switch to Normal, Web Layout, Print Layout, and Outline views by using the four View buttons in the lower-left corner of the Word window (see Figure 5.1).

FIGURE 5.1

Using the View buttons to switch among four of the views.

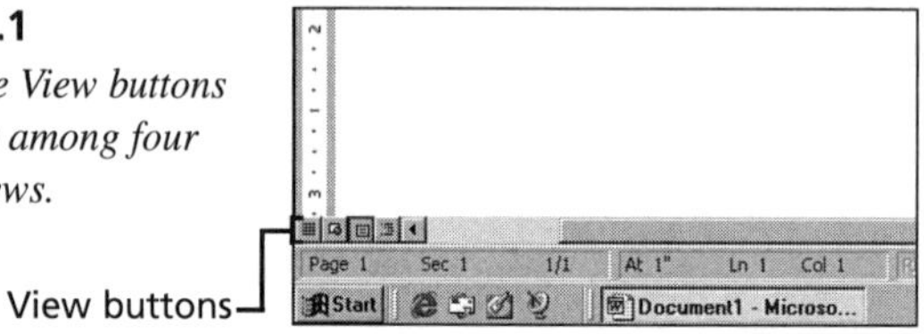

View buttons

Word remembers the view you choose for a document and uses it the next time you open the document.

Using Print Layout View

Print Layout view is the default view option, and it probably works for you most of the time. If you aren't sure whether you're using it, choose View, Print Layout or click the Print Layout View button in the lower-left corner of the Word window.

Print Layout view gives you the sense that you're typing directly onto a piece of paper (see Figure 5.2). It includes horizontal and vertical rulers so that you always know where your text appears on the page, and it shows you the top, bottom, left, and right margin areas. If you have typed text in the headers and footers (you learn how to do this in Chapter 6), it will be visible in the top and bottom margins. All page breaks (regardless of type) appear as a gap between the bottom edge of one page and the top edge of the next.

You don't have to use Print Layout view if you're typing documents with simple formatting. However, you do need to use it if you're working with more complex formatting such as columns, tables, and graphics. (These features do not display correctly in Normal view, described in the next section.)

FIGURE 5.2

Print Layout view enables you to see the margin areas of your document.

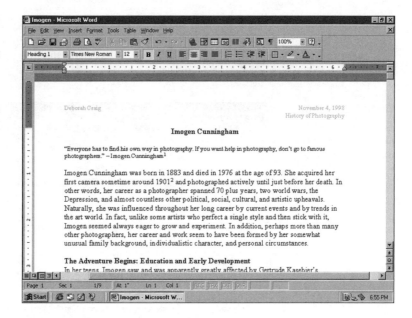

Using Normal View

In earlier versions of Word, Normal view was the default view option. Although Print Layout view is now the default, Normal view is still useful in some situations. To switch to it, choose View, Normal or click the Normal View button in the lower-left corner of the Word window.

Normal view displays only the horizontal ruler, not the vertical ruler. And it doesn't display the margin areas of the page, so you can't see headers and footers (see Figure 5.3).

One advantage of Normal view is that unlike Print Layout view, it shows you what type of page breaks are in your document. A soft page break—one that Word adds for you when the text flows on to the next page—appears as a dotted horizontal line running across the page. A hard page break—one that you insert to end a page before it's full—appears as a dotted horizontal line with the words *Page Break* on it. Figure 5.4 shows a soft and hard page break in Normal view.

Normal view also displays *section breaks*, which you have to use to apply certain kinds of formatting to only a portion of your document. You learn more about page and section breaks in Chapter 6, "Formatting Characters, Paragraphs, and Pages."

Using Full Screen View

If you like working in a completely uncluttered environment, you'll appreciate Full Screen view. To switch to this view, choose View, Full Screen. Your document window

5

enlarges to cover the entire desktop (see Figure 5.5). The title bar, menu bar, and toolbars in the Word window are temporarily hidden to give you as much room as possible to see your text. If you want to issue a menu command, point to the thin gray line running across the top of your screen to slide the menu bar into view.

FIGURE 5.3

Normal view doesn't display the margin areas of your document.

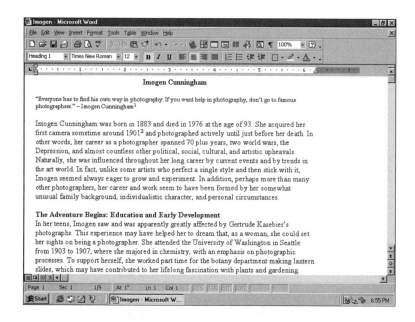

FIGURE 5.4

Switch to Normal view if you need to see what kind of page breaks are in your document.

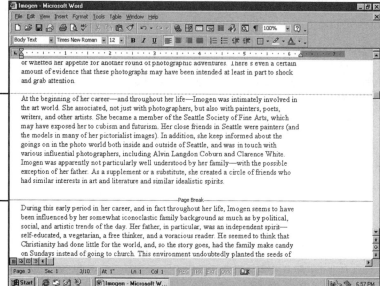

Soft page break ——

Hard page break ——

Point to the thin gray line to bring the menu bar into view.

FIGURE 5.5

Full Screen view gives you an uncluttered view of your document.

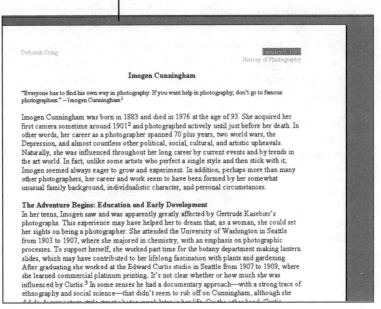

Full Screen view works in conjunction with whatever other view you are using, not in place of it. In Figure 7.5, the document is in Print Layout and Full Screen view. While you are in Full Screen view, you can switch among the other views as you like. When you are finished using Full Screen view, bring the menu bar into view and choose View, Full Screen again.

In the latest version of Word, a Reading View appears that eliminates all formatting codes and displays as much readable text as possible. You'll use the Reading View when loading long documents that you want to read more than edit.

Zooming Your Document

Word normally displays text at approximately the size it is when printed. In some situations, you might want to enlarge or shrink the text onscreen to make it easier to read, edit, and format. You change your document's magnification by adjusting the Zoom setting.

You might want to change your Zoom setting if your document has especially large or small fonts, if you're printing on a paper size other than 8 ½ by 11, or if your eyesight isn't what it used to be. When you shrink the magnification to anything less than 100%, the text appears smaller and you can see more of your document. When you enlarge the magnification to anything over 100%, the text appears bigger and you can see less of your document. Changing the magnification of your document onscreen does not affect the way it prints.

To change the Zoom setting, click the down-arrow to the right of the Zoom box at the right end of the Standard toolbar to display the Zoom list (see Figure 5.6), and then click the desired setting.

FIGURE 5.6

Choose the desired magnification setting in the Zoom list.

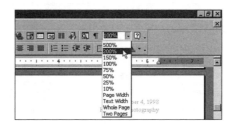

In Figure 5.7, the document has been zoomed to 200%. Word remembers the setting and uses it the next time you open the document.

FIGURE 5.7

The Zoom setting was changed to 200%.

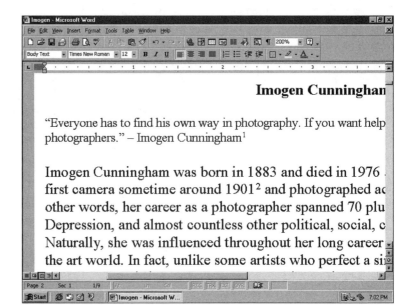

If you enlarge the magnification of your document, as shown in Figure 5.7, you may need to use the horizontal scrollbar at the bottom of the Word window to bring the right side of the document into view.

The four options at the bottom of the Zoom list also come in handy. They automatically adjust your document's magnification just the right amount to display the full width of the page (Page Width), the width of the text only (Text Width), the entire page (Whole Page), and two entire pages (Two Pages). In Normal view, the Text Width, Whole Page, and Two Pages options are not available. You can enter your own zoom magnification percentage, such as 85 in the Zoom box, to customize your viewing area.

Viewing Separate Parts of Your Document at the Same Time

With a longer document, you may find it convenient to view separate parts of it at the same time. For example, if you're typing a report that begins with a table of contents, you may want to keep it in view as you're typing later portions of the report to make sure that you're sticking to your outline.

To practice using this feature, open any document that is too long to fit onscreen. Then point to the *split bar*, the short horizontal bar directly above the up-arrow at the top of the vertical scrollbar (see Figure 5.8).

FIGURE 5.8

Drag the split bar to divide your screen into two panes.

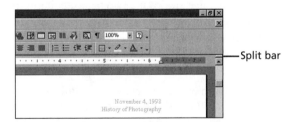

Split bar

5

When you point to the split bar, your mouse pointer changes to two horizontal lines with a vertical double arrow. Drag about halfway down the Word window. As you drag, a gray horizontal line shows where the window will be split. When the line is in the right place, release the mouse button.

Word divides the window into two *panes*. Each pane has its own rulers and scrollbars. Click in the lower pane to activate it, and then use its vertical scrollbar to scroll down in the document. As you scroll, the portion of the document displayed in the upper pane doesn't change. If you want to scroll the upper pane, click in it and then use its vertical scrollbar. The status bar at the bottom of the Word window shows you the page number of the active pane. In Figure 5.9, the first page of a 9-page document is displayed in the upper pane, and the last page is displayed in the lower pane.

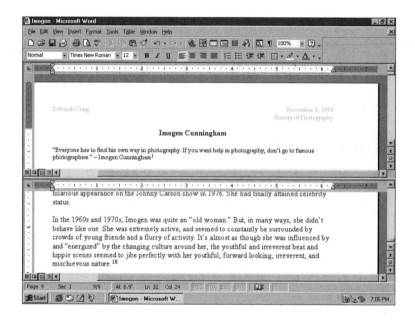

If you want to adjust the relative size of the two panes, point to the gray dividing line and drag it up or down. To remove the split, double-click the gray line or drag it all the way to the top of the Word window.

> When the Word window is split, you can drag and drop text from one pane into the other. This makes it easy to use drag-and-drop to move or copy text over long distances in a multiple-page document.

Arranging Word Documents on Your Screen

If you have more than one Word document open, you may want to display them next to one another to compare their content, or to drag and drop text between them.

To arrange your open Word documents so that all of them are visible, choose Window, Arrange All. Word tiles the documents so that they cover your entire desktop (see Figure 5.10). If you want to create more room to see your text in tiled Word windows, you can hide the rulers and place the Standard and Formatting toolbars on one row, as shown in

Figure 5.10. (To hide the rulers, choose View, Ruler. To put the Standard and Formatting toolbars on the same row, choose Tools, Customize, mark the Standard and Formatting Toolbars Share One Row check box, and click the Close button.)

FIGURE 5.10

The two open Word windows are visible at the same time.

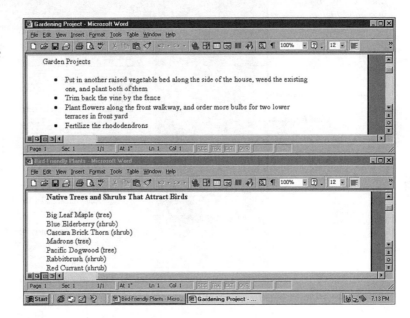

To return to viewing only one Word window, click the Maximize button in the upper-right corner of the window that you want to use.

5

Previewing a Document Before Printing

Word's Print Preview feature enables you to see what a document looks like before you send it to the printer. Using Print Preview is a great way of saving paper because you can catch things that you'd like to change before you print. To use Print Preview, click the Print Preview button on the Standard toolbar or choose File, Print Preview.

Word switches to Print Preview. When you're using this view, the title bar contains the word [Preview], and a Print Preview toolbar appears (see Figure 5.11).

To scroll through the document page by page, press the Page Down and Page Up keys. If you want to view several pages at once, click the Multiple Pages toolbar button and drag through the desired number of squares in the grid that drops down (each square represents a page). To go back to viewing one page, click the One Page toolbar button. If you want to print your document directly from Print Preview, click the Print toolbar button.

Print   Zoom   Shrink to Fit

FIGURE 5.11
*Print Preview gives
you a good idea of
what your document
will look like after it's
printed.*

Magnifier—

One Page—

Multiple Pages—

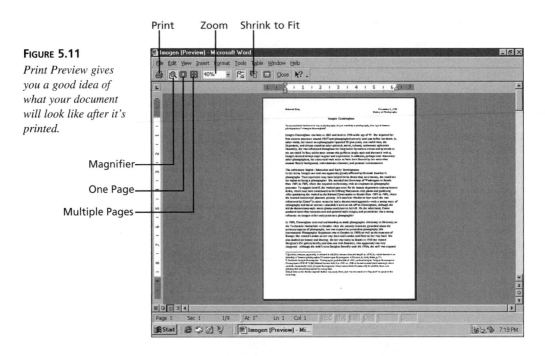

Another handy feature in Print Preview is Shrink to Fit. If you'd like your document to fit onto one page and it's spilling onto two (or you want it to fit onto two pages and it's spilling onto three, and so on), you can click the Shrink to Fit toolbar button to make it fit on one less page than it currently does. Word accomplishes this by making small adjustments to your document's formatting (reducing the font size, decreasing the amount of white space, and so on).

When you're finished using Print Preview, click the Close button at the right end of the Print Preview toolbar to return to the view you were using previously.

Printing Your Document

Word assumes that you frequently want to print a complete copy of your document, so it provides the Print button on the Standard toolbar enabling you to do just that. Clicking this button sends your document to the default printer without asking any questions at all.

If you want to customize your printing at all—by printing only certain pages or printing more than one copy, for example—you need to use the Print dialog box.

Follow these steps to print from the Print dialog box:

1. Choose File, Print or press Ctrl+P (see Figure 5.12).

FIGURE 5.12

Use the Print dialog box to customize your printing.

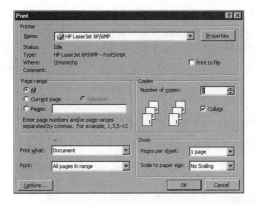

2. Check the printer listed in the Name drop-down list. If you have only one printer, you won't need to change this setting. If your computer is hooked up to multiple printers, you can select a different printer in this list.

3. Under Page Range, the All option button is marked by default. This option prints your entire document. To print only the page containing the insertion point, mark the Current Page option button. To print more than one page but not the entire document, type the page numbers you want to print in the Pages text box. Use commas to separate nonsequential pages and dashes indicate a range of pages. For example, you would type 1, 3-6, 8 to print pages 1, 3, 4, 5, 6, and 8. If you want to print only one block of text in your document, select the text before displaying the Print dialog box, and then mark the Selection option button.

4. If you want to print more than one copy of your document, enter the number in the Copies text box by typing it or clicking the spinner arrows.

5. Under Zoom, click the desired number of pages in the Pages per Sheet drop-down list if you want to print more than one document page on a sheet of paper. (You might do this to conserve paper.) Select a paper size in the Scale to Paper Size drop-down list to print on a different paper size than the one that's set for the document. (You learn how to set a document's paper size in Chapter 6.)

6. Click the OK button to send the document to the printer. (If you decide not to print, click the Cancel button.)

Printing Envelopes

Printing envelopes in Word is simple. You check the recipient's address and the return address, load your envelope in the printer, issue the command to print. Word assumes that you want to print on a standard business-size envelope, but you can choose a different envelope size if necessary.

5

You learn how to print several envelopes or labels for mass mailings in Chapter 10, "Mastering Mail Merge."

Follow these steps to print an envelope:

1. If you used Word to type the letter addressed to the recipient, open the letter now.

2. Choose Tools, Envelopes and Labels.

3. Click the Envelopes tab in the Envelopes and Labels dialog box (see Figure 5.13).

FIGURE 5.13

Use the Envelopes tab of the Envelopes and Labels dialog box to specify the addresses to print on your envelope.

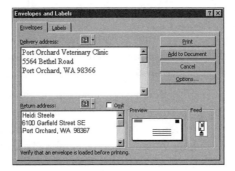

4. Word finds the address in the document you have open onscreen. Edit it in the Delivery Address box if needed.

5. Word automatically includes your return address on the envelope. If you have envelopes with a preprinted return address, mark the Omit check box.

6. If you want to print a return address, check the address in the Return Address box, and edit it if necessary.

7. If your envelope is not the standard business size, or if you want to change the font or position of the addresses, click the Options button to display the Envelope Options dialog box. Use the Envelope Size list to choose a different envelope size. To change fonts, click the Font button under Delivery Address or Return Address. To adjust the position of the return or recipient address, click the spinner arrows to the right of the appropriate From Left and From Right text boxes. When you're finished, click OK to return to the Envelopes and Labels dialog box.

8. Put the envelope in your printer and click the Print button to print it. Alternatively, you can click the Add to Document to add the envelope to the top of the current document so that it prints every time you print the document. (If you do this, remember to always have an envelope loaded when you print the document because it prints as the first page.)

> If you aren't sure how to feed your envelope into the printer, check the Feed area in the Envelopes tab of the Envelopes and Labels dialog box (see Figure 5.13). This diagram is usually correct. If it's not, check your printer's documentation for the right way to load the envelope.

9. If you changed your return address in step 6, Word asks whether you want to save the new address as the default return address. Click the Yes button if you want to use this return address in the future, or click No to use it just this once. Word finds your return address in the User Information tab of the Options dialog box. If you change it while printing an envelope, Word updates your address here. You can edit your return address and other user information at any time. To do so, choose Tools, Options, click the User Information tab, revise the information, and click OK.

Printing Labels

The steps for printing labels are very similar to those for printing envelopes. The one difference is that you'll likely need to choose another label type because labels come in such a wide variety of sizes.

Follow these steps to print a label:

1. Choose Tools, Envelopes and Labels.
2. Click the Labels tab in the Envelopes and Labels dialog box (see Figure 5.14).
3. Type or edit the address in the Address box. If you want to print your return address instead, mark the Use Return Address check box.
4. Click the Options button to display the Label Options dialog box.
5. Select the product number for your labels in the Product Number list, and click OK. (If you don't have standard Avery labels, choose a different label from the Label Products drop-down list.)

> The product number for most labels is printed on the packaging. If you can't find your labels' product number or it isn't in the Product Number list, click the New Label button in the Label Options dialog box. In the New Custom Laser dialog box (or New Custom Dot Matrix if you marked the Dot Matrix option button in the Label Options dialog box), type a name for your labels, enter their dimensions, and click OK. Your new label type is added to the Product Number list so you can choose it in the future.

5

FIGURE 5.14

Use the Labels tab of the Envelopes and Labels dialog box to specify the address to print on your label.

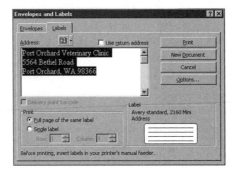

6. Mark the Full Page of the Same Label check box if you want a whole page of labels with the same address on each one.

7. If you want a single label, mark the Single Label option button, and then enter the label's row and column number.

8. Put the sheet of labels in your printer, and click the Print button to print the label or sheet of labels. (If you aren't sure which paper tray to use, check your printer's documentation.) If you are printing a sheet of labels and want to print them in the future, you can click the New Document button instead of the Print button. Word creates a separate one-page document of your labels. Save this document, print as many copies as you need, and then close it. You can open this document at any time in the future to print more of these labels.

Even though Word enables you to print a single label at a time, it is not a good idea to run a sheet of labels through a laser printer more than once. Doing so can cause labels to come off inside the printer, something that is not cheap to repair.

Summary

Word gives you all the flexibility you need for viewing and printing your documents. In addition to switching views, you can adjust the magnification of your documents, display different parts of a document at the same time, and tile open Word documents on the desktop. Before printing, you can preview your document to make sure it looks the way you want it to, and then optionally adjust your print job in a variety of ways.

CHAPTER **6**

Formatting Characters, Paragraphs, and Pages

The formatting that you can apply to individual characters—fonts, font sizes, bold, italic, underline, and so on—as well as paragraphs and entire pages is referred to as *font formatting*. You can apply font formatting to as little as one character, or as much as an entire document. Paragraph formatting includes all of the formatting that can affect, at a minimum, a single paragraph. Paragraph formatting features as alignment, line spacing, custom tabs, and indentation. Some of these you will almost certainly need at some point. *Page formatting* includes all of the formatting that affects the entire page, including margins, paper size, page numbers, and so on.

Applying Font Formatting

To make any changes to Word's default format setting, you use one of the font-formatting features. Keep these three points in mind:

- Typically, you need to select the text you want to format before issuing the formatting command.

> If you haven't yet typed the text that you want to format, you can place
> your insertion point at the location where you want to type, turn on the
> formatting options, and then type your text. The text takes on the format-
> ting you chose.

- The easiest way to tell what font, font size, font style (boldface, italic, underline), and font color has been applied to a block of text is to click in it. The options in the Formatting toolbar show you the formatting in effect wherever the insertion point is resting.

- If you want to apply the same font formatting to several blocks of text, a fast way to do it is to use the F4 key. F4, the *repeat key*, repeats whatever command you last issued. To increase the font size of several headings, for example, you could apply the new font size to the first heading, and then select the next heading, press F4, select the next heading, press F4, and so on.

Changing Fonts

The term *font* is used to refer to the typeface of your text. Each computer has a different set of fonts, depending on what software is installed and what printer you're using. Office detects what fonts you have available and enables you to select them in Word. As a general rule, it's best to use only one or two fonts in a document; any more and your document is likely to look overly busy.

The quickest way to change a font is to the use Font drop-down list in the Formatting toolbar, although you can also change fonts in the Font dialog box.

To apply a font using the Font list, follow these steps:

1. Select the text you want to change.
2. Click the down-arrow to the right of the Font list in the Formatting toolbar. The list of fonts shows you what each font looks like (see Figure 6.1). Scroll down until you find the one you want to use, and click it.

Word applies the font to the selected text. To see the change more clearly, click once to deselect the text.

Word places the fonts you use frequently above the double line in the Font list (refer back to Figure 6.1) so that you can get at them easily. Below the double line is an alphabetical list of all your fonts.

Font

FIGURE 6.1

The Font list shows you what the fonts look like. Click the one you want to use.

TrueType font

Printer font

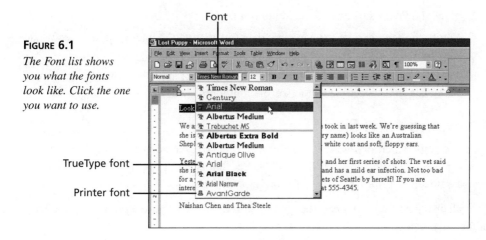

If you'd like to change other font formatting at the same time as you're changing the font, you may find it more convenient to use the Font dialog box. The dialog box gives you a "one-stop shopping" experience. All the font formatting features described here, and more, are accessible in this dialog box.

To apply a font using the Font dialog box, follow these steps:

1. Select the text you want to change.

2. Choose Format, Font or press Ctrl+D to display the Font dialog box (see Figure 6.2).

FIGURE 6.2

The Font dialog box provides access to all of the font-formatting commands.

6

3. Click the Font tab if it isn't already in front.

4. Scroll through the Font list and click the fonts that you're interested in to see what they look like in the Preview area at the bottom of the dialog box.

5. When you find the font that you want to use, select it and click OK. (Again, you may want to deselect the text to see the font more clearly.)

Changing Font Size

Font size is measured in *points*. The larger the point size, the taller the font. There are approximately 72 points in an inch, so a 72-point font is about one inch tall. Typically, business documents are written in a 10- or 12-point font.

As with changing fonts, you can change font size by using either the Formatting toolbar or the Font dialog box.

To change the font size by using the Font Size list, follow these steps:

1. Select the text you want to change.

2. Click the down-arrow to the right of the Font Size list in the Formatting toolbar, scroll down the list, and click the size that you want to use (see Figure 6.3).

Figure 6.3

Word includes commonly used font sizes in the Font Size list. Click the one you want to use.

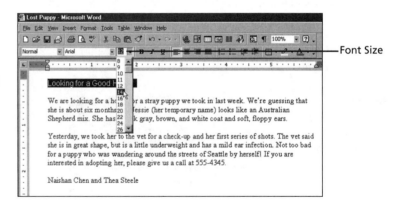

Font Size

Word applies the font size to the selected text. To see the change more clearly, click to deselect.

Applying Bold, Italic, and Underline

The most common type of font formatting other than font and font size is *font style*. This term refers collectively to boldface, italic, and underline. You can apply font styles individually, or you can apply two or more to the same block of text. For example, you could add boldface and italic to a word. Judicious use of font styles can add just the right emphasis to a document—overuse can make a document cluttered and difficult to read.

The easiest way to apply font styles is via the Formatting toolbar or a keyboard shortcut:

1. Select the text to which you want to apply a font style.

2. Click the Bold, Italic, or Underline button in the Formatting toolbar. Alternatively, you can also press Ctrl+B for bold, Ctrl+I for italic, or Ctrl+U for underline.

To remove a font style from a block of text, select the text and then click the toolbar button (or press the keyboard shortcut) again.

Changing Font Color

Changing the color of your text can brighten up a document and make key parts of it stand out. Remember that changing font color won't do much if you're printing on a black-and-white printer. (The colors print in shades of gray.) If, on the other hand, you have a color printer or your readers view the document onscreen, font colors can greatly enhance your document's appearance.

As usual, the easiest way to apply font color is to use the Formatting toolbar, as described in these steps:

1. Select the text to which you want to apply font color.

2. Click the down-arrow to the right of the Font Color toolbar button at the right end of the Formatting toolbar. A palette appears with a large selection of colors (see Figure 6.4). Pointing to a color displays a ScreenTip with the color's name. Click the one you want to use.

FIGURE 6.4

Word gives you many colors to choose from. Click the one you want to use.

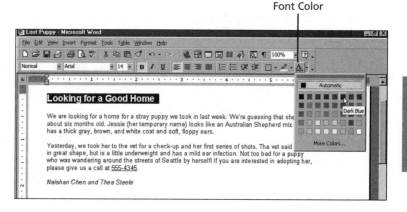

Word applies the color to the selected text. To see what it looks like, deselect the text. If you don't see a color that you want to use in the Font Color palette, click the More Colors button at the bottom of the palette to display the Colors dialog box. Click a color you like, and click OK.

Adding Effects

If you're feeling adventurous, try some of the effects available in the Font dialog box. Depending on the kind of documents you create, you may need to use one or two of these—superscript and subscript, perhaps—all the time. Other more specialized ones, such as emboss and engrave, you may never need.

Changing the Default Font Settings

If you use a different font than Times New Roman 12-point for most of your documents, you might want to change the default font. If you do, Word assumes the new font in all new documents based on the Normal template. (You can always change the font in specific documents if you choose.)

To change the default font, follow these steps:

1. Choose Format, Font to display the Font dialog box.
2. Choose all of the font options that you want for the default font.
3. Click the Default button.
4. Word displays a message box asking whether you want to change the default font, and reminding you that this change affects all new documents based on the Normal template. Click the Yes button.

Copying Font Formatting

If you have carefully applied several font formats to one block of text and then decide that you'd like to use the same combination of formats somewhere else in the document, you don't have to apply the formatting from scratch. Instead, you can use Word's Format Painter feature to copy the formatting of the original block of text and then "paint" it across the other text.

Follow these steps to copy font formatting:

1. Click anywhere in the text that has the formatting you want to copy.
2. Click the Format Painter button on the Formatting toolbar (see Figure 6.5).
3. The mouse pointer becomes an I-beam with a paintbrush attached to it. Drag over the text to which you want to apply the formatting.
4. Release the mouse button. Word applies the formatting to the selected text.

Format Painter

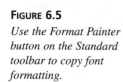

Figure 6.5

Use the Format Painter button on the Standard toolbar to copy font formatting.

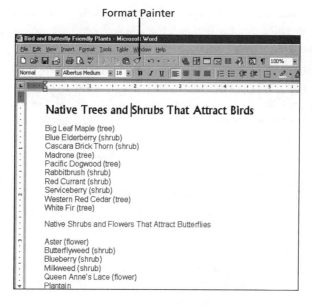

If you want to apply the same set of font formats to several blocks of text, double-click the Format Painter toolbar button in step 2. The Format Painter stays turned on while you drag over multiple blocks of text. When you're finished, click the button again to turn it off.

Removing Font Formatting

If you have applied several different font formats to a block of text and then decide you want to turn all of them off, you can, of course, select the text and then turn each one off individually. This method can be quite tedious, however, because you may have to use several dialog boxes, toolbar buttons, or keyboard shortcuts. A much faster method is to select the text and press the keyboard shortcut Ctrl+Spacebar, which strips off all font formatting and returns the formatting to Word's default.

Applying Paragraph Formatting

In addition to formatting individual characters within words, you can also format paragraphs to take advantage of Word's powerful paragraph-format features. As you're exploring the different formatting options, keep these four points in mind:

- Paragraph formatting affects individual paragraphs. If you want to apply paragraph formatting to only one paragraph, you can select the entire paragraph (by dragging

6

your mouse or clicking within the paragraph three times) or you may simply place the insertion point in that paragraph before applying the change. Word alters just that paragraph and no others.

- If you want to apply a paragraph formatting feature to more than one adjacent paragraph, select them (or a portion of all of them) first. Word considers any text followed by a paragraph mark to be a paragraph. So, for example, a three-line title contains three paragraphs. If you want to center the title, you have to select all three lines first. By the same token, if you want to make an entire document double-spaced, you have to select the whole document first (Ctrl+A selects your entire document).

- Each new paragraph you begin takes on the paragraph formatting of the previous paragraph. So you can just type and format the first one and then continue typing the remaining paragraphs.

- As with font formatting, the options in the Formatting toolbar show you the paragraph formatting that's in effect for the paragraph containing the insertion point. The same is true with the settings on the horizontal ruler. To quickly see what paragraph formatting has been applied to a paragraph, you can simply click in it, and then look at the options that are turned on in the Formatting toolbar and the ruler.

> If you find yourself applying a certain combination of font and paragraph formatting over and over, consider using a *style* to "collect" this set of formatting features into a group and apply them all at once to your paragraphs. (You'll learn about styles in Chapter 7, "Adding Styles and Templates.")

Aligning Paragraphs

Alignment refers to the way the right and left edges of a paragraph line up along the right and left margins of your document. Word gives you four alignment choices—left, centered, right, and justified—as shown in Figure 6.6.

By default, Word uses *left alignment*, which produces a straight left edge and a ragged right edge. Left alignment is usually the best choice for body text in standard business documents such as letters, memos, reports, and so on. *Center alignment* centers your text horizontally between the right and left margins. You use centering for headings and other short lines of text. *Right alignment* lines up your text at the right margin and gives it a ragged left edge. This type of alignment works well for short lines of text that you want to appear on the far-right edge of the page. Finally, you may occasionally want to use *justification*. This type of alignment makes both the right and left edges of a paragraph straight. Word makes slight adjustments to the spacing between characters to produce the straight right edge. Justified text can be a little hard on the eyes because the spacing is uneven, but it is appropriate in some situations. For example, text that is indented from both sides or arranged in columns often looks better if it's justified.

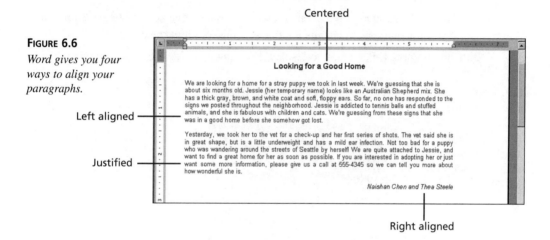

FIGURE 6.6
Word gives you four ways to align your paragraphs.

To change alignment using the Formatting toolbar, follow these steps:

1. Click in the paragraph in which you want to change alignment (or select multiple adjacent paragraphs to change the alignment of all of them).

2. Click the Align Left, Center, Align Right, or Justify button on the Formatting toolbar (see Figure 6.7).

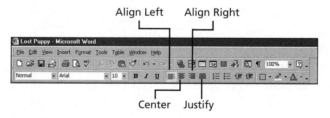

FIGURE 6.7
Click one of the alignment buttons to change alignment.

6

You can also change alignment in the Paragraph dialog box. Choose Format, Paragraph, click the Indents and Spacing tab, choose the desired option in the Alignment list, and click OK.

Changing Line Spacing

Line spacing is the amount of space between lines in a paragraph. By default, paragraphs are single-spaced. You might want to double-space a school paper or a rough draft of a report (so that you have room to scribble edits between the lines). Some people like 1.5 line spacing better than single spacing because it can make the text a little easier to read.

To change line spacing using the Paragraph dialog box, follow these steps:

1. Click in the paragraph in which you want to change line spacing (or select multiple adjacent paragraphs to change the line spacing for all of them).

2. Choose Format, Paragraph to display the Paragraph dialog box (see Figure 6.8).

FIGURE 6.8

The Paragraph dialog box gives you access to most of the paragraph-formatting commands, including line spacing.

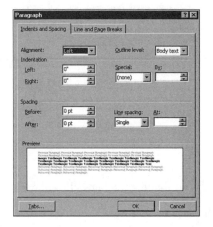

3. Click the down-arrow to the right of the Line Spacing list, and click the line spacing you want. If you choose one of the last three options, At Least, Exactly, or Multiple, you need to type an amount (in points) in the At text box.

4. Click OK.

Working with Custom Tabs

Word's default tabs are *left* tabs, meaning that they left-align text at the tab stops. The default tab stops are positioned every half-inch across the horizontal ruler. You can see them on the bottom edge of the ruler—they look like faint gray tick marks. Each time you press the Tab key, your insertion point moves to the next default tab stop, pushing over any text to the right of the insertion point.

In regular body text, the default tabs work just fine. In some situations, however, you may want to create a custom tab at the exact location on the horizontal ruler where you want to align your text. For example, if you wanted to line up several lines of text at the 3-inch mark by using the default tabs, you would have to press the Tab key six times at the beginning of each line. A much more efficient solution is to create a custom tab at the 3-inch mark. When you insert the custom tab, all of the default tabs to its left disappear. You can then press the Tab key once to bring the insertion point directly to the spot where you want to type your text.

Another advantage of custom tabs is that in addition to creating custom left tabs, you can also create right, center, decimal, and bar tabs to align text in different ways. Figure 6.9 shows a document including all five types of custom tabs.

FIGURE 6.9

You can create five types of custom tabs in Word.

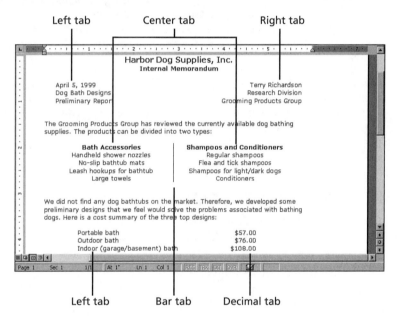

Left tab   Center tab   Right tab

Left tab   Bar tab   Decimal tab

Left tabs left-align text at the tab stop. *Right tabs* right-align text at the tab stop. *Center tabs* center text over the tab stop, and *decimal tabs* align numbers along the decimal point. *Bar tabs* create a vertical line at the tab stop. You can use a bar tab to add a vertical line between columns of text that you've aligned with the other types of custom tabs.

To create a custom tab using the ruler, follow these steps:

1. Click in the paragraph to which you want to add the tab (or select multiple adjacent paragraphs to add the tab to all of them). If you haven't yet typed the text in the paragraph, just click on the blank line where you want the custom tabs to begin.

6

2. Click the Tab Stop Indicator button at the left end of the ruler (see Figure 6.6) until you see the symbol for the tab that you want to insert. Each symbol is labeled with a ScreenTip, so you can easily tell which is which.

3. Click at the desired location on the ruler to insert the tab.

4. Repeat steps 2 and 3 to insert any additional custom tabs.

To use your custom tabs, press Tab to move to the first custom tab stop, and type your text. Press Tab to get to next tab stop (if any) and type your text. If you accidentally press the Tab key too many times, delete the extra tabs by pressing Backspace (if the insertion point is just past the tabs) or Delete (if the insertion point is just before them). Press Enter after typing the last block of text on the line, and type the remaining paragraphs that use the custom tabs.

When you work with custom tabs, you frequently need to adjust their positions on the horizontal ruler. To move a custom tab, click and drag the tab stop on the ruler to a different location. To delete a tab altogether, drag the tab drop down off the ruler and it disappears.

Indenting Paragraphs

Word's indentation feature enables you to indent paragraphs from the left and right margins. You can also create a *first-line indent*, which indents only the first line of a paragraph, or a *hanging indent*, which indents all of the lines in a paragraph except the first. Figure 6.10 illustrates all four types of indentation.

By default, Word sets a first-line indent of one-half inch when you press Tab at the beginning of a paragraph that you've already typed. This indent carries down to additional paragraphs you type, so you won't have to press Tab at the beginning of each paragraph. If you don't like this behavior, choose Tools, Options, click the Edit tab, clear the Tabs and Backspace Set Left Indent check box, and click OK.

Word provides several ways to set indents. If you want to set a left indent at a half-inch increment on the ruler, you can use the Decrease Indent and Increase Indent buttons on the Formatting toolbar (refer back to Figure 6.10), as described in these steps:

1. Click in the paragraph you want to indent (or select multiple adjacent paragraphs to indent them all).

2. Click the Increase Indent button to indent the text one-half inch. If you want to indent the text further, continue clicking this button. To decrease the indentation, click the Decrease Indent button.

FIGURE 6.10

You can indent paragraphs in four different ways.

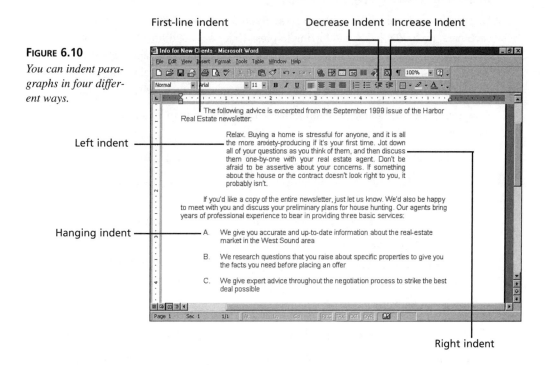

The most efficient way of setting indents is to drag the indent markers on the ruler. When no indentation is set for a paragraph, the First-Line Indent, Hanging Indent, and Left Indent markers are positioned at the left margin, and the Right Indent marker is positioned at the right margin, as shown in Figure 6.11.

FIGURE 6.11

When no indents are set, the indent markers appear at the margins.

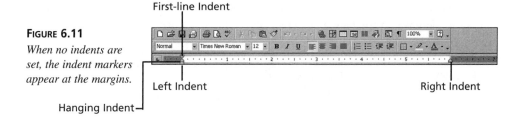

6

You can also create indents in the Paragraph dialog box. If you and your mouse don't get along, this is probably the best method for you. Select Format, Paragraph to display the Paragraph dialog box and click the Indents and Spacing tab to specify your paragraph indents.

Adding Paragraph Spacing

One way to add a blank line between paragraphs is to press Enter twice at the end of each paragraph. You can avoid having to press Enter a second time to create the blank line by adding *paragraph spacing* before and/or after your paragraphs. For example, if you are using a 12-point font, you can add 12 points of spacing below each paragraph to automatically get one blank line's worth of white space between each paragraph.

Paragraph spacing also enables you to fine-tune the amount of space above or below a paragraph to improve your document's appearance.

To add spacing before or after a paragraph, follow these steps:

1. Click in the paragraph to which you want to add spacing (or select multiple adjacent paragraphs to add the spacing to all of them).
2. Choose Format, Paragraph to display the Paragraph dialog box.
3. Click the Indents and Spacing tab if it isn't already in front.
4. Under Spacing, type a number in points in the Before and/or After text box (or use the spinner arrows to increment the spacing 6 points at a time).
5. Click OK.

Creating Bulleted and Numbered Lists

Setting off items in a list with numbers or bullets is a great way to present information clearly. Word's bulleted and numbered list features add the bullets or numbers for you, and they create hanging indents so that when text in an item wraps to the next line, it doesn't wrap underneath the number or bullet. Also, when you use the numbered list feature to create a list and then add, delete, or move items in the list, Word keeps the numbering sequential.

Word enables you to create single-level lists, or lists with two or more levels. Figure 6.12 shows single-level bulleted and numbered lists, and one multilevel list.

Follow these steps to create a single-level bulleted or numbered list:

1. Click where you want the list to start.
2. Click the Bullets or Numbering button on the Formatting toolbar (see Figure 6.13). Word inserts a bullet or number.

Bulleted list

FIGURE 6.12

You can create single-level and multilevel lists.

Numbered list ——

Multilevel list ——

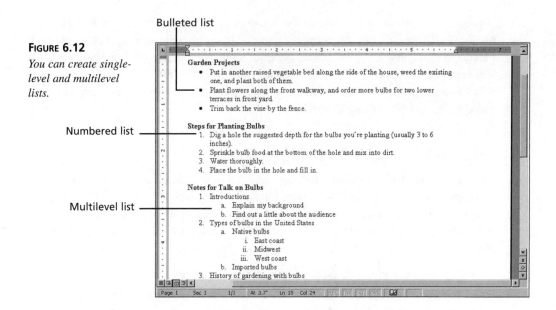

Numbering

FIGURE 6.13

The Bullets and Numbering buttons on the Formatting toolbar let you create lists quickly.

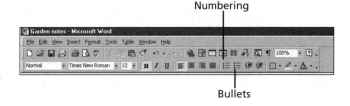

Bullets

3. Type the first item in the list, and press Enter. Word inserts a bullet or number on the next line for you. Continue typing items in your list.

4. After the last item, press Enter twice to turn off the bullets or numbers. (You can also turn off the bullets or numbering by clicking in the paragraph where you don't want the bullets or numbers, and clicking the Bullets or Numbering toolbar button again.)

To switch from numbers to bullets (or vice versa), select all of the items in the list, and then click the Bullets or Numbering button.

You may notice that Word automatically turns on the bulleted or numbered list feature as soon as you type a line of text that begins with an asterisk (*) or a number and press Enter. If you like this behavior, great. If you don't, you can turn it off: Choose Tools, AutoCorrect, click the AutoFormat As You Type tab, clear the check boxes for Automatic Bulleted Lists and Automatic Numbered Lists, and click OK.

6

If you have more than one numbered list in a document, Word starts each new list at number 1. If you want the numbering to continue from the previous list, click on the first paragraph of the new list, choose Format, Bullets and Numbering, click the Numbering tab, mark the Continue Previous List option button, and click OK. (By the same token, if Word assumes you want to continue the previous numbering and you want to restart it, mark the Restart Numbering option button.)

Applying Page Formatting

Once again, Word decides what's best for you (in a well-intentioned sort of way). It makes two main assumptions about page formatting: You want 1-inch top and bottom margins, and 1 $1/4$-inch left and right margins, and you are printing on 8 $1/2$×11-inch paper. To change these and other default page-formatting options, use the techniques described next. You need to know three things up front to understand how page formatting works:

- Page formatting is automatically applied to every page in your document.
- You shouldn't select any text before you apply page formatting. If you do, Word assumes that you want to apply the formatting to only the selected text, and it inserts *section breaks* above and below the text to make this possible (see the next point).
- If you want to apply different page formatting to different portions of a document—for example, set different margins on one page of a multipage document—you need to insert *section breaks* to divide your document into two or more sections.

You may discover that you make a particular change in almost every document you create. In these situations, you can modify the Normal template to assume the page formatting you use. To do so, display the Page Setup dialog box (File, Page Setup), set the option that you want to use, click the Default button in the lower-left corner of the dialog box, and click the Yes button in the message box that appears.

Changing Margins

The default margins are a perfectly good starting point, but you frequently encounter situations in which you need to change them. For example, you might want to narrow the margins to fit more text on the page, increase the top or left margin to make room for a preprinted letterhead, or widen the inner margins for a document that will be bound.

To change the margins using the Page Setup dialog box, follow these steps:

1. Choose File, Page Setup to display the Page Setup dialog box.
2. Click the Margins tab if it isn't already in front (see Figure 6.14).

FIGURE 6.14

Use the Margins tab of the Page Setup dialog box to change your margins.

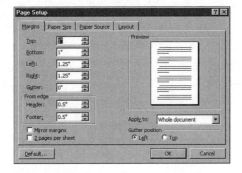

3. The value in the Top text box is highlighted. If you want to change the top margin, type a new value in inches to replace the selected value (you don't have to type the inch mark). Press the Tab key to move to the Bottom, Left, or Right text box, and type new values for any of these margins. (You can also use the spinner arrows to the right of any of these text boxes to increment the margins $1/10$ inch at a time.)
4. Click the OK button.

You can see your new margins in Print Layout view (change the Zoom setting to Page Width or Whole Page) or in Print Preview.

You can also change margins by using the horizontal and vertical rulers. To set margins this way, follow these steps:

1. Make sure you're using Print Layout view (View, Print Layout).
2. Point to the dividing line between the gray margin area and the white part of the ruler. The mouse pointer becomes a double-headed arrow, and the ScreenTip says `Left Margin`, `Right Margin`, `Top Margin`, or `Bottom Margin`, depending on which margin you're changing.

If you have trouble getting the tricky `Left Margin` ScreenTip to appear, use the Page Setup dialog box to change the margin instead.

3. Drag in the desired direction. As you drag, a vertical dashed line shows you the width of the margin. When it's the right size, release the mouse button.

6

Changing Paper Size

Word assumes that you want to print on 8 ¹/₂×11-inch paper, but it can adjust to most other standard sizes, and you can even set a custom size if you like.

To print on a different paper size, follow these steps:

1. Choose File, Page Setup to display the Page Setup dialog box.
2. Click the Paper Size tab if it isn't already in front.
3. Display the Paper Size drop-down list and choose the desired size. (If you are printing on a nonstandard paper size, choose the last option, Custom Size, and then type the width and height of your paper in the Width and Height text boxes.)
4. Click OK.

Creating Headers and Footers

A *header* appears at the top of every page, and a *footer* appears at the bottom of every page. You might want to use headers and footers to display the document title, your name, the name of your organization, and so on.

To create a header and/or footer, follow these steps:

1. Choose View, Header and Footer.

 After you have text in your header, you can double-click it when you're in Print Layout view to activate it instead of choosing View, Header and Footer.

2. Word activates the header area and displays the Header and Footer toolbar (see Figure 6.15). Note the custom tabs in the center and on the right. If you want to create a footer, click the Switch Between Header and Footer toolbar button to activate the footer area. (Click the same button again when you want to switch back to the header area.)
3. Type any text that you want to appear at the left margin. The Header and Footer toolbar provides buttons so you can place the page number, date, or time in either the header or footer if you wish.
4. If you want any text centered, press the Tab key to jump to the center tab, and type the text.
5. If you want some text to be right-aligned at the right margin, press the Tab key twice to move to the right tab, and type the text.

Center tab   Right tab

FIGURE 6.15

*The View, Header and
Footer command acti-
vates the header area
of your document and
displays the Header
and Footer toolbar.*

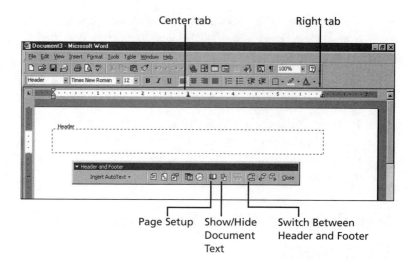

Page Setup   Show/Hide   Switch Between
             Document   Header and Footer
             Text

6. Apply any formatting that you like to text (and fields) in your header or footer by
   selecting it and using the standard formatting techniques, including the Formatting
   toolbar, the Font and Paragraph dialog boxes, keyboard shortcuts, and so on. To
   select all of the text in the header or footer, click when your mouse pointer is in the
   left margin, outside of the dashed-line that demarcates the header or footer area.

7. Click the Close button in the Header and Footer toolbar to return to viewing your
   document text.

By default, the document text is dim but visible when you're working with headers and
footers. If you like, you can hide it completely by clicking the Show/Hide Document
Text button in the Header and Footer toolbar. To bring the document text back into view,
click the toolbar button again.

Controlling Page Breaks

6

As you know, Word inserts automatic page breaks when your pages are full of text. If
you want to break a page that isn't full, you have to insert a *manual* (or *hard*) *page
break.* You might want to insert a manual page break to end a section of a report, or to
separate a title page from the rest of the document.

The steps to insert a manual page break are simple:

1. Move the insertion point to the location where you want to insert the break.

2. Press Ctrl+Enter (or choose Insert, Break, mark the Page Break option button, and
   click OK).

A manual page break looks just like an automatic page break in Print Layout view. In Normal view, however, it is labeled with the caption *Page Break*.

If you revise text above a manual page break, you likely will end up bumping the break into the wrong place in your document. If this happens, just delete it and reinsert it in the desired location.

To delete a manual page break in Normal view, click on the break and press Delete, or, if your insertion point is just past the break, press Backspace. If you're in Print Layout view, press Delete if your insertion point is immediately above the break, and Backspace if your insertion point is just after it.

Varying the Page Formatting in Your Document

Word automatically applies all page formatting to your entire document. In many cases, you need to alter this behavior. For example, you might want to vertically center the text on your title page, but not on the remaining pages. To make these kinds of changes, you have to divide your document into multiple *sections* by inserting *section breaks* at the appropriate spots. After you've done this, you can apply different page formatting in each section, independent of the others.

Word lets you create four kinds of section breaks:

- *Next page*—This section break is like a page break and a section break combined. It both breaks the page and starts a new section. An appropriate place to use a next page section break would be at the end of a title page.

- *Continuous*—This section break does not break the page. Once in a while, you may need to apply different page formatting on the same page. For example, if you want to format your document text in two columns, but want the title to be centered in the middle of the page, you can insert a continuous section break directly under the title. This enables you to keep the title and document text on the same page, but use the default single-column format for the title, and a two-column format for the text.

- *Even page*—This type of section break is most useful for longer documents that are divided into multiple parts, especially those that are bound. It forces the text in the new section to begin on the next even page.

- *Odd page*—This is the same as an even page section break, but it forces the text in the new section to begin on the next odd page.

It's easiest to work with section breaks in Normal view because the breaks are labeled onscreen. To insert a section break, follow these steps:

1. Choose View, Normal if you aren't already using Normal view.

2. Move the insertion point to the location where you want to insert the section break.

3. Choose Insert, Break to display the Break dialog box (see Figure 6.16).

FIGURE 6.16

Use the Break dialog box to insert a section break.

4. Under Section Break Types, mark the desired option button.

5. Click OK.

After you've inserted one or more section breaks in your document, you can use the status bar to keep track of which section you are in.

When your document has more than one section, all the formatting options in the Page Setup dialog box are by default applied to the section containing the insertion point. To apply page formatting to the entire document, change the setting in the Apply To list from This Section to Whole Document.

To delete a section break, use the same methods as the ones you use to delete manual page breaks (see the preceding section). To change a section break from one type to another, delete the old break, and then insert the new one.

Summary

By mixing and matching the formatting options you learned here, you can create documents that are easy to read and pleasing to the eye. In the next chapter, you learn to collect font and paragraph formatting into styles, which you can apply to your documents to give them a consistent look.

6

PART III

Making Documents Look Better

Chapter

CHAPTER 7

Adding Styles and Templates

A *style* is a collection of formatting options to which you assign a name. For example, you could create a style called *Title* that contains all the formatting—font, font size, alignment, and so on—that you normally apply to the titles of your reports. When you apply a style to text, the text takes on all the formatting that the style contains. Styles can greatly speed up the formatting process.

You will gain expertise in working with *templates*, pre-formatted documents. You'll find out how to personalize Word's templates so that you have less typing and formatting to do in the documents you create with them. You then practice creating and modifying your own templates.

Understanding Styles

If you know a bit about how styles can benefit you, what kinds there are, and where they are stored, you will feel confident about creating and using them in your documents.

The Advantages of Using Styles

Styles are advantageous for several reasons:

- They let you apply formatting quickly. Instead of applying several formatting options one at a time, you can apply them all at once by applying a style that contains all the options.
- They let you modify your formatting quickly. If you decide to make a formatting change to some element of your document, you need to update only the style you applied to that element, and the affected text throughout your document reformats instantly.
- They let you create a consistent look for all the documents that you and your co-workers create.

Styles Come in Two Flavors

Word lets you create two types of styles:

- Character styles
- Paragraph styles

Character styles can contain only font formatting, and for this reason, they are far less useful than paragraph styles. However, you might occasionally want to create a character style if a word or phrase crops up frequently in your documents and has to be formatted in a particular way. For example, company style might dictate that the name of your company always appear in an Arial, 12-point, bold font.

Paragraph styles can contain both font formatting and paragraph formatting. This makes them much more versatile than character styles. As you might expect, paragraph styles can be applied, at a minimum, to a single paragraph.

You Can Store Styles in Documents or Templates

If you create a style that will be useful only in a particular document, you can store it in that document only. It will always be available in that document, but not in any others. If, on the other hand, you want to use a style in all the documents based on a particular template, you can store the style in the template itself.

Applying Styles

The styles that are available in your document are listed in the Style list at the left end of the Formatting toolbar (see Figure 7.1).

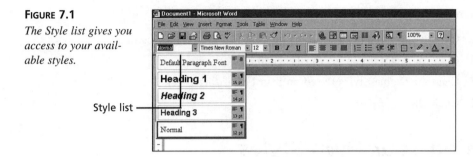

FIGURE 7.1

The Style list gives you access to your available styles.

Style list —

The style names appear with the font formatting that is specified in the style. To the right of each style name is a small gray box that shows you the alignment and font size in the style. In addition, the upper-right corner of the gray box contains an a if it's a character style, or a paragraph symbol (¶) if it's a paragraph style.

The styles in the Style list in Figure 7.1 come with the Normal template. Default Paragraph Font and Normal are the default character and paragraph styles. Heading 1, Heading 2, and Heading 3 are paragraph styles that you can use to format your headings.

To apply a character or paragraph style, follow these steps:

1. To apply a character style, select the text. To apply a paragraph style, click in the paragraph, or select multiple paragraphs to apply the style to all of them.

2. Click the Style list drop-down arrow in the Formatting toolbar, scroll down the list, and click the style that you want to apply.

To check what style you've applied in a particular location, just click in the text. The Style list in the Formatting toolbar displays the style in effect at the location of the insertion point.

Word Creates Styles On-the-Fly

If you glance at the Style list occasionally as you're typing a document, you may notice new styles suddenly appearing in the list. By default, Word creates styles for you based on the formatting that you apply in your document. Although this might be helpful for people who don't want to pay any attention to styles, it can be annoying if you want to closely control the styles in your document.

While you're learning about styles, it's a good idea to turn off this feature so that you have to contend only with styles that you've created yourself. You can always turn it back on later if you choose.

7

To turn off this feature, follow these steps:

1. Choose Tools, AutoCorrect to display the AutoCorrect dialog box.

2. Click the AutoFormat As You Type tab.

3. Clear the Define Styles Based on Your Formatting check box.

4. Click OK.

Creating Your Own Styles

To take full advantage of styles, you need to create your own. This way, you can include the exact formatting you need for the different elements in your documents. For example, if you have to type a weekly calendar of events, you might want to create one style for the names of the events, one for their descriptions, one for the date and time information, and so on. You can create new styles in two ways, as described in the next two sections.

Using the Style List in the Formatting Toolbar

The fastest way to create a style is to use the Style list in the Formatting toolbar (this technique is sometimes called *style by example*). However, using the Style list has a major limitation: Any styles you create this way will be stored only in the document, not in the underlying template, so they won't be available outside of the document. In addition, this method works to create only paragraph styles, not character styles.

To create a style by using the Style list, follow these steps:

1. Format a paragraph with all the options that you want to include in the style. For example, if you are creating a style for your body text, you might format the paragraph with a Verdana 11-point font, left alignment, and 12 points of paragraph spacing after the paragraph (so that you won't have to press Enter to create blank lines between the paragraphs).

2. Make sure your insertion point is in the paragraph, and click whatever style is currently showing in the Style list to select it.

3. Type over the selected style name with the name of your new style (it can include spaces). Figure 7.2 shows the insertion point in the formatted paragraph, and the name *Body* entered in the Style list.

4. Press Enter.

Word creates a style that includes all the font and paragraph formatting in the paragraph.

FIGURE 7.2

FIGURE 7.2

*Type a name for your
new style in the Style
list.*

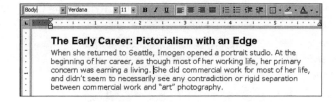

Using the Style Dialog Box

The most flexible way to create styles (either character or paragraph) is to use the Style
dialog box. When you use this method, you can instruct Word to save the style in the
template so that it will be available to other documents.

To create a style by using the Style dialog box, follow these steps:

1. Choose Format, Style to display the Style dialog box (see Figure 7.3). It doesn't
   matter where your insertion point is when you issue the command.

FIGURE 7.3

*The Style dialog box
lets you create and
modify styles.*

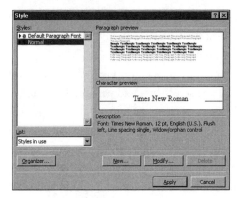

2. In the Styles list on the left side of the Style dialog box, click Normal if it isn't
   already selected. (Doing this ensures that your new style is based on the "plain-
   vanilla" Normal style.)

The option that's selected in the List drop-down list (located in the lower-
left corner of the dialog box) controls what's displayed in the Styles list. The
All Styles option displays all the styles in all your Word templates. The Styles
in Use option displays only the styles that are being used (or were used at
some point) in the current document. The User-Defined Styles option displays only the styles you've created yourself.

7

3. Click the New button to display the New Style dialog box (see Figure 7.4).

FIGURE 7.4

Use the New Style dialog box to create a new style.

4. Type a name for your style in the Name text box (type over the default name *Style1*). Leave the Style Type option set to Paragraph, unless you want to create a character style.

5. Mark the Add to Template check box if you want to add the style to the template underlying the current document. If you do this, the style will be available to other documents based on the template.

6. Click the Format button to display a list of commands that lead to all the dialog boxes in which you can select font and paragraph formatting.

7. Click the command that leads to the dialog box that contains the formatting you want to add. For example, click Font to display the Font dialog box so that you can specify the font formatting for the style. Make your selections in the dialog box, and click OK to return to the New Style dialog box.

8. Repeat steps 6 and 7 to add all the formatting that you want to the style.

9. Click OK to close the New Style dialog box, and then click the Close button to close the Style dialog box. (Don't use the Apply button to close the Style dialog box. This would apply the new style to whatever paragraph happens to contain the insertion point.)

Your new style now appears in the Style list in the Formatting toolbar.

Modifying Existing Styles

Whether you modify a style that comes with Word or one you created yourself, as soon as you make the change, all the paragraphs formatted with that style in your document automatically update to reflect the new formatting in the style. (Any text formatted with the same style in other existing documents does not get reformatted.)

Using the Style List in the Formatting Toolbar

You can modify a style using the Style list in the Formatting toolbar, just as you can when creating a style. However, the drawback to this method is that the modified style can be stored only in the document itself.

To modify a style using the Style list, follow these steps:

1. Apply the style to a paragraph, and then modify the formatting of the paragraph so that it looks the way you want it to.

2. Make sure the insertion point is in the paragraph, click the style in the Style list box (don't display the list), and press Enter.

3. Word displays a message asking whether you want to update the style to reflect recent changes or reapply the formatting of the style to the selection. Mark the Update the Style to Reflect Recent Changes option button, and click OK.

Using the Style Dialog Box

When you modify a style using the Style dialog box, you can save the modified style in the document or in the underlying template.

To modify a style using the Style dialog box, follow these steps:

1. Choose Format, Style to display the Style dialog box. (It doesn't matter where your insertion point is when you issue the command.)

2. Click the style that you want to modify in the Styles list on the left side of the Styles dialog box. (If you don't see it, choose All Styles in the List drop-down list.)

3. Click the Modify button to display the Modify Style dialog box (see Figure 7.5). Notice that this dialog box is identical to the New Style dialog box shown in Figure 7.4, with the exception of the name in the title bar.

FIGURE 7.5

Use the Modify Style dialog box to modify an existing style.

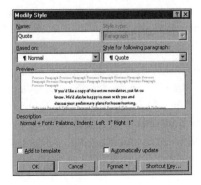

7

4. Make any changes that you want to the style. If you stored the original style in the template and want the modified style to replace the original in the template, mark the Add to Template check box. (Otherwise, the modified version is stored in the document only; the version in the template remains unchanged.)

5. Click OK to close the Modify Style dialog box, and then click Close to close the Style dialog box.

Chaining Styles Together

If you create documents in which the various text elements always appear in a particular order, you can "chain" them together so that when you press Enter to end a paragraph formatted with one style, Word automatically applies the second style to the next paragraph. Linking styles in this way can save you many trips to the Style list in the Formatting toolbar.

For example, let's say you're creating an instruction manual in which each topic is composed of a heading, an introductory paragraph, and then a numbered list of steps. And let's say you've created styles named Topic, Intro, and Steps for these three elements. You can chain the styles together so that Topic leads to Intro, Intro leads to Steps, and Steps leads back to Topic.

When you're creating or modifying a style, you can specify a style to follow by choosing it from the Style for Following Paragraph list in the New Style or Modify Style dialog box.

Basing One Style on Another

If you're creating a style that is similar to an existing one, you can base the new style on the existing one so that it gains all the formatting in the existing style. Then all you need to do is tweak the new style a little to get the formatting exactly as you want it. To base a style on another one, you select the "based on" style in the Based On list in the New Style or Modify Style dialog box.

Although this method lets you create styles rather quickly, it can cause two problems down the road. First, when you look at the description of a style that's based on another style (in the Description area of the New Style or Modify Style dialog box), it lists the "based on" style plus whatever adjustments you've made to it. For example, in Figure 7.6, the Short Quote style is based on the Quote style, so the description lists `Quote` plus the one modification (the indentation was removed). If you want to see *all* the formatting in the new style, you need to track down the content of the "based on" style—a tedious task. And if the "based on" style is itself based on another style, reach for some coffee or chocolate to cheer yourself up.

FIGURE 7.6

Think carefully before basing one style on another.

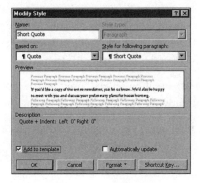

Also, if you base several styles on a style and then modify the "based on" style, *all* the other styles will change accordingly. This "ripple effect" can produce some unexpected (and often unwanted) results.

In conclusion, the most straightforward route is to base each style on the Normal style, so you can see exactly what formatting it contains and modify it without affecting other styles.

Understanding Templates

You can think of a template as a big bucket in which you store the things you need to work on a certain type of document. In addition to any formatting and text that you enter directly into a template, it can contain any combination of these items:

- Styles
- AutoText entries
- Toolbars
- Macros

The default template, Normal, is unlike other templates in that it is *loaded globally*. This is a geeky way of saying that the styles, AutoText entries, toolbars, and macros stored in the Normal template are available to *all* documents that you create, even if you base them on other templates.

7

Personalizing Word's Templates

If you have tried one of the templates that comes with Word and like the look of the finished document, it's probably worth taking a few minutes to make the template your own. Wherever possible, you can replace the `Click Here and Type` placeholder text with your personal information. For example, if you're revising a letter template, you might fill in your own return address, company name, and signature block. You can also remove any text you don't need, and modify the formatting if desired.

After you've made these changes, creating letters based on the template will be a snap because you will need to fill in only the text that changes from one letter to the next.

To personalize one of Word's templates, you create a new template based on Word's template and then modify it, as described in these steps:

1. Choose File, New to display the New dialog box.

2. Click the tab that contains the template you want to modify, and click the template. Under Create New in the lower-right corner of the dialog box, mark the Template option button. This tells Word to start a new template (not a document) based on the selected template (see Figure 7.7). Then click the OK button.

FIGURE 7.7

Word will create a new template based on the Contemporary Fax template.

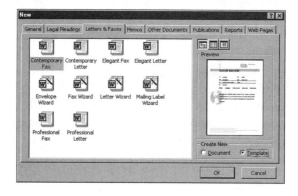

3. Word creates a new template based on the one you selected in the New dialog box. (Notice that the temporary name in the title bar begins with *Template*, not *Document*.) Fill in all the `Click Here and Type` prompts that should contain your own information, and leave the ones that you will need to change each time you use the template (see Figure 7.8).

4. Delete or revise text in the template as needed, and make any changes to the formatting that you like.

5. Click the Save button in the Standard toolbar to display the Save As dialog box.

FIGURE 7.8

*The return address
and sender have been
filled in.*

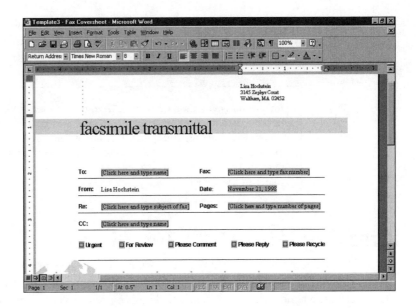

6. Because you're saving a template, Word automatically selects the Templates folder
   in the Save In list. (This folder is a subfolder of C:\Windows\Application
   Data\Microsoft.) If you save the template in the Templates folder itself, it appears
   in the General tab of the New dialog box. If this is what you want, skip to step 8.

7. If you want your template to appear in one of the other existing tabs in the New
   dialog box, create a subfolder of that name under the Templates folder. For example, to make your template appear in the Memos tab, create a Memos subfolder. If
   your template doesn't belong in any of the existing tabs, you can create a new one.
   Create a subfolder of the Templates folder with the name that you want to appear
   on the tab. A tab corresponding to this subfolder appears in the New dialog box the
   next time you display it. When you've created your subfolder, double-click it.

8. Type a name for the template in the File Name text box, and click the Save button.

Documents have an extension of .doc, and templates have an extension of
.dot. (If you don't see file extensions on your computer and you want to,
double-click the My Computer icon on your desktop, choose View, Folder
Options, click the View tab, clear the Hide File Extensions for Known File
Types check box, and then click OK.)

7

Your new template now appears in the General tab of the New dialog box, or in another tab if you saved it in a subfolder of the Templates folder. Try using the template to see whether it works as you want it to.

An alternative method of personalizing one of Word's templates is to start a new document based on the template and personalize the document. Then choose File, Save As, and specify Document Template in the Save As Type list in the Save As dialog box. Word automatically displays the Templates folder in the Save In list. Save the template in the Templates folder or in a sub-folder of this folder.

Creating Your Own Templates

If Word doesn't provide a ready-made template for the type of documents you create, or if you want more control over the appearance of your documents, you will probably want to create a template from scratch. You do this by basing the new template on the "plain vanilla" Normal template.

To create a template from scratch, follow these steps:

1. Choose File, New to display the New dialog box.

2. In the General tab, make sure the Blank Document icon is selected (this is the Normal template). Under Create New in the lower-right corner of the dialog box, mark the Template option button, and click the OK button.

3. Word starts a new template based on the Normal template. Type and format the text that you want to appear in all documents based on this template. For example, if you're creating a template for business letters, you might include the letterhead, the beginning of the salutation, and the signature block. To make the template easy to use, you might also add placeholders for text that needs to be filled in such as typing [Place Date Here] where the date should go in the target document that uses this template.

4. If you want to include styles in the template, create them now. Because you're working with the template directly, not with a document based on the template, Word saves the styles in the template whether or not you mark the Add to Template check box in the New Style dialog box.

5. When you have completed the template, choose File, Save As, and save the file in the Templates folder or a subfolder of this folder.

If you have an existing document that contains all the text and formatting you want in your template, you can save the document as a template. First remove the text that's specific to that document. Then replace the text you deleted with placeholders, and choose File, Save As. Specify Document Template in the Save As Type list in the Save As dialog box, and save the template in the Templates folder or a subfolder of this folder.

Modifying Your Templates

No matter how carefully you originally design your templates, you will sooner or later want to make some improvements.

Follow these steps to make changes to a template:

1. Click the Open button in the Standard toolbar.

2. In the Files of Type list at the bottom of the Open dialog box, select Document Templates. Then navigate to the C:\Windows\Application Data\Microsoft\Templates folder or one of its subfolders and double-click the template that you want to revise.

3. Revise your template as necessary.

4. Click the Save button in the Standard toolbar, and then close the template.

The preceding set of steps involves opening a template and making changes to it directly. This is not always necessary, however. When you close a document based on the Normal template after you've added, modified, or deleted any of the items you can store in templates (styles, toolbars, AutoText entries, and macros), Word automatically saves these changes to the template.

When you close a document that is based on any template other than Normal, Word first asks whether you want to save changes to the document (if you have unsaved changes). If you have added, modified, or deleted any of the four items you can store in templates, Word then asks whether you want to save changes to the template. Click the Yes button to retain the changes.

Attaching a Template to the Active Document

7

You may encounter situations in which you need to change the template that's attached to a document. For example, you might click the New button in the Standard toolbar and type for a while in the new document before realizing that you had meant to base the document on a template other than Normal. Or someone may give you a document that is based on an older version of a template, and you want to update the document to the current version. Word lets you change the template that's attached to the active document with a few simple steps.

To attach a different template to the active document, follow these steps:

1. Open the document to which you want to attach the template.

2. Choose Tools, Templates and Add-Ins to display the Templates and Add-Ins dialog box (see Figure 7.9).

FIGURE 7.9

Use the Templates and Add-Ins dialog box to attach a different template to the active document.

3. The currently attached template is listed in the Document Template text box. To change it, click the Attach button.

4. In the Attach Template dialog box that appears, navigate to the folder that contains the template you want to attach, and then double-click it.

5. Back in the Templates and Add-Ins dialog box, the template you selected is now listed in the Document Template text box. If you want the styles in the document to update to the ones in the newly attached template, mark the Automatically Update Document Styles text box.

6. Click OK.

The styles, toolbars, AutoText entries, and macros in the newly attached template are now available in the active document. However, if the template you attached contains any text, the text will not be copied into the document.

Loading a Template Globally

If you need to make the items in a template available in the active document, but you don't want to attach the template to the document, you can load the template globally. When a template is loaded globally, all the items it contains are available to all documents.

Follow these steps to load a template globally:

1. Choose Tools, Templates and Add-Ins.

2. Click the Add button in the Templates and Add-Ins dialog box to display the Add Template dialog box.

3. Navigate to the template that you want to add globally and double-click it.

4. In the Templates and Add-Ins dialog box, the template now appears under Checked Items Are Currently Loaded (see Figure 7.10). (You can later clear the check box next to its name if you want to temporarily unload the template, or select it and click the Remove button to permanently unload it.)

FIGURE 7.10

The templates you selected appear in the Checked Items are Currently Loaded list.

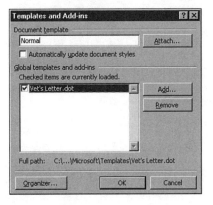

5. Click the OK button.

If you want a template to load globally every time you start Word, copy the template to C:\Windows\ApplicationData\Microsoft\Word\Startup.

7

Summary

Using styles can greatly reduce the time it takes to format (and reformat) your documents. If you work in an office, you can use styles to standardize the appearance of all the documents you and your co-workers generate. If you expect that styles will improve your quality of life, you will also benefit from templates.

Word provides templates for creating all kinds of documents. If you like one in particular, you can tweak it to make it your own. If you don't like Word's templates, or if none are designed for the type of documents you create, you can create a template from scratch so that it contains the exact text and formatting that you need. Templates can also store styles, AutoText entries, toolbars, and macros. Word gives you a variety of ways to access these items, regardless of what template they are stored in.

CHAPTER 8

Correcting Documents and Using Columns and Tables

The more you use Word, the more the shortcuts you learn here will become an essential part of your repertoire. As an added benefit, facile use of these features is a surefire way to impress your co-workers or family members. In this chapter, you will also learn how to format text in columns and tables so that you can add professional-looking documents to your repertoire.

Correcting Text Automatically

Word's *AutoCorrect* feature fixes spelling errors for you automatically. For example, if you type *hte*, AutoCorrect changes it to *the*. By default, AutoCorrect makes corrections based on suggestions from the spell checker. It also has its own list of many commonly misspelled words, and you can add your own favorite typos to the list. In addition, you can use AutoCorrect to automatically enter special symbols, long names, or phrases that you have to type frequently.

Follow these steps to add an entry to the list of words that AutoCorrect corrects automatically:

1. Choose Tools, AutoCorrect to display the AutoCorrect dialog box.

2. Scroll down the list at the bottom of the AutoCorrect tab to see what AutoCorrect knows how to fix. Word replaces the items in the left column with the items in the right column. At the top of the list are symbols, followed by a large number of commonly misspelled words.

3. To add an entry, click in the Replace text box and type the misspelling.

4. Click in the With text box and type the correct spelling (see Figure 8.1).

FIGURE 8.1

Type the misspelling in the Replace text box and the correct spelling in the With text box.

5. Click the Add button. The new entry appears in the list.

6. Click OK.

Try typing the misspelled word. As soon as you press the Spacebar or Enter, Word replaces it with the correct spelling.

> If you add an AutoCorrect entry and later decide to delete it, choose Tools, AutoCorrect, click the entry in the list in the AutoCorrect tab, click the Delete button, and click OK.

8

If you want to use AutoCorrect to insert a long name or phrase, type an abbreviation for the phrase in the Replace box, and type the full spelling in the With box. For example, you could type *nabf* in the Replace box and *National Association of Bichon Fanciers* in the With box.

If you enter an abbreviation for a long name or phrase in the Replace box, choose one that you don't ever want to leave "as is" in your document, because Word changes it to the full "correct" spelling every time you type it. (If AutoCorrect does make a change that you want to undo, however, you can always click the Undo button on the Standard toolbar or press Ctrl+Z to reverse the change.)

Inserting Standard Blocks of Text Automatically

AutoText is an extremely handy feature enabling Word to "memorize" large blocks of text. Once you've created an AutoText entry, you can insert it in your text by simply beginning to type the name of the entry. As soon as you've typed the first few characters, Word's AutoComplete feature takes over and inserts the entire block of text for you.

One of the advantages of using AutoText is that you only have to proofread the block of text once, before you create the AutoText entry. From then on, each time you insert the entry in a document, you can rest assured that it is error-free.

Creating AutoText Entries

Creating an AutoText entry is relatively easy.

1. Type the text that you want Word to "memorize," and then select it.
2. Choose Insert, AutoText, New (or press Alt+F3) to display the Create AutoText dialog box.
3. Type over Word's suggested name with your own name for the entry. (Choose a name that is at least four characters long.) See Figure 8.2.
4. Click OK.

Inserting an AutoText Entry in Your Document

Word provides several ways of inserting AutoText entries in your document. The method described in these steps is the simplest.

FIGURE 8.2

*Type a name for your
AutoText entry in the
Create AutoText dialog
box.*

Follow these steps to insert an AutoText entry in your document:

1. Click where you want to insert the entry.

2. Type the first few letters of the name. A ScreenTip appears for your entry (see
   Figure 8.3).

FIGURE 8.3

*As soon as you type
the first few letters of
an AutoText entry's
name, a ScreenTip
appears.*

3. Press Enter to insert the entry in your document.

One other convenient way to insert an entry is to type the full name of the entry and
press F3 when the insertion point is just past the name.

Finding and Replacing Text Automatically

Any time you find yourself about to embark on a time-consuming hunt through a long
document for a word or phrase, or for certain formatting, see whether Word's Find and
Replace features can do the work for you.

Finding Text

If you frequently type long documents, you have probably had the experience of
scrolling through each page trying to find all of the places where you used a particular
word or phrase. Word can help you with this process, searching for text much more
quickly and accurately than we humans can.

1. Choose Edit, Find (or press Ctrl+F) to display the Find tab of the Find and Replace
   dialog box (see Figure 8.4).

FIGURE 8.4

Use the Find tab of the Find and Replace dialog box to search for text.

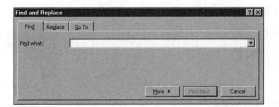

2. Type the text that you want to find in the Find What text box.

3. Click the Find Next button. Word highlights the first occurrence of the word.

4. Continue to click the Find Next button to look for more matches.

5. Click OK when Word informs you that it has found all the matches.

6. Click the Cancel button in the Find and Replace dialog box.

If you want to be more specific about what text you're looking for, click the More button to expand the dialog box and display more options (see Figure 8.5). To collapse the dialog box again, click the Less button.

FIGURE 8.5

Click the More button to expand the dialog box, and the Less button to collapse it.

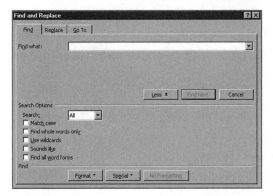

By default, Word searches the entire document for the Find What text. If you want to search up or down from the location of the insertion point, change the option in the Search list from All to Up or Down.

Replacing Text

Sometimes you not only need to find text, you also have to replace it with something else. Word's Replace feature takes the tedium out of making the same change in several places.

Follow these steps to search for text and replace it with something else:

1. Choose Edit, Replace (or press Ctrl+H) to display the Replace tab of the Find and Replace dialog box (see Figure 8.6).

FIGURE 8.6

Use the Replace tab of the Find and Replace dialog box to search for and replace text.

2. Type the text that you want to find in the Find What text box.

3. In the Replace With text box, type the text that you want to replace the Find What text.

4. Click the Find Next button.

5. Word highlights the first occurrence of the word. To replace it, click the Replace button.

6. To skip this instance without making the change, click the Find Next button.

7. Continue this process. If you don't need to confirm every replacement, click the Replace All button.

8. Click OK when Word informs you that it has found all the matches.

9. Click the Close button in the Find and Replace dialog box.

If you change your mind about a replace operation after completing it, you can click the Undo button in the Standard toolbar to undo the replacements one by one if you used the Replace button, or all at once if you used the Replace All button.

If you like, you can customize your find and replace operation by using the options in the expanded version of the Find and Replace dialog box.

Finding and Replacing Formatting

You can use Find and Replace as a quick way to search for and replace formatting in your document.

To modify formatting with Find and Replace, follow these steps:

1. Display the Replace tab of the Find and Replace dialog box, and click in the Find What text box. (If the dialog box isn't already expanded, click the More button.)

8

2. Click the Format button, and click the command that leads to the formatting option you want to search for. For example, if you want to search for boldface, click the Font command.

3. Select the desired formatting option in the dialog box that appears, and click OK.

4. The formatting is now listed beneath the Find What box.

5. Click in the Replace With text box and use the Format button to specify the formatting that you want to replace the Find What formatting. If you want to strip off the Find What formatting without replacing it, choose the default formatting. For example, to remove boldface, you would choose Not Bold in the Font Style list in the Font dialog box.

6. Continue with the usual replace procedure.

If you like, you can combine formatting and text in the Find and Replace dialog box. For example, you could type the words *Puget Sound* in the Find What text box, and then type *Puget Sound* in the Replace With text box and specify a single underline. This would search for and underline every instance of *Puget Sound* in your document.

Inserting Symbols and Special Characters

Many everyday documents, such as letters and memos, require special characters here and there. For example, you might need to use the trademark symbol (™), a long dash (—), or the ellipsis (…]). Word inserts many of these symbols for you automatically as you type. If it doesn't insert the one you need, you can likely find it in the Symbol dialog box.

To see what symbols Word inserts automatically, first choose Tools, AutoCorrect to display the AutoCorrect dialog box, and click the AutoCorrect tab. As you saw in the "Correcting Text Automatically" section, when you type the characters in the left column, Word replaces them with the symbols on the right. Next, click the AutoFormat As You Type tab. The Replace As You Type options in the middle of the dialog box insert many symbols for you as well (see Figure 8.7). Click the Cancel button to close the AutoCorrect dialog box.

To insert a less commonly used symbol, follow these steps:

1. Click where you want the symbol to go, and choose Insert, Symbol (see Figure 8.8).

2. Click the Symbols tab if it isn't already in front. Look through the symbols in the grid. If you want to see one more clearly, click it to magnify it.

FIGURE 8.7

*The Replace As You
Type options insert
many symbols for you
as you type.*

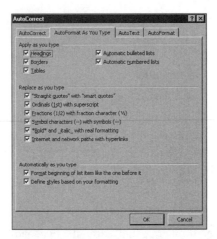

FIGURE 8.8

*The Symbol dialog box
lets you insert all sorts
of symbols.*

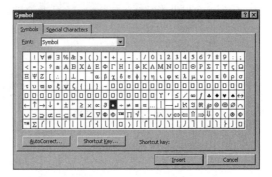

3. If you don't see the symbol you want, display the Font drop-down list, and choose
    a different font set.

4. To insert a symbol, double-click it, and then click the Close button.

Organizing Your Outline

If you have applied heading styles (or outline levels) to the headings in your document,
you can use Outline view to examine and modify the heading structure of your document.

To use Outline view, follow these steps:

1. Choose View, Outline, or click the Outline View button in the lower-left corner of
    the Word window.

2. Word switches to Outline view and displays the Outlining toolbar. Headings that
    contain subheadings and/or body text have plus signs to the left of their names.

Those that are currently empty have minus signs. To collapse the outline down to your top-level headings, click the Show Heading 1 button in the Outlining toolbar (see Figure 8.9).

3. To further expand the view of your outline, click the desired Show Heading button. (For example, to display the top three heading levels in your document, click the Show Heading 3 button.)

4. To expand an individual heading to see all of its subheadings, click the plus sign to its left to select it (the mouse pointer changes to a four-headed arrow when you point to the plus sign), and then click the Expand button in the Outlining toolbar. To collapse the view of a heading, select it and click the Collapse toolbar button.

FIGURE 8.9

Use the Outlining toolbar to organize your document's outline.

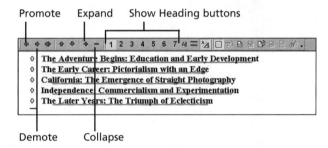

Promote   Expand   Show Heading buttons

Demote   Collapse

5. To restyle a heading to demote it one level or promote it one level, select it and then click the Promote or Demote buttons in the Outlining toolbar. Word applies the appropriate heading style. For example, if you demote a heading formatted with the Heading 2 style, Word reformats it with the Heading 3 style.

6. To move a heading (along with all the subheadings and body text it contains) to a new location in the document, drag its plus sign. As you drag, a horizontal line indicates where the heading will appear. When the line is in the right place, release the mouse button.

7. When you're finished using Outline view, use the View menu or the View buttons to go to another view.

If you want to print an outline of your document, switch to Outline view, collapse your outline to the level that you want to print, and click the Print button in the Standard toolbar.

Working with Columns

If you plan to produce newsletters, bulletins, journal articles, and so on, you'll appreciate Word's capability to format text in multiple columns. When you use this feature, the text snakes from column to column (see Figure 8.10). After you've formatted your text in columns, changing the number of columns is a breeze.

FIGURE 8.10

This document is formatted in two columns.

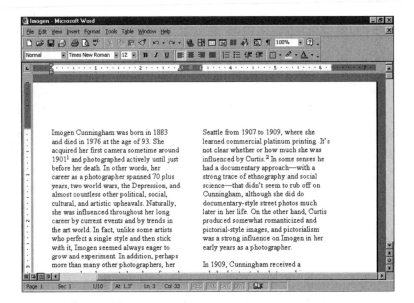

If you want to create columns of text that *do not* wrap from one column to the next, use either custom tabs or a table.

Creating Columns

Columns fall into the page formatting category. As with other page formatting, columns apply to your entire document unless you insert *section breaks* around the text that you want in columns. For example, you might do this is if you want a title above the columns that is centered in the middle of the page (see Figure 8.11). To do this, you need to insert a continuous section break between the title and the remainder of the document.

You can then leave the default (single) column formatting in the first section, and apply two or more columns to the rest of the text.

Column Width marker

FIGURE 8.11

A continuous section break separates the title from the rest of the text.

There is a continuous section break here.

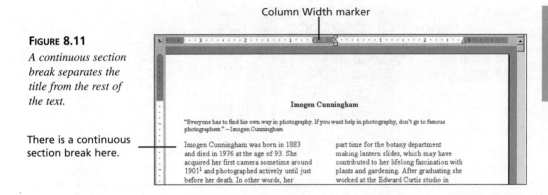

Follow these steps to format your text in columns.

1. Make sure you're using Print Layout view (choose View, Print Layout). Columns don't display accurately in Normal view.

2. If you have inserted section breaks, make sure your insertion point is in the section where you want to apply the columns. If you're applying columns to the entire document, your insertion point can be anywhere in the text.

3. Click the Columns button on the Formatting toolbar, and click the number of columns that you want in the grid that drops down (see Figure 8.12).

FIGURE 8.12

Click the number of columns that you want in the grid attached to the Columns button in the Formatting toolbar.

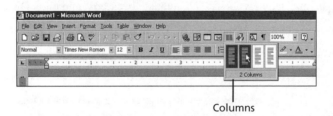

Columns

Word creates the number of columns that you specified. If you decide to change the number of columns in your document, follow these steps again. To remove columns, click the leftmost column in the grid in step 3.

Modifying Columns

Follow these steps if your columns need to be a specific width or if you want to add a vertical line between the columns:

1. Click anywhere in the multiple-column text, and choose Format, Columns to display the Columns dialog box (see Figure 8.13).

FIGURE 8.13

*You can make changes
to your column format-
ting in the Columns
dialog box.*

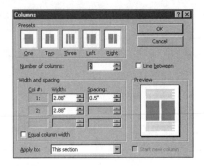

2. If you see a format under Presets at the top of the dialog box that matches what you want, click it.

3. If you have specific requirements for column widths, first clear the Equal Column Width check box. Then enter the desired settings for each column under Width and Spacing. (*Spacing* refers to the amount of space between columns.)

4. To add vertical lines between your columns, mark the Line Between check box.

5. When you have made all your selections, click OK.

Columns sometimes look better if the text is justified so that it has a straight right edge. If you do justify your text, it will probably look best if you hyphenate it as well to reduce gaps between words. To apply hyphenation, choose Tools, Language, Hyphenation, mark the Automatically Hyphenate Document check box, and click OK.

If you need to force a column to break in a particular place, move the insertion point there, choose Insert, Break, mark the Column Break option button, and click OK.

To balance the length of your columns on the last page of a document, insert a continuous section break at the very end of the document. (Press Ctrl+End to move to the end of the document, choose Insert, Break, mark the Continuous option button, and click OK.)

Working with Tables

Word's table feature gives you a wonderfully flexible way of aligning text in a grid of rows and columns. You enter text into the individual boxes in the grid, which are referred to as *cells*. You can create a table that looks table-ish, like the one shown in Figure 8.14.

But you can also create tables that are "invisible" by hiding the gridlines between cells. The résumé shown in Figure 8.15 is actually typed in a table, but the gridlines have been hidden so that it's not obvious.

FIGURE 8.14

This table doesn't disguise its true nature.

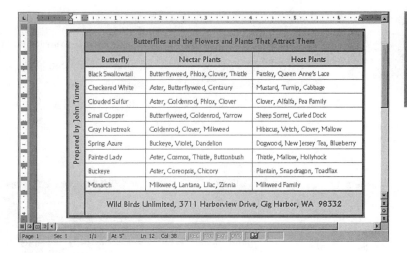

FIGURE 8.15

Tables don't have to look like they belong in a scientific paper.

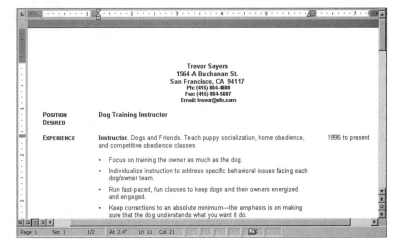

Creating a Table

Word gives you two methods for creating tables. With the standard method, you tell Word to create a table with a particular number of rows and columns, and then revise it from there. With the second method, you "draw" the table with your mouse. The first method is a little faster, but the second is better for creating a more complex table such as the one shown earlier in Figure 8.5.

Using the Standard Method

To create a table using the standard method, you can either use the Insert Table button on the Standard toolbar or choose Insert, Table; the end result is the same. In these steps, you use the Insert Table toolbar button because it's a little more efficient.

Follow these steps to insert a table with the standard method:

1. Move the insertion point to the place where you want to insert the table.

2. Click the Insert Table button on the Standard toolbar.

3. The squares in the grid that drops down represent cells. Drag through the approximate number of rows and columns that you want (see Figure 8.16), and then release the mouse button.

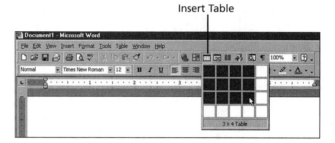

FIGURE 8.16

Drag through the number of rows and columns that you want to start off with.

A table appears in your document.

Drawing a Table

To draw a table, you use the Draw Table button on the Tables and Borders toolbar. (This tool is available in Print Layout view; it isn't in Normal view.) Although you can start by drawing a single cell and then add on, it's usually more straightforward to draw the outline of a table and then fill in the rows and columns. This method of creating a table is extremely flexible; if you can envision a design for your table, you can almost certainly create it.

To draw a table, follow these steps:

1. Make sure you're in Print Layout view, and then click the Tables and Borders button on the Standard toolbar to display the Tables and Borders toolbar.

2. Click the Draw Table button if it isn't already selected (pushed in). Your mouse pointer now looks like a small pencil when it's over your document.

3. Display the Line Style list and choose a line style for the outside border of your table.

4. Display the Line Weight list and choose a line weight for the outside border of your table.

5. Click the Border Color button and click a color for the outside border of your table in the drop-down palette.

6. Starting in the upper-left corner, drag diagonally down and to the right, releasing the mouse button when the outline is the right size (see Figure 8.17). Word creates the outside border of your table.

8

Draw Table   Line Style   Border Color

FIGURE 8.17

Drag until the outline of your table is approximately the right size.

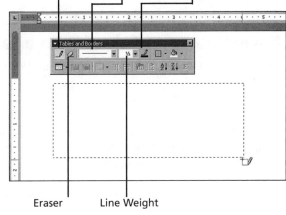

Eraser   Line Weight

7. Now repeat steps 3–5 to choose what kind of inside lines you want, and draw them with the Draw Table tool (see Figure 8.18). If you want to remove a line, click the Eraser toolbar button and then draw over the line. When you release the mouse button, the line disappears.

FIGURE 8.18

Draw the inside lines in your table.

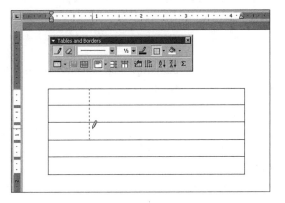

You can draw lines to divide up the inside of the table however you like. You are not restricted to a standard grid. You can create cells of different sizes depending on what you're using the table for. Word even lets you draw diagonal lines.

8. Click the Draw Table button to turn it off, and enter the text in the table (see the next section).

Typing, Navigating, and Selecting in a Table

Typing, navigating, and selecting in a table works much like you might expect, with a few twists.

Typing Text in a Table

When you type text in a cell, if the entry is too wide to fit in the cell, Word automatically wraps the text to the next line and increases the row height. In Figure 8.19, the text was allowed to wrap within cells, and the row height adjusted accordingly.

FIGURE 8.19

Unlike in a spread-sheet program, Word wraps text in cells automatically.

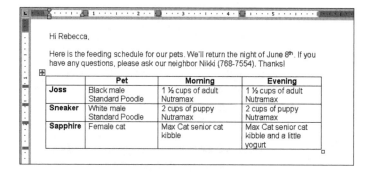

Pressing Enter in a cell ends the paragraph and adds a blank line to that row. (If you accidentally press Enter, press Backspace to remove the blank line.)

 If you want to insert a tab within a cell, press Ctrl+Tab instead of Tab. (Pressing the Tab key by itself just selects the contents of the cell to the right.)

Navigating in a Table

Navigating in a table with the mouse is just a matter of clicking in the cell you want to move to. To navigate with the keyboard, refer to Table 8.1.

TABLE 8.1 Keyboard Techniques for Moving the Insertion Point in a Table

Navigation Technique	Moves the Insertion Point
↓	Down one row
↑	Up one row
→	One cell to the right, or character by character to the right if the cell contains text
←	One cell to the left, or character by character to the left if the cell contains text
Tab	One cell to the right; if the cell to the right contains text, it will be selected
Shift+Tab	One cell to the left; if the cell to the left contains text, it will be selected

Selecting Parts of a Table

Selecting is a big deal in a table. In many cases, you have to select the part of the table that you want to affect before issuing a command. For this reason, it's worth taking a few moments to practice the various selection techniques outlined in Table 8.2. Before you do, check to make sure the Draw Table and Eraser buttons in the Tables and Borders toolbar are turned off.

TABLE 8.2 Selection Shortcuts in a Table

Amount Selected	Technique
One cell	Point just inside the left edge of the cell. When the mouse pointer becomes a black arrow, click once.
A group of cells	Select the first cell and then drag over the additional adjacent cells.
One row	Rest the mouse pointer outside of the left border of the table—it should be a white arrow angled toward the table. Click once. (If you've increased the row height or you drew your table, only the top of each cell in the row becomes highlighted. Don't worry; the row is selected.)
Multiple rows	Select the first row and then drag straight up or down to add rows to the selection.
One column	Rest the mouse pointer on the top border of the column. When it changes to a small downward-pointing arrow, click once. You can also Alt+click anywhere in the column.
Multiple columns	Select the first column and then continue dragging to the right or left to add columns to the selection.
Entire table	Click the four-headed arrow icon just outside the upper-left corner of the table. (This icon appears only when the Draw Table and Eraser tools are turned off.)

Changing the Structure of a Table

As you enter text in a table, you will almost certainly need to change its structure. Here you learn the most common adjustments that you'll need to make. As you experiment with these techniques, keep in mind that Word does not prevent you from making a table too wide to fit on the page. If you're adding columns and increasing column widths, check periodically to make sure that table isn't running off the page. (You have to check in Print Layout view or Print Preview—Normal view won't do the trick.)

 Most of the commands in the Table menu are active only when the insertion point is in a table.

Adding and Deleting Rows and Columns

If you want to add a row at the end of the table, click anywhere in the lower-right cell in the table, and press the Tab key.

To add a row in the middle of the table, select the row below the location of the new one, and click the Insert Rows button on the Standard toolbar. (The Insert Table button turns into Insert Rows when a row is selected.) If you want to add two or more rows, select that number of rows before clicking the Insert Rows button.

To insert a column, select the column to the right of where the new one will go, and click the Insert Columns button on the Standard toolbar. (The Insert Table button turns into Insert Columns when a column is selected.) Again, you can add two or more columns at once by selecting that number before clicking the Insert Columns button.

If you want to delete a row or column, select it first, and then choose Table, Delete, Rows or Table, Delete, Columns (or right-click the selected row or column and choose Delete Rows or Delete Columns).

Merging and Splitting Cells

When you merge cells, they become one larger cell. You might, for example, merge all the cells in the top row of a table to create a large cell in which to type a centered title. You can merge cells that are horizontally or vertically adjacent to one another. To merge cells, first select them, and then click the Merge Cells button in the Tables and Borders toolbar.

8

Merging cells is not the same as hiding the lines that separate them. When you merge cells, they become one. When you hide the lines, the cells remain separate.

You can also split a cell into two cells. To do so, click in the cell and then click the Split Cells toolbar button.

Another way to merge cells is to erase the lines between them with the Eraser tool in the Tables and Borders toolbar. And you can split a cell by drawing a line through it with the Draw Table tool.

Formatting a Table

Formatting a table can take far longer than creating it in the first place. Try not to overdo it. If your table is plastered with wild colors, fancy lines, and flamboyant fonts, the text it contains will be almost impossible to read. Also, be careful to select the exact cells that you want to format before issuing a command, and remember that you can always use Undo if you make a change that you don't like.

At the risk of stating the obvious, you can apply all the regular font and paragraph formatting in a table. Select the part of the table that you want to affect, and then use the familiar options in the Formatting toolbar, Font and Paragraph dialog boxes, and so on. The next four sections describe formatting that's specific to tables.

Changing the Appearance of Lines and Adding Shading

To change the appearance of the lines in your table, choose the desired options in the Line Style, Line Weight, and Border Color lists in the Tables and Borders toolbar. (If you want to hide the lines, choose No Border in the Line Style list.) Then turn on the Draw Table tool, if necessary, and draw over the lines you want to affect.

To apply shading, select the desired part of the table, display the Shading Color list in the Tables and Borders toolbar, and click the desired color.

Resizing Columns, Rows, and the Entire Table

To adjust a column's width, drag its right border. To adjust a row's height, drag its bottom border. (When you point to any line in a table, the mouse pointer changes to a double-headed arrow to remind you that you can drag to resize.)

If you want to make multiple rows the same height, or multiple columns the same width, select the rows or columns, and then click the Distribute Rows Evenly or Distribute Columns Evenly button on the Tables and Borders toolbar.

To proportionally resize the entire table, make sure the Draw Table and Eraser tools are turned off, and point to the small square just outside the lower-right corner. Then drag diagonally up and to the left to shrink the table, or down and to the right to enlarge it. If you don't see this square, make sure the Draw Table and Eraser tools are turned off, and rest the mouse pointer inside the table.

Adjusting the Position of the Table on the Page

To move your table around on the page, drag the four-headed arrow icon located just outside the upper-left corner of the table.

Aligning Text and Changing Its Direction

To change the vertical/horizontal alignment of text in your table, select the cells whose alignment you want to change, display the Align list, and click the desired option. To change the direction of text from the default left-to-right to either bottom-to-top or top-to-bottom, select the cell and then click the Change Text Direction button one or more times (see Figure 8.20).

Change Text Direction

FIGURE 8.20

Use the Align and Change Text Direction tools to play with the appearance of text in a table.

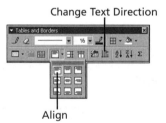

Align

Sorting Rows in a Table

The fastest way to sort rows in a table is to use the Tables and Borders toolbar. Click in the column that you want to sort by, and click the Sort Ascending or Sort Descending button. Word assumes that you want to sort all rows but the first. If you want to include the first row, click in the column to sort by, choose Table, Sort, mark the No Header Row option button, and click OK.

If you have entered numbers in a column, you can have Word total them automatically. Click in the last cell in the column and then click the AutoSum toolbar button to insert a field that sums the numbers above. If you later

8

change some of the numbers, remember to update the field. (It won't update automatically.)

Summary

If you do use even a few of these editing shortcuts, you can greatly reduce, or even eliminate, the tedious and repetitious typing that often goes along with word processing.

The Columns feature is the way to go if you want your text to wrap from one column to the next. For all other documents in which you want text to line up in columns, use custom tabs or tables. You saw here how Word makes tables so easy to add and format.

CHAPTER 9

Inserting Graphics, Drawing Shapes, and Creating Text Effects

One of the perks of using a powerful word processing program is that you get to put pictures in your documents. Graphics help break up the text, convey meaning, and grab the reader's attention. Plus they are just plain fun to work with. Here, you start by learning how to insert an image in your document. This could be a piece of clip art, a photograph or image that you've scanned, a drawing you created in another program, or an image you found on the Web. You then learn how to draw shapes and use WordArt to create special effects with text.

Inserting Images

Word lets you insert images from a variety of sources. You can pull them from the Clip Gallery, or from any folder on your own computer or network.

And if you have a scanner or digital camera, you have the option to import images directly from the scanner or camera software into Word.

Inserting Images from the Clip Gallery

The Microsoft Office CD contains a Clip Gallery of stock clip art images you can use in your documents. Although functional, they are nothing to write home about. However, you can also use the Clip Gallery as a jump-off point to browse a larger gallery of clip art at Microsoft's Web site, and you can use it to catalog all the images you gather from various sources, so you have them all in one place.

To insert a piece of clip art from the Clip Gallery, follow these steps:

1. Move the insertion point to the approximate place where you want to insert the graphic.

2. Place the Microsoft Office CD in your CD-ROM drive, and choose Insert, Picture, Clip Art to display the Insert ClipArt dialog box (see Figure 9.1). If the Drawing toolbar is displayed, you can click its Insert Clip Art button as well. (If you use Word XP or later, you control the Clip Art images from the Word Task Pane that appears to the right of your screen.)

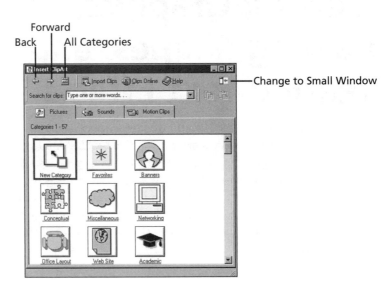

FIGURE 9.1

The Insert ClipArt dialog box lets you browse the images in the Clip Gallery and insert them into your document.

3. In the Pictures tab, scroll through the categories of images and click one that you want to browse.

4. To return to the list of categories, click the All Categories button. To move backward and forward among categories you've already browsed, click the Back and Forward buttons.

5. If you know what type of image you're looking for, type a descriptive word or two in the Search for Clips text box, and press Enter. Word displays the images that most closely match your keywords.

6. When you find an image that you want to use, click it.

7. A small toolbar appears above the image. Click the Insert Clip button (see Figure 9.2). (You can also right-click the image and click Insert in the context menu.)

FIGURE 9.2

Click the image that you want to insert, and then click the Insert Clip toolbar button.

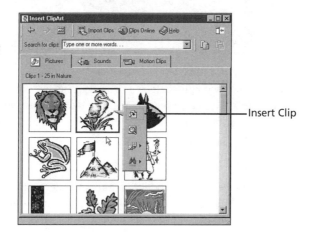

Insert Clip

8. Insert additional images if you like (you may have to drag the dialog box out of the way to see the images in your document), and then click the Close button in the upper-right corner of the Insert ClipArt dialog box.

The graphic is inserted in your document (see Figure 9.3). Don't worry if the image is not the right size, drag one of the eight resizing handle boxes on the image to resize it.

Searching for Clip Art Online

If you don't find a suitable clip-art image in the Insert ClipArt dialog box, you can click the Clips Online button at the top of the dialog box to connect to Microsoft's Clip Gallery Live Web site. After you click this button, you may see a message box telling you to click OK if you have access to the Web and want to browse additional clips. And, depending on your Internet connection, you may also be prompted to connect. Word then launches your browser and takes you to the site.

FIGURE 9.3

After you've got the image in your document, you'll have to do a little tinkering to get its size, position, and appearance just right.

The first Web page you'll see at the site is an end-user license agreement for using the images at the site. Click the Accept button. You can then browse Microsoft's collection of images and download them for free. This set of images is continuously updated, so you might want to check back periodically to see what's new.

Importing Images to the Clip Gallery

You can use the Clip Gallery as a "binder" of sorts to collect all your images in one place. Word gives you three options for how you want to import an image to the Clip Gallery:

- Leave the image in its current location and copy it to the Clip Gallery. Use this option if you want to be able to access the image in its current folder on your computer or network.

- Move the image to the Clip Gallery. You might choose this option if you are short on disk space. This option is not available if the image is on a network drive.

- Leave the image in its current location and ask the Clip Gallery to retrieve it from that location when you issue the command to insert the image. Use this option if you frequently access the image in its current location, but want to be able to access it from the Clip Gallery once in a while.

Follow these steps to add an image to the Clip Gallery:

1. Choose Insert, Picture, Clip Art to display the Insert ClipArt dialog box.
2. Click the Import Clips button at the top of the dialog box.
3. In the Add Clip to Clip Gallery dialog box, choose one of the three option buttons at the bottom of the dialog box.
4. Navigate to and select the image (see Figure 9.4), and click the Import button.

FIGURE 9.4

Select the image that you want to add to the Clip Gallery in the Add Clip to Clip Gallery dialog box.

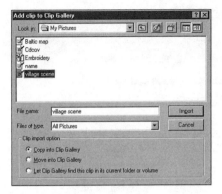

5. The Clip Properties dialog box appears (see Figure 9.5). Type a short description of the image in the Description of This Clip text box. This description is used to label the image in the Clip Gallery.

FIGURE 9.5

Use the Description tab to enter a name to identify your image in the Clip Gallery.

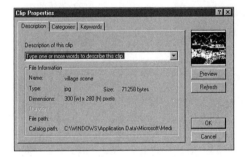

6. Click the Categories tab, and mark the categories in which you want this image to appear (see Figure 9.6). To create a new category, click the New Category button, type the name of the category in the New Category dialog box, and click OK.

7. Click the Keywords tab. You use this tab to enter the keywords that will pull up this image when you perform a search in the Clip Gallery. Click the New Keyword button, enter a keyword in the New Keyword dialog box, and click OK. Repeat this step if you want to add more keywords (see Figure 9.7).

8. Click OK in the Clip Properties dialog box.

The image now appears in the Clip Gallery. If you want to change any of the information that you entered in steps 5–7, right-click the image and choose Clip Properties in the context menu. To remove the image from the Clip Gallery, right-click the image and choose Delete.

FIGURE 9.6

Use the Categories tab to categorize your image in the Clip Gallery.

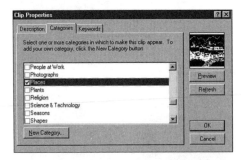

FIGURE 9.7

Use the Keywords tab to enter keywords you can use to search for this image in the Clip Gallery.

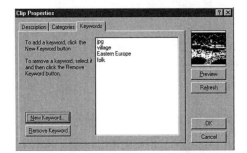

Inserting Images from Other Locations

If the graphic that you want to use is not in the Clip Gallery, but is sitting in a folder on your computer or network, you can insert it in your document. Word can handle graphics files in all sorts of formats, including (but not limited to) BMP, EMF, EPS, PNG, GIF, JPG, PCX, PICT, PING, and WMF. (If these formats don't mean anything to you, don't worry about it. Chances are, Word will be able to use your graphics file without a problem.)

If you want to insert a graphic from a folder on your hard disk or network instead of from the Clip Gallery, follow these steps:

1. Move the insertion point to the approximate place where you want to place the image.
2. Choose Insert, Picture, From File. (Or, if the Picture toolbar is showing, click the Insert Picture toolbar button.)
3. In the Insert Picture dialog box, navigate to and select the desired graphics file (see Figure 9.8). You might want to display the Views list and choose Preview to display a preview of the selected image in the right side of the dialog box.
4. Click the Insert button to insert the image in your document.

FIGURE 9.8

Select the graphics file that you want to insert in the Insert Picture dialog box.

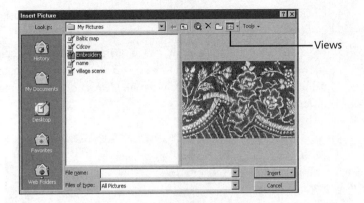

Views

Inserting Scanned Images and Digital Photographs

Word knows how to "talk" to the software that manages scanners and digital cameras. If you have one of these gadgets (they are known as *TWAIN* devices), you can easily insert a scanned image or digital photograph into your Word document, without first saving it as a separate graphics file on disk.

To insert a scanned image or digital photograph from the scanner or camera, follow these steps:

1. Choose Insert, Picture, From Scanner or Camera.

2. In the Insert Picture from Scanner or Camera dialog box (see Figure 9.9), select the camera or scanner that you want to use in the Device list.

FIGURE 9.9

If you have more than one TWAIN device, select the one you want to use.

3. Depending on the software that runs your scanner or camera, the Insert button and the associated Web Quality and Print Quality option buttons may be active or dim. If they're active, the software knows how to send an image to Word with no more participation from you after this dialog box. Select Web Quality (poorer) or Print Quality (better), click the Insert button, and wait for the image to appear in your document. If these buttons are dim, as they are in Figure 9.9, continue with the next two steps.

4. Click the Custom Insert button to launch the software you use for your scanner or camera.

5. Issue the command to scan the image or import it from the camera. Figure 9.10 shows the main program window for software that runs a scanner. Unless you're using the exact same software program (*PaperPort*), your window will look different.

FIGURE 9.10

Use the software that manages your TWAIN device to scan or import the image.

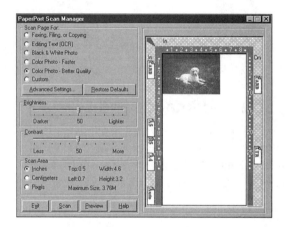

After a moment, the image appears in your document (see Figure 9.11).

FIGURE 9.11

The image appears in your document as soon as it's scanned or imported.

Deleting Images

To delete an image, click it to select it and then press the Delete key. When an image is selected, small squares (called *selection handles*) appear around its edges. Depending on the situation, the squares are either black, as they are in Figure 9.12, or white.

FIGURE 9.12

To delete an image, select it and then press Delete.

Drawing Shapes

Sometimes you don't need a complex graphic in your document—you just need something simple, such as an arrow or a box. Word's Drawing toolbar lets you quickly draw all manner of arrows, rectangles, ovals, callouts, banners, and so on. (You can also create text boxes, which are discussed at the end of this section.) Figure 9.13 shows one example of a drawing you can create with Word's drawing tools.

FIGURE 9.13

This floorplan is a simple example of what you can create with Word's drawing tools.

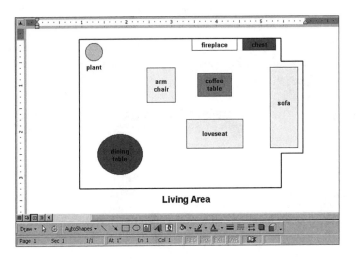

1. Click the Drawing button on the Standard toolbar.
2. The Drawing toolbar appears docked at the bottom of the Word window by default. In Figure 9.14, it has been moved and is floating over the Word window.

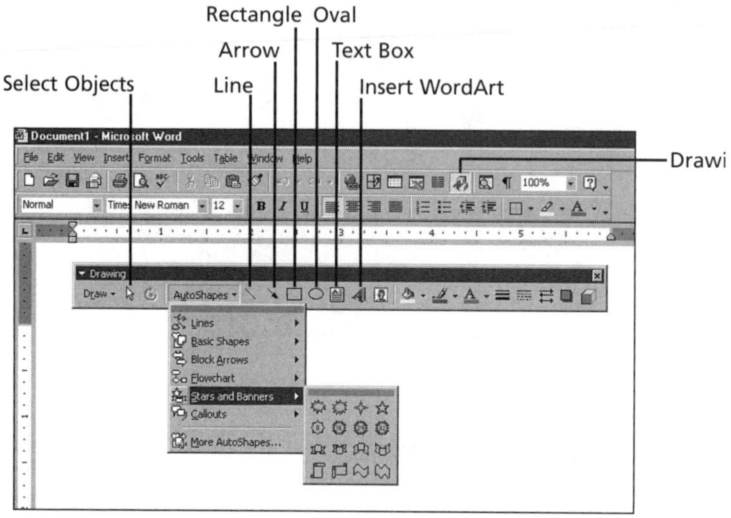

Rectangle Oval

Arrow   Text Box

Select Objects   Line   Insert WordArt

FIGURE 9.14

Click the Drawing button on the Standard toolbar to display the Drawing toolbar.

Drawi

3. Click the drawing tool that you want to use. The tools for basic shapes (lines, arrows, boxes, and so on) are available directly on the toolbar. If you want a more unusual shape, click the AutoShapes button, point to the category that you want to use, and click the shape in the submenu. In Figure 9.14, the Stars and Banners submenu is displayed.
4. Point with the crosshair mouse pointer to the upper-left corner of the area where you want to draw the shape, and drag diagonally down and to the right (see Figure 9.15).

FIGURE 9.15

Drag to create the shape.

5. Release the mouse button to finish drawing the shape.

If you plan on drawing several objects using the same tool (for example, you want to draw several lines), *double-click* the button in step 3. It will stay turned on as long as you want to use it. When you're finished, click it again to turn it off. (This does not work for the tools in the AutoShapes menu.)

If you are using the Rectangle tool and want to draw a perfect square, hold down the Shift key as you drag. This also works with the Oval tool to get a perfect circle, the Star tool to get a perfectly proportioned star, and so on.

9

To delete a drawing object, click it. It will gain small white squares (selection handles). (If it doesn't, click the Select Objects button in the Drawing toolbar and then click the object again.) Then press the Delete key.

One drawing object that deserves special attention is the text box. The Text Box tool on the Drawing toolbar lets you draw a rectangular box in which you can type text. Putting text in a text box gives you control over the position of the text in your document because you can drag the text box around just as you do other drawing objects. In Figure 9.13, you saw that the text labels in the diagram were all created with text boxes. (Their borders were removed, and they were placed on top of other drawing objects.)

To create a text box, click the Text Box tool, drag to create a rectangle of about the right size, and then release the mouse button. An insertion point appears in the box to let you type text (see Figure 9.16).

FIGURE 9.16

When a text box is selected, an insertion point appears in it to let you type.

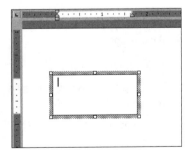

After you've typed your text, you can apply all the usual font and paragraph formatting to it. In addition, you can format the box itself, adjusting the appearance of the borders, changing the fill color, and so on.

In addition to creating text boxes with the Text Box tool, you can type text into any drawing object (with the exception of lines and arrows) by right-clicking it and choosing Add Text in the context menu. An insertion point appears in the object. Type the text as you would in a text box.

Creating Special Effects with WordArt

When you add graphics to a document, you aren't limited to working with images separate from your text. *WordArt* lets you add flair to your text itself. It's perfect for creating splashy headings and titles. You start with a basic "look" for your word or phrase, and then tweak it to get the exact effect you want. After you've added a WordArt image, you can resize it, add borders, and so on. Figure 9.17 shows a heading created with WordArt.

FIGURE 9.17

You can create a variety of effects with WordArt.

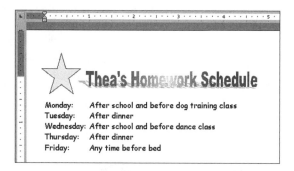

To create a WordArt image, follow these steps:

1. Click where you want the WordArt image to go.

2. Choose Insert, Picture, WordArt. (If your Drawing toolbar is displayed, you can also click the Insert WordArt button on this toolbar.)

3. The WordArt Gallery dialog box opens (see Figure 9.18). Click the look that you want to start with, and click the OK button.

4. The Edit WordArt Text window appears.

5. Type the text for your WordArt image, replacing the Your Text Here placeholder text (see Figure 9.19). Your text won't take on the look you chose in step 3 until it's inserted in the document.

6. Use the Font and Size lists and the Bold and Italic buttons to make additional adjustments to the text.

7. Click the OK button.

FIGURE 9.18

Choose the WordArt style that most closely matches what you want.

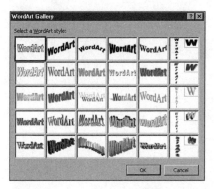

FIGURE 9.19

Type the text that you want to use in the Edit WordArt Text window.

The WordArt image appears in your document. To revise the WordArt text or change its appearance after you've created the image, use the WordArt toolbar. This toolbar appears as soon as you insert a WordArt image. If you don't see it, choose View, Toolbars, WordArt.

Summary

You can insert existing images into your documents—via the Clip Gallery or from another location on your computer or network—or you can create new images with the drawing tools or WordArt.

PART IV

Using Word to Manage Documents

Chapter

CHAPTER **10**

Generating a Mass Mailing

When you want to send a letter to a large number of people, Word's mail merge feature lets you sidestep the tedious task of personalizing the document for each recipient. You prepare two documents: the form letter and a list of the recipients' names and addresses. Word then "merges" the information from the list into the form letter to generate the mass mailing.

Understanding Mail Merges

Before you start the mail merge process, you need to understand the two documents that make up a mail merge:

- *Main document*—This is the actual document that you are producing. It can be a form letter or label. The main document contains the text and formatting that stays the same for each copy of the letter, as well as *merge fields*, which "hold places" that tell Word where to insert individual pieces of information from the *data source*.

- *Data source*—This is the file that contains the data you will merge into the main document. It is organized into *records*, one for each recipient. Each record is composed of individual fields for specific pieces of information, such as first name, last name, address, and so on.

Starting the Main Document

In this first phase of the mail merge process, you tell Word which document you want to use as the main document.

Follow these steps to start your main document:

1. If you have an existing letter that you want to use for your form letter, open it now, and delete any parts of it (such as the name and address) that you don't want to include in the form letter. If you want to start a letter from scratch, start a new, blank document.

2. Save the document (use File, Save As if you've opened an existing document) with a name such as *Form Letter - Main* to remind you that it is a main document.

3. Choose Tools, Mail Merge to display the Mail Merge Helper dialog box.

4. Click the Create button, and click Form Letters in the drop-down list (see Figure 10.1).

FIGURE 10.1

Use the Mail Merge Helper dialog box to start your mail merge.

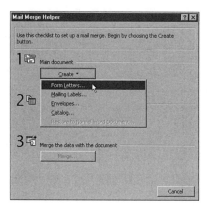

5. Word displays a message box asking whether you want to use the active document as your main document or start a new document.

The Mail Merge Helper dialog box appears again with information about the main document listed under the Create button. Continue with the next section.

Creating and Saving the Data Source

In this second phase, you tell Word which document you want to use as your data source. You can either create a new one or open an existing one.

The key step in creating a data source is telling Word which fields you want to use. Typical fields are first name, last name, company, address, city, state, ZIP code, and so on. Include a field for any piece of information that you might want to include in your main document. For example, if you want to refer to the recipient's job title in your form letters, be sure to include a job title field. (When you are entering your records, as described in the next section, you can always leave a field blank if you don't have that piece of data for a particular recipient.)

Follow these steps to create and save the data source:

1. Click the Get Data button in the Mail Merge Helper dialog box, left open from the previous section, and choose Create Data Source in the drop-down list (see Figure 10.2).

10

FIGURE 10.2

Choose Create Data Source to create a new data source.

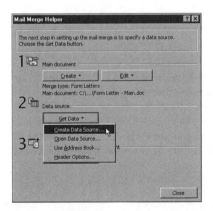

2. The Create Data Source dialog box appears (see Figure 10.3). To remove a field that you don't want, click it in the Field Names in Header Row list, and then click the Remove Field Name button.

3. To add a field, first replace the contents of the Field Name text box with the name of the field you want to add. Then click the Add Field Name button to add the name to the Field Names in Header Row list. (This button becomes active as soon as you type text in the Field Name text box.) No spaces are allowed in field names.

FIGURE 10.3

Use the Create Data Source dialog box to define the fields you want to use in your data source.

The order of the fields in the Field Names in Header Row list determines the order in which they will appear when you enter the data later on. If you want to adjust the position of a field in the list, click it and then use the Move arrows to the right of the list to move it up or down.

4. When your list of fields is the way you want it, click OK.

If your mailing list contains a lot of addresses with building or department names, suite numbers, and so on, keep the Address2 field to use for this information. The Salutation field is a good one to add to a data source. Use it to store the name that will appear after *Dear* in the letter. This lets you adjust the way you address a letter depending on the recipient. For example, if a person's FirstName field contains *Elizabeth* and the LastName field contains *Larson,* you can enter *Liz* in the Salutation field if you know the recipient well, or *Ms. Larson* if you want to be more formal.

5. Word displays the Save As dialog box to let you save your data source. Save it with a name that will remind you that it's a data source, such as *Mailing List and Data Source*.

6. When Word asks what you want to do next, click the Edit Data Source button.

The Data Form appears to let you enter data in your new data source. Continue with the next section.

If you already have a table of names and addresses in a database program such as Access, you may be able to use that table as your data source. In step 1 in the previous list, click Open Data Source instead of Create Data Source, display the Files of Type list in the Open Data Source dialog box, and click the appropriate file format. Locate and select your database, and then click the Open button.

Entering Records into the Data Source

In this third phase, you enter the records in your data source. Luckily, you have to do this only once—in the future, you can use the same data source with other main documents.

1. The blank Data Form that appeared at the end of the previous section contains text boxes for all the fields that you defined for your data source.

2. Enter the information for the first person in your mailing list, using the Tab key to move from field to field.

3. Click the Add New button to add the next record (see Figure 10.4).

FIGURE 10.4

Add your records one by one to your data source.

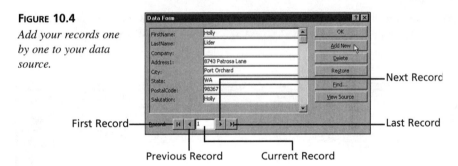

Next Record

First Record

Previous Record   Current Record

Last Record

Be careful not to click the OK button at this point. If you do, Word assumes you are finished entering records and closes the Data Form. If this happens, click the Edit Data Source button at the far-right end of the Mail Merge toolbar to redisplay the Data Form.

4. Word clears the Data Form to let you enter record 2. Continue entering records.

5. The Record arrows let you move forward and back in your data source so that you can review and revise records you've already entered.

6. When you've finished entering all the records, click the OK button.

Your main document appears onscreen. Continue with the next section.

Completing the Main Document

In this fourth phase, you finish the main document. This entails typing and formatting the text (if you started your main document from scratch) and inserting the merge fields that tell Word where to insert the data from your data source.

Follow these steps to complete the main document:

1. Word has displayed your main document. Notice the Mail Merge toolbar directly under the Formatting toolbar. This toolbar automatically appears in main documents—you'll learn how to use many of its buttons in the remainder of this chapter.

2. Type and format the text that stays the same in all the form letters, including the letterhead (unless you're using preprinted letterhead), the body of the letter, and so on. If you opened an existing document in "Starting the Main Document," confirm that you've deleted all the personal data (the name, address, salutation, and any text in the body of the letter that's specific to the recipient).

3. Place the insertion point on the line where the address block will go, and click the Insert Merge Field button in the Mail Merge toolbar. In the list that appears, click the first field in the address block, usually Title or FirstName (see Figure 10.5).

FIGURE 10.5

The Insert Merge Field button lists all the fields in the attached data source.

Mail Merge toolbar ⌐

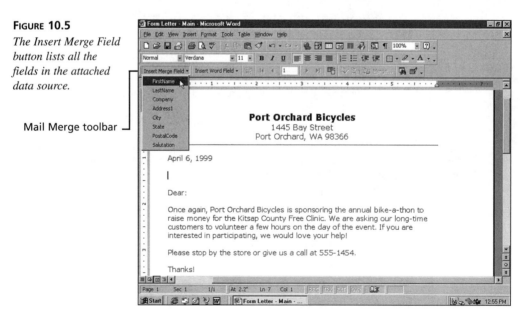

4. Word inserts the merge field surrounded by chevron brackets. Insert the remaining merge fields in the address block, pressing Enter and adding spaces and commas

where necessary. If you have a salutation field, add it after *Dear*, and follow it with
a colon or comma (see Figure 10.6).

Figure 10.6

*Add all of your merge
fields to your main
document.*

Merge fields ——

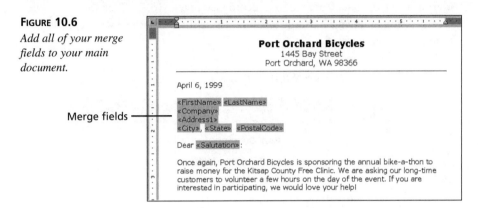

5. Save the main document, and leave it open for the next section.

When you close the main document (either before or after performing the
merge), Word may ask whether you want to save the data source attached
to the main document. You'll see this message box if you have any unsaved
changes in your data source. Click the Yes button. Otherwise, you'll lose any
changes you've made to your data source (this could mean hours of typing if
you've added a lot of records). If you have unsaved changes in your main
document, you will then be asked to save it as well. Click Yes again.

If you later want to convert your main document back to a normal Word
document, open it, choose Tools, Mail Merge. In the Mail Merge Helper dialog box, click the Create button, and choose Restore to Normal Word
Document. In the message box that appears, click the Yes button, and then
click the Close button in the Mail Merge Helper dialog box.

Running the Merge

In this final phase of the mail merge process, you merge the main document with the
data source to produce your letters. The first two steps in the following list are
optional—they let you confirm that the data will merge correctly before you actually perform the merge.

1. After completing step 5 in the previous section, click the View Merged Data button on the Mail Merge toolbar.

2. Word displays the data from the first record (see Figure 10.7). Click the Next Record button on the Mail Merge toolbar. (These Record buttons work exactly like those in the Data Form.)

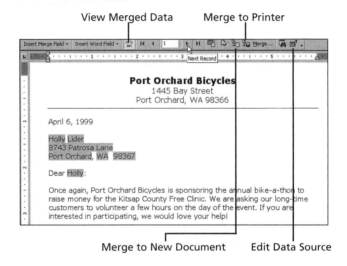

FIGURE 10.7

Optionally use the View Merged Data button to check for errors in your data and merge fields.

3. Word displays the data from the next record. Look at a few more to see whether the data is merging correctly. If you find any mistakes in the data, click the Edit Data Source button to display the Data Form, revise the data, and then click OK. When you're finished, click the View Merged Data button again to turn it off.

4. Click the Merge to New Document button on the Mail Merge toolbar to merge the documents.

If you're merging a large number of letters, you may want to click the Merge to Printer button instead. This button also performs the merge, but the letters are sent directly to the printer instead of appearing onscreen in a new document. (A document containing hundreds of merged letters would be hundreds of pages long, and if your computer doesn't have much memory, it may balk at the task of displaying the document onscreen.)

5. The merged letters appear in a document entitled *Form Letters1* (see Figure 10.8). Scroll down the document. The letters print on separate pages because Word

separates them with next page section breaks. (If your main document is a multiple-page letter, the section break comes at the bottom of the last page of each letter.) Click the Print button in the Standard toolbar to print the letters.

FIGURE 10.8

The Form Letters document contains all your merged letters, separated by next page section breaks.

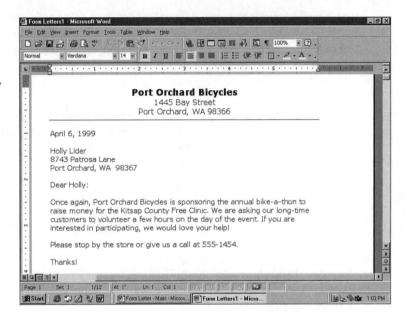

6. Close the *Form Letters1* document without saving it. (You don't need to save the merged letters because you can always run the merge again.) Then click the taskbar button of the main document to switch to it if necessary, and close it as well.

Everything else you can do with mail merge builds on the procedure you've just completed.

Running Subsequent Merges

When you want to merge the same main document and data source in the future, just open the main document with the usual File, Open command, and click the Merge to New Document or Merge to Printer button in the Mail Merge toolbar. That's all there is to it.

If you want to merge an existing main document with a different data source than the one you used with it previously, you can attach a new data source. Open the main document, choose Tools, Mail Merge, and click the Get Data button.

Then, if you want to create the new data source from scratch, choose Create Data Source and continue with the steps described earlier to run the merge (starting with "Creating and Saving the Data Source").

If you want to attach an existing data source, click Open Data Source, select the data source in the Open Data Source dialog box, and click the Open button. Back in the Mail Merge Helper dialog box, click the Merge button, and then click the Merge button again in the Merge dialog box to run the merge.

> If you attach a data source that has different field names than the ones referenced in the merge fields in your main document, you'll get errors when you try to run the merge. To prevent this from happening, check the merge fields in your main document. If they don't match the data source, delete them and insert them again using the Insert Merge Field toolbar button (this button always displays the merge fields in the currently attached data source).

Editing Your Data Source

The easiest way to edit an existing data source is to open it through the main document to which it is attached.

Follow these steps to edit your data source:

1. Open the main document.
2. Click the Edit Data Source button at the far-right end of the Mail Merge toolbar to display the Data Form.
3. Edit the records. You can revise and delete existing records, and add new ones.
4. When you're finished, click OK.
5. Save the main document, and click Yes when Word asks whether you want to save the data source.

The one drawback to this method is that it's easy to forget to save the data source in step 5. If this feels risky and you want more control over saving the data source, you can open and edit your data source directly instead of using the Data Form.

Word actually stores your data source in a Word table. To view this table, click the View Source button in Data Form, or choose File, Open and open your data source file.

In a data source table, each field is a column, and each record is a row (see Figure 10.9). Word provides the Database toolbar at the top of data source files to let you easily revise your data.

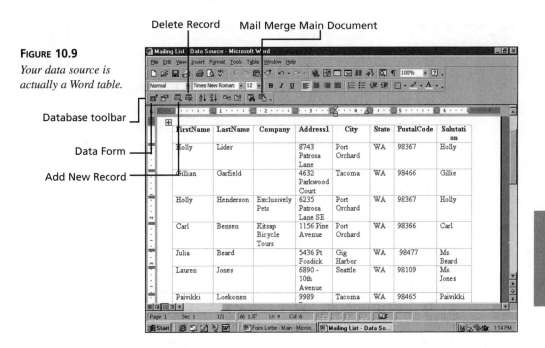

FIGURE 10.9
*Your data source is
actually a Word table.*

You can add or delete a record by adding a row and filling in the data for the record, or selecting the row that contains the record and deleting it. However, it's a little faster to use the Add New Record and Delete Record toolbar buttons. When you click the Add New Record button, Word automatically adds a blank row at the bottom of the table. When you click the Delete Record button, Word deletes the row containing the insertion point.

If you like entering data through the Data Form better than typing it directly in the data source table, click the Data Form toolbar button. If you want to view the main document to which the data source is attached, click the Mail Merge Main Document toolbar button.

The Database toolbar provides the same Sort Ascending and Sort Descending buttons as those in the Tables and Borders toolbar. You can use them to sort your table by the field (column) in which you want the merged letters to appear the next time you run your merge.

If you make changes in your data source table, remember to save it before closing.

Merging Envelopes and Labels

Chances are that you usually need to print envelopes to go with your form letters. When you merge addresses onto envelopes, the five basic steps of performing a mail merge (described earlier) stay the same. However, two aspects of the process are slightly different:

- The main document is an envelope instead of a form letter.
- It's easier to merge envelopes from the Mail Merge Helper dialog box than from the Mail Merge toolbar in the main document.

Before you practice these steps, note that if you have an envelope tray on your printer that holds a stack of envelopes, it will be much simpler for you to merge labels. (To merge envelopes without an envelope tray, you would have to feed each envelope manually.)

Follow these steps to merge envelopes:

1. Start a new document, and save it with a name such as *Envelopes - Main*. This is your main document.
2. Choose Tools, Mail Merge to display the Mail Merge Helper dialog box.
3. Click the Create button under Main Document, and then choose Envelopes.
4. Word asks what document you want to use as your main document. Because you've already started the main document, click the Active Window button.
5. Click the Get Data button, and then click Open Data Source. In the Open Data Source dialog box, navigate to and select your data source, and then click the Open button.
6. When Word informs you that it needs to set up the main document, click the Set Up Main Document button.
7. Word displays the Envelope Options dialog box (see Figure 10.10). Change the envelope size if necessary, and then click OK.

FIGURE 10.10

Use the Envelope Options dialog box to tell Word what kind of envelopes you're using.

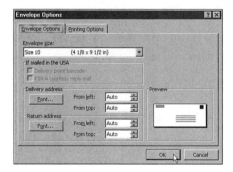

8. Word displays the Envelope Address dialog box to let you insert the merge fields in the envelope. Use the Insert Merge Field button to insert all the fields in their proper positions, pressing Enter at the end of the lines, and inserting commas and spaces as necessary (see Figure 10.11). Then click OK.

FIGURE 10.11

Insert the merge fields that you want to use on your envelope.

9. Word redisplays the Mail Merge Helper dialog box, and the Merge button is now active. You'll also see the envelope appear in the Word window behind the dialog box. Click the Merge button to display the Merge dialog box.

10. Be sure New Document is selected in the Merge To list unless you want to merge directly to the printer, and click the Merge button to run the merge.

11. Word merges the envelopes into a document named *Envelopesl*, shown in Figure 10.12 in Print Layout view. Scroll through the envelopes to make sure there aren't any problems, make sure your envelopes are properly loaded in your printer, and then print using the standard methods. You can close this document without saving it. (To generate the envelopes again, just rerun the merge.)

FIGURE 10.12

The merged envelopes appear onscreen after you run the merge.

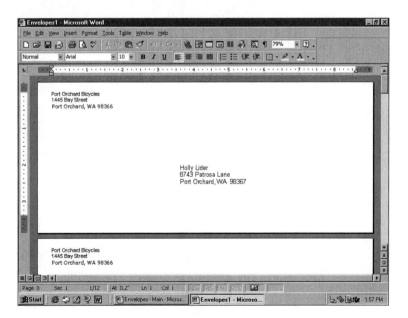

12. Click the taskbar button of the main document (your envelopes) if necessary to switch to it. Then save and close it.

> Word automatically prints the return address on merged envelopes. If you want to omit it, use either of these rather clunky workarounds: Before you run the merge, choose Tools, Options. Click the User Information tab. Delete the address under Mailing Address, and click OK. After you've merged and printed the envelopes, retype the address in the User Information tab. Alternatively, you can click Cancel in step 9 to close the Mail Merge Helper dialog box before clicking the Merge button. Delete the return address from the main document, and choose Tools, Mail Merge to go back to the Mail Merge Helper dialog box. Click the Merge button and continue with the steps.

Summary

You should now have a good feel for how to run a merge, although it will probably take a little practice to feel completely comfortable with the process. If you veer off the beaten path and become perplexed, come back to the procedure described here to solidify your understanding of the basic steps.

CHAPTER 11

Collaborating on Documents

Now that networks and email are commonplace, companies are equipped to let people collaborate on documents without printing them out. For example, you can write the rough draft of a document and send it to a colleague for review. This person edits the document onscreen and then sends it to a second person, who adds more revisions before emailing the document back to you. After you receive the edited copy, you incorporate your colleagues' suggestions and finalize the document.

Using the Highlighter

Word's *highlight* feature lets you mark up your document onscreen just as you would use a highlighter pen to mark up a printed document. Highlighting is designed for use on documents that you'll edit onscreen, but it will also print out. If you don't have a color printer, highlighting prints in a shade of gray.

To use the highlighter, follow these steps:

1. Click the down arrow to the right of the Highlight button on the Formatting tool-bar, and click the color that you want to use in the palette that appears (see Figure 11.1).

Highlight

FIGURE 11.1

You can choose among many highlighter colors.

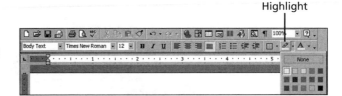

2. The I-beam takes on the shape of a highlighter pen. Drag across the text that you want to highlight, and then release the mouse button.

3. The text is now highlighted with the color you chose (see Figure 11.2). Highlight any other text you like, and then click the Highlight button again to turn the feature off.

FIGURE 11.2

Highlight text to call attention to it.

Our clinic is working hard to increase the percentage of dogs and cats in South Kitsap who get regular immunizations. To this end, we are donating our services to run a series of low-cost vaccination clinics at local pet stores. We are currently looking for a store that is willing to host this clinic for one weekend in July. If you are interested, please give us a call at 769-6674.

The Highlight button shows the color that you most recently selected from the palette. If you want to use that color, click the button itself in step 1 instead of choosing a color in the palette.

Another way to apply highlighting is to select the text and then click the Highlight button (or display the palette and choose a different highlight color).

To remove highlighting, select the text, display the Highlight palette, and choose None.

Working with Comments

You may, at times, want to write notes in a document (either to yourself or to other authors) that don't print out. Word's *Comment* feature lets you add comments that reference particular blocks of text, and track comments from multiple authors.

If you work extensively with comments, you'll appreciate the buttons in the Reviewing toolbar (choose View, Toolbars, Reviewing), shown in Figure 11.3. If you use Windows XP or later, the Reviewing toolbar shows slightly different icons from those shown in Figure 11.3.

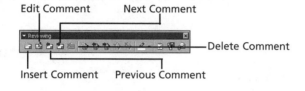

FIGURE 11.3

The Reviewing toolbar contains buttons for working with comments.

To add a comment to a document, follow these steps:

1. Select the text that you want to comment on.

2. Click the Insert Comment button in the Reviewing toolbar. (You can also choose Insert, Comment or press Alt+Ctrl+M.)

3. Word highlights the text you selected, opens the comment pane at the bottom of the document window, and inserts a reference mark for the comment in the document and in the comment pane. Type your comment in the comment pane (see Figure 11.4).

FIGURE 11.4

Type your comment about the highlighted text in the comment pane.

Comment pane

4. Click the Close button at the top of the comment pane.

The reference mark is made up of your initials and a sequential number. It is formatted as *hidden text*, so it appears onscreen only when the comment pane is showing or the Show/Hide button in the Standard toolbar is turned on. The dotted underline under reference marks (see the reference mark [TL1] in Figure 11.4) just indicates that it's hidden text.

11

Word closes the comment pane. When the Show/Hide button is turned off, the reference mark is hidden from view. You can tell where the comment is, however, because the text that you selected is still highlighted.

To read a comment, rest the mouse pointer over the highlighted text. In a moment, a ScreenTip appears with the name of the person who wrote the comment and the comment itself (see Figure 11.5).

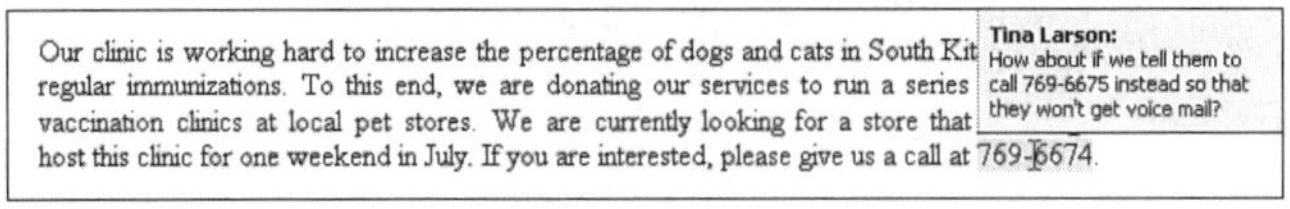

FIGURE 11.5
Rest your mouse pointer over highlighted text to read the associated comment.

Our clinic is working hard to increase the percentage of dogs and cats in South Kit... **Tina Larson:** How about if we tell them to call 769-6675 instead so that they won't get voice mail? regular immunizations. To this end, we are donating our services to run a series vaccination clinics at local pet stores. We are currently looking for a store that host this clinic for one weekend in July. If you are interested, please give us a call at 769-6674.

To move from one comment to the next in a document, click the Next Comment and Previous Comment buttons in the Reviewing toolbar.

To edit your comments, click the Edit Comment button in the Reviewing toolbar (or right-click the highlighted text of any comment and choose Edit Comment in the context menu). Word opens the comment pane to let you revise the comment text. When you are finished, click the Close button at the top of the comment pane.

To delete a comment, click to the left of the comment and click the Delete Comment button in the Reviewing toolbar (or right-click the highlighted text and choose Delete Comment from the context menu).

Tracking Changes to a Document

The cornerstone of Word's collaboration features is *track changes*. This feature lets you track the revisions (insertions, deletions, and a few formatting changes) that are made to a document. When the feature is turned on, any text you insert in the document is displayed in color with an underline. Text you delete is shown in color with strikethrough. If more than one person edits a document, each person's changes show up in a different color. When you are ready to finalize a document, you can go through and accept or reject each tracked change.

As you work with tracked changes, you may want to use the buttons in the Reviewing toolbar, as shown in Figure 11.6.

Tracking Your Changes

To turn track changes on (or off), click the Track Changes button in the Reviewing toolbar. The TRK indicator in the status bar at the bottom of the Word window is dark when track changes is turned on. (You can also double-click the TRK indicator, press

Ctrl+Shift+E, right-click the TRK indicator and choose Track Changes from the context menu, or choose Tools, Track Changes, Highlight Changes, and mark or clear the Track Changes While Editing check box.)

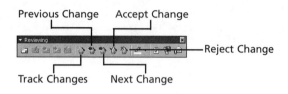

FIGURE 11.6
The Reviewing toolbar contains buttons for working with tracked changes.

After you've turned on track changes, revise your text as you normally do. If more than one person has edited a document and you want to see who made a particular change, rest your mouse pointer over the revision. A ScreenTip appears that lists the name of the person who made the edit, and the date on which it was made (see Figure 11.7).

FIGURE 11.7
When you rest your mouse pointer over a tracked change, Word tells you who made the change and when.

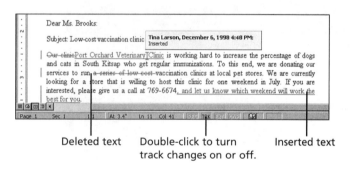

One of the advantages of using track changes is that you can hide the changes to see how the text would flow if you accepted all of them. To do so, choose Tools, Track Changes, Highlight Changes to display the Highlight Changes dialog box (see Figure 11.8), clear the Highlight Changes on Screen check box, and click OK.

FIGURE 11.8
Clear the Highlight Changes on Screen check box to hide the tracked changes.

Figure 11.9 shows the same text as you saw in Figure 11.7, but the tracked changes are hidden. Hiding changes does not turn off the track changes feature. If you like, you can edit the document while changes are hidden, and Word continues to track your edits.

When you next mark the Highlight Changes on Screen check box, you will see all the revisions you made when changes were visible and when they were hidden.

FIGURE **11.9**

Hiding tracked changes is a great way to see how the text would read if the changes were all accepted.

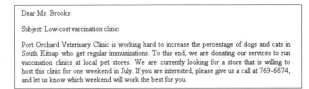

Understanding the Colors of Tracked Changes

By default, Word assigns a different color to each person (author) who edits a document. To see how this works, choose Tools, Options to display the Options dialog box, and click the Track Changes tab (see Figure 11.10).

FIGURE **11.10**

The Track Changes tab of the Options dialog box lets you change the settings for track changes.

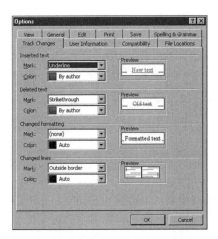

For the colors to work properly, you have to use the default setting of By Author in the Color lists under Inserted Text and Deleted Text. You can't choose a particular color for your revisions; when you edit a document with track changes turned on, Word assigns you the next available color in its color palette. If you choose a specific color in the Color lists, all authors' edits will appear in that color, which defeats the purpose of using track changes.

Helping Word Recognize Different Authors

Word recognizes the different authors who work on a document by checking the name that's listed in the Name text box in the User Information tab of the Options dialog box (choose Tools, Options), as shown in Figure 11.11.

FIGURE 11.11

Make sure your user information is current before using track changes.

Before you use track changes, you should check the User Information tab and make sure that your name is entered correctly. If it isn't and you revise a document with track changes turned on, other people who review the document after you will assume that your edits were made by whomever happens to be listed in the User Information tab.

In some cases, you may need to edit a document twice. If you want your edits on separate passes to appear in different colors, change the name in the User Information tab before you begin your second pass. For example, you could enter *Tina Larson (first pass)* in the User Information tab before beginning your first pass, and then change it to *Tina Larson (second pass)* before beginning your second pass.

Accepting and Rejecting Tracked Changes

When you have finished editing a document with track changes, you need to go through and decide whether to accept or reject each of the revisions. If you accept an insertion, the inserted text becomes part of the document. If you accept a deletion, the text is removed.

Follow these steps to accept or reject the changes in a document:

1. Press Ctrl+Home to move to the top of the document.
2. Click the Next Change button in the Reviewing toolbar to find and select the next change.
3. Click the Accept Change or Reject Change toolbar button.
4. Click Next Change again, and continue accepting or rejecting changes until Word informs you that it found no tracked changes in the document.

You can also accept and reject changes in the Accept or Reject Changes dialog box. Choose Tools, Track Changes, Accept or Reject Changes, click the Find buttons to move from one change to the next, and click the Accept or Reject buttons to accept or reject them. One advantage of using this dialog box is that it lists the author and date of each change as you're reviewing the document. Another advantage is that it includes Accept All and Reject All buttons, which you can use to accept or reject all of the changes in a document without reviewing them one by one.

Protecting Documents from Being Revised

You might want to keep your document (or template) from being revised by other people. If you turn on this type of protection, other people can open and edit your document, but they can't overwrite the original document with their revised version. Instead, they are prompted to save the edited document under a different name and/or location.

To protect your document from revisions, follow these steps:

1. With the document onscreen, choose File, Save As.
2. Click the Tools button at the top of the Save As dialog box, and click General Options.
3. In the Save dialog box, type a password in the Password to Modify text box. Passwords can be up to 15 characters long, and they are case sensitive.
4. Click OK.
5. Retype the password in the Confirm Password dialog box, and click OK again to return to the Save As dialog box.
6. Finish saving the document.

The next time you open the document, the Password dialog box appears. If you know the password to modify the document, you can enter it and click OK. Otherwise, you have to click the Read Only button to open the document.

If you open the document as a read-only file, the label [Read-Only] appears in the title bar to remind you that if you revise the document, you will have to save the edited document under a new name.

If you enter a password in the Password to Open text box, the user can't even open the document without the password. The Read-Only Recommended check box is the lightest level of protection. If you mark it, Word suggests that the user open the document as a read-only file, but doesn't require him/her to do so. (You would most likely use this check box instead of requiring either type of password.)

Saving Different Versions of a Document

If you need to create several versions of the same document (several versions of your résumé, perhaps), you might want to keep them all in one place under the same filename instead of saving them as separate documents. Word's versioning feature lets you save multiple versions of a document under the same name. For each version, Word stores information about who created it, when it was created, and a brief description of it.

To save a version of a document, follow these steps:

1. Open the document, and revise it to create the version that you want to save.
2. Choose File, Save As.
3. Click the Tools button at the top of the Save As dialog box, and click Save Version.
4. In the Save Version dialog box, type a brief comment about the version that's onscreen.
5. Click OK.

When you later want to open a particular version of a document, first open the document, and then choose File, Versions to display the Versions dialog box. This dialog box lists any versions of the document that you have saved with the versioning feature. Select the one that you want to work with, and click the Open button.

11

Summary

Collaborating on documents with other people has plenty of rewards, but it can be frustrating if you lose track of who made what changes when. Word's collaboration features can bring some semblance of order to an essentially messy process. Now that you know what features Word has to offer, you'll be better able to decide whether and how you and your colleagues might work on Word documents as a team.

CHAPTER 12

Using Other Office Data with Word

If you use other Office applications and want to use data from them in your Word documents, you'll learn some useful techniques here. You can integrate Office applications in many ways. In this chapter, you'll see how to use Excel and PowerPoint to integrate those programs' data with Word data.

Inserting Data from Excel Worksheets

If you want to insert data from an Excel worksheet, you can, of course, copy it into a Word document with the Copy and Paste commands. (Select the desired cells in Excel, issue the Copy command, switch to the Word document, click at the desired location, and issue the Paste command.)

When you use this method, Word puts the Excel data in a table, which you can format and modify with the table and column techniques you learned in Chapter 8, "Correcting Documents and Using Columns and Tables." In Figure 12.1, the data in the table was pasted from an Excel worksheet.

Figure 12.1

Excel data that you insert with the Copy and Paste commands appears in a Word table.

This method has two drawbacks. First, the Excel formulas are converted to plain numbers, so they won't update if you revise any of the numbers in the table. Second, no link exists between the pasted data in the Word document and the original data in the Excel worksheet, so revising the data in Excel does not update it in Word.

One way to avoid these shortcomings is to *link* the pasted data in Word to the original data in the Excel worksheet. Then whenever you update the data in Excel, it is automatically updated in the Word document.

To insert linked data from Excel into your Word document, follow these steps:

1. In Excel, select the cells that you want to copy to Word and issue the Copy command.

2. Switch to the Word document, move the insertion point to the desired location, and choose Edit, Paste Special to display the Paste Special dialog box.

3. Mark the Paste Link option button, choose Microsoft Excel Worksheet Object in the list in the middle of the dialog box (see Figure 12.2), and click OK.

Figure 12.2

Choose Paste Link in the Paste Special dialog box to link the pasted data with the original data in Excel.

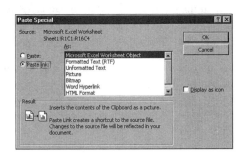

4. Switch back to Excel, press Escape to turn off the marquee around the copied data, and then close the workbook.

The data is pasted into Word as an object, as shown in Figure 12.3 (note the selection handles around the data).

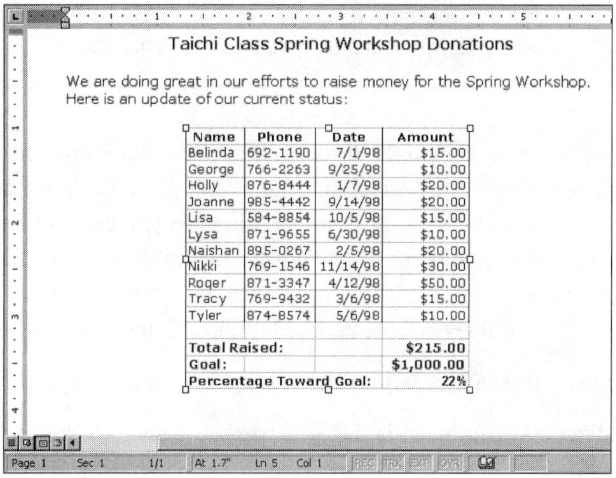

Name	Phone	Date	Amount
Belinda	692-1190	7/1/98	$15.00
George	766-2263	9/25/98	$10.00
Holly	876-8444	1/7/98	$20.00
Joanne	985-4442	9/14/98	$20.00
Lisa	584-8854	10/5/98	$15.00
Lysa	871-9655	6/30/98	$10.00
Naishan	895-0267	2/5/98	$20.00
Nikki	769-1546	11/14/98	$30.00
Roger	871-3347	4/12/98	$50.00
Tracy	769-9432	3/6/98	$15.00
Tyler	874-8574	5/6/98	$10.00
Total Raised:			$215.00
Goal:			$1,000.00
Percentage Toward Goal:			22%

FIGURE 12.3
Your Excel data appears as an object in Word.

To edit the data in Excel, double-click the linked object in your Word document. In a moment, the associated worksheet opens in Excel with the linked cells selected (see Figure 12.4). When you revise the data in Excel, it is instantly updated in the Word document. (You can't edit the linked data in the Word document.)

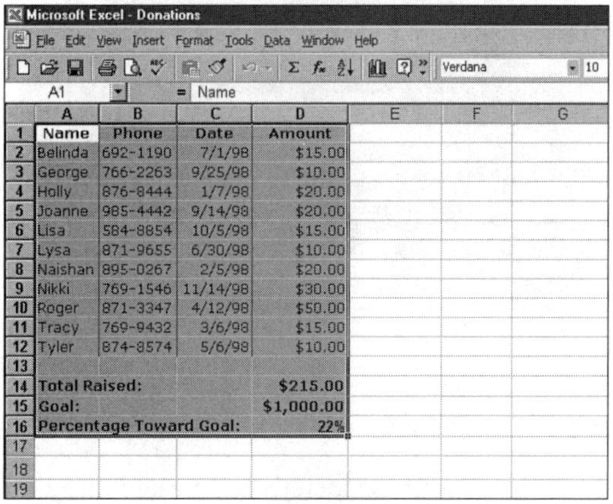

	A	B	C	D
1	Name	Phone	Date	Amount
2	Belinda	692-1190	7/1/98	$15.00
3	George	766-2263	9/25/98	$10.00
4	Holly	876-8444	1/7/98	$20.00
5	Joanne	985-4442	9/14/98	$20.00
6	Lisa	584-8854	10/5/98	$15.00
7	Lysa	871-9655	6/30/98	$10.00
8	Naishan	895-0267	2/5/98	$20.00
9	Nikki	769-1546	11/14/98	$30.00
10	Roger	871-3347	4/12/98	$50.00
11	Tracy	769-9432	3/6/98	$15.00
12	Tyler	874-8574	5/6/98	$10.00
13				
14	Total Raised:			$215.00
15	Goal:			$1,000.00
16	Percentage Toward Goal:			22%

FIGURE 12.4
Any changes you make to the data in Excel are immediately reflected in your Word document.

If the Word document isn't open when you revise the data in Excel, it's updated the next time you open the document.

If you move the Excel workbook that contains the source data, you have to tell Word where to find it. To do so, select the linked object in Word, and choose Edit, Links to display the Links dialog box. Click the Change Source button, navigate to and select the workbook in the Change Source dialog box, click the Open button, and then click OK.

Another option is to embed the Excel data in your Word document. When you use this technique, double-clicking the embedded object displays the Excel interface—menus, toolbars, and so on—within the Word window, so you can use Excel controls to revise the data without ever leaving Word. When you embed data, the Excel data "lives" in the Word document and is not linked to original data in Excel. When you edit the data in the Word document, it does not get updated in the original Excel worksheet, and vice versa.

To embed Excel data in a Word document, follow these steps:

1. In Excel, select the cells that you want to copy to Word and issue the Copy command.

2. Switch to the Word document, move the insertion point to the desired location, and choose Edit, Paste Special to display the Paste Special dialog box.

3. Mark the Paste option button, choose Microsoft Excel Worksheet Object in the list in the middle of the dialog box (see Figure 12.5), and click OK.

FIGURE 12.5

Choose Paste in the Paste Special dialog box to embed the pasted data in the Word document.

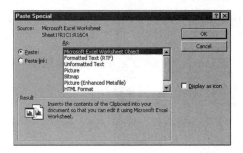

4. Switch back to Excel and press Escape to turn off the marquee around the copied data, and then close the workbook.

Just as when you link the data, embedded data is pasted into Word as an object. However, Word responds differently when you double-click an embedded object. Instead of displaying the source data in Excel, it displays the Excel interface in the Word window, as shown in Figure 12.6.

FIGURE **12.6**

FIGURE 12.6

*You can use Excel
controls to edit the
embedded data in your
Word document.*

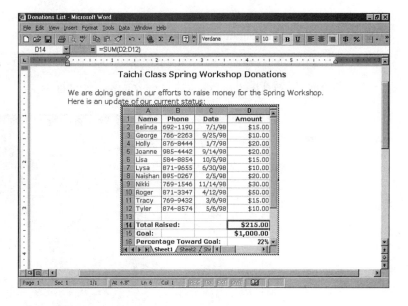

You can also start an embedded Excel worksheet from scratch in your
Word document instead of beginning with data that you pasted from an
existing Excel worksheet. To do so, click the Insert Microsoft Excel Worksheet
toolbar button in the Standard toolbar, drag across the number of cells that
you want to start out with in the drop-down grid, and release the mouse
button.

12

Inserting PowerPoint Presentations and Slides

You can, of course, use a no-frills approach to getting text and slides from a PowerPoint
presentation into your Word documents. Simply use the standard Copy and Paste commands. If you go this route, your pasted data maintains no link to the source data in the
PowerPoint presentation. If you want to get a little fancier, try one of the other options
described here.

If you want to export a PowerPoint presentation to a Word document, you can issue a
command in PowerPoint to create a write-up of the presentation in Word. When you do
this, you can choose to paste the slides in the *write-up* as embedded or linked objects. If
you embed the slides in the Word document, they are not linked with the original presentation. When you double-click one of the slides, the PowerPoint interface appears in the
Word window. In contrast, if you link the slides, double-clicking one of them in the Word

document opens the source slide in PowerPoint. If you edit the slide in PowerPoint, you can tell Word to update it in the write-up.

Follow these steps to create a write-up of your presentation in a Word document:

1. Start PowerPoint and open the presentation (see Figure 12.7).

FIGURE 12.7

Open the presentation that you want to export to a Word document.

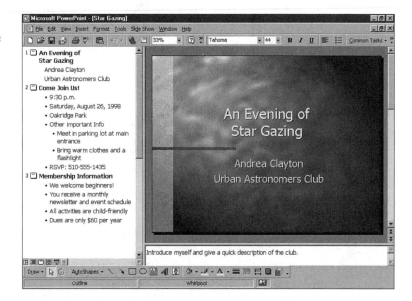

2. Choose File, Send To, Microsoft Word to display the Write-Up dialog box (see Figure 12.8).

FIGURE 12.8

The Write-Up dialog box lets you choose how you want the presentation to look in Word.

3. Mark the option button under Page Layout in Microsoft Word that most closely matches the layout you want to use.

4. Mark the Paste option button to embed the slides in the Word document, or mark the Paste Link option button to link them to the original slides in PowerPoint.

5. Click OK.

In a moment, the presentation appears in a Word document (see Figure 12.9). Note that Word has placed it in a table, so you can modify its appearance.

FIGURE 12.9

The PowerPoint presentation appears in a Word table.

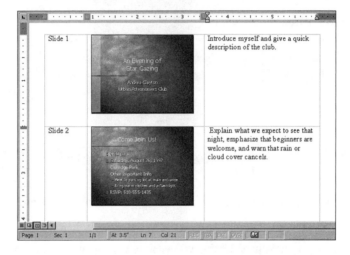

If you chose Paste in step 4, each slide in the Word document is an embedded object. When you double-click a slide, the PowerPoint controls appear in the Word window, as shown in Figure 12.10.

If you chose Paste Link in step 4, each slide in the Word document is an object that's linked to the original slide in PowerPoint. To edit the slide in PowerPoint, double-click it in the Word document. Unlike linked Excel data, linked PowerPoint slides don't update instantly when you modify them in PowerPoint. To update the slide object in Word, select it and press F9.

To ensure that the most current version of the slides always prints, choose File, Print in Word, click the Options button in the lower-left corner of the Print dialog box, mark the Update Links check box, and click OK. Back in the Print dialog box, click OK to print or Close to close the dialog box without printing.

In addition to exporting an entire PowerPoint presentation to a Word document as a write-up, you can also insert individual slides, either as linked or embedded objects.

12

FIGURE **12.10**

You can use PowerPoint controls to edit the embedded slides in your Word document.

PowerPoint controls

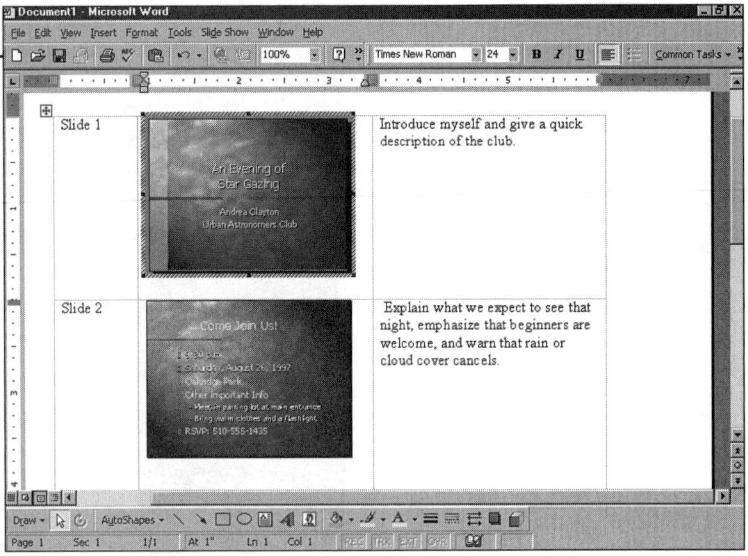

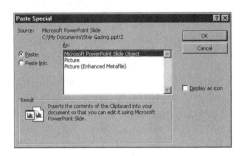

Follow these steps to insert an individual slide in your Word document:

1. In PowerPoint, choose View, Slide Sorter to switch to Slide Sorter view.

2. Right-click the slide that you want to copy to Word, and choose Copy.

3. Switch to the Word document, move the insertion point to the desired location, and choose Edit, Paste Special to display the Paste Special dialog box.

4. Mark the Paste or Paste Link option button, and choose Microsoft PowerPoint Slide Object in the list in the middle of the dialog box (see Figure 12.11), and click OK.

FIGURE **12.11**

Choose Paste or Paste Link in the Paste Special dialog box to embed or link the pasted slide in the Word document.

If you have linked PowerPoint slide objects (either in a write-up or individual slides) in a Word document, make sure to select the slides and press F9 to update them if you edit the source slides in PowerPoint. Also, you need to tell Word if you move the source presentation. Select all the slide objects in the Word document by holding the Ctrl key and clicking each object you want to select, then choose Edit, Links to display the Links dialog box. Select the objects in the Links dialog box (drag to select more than one), click the Change Source button, select the source presentation in the Change Source dialog box, click Open, and then click OK.

Summary

You just learned how to enhance your Word documents with material that you created in other Office applications. The general principles of linking and embedding are not limited to Microsoft Office programs—they apply to all Windows applications. Feel free to take ideas from this chapter and experiment with bringing data from other applications into your Word documents, or bringing Word text into documents in other applications.

12

CHAPTER 13

Using Word with the Web

Word gives you a host of options for integrating Word and the Web. You can turn Word documents into Web pages, turn Web pages into Word documents, and create Web pages from scratch in Word. And if you are responsible for making Web pages accessible to other people on an intranet or Internet site, you can even handle this task from the Word window.

Converting Word Documents to Web Pages

If you have information in a Word document that you want to let a large number of people read, you can convert the document to a Web page and then post the page on a Web site, the Internet, or your company intranet. Before you convert your document, however, check with your network administrator to see whether it's necessary. In some cases, you can put Word documents on company intranets without changing the document format at all.

Follow these steps to save a Word document as a Web page:

1. Open the Word document that you want to convert or create a document now (see Figure 13.1).

2. Choose File, Save As Web Page to display the Save As dialog box.

3. Optionally click the Change Title button to revise the title that will appear in the title bar for the page. Then specify a name and location for the page (see Figure 13.2), and click the Save button.

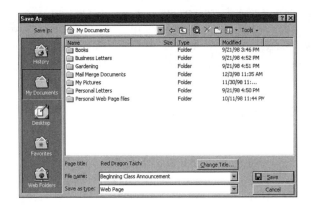

4. You may see a message such as the one shown in Figure 13.3 stating how Word will modify formatting that can't be rendered in a Web page. If this modification is okay, click the Continue button.

FIGURE 13.3

Word tells you it can't convert all the formatting in the Word document.

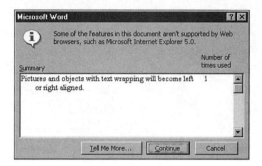

5. The newly converted Web page appears in the Word window (see Figure 13.4). Word automatically switches to Web Layout view (View, Web Layout) whenever it displays a Web page.

FIGURE 13.4

Word displays your Web page in Web Layout view.

Red Dragon Taichi

Taichi is an internal martial art founded in China. It is called an "internal" martial art because its training focuses on relaxation, alignment, and energy cultivation instead of strength training and athletic conditioning. You can think of Taichi as a moving form of yoga and meditation combined. The movements are performed smoothly, softly, and gracefully.

A new 8-week beginning class is starting on November 9. The class meets Mondays and Wednesdays from 5:30p.m. to 7:00p.m., and the cost is $22.50 per month. The instructor, Roger Cloutier, has been practicing Taichi for 29 years and has extensive teaching experience. Classes are easygoing and fun. For more information, call the Givens Community Center at 337-5733.

6. If you want to see what the page will look like when viewed in a browser, choose File, Web Page Preview.

7. Your browser opens and displays the Web page. In Figure 13.5, the Web page is displayed in Internet Explorer. Close your browser when you're finished viewing the page.

13

FIGURE 13.5

*You can view your Web
page in your browser
to see how it will look
to others.*

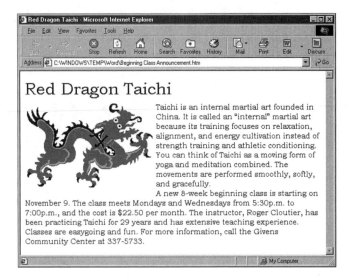

Converting Web Pages to Word Documents

Once in a while, you may want to save a Web page as a Word document. Perhaps you found a recipe on a Web site and want to edit the text in Word, or you discovered a Web page about woodworking and want to take advantage of Word's formatting and printing capabilities to spruce it up a bit. When you convert a Web page to a Word document, Word does its best to preserve the formatting in the page.

Follow these steps to save a Web page as a Word document:

1. Display the Open dialog box, type the address for the Web page in the File Name text box, and click the Open button. (Make sure to include the `http://` at the beginning of the address in the File Name text box.)

2. Word prompts you to connect to the Internet if necessary, and then opens the Web page in the Word window (see Figure 13.6). Choose File, Save As to display the Save As dialog box.

3. Choose a location for the document, and type a name in the File Name text box.

4. Display the Save As Type list and select Word Document.

5. Click the Save button.

The Web page is saved as a Word document, and all the graphics are included in the document itself.

FIGURE 13.6

Word can display Web pages as well as Word documents.

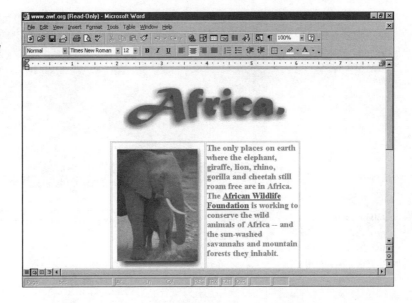

Step 1 in the previous steps describes how to open a Web page directly from the Internet. You could also use your browser to save the page to your hard disk, and then open it from your hard disk. If you use this latter method, make sure to select All Files in the Files of Type list in the Open dialog box so that the Web page will be visible. (By default, Word shows only Word documents in the Open dialog box.)

Creating Web Pages in Word

Word gives you a variety of ways to create Web pages—and you don't have to be a professional Web page designer to make them look good. In this section, you get a taste of creating a Web page from scratch. For practice, you'll create a "personal Web page" and use one of Word's many themes ("looks") to give the page some visual flair.

To create a Web page with a theme, follow these steps:

1. Choose File, New to display the New dialog box.

2. Click the Web Pages tab, click the Personal Web Page icon, and then click OK (see Figure 13.7).

3. The default Web page opens (see Figure 13.8). The hyperlinks under Contents (Work Information, Favorite Links, and so on) lead to locations in the same page. To make the page more visually appealing, choose Format, Theme.

13

FIGURE 13.7

Select Personal Web Page to practice creating a Web page in Word.

FIGURE 13.8

Word creates the Web page with plain formatting and placeholder text.

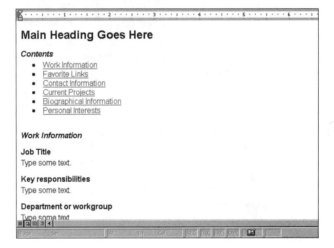

4. In the Theme dialog box, click a few themes in the Choose a Theme list. You can preview each theme in the Sample of Theme area. When you find one that you like, select it (see Figure 13.9) and click OK.

5. Word applies the theme to the Web page. Select all the placeholder text and replace it with your actual text (see Figure 13.10). Then save and close the page.

FIGURE 13.9

Choose a theme that is visually appealing to you.

FIGURE 13.10

Replace the place-holder text with your content.

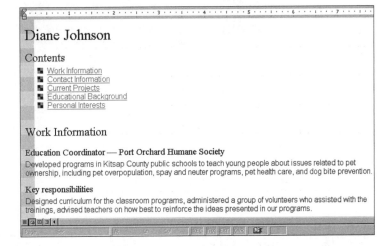

Making Your Web Pages Available to Others

13

To make your Web pages visible to others, you have to copy (*upload*) them to the Internet Web site or intranet site where they will "live." You can do this in the Save As dialog box. Choose File, Save As, and then click the Web Folders icon on the left side of the dialog box. If you see the location you want, select it and then click the Save button. If you don't see the right location here, you can specify the location yourself.

You typically upload pages to a Web or intranet site via a *protocol* called *FTP*, for *File Transfer Protocol*. So telling Word where you want to upload your Web pages involves defining an FTP location. You have to do this only once. From then on, you will be able to choose the FTP site in the Save As dialog box.

Follow these steps to set up an FTP location for uploading your Web pages to a Web site on an intranet or the Internet:

1. Choose File, Save As, and then select Add/Modify FTP Locations in the Save In list (see Figure 13.11).

FIGURE 13.11

Use Add/Modify FTP Locations in the Save In list.

2. Word displays the Add/Modify FTP Locations dialog box. Type the name of the site in the Name of FTP Site text box. Most FTP sites begin with *ftp*. (If you aren't sure of the name, ask the system administrator at the site.)

3. If you don't have a personal account at the site, mark the Anonymous option button. If you do, mark the User option button, and enter your username and password. Then click the Add button to add the site to the list of FTP sites at the bottom of the dialog box and click OK.

Many companies let people who don't have personal accounts log in to their FTP site as anonymous users. Anonymous users have access to only certain public areas of a site, and they may not be permitted to upload files at all.

4. The new FTP location now appears in the Save In list (and in the Look In list in the Open dialog box). Select it if necessary, and then click the Open button.

5. Word connects to the Internet (or your intranet) if you aren't already online, and displays the contents of the folders at the FTP site.

6. Navigate to the folder in which you want to save the Web page, type a name for it in the File Name text box (use all lowercase), and click the Save button.

Word saves your Web page at the FTP site. It is now in a location where other people can access it via their browsers. If you need help with this process, ask your network or system administrator.

Summary

You just took a tour of Word's Web-related features. You now have the skills to create simple Web pages and make them available to your friends and co-workers.

13

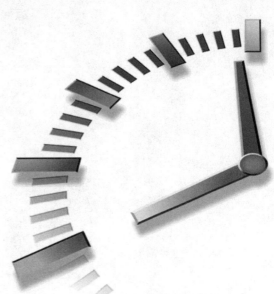

PART V

Managing Contacts, Email, and Tasks in Outlook

Chapter

CHAPTER 14

Touring with Outlook

If you're like most people, the first thing you want to know when you get something new is "What can it do?" This chapter puts Outlook through its paces to give you a quick idea of what it can do and how it can help organize and simplify certain aspects of your life. You'll first be introduced to various components of Outlook without examining them in depth. This will be the grand tour.

What Can Outlook Do for Me?

Information: You can't live with it; you can't live without it. So the only rational course is to try to manage it. Outlook's central mission is to help you get a handle on a good chunk of the onslaught of information that confronts you each day. Outlook is designed to be the centerpiece of your computerized workplace. Outlook combines email, scheduling, and management of contacts, tasks, and notes. Outlook can also keep track of your use of other Office applications. Each day, Outlook Today greets you with a summary of what's on tap.

Outlook can help simplify and organize certain aspects of your life, assuming that you are willing to invest a little time to take advantage of the tools provided. Among other things, Outlook can

- Automatically organize your incoming and outgoing email and faxes, including routing unwanted junk mail directly into the electronic trash bin.
- Keep track of and schedule events and appointments—online and otherwise, one-time and recurring.
- Keep track of your work with Office applications.
- Help you coordinate work with other Outlook users by providing a common medium for engaging in a productive electronic dialogue; this includes sharing data over LANs, WANs, and the Internet.
- Be your electronic social secretary, keeping track of Girl Scout meetings, shopping lists, family reunion details, weddings, anniversaries, birthdays, holidays, and mail to and from Grandma.
- Manage multiple email accounts in a single Personal Folders file, saving you the work of coordinating information from diverse sources.
- Handle business and personal data, simultaneously, while giving you the tools to keep business and private matters organized and separate.

What Can't Outlook Do for Me?

Although Outlook is nicely integrated with the rest of Microsoft Office, it cannot take the place of other Office components. Outlook is not a word processor—although it seems to come close sometimes, and it does appear to have taken over the role of creating much routine office and personal correspondence. Outlook is more decidedly not a spreadsheet, database, or presentation manager. However, through *OLE* (object linking and embedding) and integration, Outlook gets along well with its Office siblings—Word, Excel, and PowerPoint.

Outlook's Personalized Menus and Toolbars

A few years ago, Microsoft began adding features to Office and other applications to help the software adapt to the way you work. It's called *IntelliSense*—software that senses how you work and adapts to your style. Office supports IntelliSense features, personalized menus and toolbars, just as Word does. In a nutshell, Outlook's menus and toolbars keep track of which features you use most often and give them a prominent place. Features used less often (or not at all) gradually slink out of sight.

Start Outlook so that you can see some of this functionality in action. With Inbox displayed, click View in Outlook's main menu. Notice the double arrows at the bottom of the View menu, as shown in Figure 14.1. This tells you that additional commands are hidden at the bottom. If you leave the View menu open for about five seconds, it automatically expands. To see the additional choices even sooner, click the double arrows.

To see the full list of choices immediately, double-click the main menu item instead of single-clicking. The keyboard equivalent is to press the hotkey (for example, Alt+V for View) twice instead of once. Or you can activate any menu item by using its complete hotkey sequence, even if the corresponding item is hidden. For example, Alt+V followed by S (View, Status Bar) toggles Outlook's status bar, even if Status Bar is not visible on the personalized menu.

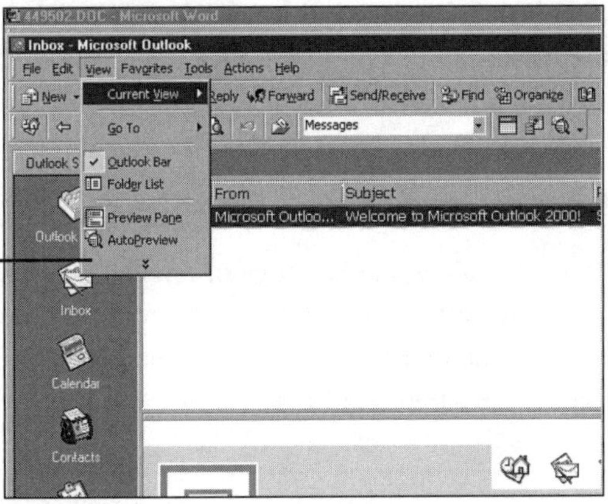

FIGURE 14.1
Personalized menus move seldom-used commands out of sight.

Expand menu

When a toolbar contains more icons than you can display at one time, a double arrow appears at the right as you've seen in Word's menus. Click the double arrow to display the rest of the choices.

If you'd rather see the full menus all the time, choose Tools, Customize, and then click the Options tab. Deselect Menus Show Recently Used Commands First to turn personalized menus off (see Figure 14.2).

In fact, to ensure that the screen shots in this book are as consistent as possible, this book assumes that you've done the following:

- Turned off personalized menus
- Turned on the Advanced toolbar

14

FIGURE 14.2

Uncheck Menus Show Recently Used Commands First while reading this book!

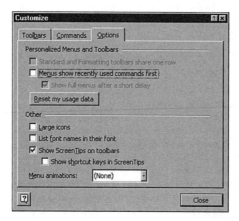

If you turn off personalized menus, most of what you see onscreen will agree with what you see in this book. Similarly, turning on the Advanced toolbar will make your screen agree with ours, as well as giving you quick access to many features described in this book. To display the Advanced toolbar, right-click any menu or toolbar and choose Advanced.

Using Shortcuts on the Outlook Bar

The *Outlook Bar* is located along the left edge of the Outlook window. By default, it contains shortcuts to frequently used folders. Information for each Outlook component (mail, contacts, calendar, and others) is kept in a separate folder. The shortcuts in the Outlook Bar are simply icons pointing to the various folders.

While Outlook Bar shortcuts can include shortcuts to Windows file system folders (subdirectories), Outlook folders such as Inbox, Outbox, Calendar, and so on are not actually folders in the Windows file system. They are instead subsets of your personal folder file (.pst) or offline folder file (.ost).

If you use Outlook XP or later, the Outlook Bar looks hardly anything like the one shown here (this is the Outlook 2000 version). The folders are grouped differently in Outlook XP but you access virtually all of the concepts you master in this text in the same way.

The Outlook Bar contains three groups of shortcuts—Outlook Shortcuts, My Shortcuts, and Other Shortcuts—each of which can be modified to meet your needs. You can create shortcuts to specific files, URLs, and other resources.

> *URL* stands for uniform resource locator. In popular parlance, a URL is a Web address (for example, www.samspublishing.com). Technically, the URL includes the protocol as well, such as ftp or http (for example, http://www.samspublishing.com).

Outlook Shortcuts

The default Outlook Shortcuts group usually contains seven icons:

- *Outlook Today*—Summary of pending appointments, tasks, and recent emails
- *Inbox*—Email you've received
- *Calendar*—Scheduling of appointments, meetings, and events
- *Contacts*—Address and phone list
- *Tasks*—Keep track of work
- *Notes*—Electronic yellow sticky notes
- *Deleted Items*—Outlook items you've deleted

Depending on your screen resolution and whether Outlook is maximized, you may not be able to see all the shortcut icons at once. If you see an arrow near the top or bottom of the Outlook Bar, you can click it to view the other icons.

My Shortcuts

To see the second set of shortcuts, click on the My Shortcuts bar near the bottom of the Outlook Bar. Outlook displays a different set of icons. By default, you should see the following:

- *Drafts*—Unsent messages that are being composed.
- *Outbox*—Undelivered messages.
- *Sent Items*—Delivered messages.
- *Journal*—A log of Outlook and Office activities.
- *Outlook Update*—A URL that points to a Microsoft Outlook Update site so you can download patches and features that Microsoft might make available over the Internet.

14

Other Shortcuts

The last set of shortcuts, Other Shortcuts, contains icons used to open the following:

- *My Computer*—The Windows file system
- *My Documents*—Default location for storing Microsoft Office files
- *Favorites*—Shortcuts you create to documents, files, folders, and URLs

You can customize and rearrange all three of these shortcut areas as well as add and delete folders and other items. To get started navigating Outlook, follow these steps:

1. Make sure that only the Outlook Shortcuts bar is at the top of the Outlook Bar. Click Outlook Today. The screen changes, as shown in Figure 14.3. You might want to make this your starting screen, rather than the Inbox. You'll learn how to make such changes shortly.

FIGURE 14.3

The Outlook Today screen can be used as a table of contents, leading to other functions logically used in conjunction with Outlook.

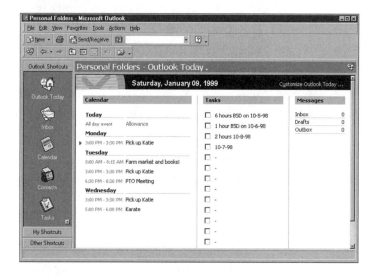

2. You've already looked at the Inbox screen (where email is stored), so click the Calendar shortcut. Your screen should be similar to the one shown in Figure 14.4 (you might also see the TaskPad in the lower-right corner).

3. At some time during your work with Outlook, you may not be able to see the shortcut icon you need. Remember, use the up or down arrow on the Outlook Bar to see additional icons. Now, click the Contacts icon. (If you're a new Outlook user, your list might be empty. You'll remedy that a little later.) Your screen should be similar to the one shown in Figure 14.5.

4. Now that you have an idea of how to move between Outlook components, check out each one. Then return to the Outlook Today screen.

FIGURE 14.4

The Calendar allows you to set dates and times for appointments, events, and meetings.

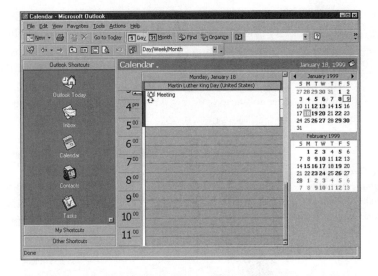

FIGURE 14.5

Contacts is an extremely powerful phone book and address book.

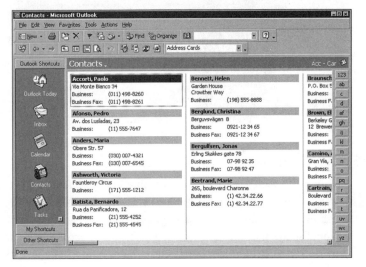

Outlook Today

The Outlook Today page provides a preview of the current day (as well as several days in the future). You can see a summary of your appointments for the day, a list of scheduled tasks, and even a listing of your new mail messages (email, fax, and other kinds of computer-controlled messages). Outlook Today serves as an electronic briefing room where you can see the big picture and decide how to organize your day. The Outlook Today page can be set as the first folder to open when you start Outlook. Many users find this more helpful than having the Inbox open first.

14

To change the default opening page to Outlook Today, click the Customize Outlook Today button. By default, it's in the upper-right corner of the Outlook Today window. However, it can change locations, depending on options you choose, so you might need to hunt for it later. The Customize Outlook Today page, shown in Figure 14.6, is displayed. Check the When Starting, Go Directly to Outlook Today box. Then click Save Changes to return to Outlook Today. From now on, Outlook Today will be the opening page when you open Outlook.

FIGURE 14.6

The Outlook Today Options box allows you to set Outlook Today as your beginning screen in Outlook.

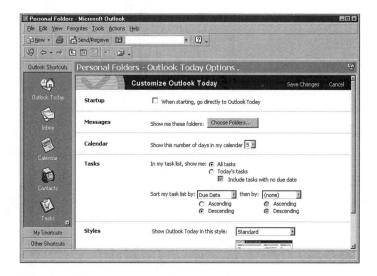

Using the Inbox for Email

The Inbox is a storage folder for incoming mail. By default, the Inbox window is divided into two panes. The top pane contains a listing of multiple messages in message view (each message is displayed as a single line of text). Beneath that is the Preview pane, which displays the text of the message. The lower scrollbar on the right side of the window is used to scroll through the selected message. If you have more messages than can be displayed in the upper window, you can use the upper scrollbar to scroll through them.

You can modify the height of the upper and lower windows by dragging the dividing bar that separates them. Move the mouse pointer over the bar. When the pointer turns into a horizontal line with a double-headed vertical arrow, you can drag the boundary up or down to adjust the size of the windows.

Keeping a Calendar

Now that you've had a brief look at the Calendar, let's enter some data and see how it interacts with other Outlook modules. Outlook integrates Calendar data with other Outlook components, so making a change in one module affects the display in other modules. You can make a calendar entry by following these steps:

1. Click the Calendar shortcut on the Outlook Bar. As shown back in Figure 14.4, the day is divided into half-hour segments. (Later, you'll learn how to control the segment length.) Click on the 12:00 p.m. bar. The entire half-hour segment turns blue. Type "Lunch at the SalaDeli with Karen Sandusky" and press Enter.

2. In the Calendar window in the upper-right corner, click on the day on either side of the current day. Notice that today's date is boldfaced. That means that an appointment has been entered. Click the current date again.

3. This is a business lunch, so a half hour probably isn't enough time. While you're here, hover the mouse pointer over the appointment. If the text is too long to display in full, hovering the mouse pointer over the item will display the full text as a popup ToolTip. To extend the time of this appointment, point to the bottom of the segment (it's outlined in blue). The cursor changes to a double-headed vertical arrow. Drag the bottom of the box down until two segments are filled (the time between 12:00 and 1:00) to allocate a full hour.

4. Click the Outlook Today icon. Your screen should be similar to the one shown in Figure 14.7. If you have already used Outlook, you may have additional entries displayed.

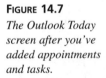

FIGURE 14.7
The Outlook Today screen after you've added appointments and tasks.

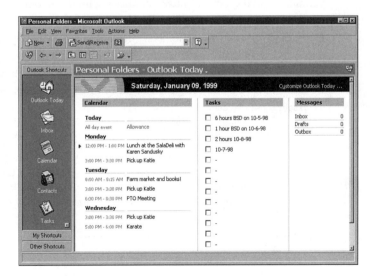

14

Working with Contacts

The Contacts module of Outlook acts as a high-performance telephone and address book. Not only can you enter basic information about each person, but you also can add information about their family or business and document each interaction you have with them. As always, feel free to substitute actual data for the data you see in the next steps as you follow along.

1. Click the Contacts icon on the Outlook Bar. If you haven't yet created or imported any contacts, no information will be displayed. Note the index tab at the right, which resembles the side of a personal address book.

2. Click the New Contact button (the leftmost button on the Standard toolbar). Your screen is now similar to the one shown in Figure 14.8. For now, you'll just enter some basic data.

3. Click in the Full Name text box. Type Katherine Madison. You can move to the next field by pressing the Tab key (or press Shift+Tab to move to the previous field), or you can click in the field where you want to enter data. Press Tab to move to the Job Title field. In the Job Title box, type CEO. Press Tab.

4. Look in the File As text box. You'll see that Outlook automatically files the name by last name, followed by first name. The drop-down arrow allows you to file the information by first name instead. Alternatively, you can file the contact using some other name, such as the name of the company. Type Forklift Computing in the Company field. Press Tab three times to move to the Business phone field. Type 703-555-4321. Press Tab until the insertion point is in the Address box. Note that you might get the Check Phone Number popup if Outlook regards the telephone number as ambiguous in some way. You can click OK or Cancel, as appropriate. Depending on your international settings, after you tab away from the Business phone field, Outlook sometimes reformats it by putting the area code in parentheses. In the Address box, type 1234 Industrial Drive. Press Enter. Type Alexandria, VA 22308 and press Tab four times to move to the E-mail text box. Type kmadison@forklift.com.

Depending on your settings, you might receive the Check Address dialog box when you press Tab after entering the address. If this always happens to you, you might consider entering the address in the Check Address dialog box to begin with. Click the Address button to display the Check Address box.

FIGURE 14.8

This screen is used to input contact data.

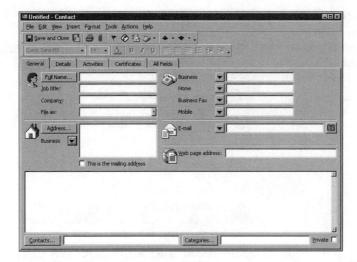

5. So far, you have entered information only on the General tab. Click each of the other four tabs (Details, Activities, Certificates, and All Fields) to see the other types of information that can be stored. Click the Save and Close button on the toolbar. The screen now contains the basic contact information you entered. Notice that not all fields are visible from this screen (such as Job Title and Company). To open the contact information, simply double-click anywhere on it. Press Esc to dismiss the contact without making any changes.

Assigning and Managing Tasks

If you want to add tasks or add more information, you can use Outlook's Task Manager module. Here you can change the status, the due date, and the current percentage completed, and you can assign the task to a specific category. You can even prioritize each task. The following steps introduce you to Outlook's task-entering feature.

1. Click the Tasks icon on the Outlook Bar. Click the box below the subject to enter a new task. Type `Call George about documentation for the loan model`. Press Enter.

2. Click under Subject to enter a new task. Type `Call Linda and Forrest about concert schedule`. Click in the Due Date field. You can either type a date directly or click the drop-down arrow to choose a date from a calendar. This time, type `12/12/99`. Press Enter.

3. To see the full list of possibilities for the task, double-click anywhere on the task. The Task dialog box for the specific task is displayed, as shown in Figure 14.9. You may have to resize the window to see all of it. Click to see the Details tab information, and then click the Task tab.

14

FIGURE **14.9**

The Task tool lets you create, specify, and assign tasks.

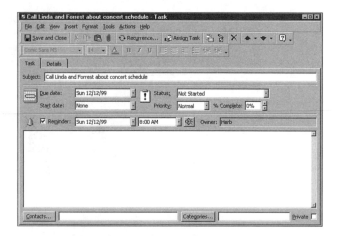

4. Click the Categories button at the bottom of the Task dialog box. The Categories dialog box, shown in Figure 14.10, is displayed.

FIGURE **14.10**

Use the Categories dialog box to assign and create categories for tasks.

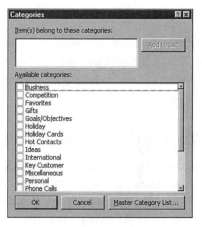

5. Type Research in the Item(s) Belong to These Categories box and click the Add to List button. Click the Business category. Business, Research is now displayed in the Category field for this task. This also adds Research to the master list. To manage the list of categories, click the Master Category List button. Here you can also delete categories, as well as add categories or reset the list to the default. Click OK to close the Categories box, and then click Save and Close to close the task.

Keeping a Journal

Journal is a semiautomatic diary. It can be used to track phone calls you make, track the time you spend working on a specific project, and even automatically log the time you spend working in each Office application. Like most Outlook tools, Journal can be customized to fit your needs and the way you work.

Using Outlook Notes

Do you have pieces of scratch paper or sticky notes all over your office (or your car, or your home)? You know that you wrote down the information that you need somewhere. The question is, where? The *Notes* feature of Outlook can help clean up your sticky-note problems.

If you're compulsive about writing things down, and if the very act helps you remember, Outlook's Notes feature probably won't solve the litter problem in your office. But it's worth a shot, right?

Click the Notes icon on the Outlook Bar. The Notes window shown in Figure 14.11 contains a handful of notes. Yours might be blank. In the next few steps, you will create three notes and then search to find the information you need.

FIGURE 14.11

The Notes module can contain hundreds or even thousands of notes, which can be easily searched, categorized, and sorted.

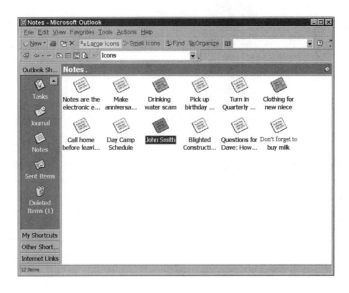

1. Click the Notes icon on the Outlook Bar. The screen should be similar to the one shown in Figure 14.9. Depending on how Outlook was installed, you might have an introductory note created during installation.

14

2. To create your first note, click the New Note button on the left edge of the Standard toolbar. A yellow note appears on the screen with the insertion point already positioned. Type `Don't forget to buy milk`, and press Enter. If you type additional text, the first line (up to where you press Enter) becomes the title. Close the note by clicking the Close button.

3. Create two more notes. Click the New Note button and type `Ask IDSK about connection rates 800-555-6789`. Close the note. Click the New Note button again and type `Questions for Dave: How much will it cost; how long will it take; and when can he start?` Close the note. As shown in Figure 14.12, if you don't explicitly create a title by pressing Enter, the entire text is used as the note title. Otherwise, only the title is displayed.

FIGURE 14.12

If you don't press Enter, the entire note can be interpreted as the title.

Contacts, tasks, and journal entries are normally used for permanent information, whereas the information in Notes usually is temporary. After something temporary makes the transition to permanent, you can quickly convert a Note into a different kind of Outlook item. For example, to convert a note into a task, drag the note to the Outlook Bar and drop it onto the Tasks icon (if the Folder List is open, drop it onto the Tasks folder). The Task window opens with the note title already included in the subject and the note title and body in the text area. Fill in the fine print and click Save and Close. You can convert a task into a note, too.

4. With only a few notes, it's simple to see what each one contains. But what if you have 300 notes to search through? It's still pretty simple. Click the Find button on the Standard toolbar. Type something you remember about the note (for example, "rate") and click Find Now. The IDSK note is displayed, as shown in Figure 14.13.

5. Close the Find box by clicking the Close button in the upper-right corner, just to the right of the Advanced Find command.

FIGURE 14.13

The Find option helps you find the needle in the computerized haystack.

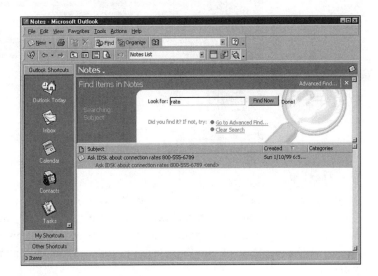

Managing Deleted Items

Luckily, deleting items in Outlook is not necessarily permanent. In the next few steps, you'll see how to delete a note and then recover it.

1. If necessary, click the down arrow in the Outlook Bar until you can see the Deleted Items icon. Back in the Notes folder, make sure that the IDSK note is highlighted and then press Delete. There are myriad ways to delete notes, but we won't cover all of them here.

2. In the Outlook Bar, click Deleted Items to see the contents. Any previously deleted items are shown in the upper half of the window. The item highlighted in the upper half of the window—usually the most recently deleted item—is displayed in the lower portion of the window, as shown in Figure 14.12.

3. To undelete the item, drag the note icon on the left side of the selected item in the upper half of the window to the appropriate folder in the Outlook Bar (in this case, the Notes folder). Click the Notes folder again. The IDSK note has been restored.

14

FIGURE **14.14**

The highlighted item in the upper half of the window is displayed in the lower half.

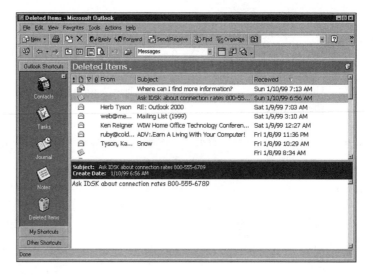

Summary

You've now sampled the sights of Outlook. Outlook offers many tools to help organize your life—business and personal. However, to get the most from Outlook, you must use it regularly and keep the information updated. In the next few chapters, you'll learn the real power behind Outlook and find many tips for easily integrating it into your normal workday.

CHAPTER **15**

Managing Outlook Folders

During this chapter, you learn about the standard configuration of Outlook and how to modify it to fit your needs. You'll learn about folders and how to fit them for the way you work. Finally, you'll learn where to go to make additional changes to Outlook's look and feel. In this chapter, you'll learn where the important controls are, and later chapters cover configuration options in more detail.

Working with Folders

As you use Outlook to create more and more tasks, notes, appointments, email messages, and other items, and as mail starts to arrive from others, you might find it useful to create other folders to better organize your information.

For example, you might want to organize data by project or by the type of contact. Sent Items is a useful concept. However, mail you sent to Aunt Jane probably doesn't belong in the same folder as mail you sent to the IRS.

You can create folders, change their names, arrange them in a different order on the Outlook Bar, copy them, and even delete them. By learning to manipulate the Outlook folders on your hard drive, you will find it easier to organize your information. Figure 15.1 shows a sample view of a folder structure.

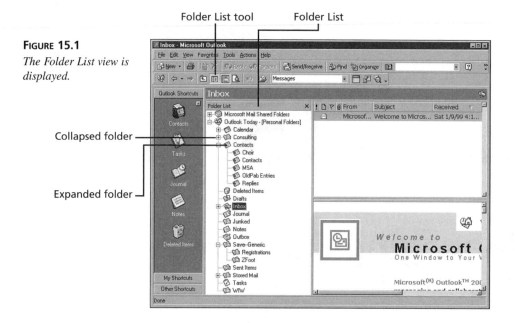

FIGURE 15.1
The Folder List view is displayed.

There are several ways to display the folder structure:

1. Click the folder name button (for example, Inbox) at the top of the viewing pane. This drops down the folder list. Click the folder name again or press Esc to remove the folder list.

2. After clicking the folder name button, while the folder is displayed, click the push pin as indicated. The push pin is located where you would normally find the close box. When you click the push pin, it changes to the Close icon. The pane at the right resizes to display field headers correctly.

3. Choose View, Folder List.

4. Click the Folder List tool on the Advanced toolbar, shown in Figure 15.1.

In Figure 15.1, there are several folders within the main folder. These are called *subfolders*. The term subfolder is relational. When looking upward in the folder hierarchy, you might think of the Contacts folder, for example, as a subfolder. When looking downward, however, if Contacts is subdivided into other folders, you tend to think of Contacts as a folder.

The master container or folder for all of your Outlook data usually is a single file named Outlook.pst or Mailbox.pst. The folder structure you create within Outlook does not show up on your hard disk. The structure is completely internal to the .pst files. If you want to selectively copy contacts, messages, or other Outlook items from one place to another, you'll need to use Outlook rather than the Windows Explorer.

A *profile* is a group of settings that defines a specific combination of Outlook services (email, fax, address books, personal folder files, and so on). Typically, you need only one profile. However, workgroups, families, and individuals often can use profiles to help further organize their use of Outlook. Profiles are available only in Corporate or Workgroup mode and are created by using the Mail icon in the Windows Control Panel.

Folder List Symbols

When the Folder List is displayed, as in Figure 15.1, notice that some of the folders have minus signs, some have plus signs, and others have no symbol at all. The presence of a plus or minus sign indicates that the folder contains subfolders. If the plus sign is displayed, the subfolders are collapsed (not displayed). If the minus sign is displayed, the subfolders are expanded (displayed). If there is no symbol next to the folder name, the folder contains no subfolders. If you've used Windows Explorer, you're already familiar with the hierarchical use of – and + to indicate expanded and collapsed.

You can use the –/+ icons to control the level of folders displayed at any time. Clicking a minus icon collapses the folder; that causes all subfolders to be hidden. The symbol changes to a plus to indicate there are subfolders that are not displayed. Clicking a plus icon expands the folder, displaying the next level of subfolders under that folder.

Creating a Subfolder

The purpose of the Folder List is to allow you to organize how your information is stored so that you can access it quickly and efficiently. You can direct Outlook to store various types of information in specific folders.

There are several ways to create a subfolder. Choose a method that fits the way you work, at the time you need it. If the Folder List is displayed, select the folder (for example, Inbox) in which you want to create a subfolder:

- Right-click the folder name for which you wish to create a subfolder, and choose New Folder.
- Click the drop-down arrow to the right of the New button on the Standard toolbar and click Folder (note the shortcut key, Ctrl+Shift+E).

- Choose File, New, Folder from the menu bar.
- Choose File, Folder, New Folder from the menu bar.

In the next few steps, you'll get a chance to practice changing the view, expanding and collapsing folders, and creating a subfolder to store additional information. The skills you learn in the next few minutes will be ones that you will continue to use as your Outlook skills increase.

1. Open Outlook if it isn't already open.

2. If it isn't already selected, click the Inbox icon in the Outlook Bar. It doesn't matter if there are any messages in the Inbox.

3. Click the Inbox name in the folder banner (the title bar for the Inbox). The Folder List is displayed over the top of the Input window, as shown in Figure 15.2.

Folder
Banner   Push pin

FIGURE 15.2

The Folder List appears temporarily.

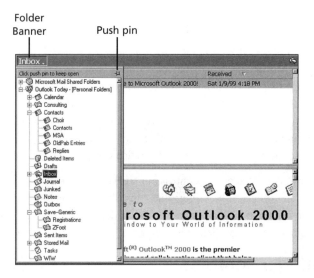

4. Right-click the first level folder (it might be called Personal Folders, Outlook Today, Internet Folders, or another folder name). Nothing happens. That's because the current view of the Folder List view is just a drop-down list; it's for selecting a folder only. Click the push pin (using the left mouse button) to display a functional Folder List with which you can actually work. The push pin changes to a close box.

5. Right-click the Tasks icon in the Folder List. From the pop-up menu, choose New Folder. The Create New Folder dialog box is displayed, as shown in Figure 15.3.

FIGURE 15.3

Use the Create New Folder dialog box to create a subfolder inside an existing folder.

6. Click the drop-down menu on the right side of the Folder Contains text box. Notice that a folder can contain only one of six item types: Appointment, Contact, Journal, Mail, Note, or Task. Click the Task option. In the Name text box, type Outlook Tasks.

7. To change the folder where the subfolder is attached, click a different position in the Select Where to Place the Folder display. In this case, choose the Tasks folder, and then click OK. If the Outlook Bar is displayed, the Add Shortcut to Outlook Bar? dialog box pops up, as shown in Figure 15.4. If you don't want to view this dialog box again, click the Don't Prompt Me About This Again option. In this case, you don't want a shortcut, so click No. If you say Yes, the shortcut will be added to the My Shortcuts group.

FIGURE 15.4

The Add Shortcut to Outlook Bar? dialog box is used to automatically add a folder shortcut to the My Shortcuts group on the Outlook Bar.

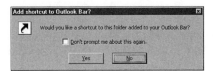

 After you create a folder, you can make it a shortcut on the Outlook Bar by dragging it from the Folder List to the desired position on the Outlook Bar.

8. Click the Outlook Tasks folder icon in the Folder List. (If you click the right mouse button, a menu opens instead of displaying the new Task list.) The folder banner now reads Outlook Tasks. A new (currently empty) Task list shows up in the right window.

9. Click in the Click Here to Add a New Task text box. Type `Learn to copy a folder`. Press Enter. The task appears in the Task list.

Copying or Moving a Folder

When you copy a folder from one place in the main folder to another, any items in the folder are also copied. When you move a folder, the items are also moved to the new position. When you copy a folder, you end up with two folders (which take up twice as much space as one). Moving a folder from one place to another means that the folder is no longer in the original location.

To move a folder, simply drag it from its current position into the new folder. For example, if you want it to be a subfolder of the Inbox folder, drag it onto the Inbox icon. To copy a folder from one position to another, press Ctrl and drag the folder to the new position. Alternatively, drag using the right mouse button and you'll be prompted to Move, Copy, or Cancel.

You can also copy or move a folder by highlighting it and choosing Edit, Move to Folder (Ctrl+Shift+V) or Edit, Copy to Folder.

If you use the Edit, Move to Folder or Edit, Copy to Folder method (from Outlook's main menu), the Move (or Copy) Folder dialog box is displayed. Click the destination folder. The Move Folder dialog box is then displayed. If you want to create an additional folder as the destination folder, click the New button.

Renaming a Folder

The simplest way to rename an existing folder is to select the folder icon (the name appears blue) in the Folder List and press the F2 key. The folder name text box is highlighted (selected). While the folder name is highlighted, any text you type replaces the existing name. Or, you can press the left or right arrow key to clear the selection, and then use normal editing keys to modify the existing name.

To add a shortcut to an Outlook Bar group that isn't currently open, drag the item onto the group name and hesitate a moment. The group will open. You can then finish dragging to the desired location.

Adding a Folder to the Outlook Bar

In some cases, you might want to add a shortcut to the Outlook Bar. The easiest way to do that is to drag the folder icon onto the Outlook Bar. You can then drag it up or down to position it between existing icons or move it to the top or bottom of the Outlook Bar.

Adding File System Shortcuts

The Outlook Bar can also be a container for shortcuts to file system items such as files, folders, and URLs. Follow these steps to see how to add an item to the Outlook Bar:

1. If necessary, display the Outlook Bar, and click the Other Shortcuts group.

2. In the Outlook Bar, notice My Documents and Favorites. If you have files or shortcuts in either of those two folders, you can add those items to the Outlook Bar. Click Favorites. In the right pane (the far-right pane if your Folder List is still displayed), find an item you want in the Outlook Bar and drag it into the Other Shortcuts group.

3. Click My Computer. Notice that the file system is displayed, similar to what you see if you click My Computer on the desktop. From here, you can display any file or folder on your computer.

4. Right-click C: and observe the Add to Outlook Bar option. If you click this option, a shortcut to C: will be added to the Outlook Bar.

5. In the right pane, double-click any drive to display the contents of that drive. Double-click any displayed folder to display subfolders. Right-click any folder and select Open to open it in a new Outlook window. Double-click any file to open it just as you would in Windows Explorer. You can create shortcuts to any file or folder simply by dragging it to the Outlook Bar.

Deleting a Folder

To delete a folder from the Folder List, select the folder icon and press the Delete key, click the Delete button on the toolbar, or right-click and choose Delete "File Name". Outlook prompts for you to confirm the deletion and, in the process, reminds you that deleting sends the folder to the Deleted Items folder.

Remember, if the folder icon isn't selected, you won't be able to delete the folder (or do anything else with it).

Personalizing Outlook

From Outlook's Tools, Options menu, you can see how to make Outlook work even harder for you.

Choose Tools, Options to display the Options dialog box shown in Figure 15.5. The Options dialog box will have differing numbers of tabs, depending on your installation mode. Figure 15.5 shows seven tabs that normally appear in C/W (Corporate/Workgroup) mode. Depending on your installation, you might see more or fewer tabs. For example, if you have Exchange Services installed, you'll have an eighth tab, Delegates. If you don't have Internet E-mail installed, that tab will be missing.

Initially, you might find that most of the settings are acceptable. In this section, only a few of the options will be covered. Others are seldom used.

FIGURE 15.5

The Options box is used to personalize Outlook to meet your needs—shown here in Corporate/Workgroup mode with Internet E-mail installed.

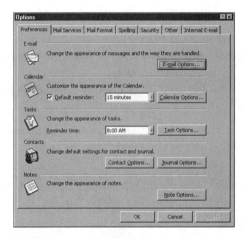

Personalizing Email Options

The E-mail options control the basic behavior of the Inbox and how you work with messages. Choose Tools, Options, Preferences tab, and click E-mail Options (see Figure 15.6). It is divided into two parts: Message Handling and On Replies and Forwards. The very first option controls what Outlook does after you move or delete an open message. The choices are

- Open the previous item (default)
- Open the next item
- Return to the Inbox

After using Outlook for a while, you will get a feel for which of these behaviors is most useful to you.

Other Message Handling options include:

- Close original message on reply or forward (unchecked by default)—If you typically find that you don't need to look at the original message after you send a reply or forward, this option saves you the work of having to close the original. If,

however, you usually find yourself having to reopen the original message, this
option will be an annoyance.

FIGURE 15.6

*E-mail Options lets
you control how mes-
sages are handled
(shown in
Corporate/Workgroup
mode).*

- Save copies of messages in Sent Items folder (checked by default)—In a work
  environment, you typically need to keep copies of most email you send, making
  this option essential. In a home environment, you might not want to keep email
  you send. If you do keep this option checked, you can always cull out sent items
  you don't want to keep or, better still, use the Rules Wizard to organize and delete
  outgoing (as well as incoming) messages.

- Display a notification message when new mail arrives (unchecked by default)—
  With this option enabled, Outlook pops up a notification dialog box each time new
  mail arrives. If you get tons of mail, you will quickly tire of this option. On the
  other hand, if you're expecting something crucial, you might want to enable this
  option on an as-needed basis.

- Automatically save unsent messages—This option automatically saves unsent messages in the Drafts folder (by default). This provides an insurance policy if Outlook
  crashes or if the lights go out. It also lets you save a message in mid-composition
  when you're not finished, for example, when it's time to shut down for the day or
  when you need to do additional research before completing a message. Click
  Advanced E-mail options to change the folder where unsent messages are saved, as
  well as how often Outlook automatically saves drafts in progress.

You've already had a glimpse at the Advanced E-mail Options dialog box, shown in
Figure 15.7. You might never need to change them, but they can be useful.

FIGURE 15.7

*The Advanced E-mail
Options dialog box
allows you to further
refine Outlook's mail
handling behavior
(C/W mode).*

Tracking lets you know when messages are delivered (but not necessarily when they get read). By default, messages aren't tracked. Click the Tracking Options button to display the Tracking Options dialog box.

Looking at the lower half of the E-mail Options dialog box, you can control the appearance and content of forwarded mail and replies. Under When Replying or When Forwarding, click the drop-down arrow to see the array of choices. You can also prefix each line of an original message with a mark of your choice, as well as mark your own comments with your initials or some other indicator.

Automatically Add People to Contacts

If you use Outlook in Internet Only mode, you will have an additional option at the bottom of the E-mail Options dialog box—Automatically Put People I Reply to In. Selecting this option automatically adds people to whom you send mail to your Contacts folder.

Choosing Calendar Options

The Calendar options allow you to establish the days and times that you work. Choose Tools, Options, Preferences tab. Note that you can set the default time for appointment reminders. If you typically find yourself resetting the reminder time to an hour or some other time, change the setting here to save yourself work later. Click the Calendar Options button to display the dialog box shown in Figure 15.8.

Selecting Task Options

Choose Tools, Options, Preferences tab, and click Task Options to display the dialog box shown in Figure 15.9. Drop-down menus allow you to choose the colors for Overdue and Completed tasks. Choose the desired colors and click OK to return to the main dialog box. Back in the main Options dialog box, Reminder Time lets you specify the time that you will be reminded about tasks due each day.

FIGURE 15.8

The Calendar Options dialog box allows you to set your personal schedule.

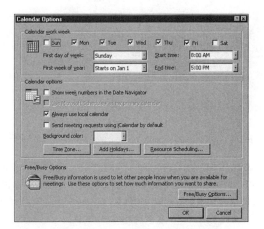

15

FIGURE 15.9

The Task Options dialog box allows you to set the display colors for overdue and completed tasks.

Controlling Contacts Display

The Contact Options button is used to control the way contact names are displayed and the order in which contacts are filed or sorted. The Contact Options dialog box, shown in Figure 15.10, provides pull-down controls for choosing display and sorting options.

Controlling the Journal

Properly used, the Journal can automatically keep track of Outlook and Office "events"—email messages, meeting activities, task activities, along with time spent working on Office documents. The Journal Options dialog box is used to control which "events" Outlook keeps track of.

Figure 15.10

*Contact Options lets
you choose how names
are displayed and
filed.*

Setting the Options for Notes

The final option on the Preferences tab of the Options dialog box is controlling the Notes
feature—choose Tool, Options, Preferences tab, Note Options. Outlook's Notes are like
electronic yellow sticky notes you can write as ideas occur to you. As shown in Figure
15.11, Notes Options lets you control color, size, and font.

Figure 15.11

*Control of the Notes
feature is fairly lim-
ited. You can set the
color, size, and font
used.*

Mail Delivery (Internet Only Mode)

If you use Outlook in Internet Only mode, the Mail Delivery tab shows up in the Options
tab instead of Mail Services. Shown in Figure 15.12, this dialog box is divided into three
sections:

- *Accounts Manager*—Lets you select and define mail and directory service
  accounts.
- *Mail Account Options*—Lets you control sending and receiving of email.
- *Dial-up Options*—Lets you control Outlook's use of Dial-up Networking (which is
  set up through Start, Programs, Accessories, Communications, Dial-Up
  Networking).

A number of options shown in the Mail Delivery tab in Internet Only mode
are available in the Internet E-mail tab when set up in Corporate/Workgroup
mode.

Note the Reconfigure Mail Support button at the bottom of the Mail Delivery options dialog box. This button lets you switch between Internet Only and Corporate/Workgroup modes. If you're set up in C/W mode, this button is located in the Mail Services tab.

FIGURE 15.12
The Mail Delivery tab is used in Internet Only mode.

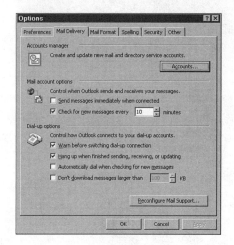

Mail Format

The Mail Format Options dialog box, shown in Figure 15.13, is divided into three sections:

- *Message Format*—This option group lets you choose among HTML, RTF (rich text formatting), and Plain Text.
- *Stationery and Fonts*—This option group lets you specify the fonts for viewing email and—when using HTML or RTF—the fonts for sending email, as well. Note that font and signature settings are unavailable when Word is selected as the email editor.
- *Signature*—This option lets you set up custom *signatures* to be added to messages you compose.

Setting the Options for Spelling

Spelling options can be set to reflect your personal preferences. One option that is generally turned off that you will want to turn on is the command to always check spelling before sending a message.

Establishing Other Options

The Other tab is divided into three parts, as shown in Figure 15.14.

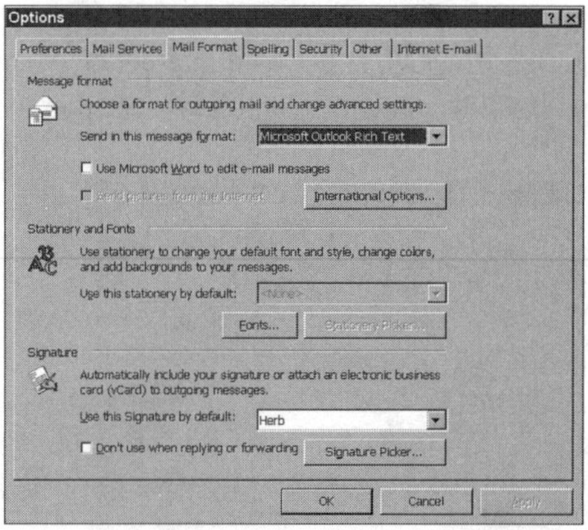

FIGURE 15.13

Mail Format Options lets you choose how email is formatted for sending and for display.

FIGURE 15.14

The Other tab of the Options dialog box allows you to control when the Deleted Items folder is emptied, the frequency of AutoArchive, and the look of the Preview pane (figure shown in Corporate/Workgroup mode).

- *General*—Lets you tell Outlook to automatically empty the Deleted Items folder when exiting. Also provides access to Advanced options, which lets you set Outlook's startup folder, warning behavior when deleting, and other options. Click the Advanced Options button and explore the options and settings on your own.

- *AutoArchive*—The AutoArchive button lets you specify Outlook's archiving behavior. Additional settings can be accessed by right-clicking a folder and choosing Properties, AutoArchive tab (except for Contacts and Outlook Today).

- *Preview Pane*—The Preview Pane button lets you configure the appearance and behavior of the *Preview pane* where the top part of your email messages appear so you can skim through your messages. To turn the Preview pane on and off, use View, Preview Pane or use the Preview Pane button on the Advanced toolbar.

Summary

You learned in this chapter how to control the configuration of Outlook. You learned to create new folders, delete them, rename them, and move and copy them, and you examined some of the available configuration options.

15

CHAPTER 16

Working with Outlook Contacts

If you keep your contacts in Outlook, you can consolidate most (if not all) of your email, tasks, notes, appointments, and contact information into a single information manager. Outlook lets you organize phone numbers, addresses, and demographic data in an easy-to-handle database. You can add a new friend, business associate, or your Congressperson in the matter of a few keystrokes, categorizing the data so you can easily recall it in the future.

Putting Contacts into Action

The Contacts folder is a good place to start when you begin using Outlook. You should enter all your contacts' information first because so many other features interact with the Contacts database. If you want to send an email or fax, schedule a meeting, or send a task request to someone, it is easier if you have the right data in your Contacts database.

You can view your contacts in a number of different ways, but the most common view is the Address Card view, shown in Figure 16.1. If you use Outlook 2003 or later, you'll see a place to import a digital picture of your contact.

Figure 16.1

The Address Card view in the Contacts folder shows you partial information for several contacts at once.

New Contact button

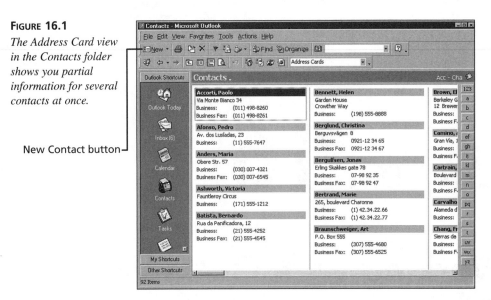

Outlook offers the usual business card and Rolodex fields, such as addresses, phone numbers, and email addresses. It also offers some not-so-common fields, such as anniversary date, government ID number, and ISDN number.

Managing Your Contacts Database

You can access the Contacts area of Outlook in a variety of ways:

- Click the Contacts icon in the Outlook Bar (it looks like a manual business card filing system).
- Click Contacts in the Folder list.
- Choose View, Go To, Contacts from the menu.

Entering a new contact is a very simple procedure and will help acquaint you with how Outlook works. The information you enter here is usable in other areas of Outlook, as well as in other Office applications.

There are several ways to add a new contact to your database:

- Press Ctrl+Shift+C to display a new Contact form from any other area of Outlook.
- When you're in any folder other than Contacts, choose File, New, Contact.

- When you're in the Contacts view, click the New icon on the Standard toolbar.

- When you're in the Contacts view, press Ctrl+N.

- Double-click on a blank area of the Contacts desktop.

- Right-click the Contacts area and choose New Contact.

Once Outlook displays a new Contact form, you can enter all the information that you have about that person or business.

16

When you enter birthdays or anniversary dates in the appropriate fields, those dates will automatically be entered in the Calendar component of Outlook. They appear on your calendar as recurring events. If you want Outlook to remind you to buy a gift or send a greeting card, just double-click on the reminder in the calendar and drag it onto the Tasks icon. When the Task form appears, you can set an alarm for yourself. Click the Save and Close button. You can also double-click the appointment itself and set the reminder.

Name Notes

In the Full Name text box, enter the name as you normally would. If you enter Herbert L. Tyson in the Full Name text box, it's automatically stored in the File As text box as Tyson, Herbert L. when you press Tab to move to the next field.

In most cases, this filing method is fine. But what happens if you enter Dr. James E. Smith, Jr. in the Full Name text box? Outlook is smart enough to store it as Smith, James E. But what happened to the rest of the information?

Now for the really clever part. So far, you've entered text into the Full Name text box, but notice that Full Name is also a button. Click on this button to display the Check Full Name dialog box, as shown in Figure 16.2.

FIGURE 16.2

The Check Full Name dialog box allows you add a title and suffix if needed.

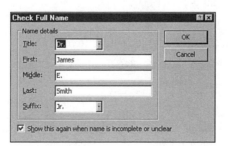

Before you begin entering the names of co-workers and friends into your Contacts database, work through the following exercise to enter data for the first of your contacts—yourself. You'll create a new contact for yourself and learn the purposes of the most common fields. By becoming familiar with how everything works now, you can save time later. Follow the next few steps to learn how to add a new contact to Outlook.

1. Start Outlook. Click the Contacts icon in the Outlook Bar. Click the New Contact button on the left edge of the Standard toolbar. A blank Contact form named Untitled - Contacts is displayed.

2. Notice the blinking cursor (the insertion point) in the Full Name text box. Type in your name: first name, middle initial, last name—without commas.

3. Fill in the rest of the information on the General tab. As you move around on this tab, Outlook might prompt you to check information you've typed. Outlook does this whenever it detects any ambiguity in your data entry.

4. When you've entered the data about yourself, click the Save and Close button on the toolbar to close the Contact form and return to the Address Card view. Your information is now entered in the Contact database (which actually is your Outlook .pst file).

There are five tabs on a typical Contact Entry form: General, Details, Activities, Certificates, and All Fields. Each of these tabs represents a form for the contact that is used to store specialized information.

Deleting a Contact

You can delete a contact in several different ways. The method you choose will probably depend on what you're doing at the moment. You can use any one of the following methods, all of which assume you're in the Address Card view (where you can see multiple entries at once):

- Select the contact, right-click on it, and choose Delete from the drop-down menu.
- Select the contact and choose Edit, Delete.
- Select the contact and press Ctrl+D.
- Select the contact and press the Delete key.
- Drag and drop the contact onto the Deleted Items folder.
- Select the contact and click the Delete button on the toolbar (it looks like an "X").

Know when your Deleted folder is going to be emptied. Your deleted contacts go to the Deleted folder until that folder is emptied. You can check by choosing Tools, Options and clicking the Other tab in the Options dialog

box. If there's a check mark in the Empty the Deleted Items folder upon exiting box, the folder is emptied every time you exit Outlook.

Opening a Contact

You can also edit a contact entry in several ways. Again, the method you choose will
probably depend on what you're doing. Here are a few ways of opening a contact:

- In the Contacts window, double-click anywhere on the contact you want to edit.
- Right-click on the contact you want to open and choose Open from the drop-down
  menu.
- Select the contact and press Enter.

Modifying a Contact

Contact information can also be modified in Address Cards view. Click on the field you
want to change and make the modification. Note that you cannot change the name of the
contact in this way, but any other displayed fields can be changed. Many of the fields are
not available from the Address Cards view, so you might need to use the Detailed
Address Cards view to make changes. On the Advanced toolbar, drop down the list of
views and choose Detailed Address Cards.

Gaining More Control Over Your Contacts

For the next few sections, you'll see an overview of the helpful contact features.

General Tab: Categorizing Your Contacts

At the bottom of the General tab of the New Contact form, there's a place to list categories applying to each contact. When you work on many different projects or with many
groups of people, the category function is a great tool. Each contact can belong to any
number of different groups or categories. As your Contacts database grows, you can filter
your contacts by categories.

According to Microsoft, "A filter is an easy way to view only those items or files that
meet conditions you specify."

When the Categories button is clicked in the Detailed Address Cards view, a checklist of
available categories is displayed, as shown in Figure 16.3. You can use one of these categories or create your own categories by going into the Master Category List at the bottom of the list box and adding your own.

FIGURE 16.3

The Categories dialog box allows you to choose from predefined categories or create your own.

Details Tab: Keeping Track of the Small Stuff

As with the General tab, it isn't necessary to fill out all of the fields on the Details tab. For that matter, you don't even need to use the Details tab. However, if you'd like to add a personal touch to your phone calls, this can really impress your customers. For example, on your next call you might ask, "Isn't your anniversary next week? Are you and Mike doing anything special?"

Activities Tab: Contacts with Your Contacts

By clicking the third tab in the Contact entry form, you can display information about activities conducted with your contacts. Once you delete an email item and empty it from Deleted Items, it will no longer show up in the Activities tab.

Certificates Tab: May We See Some ID, Please?

Certificates (also called digital IDs) are files that are issued by a certified security authority, such as VeriSign, or by your administrator. These certificates are used to send security-related information over the Internet. In order for the certificates to work, both the sender and the receiver must have a valid and current certificate (certificates have expiration dates). Even so, you can still decrypt messages sent to us after your certificate has expired. You can learn more about digital certificates at http://www.verisign.com, VeriSign's Web site.

All Fields Tab: Seeing the Whole Picture

The final tab on the Contacts form is All Fields. On this tab, you can choose the fields you want to view from a drop-down list. The different fields and their corresponding entries are shown in a table format. You can enter information about a contact in this window, and you can select fields and copy information as well. When you copy cells from this view and paste them into a Word document, for example, the information is separated by tabs.

You can also use the All Fields tab to create new fields for a contact. Click the button marked New at the bottom-left corner of the form. Before you create a new field, remember that Outlook already offers four user fields that you can customize to meet your needs. View these user fields by choosing Miscellaneous fields from the drop-down list. Although you can add any information to the four user fields, you can't change their names or properties.

Displaying Contacts in Different Views

The default view for contacts is the Address Card view. Both the Address Card view and the Detailed Address Card view are easy formats to work with, especially if you have many blank fields within each contact entry. These two views don't display blank fields unless you specify otherwise and modify the views. Both views are shown in Figure 16.4, with detailed address cards on top and plain address cards on the bottom. If you display the Advanced toolbar (right-click any toolbar and choose Advanced), you can readily switch between different views.

FIGURE 16.4

Address Card and Detailed Address Card views hide the blanks so you see only data.

Detailed Address Card view

Address Card view

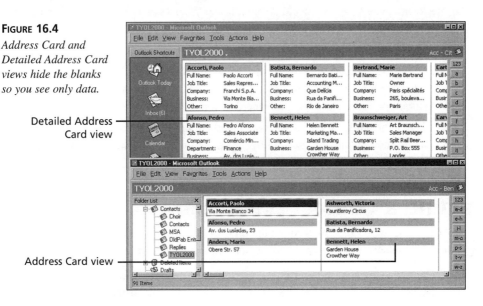

> You can open multiple instances of Outlook simultaneously. Hence, you can see your calendar, contacts, and email at the same time (if your screen is large enough and your eyesight is good enough). In the Outlook Bar or Folder List, right-click the module you want to see and choose Open in New Window. To display them side-by-side, Ctrl+click each icon on the Windows taskbar, right-click any of the selected icons, and choose Tile Horizontally or Tile Vertically.

Switching Among Views

In addition to the two predefined Address Card views, you can also switch between different table views. In the Contacts folder, there are seven predefined views. To choose a different view, click the drop-down arrow next to the current view on the Advanced toolbar, and then select one of the views in the drop-down list. The list offers different views that have already been defined by the creators of Outlook.

Deleting an Outlook Folder

Deleting a folder is a two-step process. First delete the folder itself, and then delete the shortcut that points to the deleted folder (assuming a shortcut was created). The following steps show you how you would delete a folder Contacts named *TYOL*. Substitute the name of your folder you wish to delete for TYOL.

1. If necessary, click the Folder List tool on the Advanced toolbar to display the Folder List. Expand the Contacts folder again, if necessary, and click on the TYOL folder. Press the Delete key, or click the Delete button on the Standard toolbar. Outlook prompts you to confirm the deletion. Click Yes.

2. Display the Outlook Bar, if necessary, and click My Shortcuts. Right-click the TYOL Shortcut and choose Remove From Outlook Bar. When prompted to confirm, click Yes.

Creating a Contact Database

The following steps take you through the process of creating a new Contacts folder and adding 10 contacts. This will give you a Contacts database to work with.

1. Click the Contacts shortcut on the Outlook Bar. Choose File, New, Folder. The Create New Folder dialog box, shown in Figure 16.5, is displayed.

2. In the Name text box, type India Contacts. Make sure that the Folder Contains text box reads Contact Items. The Contacts folder should be selected in the Select

Where to Place the Folder window. Click OK. When you're asked if you want to add a shortcut to the Outlook Bar, click Yes.

FIGURE 16.5

The Create New Folder dialog box is used to create a place to store the contacts you're going to create.

3. Click the My Shortcuts icon in the Outlook Bar. Click the India Contacts icon. No data is currently contained in this folder.

Adding the First Contacts

In the following steps you'll enter 10 contacts, all from different fictitious companies. Besides the basic data, you'll also enter some keywords and other information that you can later use to examine Outlook's Contacts capability.

1. Click the New Contact button on the left end of the Standard toolbar.

2. Enter the data shown in Table 16.1, including full name, company, business address, and business phone numbers. After you enter the data for each contact, click the Save and New button on the toolbar (just to the right of the Save and Close button). That saves the current contact and displays a blank form.

TABLE 16.1 Data for the India Contacts Folder

Linda Terry	Alana Ekatiron
Kelly Flippers	Sisters and Others
3256 South Jemison	524 Hargis Lane
Douglas, VA 23354	St. Louis, MO 63105
(804) 555-6784	(314) 555-2288
(804) 555-6701	(314) 555-9881

TABLE 16.1   continued

George Renttek	Joanna Toodha
Art Time	Paint, Inc.
13558 Anteres	12322 Main Street
Court Englewood, CO 80111	Hollywood, CA 90028
(303) 555-7415	(213) 555-2224
(303) 555-7488	(213) 555-7841
Lois Herbert	Robert Williams
Mania Fish Company	Jazz Gitboxes, Inc.
1801 Stratford	6300 Iris Way
Hampton, VA 23664	Aurora, CO 80013
(757) 555-8800	(303) 555-3369
(757) 555-8701	(303) 555-8433
Ali Reyas	Mollye Sniktaw
Artful Manufacturing	ArtFirst
7314 Booth	244 Nicobar
Klamath Falls, OR 97602	Lancaster, CA 93534
(503) 555-6991	(805) 555-9898
(503) 555-9898	(805) 555-7461
Katie Nerak	Robert George
Soft-Serve Freezies	Felt Artist Supplies
8654 Sleepy Hollow Road	84 North Oak
Alexandria, VA 22310	Sandusky, OH 44870
(703) 555-1122	(419) 555-9355
(703) 555-1213	(419) 555-5000

3. When you've entered the last contact, click Save and Close on the toolbar. This
   returns you to the Address Cards view.

Add a Contact from the Same Company

If you're building a large contact database, you'll probably be entering several contacts
from the same company. Rather than repeatedly entering the same data, you can tell
Outlook to automatically enter the required data for that company. Select a contact that
represents that company and choose Actions, New Contact from Same Company. You
can do this from the Address Cards view or from the Opened Card view.

Understanding Categories and Items

You can add categories to any item: email, task, notes, and others. These items can then be grouped. For example, if you're entering your holiday card list, you can group all of the contacts connected with the list, any tasks you've assigned them, memos, and other related items into subfolders of a single folder.

Adding categories to contact items is only the beginning of a powerful process that allows you to quickly look at all items in a specific category.

16

Adding Categories to the Contacts

You can assign numerous predesignated categories to each contact. Outlook provides nearly two dozen of these categories. Also, you can create as many additional categories as you need in the Master Category dialog box.

Categories are important for grouping and filtering contacts. When you filter contacts, you tell Outlook to display only the contacts that meet specific criteria. For example, if a dozen contacts are participants in a committee you're chairing, you can tell Outlook that you want to write a memo to only those contacts.

Adding Standard Categories

Categories can be added from the Address Cards view or from any open contact. Usually, you'll find it best to add categories to an open contact because you can immediately see that the category has been added correctly. If you add a category or categories to a contact from the Address Cards view, you probably won't be able to see it unless you've modified the view to include the Category field.

To add a category to a contact from the Address Cards view, begin by clicking the contact. If you want to add the same category to multiple, nonconsecutive contacts at the same time, click the first contact and hold down Ctrl while clicking on all other contacts desired. To select multiple, consecutive contacts (for example, if you've sorted your contacts by company name), click the first one, press Shift, and click the last one. All contacts between the first and last one are automatically selected. Right-click any selected contact and choose Categories to display the Categories dialog box, shown in Figure 16.6.

To assign categories to selected contacts, click on the check box next to each category name. Choose any categories that apply to the selected contacts. When you've finished, click OK. Each selected category is assigned to the selected contacts.

Categories can also be assigned from the open Contact view. Double-click the contact to open it. Click the Categories button at the bottom of the window—you might need to expand the Contact window to see the buttons at the very bottom. When you select the category or categories and click OK, they're added to the text box to the right of the Categories button in the Contact window.

FIGURE 16.6

The Categories dialog box allows you to assign any existing categories, whether built-in or user-created.

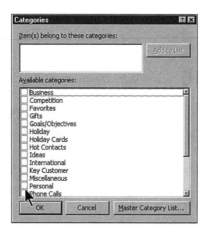

Adding and Deleting Custom Categories

As indicated previously, you aren't limited to the categories offered by Outlook. To create a new category, open the Categories dialog box and click the Master Category List button. The Master Category List dialog box allows you to create new categories and use them in grouping your contacts and other items.

To create a new category, simply type the name in the New Category text box and click Add. You can create as many categories as you need. When you're finished, click OK to return to the Categories dialog box, where all of the new categories are displayed. You can now select any of the new categories.

You can also individually delete any categories in the Master Category List dialog box—including predefined categories. Select the category to be removed and click Delete.

Providing Additional Information About a Contact

Although you may not do a lot with the Details tab, you should be aware of it. You can use it to your advantage, particularly in cases where you need to recall personal information about a contact.

To view the Details tab, open any contact and click the Details tab. It's shown in Figure 16.7.

FIGURE 16.7

The Details tab is used to record more detailed information about a contact.

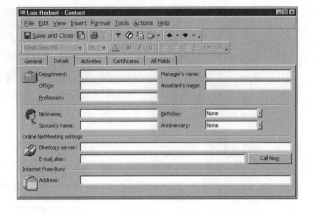

Manipulating the Contacts

It's difficult to illustrate the power of Outlook's Contacts feature without putting a lot of work into expanding a fictional database. The sample India Contacts database you created earlier is very small, but most of your databases will contain dozens or even hundreds of entries. In the India Contacts database, you can easily scan the contacts to find the ones you need. As your database grows, however, this method of finding contacts will become unrealistic.

Finding a Contact

Finding a contact can be a big challenge when you're working with a large database. By using Outlook's Find and Advanced Find features, you can quickly find the information you're looking for.

From the Address Cards view, click Find on the Standard toolbar to open the Find dialog box, as shown in Figure 16.8. In this basic Find dialog box, only the Name, Company, Addresses, and Category fields are searched by default. This points up the importance of using categories—since Category is so readily available for searching! Placing a check mark in the Search All Text in the Contact option box instructs Outlook to search all of the text fields.

Using the Advanced Find Feature

Advanced Find can be used with contacts even if you remember only a portion of the information (such as the spouse's name).

There are at least three ways to start Advanced Find:

- Click Advanced Find in the upper-right corner of the regular Find pane.
- Choose Tools, Advanced Find.
- Press Ctrl+Shift+F.

FIGURE 16.8

The Find dialog box is opened above the Address Cards view.

Figure 16.9 shows a sample Advanced Find dialog box. From here, you can search for information contained nearly anywhere in Outlook. Take a few minutes and explore some of the Find options on the Contacts, More Choices, and Advanced tabs.

FIGURE 16.9

The Advanced Find dialog box allows you to search many additional features and modules of Outlook to find exactly the information you need.

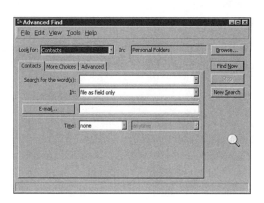

Dialing a Contact

If you want to have Outlook dial the phone for you, right-click the contact you want to call and choose Call Contact. The New Call dialog box is shown in Figure 16.10. Note the option to create a journal entry at the start of the call. To start the call, click Start Call. When you're prompted, take the phone off the hook, click Talk, and begin your call.

16

FIGURE 16.10

In the New Call dialog box, you can have Outlook dial a contact's telephone number.

Display Different Printing Options

There are several default ways to print your contact list:

- Card—All cards from top to bottom on the page, two columns wide, with blank cards printed at the end and with letter tabs and headings.
- Small Booklet—All cards on two sides of a sheet of paper, eight cards per sheet, in landscape orientation. You can cut and staple to make a booklet.
- Medium Booklet—All cards on two sides of a sheet of paper, four booklet pages per sheet, in portrait orientation. You can cut and staple to make a booklet.
- Memo—Selected items are printed one at a time in the form of a memo. Attachments are printed as graphics.
- Phone Directory—Names and phone numbers for all contact items from top to bottom on the page, with letter tabs and headings. If you have enough records, the Phone Directory view is printed in two columns.

To print your contact list, click the Print tool (Ctrl+P) on the Standard toolbar. In the Print Style panel, choose the method for printing.

For customized print styles, view the online help files. Search for Print Style.

Summary

You've learned what the Contacts component can do for you. You read about how to manage contacts and perform the basic tasks associated with the Contacts feature, such as adding, opening, deleting, and importing contacts. You also learned how to assign your contacts categories. As your Contacts database grows, you can easily locate specific groups of people for mailing, faxes, phone calls, and anything else you want to do with contacts.

CHAPTER 17

Emailing with Outlook

The development of email is one of the most significant advances of the computer age. (The United States Postal Service is often referred to as *snail mail* now)

With a few keystrokes and a click of your mouse, you can send messages that are delivered within seconds (depending on how well your mail server and the Internet are working), and you can receive a reply within a matter of minutes.

You can have Outlook sort your email by the name of the sender, the date the message was received, or a number of other elements. No matter how you want to digest or process information, Outlook can present it to you in a way that's ready to use. Just think of how much time that can save you.

 Outlook requires some the features and files in Internet Explorer. So even if you never use Internet Explorer, if you use Outlook, you nonetheless need Internet Explorer.

What Is the Inbox?

Outlook's Inbox does more than just provide email retrieval. It organizes your information, can tell you what is high (or low) priority, and can even tell you when one of your meetings has been canceled or moved.

Be careful about giving out your email address. After you make it onto any of the mass junk email address lists, it's virtually impossible to get removed. Users often resort to having to change their email addresses—and that's almost never convenient.

The following steps show you ways to customize your Inbox so that it works the way you want to work.

1. Start Outlook.

2. On the Outlook Bar, select Inbox. As shown in Figure 17.1, the Inbox is displayed. By default, the Inbox screen is divided into two parts. The top half of the screen displays summary information about each piece of email. The bottom half displays the preview showing the text of the selected email message. If you use Outlook 2000 or later, the preview pane (if displayed) might appear on the right side of your Outlook program window.

In the Outlook Bar, the (1) next to Inbox means that Inbox contains one unread message.

3. On the Column Heading bar click the From box. This directs Outlook to sort your email messages alphabetically, based on the name of the sender. Notice that Outlook has placed a small arrow in the From column heading. This arrow tells you whether Outlook is alphabetizing the information in ascending (A to Z) or descending (Z to A) order. If the arrow is pointing up, the email is sorted in ascending order. To change the order to descending, simply click the From column heading again. The arrow will point down and the email will be reorganized in descending order.

4. Click the Received column heading. This sorts your email by the date of receipt rather than by the sender's name. Click a second time to reverse the sort order. Also notice that you can organize your mail by importance, icon, flag status, attachment, or subject simply by clicking on the appropriate column heading.

FIGURE 17.1

The default Inbox lists all emails you have received in the top box and displays the text of the selected email in the bottom box.

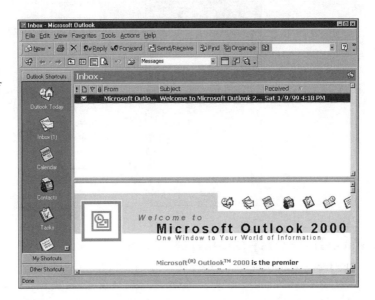

17

Do you keep a lot of messages in your Inbox? If you do, you can save your-self some aggravation by reverse-sorting by Received date. This causes the most recent messages to display at the top of the list.

Inbox Symbols

Understanding the various symbols in the Inbox enables you to organize your email effectively and understand the general nature of the email even before you read it. For instance, some symbols indicate whether the email is of high priority, and others tell you whether a file is attached to the email. Figure 17.2 provides a list of the various Inbox symbols and their descriptions.

Figure 17.2

The various symbols used in the Inbox.

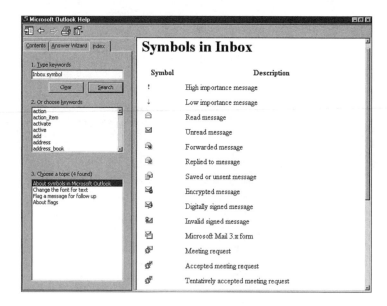

Customizing Your Inbox

The Inbox window doesn't have to look exactly like the way it appears on your screen now. You can change the way it looks to suit your tastes or needs. Remember that you can close the Outlook Bar on the left side of the screen by right-clicking an empty area on the bar and choosing Hide Outlook Bar. To redisplay the bar, choose View, Outlook Bar from the menu.

You can turn the toolbars on and off, just as you can in any other Office program. Right-click anywhere on the toolbar and click Standard to toggle the display of the Standard toolbar.

Additionally, you can change the height or width of any window pane. Move the cursor over any window edge and drag it to a new position.

Finally, you can change the width of the column headings in the Column Heading bar. Move the cursor onto the edge of any column, and drag it to the new position. When you quit Outlook and return, the sizing changes remain active.

Importing Account Settings

Outlook imports certain email account settings and email when you install Outlook. If you have email or account settings that were not imported on installing Outlook, you can do it now by choosing File, Import and Export. This starts the Import and Export Wizard, shown in Figure 17.3. You can import Internet Mail account settings. Just make your choice and follow the wizard's directions.

FIGURE **17.3**

The Import and Export Wizard allows you to import Internet settings and messages from other programs.

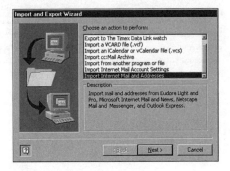

17

Importing Existing Mail

If you previously used another program for email, you can also import messages by using the Import and Export Wizard. Choose File, Import and Export; select Import Internet Mail and Addresses; and follow the instructions.

If you import information from another program, it remains intact in the original program. It is not physically moved into Outlook, only copied. Keep this in mind if you have limited disk space and tons of data.

Composing a Mail Message

Take a moment to think about a conventional "snail mail" letter. Each letter needs a delivery address where it will be sent, a return address, the body of the letter, and, of course, a signature. Email composed using Outlook has many of the same elements and a few more to make the email more useful. For instance, email includes a Subject line that cues the recipient to the subject matter of the email. In addition to the standard components of an email message, email created with Outlook can also tell the recipient whether the message is of high or low importance and whether a file has been attached to the message.

The next few steps take a look at each component of Outlook email and shows you how to create, address, and send email. Additionally, you'll learn to modify several of Outlook's options that enable you to track your message to its final destination.

1. Select the Inbox if it is not already displayed.
2. Click the New Mail Message button on the toolbar (or press Ctrl+Shift+M). The Untitled - Message dialog box, as shown in Figure 17.4, is displayed.

FIGURE 17.4

The Untitled -
Message dialog box is
used to create a new
piece of email. "(Rich
Text)" indicates that
this message can be
formatted.

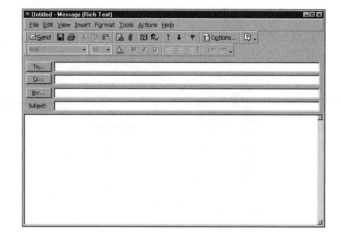

You can use Microsoft Word as your email editor, and if you have already set this option, your screen will be slightly different from the one shown in Figure 17.4.

Using Your Contact List to Address Email

Whom you send your message to is often as important as the message you send. Accidentally sending a copy of your personal email to your boss is usually not a good idea, and emailing documents to the wrong client can be equally disastrous. It is very important that you carefully address your message.

In the following steps, you'll learn to address the new email. You'll also discover how to send a carbon copy, and even a blind carbon copy, to other users.

1. Click the To button so that you can specify an address for your mail. The Select Names dialog box, shown in Figure 17.5, displays all the email addresses in the default address book. Use the drop-down list, shown in Figure 17.6, to select a different address book, such as Personal Address Book, Postoffice Address List, or any Contacts subfolders.

2. In the Type Name or Select from List box, you see names and email addresses. You might also have some telephone numbers or other information in the list. You might need to scroll up or down to find the desired name. Highlight the name and click the To-> button. Outlook places that name in the Message Recipients box. Click OK.

FIGURE 17.5

The Select Names dia-log box lists all the names with email addresses in the default address book (figure shown in Corporate/Workgroup mode).

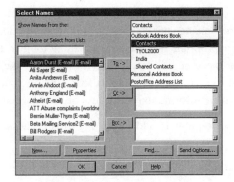

You can also type the names of the recipients directly into the blank boxes next to each field. Outlook then attempts to match the names you type with the entries in all of your address books. If it does not recognize a name from an address book, finds duplicate or ambiguous addresses, or determines that the address is not a proper Internet address, Outlook notifies you of the problem and asks you to select a name from the address list or enter a new address.

If Outlook doesn't recognize the name, it underlines it in red. Right-clicking the name displays a list of names to choose from (assuming that any of the names in the database is a match). If Outlook displays the name with a dotted green underline, that means there are other alternative addresses available, but Outlook is using the address you used last time. Right-click the name to see the alternatives.

3. Click the Cc: button and select another recipient to whom you would like to send a carbon copy of the email. Keep in mind that all recipients then receive a copy of all recipients' email addresses.

   You can also designate recipients to receive blind "carbon copies" of your message by placing their names in the Bcc: box. Addresses in the Bcc field are not visible to message recipients. Use this technique to protect recipients' privacy.

4. Click OK to close the Select Names dialog box.

Formatting Your Message

For messages sent in Rich Text Format (the factory-installed default when working in Corporate/Workgroup mode) or HTML format, Outlook allows you to format your email

17

much in the same way you format a document created in Microsoft Word. You can format text's color, font size, enhancements (such as bold, italic, or underline), and font simply by choosing the appropriate box on the Formatting toolbar. Remember, however, that the recipient of your message will not see the formatting if she is using an email editor that does not support formatting. Therefore, before sending your message, be sure that it accurately conveys the information regardless of your formatting.

The following steps show you how to add formatting to your messages.

1. In the Subject field, type e-mail is handy. Press Tab to move the insertion point into the message window.

2. Type It's nice to know how to create e-mail using Outlook. In the text message area. Press Enter.

3. Highlight the word Outlook and click the Bold button (or press Ctrl+B).

4. Highlight the entire sentence and click the Font Color button. Choose Lime as the text color. (You won't see the color change until you deselect the text.)

Adding a Custom Signature to Your Message

Another way to customize your email is to add a custom *signature* to your message. Although this option is not actually your signature, it is a custom-formatted version of your name that adds personality—and sometimes information—to your messages. The following steps explain how to create and format a signature.

1. Use the taskbar to display the main Outlook Inbox window.

2. Choose Tools, Options, Mail Format tab. Note that the Use Microsoft Word option should be unchecked and the default format should be set to Microsoft Outlook Rich Text format; click Signature Picker.

3. To create a new signature, click New, which displays the Create New Signature Wizard shown in Figure 17.6. Type a descriptive name for the signature (for example, *Work Signature*, *URL Signature*) in the space numbered as 1. Leave item 2 set as Start with a Blank Signature, and click Next.

4. In the Edit Signature box type the signature as you want it to appear. To apply font formatting, select the part of the signature you want to format (select the whole signature by using Ctrl+A). Click the Font button and apply the desired formatting. To apply paragraph formatting, move the insertion point into the target line and click the Paragraph button. Paragraph formatting is applied to the entire current line in the signature. Again, press Ctrl+A to apply paragraph formatting to the entire signature.

FIGURE 17.6

The Create New Signature Wizard helps you create a new signature.

5. When done, choose Finish and then OK to save the signature and return to the Options dialog boxes. Here, set Use This Signature by Default to the signature you just created. If you want the signature included in all messages, remove the check next to Don't Use When Replying or Forwarding. Click OK; then switch back to the email message you were composing.

6. The signature will automatically be inserted into future messages. To place it into this message, set the insertion point where you want it to appear, and click the Insert Signature button on the Standard toolbar; click the signature you just created.

Checking the Spelling in Your Message

To check the spelling before sending your message, choose Tools, Spelling (or press F7).

Sending the Message

After you have chosen your recipients, created the message, added your files and signature, and checked the spelling, you are ready to send your message. To send the message, simply click the Send (Alt+S) button and away it goes.

Although you may have sent the message, it first goes into your Outbox. Assuming that your local mail server is available, it then goes there. If you don't have a connection to your server (such as having to use a modem to dial up your server), the message sits in your Outbox folder until you establish a network connection. The server may send your message immediately, or it may be programmed to send at various intervals. Depending on network (Internet and other networks) activity, the message may be delivered to the server immediately, or it may take several minutes or even hours. Then the receiving server has to decide when it has time to post your message to the recipient. Normally, you won't notice a delay, but you should be aware of what happens when you click the Send button.

Checking for New Mail

To check for new mail, simply click the Send and Receive button on the toolbar. This command instructs Outlook to check all the services specified in the Options dialog box under the Mail Services tab (in C/W mode; in IMO mode, accounts are listed in Tools, Accounts).

You can tell Outlook to automatically check your email accounts after a specified interval. In the main Outlook window, choose Tools, Options. Depending on which mode (Internet Only or Corporate/Workgroup) is installed, this setting is found either in the Internet E-mail tab or in the Mail Delivery tab. In case your modem is not connected when Outlook attempts to receive subsequently, you would also need to check the Automatically Dial and/or Check Internet Explorer options if you use a modem.

Opening the Mail

Now that you know how to create and send email, it is highly likely that soon you'll start receiving replies. Therefore, it's a good idea to familiarize yourself with the process of reading, printing, and managing the email you receive.

Reading Your Messages

Reading a message in Outlook is simple. If the Preview pane (on the Advanced toolbar) is open, just highlight the message you want to read in the top portion of the Inbox, and scroll through the text that is displayed in the bottom portion of the Inbox. What could be easier?

To open a message in its own window, just select it and press Enter (or double-click it, or press Ctrl+O). The message opens and you can choose to reply to the sender, reply to all addressees, forward the message, or select from a multitude of other options.

Printing a Message

Printing an email with Outlook is almost as easy as reading your mail. An email message can be printed in various ways, including these two:

- Select the mail message and choose File, Print. In the Print dialog box, you can choose to print not only the message but any attachments as well. (*Attachments* are separate files that tag along with email messages.) To print the attachments, find the option at the bottom left of the Print dialog box, and place a check mark in the check box for printing the attachments.

- From the Inbox, right-click on any mail message and choose Print from the drop-down list of options.

Saving a Message As a File

At times you might want to save an email message as a file. Doing this does not remove the message from Outlook, it simply creates a file with the format you choose in the Save As dialog box. Your choices for formats are Text Only (*.TXT), Outlook Template (*.OFT), Message Format (*.MSG), and, for HTML messages, HTML (*.HTM).

Replying and Forwarding

Replying to and *forwarding* messages are similar tasks. Forwarding a message means that you send it to someone who wasn't originally listed as a sender or recipient of the original message. Replying means answering the email.

To reply to a message, simply highlight the message and decide whether you want to reply to just the original sender or to everyone who received the original email. If you want to reply only to the original sender, click the Reply button on the toolbar. If, however, you want to reply to everyone who was on the original sender's recipient list, click the Reply to All button. You can also use the Reply and Reply to All buttons on the toolbar when the message is open.

To forward a message to someone who was not on the original recipient list, simply click the Forward button and choose the person to which the message is to be sent.

Deleting Messages

Be sure to go through your messages regularly and delete those that are no longer needed. Deleting messages with attached files saves room on your hard drive or your network's mail server. You can delete items from your Inbox in several ways, including:

- In the Inbox, right-click on the email message and choose Delete from the drop-down list of options.

17

- Click the Delete button on the Standard toolbar of an open message.
- Highlight the message you want to delete, and click the Delete button on the toolbar.

You should note that the messages aren't really deleted until they've been removed from the Deleted Items folder.

Resending a Message

One occasion in which you may want to resend a message is when an external mail server has returned it to you as undeliverable. The message sometimes will have quite a bit of extra information, which really won't mean much to you. If it's clear that you used the wrong email address, click the Send Again option. This option reopens the original email message. Supply the correct address and click Send.

Attaching a File to Your Email Message

Sometimes, you'll want to send something you can't put into a regular email message. Maybe you have some baby pictures, a MIDI file, or even a collection of email messages you want to send to somebody.

Attaching a file is easy:

1. Press Ctrl+Shift+M to start a new email; fill in the To:, Subject:, and other header information.
2. Type a message describing the attachment and any special instructions.
3. Click the Insert File tool on the Standard toolbar, to display the Insert File dialog box.
4. Use Look In: and other controls to find the desired file or files. If you have multiple files to attach, you can use standard Windows selection techniques (click on the first item and then Ctrl+Click on additional items) to select multiple files, as shown in Figure 17.7.
5. Click the drop-down arrow on the Insert button and observe the choices. The default Insert is the same as Insert As Attachment. The other options are as Text and Shortcut. The Text option inserts the contents of the file into the email. The Shortcut option creates a Windows shortcut. That option might not be useful if the recipient is not on the same network as you. To insert the file as a normal attachment, skip the drop-down arrow and click Insert.

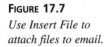

FIGURE 17.7
Use Insert File to attach files to email.

Saving an Attachment

When you receive an attachment, you usually will want to put it into your file system somewhere so that you can use it. You have at least three options for saving an attachment:

- Right-click the attachment and choose Save As.

- Drag the attachment from an open message window to the Windows Explorer (or to the file system when accessed from within Outlook via My Computer or Personal in the Outlook Bar).

- From an unopened message window, choose File, Save Attachments, and click the attachment you want to save.

Summary

Learning to create, send, and manage your email can open a whole new avenue of communications for you. Understanding the most effective way to create and manage your email can also increase productivity by cutting down on the amount of time you spend waiting for replies.

CHAPTER 18

Scheduling with Outlook's Calendar

You'll now take a look at what many consider Outlook's most useful feature: the Calendar.

Overview of Features

Besides its capability to display the various calendar views, Outlook's Calendar tool also helps you keep track of your time by setting appointments, holidays, and meeting dates. Calendar can perform these tasks:

- Set detailed appointments for any time of day. These appointments can be categorized by the criteria you set (business meeting, school event, or family event, for example). You can easily set Calendar to remind you of impending appointments with an onscreen message or even with a reminder sound.

- Create all-day events on your schedule. Similar to appointments, scheduling events allows you to quickly block out days of time, rather than just hours. You can even indicate how reachable you are (free, busy, tentative or out of the office) and whether the appointment time and date is firm or tentative.

- Plan meetings with associates—in your office or over the Internet—who also use Outlook. Calendar's Meeting Planner can search each person's calendar and automatically set a meeting time that is convenient to all, and it can even notify everyone who needs to attend the meeting.

- Make setting recurring appointments, meetings, and events a snap. If you need a nudge to pick up your daughter every day at 3:00 p.m., Calendar can set reminders for you with just a few clicks.

Starting the Calendar

As with so much of the Microsoft get-there-from-anywhere paradigm, you can access Calendar in more than one way. The main way to start Calendar is from within Outlook itself. From any part of Outlook, click the Calendar icon in the Outlook Bar or the Calendar folder in the Folder list, depending on the view you have displayed. From the menu, choose Go, Calendar.

Going Through the Grand Tour

When Calendar is displayed, you see the default Calendar screen, shown in Figure 18.1. Your screen might look slightly different; for example, your Calendar view might not include the TaskPad, and the date will most certainly be different.

Calendar, like all the other Outlook tools, has dynamic menus and toolbars. As the situation changes, so do the tools available on the toolbars and menus. What displays is actually dictated by two criteria: the Outlook module you are using and the view you are in. Calendar has seven built-in views—which you can select from the Current View dropdown arrow in the Advanced toolbar—with the toolbars varying slightly for each view.

In the default Day/Week/Month view, the Information Viewer has three panes: the Daily Appointment Calendar, the Date Navigator view of the current and next month, and the TaskPad.

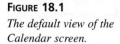

Figure 18.1

The default view of the Calendar screen.

Date Navigator

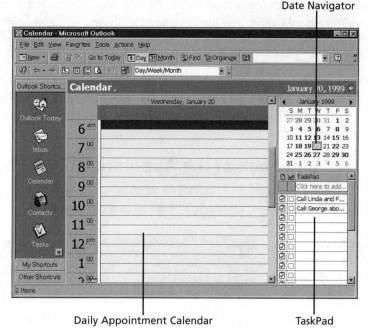

Daily Appointment Calendar   TaskPad

18

Customizing Calendar

Outlook defaults to a workday of 8:00 a.m. to 5:00 p.m., Monday through Friday. But what do you do if your workday is 7:00 a.m. to 4:00 p.m.? Or third shift, Sunday through Thursday from 11:00 p.m. to 7:00 a.m.? You can customize Calendar to define when your workday and workweek begin and end.

To change the specific workday parameters, choose Tools, Options, click the Preferences tab, and click the Calendar Options button.

In the Calendar workweek section, click the appropriate days' check boxes to match your workweek. You can enter the first day of the week from the drop-down list or directly type the day. You can also designate the first week of the year, just in case you work a fiscal year rather than a calendar year.

Enter the start times and end times of your day either by using the drop-down lists or by directly entering the times into each field.

Creating a New Appointment

Naturally, there's more than one way to begin the process of setting an appointment. However, all roads lead to the same place: the Appointment window.

The easiest way to begin is to click the New Appointment button on the far-left side of the standard Calendar toolbar. The menu command is Actions, New Appointment. If you like to use shortcut keys, you can press Ctrl+N to activate the New Appointment window.

If you are in Outlook but not in Calendar, and you need to set an appointment, select the Appointment command in the Standard toolbar's New Items drop-down box. This list also displays Ctrl+Shift+A as the shortcut key for activating the New Appointment window. You can always start a new appointment from anywhere within Outlook by pressing Ctrl+Shift+A.

A Quick Look at the Appointment Window

As shown in Figure 18.2, the Appointment window offers menu commands and toolbar functions to help you set appointments as easily as possible.

FIGURE 18.2

The Appointment window displays as Untitled until you complete the Subject field.

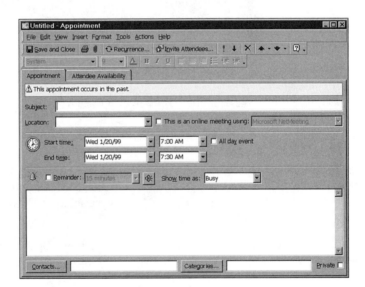

Time and Date Errors

When you first create a new appointment, you might see a warning (located just above the Subject line) which states that the appointment occurs in the past, as shown in Figure 18.2. This is because, by default, Outlook assumes that the appointment you want to schedule is for the time and date highlighted in the current appointment window. If the current time is after the highlighted time, the appointment occurs in the past. Don't worry about this error message; you'll learn to fix it shortly. Actually, although this might seem like an extra step, it keeps you from accidentally scheduling appointments in the past.

Defining the Appointment Subject

Keep the subject short and to the point. Save detailed explanations for the Note box near the bottom of the Appointment window. After you type a subject and leave the Subject field, the window title changes from Untitled to whatever subject you typed.

Entering the Location

Unless your appointments are always at the same place, it's wise to note where meetings and events will be held. This field is especially helpful for offsite events. The nice thing about the Location field is that it is actually a drop-down list box that remembers the last 10 locations you entered into this field. This is great for office appointments, because these tend to occur in the same places. After a short while, the drop-down list should contain a customized list of most of the places your appointments are likely to occur.

Entering Dates

To save you from typing dates and times, Calendar's drop-down boxes in date fields enable you to use the mouse to set up the appointment's date and time. Click the drop-down arrow next to the date field in the Start Time line to see a calendar of the current month. Click any day in the displayed month to choose the day for your appointment. The current date always appears enclosed in a red box. If you want to move to a different month, click the back (left) or forward (right) arrows in the top corners of the calendar. Also, anytime you want to move quickly back to your present position in the space-time continuum, simply click the Today button on the bottom of the calendar.

You can also type dates in the normal format, for example:

12/12/04

12/12/2004

December 12, 2004

18

> Outlook understands major holidays that occur on the same date each year (such as Christmas) but not variable holidays (such as Easter or Hanukah).

Setting Times

The Start Time drop-down box displays times in half-hour intervals starting at 12 a.m. By default, Outlook assumes that the appointment duration is one-half hour.

Set the appropriate date and start time for the appointment. Generally, you can skip the End Time date field (appointments generally last less than one day) and click the drop-down arrow for the End Time field. A list of half-hour intervals is displayed, now with duration notations next to them. If you know the specific time your appointment will end, you can click that time, or if you just know the duration of the appointment, you can search for the correct duration time without doing the mental calculations to determine the actual end time.

In the next few steps, you set an appointment to surprise one of your office workers, Kevin, with a 40th birthday party tomorrow. The party is at 2:00 p.m. in the cafeteria. You are the person responsible for getting Kevin there.

1. Open Outlook if it isn't already open. Click the Calendar folder in the Outlook Bar or Folder list.

2. Press Ctrl+Shift+A to display an Untitled-Appointment window.

3. In the Subject text box, type `Kevin's Birthday Party`.

4. In the Location text box, type `Cafeteria`.

5. Display the calendar for the start date and click the next business day.

6. Click the Start Time drop-down arrow and choose 2:00 p.m. to set the start time (making sure you click the second 2 rather than the first 2, so you choose p.m. rather than a.m.). When you finish entering the date and time, notice that in the End Time fields, the end date and end time change to the same date and a half-hour later than the time in the Start Time fields. This saves steps in setting up the end time, provided that the event is supposed to last the default half hour.

7. If the party is scheduled to last only a half hour, this appointment's times would now be set. However, Kevin and his coworkers are a bit more fun than that, and they plan to party about an hour and a half. This party will last 1.5 hours, so choose 3:30 p.m. (1.5 hours) as the end time. You can use the drop-down arrow with the mouse; or, if your fingers are already on the keyboard, tab down to the End Time field and tap the down-arrow key twice to advance from the default 2:30 to 3:30.

8. Your Appointment screen should be similar to the one in Figure 18.3. With the subject, location, date, and time completed for Kevin's party (the minimum amount of information you need in order to set up an appointment), click the Save and Close button.

More Ways to Set Appointments

You can set your times and create a new appointment in other ways as well. Instead of using the Appointment window to set the dates and times, you can use Calendar itself:

1. Move to the day on which you want to set up the appointment by clicking the new date on the Date Navigator; scroll to the desired time in the Calendar.

FIGURE 18.3

The basic appointment information for Kevin's party has been entered.

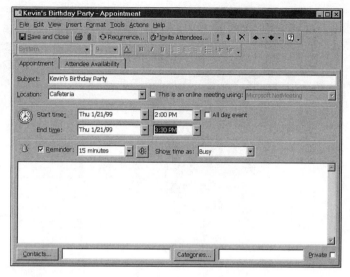

2. Double-click the half-hour block of time in the daily calendar to indicate when the appointment will begin.

3. The Appointment window pops up with the correct date and time for a half-hour appointment already entered. Change the duration if necessary.

Editing Appointments

In a perfect world, after you set an appointment, that would be it. No changes, no conflicts, nothing to disturb your inner harmony. But nothing is settled until it's over. And, even then, it's still not finished. Look at Figure 18.4 for a case in point.

This schedule, which easily could have been created over a number of days, has some conflicts that need to be resolved. If the appointment creator had been paying attention as these appointments were created, this might not have happened. When an appointment is created, Calendar warns you if the appointment conflicts with another, or if it is immediately adjacent to another (see Figure 18.5).

Changing Appointment Start and End Times

You can change an appointment's beginning or ending time by opening the item and changing the time in the Start Time and End Time boxes. An easier way is to drag the top or bottom boundary to the new starting (top boundary) or ending (bottom boundary) time.

FIGURE 18.4

This day has some scheduling conflicts.

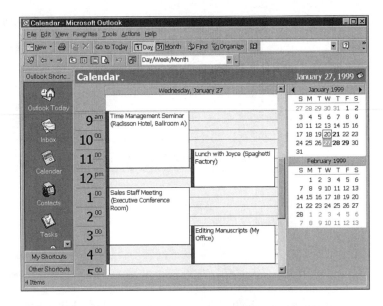

FIGURE 18.5

Conflicting appoint-ments give this warn-ing message.

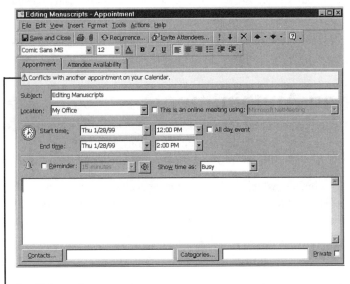

Conflict warning message

Moving an Appointment

To move an appointment, click on it and drag it to the new time block.

Changing Appointment Dates

Date conflicts are a little tougher to resolve than time conflicts, although they really aren't difficult either. In the example shown in Figure 18.4, the seminar is mandatory, and the lunch partner cannot change her lunch time. She can, however, have lunch at the same time on Thursday. You could simply double-click the item (or the item's move handle, if it is already selected) to open the Appointment window and type the new date. However, there is an easier way to make this change. Click the move handle on the item to be changed (remember, the move handle is the thick blue line along the left edge of the item). Drag the item onto the correct date in the Date Navigator (at the right of the Calendar). The item is automatically moved from the current date to the new date. All other information, including time and location, remains unchanged.

Changing the Subject

During the course of rechecking the schedule created earlier, you become aware of another error: The conference call next Thursday is to London, not Sandusky. This is good to know because you have to consult a completely different set of notes for the London meeting and adjust for the different time zone. You can change the subject by using one of the following methods:

18

- Double-click the item (or the item's move handle if the insertion point is inside the item) to open its Appointment window and change the subject.
- Change the subject by clicking once on the appointment item in the Calendar. All but the subject information disappears, allowing a direct edit. When any other part of the screen is clicked, the new information is saved.

Moving to a New Location

As you have seen, when a location is initially added to an appointment, it is displayed in the Daily view in parentheses, directly following the subject. If you click the item in the Daily view, the location disappears. It cannot be edited from here. If you find that the location is incorrect, you have only one method to change the location of an appointment: You must open the item and change the location in the Location text box.

Deleting an Appointment

If you decide that you do not have to go to your doctor's appointment because you are feeling much better, you can delete the appointment. (Outlook isn't smart enough to call your doctor and cancel the appointment, so you'll have to do that yourself.) You can delete an appointment in one of several ways:

- Double-click the item's move handle to open its Appointment window. Click the Delete button on the Appointment's toolbar.
- From the Daily view, single-click the item, and then click the Delete button on the Calendar's Standard toolbar.
- From the Daily view, single-click the item, and then press the Delete key on the keyboard.
- From the Daily view, right-click the item and choose Delete.

Handling Events

Outlook refers to any appointment that lasts 24 or more hours as an *event*. Scheduling events is much the same as handling appointments. In fact, the procedures are virtually identical, except for one thing: In the Appointment window, just to the right of the Start and End Time fields, you see the check box All Day Event. When this is checked, the start and end times disappear, because the event now stretches over the entire day. You should also see a purple (out of office) border along the left edge of the whole day, between the times and the text area of the Calendar.

In the Date Navigator, click the date for your Ottawa tour, and scroll—if necessary—so that the Ottawa tour appointment is visible. Double-click the appointment and change this to an all-day event by putting a check mark next to All Day Event. The time shows as Free, which is the default. Change it to Out of Office. Click the Save and Close button. Figure 18.6 shows how an event looks in the daily calendar. Notice that the event is displayed as a fixed banner at the top of the daily calendar. To edit, move, or delete an event, use the same techniques used for appointments.

Sending Events and Appointments to Others

You can send events, appointments, and cancellations to other Outlook users. When an event is canceled, Outlook sends cancellation notices to anybody who has been *invited* to an event or appointment. So if you and your doctor use Outlook to schedule medical appointments, Outlook might actually be smart enough to let your doctor know that the appointment was canceled, even if it isn't actually going to pick up the phone.

Note that an event with invitations is called an *invited event*, and an appointment with invitations is called a *meeting*.

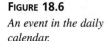

FIGURE 18.6

An event in the daily calendar.

The following steps show you how to invite others to appointments or events.

1. Begin by opening any appointment you created earlier.

2. Notice that the appointment has two tabs: Appointment and Attendee Availability. Click the Attendee Availability tab.

3. At the moment, you are the only attendee, as the one who created the appointment. Click Invite Others to display the Select Attendee and Resources dialog box, shown in Figure 18.7.

4. Choose the attendees you want to invite, noting that there are three categories: Required, Optional, and Resources. Click OK when you're done. Invitations will be sent to the Required and Optional attendees. To avoid sending an invitation to any given attendee, click the envelope next to the attendee's name in the All Attendees list, and choose Don't Send Meeting to this Attendee.

5. Note that the Save and Close button on the Standard toolbar has been replaced by Send. Note also that the appointment has now changed into a meeting. Once you invite others to an appointment, it becomes a meeting. Click Send to finish the appointment and to send notices to the different invitees.

Responding to an Invitation

When you send an invitation, required invitees will receive an email that displays as an appointment, as shown in Figure 18.8. To respond to an invitation, click Accept, Tentative, or Decline. Choosing Accept or Tentative adds that appointment to your calendar. Your response is also sent via email to the appointment or event originator. A notation then shows up in the originator's calendar indicating that a response has been received. The person can then plan accordingly.

FIGURE 18.7

Invitees will be notified by email of the meeting and any subsequent changes (figure shown in Corporate/Workgroup mode).

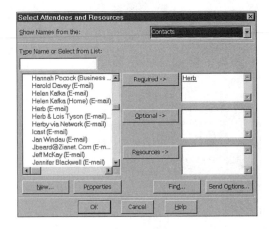

FIGURE 18.8

The Accept, Tentative, and Decline buttons send email back to the host.

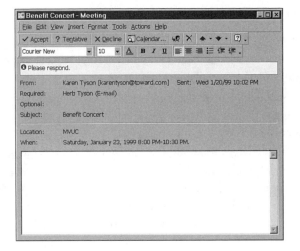

Canceling an Appointment

Suppose that you and your doctor conduct scheduling by using Microsoft Outlook. If you cancel your appointment via Outlook, an email to that effect is sent to your doctor. When you delete an appointment that has invitees, you can choose to delete the appointment and send a cancellation notice, or just delete without sending a notice. Choosing the delete/cancel option displays the appointment onscreen; click Send to complete sending a cancellation notice.

When you receive a cancellation notice, you are presented with an opportunity to remove that appointment from your calendar. Click Remove from Calendar to move the appointment into the electronic wastebasket.

Recurring Items and Events

Often, you will find that certain events take place on a regular basis, such as that pesky Friday-afternoon team meeting or the quarterly staff meeting. If your events have a specific pattern (the second Thursday of the month, for example), you can make them *recurring*.

You display the Appointment Recurrence dialog box, shown in Figure 18.9, by choosing Actions, New Recurring Appointment. If you selected the starting date and time in the Daily view before opening the dialog box, the start date and start and end times are already inserted. Or you can right-click the desired time and choose New Recurring Appointment (or Event or Meeting).

> You can choose New Recurring Appointment or New Recurring Meeting. The difference is that the latter requires you to enter the names of meeting invitees.

18

Using the Appointment Recurrence dialog box, you can choose to have the appointment recur daily, weekly, monthly, or yearly. Set the Recur Every text box to define the frequency of the appointment. Select the day (or days) of the week on which the appointment is to occur.

FIGURE 18.9

The Appointment Recurrence dialog box.

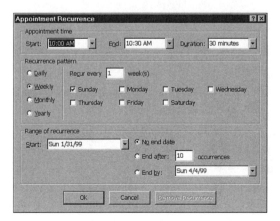

In the lower area, you can specify the start date, and whether the meetings will occur only a specific number of times (for example, in the case of a six-week class). If the appointment recurs indefinitely, choose the No End Date radio button. If a specific number of recurrences is known, this value can be entered in the End After: *X* Occurrences field. If a specific end date is known, enter this value in the End By field.

Adding Holidays or a Recurring Event

When you're entering a recurring event, the steps are almost identical to those for entering a recurring appointment. The only difference is that you need to click the All Day Event check box before you click Save and Close.

Holidays are one form of recurring events. Adding them to your Calendar is a snap as the following steps demonstrate.

1. Choose Tools, Options, Calendar Options to display the Calendar Options dialog box.

2. Click the Add Holidays button. The Add Holidays to Calendar dialog box appears (see Figure 18.10).

FIGURE 18.10

The Add Holidays to Calendar dialog box.

3. Locate the United States option (or whichever country you live in) and place a check mark next to it. (It is probably already checked.) You may want to add other countries or holiday sets. Click OK. Calendar imports all the holidays for the selections you have checked.

4. Click OK to exit Calendar Options and OK again to return to the Daily view.

Repeating an Existing Appointment or Event

Once in a while, the need arises to make an appointment repeat indefinitely or for a number of consecutive days. So you need to repeat the all-day event and stretch out your travel time. This technique works for any appointment as the following steps show.

1. Open the Appointment window for the appointment by double-clicking the event in the Calendar window.

2. On the Standard toolbar, click the Recurrence button (the one with two arrows in a circle). This selection opens the Appointment Recurrence dialog box.

3. Click the Daily Recurrence Pattern radio button and then the Every *X* Day(s) radio button.

4. In the Range of Recurrence section, set the End By date to be one week after your departure date (type 1 week into the End By field). The settings should be similar to those shown in Figure 18.10.

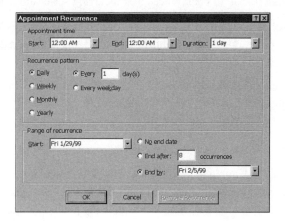

FIGURE 18.11

Appointment Recurrence settings are a real work saver.

18

5. Click OK to close the Appointment Recurrence dialog box; then click Save and Close.

6. Click the other days on which you will be gone. Each is now blocked out as a recurring event.

Editing a Recurrence

Editing a recurring item is much the same as editing any item in Calendar. But when you first double-click the item's move handle in the Daily calendar, Calendar displays an exclamation dialog box asking whether you want to edit the entire series or just that item. Use caution here because if you want to edit only one occurrence of the item, you could inadvertently change the entire series' information.

From here, proceed to edit the item or series as you normally would edit a single item. Entering the occurrence results in a change being made only to that specific item. If you edit the series, changes made are applied to every single occurrence of the appointment or event.

Removing a Recurrence

When an appointment that was supposed to repeat changes to a one-time-only event, Calendar gives you a way to make this change. Double-click the single appointment you want to keep. Choose the Open the Series radio button and click OK. Click the Recurrence button once more to open the Appointment Recurrence dialog box. The Remove Recurrence button is displayed. If you click this, all other occurrences of this series except the date currently showing will be removed.

Deleting All Occurrences of a Recurring Item

If you want to get rid of all occurrences of a recurring series, do one of the following:

- Double-click to open the item, and choose Open the Series. Click the Delete button on the Standard toolbar. In Confirm Delete, choose Delete All Occurrences.

  Or

- Right-click the item and choose Delete. In Confirm Delete, choose Delete All Occurrences.

Summary

By now, you should be able to see just how easy it is to set and edit appointments and events—and to send appointments and events to others. Recurring appointments and events, the bane of anyone with a nonelectronic day planner, are simple to create as well. Calendar also enables you to set up meetings.

CHAPTER 19

Managing Tasks

At work your projects are broken down into specific tasks, in addition to your daily and weekly repetitive tasks that somehow pile up overnight. At home there are the family-related tasks such as the Monday afternoon Girl Scout meetings with the new patches needing to be sewn on the vest immediately, trying to find a sitter for Saturday night, and all the regular chores too. You also have the home-related tasks such as mowing the lawn, grocery shopping, and picking up the dry cleaning.

Now, even with task lists and sticky notes, how do you find time to get it all done? Task management and time management are the focus of this chapter.

What Is a Task?

You might be skeptical of time management and personal organizers. However, the Tasks feature can make a believer of you by doing the following:

- Allowing you to create and maintain lists of things to do, as well as track tasks by project, by the people involved, and by priority.

- Letting you maintain lists of recurring tasks that either occur on specified dates or occur a certain time after the preceding occurrence of the task is completed.

- Allowing delegation of tasks and task management to other people, for those times when you're too busy to do it yourself.

- Accepting task assignments from others. This is certainly not fun, but at least Tasks makes it easy by enabling you to integrate a new incoming task into your list of things to do.

All of this, naturally, begs the question: What is a *task*? Basically, a task is anything that requires somebody's action. Are appointments tasks? Semantically, most certainly. In Outlook, they're different things, but there's no reason appointments can't become tasks, and vice versa. Even Journal entries correspond to work you've done. If you need to track work you do for clients, perhaps Journal entries should become tasks, too.

Starting the Task Screen

Accessing the Tasks screen in Outlook is much the same as using any of the other tools.

You can start Tasks by taking one of the following actions:

- Clicking the Tasks icon in the Outlook Bar.
- Clicking the Tasks folder in the Folders list.
- Choosing View, Go To, Tasks.

The Tasks Screen

The Tasks screen is not flashy. That might be why many Outlook users ignore it. As you can see in Figure 19.1, the Information Viewer section of the Outlook screen is filled with a simple-looking, columnar table. But you know by now that in Outlook, such things are never quite as simple as they look. If they were, this book would be very short. Depending on what you've been doing, your task screen might be a little different.

This particular view of Tasks is the Simple List view. The Icon column shows the type of Outlook item. Most of the time, the plain Task icon will be present here, although assigned tasks are symbolized in this column as well (the first task in Figure 19.1 is an assigned task, denoted by the hand icon).

The Subject column describes the task: Take out the trash. Get Dave the Top Ten List by 5:30. Launch the Mars probe. These are all good examples of task subjects. The subject should include enough information to tell you at a glance what the task is. You can add more information in the Note box at the bottom of the Task screen when an individual task has been opened.

Figure 19.1

*The Tasks screen is
one method of
inputting tasks.*

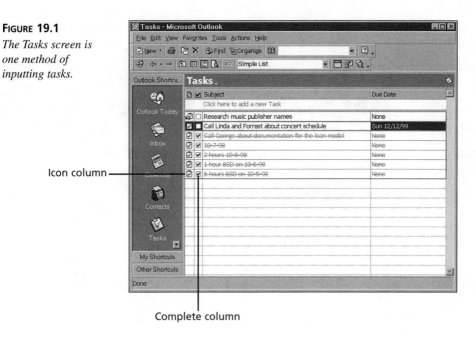

Icon column ——

Complete column

The Date Due column displays the date the task should be completed. Not all tasks have
due dates. Tasks that do not have due dates are indicated by *None*.

Creating a Task

Tasks can help you organize your busy life—business and personal—especially in our
upcoming example, in which your family is soon to be enlarged.

The following few pages follow a working parent-to-be. Over the next few months a lot
must be done to prepare for the new arrival. For you to get everything done without waiting until the last minute, a task list will really be handy.

To create a task list, you can activate the New Task window (also called the Task tool) in
several ways. When in the Tasks view

- Click the New Task button on the far-left end of the Standard toolbar.
- Use the shortcut keys Ctrl+N.
- Choose Actions, New Task.
- Double-click the Click Here to Add a New Task in the Task Entry Row button.
- Press Ctrl+Shift+K from anywhere within Outlook (this is my favorite method).
- Double-click an empty line in the Task list, or right-click and choose New Task.

After you employ any one of these methods, the New Task screen is displayed, as shown in Figure 19.2.

FIGURE 19.2

The New Task screen is used to enter more detailed data than can be entered from the simple view.

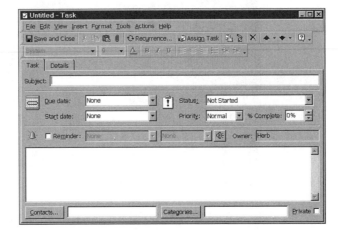

The Subject line should be simple and to the point. Extra information can be added in the Note box at the bottom of the Task tool as needed.

The next information group is the Due Date field. The default is None. By clicking the drop-down arrow, you see the Date Navigator box. The current date is highlighted. Select the date by which you want to complete the task, or leave it at None. For the current date, either click the Today button or click the current day's date on the Date Navigator. To choose another date, click the appropriate date in the Date Navigator. Also, you can just type the correct date directly over None.

The Start Date field works in much the same way as the Due Date field. It is used to establish the date on which the task will begin. This date can be immediately or some time in the near future. If the task is already in progress, the start date might be in the past.

The next field is the Status field. How is the project going? Has it begun? This is what Outlook means by Status. In the Status field, there are five choices: Not Started, In Progress, Completed, Waiting on Someone Else, and Deferred. After the task is underway, depending on how you use Tasks, you might need to open the task and change the status from time to time.

Another drop-down list box lists three Priority choices: High, Normal, and Low.

The next field, % Complete, is another way to think about status—like most of the Task fields, it too is optional. In certain situations pinning down a percentage value is tricky.

When the task is more segmented or can be easily measured, however, it's helpful to use this field. For instance, when writing a specific number of chapters in a book, an author could change the percentage of chapters completed and submitted to the editor by either directly entering the percentage or using the spin buttons to the right of the field to increase or decrease the percentage. You might also think in terms of budget. When you're executing a project, you might think of % Complete as % Spent.

In the following steps, you practice entering several tasks that are of concern to the expectant parents.

1. By using any method, open an Untitled Task window.
2. Type Purchase baby crib in the subject line.
3. Insert the date three months from now as the due date. You can just type 3 months and press Tab.
4. Enter today as the start date.
5. Choose the In Progress option for the Status field.
6. Leave Normal as the priority for now. (Normal is the default priority.)
7. Click Save and Close.
8. You might need to drag the column headings so that the widths are similar to those shown in Figure 19.3. Position the mouse pointer between adjacent column headings such that a two-headed sizing arrow appears, and drag to the left or right to change the relative widths of the adjacent columns.

FIGURE 19.3

A single task has been entered and the column widths have been adjusted.

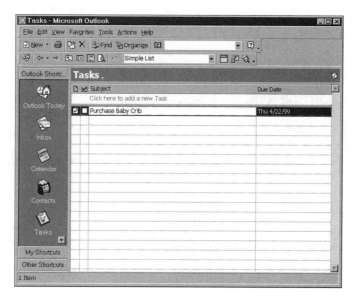

19

9. Over the course of the next few months, a lot of other tasks will need to get done before the baby arrives home. Take the next few minutes and enter the tasks noted in Table 19.1.

> You can enter and edit tasks from the TaskPad rather than opening an Untitled Task window for each entry. Clicking the entries for Due Date and Status brings up drop-down arrow lists to facilitate selection of possible choices.

TABLE 19.1 Data for Task Entry

Priority	Subject	Status	Due Date	% Complete
Normal	Arrange for diaper service	Not Started	3 mo.	0
Normal	Decorate baby room	In Progress	3 mo.	10
High	Time off work, HR paperwork	In Progress	1 mo.	25
High	Choose a pediatrician	Waiting on Someone Else	1 mo.	25
High	Select a baby name	In Progress	3 mo.	25

Your tasks should look similar to the ones shown in Figure 19.4.

Creating a Task Automatically

You may get a lot of email that contains urgent matters that require efficient processing to keep your world from collapsing. You know—things such as, "Could you get me a copy of that song?" or "Can you finish three more chapters by Friday?" Messages such as these can be converted to a task quite easily.

1. Click Inbox and select the appropriate message. Using the left mouse button, drag-and-drop the message onto the Task icon (or into the Task folder).

2. When the New Task tool appears, fill in the appropriate information (priority, due date, and so on).

3. Click Save and Close.

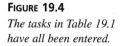

FIGURE 19.4

The tasks in Table 19.1 have all been entered.

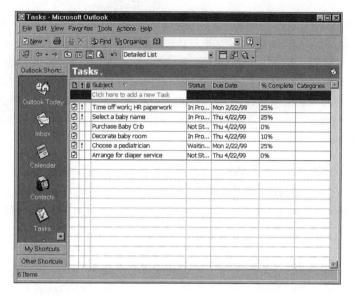

Finishing a Task

There's no greater satisfaction than a job well done, but how do you tell Tasks you're done? There are four ways:

- When the Complete column is in view, as in the Simple List view, click the check box next to the finished task to mark that task as completed (clicking the check box toggles the check on and off).

- In Detailed List view, click the Status field and choose Completed, or enter 100% into the % Complete field.

- In the Task tool, choose Completed in the Status field or enter 100% in the % Complete field.

- In the Task tool, click the Mark Complete button on the toolbar.

After you have marked a task complete, it does not disappear from the Simple List view. Rather, it changes to a lighter, strikethrough text. This helps you keep track of the recent things you've accomplished.

In the Active Tasks view, however, tasks disappear when they are marked complete. Although the tasks are still in the folder, to see them you must switch to the Simple List view. Later you will learn to completely delete a task.

19

Editing a Task

Editing a task is not difficult. If the item you want to edit is visible in the Information Viewer, you can edit it directly without opening the Task tool. In the next exercise, you'll learn to add a reminder date.

When you want to do more detailed editing, double-click on any task in the Information Viewer. This opens that task's Task tool. Editing any of the fields on the Task tab is the same as creating the task.

Deleting a Task

As I've mentioned, when tasks are completed, they do not just vanish into the air. They stick around, reminding you of all the good work you've accomplished.

You can keep tasks around until they are auto-archived, but you might want to clean house and sweep out these old tasks sooner than that. You might even need to delete a current task if someone else has taken it over and you are no longer responsible for its completion. In any case, to delete a task, highlight the task in question and then click the Delete button on the Standard toolbar in Tasks or on the Task tool toolbar if the Task Detail screen is open.

Checking Task Status

Usually you'll want to use the task-status capability at work because work tasks tend to be more segmented and easier to track. If your boss has access to your calendar, he can use the Status section to check the progress of a task he has assigned to you without having to call you into his office.

Summary

You have learned some ways to manage your time and your life better. You will find that tracking all of your tasks will become a habit, and you will be much more organized after using this feature for a while. Not only will you know what you need to complete and what you have already done, but you also will be able to keep a close eye on all those tasks and projects you ask other people to take care of.

PART VI

Making Outlook Work the Way You Do

Chapter

CHAPTER 20

Customizing Outlook

If you look carefully at all of the Outlook screen shots in this book, you might even notice an occasional menu view where Define Views and other commands are on the main menu to the right of Help. In this chapter, you'll learn how they got there. You'll also become a master at adding, moving, and removing menu and toolbar items. You'll become so confident that you won't hesitate to add a command to the menu or a toolbar for a special project—and then remove it when you're done.

Personalized Toolbars and Menus

You can turn off Outlook's personalized menus and toolbars if you prefer to see full menus. To turn them off, choose Tools, Customize, and click the Options tab. Make sure you deselect the check box called Menus Show Recently Used Commands First, as shown in Figure 20.1.

FIGURE 20.1

Use the Customize dialog box's Options tab to turn off personalized features.

Tooling Around with Toolbars

The key to customizing Outlook's menus and toolbars is knowing what you have to work with. First, you need to explore an often-overlooked aspect of toolbars. Display the Advanced toolbar, if it's not already displayed. Right-click any toolbar or menu and choose Advanced. Look at the right end of the Advanced toolbar. You should see a downward-pointing black triangle. Click that triangle, and then click Add or Remove Buttons to display the view shown in Figure 20.2.

FIGURE 20.2

For quick customizing, use Add or Remove Buttons to selectively turn toolbar buttons off and on.

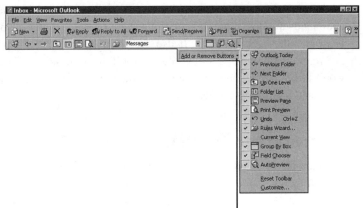

The More Buttons tool

To hide toolbar buttons that you do not need to see, follow these steps:

1. Display the Inbox, and then click the More Buttons tool at the right end of the Advanced toolbar and click on Add or Remove Buttons to display the list shown in Figure 20.3. (Notice that all of the items are checked. That means that all of the default buttons are set to appear.)

2. Remove the checks next to Previous Folder and Next Folder. Observe the toolbar as you do this. When you remove a check, the toolbar icon corresponding to that item disappears. Even though you've now hidden those items, they'll still be displayed as choices each time you display the list shown in Figure 20.2.

3. The list of tools now appears as shown in Figure 20.3. Notice that there are no checks next to the two removed tools. Click each tool to restore it to the menu.

FIGURE 20.3

Use the More Buttons tool to hide buttons you never use.

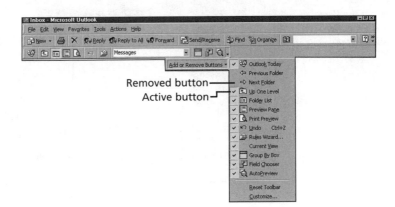

Do you like the toolbars where they are? If so, that's great. If not, why not move them somewhere else, as the following steps demonstrate (see Figure 20.4):

1. Move the mouse pointer over the bar (the Move handle) at the left end of any menu or toolbar (or the top end, if the menu or toolbar is displayed vertically) so that a four-headed arrow appears.

2. Using the left mouse button, drag the toolbar or menu to the desired position and release the mouse button.

3. To anchor the toolbar or menu to one of the four sides, drag it so it snaps into place. To float the toolbar or menu, drag it to an open space away from the four sides of Outlook's window.

4. Floating toolbars and menus can be resized into any rectangular shape. When you hover the mouse pointer over any of the four sides of a floating toolbar, the mouse pointer becomes a two-headed resizing pointer. Use the left mouse button to widen or narrow that dimension.

20

To return a floating toolbar to its last-anchored position, double-click its title bar.

Web toolbar

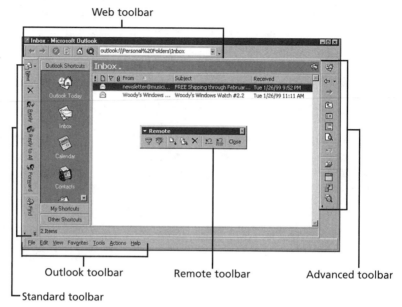

Figure 20.4

The menu and toolbar aren't welded to the top of the Outlook screen (shown in Corporate/Workgroup mode; the Remote toolbar is not available in IMO mode).

Outlook toolbar   Remote toolbar   Advanced toolbar

Standard toolbar

Displaying, Resetting, and Creating New Toolbars

You've already seen how to choose which toolbars to display by right-clicking any menu or toolbar. That technique is useful for turning a single toolbar on or off, but it's tedious when you want to manipulate multiple toolbars at the same time. For more control, right-click a toolbar, choose Customize, and click the Toolbars tab to display the Customize dialog box shown in Figure 20.5. The Standard, Advanced, and Menu Bar toolbars are enabled. The Web and Remote toolbars are turned off.

Figure 20.5

Use the Customize dialog box's Toolbars tab to turn on/off multiple toolbars at the same time.

While you're here, use the New button to create a brand new toolbar. For example, you can create customized toolbars for different projects. Suppose you go through design

phases. You can create a customized toolbar that contains just the design tools you need by following these steps:

1. Right-click any toolbar or menu and choose Customize (or choose Tools, Customize from Outlook's main menu).

2. In the Toolbars tab, click New.

3. Type a new name for the toolbar and click OK.

4. As shown in Figure 20.6, the new toolbar appears to the left of the Customize dialog box, which now includes My Toolbar on the list. You'll learn how to add commands to it in a moment.

FIGURE 20.6

My Toolbar has been added to the Toolbars list and now appears as a floating toolbar.

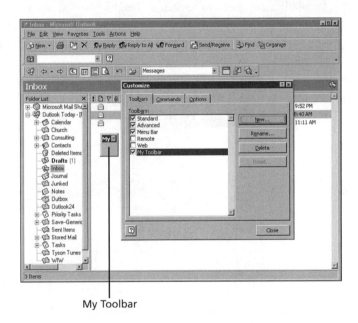

My Toolbar

After you've added the new toolbar, a couple of changes occur inside the Customize dialog box. Notice that with My Toolbar selected, the Rename and Delete buttons are now available. You cannot delete or rename the built-in toolbars, but you can rename and delete those you create. Keep the Customize dialog box onscreen as you begin the next section.

20

Adding Tools and Commands to a Toolbar

Outlook lets you add tools and commands to any toolbar or menu—including toolbars you've created. In the previous section, you created a new toolbar called *My Toolbar*. In this section, you'll learn how to populate that toolbar.

If you jumped to this section from elsewhere in the book, right-click any toolbar or menu and choose Customize. If you didn't do it before, click New and create a new toolbar named My Toolbar.

In the following steps, you'll create a customized toolbar by adding commands from the Customize dialog box and copying commands from existing toolbars. This customized dialog box will contain tools for creating each of Outlook's items (new message, new contact, new task, and so on).

1. Right-click any menu or toolbar and make sure that My Toolbar is displayed, if it's not already. Then right-click any menu or toolbar and choose Customize.

2. Click the Commands tab to display the commands shown in Figure 20.7.

FIGURE 20.7

The Commands tab provides access to all of Outlook's commands.

3. Under Categories, make sure File is selected. Under Commands, locate Appointment. Move the mouse pointer over Appointment. Using the left mouse button, click and drag Appointment into My Toolbar, and then release the mouse button. My Toolbar should now appear.

4. Now drag Meeting Request into My Toolbar. As you add items, you might need to reposition My Toolbar so you can see where you're putting the items.

5. Add tools for each of the other types of Outlook items: Mail Message, Contact, Task, Task Request, Journal Entry, and Note. You'll probably need to scroll through the list of commands to find them all.

6. Add Outlook's Advanced Find to My Toolbar, too. In Categories, click Tools. Then scroll down the list of commands to Advanced Find and drag it to My Toolbar.

7. Suppose you're thinking about replacing the Advanced toolbar with My Toolbar. You might want to include some of its commands on My Toolbar. With the Customize dialog box still displayed, press the Ctrl key and use the left mouse button to drag/copy the Current View tool from the Advanced toolbar to My Toolbar. Notice the + next to the command as you drag. This tells you that you're copying the tool rather than moving it. If you release the Ctrl key, you'll move the Current View tool rather than simply copying it. My Toolbar should now appear as shown in figure 20.8.

8. Click Close to complete the customization.

Display the Customize dialog box again and choose the Toolbars tab. With Standard selected, notice that the Reset button is available. This is because the Standard toolbar has a default configuration that you can restore. Now click on My Toolbar. The Reset button is no longer available. That's because user-created toolbars don't have default configurations. The default is nonexistence, which you can bring about by choosing Delete. You can also rename toolbars you create.

Current View tool on the Advanced toolbar

FIGURE 20.8

You can copy commands between toolbars and menus.

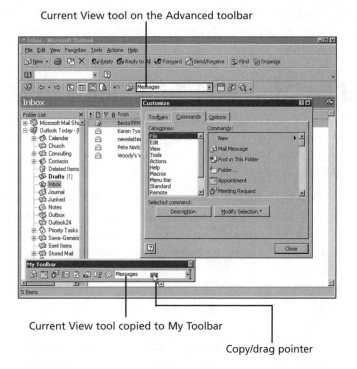

Current View tool copied to My Toolbar

Copy/drag pointer

20

> Although this discussion focuses on tools, you can add commands just as easily. The only real difference between a tool and a command is that one has an icon and the other doesn't. If you find commands without icons in the list of commands, just drag them where you want them.

Removing Tools and Commands from Toolbars

You can remove an item from a toolbar by dragging it off the toolbar while the Customize dialog box is onscreen. However, there's an easier way. You're about to learn a power-user technique that works throughout Office applications as the following steps show.

1. Move the mouse pointer over a tool you want to remove. The tool will be recessed as if it were being pushed.

2. Hold down the Alt key. Using the left mouse button, click and drag the tool away from all toolbars so that an X appears. Release the mouse button to complete the removal.

Adding Tools and Commands to Menus

You can also add tools and commands to menus. The technique is similar to that for modifying toolbars, but it might require steadier hands for drilling down to the menu level you want. The following steps walk you through the adding of tools and commands to Outlook menus.

1. Right-click any menu and choose Customize. Click the Commands tab.

2. Put the Define Views command onto a more prominent spot on the menu. In Categories, choose View, and in Commands, find Define Views. Notice that the commands aren't in alphabetical order. Fortunately, Define Views is close to the top.

3. Using the left mouse button, drag Define Views to the menu bar and drop it between Actions and Help.

4. With the Customize dialog box still open, drag any command from the dialog box to the Tools menu—but don't release the mouse button. Drag the command down to any item that has a black right-pointing triangle (which indicates that a menu contains additional items). That item opens. You could now drag the command to

any location in the menu and drop it. But don't. Instead, press Esc to cancel the drag. Click Close.

Creating a New Menu

If you have many commands to add to the menu, perhaps you need to add a new top-level menu, similar to File, Edit, View, and so on. The following steps show you how to add a new menu item for all of the tools and commands you're going to want to access after exploring the Commands tab in the Customize dialog box.

1. Right-click any Outlook toolbar or menu and choose Customize.

2. In the Toolbars tab, make sure Menu Bar is checked, and then choose the Commands tab.

3. In Categories, scroll to the bottom of the list and choose New Menu. In the list of commands, the only item displayed is New Menu. Using the left mouse button, drag New Menu to the menu, just to the right of Help, as shown in Figure 20.9.

New menu

FIGURE 20.9

The new item has been added to the menu bar.

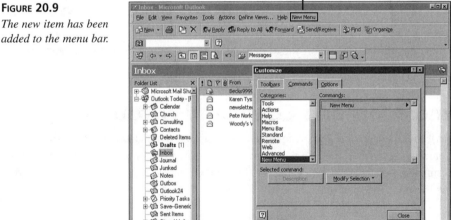

20

4. Right-click New Menu to display its settings menu. In the Name box, type a new name, such as Tools&1, as shown in Figure 20.10. If you want to access this menu by using a hotkey, put & before the hotkey character. Make sure you choose a character that's not already in use. Press Enter to complete the name change.

Figure 20.10
Use New Menu's settings to change the name to something more useful.

Hotkeys are Alt+*character* combinations, such as Alt+F (File) and Alt+V (View). When you're seeking unused characters, numbers are a good bet. For example, "Tools&1" would be accessible by pressing Alt+1.

Removing Tools and Commands from Menus

Removing menu items isn't quite as easy as removing toolbar items. Hold down the Alt key, drag the unwanted item off the toolbar so that an X appears, and then release the mouse button.

Moving Tools and Commands Around

The Alt trick is handy for removing unwanted tools and commands, but it's also useful for rearranging the furniture. To move any top-level menu command or any toolbar tool or command, press the Alt key. Using the left mouse button, drag the tool or command to a new location, and then release the mouse button.

Summary

In this chapter, you've learned how to use Outlook's toolbars and menus. Now you can create exactly the working environment you need. Tools, Customize, Commands is your hardware store—and the menus and toolbars are your workbench.

CHAPTER 21

Combining Outlook and the Other Office Products

Microsoft Office integrates its programs with each other as much as possible so that their uses when combined are far greater than those for each module when used individually. Some of the integrative methods are fairly obvious, thanks to document object linking and embedding (OLE). Other aspects of the integration are more subtle. Such is the integration between Outlook and the Office programs. Some of the possibilities are obvious, such as WordMail. Some are subtle. For example, you can schedule a meeting from the middle of a PowerPoint slide show. This chapter shows you several ways to integrate Outlook with the other Office programs.

Outlook and Word

Word and Outlook have the most levels of interaction. Using both programs, you can send email messages, create mail merge documents, and generate tasks.

Using Word As Your Email Editor

When you send email messages from Outlook's Inbox, Outlook provides tools you can use to format your message. You can apply bold, underline, or italic formatting, change the text's font and size, and create bulleted lists. These basic formatting options usually are all you'll need for your email.

Sometimes, though, you might prefer additional word and document processing tools, such as AutoCorrect, AutoText, Drawing tools (such as Word's Drawing toolbar), and automatic spelling and grammar checking as you type. Or perhaps you need extensive formatting with tables, automatic numbering, or other features you find easier to use in Word. When the need arises, Outlook gives you this option. (Outlook XP and later supports AutoCorrect, AutoText, and Drawing tools.)

If you send formatted email from Word directly, and not as an attachment, Word sends the email in HTML format. You also get the same result in Outlook when you select HTML as the default format and opt to use Word as the email editor. An Outlook user receiving such an email might see a prompt similar to that shown in Figure 21.1. In this instance, Outlook needs to run an HTML script in order to interpret WordArt formatting embedded in that HTML message. Scripts are one vehicle for spreading email viruses so many users never run them, or their antivirus software disables the scripts. Therefore, formatting with WordArt may not be seen by all your recipients so don't overuse the ability to format email. Plain text is always safe to send and is always allowed through antivirus programs.

FIGURE 21.1

Outlook warns you about HTML scripts when you open certain HTML-formatted email messages.

If you do decide to use Word as your regular email editor—with the advantages of AutoCorrect, automatic spell checking as you type, and other features—you need to inform Outlook. Click Tools, Options. In the Options dialog box, click the Mail Format tab, as shown in Figure 21.2. Click Use Microsoft Word to edit email messages, and then click OK.

The next time you create a new mail message, you might see a little message box that says Starting Word as your e-mail editor, followed by a brand new message window that looks similar to Outlook's message window, but that is Word instead (see Figure 21.3). Word defaults to Outlook's default format set using Tools, Options, Mail Format.

FIGURE 21.2

Choosing Word as your email editor provides a wider variety of formatting options.

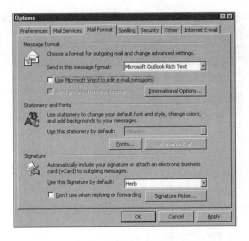

FIGURE 21.3

The super-deluxe WordMail Message tool.

Check names

Send   Address book   Importance: High   Importance: Low

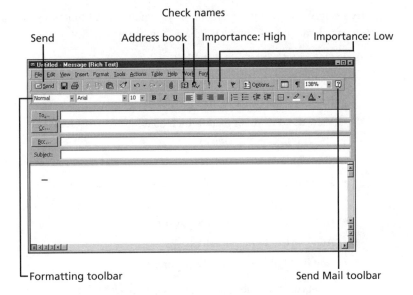

Formatting toolbar   Send Mail toolbar

Look at the toolbars in Figure 21.3 again. There are a lot more tools on them than on the Outlook toolbars. To see the difference, compare Figure 21.3 with Figure 21.4, which shows a standard Outlook message window.

Tools of the Trade

You can see that the toolbars and menus of the WordMail Message tool have more in common with Word than with Outlook. The Formatting toolbar has been expanded to match the one in Word, and the Standard toolbar has been replaced with the Outlook Send Mail toolbar.

21

FIGURE 21.4

*The mild-mannered
Outlook Message tool.*

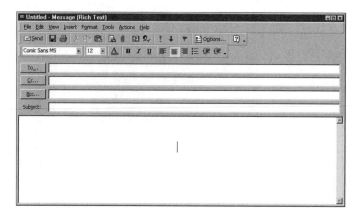

Different Strokes for Different Buttons

By using Word as your email editor, you gain several functions that aren't available in
the standard Outlook message editor. You can do the following:

- Use AutoCorrect and AutoText
- Use your keyboard customizations
- Have full use of table features
- View the document map (which enables you to quickly navigate a long document
  containing heading styles)
- Show/hide hidden marks (such as spaces and paragraph marks)
- Zoom in and out (make the contents appear larger or smaller without changing the
  size of the window)
- Use character and paragraph formatting styles
- Add borders to paragraphs
- Add highlighting to words or phrases

As you can see, there are many advantages to using Word as your email editor (provided
that your correspondents can decipher Word's version of the message, of course). You
can also click the Options button to open the Message Options dialog box, shown in
Figure 21.5. Here you can set several features of your email message. Note that these
options are also available without using Word.

As for the rest of the buttons and fields, you'll find that they function like Word's
Standard and Formatting toolbars. In addition, the To:, Cc:, and Subject: fields work
exactly like those in Outlook's Message window.

FIGURE 21.5

The Message Options dialog box enables you to customize your message (shown in Corporate/Workgroup mode).

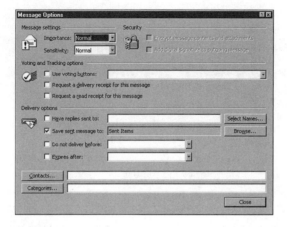

When you use Word as your default email editor, it defaults to the format you choose from Outlook's menu under Tools, Options, Mail Format. Word's formatting tools work fine no matter which format you choose. However, if plain text is set as Outlook's default, any formatting you apply from within Word will be lost when the message is sent.

Creating Tasks

In addition to using both Word and Outlook to create your email, you can use other Outlook options from other Office modules.

Back when you were learning how to create tasks in Chapter 19, "Managing Tasks," you might have thought, "Sure, tasks are useful, but it doesn't seem very productive to stop what I'm working on, switch to Outlook, and create a task." Unfortunately, this is true. No one likes to have his train of thought interrupted.

So why do it? Fortunately, with Word, you can create a task from any Microsoft Office document in which you're working. The new task will even have the open document linked to it for more convenience as these steps demonstrate:

1. In a previously saved document, right-click any toolbar in Word.

2. Select the Reviewing toolbar from the menu.

3. On the Reviewing toolbar, click the Create Microsoft Outlook Task button, as shown in Figure 21.6.

4. A Task window appears with the open filename in the subject field, a shortcut to the document, and the current paragraph from the Word document in the note box. Finish filling in the rest of the task information, and then click Save and Close.

21

Create Microsoft Outlook Task button

FIGURE 21.6

Creating a task in Word is as simple as pointing and clicking.

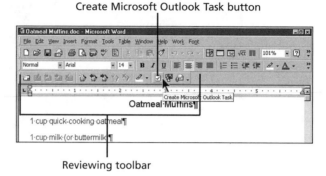

Reviewing toolbar

If you create a lot of these document-related tasks, you can copy the Reviewing toolbar's Task button into either the Standard or Formatting toolbar. Then you'll have the tool present all the time. To copy the button, you must have the Reviewing toolbar displayed, as well as the destination toolbar. With the Alt and Ctrl keys depressed, use the left mouse button to drag a copy of the Task tool to the desired location on the target toolbar.

When you close Word, you might be asked to save changes to the current template. Say Yes to save the change you just made.

Outlook and Excel

Excel's worksheet files can be used in much the same way as Access data files. Choose File, Send To from Excel's menu and use the new Office Envelope feature to email a spreadsheet to someone. In addition, you can use Excel and Outlook together to create workbook-related tasks and to share data. The following steps show you how to create an Outlook task in Excel:

1. Open Microsoft Excel.

2. Right-click any toolbar.

3. Select the Reviewing toolbar from the menu.

4. On the Reviewing toolbar, click the Create Microsoft Outlook Task button.

5. As with Word, a Task tool appears, and you can fill in the necessary information. Click Save and Close to complete the task.

If you anticipate creating a lot of workbook-related tasks, use the tip suggested in the previous section, and move the Task button to Excel's Standard or Formatting toolbar.

You can also use Office's new Envelope feature to email an Excel spreadsheet in HTML format, as the following steps show.

1. In Excel, open the worksheet you want to send and click the E-mail button on the Standard toolbar. This adds normal email headers to the top of the Excel window.

2. Use the To:, Cc:, and other header fields as you would for email sent using other techniques.

3. Click Send this Sheet. This sends the current worksheet in HTML format.

> When you send a complex HTML document that contains graphics such as charts, you should preview what you're sending to make sure it will appear as you want. Before you send it to somebody else, send it to yourself first. After verifying that it looks correct, repeat the procedure to send the file.

Outlook and PowerPoint

When you look at Outlook and PowerPoint, no two applications of Office could seem to be more different. One's a personal information manager, and one's a slide show maker. How can there be any commonality between them? Remember that PowerPoint is not just a "slide show maker." It's a business presentation tool, and that one word— *business*—is its common connection with Outlook.

After you have created a presentation in PowerPoint, one of your options is to use a computer monitor to project the presentation. While the presentation is being made, PowerPoint's Meeting Minder can take notes, schedule a meeting, or create a task. It's those last two capabilities that relate directly to Outlook.

Scheduling a Meeting

Scheduling a meeting with PowerPoint's Meeting Minder is simple. Click Tools, Meeting Minder. PowerPoint opens the Meeting Minder dialog box, as shown in Figure 21.7.

When you click the Schedule button, a untitled Appointment window appears. Using this, you can quickly schedule a meeting without switching to Outlook.

Creating Tasks

As with Word and Excel, you can create an Outlook task in PowerPoint by clicking the Create Microsoft Outlook Task button on the Reviewing toolbar. As with the other modules, fill in the necessary information and click Save and Close when you're finished.

21

FIGURE 21.7

Creating a meeting in PowerPoint is simple.

You can also use the Meeting Minder to create some tasks. Click the Action Items tab and enter the task's subject into the Description field and the due date and assignee into their respective fields. When this information is entered, click the Add button.

You can add as many action items as you desire. When you're finished, don't click the OK button. Click the Export button instead. This will activate the Meeting Minder Export dialog box, shown in Figure 21.8.

FIGURE 21.8

You can export Meeting Minder Action items from PowerPoint into a Word document or directly into Outlook.

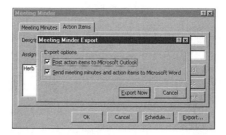

This dialog box offers two choices: You can export meeting minutes and action items to a Word document, or you can export just the action items to Outlook. If you check the latter option and click Export Now, the action items will be placed directly into Outlook's tasks.

Summary

This chapter focused on Outlook's capability to interact and share data with the other Microsoft Office modules. With the capability to share data and email tools and to create tasks from most of the Office programs, Outlook is truly an integral part of the Office family.

PART VII

PowerPoint Presentations for Your Audience

Chapter

CHAPTER **22**

Mastering PowerPoint Basics

You're about to become a master at presentations. A *presentation* is a structured delivery of information. Teachers, professors, politicians, and sales representatives make a living delivering informative presentations. If you want to create powerful multimedia presentations quickly, you've picked up the right book. Knowing the ins and outs of PowerPoint will ensure that your message is properly presented, well received, and remembered long after you've left the room.

What PowerPoint Is All About

PowerPoint helps you structure the ideas and information that you want conveyed to your audience. With it, you can add visual images, animation, supporting documents, and audio recordings to enhance your presentation. For example, you can easily do the following:

- Turbocharge that tired old training speech with animation and sound clips

- Visually demonstrate the importance of the yearly budget numbers by incorporating charts, tables, and high-impact graphics
- Impose structure on a presentation so the audience grasps the message
- Post the presentation on the World Wide Web so others can review it
- Generate an outline for your presentation
- Create audience handouts and speaker's notes

PowerPoint includes several templates that supply a presentation framework for many common topics. The task of building multimedia slides isn't a chore with PowerPoint because it has many of the formatting and content-creation tools built into other Office products. It also includes a rich library of clip art and sound files to jazz up the text. PowerPoint has drawing capabilities that enable you to create a dynamic presentation by including animation and action buttons in the presentation. In addition to slide-creation tools and navigation features, different slide perspectives are available to help you structure your ideas into a coherent presentation.

After you have reviewed your presentation and are ready to publish the content, PowerPoint supports a variety of display media. You can deliver your presentation with overhead projectors and transparencies (black-and-white or color), with 35mm slides, on the Internet, or simply onscreen. By combining PowerPoint with your presentation subject and this book, you will enjoy learning to use PowerPoint to create fantastic presentations.

Starting the AutoContent Wizard

Every time you start PowerPoint, the PowerPoint dialog box is displayed, as shown in Figure 22.1. You can use it to choose the method for starting your PowerPoint session. The main choices are creating a new presentation or opening an existing presentation.

 The PowerPoint dialog box shows up only when you first start a PowerPoint session. After its first appearance, it disappears. You don't see it again until you exit PowerPoint and start a new session.

The first option in the PowerPoint dialog box list is the *AutoContent Wizard*, the best method for starting a presentation if you're new to PowerPoint. It's also a great tool to use if you need to create a presentation quickly. The AutoContent Wizard is a guide composed of several screens that help you create professional presentations. It leads you through a series of questions so you can choose the best layout for your presentation.

22

You can select from several predefined content templates. The AutoContent Wizard supplies not only the design for your presentation, but also ideas, starter text, formatting, and organization. It's an excellent tool to use if you don't know where to start.

FIGURE 22.1

The PowerPoint dialog box enables you to choose different layouts for your slides.

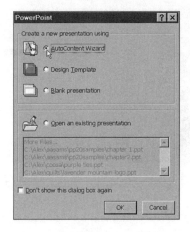

When the AutoContent Wizard starts, the first screen displayed is the start screen, shown in Figure 22.2. It provides explanatory text that introduces you to the AutoContent Wizard. Look over the text, and then click the Next button. That advances you to the next screen in the AutoContent Wizard.

FIGURE 22.2

The start screen of the AutoContent Wizard enables you to begin using the wizard.

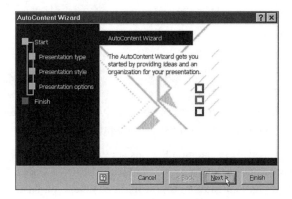

The second screen in the wizard defines the presentation type. You use this screen to select the type of presentation you're going to create. You can scroll through the list of all the available types or click a category button to narrow the list of choices. If you don't see a presentation type that fits your needs, just click the General button and select the Generic presentation type. For example, if you were going to create a presentation on basket weaving, an unsupported topic, click the General button and select the Generic presentation type, as shown in Figure 22.3. After you have selected a presentation type, click the Next button.

FIGURE 22.3

The AutoContent Wizard's presentation type screen is shown with the Generic presentation type selected.

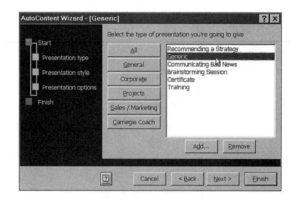

The AutoContent Wizard's third screen contains the Presentation style options, as shown in Figure 22.4, where you select the target output format for your presentation. You have five choices:

- *Onscreen presentation*—Use this option when you give your presentation using an onscreen projector hooked to a computer (usually a laptop). You will then show your presentation using PowerPoint on the computer.

- *Web presentation*—Use this option for Internet or kiosk presentations.

- *Black and white overheads*—This option is used when you will print without color onto slide transparencies.

- *Color overheads*—Color overheads are similar to black-and-white overheads, only with color.

- *35mm slides*—Use slides when you will give your presentation with the use of a slide projector (just like Dad's vacation presentation).

The next screen is the Presentation options screen, as shown in Figure 22.5. Here you get to give your presentation a title, and include a footer if you want. Simply click in the appropriate text box and enter your information. When you have completed this screen, click the Next button.

The title of your presentation will be placed on the title slide of your presentation. The title slide is the first slide in your presentation.

FIGURE 22.4

The Presentation style screen of the AutoContent Wizard gives you many different display options.

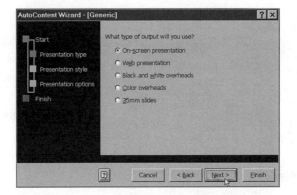

After you have set the Presentation style for your presentation, click the Next button.

FIGURE 22.5

In the Presentation options screen, you can choose to let PowerPoint enter the title, footer, date, and slide number automatically.

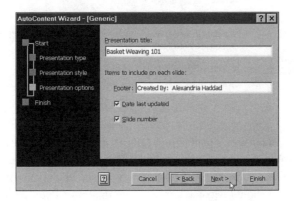

The last AutoContent Wizard screen is the finish screen. The AutoContent Wizard has finished its question-and-answer session, so it's time to generate the presentation file. If you need to change any previously set options, now would be a good time. You can use the Back button to go backward through the wizard screen by screen and change any option you want. You can also just cancel the whole darn thing and go to lunch. If you've decided to take the plunge, all you need to do is click the Finish button to view your generated presentation.

What You See Onscreen

Now that you have finished with the AutoContent Wizard, you will see your presentation in Normal view, as displayed in Figure 22.6. The PowerPoint screen also displays several toolbars, a color view of your presentation, and the helpful Office Assistant.

Figure 22.6

The presentation is shown as it appears in the Normal view.

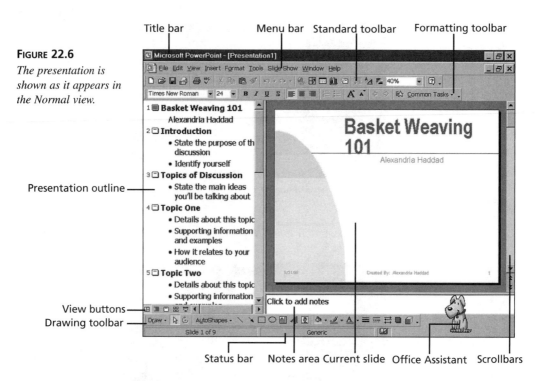

The presentation outline is made up of sample slides that have been generated by the AutoContent Wizard. The slides have suggestions that indicate the type of information to be entered on each slide. Before you begin to customize the presentation with specific information, you should become familiar with the PowerPoint screen elements and what they can do for you.

The Bars

There are several bars on your screen, and they all have a different job to do (but they don't serve any stiff drinks). The following sections give you a brief description of each bar type, starting from the top of the screen and working down.

Title Bar

The title bar sits at the top of your screen. Its job is to display the title of the application you're using and your presentation's name. Because you haven't yet saved your presentation and given it a name, the title is a generic name. Presentation1 is the default name for the first unnamed presentation created in this PowerPoint session. The next unnamed presentation would be Presentation2, and so on. The title bar also holds the Minimize, Restore/Maximize, and Close buttons on the far right for the application (PowerPoint).

Menu Bar

The menu bar is where you can choose PowerPoint commands. The menu bar also contains the Minimize, Restore/Maximize, and Close buttons on the far right. These buttons will affect the presentation window, but not the PowerPoint software as the buttons on the Title bar control the software. Most of PowerPoint's commands can be found in the drop-down menus under one of the main menu titles: File, Edit, View, Insert, Format, Tools, Slide Show, Window, and Help. After you click on any main menu title, you can view other drop-down menus by simply sliding the mouse pointer over a title, and the corresponding menu will open. Take a few minutes to familiarize yourself with the menu by clicking on File and reading the commands (don't click on anything in the drop-down menu, just read); then continue across the menu bar until you have completed reading the Help menu. To close the menu, either click the menu title again, click outside the drop-down menu, or press the Esc key once. If you have a menu plus a submenu open, such as File, Send To and the subsequent submenu that appears, you will need to hit Esc once for each menu displayed to close them.

Toolbars

PowerPoint comes with several toolbars. You can customize any toolbar or even create your own using the Tools, Customize menu option. The three main toolbars are the Standard, Formatting, and Drawing toolbars. You can display or hide any toolbar by using the following steps:

1. Choose View, Toolbars from the menu. A submenu appears listing the available toolbars.

2. Click the toolbar name you want to display or hide. A checkmark indicates that a toolbar is currently displayed.

The Standard toolbar has buttons for the most common tasks you perform in PowerPoint, such as saving, printing, or spell checking a presentation.

The Formatting toolbar has buttons that make formatting a snap. You use most of the buttons to format text, such as changing the font type or size, making your text bold or italic, turning bullets off, and so on.

The Drawing toolbar sits at the bottom of your screen. It contains buttons that are used—you guessed it—when you are working with drawing objects. Many of the commands are not available except from the Drawing toolbar.

Scrollbars

Scrollbars are used to scroll through the current presentation. When you drag the scroll button on the vertical scrollbar, PowerPoint displays a ScreenTip that indicates which slide you're going to display.

Status Bar

The PowerPoint status bar is the bar at the bottom of the PowerPoint window. It displays three pieces of information:

- The slide (page) you're currently working on and how many slides are included in the entire presentation.
- The type of the current presentation design.
- Whether Spell Check As You Type is active. If it is active, you will see a small icon that looks like a book with a red checkmark. If it is not, you will see nothing in the third section of the status bar.

Presentation Perspectives

After you have finished answering the questions posed by the AutoContent Wizard, you see the sample presentation displayed in Normal view. Other views are available when you need them. PowerPoint has six different ways to view your presentation:

- Normal view
- Slide Sorter view
- Notes Page view
- Slide Show view
- Outline view
- Slide view

Each view has a different function. The different views are described in the following sections. To switch views, you can use either the View menu or the view buttons in the lower-left corner of the PowerPoint window.

Normal View

Normal view is a combination of Outline, Slide, and Notes Page views. This is a new view for PowerPoint, as shown in Figure 22.7. You can resize each frame of the view by dragging the frame border to a new location. Normal view facilitates getting your presentation finished in the shortest possible time. This is the view you see first in PowerPoint. You can switch to Normal view by selecting View, Normal from the menu, or by clicking the Normal view button in the lower left of the screen.

Slide Sorter View

The Slide Sorter view displays a miniature of each slide in your presentation, as shown in Figure 22.8. Use the Slide Sorter view when you want to add some polish to a

22

presentation. You can add transitions to your presentation or use the Slide Sorter view to easily move, delete, and copy slides. You can switch to Slide Sorter view by selecting View, Slide Sorter from the menu, or clicking the Slide Sorter view button in the lower left of the screen.

FIGURE 22.7

Normal view combines Outline, Normal, and Notes Page views to give you an overall look at your slide.

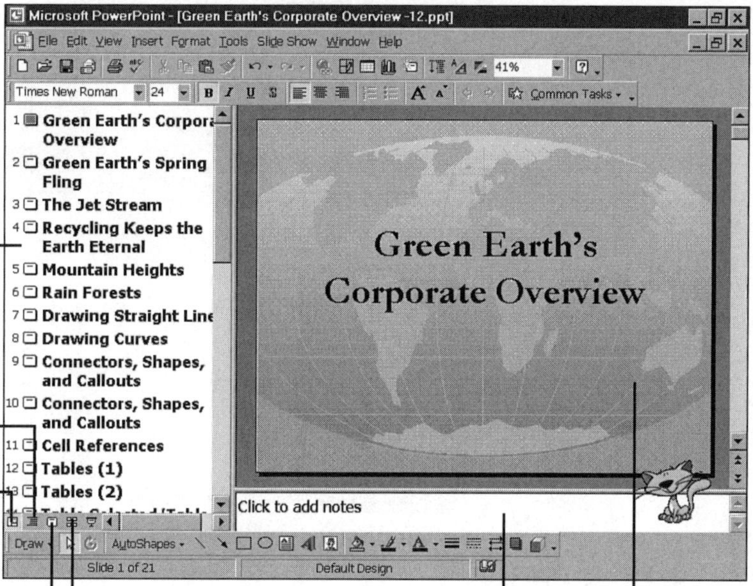

Outline Pane

Outline View

Normal View

Slide Sorter   Slide Show   Notes Pane   Slide Pane

Slide Show View

Slide Show view is the mode in which to operate if you want to display your presentation onscreen or preview it for further editing. To move from slide to slide, simply click the mouse until you reach the end of your presentation. You can start the Slide Show by selecting View, Slide Show from the menu, or clicking the Slide Show button in the lower left of the screen. You can cancel a presentation before its conclusion by pressing Esc.

If you want to see the entire presentation from slide one to the end of the presentation, select View, Slide Show from the menu. If you click the Slide Show button (in the lower-left corner of the screen), your presentation begins from the current slide.

Outline and Slide View

The Outline and Slide views are simply larger views of the Normal view panes. They enable you to work in the selected view, sized for the whole screen. If you need only to edit text, you may find it helpful to use the Outline view. When you are working strictly with graphics, Slide view might prove more beneficial.

FIGURE 22.8
You can see the different slides that comprise your presentation in Slide Sorter view.

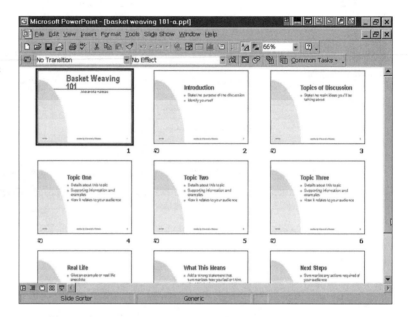

Notes Page

This view displays the slide and the notes area as they would print on a page if you chose to print notes pages. You can use the Notes Page view to add notes to the slides in your presentation, just as you can add notes in the Normal view. Simply click the notes area and type your notes. You can also add graphics to your notes in the Notes Page view.

Displaying Slides

There are several ways to navigate from slide to slide when you're editing your presentation. The method you choose depends on what view is currently active and whether you prefer using the keyboard or the mouse.

Using the Keyboard

Table 22.1 lists keyboard navigation techniques you can use to display different slides in your presentation.

TABLE 22.1   Common PowerPoint Navigation Keys

Key Combination	Movement
PgUp	Positions you back one slide at a time
PgDn	Positions you forward one slide at a time
Ctrl+Home	Positions you at the beginning of the presentation
Ctrl+End	Positions you at the end of the presentation

Zooming

At times, you might find that you need to change the onscreen magnification of a slide. Magnification is commonly referred to as *zoom*. When you start working with the drawing tools or want to create speaker notes, the capability to zoom in and out of a slide is extremely important. To change the zoom options, follow these steps:

1. Choose View, Zoom from the menu to open the Zoom dialog box.

2. Select the appropriate zoom percentage, as shown in Figure 22.9.

3. Click OK.

FIGURE 22.9

Selecting the zoom percentage in the Zoom dialog box.

Customizing the Sample Slides

You now should be familiar with all the PowerPoint screen elements and know how to move between your presentation slides. Now you're ready to learn how to customize the generic presentation. The standard sample text previously generated by the AutoContent Wizard needs to be replaced with your specific information. You may find that editing the outline is the easiest way to go.

Editing the Outline

The AutoContent Wizard's sample text serves as a guide that gives you an idea of what content should be displayed on each slide. These are only suggestions, however; you can display any message you want in your presentation. PowerPoint's Outline view makes editing slide content very easy. Simply type your own words into the presentation outline and delete the sample text created by the AutoContent Wizard. The modified text automatically appears on the appropriate slide. As you type in the outline, the slides will change to reflect your input.

Editing the Slide

You can also edit the text directly on the slides. Editing slides is easy when you understand the basics of working with text objects. To edit a text object, just click the text you want to edit and start typing. PowerPoint displays a cursor, shown in Figure 22.10, showing you where to add and delete text. You might need to move the cursor to the correct position before you edit the text. Use the arrow keys on the keyboard to reposition the cursor.

FIGURE 22.10

Slide one of the Basket Weaving 101 presentation with the title object selected.

Adding Speaker Notes

PowerPoint not only helps you create your presentation, but also assists in creating speaker notes, which are paragraphs that serve as your reference material when you give your presentation. You can type speaker notes into your presentation while in Normal view. The notes will print only when you print notes pages. To add speaker notes, follow these steps:

1. In Normal view, display the slide to which you want to add notes.
2. Click in the notes frame (lower right, under the slide), as shown in Figure 22.11.
3. Type your notes.
4. Click any area outside the slide (any gray area) when finished.

FIGURE 22.11

Adding speaker notes is as easy as adding text to your slide.

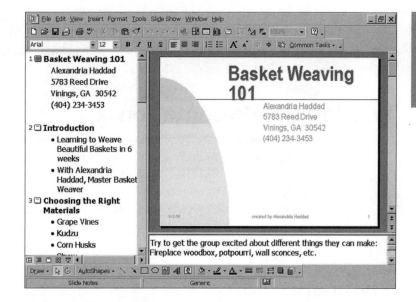

22

Spell Checking the Presentation

While you have been busy typing all the important information for your presentation, PowerPoint has been making sure you're spelling the words correctly. You might have noticed the automatic spell check at work when a red wavy underline is displayed beneath a misspelled word. This line appears every time you misspell a word. You can fix your spelling immediately when PowerPoint tells you a mistake has been made, or you can wait until you have finished typing and run a complete spell check. If you've used Microsoft Word before, you will recognize the spell checker in PowerPoint. You can spell check your presentation in one of several ways, including the following:

- Choose Tools, Spelling from the menu.
- Click the Spelling button on the standard toolbar.

With either method, the Spelling dialog box opens and your spell check begins.

Every misspelled word or word that's not recognized by the spell checker is highlighted in the Not in Dictionary box. PowerPoint usually makes an appropriate suggestion in the Change To box about how the spelling of the word should be changed. PowerPoint sometimes gives you a whole list of suggestions to choose from in the Suggestions list box. To modify the spelling, simply click the correct word, and then click the Change button.

If the word is spelled correctly, but PowerPoint doesn't recognize it as a "real" word, you can tell PowerPoint to ignore the word by clicking the Ignore button. You have a other options when you run the spell checker just as you do in Word and the other Office programs.

Printing the Presentation

When you have finished editing the presentation contents, you can print your presentation by selecting File, Print from the menu. In the PowerPoint Print dialog box, you can select what pages to print, what slide content to print, and how many copies to print. You can also choose to print all the presentation's slides, just the current slide, or a specific combination of slides. You have even more options for determining the contents to be printed. For example, you can print the slides, speaker notes, handouts, or the presentation's outline.

Summary

This chapter is jam-packed with information. You have learned how to create a presentation by using the powerful AutoContent Wizard. You've also learned about the screen elements, how to use them, and how they can help you get your work done a little more quickly. PowerPoint has many different views for you to display your slides, and each view helps you perform different tasks.

You can quickly move to another slide in your presentation by using the mouse or the keyboard, and zooming allows you to view a slide either close up or from a distance, depending on your needs. After you have created an initial presentation using the AutoContent Wizard, you can edit the content of the sample slide using either the Outline or Slide in Normal views.

CHAPTER **23**

Diving into PowerPoint Presentations

Now that you have created your first presentation, you need to save it and learn the steps for reopening it later. After you save your presentation document, you can give it to colleagues so they can add some final comments or modifications. Here are a few questions that can come up when you're working with files:

- Where is my presentation file located on my computer?
- How do I open the file?
- What concepts and tasks make up file management?

These questions and other intriguing issues are answered in this chapter. This chapter also covers how to create a new presentation in your own unique format.

A Few Words on How a PC Stores Presentations

The best way to visualize the physical and logical storage of files is to correlate computer concepts with real-world objects, which makes Windows file management much easier to understand. The Windows interface uses disk drives, folders, subfolders, and documents for file management.

A disk drive is analogous to an office filing cabinet. Like a filing cabinet, a disk drive is used to store documents that can contain presentations, spreadsheets, or databases. Each disk drive has a unique name. Typically, you access drives by referring to a corresponding letter, such as A, B, C, D, and so on. Each letter represents a distinct container—a separate filing cabinet—that's used to store information in your computer. Usually, the A: or B: drive is reserved for removable media, such as floppy disks. The C: drive letter designates your computer's hard drive. Other letters commonly represent additional drives—the D: drive can be assigned to the CD-ROM drive, and any additional letter in the alphabet is probably a remote networked drive.

You can understand the folder and subfolder components by expanding the filing cabinet analogy. A filing cabinet has drawers with green hanging file folders in them; these folders might contain smaller manila folders used to store paper documents in an organized fashion. The folder and subfolder concepts correspond to the green hanging folders and manila folders, respectively. As in the real world, you can store document files in either folders or subfolders. In Figure 23.1, the document path `C:\My Documents\PowerPoint\ZT Relocates.ppt` has been broken down to correlate it with real-world objects.

FIGURE 23.1

A computer document can be compared to objects in a filing cabinet.

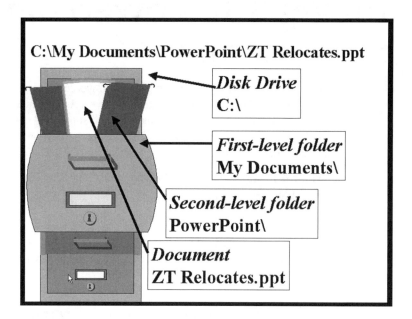

Saving a Presentation

Saving your work is one of the most important tasks you do when you work with PowerPoint. Until you save your work, it doesn't exist in a permanent form. Saving is extremely easy, and you should do it often. When you save a presentation, you must provide a filename for the document that should indicate the presentation's contents. By using an easy-to-remember filename, you can readily locate the presentation in future PowerPoint sessions.

PowerPoint also includes options for saving your presentation in other formats. For example, you can save a presentation to the HTML (HyperText Markup Language) format so the presentation can be viewed through a standard Web browser, such as Internet Explorer or Netscape. You can post the presentation on the Internet so it's accessible for anyone who can reach your Web site. You also can save a presentation with information about its runtime characteristics. If you want to distribute the electronic presentation document to an audience, save it in Slide Show view.

There are two types of save operations: Save As or Save. For an unnamed presentation that hasn't been previously saved, both options work in exactly the same way. However, after a presentation has been given a document name, the options work a little differently. Save As lets you specify a new document name and location. The Save operation simply updates the presentation with the same name in the current location, with no questions asked.

The Save button on the standard toolbar works much like the Print button. You won't see anything happen, but your file will be saved using the Save command.

You should use the Save As command when you save a file for the first time. Save As is also used when you want to give a presentation a new name or you want to save it in a different location or folder. You can quickly save a presentation to a floppy disk with the Save As operation by specifying the appropriate drive letter. To save your presentation for the first time or to give a presentation a new name, follow these steps:

1. Choose File, Save As from the main menu. This opens the Save As dialog box.

2. In the File Name box, enter a name for your presentation.

3. To save the presentation to a floppy disk or a different folder, select the appropriate location from the Save In drop-down list.

4. Click Save.

Your filename can have up to 255 alphanumeric characters and can also contain the space character, as shown in Figure 23.2.

Choose drive and/or folder here

FIGURE 23.2

*Saving your presenta-
tions is easy in the
PowerPoint Save As
dialog box.*

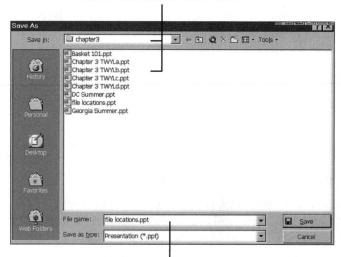

Type name of presentation here

After you save your presentation, the filename appears in the PowerPoint application's
title bar instead of the generic PresentationX label. PowerPoint also automatically
assigns the .PPT extension to the end of your filename.

The .PPT extension at the end of the filename tells Windows that your file is
a PowerPoint presentation.

You might not see the .PPT extension, depending on the system options
that have been initialized for your operating system.

Changing the Drive or Folders

By default, PowerPoint saves all your presentations on the C:\ disk drive in the My
Documents folder. If you want to save a presentation on a different disk drive (such as a
floppy disk) or in a different folder, you must indicate the new location by selecting an
alternative disk drive and folder from the Save In list box. For example, to save the presentation to the A:\ drive, click the down triangle next to the Save In list box and select
the 3 1/2 Floppy (A:) option from the list.

If you want to save a presentation in a different folder on your C:\ drive, you must first
select the (C:) option from the Save In list box. You can then open a folder and subsequent subfolders by double-clicking the appropriate folder icon until you reach the location in which you want to save your presentation.

Using the Save Command

To quickly protect your work, use the Save command to periodically update your presentation document. A good rule of thumb is to save every 10 minutes, or after every major modification. Saving takes only a moment, so do it often. If your computer inadvertently crashes between saves, you have a better chance of retrieving all your hard work. You can save and update your presentation in one of two ways:

- Choose File, Save from the menu
- Click the Save button on the toolbar

23

Closing a Presentation

Closing a presentation takes it out of sight and mind. Before you go to lunch or leave for the day, it's best to close your presentation. You can do this in one of two ways:

- Choose File, Close from the main menu
- Click the document Close button on the menu bar

After you have closed a presentation, you have three options available:

- Open an existing presentation
- Start a new presentation
- Exit PowerPoint

Each of these options is covered in the following sections.

Opening an Existing Presentation

You can open any PowerPoint presentation that has been previously created and saved to view or modify it. Opening a presentation is a simple process. In fact, it's almost the same as the steps you use to save a presentation. The only requirement is that you supply the saved presentation's location (drive and folder/subfolders). In PowerPoint, you can see a preview of the presentation file before it's officially opened. Figure 23.3 shows the Open dialog box with the Preview option. Use the following step to open a PowerPoint presentation:

1. Choose File, Open from the menu.

Or, do the following:

1. Click the Open button on the standard toolbar.
2. Select the correct drive or folder.

To open a presentation document that's in a different location, select the drive or folder from the Look In drop-down list.

3. Select the presentation name from the file list. To see a preview of the presentation (if one is not showing), click the Views button on the Open Dialog Box toolbar (to the right of the Look In textbox) and choose Preview.

4. Click Open.

FIGURE 23.3

You can preview your PowerPoint file in the Open dialog box.

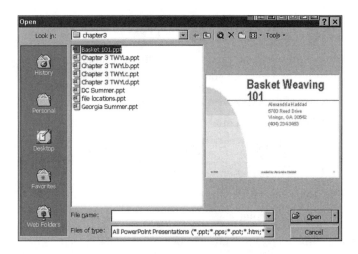

PowerPoint "remembers" the last four files you have worked on. A quick way to open a presentation you have been working on recently is to select the filename from the bottom of the File menu.

Selecting and Opening Multiple Files

With PowerPoint, you can work on one presentation at a time or open several concurrent sessions. To open several presentations at once, follow these steps:

1. Choose File, Open from the menu to display the Open dialog box.

2. From the displayed list of files, select the files you want to open.

> To select multiple contiguous files, click the first file, hold down the Shift key, and click the last file. All files will be selected.
>
> To select multiple noncontiguous files, click the first file, and then hold down the Ctrl key while you click each subsequent file. Only the files you clicked will be selected.

23

3. Click the Open button to open all the selected presentations.

When you have multiple presentations open, you should use the Window menu item to switch between presentation documents. See the "Navigating Open Presentations" section of this chapter for more information.

Starting a New Presentation

Starting a new presentation when you first open the PowerPoint application is an easy technique to grasp. When you want to create a new presentation in the middle of an active PowerPoint session, the steps are a little different. You still have the same three options for your new presentation, but they are found in different places and are activated with different commands. The following sections explain where to find each of the options that are initially displayed in the PowerPoint dialog box.

AutoContent Wizard

During your PowerPoint session, the friendly AutoContent Wizard has gone into hiding. But don't worry—you can still find it in the New Presentation dialog box. To start a new presentation using the AutoContent Wizard, follow these steps:

1. Choose File, New from the menu to open the New Presentation dialog box.
2. Click the General tab, if it is not already displayed.
3. Click the AutoContent Wizard, as shown in Figure 23.4.
4. Finally, click OK to start the wizard.

Presentation Design (or Template)

When you first create a presentation, choosing the Template option is appropriate if you don't need any help with the logical flow of the ideas in the presentation, especially if you already know the content each slide will contain. Templates allow you to focus on creating the presentation message without worrying too much about the presentation's overall style. The template, which can also be called a presentation design, supplies the artistic theme or style for the slides. The template you choose defines the choice of colors, background graphics, and fonts. This is an excellent choice if you will be giving your presentation on a large screen. Professional commercial artists have created most of these designs. As much fun as PowerPoint is, you may not have the time to create the entire content for a presentation and worry about the design elements, too. Follow these steps to select an appropriate presentation design for your message:

1. Choose File, New from the menu to open the New Presentation dialog box.
2. Click the Design Templates tab (see Figure 23.5).
3. Select an appropriate design.
4. Click OK.

FIGURE 23.4

The New Presentation dialog box with the AutoContent Wizard selected.

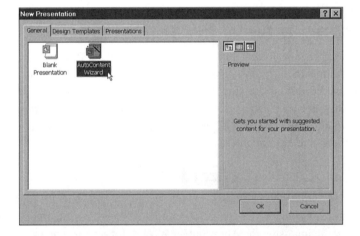

FIGURE 23.5

The Design Templates tab of the New Presentation dialog box gives you many design options.

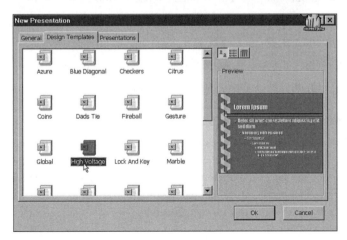

The first few times you select a presentation design, it's a good idea to pre-view all the designs you have available. You can preview a presentation design template either by clicking once on each design name or by using the arrow keys on your keyboard to highlight each design. You should also realize that the number of designs available on a computer varies. For example, Bob might have downloaded some extra design sets from the Microsoft Web site.

23

Blank Presentation

The final option available for creating a new presentation is to start a blank presentation. A blank presentation has no color, no design, and not a shred of fancy stuff. PowerPoint leaves all the slide formatting up to you. Unless you need to design a very specialized presentation—for example, when you're using your company's colors, logo, and font choices—you probably would do better choosing from one of the preformatted design Templates. If you need to create a presentation design for your company's use, use the blank presentation option. In general, though, when you start from a blank presentation, you could find yourself putting much more work into a presentation than necessary. Choose the AutoContent Wizard or a premade presentation design, if possible. However, when you need a blank canvas to create an exceptionally unique slide, follow these steps to start a new blank presentation:

1. Choose File, New from the menu to open the New Presentation dialog box.
2. Click the General tab.
3. Select Blank Presentation.
4. Click OK.

When you want to start a new blank presentation, you can also click the New button. However, if you want to select a presentation design or use the AutoContent Wizard, use the File, New menu command and save yourself some time.

Navigating Open Presentations

You can start a new presentation without closing the currently active presentation. Having several presentations open at once in PowerPoint is a great way to copy information from one presentation to another and compare different presentations, and has numerous other advantages. If you use this feature, you need to know how to switch between the presentations. At first, having several presentations open at one time may seem a little confusing—it's like having several projects on your desk at one time. You may not be working on them all at once (or you may be), but you need to have them all available to you throughout the day. Just like switching from one project to another on an actual desk, PowerPoint enables you to do the same thing with presentations.

Any presentation you might have open will be listed in the Window menu. You need only select the actual presentation name from the list. As you can see in Figure 23.6, there are currently three open presentations. The presentation your attention is currently focused on is called the active presentation window, which has a checkmark by its name. To switch presentations, simply select the presentation by name and—presto—you're now billing some other client for the work!

The Window menu has a few other options worth mentioning here. The New Window, Arrange All, and Cascade items all play important roles in the quest for seamless presentation navigation.

1. Click the Window menu title.

2. Click the presentation you want to switch to.

FIGURE 23.6
*The Window menu
shows three presenta-
tions currently open.*

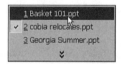

Summary

You now know the fundamentals that allow you to create, print, show, and save a basic presentation. You could put this book down now if that were all you needed to know, but the fun has just begun. You wouldn't really be happy just knowing the basics; the excitement of PowerPoint starts after learning how to change colors, insert clip art, add WordArt, and add animation to a presentation.

CHAPTER 24

Working with Slides and Text

During this chapter, you learn how to work with the building blocks of a presentation: the slides.

You may have already noticed that PowerPoint deals with text in a manner that's slightly different from Word. When you enter text in PowerPoint, you're not only entering the text on a slide, but you're also entering the text into a text object. It's very important to understand that you're not only working with text, but also the underlying object.

Using AutoLayout

When you start a new presentation using either the Design Template or Blank Presentation option, the first screen you see is the New Slide dialog box (see Figure 24.1). You should also see it every time you insert a new slide. The box asks you to select an AutoLayout, which is a preliminary, draft layout for that specific slide. All the AutoLayout formats except Blank have placeholders for different types of PowerPoint objects. PowerPoint has

24 AutoLayout designs from which you can choose, including Title Slide, Bulleted List, Chart, Text & Clip Art, and many others.

Select an AutoLayout

FIGURE 24.1

You can select a slide format from the New Slide dialog box.

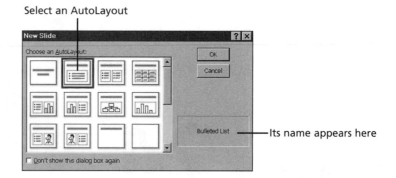

Its name appears here

Creating a Title Slide

The *Title Slide* is the very first presentation slide your audience sees, so it sets the tone for the rest of the presentation. The AutoContent Wizard automatically creates the Title Slide. When you do not use the AutoContent Wizard, you need to create a Title Slide for your presentation by selecting the Title Slide AutoLayout. After creating a title slide, enter your title slide information by simply clicking the title or subtitle *placeholder* and entering the appropriate text.

A placeholder is a box with dashed lines on a slide, which contains instructions such as Click to add title or subtitle or text, as shown in Figure 24.2. For objects, the placeholder will say, Double-click to add table (or chart, org chart, clip art, object, or media clip).

An *object* is any item that you edit or add to a PowerPoint presentation; text, clip art, chart, and so on. This is unlike a word processor, where you work with mostly text. You work with text in PowerPoint, too, but the text is contained in text object placeholders. There are other objects, such as clip art objects and drawing objects.

Title object

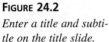

FIGURE 24.2
Enter a title and subtitle on the title slide.

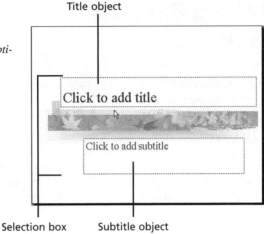

Click to add title

Click to add subtitle

Selection box   Subtitle object

24

Undoing Your Mistakes

If an action doesn't give you the effect you want, you can reverse it. To go back one step, you can either choose Edit, Undo from the menu or click the Undo button on the standard toolbar. Right next to the Undo button is the Redo button. Redo undoes your undo (for all of us who get trigger-happy).

Adding New Slides

Unlike working with a word processing application, you have to explicitly add each new page (slide) in PowerPoint that you want to include in your presentation. Several different methods for adding a new slide are available. To create a new slide, simply use one of the following methods. Try each method until you find the one that works best for you.

- Choose Insert, New Slide from the main menu.
- Press the Ctrl+M key combination.
- Click the New Slide button on the Standard toolbar.
- Select Common Tasks, New Slide from the Formatting toolbar.

PowerPoint adds a new slide after the slide that is currently displayed, as opposed to the end of the presentation. You can easily move slides around later.

Creating and Using Bulleted or Numbered Slides

Most presentations you create contain at least one list of key points. The bulleted list presents this information in a manner your audience can easily understand. You can enter text in a bulleted slide either in the Outline or Slide pane.

An impressive feature of PowerPoint is its capability to AutoFit text to fit the placeholder. For example, if your bulleted list becomes a bit too long, PowerPoint will automatically resize the text to fit the placeholder. This also works in reverse; if you delete some items, PowerPoint will enlarge the text up to the original size.

PowerPoint now enables you to use numbered lists in addition to bullets. To use numbers instead of bullets, select the entire text object and click the numbering button on the Formatting toolbar.

Entering Bulleted Text in the Slide Pane

It's very simple to enter and modify bulleted text in the Slide pane. You can quickly promote (move up in the hierarchy) or demote (move down in the hierarchy) bullet items. To create a multilevel bulleted list as shown in Figure 24.3, use the following steps:

1. Click on the text object Click to add text.
2. Type your first item (a first-level bullet) and press Enter.
3. Press the Tab key to demote the next bullet to a second-level bullet.
4. Type the desired text, press Enter, and repeat as needed. Press Enter after the last item. A second-level bullet will be created.
5. To promote the bullet to the first level, press Shift+Tab. Type the desired text and press Enter.
6. Repeat steps 3–5 until your list is complete. Do not press Enter after the very last bullet. If you do, either press Backspace or use the Undo feature.
7. Click anywhere outside the bulleted object to deselect the object.

The bullet character for each level is determined by the presentation design that is chosen when you first created the presentation. You can edit the bullet style, color, and size can be edited, if desired.

FIGURE 24.3

A bulleted slide can support multiple bullet levels.

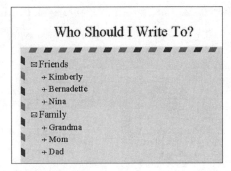

Entering Bulleted Text in the Outline Pane

You can also enter bulleted text in the Outline pane almost as easily as you can in Slide view. To enter text in Outline view, use the following steps:

1. On a new slide, type the title of the slide and press Enter. PowerPoint then adds a new slide.

2. Press the Tab key to convert the new slide to a first-level bullet.

3. Type the desired text, a first-level bullet, and press Enter.

4. Press the Tab key to demote the next bullet to a second-level bullet (if desired—if not, skip steps 5 and 6).

5. Type the desired text, press Enter, and repeat as needed. Press Enter after the last item. A second-level bullet will be created.

6. To promote the bullet to the first level, press Shift+Tab.

7. Type the desired text and press Enter.

8. Repeat steps 3–7 as necessary.

When you complete the list, you can press Shift+Tab to create a new slide if desired or press Backspace to delete any unwanted bullets.

Moving Slides

When you insert slides, the order of your presentation can become a bit messy. Never fear, though; there's a way to move your slides around quickly and easily. You can use the Outline pane or switch to Slide Sorter view. In the Outline pane, use the following steps:

1. Place your mouse pointer on the slide icon for the slide you want to move. The mouse pointer looks like a four-headed arrow when it's over the slide icon.

2. Drag the slide icon to the new location.

PowerPoint displays a horizontal line, shown in Figure 24.4, that indicates the final destination for the moved slide.

FIGURE 24.4

Moving a slide in the Outline pane is quick and easy.

Horizontal line indicates where slide will be moved

Drag this icon to move a slide

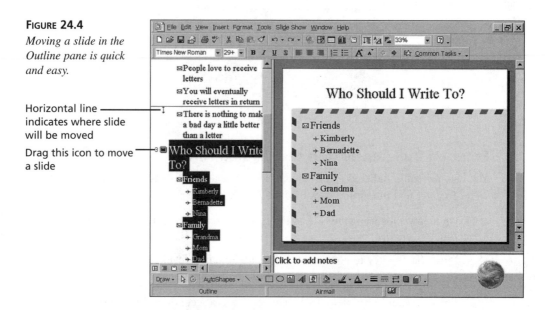

You can also move slides while you're in Slide Sorter view, which can be a bit easier than the previous method. Simply switch to Slide Sorter view and drag the slide to the new location. It couldn't be easier to rearrange your thoughts or your slides, so let's get moving.

The duplicate slide is inserted after the original. Don't worry—you can always move the slide to a different location if you want.

Deleting Slides

There may come a time when a slide is no longer necessary for your presentation. For example, the slide that covers the reasons you don't write to your mother (she can't cook, she made you wear saddle shoes, she imposed a 9 p.m. curfew on you, and so on). To make the slide disappear, simply delete it by using these two simple steps:

1. Display or click the slide you want to delete.
2. Choose Edit, Delete Slide from the menu.

Changing a Slide's Layout

With PowerPoint, you can change a slide's layout template anytime. This feature is especially useful if, for example, you decide you would like to add a chart to a bullet list. To change the layout of a slide, follow these steps:

1. Click the slide you want to change.

2. Choose Format, Slide Layout from the menu to open the Slide Layout dialog box.

3. Select a new layout.

4. Click the Apply button.

> When you change a slide's layout, you're actually applying the layout's specific formatting to the slide. Although you won't lose any presentation information previously typed into a slide (or any objects that have been previously added), you might lose formatting modifications you have made to the text. This process can also be used to reapply the same layout to a slide, just in case you really mess up the formatting.

24

Changing the Presentation's Design

You can change your presentation's design at any time by following these steps:

1. Choose Format, Apply Design Template from the menu to open the Apply Design dialog box.

2. Select a new design for the presentation.

3. Click the Apply button. The new design is then applied to every slide in your presentation.

> Changing the document's presentation design is similar to changing the layout of an individual slide. When you apply the presentation design's formatting to your presentation, your slides won't lose any text or objects you have entered; however, the formatting may change.

Text Objects Versus Text Boxes

PowerPoint supports various methods for entering text on a presentation slide. In the Slide pane, simply click the placeholder and type the text. In the Outline pane, position the blinking cursor where you want the text to appear and start typing.

Another method is to insert a text box on the slide and type your text in the box. This is not recommended, however, as the text is not included in the outline, nor in a spell check.

When you enter text in the Outline pane, PowerPoint automatically creates the text object placeholder if there is not one already, and enters the text into the placeholder. Before you enter text in the Slide pane, there must be a placeholder available. If you don't have a text placeholder available, either enter text in the presentation's Outline view or change the slide's layout.

Selecting Text and Text Objects

Before you can move text or change any of the text attributes, you need to know how to select text. Most of the objects and elements that have been selected up to this point have been triggered by simply clicking on the item you want to select. When you're working with text information, the process is slightly different. You will need to either edit only a portion of the text, or apply a formatting option to all of the text. Text is selected when it's highlighted in black just as it is in Word and the other Office programs.

Rearranging Text and Text Objects

Once you select text, you can start moving and copying it. You can rearrange snippets of text, or you can relocate an entire text object. Being able to copy and move text is a feature that makes Microsoft Office applications so much more productive than pen and paper.

Moving or Copying Text and Text Objects

You move and copy text in PowerPoint just as you do in virtually all other Windows applications. You can move or copy text from either the Slide or Outline pane, depending on your preference. Four basic steps are involved, but one step differs depending on whether you want to move or copy the text. To move or copy text, simply select the text and drag the text to its new location and release your mouse button. You also can copy or cut the selected text to the Office Clipboard and paste the test elsewhere.

Moving Text Objects on a Slide

When you move and copy text objects to different slides, they usually do not end up in the position that you had envisioned. You may need to move them around. You may also find that at times the AutoLayouts available do not meet the exact layout specifications for your presentation.

To move text objects on a particular slide, use the Slide pane and just use the mouse to drag the object to the desired location on the slide.

Changing Text Properties

PowerPoint supports the font-formatting techniques you mastered in Word (see Chapter 6, "Formatting Characters, Paragraphs, and Pages") such as bold, italics, colors. In addition, you can select the font styles you want to use in your presentations.

Before you change any font attributes, you must first select the text that will be affected by the change. To change the font for a portion of text—for example, just the one word you want in bold—select just that one word. To change the font for an entire text object—if you want the entire title a bit bigger, for instance—select the text object.

24

Working with Bulleted Text

When you have slides with bulleted text, there are a few tricks you can use to achieve a professionally coordinated presentation. In PowerPoint, your slides can have up to five bullet levels. Each level can have a different bullet character, and each descending level is automatically defined with a font size smaller than the preceding bullet level. The two most common operations people want to perform with bulleted text are to modify the bullet symbols (Bob wants checkmarks instead of smiley faces, for example) and to change the relative font size.

Changing Bullet Symbols

Changing the style of a bullet is fairly simple. The biggest hurdle to overcome is not to get overwhelmed by all the different symbol choices. Keep your audience and presentation subject in mind when choosing bullet symbols. The bullets in Figure 24.5, for example, are congruent with the computer theme for this book. You may also want to use a numbered list instead of bullet symbols. To change the bullet style, use the following steps:

1. Click on the line where you want the bullet symbol changed.
2. Choose Format, Bullets and Numbering from the menu.
3. Click the Bulleted tab on the Bullets and Numbering dialog box, if it is not already displayed as shown in Figure 24.6.

FIGURE 24.5

Pictures as well as the usual bullet dots can add interest to your slides.

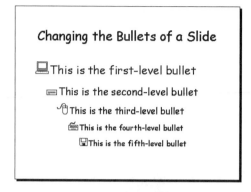

FIGURE 24.6

Use the Bullets and Numbering dialog box to create custom bullets for your slides.

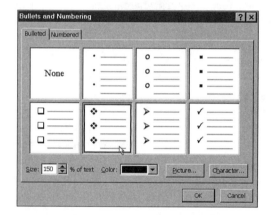

4. Click one of the seven predefined bulleted styles.

5. Change the color or size of the bullet symbol, if you want.

6. Click the OK button.

Repeat these steps for each bullet item you want to change, or you can select all the bullet items to make a global change.

If you do not like any of the pre-existing bullet styles, there are hundreds of other bullet characters or pictures to choose from. To choose a completely different character or picture, use the following steps:

1. Click on the line where you want the bullet symbol changed.

2. Choose Format, Bullets and Numbering from the menu.

3. Click the Bulleted tab if it is not already displayed.

4. Click the Character button.

5. Select a font from the Bullets From drop-down list.

6. Click a symbol from the symbol grid.

7. Change the color or size of the bullet symbol, if you want.

8. Click the OK button.

Line Spacing

When you want to create more distance between lines of text or bullet points, don't press the Enter key an extra time. PowerPoint gives you a much simpler option for changing the line spacing that also gives you much more control than pressing Enter and adding an extra blank line. The Line Spacing option affects any lines of text you have previously selected. You can set the measurement for line spacing in number of lines or by points.

Point size is the unit of measurement typically used for fonts. One point is $1/72$ inch. Therefore, 72 points is 1 inch, 36 points is $1/2$ inch, 18 points is $1/4$ inch, and so on. Follow these steps to change the line spacing for selected text:

1. First, select the lines to modify.

2. Choose Format, Line Spacing from the menu to open the Line Spacing dialog box.

3. Select the amount of space you want between lines of text.

4. Select the unit of measurement for the line spacing.

5. Click the OK button.

Changing Text Object Attributes

This next section covers how the text object affects the text contained in it and how to control the text object itself. Each of the following sections explains a different option or feature, and the title object is used as the sample object.

Adding a Border or Fill

The first feature is adding a border or fill (shading) to your text object, which is a great way to make text stand out from the crowd. Figure 24.7 shows how a text object can be formatted with borders and shading.

Gradient fill is a very cool special effect that you can use with almost every PowerPoint object. With a gradient fill effect, one color gradually fades into black, white, or another color. PowerPoint also has several preset color schemes from which you can choose. To add a border or fill to a text object, follow these steps:

24

1. Click anywhere in the text object to which you want to add a border or fill to select it.

2. Choose Format, Placeholder from the menu (the last option in the Format menu), to display the Format AutoShape dialog box.

3. Select the Colors and Lines tab.

4. If you want to add a fill, select an option from the Color drop-down list in the Fill section.

5. If you want a border, select a line color from the Color drop-down list in the Line section of the dialog box.

6. Change the Style, Dashed, and Weight options for the border, if you want.

7. Click the Preview button to preview your changes before accepting them.

8. Click the OK button when you're finished.

FIGURE 24.7

A text object shown with a border and a gradient fill.

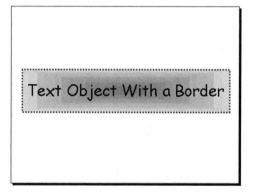

Setting the Text Anchor Point

When you're trying to get the best look for your presentation, you can control how the text is anchored within a text object, especially when you have used a border or fill option. The text anchor point is the point where the text sits in the object. Text can be anchored to an object position at the top, middle, bottom, top center, middle center, or bottom center. Figure 24.8 shows two text objects, each with a different anchor point. If you need to change the anchor point, follow these steps:

1. Select the text object.

2. Choose Format, Placeholder from the menu.

3. Select the Text Box tab.

4. Select a new anchor point from the Text Anchor Point drop-down list.

FIGURE 24.8

Message text is anchored to the middle and bottom of the text box.

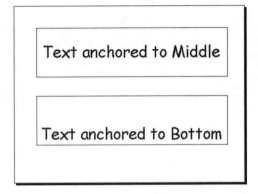

5. Click the Preview button to see a preview of your change.

6. Click the OK button.

Using Find and Replace

You can use the PowerPoint Find option to quickly locate a phrase or word in your presentation. PowerPoint searches all the text objects—including all slides and speaker's notes—in your presentation for the text you specify. It is best to use this option in Normal view. Simply select Edit, Find or Edit, Replace to locate specific text within your presentation and change that text if you wish to do so.

Summary

You should now be familiar with creating a new presentation and a title slide. You know how to add new slides to your presentation and create, edit, and expand a bulleted slide, so duplicating, moving, and deleting slides should now be easy tasks.

You should now be comfortable working with any type of PowerPoint text object and know the difference between a text object and a text box. After you select a text object or just a snippet of text, you can move or copy it to any location. You have seen how to enhance your presentation by changing any text properties you want. PowerPoint makes it easy to modify bulleted text with a host of tools and options available to you. You can change the bullet symbol used for each level of text, increase or decrease the font size in proportion to the rest of the text, and change the line spacing, if needed.

PART VIII

Making Your Presentations Shine

Chapter

CHAPTER 25

Customizing Your Presentation

Once you produce your presentation, you'll want to modify and polish your presentation to make it the best it can be. In this chapter, you will learn how to create a custom color scheme. You will also create custom backgrounds for your slides. After polishing your presentation, you will want to produce speaker's notes so you can lead your presentation without a flaw. In addition, you may want to print handouts of the presentation for your audience.

Customizing the Color Scheme

When you choose one of PowerPoint's presentation designs or presentation templates, you aren't required to choose coordinating colors for the slide objects. Each design and template has eight coordinating colors for the background, regular text, title text, fills, and accents. The color scheme affects every slide in your presentation. If you want to change the colors for your entire presentation, there's no need to go to each slide and change everything one item at a time. PowerPoint can easily do this for you.

There might also be times when you don't need any color, such as when your presentation will be given on an overhead projector or printed in black and white. You don't want to lose all the panache that the template gives you, but you do need to sell your ideas clearly. PowerPoint gives you the option of showing the presentation in black and white.

At other times, you may want to use your own custom colors, rather than the standard color scheme. When situations such as these arise, you have two options: You can choose from one of the standard color schemes already created, or you can create your very own custom color scheme.

Keep the format of your presentation in mind when deciding on a color scheme. Will you be presenting using an overhead projector with slide transparencies, a laptop and projector, or 35mm slides? Each of these options—in addition to your target audience—will determine the proper color scheme for your presentation. Use color schemes with light or nonexistent backgrounds for overhead projectors, and darker backgrounds for slide shows (either projectors or 35mm).

Standard Color Schemes

Each presentation design or template has a standard color scheme that is first displayed when you create the presentation. You can also select from at least one other predesigned color scheme, and a black-and-white scheme, as shown in Figure 25.1.

 Many of the template designs have more than one color scheme from which to choose. Use the black-and-white scheme for those occasions when you can't use a color printer and need to generate a presentation on transparencies or handouts.

To select another predesigned color scheme for the entire presentation, follow these steps:

1. Choose Format, Slide Color Scheme to open the Color Scheme dialog box.
2. Click the Standard tab.
3. Click any color scheme; the black-and-white color scheme is usually the top-right color scheme.
4. Click the Preview button to see a preview of the selected scheme.

Use these color schemes   Use the black-and-white scheme
for transparencies   when no color is needed

FIGURE 25.1

*The Color Scheme
dialog box gives you
several color scheme
choices.*

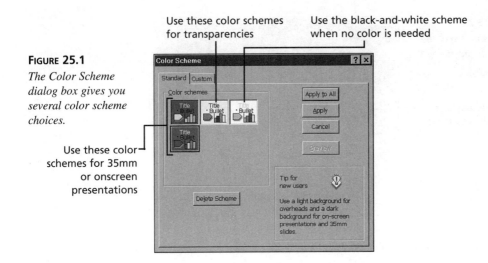

Use these color
schemes for 35mm
or onscreen
presentations

You may need to move the dialog box out of the way to see the preview. To
move a dialog box, place the mouse pointer in the title bar of the dialog
box, click and hold down the mouse button, and drag the box to another
location.

25

5. Click the Apply to All button to accept the change.

When you're selecting a color scheme, PowerPoint also enables you to change the color
scheme for just one individual slide. This feature lets you add emphasis to a specific
slide.

To change the color scheme for just one slide, use the previous steps and click Apply
instead of Apply to All.

Custom Color Schemes

If you don't like any of the standard color schemes, you can always create your own custom color scheme. When you create a custom color scheme, you can select a custom
color for the following eight options: Background, Text and Lines, Shadows, Title Text,
Fills, Accent, Accent and Hyperlink, and Accent and Followed Hyperlink. As you select
a new color for each of these eight options, PowerPoint shows you a preview of what
your choice will look like. Figure 25.2 shows the Custom tab of the Color Scheme
dialog box.

FIGURE 25.2

The Custom tab of the Color Scheme dialog box.

Change any of these options to create a custom color scheme

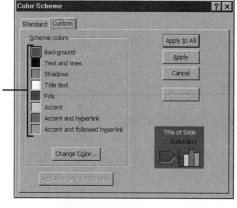

To create a custom color scheme, follow these steps:

1. Choose Format, Slide Color Scheme from the menu.

2. In the Color Scheme dialog box, click the Custom tab.

3. Click the color box of the feature you want to change in the Scheme Colors section.

4. Click the Change Color button.

> The name of the color box you select in step 3 determines the name of the Color dialog box. Figure 25.3 shows that the Background color box was selected before the Change Color button was clicked.

5. Select a standard color, as shown in Figure 25.3, from the Background Color dialog box, or choose a color from the Custom tab.

6. Click the OK button.

7. Repeat the preceding steps for each feature you want to customize.

8. Click the Preview button to see a preview.

9. Click the Apply or Apply to All button to accept the change.

> If you want to change the color scheme for only one slide, you must first display the slide.
>
> If you want to create a custom color, use the Custom tab in the Background Color dialog box. You can then either drag the crosshair and scroll arrow to

select a color, or be more scientific and type in the number (0–255) for the Red/Green/Blue and Hue/Saturation/Luminance color component options.

FIGURE 25.3

The Background Color dialog box offers you many color choices in the Standard colors tab.

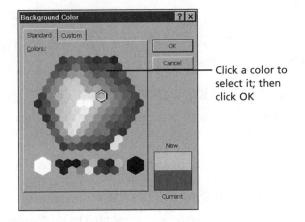

Click a color to select it; then click OK

After you have created a color scheme, you can add that color scheme to the standard list. That can save you time in the future if Bob wants to use the same colors over and over and over.

Follow these steps to save a custom color scheme:

1. Choose Format, Slide Color Scheme from the menu.
2. Click the Custom tab.
3. Create a custom color scheme by changing the Scheme Colors.
4. Click the Preview button to see a preview.
5. Click the Add As Standard Scheme button.

Customizing the Background

PowerPoint allows you to not only change the color scheme of your slides, but also change the appearance of the presentation or slide background. If you want to change the background, you have many options available: color, shade, pattern, texture, or picture (such as a watermark image on your slide's background).

25

Although you can choose from all these background options, you can use only a single type of background for a specific slide. For example, you can have either a gradient shaded background or a picture as the background, but not both.

Just as you can change the color scheme, you can change the background for only one slide or for the entire presentation.

Changing the Background Color

In addition to changing the background color through the Custom tab of the Color Scheme dialog box, PowerPoint has a quick way to change the background color with the Format, Background command. You can change the background color for just the current slide or for all the slides in your presentation.

To change the background color, follow these steps:

1. Choose Format, Background from the menu. The Background dialog box displays.

2. Click the drop-down list in the Background Fill section of the dialog box, as shown in Figure 25.4.

FIGURE 25.4

You can select many options for your presentation backgrounds using the Background dialog box.

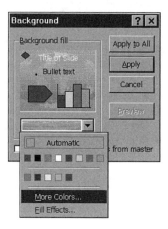

3. Click one of the color boxes.

   or

4. Click More Colors and select another color from the Colors dialog box.

5. Click the OK button (from the Colors dialog box).

6. Click the Preview button to see a preview.

7. Click the Apply or Apply to All button to accept the change.

If your slides have graphics, and you want to change only the background color (not add gradient shading or use a pattern), try changing the background color by using the Format, Color Scheme command. When you create the custom color scheme, change only the background color. Although you can change the background color by using the Format, Background command, this option doesn't give you a good display when slides have certain graphical elements.

Changing the Fill Effects

One way to add special effects to a slide is to modify the fill effects for the background. You have four options for the background fill:

- Gradient
- Texture
- Pattern
- Picture

Each option, when used skillfully, can visually enhance a presentation or slide and add emphasis for a particular topic of discussion.

Gradient

Gradient shading is the most frequently used fill effect, not only for the slide background, but for drawing shapes as well. This effect can produce a dazzling visual display. For example, you could gradually transform one solid color into a lighter or darker color, fade two colors from one to the other, or use preset PowerPoint gradient choices with exotic names, such as Early Sunset or Rainbow. Gradient shading also includes six different shading styles, most of which have four different variants to choose from.

To select a gradient shading option for the background, use these steps:

1. Choose Format, Background from the menu to display the Background dialog box.

2. Select Fill Effects from the Background Fill drop-down list.

3. In the Fill Effects dialog box, click the Gradient tab, as shown in Figure 25.5.

4. Select a color option, such as Preset, from the option buttons in the Colors section.

5. Select one of the option buttons, such as Horizontal or Vertical, in the Shading Styles section.

25

FIGURE 25.5

The Gradient fill options offer many dynamic possibilities for your presentation.

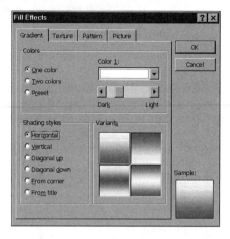

6. Select an option (most shading styles have four) in the Variants section; the one you pick is displayed in the Sample box.

7. Click the OK button.

8. Click the Preview button to see a preview.

9. Click the Apply or Apply to All button to accept the change.

Preparing Speaker's Notes

When you create a presentation, you have done only half the job. Eventually, you have to go before an audience and speak! Showing the slides isn't enough; you need to extrapolate the information on each slide and present it to your audience. What will you say? You've created a stupendous presentation using PowerPoint, but now you need to create some notes pages for the verbal part of the presentation. Unlike other presentation programs, PowerPoint makes it very easy to create speaker's notes. You can do that by using the notes pane in the Normal view.

To create speaker's notes in Normal view, use the following steps:

1. Display the slide to which you want to add notes.

2. Click the Notes pane.

3. Type your notes.

4. Click the Slide or Outline pane when finished.

You can also use the Notes Page view as in previous versions of PowerPoint. Select View, Notes Page from the menu. Click the Notes placeholder and type your notes. Usually the placeholder for your notes is so small that you can't see what you're typing. You might want to zoom in to 75% or 100% for a more legible display. Change back to Normal view when you are finished.

The Notes pane can be resized if needed. Place the mouse pointer on the Notes pane border until it looks like a double arrow, and drag the border to a different size. Release the mouse button when finished.

Printing Speaker's Notes

Typing your speaker's notes is only half the battle; you will eventually want to print out those notes. You can print notes only when you select the Notes Pages option from the Print dialog box (see Figure 25.6).

FIGURE 25.6

Use the Print dialog box to print speaker's notes.

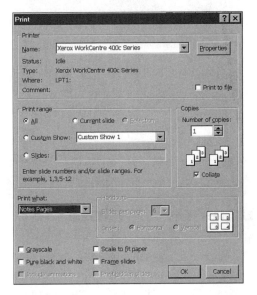

25

To print speaker's notes, follow these steps:

1. Choose File, Print from the menu to display the Print dialog box.

If you want to print speaker's notes, do not click the Print button because that prints your entire presentation, no questions asked. You need to specify that you want to print speaker's notes in the Print dialog box.

2. In the Print What drop-down list, select Notes Pages.

3. Change any other options needed.

4. Click the OK button.

PowerPoint prints a miniature of each slide on the top half of the page, with the corresponding speaker's notes on the bottom half, as shown in Figure 25.7.

FIGURE 25.7

Speaker's notes show the appropriate slide with the applicable notes.

Preparing Audience Handouts

Now that you have finished your speaker's notes, wouldn't it be nice to have a printout of your presentation? Audience handouts are useful to keep the audience in step with your presentation. They also can be used to facilitate note-taking. Printing audience handouts couldn't be easier, and you can select the number of slides you want to appear on each printed page. Audience handouts are a nice souvenir to give out. They are great to take notes on and to help your viewers stay on track during your presentation. Keep this fact in mind: People retain 10% of what they hear, 30% of what they hear and see, and 70% of what they hear and see when they have something tangible to remind them, like handouts.

To print audience handouts, use the following steps:

1. Choose File, Print to open the Print dialog box.

2. In the Print What drop-down list, select Handouts.

3. In the Handouts area, select the number of slides per page (2, 3, 4, 6, or 9).

4. Select the order in which to print the slides, either horizontal or vertical.

5. Change any other options you want.

6. Click the OK button.

> If you want your audience to have some room on the handouts where they can write their own notes, use the 3 Slides per Page option. This option prints three slides on the left side of the page with lines on the right side for taking notes.

> Unless you're printing color audience handouts, make sure the Black and White option in the Print dialog box is checked. Otherwise, you will have some very dark printouts. When you print audience handouts in black and white, PowerPoint prints only the basic information from each slide. All of the text, some of the graphics, and usually none of the background options are printed.

25

Summary

Even though PowerPoint creates excellent initial presentation designs, the customization work you add will make the difference between a captivating presentation and just another canned speech. This chapter has demonstrated some useful features to help you create a great presentation. Adding a custom color scheme or background can make your presentation stand out, and printing speaker's notes and handouts for your audience is an easy step that shows your preparation for the presentation.

CHAPTER **26**

Understanding Slide Show Basics

Now that you have created and edited several presentations, you're finally ready to show off all your hard work. This chapter discusses what you need to know to finalize your presentation and get your slide show up and running.

Viewing the Presentation

Viewing your presentation is the easy part, but deciding which option to use can be a bit more difficult. Although there are several ways to view a presentation, you'll learn just two options in this chapter:

- Starting the slide show in PowerPoint
- Saving a presentation so that it always starts as a slide show

Starting the Slide Show in PowerPoint

During the initial presentation design, you need to start and view your presentation in PowerPoint. Doing so gives you the opportunity to fine-tune your presentation and add timings, transitions, and any other finishing touches to your show. To start a slide show in PowerPoint, you have four main options:

- Choose View, Slide Show from the menu
- Choose Slide Show, View Show from the menu
- Choose Slide Show, Rehearse Timings from the menu
- Click the Slide Show View button

Each option gives you basically the same result, with a few minor differences. You can view the entire presentation from start to finish, clicking the mouse to advance to the next slide. The Rehearse Timings option gives you the opportunity to rehearse your presentation. While you are rehearsing, PowerPoint will keep track of the amount of time spent on each slide, and the total amount of time for the entire presentation. Figure 26.1 demonstrates PowerPoint Rehearsal toolbar during such a rehearsal.

The Rehearsal toolbar displays to show you the time spent on each slide. You can click the Next button to advance to the next slide. There is even a Repeat button if you want to start over on a particular slide. The Pause button enables you to pause the presentation, say to take an important phone call, and then you can resume the rehearsal without having to start all over again.

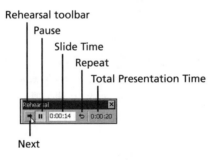

FIGURE 26.1

Use the Rehearsal toolbar option to view and rehearse your slide show while recording timings for each slide.

When you click the Slide Show View button, you usually start the slide show from the currently displayed or active slide. If you want to start the presentation from the beginning, go to the first slide before going into Slide Show view.

To create a shortcut on your desktop, follow these steps:

1. Find the file by using My Computer.

2. Right-click the file and drag it to your desktop.

3. Release the mouse button and select Create Shortcut(s) Here.

4. To run the show, simply double-click the icon.

Setting and Using the Slide Show Settings

When you view a slide show, you have several options for its display, most of which are available in the Set Up Show dialog box (see Figure 26.2). From this dialog box, you can choose whether the show is going to be presented by a speaker, browsed by an individual, or run at a kiosk. You can also determine which slides or custom shows to display, how the slides should advance, and the default pen color (explained in the following section, "Using the Pen").

FIGURE 26.2

The Set Up Show dialog box determines how the slide show will be displayed.

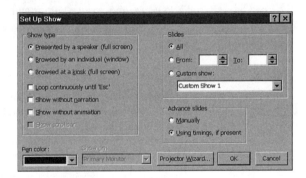

26

To change any show settings, follow these steps:

1. Choose Slide Show, Set Up Show to display the Set Up Show dialog box.

2. Change any options needed.

3. Click the OK button.

If you have a laptop and will be using a projector to display your presentation, PowerPoint has a Projector Wizard to help with the setup of the projector. Simply click the Projector Wizard button in the Set Up Show dialog box, and follow the instructions. PowerPoint will attempt to detect your projector and configure everything for you.

Using the Pen

When you're viewing a presentation, you have the capability to temporarily annotate each slide by turning your mouse pointer into a pen. This is a great feature when you have audience participation. To display the pen during a slide show, select one of the following options:

> If you plan on annotating a slide show, it's usually best to manually advance each slide.

- Press Ctrl+P.

  or

- Right-click and select Pointer Options, Pen from the Menu.

- To use the pen, simply hold down the left mouse button and write or draw annotations by moving the mouse. The annotations you make during the slide show aren't permanent, so they disappear for the next show.

> It's a good idea to get some practice using the pen before the actual slide show. Sometimes your annotations can end up as illegible handwriting. Typically, the pen is used to underline or emphasize a specific point during your presentation. A good trick to use to draw straight lines is to hold down the Shift key while you're drawing lines. This keeps your lines straight.

To change the pen back to the pointer arrow, use one of these methods:

- Press Ctrl+A.

  or

- Right-click and select Pointer Options, Arrow from the menu.

Slide Sorter View

When you're adding all the finishing touches to your slide show, you'll find that the Slide Sorter view is the most useful. Slide Sorter view allows you to view several slides simultaneously. You can move slides around, add and view the timings for individual slides, hide slides, add transitions, and include animation. Slide Sorter view has its own unique toolbar with buttons that make most tasks just a click away.

While in Slide Sorter view, you may see little icons underneath the individual slides. The icons represent transitions, animation, hidden slides, and timings that have been added.

Moving Slides

When you need to rearrange your slides, Slide Sorter view is the place to do it. If possible, set the zoom control so that you can see the slide you want to move and the destination position, as shown in Figure 26.3.

Line indicates new
position of slide

FIGURE 26.3

You can easily move a slide to any position in the presentation.

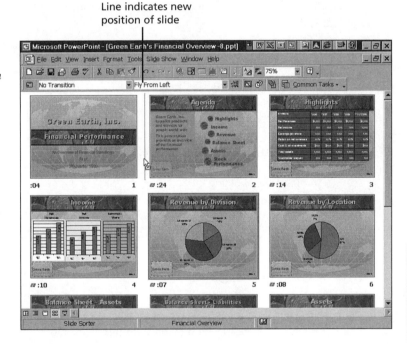

To move a slide, follow these steps:

1. Place your mouse pointer on the slide you want to move.

2. Hold down the left mouse button.

3. Drag the mouse pointer to the new position; you should see a vertical line indicating the placement of the slide.

4. Release the mouse button.

Timing

When you want a presentation to run on its own, or a slide show that advances from slide to slide without using the mouse or keyboard, you must set timings for each slide.

You can either make an educated guess as to how long the slide should be displayed (custom timings) or rehearse your presentation and have PowerPoint record the duration (rehearsed timings) before you advance to the next slide, as discussed earlier in this chapter.

It's easiest to set custom timings while you're in Slide Sorter view. To set custom timings for your presentation, follow these steps:

1. Select the slide or slides you want to set timings for.

2. Choose Slide Show, Slide Transition from the menu. The Slide Transition dialog box displays.

3. Under Advance, click the Automatically After check box.

4. Type the number of seconds you want the slide to be displayed onscreen.

5. Click the Apply button.

> To select a slide, just click on the slide. To select multiple noncontiguous slides, hold down the Ctrl key and click on each slide you want to select. You can select a contiguous group of slides by clicking on the first slide of the group, holding the Shift key, and clicking on the last slide of the group.
>
> If you want to set the same show timings for all the slides in your presentation, click the Apply to All button in the Slide Transition dialog box.

Rehearse Timings

You can also rehearse your presentation and have PowerPoint automatically add timings for each of your slides. While you're rehearsing your presentation, PowerPoint displays the Rehearsal toolbar as shown previously in this chapter.

To rehearse your presentation and add automatic timings, use the following steps:

1. Choose Slide Show, Rehearse Timings from the menu.

2. Practice your entire presentation as though you were in front of your audience. Click the next button to advance to the next slide and record the time for the current slide.

3. At the end of the show, click the Yes button to record your timings and use them when you view the show.

PowerPoint will display your slides in Slide Sorter view so that you can either edit them or rehearse your show to get new timing values.

Hiding a Slide

Sometimes when you're creating a presentation, you might not be sure whether a piece of information is relevant. Of course, you always want to be prepared (even if you're not a Boy Scout), no matter what might come up. If you have a slide that doesn't need to be shown, you can always leave it in the presentation file, but hide it from the show by following these steps:

1. Select the slide you want to hide.
2. Choose Slide Show, Hide Slide from the menu.

   or

3. Click the Hide Slide button from the Slide Sorter toolbar.

 If you're hiding slides, you might not want to have them numbered automatically. Although PowerPoint doesn't display a slide that has been hidden, it doesn't renumber the slides automatically.

Creating a Summary Slide

Creating a summary slide quickly is a great feature of PowerPoint. PowerPoint creates the summary (or agenda) slide from the titles of the slides you select.

To create a summary slide, follow these steps:

1. Switch to Slide Sorter view.
2. Select the slide(s) that you want included in the summary.
3. Click the Summary Slide button on the Slide Sorter toolbar.

26

PowerPoint creates the summary slide in front of the first slide selected. Move the summary slide to the end to close your presentation powerfully.

Summary

You have now completed your PowerPoint presentation from design to delivery. Creating a slide show is the finishing touch to your hard work. It's important to apply creativity and thought to the slide show and remember that you're judged on the pacing as well as the overall design of the presentation. It is important to keep in mind that you are what is most important; your presentation is a tool that you are using to help convey your ideas to your audience. The star of the show should not be the presentation itself.

CHAPTER 27

Drawing Objects in Presentations

You now are ready to learn about different drawing options available in PowerPoint. Text box and WordArt objects are considered drawing objects, even though they contain text. This hour covers these text drawing objects and using the guides to position objects.

PowerPoint supplies drawing tools that inspire unlimited creativity. Here you learn the fundamentals of creating eye-catching graphics using PowerPoint. Better than oils and canvas, PowerPoint and a high-resolution monitor enable you to experiment with unique digital effects. If you have the time, creating custom drawing objects in PowerPoint is an energizing, artistic experience. Exciting drawing features are available in PowerPoint.

Text Boxes

You have already been adding text to your slides using the preplaced text object placeholders. These placeholders have been the primary vehicle for your text additions. When you need text added to your slide outside the placeholders, use the Text Box tool on the Drawing toolbar.

When you add a text box to a slide, it behaves in one of two ways:

- As a label, as shown in Figure 27.1, in which the text within it doesn't word wrap. This option is useful when you need a short caption for a chart or a graphic image.

FIGURE 27.1

Text labels for charts help describe the information presented.

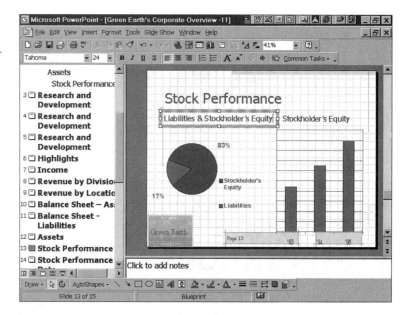

- As a word processing box, as shown in Figure 27.2, in which the text within the text box does word wrap. The text box can expand, if necessary.

    1. Click the Text Box tool on the Drawing toolbar.

    2. Click on the slide where you want to position the text label.

    3. Start typing.

Be careful when typing text labels. Don't type too much text, or the text box will run off the slide. When there's a chance you might have too much information, create a word processing box instead. If the text does overrun the edge, you can either add hard returns manually or resize the text box object.

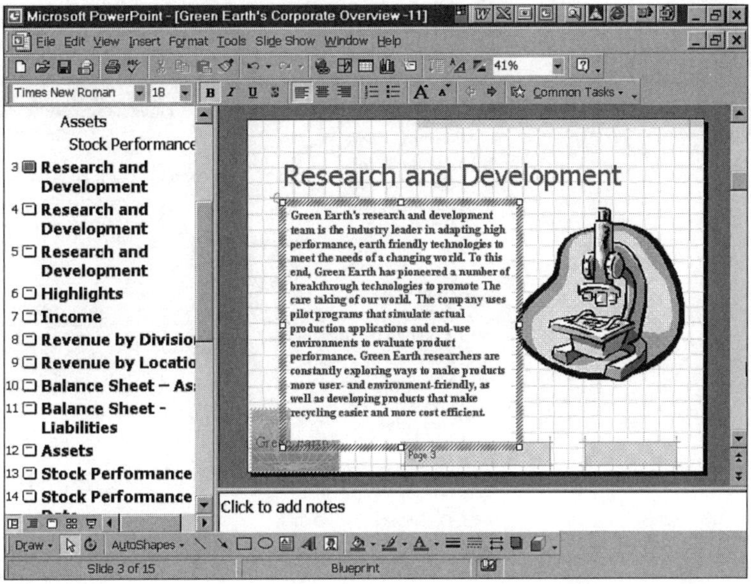

FIGURE 27.2

Use a word processing text box when you want to add a lot of text.

Formatting a Text Box

You can add many special effects to a text box for emphasis and impact, such as including a fill or border. PowerPoint also enables you to control the size and position of the text box and change the text anchor point and internal margins of the text. All these options are available in the Format Text Box dialog box.

Adding a Fill or Border

By adding a border or fill to your text box, you can really make the text stand out. Figure 27.3 illustrates how a text box can be formatted by using the fill and border options.

1. Select the text box you want to format.
2. Choose Format, Text Box from the menu to display the Format Text Box dialog box.
3. Click the Colors and Lines tab.
4. Select a color or fill option from the Color drop-down list in the Fill section.

Use the Fill Effects option from the Color drop-down list to apply a gradient or other fill effect to your text object. Although it's easy to get carried away with all the special effects, just remember that the text is what you want the audience to focus on, not the fancy formatting.

27

FIGURE 27.3

*Format a text box with
a fill and a border to
draw attention to the
text.*

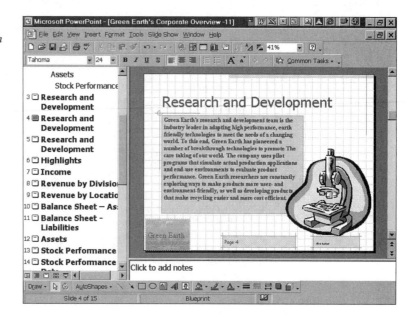

5. If you want a border, click the Color drop-down list under the Line section.

6. Change the Style, Dashed, and Weight options for the line, if you want.

7. Click the Preview button to preview your changes before accepting them.

8. Click the OK button when you're finished.

Moving a Text Box

After you create your text box, you might decide later that it needs to be moved to
another location on the slide. PowerPoint has two options for moving the text box. You
can either drag the text box to a desired position or set an exact position in the Format
Text Box dialog box. To drag a text box to a new location, use the following steps:

1. Click once on the text box to select it.

2. Place the mouse pointer on the box's border so you can see the move pointer.

3. Click and hold down the left mouse button.

4. Drag the box to the new location.

5. Release the mouse button.

When you know exactly where you want the text box to be placed on a slide, you can
use the Position tab in the Format Text Box dialog box. You must measure the position
from either the top left corner or the center of the slide.

Changing the Size of a Text Box

Usually, a text box is set to automatically fit the size of the text that it contains. However, on occasion, as in Figure 27.4, you may need the text box to be smaller or larger than the automatic size given by PowerPoint. In this example, because of the border and shading, the overall look would be greatly improved by making the text box a smidgen smaller. To resize the text box manually, you must first turn off the automatic resizing feature.

FIGURE 27.4

If a text box is too small, simply resize it.

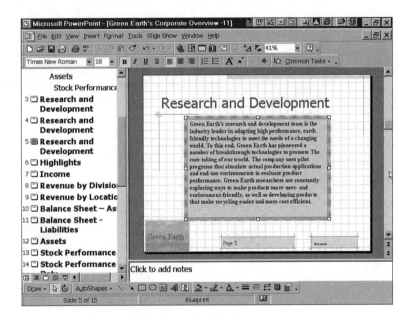

1. Click once on the text object to select it.
2. Choose Format, Text Box from the menu. The Format Text Box dialog box opens.
3. Click the Text Box tab.
4. Uncheck the Resize AutoShape to Fit Text option.
5. Click the OK button.
6. Drag the appropriate resizing handle to resize the text box.

27

Formatting the Text in a Text Box

You can format the text in a text box by using the Format Font dialog box or by selecting any of the text formatting tools on the Formatting toolbar. Make the text bigger or smaller, select a new font face, or change the color. So many font choices, so little time! To format text in a text box, follow these steps:

1. Select the text you want to format. If you want to format all the text in the text box, click once on the text box to select it and a second time on the text box border to select the entire text box.

2. Choose Format, Font from the menu to open the Font dialog box.

3. Change any options you want.

4. Click the Preview button to see a preview of your changes before accepting them.

5. Click the OK Button.

Using WordArt

The WordArt feature included with PowerPoint enables you to create dynamic text drawings. Create a new logo or heading by using any of the hundreds of formatting combinations available to you with WordArt. Special effects and other embellishments are only a click away. There are many exciting features, such as 3D effects, shadows, and textured fills. WordArt also gives you several predefined shapes for your text as shown in Figure 27.5.

FIGURE 27.5

Use WordArt in your presentation slides to create a dramatic effect.

When you create WordArt, the text is changed to a drawing object, so it is not included in a spell check or the Outline view. Keep a dictionary close at hand, just in case you need to check the spelling of a word. A spelling error on a letter will seem like nothing, compared to a spelling error in a presentation that is magnified to two feet or more!

1. Select Insert, Picture, WordArt from the menu to open the WordArt Gallery, or click the WordArt button on the Drawing toolbar.

2. Select a style from the WordArt Gallery as shown in Figure 27.6. Don't pay attention to the color of the WordArt, as this can, and probably will, be changed later.

FIGURE 27.6

The WordArt Gallery has several dozen samples for you to choose from.

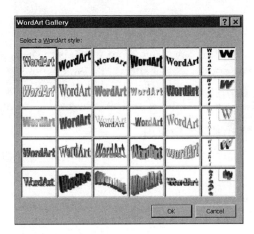

3. Type your text.

4. Change the font style and/or font size, if desired.

5. Add bold or italic, if desired.

6. Click the OK button.

The WordArt object will be added to the middle of your slide, ready to be resized and repositioned as necessary. To resize WordArt, follow these steps:

1. Click once on the WordArt to select it.

2. Position the mouse over any white sizing handle.

3. Hold down the left mouse button and drag the sizing handle to a new location.

4. Release the mouse button.

To move the WordArt object, follow these steps:

1. Position the mouse pointer on the WordArt object (the middle of the object works well).

2. Click and hold down the left mouse button; you should see a move pointer.

3. Drag the WordArt object to a new location on the slide.

4. Release the mouse button.

27

To edit the text in a WordArt object, follow these steps:

1. Double-click the WordArt object.
2. Edit the text.
3. Click the OK button.

Using the WordArt Toolbar

When you click on a WordArt object, the WordArt toolbar usually appears. Use this toolbar to add or change any of the special effects of a WordArt object. Some of the features you can change are the WordArt object's shape and format. You can also rotate the WordArt object and switch the text to a vertical or horizontal orientation.

Changing the WordArt Shape

There are 40 custom shapes you can use for your WordArt object. To change the shape, follow these steps:

1. Select the WordArt object.
2. On the WordArt toolbar, click the WordArt Shape button.
3. Click a new shape.

Formatting WordArt

You can format WordArt in the same manner as any other object. You can change the color and line options for the WordArt. The Fill option is an excellent method for coloring the WordArt object and making it stand out. To add color and fill to a WordArt object, follow these steps:

1. Select the WordArt object you want to format.
2. Click the Format WordArt button on the WordArt toolbar to display the WordArt Gallery.
3. Click the Colors and Lines tab.
4. Select a fill option from the Color drop-down list.
5. If you want, select Color, Style, Dashed, and Weight options for a border.
6. Click the Preview button to preview your changes before accepting them.
7. Click the OK button when you're done.

Figure 27.7 illustrates vertical WordArt. To make the WordArt text vertical instead of horizontal, use the following steps:

1. Select the WordArt object you want to change.
2. Click the WordArt Vertical Text button on the WordArt toolbar.

You can easily rotate WordArt by using the Free Rotate button on the WordArt toolbar; just follow these steps:

1. Select the WordArt object you want to rotate.

2. Click the Free Rotate button on the WordArt toolbar. You should see four green rotate handles in each corner of the WordArt object.

3. Place the mouse pointer on any green rotate handle, hold the left mouse button down, and drag to rotate the WordArt object.

4. Release the mouse button when the WordArt object is in the position you want.

FIGURE 27.7

Use the WordArt vertical text option to display the text on the side of a slide.

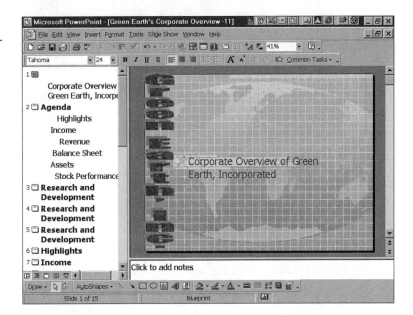

Drawing AutoShape Objects

When you look at Figure 27.8, you probably see a Manhattan cocktail with a cherry. But really, the figure consists of two trapezoids, a rectangle, an oval, a circle, and a curved line. Each of these objects has also been formatted to create a particular effect.

27

Even though you can't tell at a glance, the shapes in this picture have also been grouped to interact as a single vector graphic.

Vector graphics are a type of graphic image composed of grouped shapes. The shapes are
stacked in an order that creates a picture in the mind's eye. Think back to when you were
in kindergarten. Remember cutting out a bunch of circles, squares, and triangles? After
gluing the shapes together, you had formed a picture of a house underneath clouds.
Vector graphics work by the same principles.

Lines

PowerPoint has six line styles to choose from: three straight and three curved. Each line
style can also be formatted with many options. PowerPoint always has the type of line
you need for a project. The line, arrow, and double-arrow options all draw straight lines.
To draw a line, use the following steps:

1. Select AutoShapes, Lines from the drawing toolbar to display the Lines submenu.

2. Click a line style: Line, Arrow, or Double Arrow.

3. Move the mouse to the area on the slide where you want the line to start. The
   mouse pointer should look like Figure 27.9, a thin cross (also called a crosshair).

FIGURE 27.9

*The mouse pointer is
ready to draw a line.*

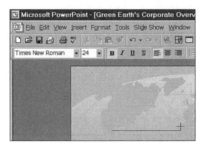

4. Click and hold down the left mouse button.

5. Drag the mouse to the location where the line should end, and then release the mouse button.

> If you selected Arrow, the arrow appears on the end of the line where you release the mouse button. Therefore, if you're drawing a line from left to right, the arrow appears on the right end of the line. Depending on the settings, the arrow might be so small that you can't see it. The later section, "Using Arrowheads," gives more information on formatting arrowheads.

> If you want to draw a straight, or constrained, line, hold down the Shift key while dragging. This method keeps the line constrained to 15-degree angles and makes drawing less tedious.
>
> Holding down the Ctrl key while dragging causes the line to draw in both directions from the starting point.
>
> Use Ctrl+Shift while dragging the mouse to get a straight line drawn in both directions.

Connectors

A *connector* is a valuable, time-saving drawing object used to visually connect two points. Using connector lines instead of normal lines is helpful when you move an object, because the lines stay connected (hence the name *connectors*). To connect any object, use one of PowerPoint's three types of connector lines: straight, angled, or curved. Follow these steps:

1. Select AutoShapes, Connectors from the drawing toolbar to display the Connectors submenu.

2. Click the type of connector you want.

3. Position the mouse on the first object to connect.

4. Click a blue connection site.

5. Move the mouse to the second object and click a connection site.

After you have connected two objects, the connection lines show locked connectors as red squares. If a connector isn't locked to an object (unlocked), the connector is shown as a green square. You can also use the yellow adjustment controls to "snake" the connector the way you want.

27

The rest of the AutoShape options behave in basically the same manner. The main difference between the objects is the specific shape. There are many closed shapes that can be easily drawn and grouped to create almost any kind of picture. Remember the sample cocktail shown at the beginning of this chapter? Your drawing can be very simple or extremely complex—enough to create an intricate work of art.

Follow these steps to draw an AutoShape:

1. Select AutoShapes from the drawing toolbar to open the AutoShapes submenu.
2. Select Basic Shapes, Block Arrows, Flow Chart Symbols, Stars and Banners, or More AutoShapes to open the corresponding submenu.
3. Select a shape.
4. Click and hold the left mouse button on the upper-left corner of the imaginary box, and then drag to the lower-right corner of the imaginary box.
5. Release the mouse.

Callouts

A *callout* is a text description for part of a graphical image. Callout objects are useful AutoShapes when you need to use text with a connecting line back to an object. For example, you might need to describe a particular object, as shown in Figure 27.10. To create a callout, use the following steps:

1. Select AutoShapes, Callouts from the drawing toolbar to open the Callouts submenu.
2. Click the callout you want.
3. Click where you want the callout to be attached and drag to the size you want.
4. Type the text for the callout.

FIGURE 27.10

Use callouts to attach text to the object you are referencing (like comics in the newspaper).

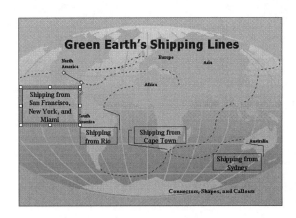

Action Buttons

Action buttons, the last available option on the AutoShapes menu, enable you to create navigation buttons like the ones you see displayed on World Wide Web pages. You draw these buttons just as you do any other AutoShape. When you release the mouse button, PowerPoint displays the Actions Settings dialog box, where you can set the specific action you want the button to perform.

Adding Text in Drawing Objects

You can add text quickly and easily to almost any AutoShape except lines. Do not draw an AutoShape and then create a text box for text. This creates two separate objects: the AutoShape and the text box, which will cause you unnecessary problems later when you need to move or resize the AutoShape.

To avoid any potential problems, simply select the shape you want to add text to and then start typing. It is almost too easy! The text is automatically centered in the AutoShape and can be formatted in the same manner as other text objects.

Formatting Drawing Objects

Do you want color? Lines? What type of arrows do you want on your lines? Do you need the arrow to be placed at the other end of the line? The drawing objects you have learned to draw in this hour can be formatted in so many different ways. PowerPoint is like that famous fast-food chain—yes, you can have it your way!

Working with Shapes

The shape of AutoShape objects can easily be formatted with color and lines, which is discussed in this section. The Manhattan cocktail pictured at the beginning of this chapter had different color and line options set for each object. The three shapes that made up the glass were colored white, with no lines. The liquid was colored light brown and enhanced with gradient shading and no lines. The cherry, colored red, had gradient shading and no lines, and its stem was a single curved line that was three points thick.

If you have entered text into an AutoShape, you can format its appearance just as you would any other text object. You can use the Format Font dialog box or any of the text formatting tools on the formatting toolbar. You can also move or resize an AutoShape just as you would any other object in PowerPoint.

Using Colors and Lines

You can add or change the color and lines of any AutoShape. How you combine these options depends on the effect you want. At first, it might seem as though it takes a while

27

to figure out how to get a certain special effect, but eventually you will find yourself seeing every object in your home as a combination of PowerPoint AutoShapes with color
and lines. To change or add color or lines to any AutoShape, follow these steps:

1. Select the AutoShape you want to format.

2. Choose Format, AutoShape from the menu to open the Format AutoShape dialog
   box.

3. Click the Colors and Lines tab.

4. Click the Color drop-down list, as shown in Figure 27.11, and select a fill color or
   effect.

FIGURE 27.11

*Select a fill color or
effect from the Color
drop-down list.*

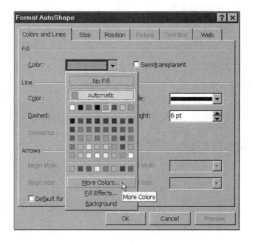

5. If you want a border, click the Color drop-down list under the Line section and
   select a color (or No Line to omit a border).

6. Change the Style, Dashed, and Weight options for the line for different effects.

7. Click the Preview button to preview your changes before accepting them.

8. Click the OK button when finished.

Working with Lines

There are hundreds of ways to format a line. PowerPoint offers you choices for changing
the look for any type of line you might have drawn. The following sections cover the
available options for these attributes:

- Line styles
- Color
- Thickness

- Arrowheads
- Connectors

Formatting Line Styles

All the lines you draw can be formatted with many options for just the right look. You can change the line color, select one of PowerPoint's dashed line styles, or choose a custom line pattern. You can also change the line's thickness simply by changing the line weight to a larger point size. On the Green Earth's Shipping Lines slide, the connector lines have been formatted as dashed lines, only .25 point thick. To change the line style, use the following steps:

1. Select the line you want to format.
2. Choose Format, AutoShape from the menu to open the Format AutoShape dialog box.
3. Click the Colors and Lines tab.
4. Under the Line section, select a color or pattern option from the Color drop-down list.
5. Change the Style, Dashed, and Weight options for the line for different effects.
6. Click the Preview button to preview your changes before accepting the modifications.
7. Click the OK button when finished.

Using Arrowheads

You can easily add or edit arrowheads on a line. You might realize that you need arrowheads or that an arrowhead ended up on the wrong side of the line after you drew it. You also have several arrowhead styles to choose from.

The option of adjusting the arrowhead size without changing the line's thickness is a new feature in PowerPoint. Not only can you adjust the size, but for double-arrowhead lines, you can also have a different style and size for each end of the line! Figure 27.12 illustrates a line with different arrowhead styles and varying sizes for each end of the line.

1. Select the line you want to format.
2. Choose Format, AutoShape from the menu to open the Format AutoShape dialog box.
3. Click the Colors and Lines tab.
4. Under the Arrows section, select a begin style or end style of arrow for the line.
5. Select a begin size and/or end size for each arrow style.

27

FIGURE 27.12
PowerPoint offers different arrowhead styles.

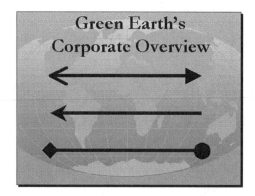

6. Click the Preview button to preview your changes before accepting them.

7. Click the OK button when finished.

Using Connector Lines

Connector lines can also be formatted with all the options previously discussed. In addition to the standard formatting options, you can change the connector line style, if you want. The connector can have the following styles:

- Straight
- Elbow
- Curved

Follow these steps to change the Style of a Connector Line:

1. Select the line you want to format.

2. Choose Format, AutoShape from the menu to open the Format AutoShape dialog box.

3. Click the Colors and Lines tab.

4. Under the Line section, select the connector style you want from the Connector drop-down list.

5. Click the Preview button to preview your changes before accepting them.

6. Click the OK button when finished.

Summary

Drawing objects allow you to add depth to your presentation and more clearly define your message. In this chapter, you have learned how to create text objects, use the WordArt program, and follow the steps for using the guides to position objects.

You have now mastered options for drawing and formatting AutoShapes in PowerPoint, and you were introduced to the concept of using the AutoShape features available with PowerPoint to create a picture. You saw a picture with simple formatting created with AutoShape lines and shapes.

You also learned how to draw straight, curved, and connector lines; explored the quick, easy methods available for drawing any other AutoShape; and learned how to make an AutoShape take on new and exciting dimensions by simply changing the color, fill, line, and other options found in the Format AutoShape dialog box.

27

PART IX

Jazzing Up PowerPoint Presentations

Chapter

CHAPTER 28

Working with Tables

Tables are a great way to convey information that would best be formatted in rows and columns. Some examples include calendars, forms, itineraries, and meeting agendas. You have seen several examples of tables throughout this book.

Creating a Table

There are two basic ways to create a table in PowerPoint. You can either use the AutoLayout feature, which has a predesignated placeholder for a table, or you can insert a table into any slide when and where you need one.

Using the Table AutoLayout

When you want to create a slide that contains only a table for your presentation, use the AutoLayout feature. This is the easiest method available. Using the table AutoLayout feature provides you with a predesignated placeholder for a table object. To create a table slide using the table AutoLayout, use the following steps:

1. Insert a new slide by selecting Insert, New Slide from the menu (or any way you like). Select the Table AutoLayout from the New Slide dialog box.

2. Select the Table layout and click the OK button.

3. Click the title placeholder and enter a title for the slide (if desired).

4. Double-click the table placeholder to display the Insert Table dialog box.

5. Enter the number of columns and rows desired, as shown in Figure 28.1.

FIGURE 28.1

Select the number of columns and rows for your table.

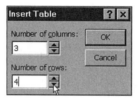

6. Click the OK button.

Inserting a Table in a Slide

When you already have a slide created and want to display a table in addition to other objects, you can use the Insert menu to create the table. To insert a table into any slide, use the following steps:

1. Display the slide where you want to insert a table.

2. Select Insert, Table from the menu to display the Insert Table dialog box.

3. Enter the number of columns and rows desired.

4. Click the OK button.

After you have inserted a table, PowerPoint should be ready for you to insert text and edit the table. This is referred to as *table edit mode*. The mouse pointer will look like a little pencil, and you should see the Tables and Borders toolbar. To exit quickly from table edit mode, click anywhere outside the table.

Parts of a Table

Before you jump right in and start entering data into your table, let's take just a minute to understand the parts of a table. A table is made up of rows and columns. The *rows* are drawn using horizontal lines, and the *columns* are drawn using vertical lines. At every intersection of a row and column is a *cell*.

Although PowerPoint does not label the rows and columns, it is sometimes helpful to do so. Some people reference cells by indicating the row and column the particular cell is in, such as "The information in row 3, column 3 demonstrates the need for more education in vaccination." Another method used is to designate each row by a number and each column by a letter. This is the method used in the PowerPoint chart program and in many spreadsheet programs, such as Excel. This naming process makes it easy to reference the individual cells. Although PowerPoint does not reference cells in this manner, Figure 28.2 shows a table with the cell references typed in.

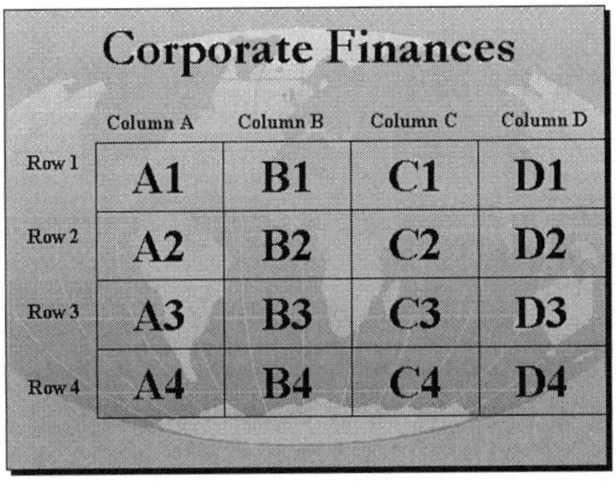

Figure 28.2

The columns, rows, and cells can be easily referenced by letters and numbers.

Corporate Finances			
	Column A	Column B	Column C	Column D
Row 1	A1	B1	C1	D1
Row 2	A2	B2	C2	D2
Row 3	A3	B3	C3	D3
Row 4	A4	B4	C4	D4

Navigating a Table

Before you can enter text in a specific cell, you must first position the blinking cursor in that cell. You have several options available to you:

- Click with the mouse in the cell.
- Use the up-, down-, left-, or right-arrow keys on the keyboard.
- Press the Tab key to move the cursor to the next cell.
- Press the Shift+Tab key combination to move the cursor to the previous cell.

Using the Tab key or Shift+Tab key combination is a quick way to move the cursor to another cell in a table. However, PowerPoint is actually selecting the entire cell when you use this method. This is not really apparent, nor does it matter if there is no text in a cell.

However, if you have information already entered in a cell, this could potentially cause a problem. When a cell is selected and you start typing, you replace the current contents with the new data you are typing. If this happens to you, use the undo button right away. To avoid this problem, use the mouse or the arrow keys to navigate a table.

28

If you press the Tab key while in the last cell of the table, you will add a row to the end of the table. If you don't want the additional row, just click the undo button on the standard toolbar.

Entering Text

After a table has been inserted into a slide, you can enter the text that you want the table to display. To enter text in a table, simply position the cursor in the appropriate cell and begin typing.

Formatting Text in a Table

Formatting text that is in a table is pretty much the same as formatting any other text object. There are one or two tricks, however, that make this task a little easier. There is even an option to center the text vertically in a cell in addition to the standard center option.

Selecting the Table, Columns, Rows, or Cells

The best shortcut to formatting text in a table is to select the entire column or row you want to format (you can even select multiple columns, rows, or cells or the entire table to format). Table 28.1 lists available selection options.

TABLE 28.1   Selecting Parts of a PowerPoint Table

Table Part	How to Select
Table	Click in the table and then select Table, Select Table from the Tables and Borders toolbar.
Row	Click in the row and then select Table, Select Row from the Tables and Borders toolbar.
Column	Click in the column and then select Table, Select Column from the Tables and Borders toolbar.
Cell	Click in the cell. To select multiple cells, drag through them using the mouse. Use this method to select multiple rows or columns as well.

1. Select the text, cells, rows, or columns you want to edit.
2. Choose Format, Font from the menu, to display the Font dialog box.
3. Make any changes you want from the Font dialog box.
4. Click the OK button.

You might want to change the alignment of the text in the cells of your table. To change the alignment, use the following steps:

1. Select the cells where you want to change the alignment.

2. Select Format, Alignment to open the Alignment submenu. Choose Align Left, Center, Align Right, or Justify from the menu.

You can also vertically align text in a cell, either at the top, center, or bottom of the cell. The center option frames the text nicely in the cell and gives a much more professional appearance. To vertically align text in a cell, use the following steps:

1. Select the cells where you want to change the alignment.

2. Click either the Align Top, Center Vertically, or Align Bottom button from the Tables and Borders toolbar, as shown in Figure 28.3.

FIGURE 28.3

Select a vertical alignment option from the Tables and Borders toolbar.

Selecting Cells, Rows, Columns, and the Entire Table

Before you can truly customize the look of the table, you should take a moment to consider how you want the final product to look. Figures 28.4 and 28.5 show the same information in two tables with completely different looks.

FIGURE 28.4

A Green Earth table with custom formatting.

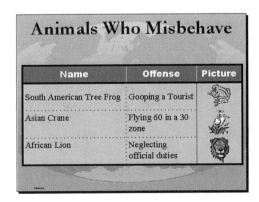

28

FIGURE 28.5

The same Green Earth table with different formatting.

When you create custom tables, you may want to format the entire table or parts of that table. To format a part of a table, you select the part you want to format.

Selecting Tables Properly

When the table is selected, nothing is highlighted. The table placeholder border will change from diagonal dashed lines to a dotted line.

When the table is selected, all formatting changes—that is, border, shading, font, and so on—will affect the entire table.

To select multiple columns, rows, or cells, use the mouse to drag through the items you want to select.

You can also select a column by placing the mouse pointer above the column (so that the pointer becomes a down-pointing black arrow, as shown in Figure 28.6) and clicking.

Column selection

FIGURE 28.6

When the mouse changes to a down arrow, you can select a column.

Animals Who Misbehave

	Name	Offense
	South American Tree Frog	Gooping a Tourist
	Asian Crane	Flying 60 in a 30 zone
	African Lion	Neglecting official duties

Inserting and Deleting Columns and Rows

You can add extra columns or rows easily to a table at any time. When you add extra columns or rows to a table, the table object will probably become bigger than the slide. You may need to resize the table so that it will fit.

Inserting and Deleting Columns

To insert a column to the left of the current insertion point's position, position the cursor (insertion point) in a cell to the right of where you want the new column. Then simply select Table, Insert Columns to the Left from the Tables and Borders toolbar.

To insert a column to the right of the current insertion point's position, position the cursor (insertion point) in a cell to the left of where you want the new column. Now you should select Table, Insert Columns to the Right from the Tables and Borders toolbar.

To insert more than one column, select the number of columns you want to insert. For example, to insert two columns, you should select two columns and then select Table, Insert Columns to the Left (or Right) from the Tables and Borders toolbar.

Deleting a column is comparably easy. To delete a column, click in any cell in the column you want to delete. Now select Table, Delete Columns from the Tables and Borders toolbar.

Inserting and Deleting Rows

Inserting rows is just as simple. To insert a row above the current insertion point's position, position the cursor (insertion point) in a cell below where you want the new row. Now from the Tables and Borders toolbar, select Table, Insert Rows Above.

To insert a row below the current insertion point's position, first position the cursor (insertion point) in a cell above where you want the new row. Now go to the Tables and Borders toolbar and select Table, Insert Rows Below.

Deleting a row is comparably easy. To delete a row, first click in any cell in the row you want to delete. Now, from the Tables and Borders toolbar select Table, Delete Rows.

28

Adjusting the Size and Position of the Table, Column Width, and Row Height

After inserting columns or rows, you might find that the table is too big for the slide. You have several choices: Resize the entire table, adjust column widths, adjust row heights, or use a combination of each of these tasks. To resize the entire table to fit on the slide, use the following steps:

1. Click the table and select Table, Select Table from the Tables and Borders toolbar.

2. Place the mouse pointer on any resizing handle (the lower right works great) and drag the handle to fit the table on the slide, as shown in Figure 28.7. The mouse pointer changes to a two-headed arrow when it's over the handle.

3. Repeat step 2 as necessary.

FIGURE 28.7

Adjust the table size by dragging the resizing handles.

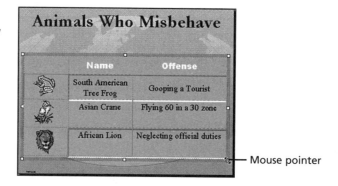

Mouse pointer

To adjust the width of a column, simply place the mouse pointer on a border line of a column, so that the mouse pointer changes to a double-headed arrow pointing left and right. Then click and drag the border to the desired column width.

To change the height of a row the procedure is almost the same. First place the mouse pointer on a borderline of a row, so that the mouse pointer changes to a double-headed arrow pointing up and down. Now click and drag the border to the desired row height.

Moving a Table

After a table has been resized, you may want to reposition it on the slide. To move a table, position the mouse on the left, right, or bottom placeholder border (the mouse pointer changes into a four-headed arrow). Then click and drag the table to the desired location.

Adding Impact with Custom Borders and Shading

When you really want to dazzle your audience and make them sit up and pay attention, customize the table with borders and shading. The table in Figure 28.8 shows a table that has been formatted with customized borders and shading.

FIGURE 28.8

A table with customized borders and shading draws the attention of an audience.

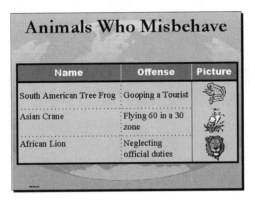

When you create a table in PowerPoint, it is usually formatted with a border around each cell and no fill (or shading). Changes made to the border and fill style affect only those cells that are selected. This enables you to have different borders and fill styles for different table elements, as shown previously. Changing the border or fill style of a table is easy to do. You have two choices: Use the Format Table dialog box or use the Tables and Borders toolbar buttons.

The following steps illustrate making changes using the Format Table dialog box. This dialog box offers a few additional options that are not available from the Tables and Borders toolbar.

If you want to change the border or shading style for the table, use the following steps:

1. Select the cell, row, column or table you want to format.

2. Chose Table, Borders and Fill from the Tables and Borders toolbar to open the Format Table dialog box.

3. Click the Borders tab in the Format Table dialog box if it is not currently displayed.

28

4. Select a border style, color, and width.

5. Click the diagram borders or buttons to change the border style.

 If you click the buttons, you need to click twice. The first click turns the border off, and the second click turns it back on with the new style settings.

6. Click the Preview button to see a preview of your changes.

7. Click the Fill tab.

8. Select a fill color from the fill drop-down list.

9. Click the Preview button to see a preview of your changes.

10. Click the OK button when finished.

Summary

In this chapter, you learned how to create a table in a PowerPoint slide. There are two methods available: using the table AutoLayout or inserting a table. Navigating within a table is easy by using the mouse or arrow keys on the keyboard. You can now enter and edit text that has been added to a table. Setting the alignment of text is also easy when you use the buttons available on the Formatting toolbar and the Tables and Borders toolbar.

Once you create a table, you're ready to modify and customize it. You can insert or delete columns and rows. You also can adjust the width of columns, the height of rows, and the size of a table. Simple changes to a table's border and shading options can add impact to your table.

CHAPTER 29

Multimedia and PowerPoint

This chapter introduces you to the basics of inserting multimedia elements into a PowerPoint presentation. This chapter expands on what you learned previously and enhances your PowerPoint presentations with photos, sound, music, narration, and video.

What Is Multimedia?

Multimedia is sound, pictures, and video that can be used in a presentation to dazzle and entertain an audience. You use multimedia objects, such as clip art, photos, pictures, sound clips, music files you may have on your computer, music or other CD tracks, custom soundtracks, voice narration, and video—in other words, the things that make people say "ooh" and "aah" as you present your PowerPoint slide show.

Other than a gratifying audience response, why would you want to add these fancy multimedia objects to your PowerPoint presentation? After all, you might already have some nice clip art built into your slide show. You can add more piz-zazz to your presentation by incorporating multimedia files. It's been said that a picture is worth a thousand words, so imagine how much more you can say when you can add a photo, music, or video clip to your presentation!

Inserting Sound Files

With slides of information, clip art, and pictures, PowerPoint presentations are effective by themselves. However they can be even more attention-grabbing with sound effects added to the presentation. These sound effects can come from many sources, including a prerecorded sound file, a music track from a CD, or a custom narration for your presen-tation. To use sound files effectively, you must have the proper hardware installed on your computer and the computer that will be used to give the presentation: a sound card, speakers, and a microphone to record narration. If you will be playing a music CD, your computer will also need a CD-ROM drive. Most new computers and many laptop com-puters have everything you need built-in, so they should be able to play sound effects.

> PowerPoint recognizes different types of sound files. The more popular of these are WAV, which are more like real recordings of actual sounds, and MID, which are *MIDI* (*musical instrument digital interface*) music files. Depending on your computer's sound card, these files can sound like either an organ or a full-size orchestra.

Inserting Sound Files from the Clip Gallery

PowerPoint's Clip Gallery might also include a few sound clips that you can include in your presentation. You maneuver through the Clip Gallery the same way you browse for clip art.

> If you find that there are no sound files in the Clip Gallery, never fear—the next few sections cover how to find files on your computer. You can also download some really fantastic sounds from the Web at Microsoft's Clip Gallery Live site. You may need to come back to this section.

To browse the Clip Gallery, use the following steps:

1. Select Insert, Movies and Sounds, Sound from Gallery from the menu. This opens the Insert Sound dialog box, as shown in Figure 29.1.

Import clips from disk   Forward button

FIGURE 29.1

You can insert sounds by using the Insert Sound dialog box.

Back button

Categories

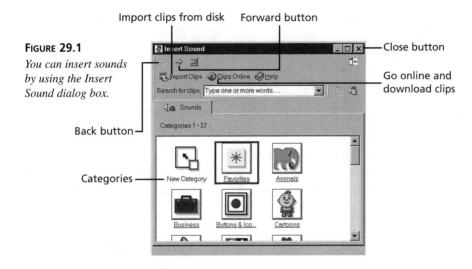

Close button

Go online and download clips

2. Click a Category button (such as Downloaded) to display a list of the sound clips available for that category.

3. Use the Back and Forward navigation buttons, as shown, to help in the viewing of the gallery categories.

4. When you are done browsing, you can insert a sound clip, import a sound clip into the gallery, go to the Web to download sound clip(s), or close the gallery. These options are discussed in detail in the following sections.

When you find a sound clip that you want to play in your presentation, inserting it into your presentation is as easy as inserting a clip art image.

To insert a sound clip from the Clip Gallery, use the following steps:

Skip steps 1–3 if you have already been browsing the Clip Gallery.

1. Select Insert, Movies and Sounds, Sound from Gallery from the menu to open the Insert Sounds dialog box of the Clip Gallery.

2. Click a Category button to display a list of the sound clips available for that category.

3. Use the Back and Forward navigation buttons, as shown, to help in the viewing of the gallery categories.

4. Click the sound clip you want to insert and the Pop-up menu will display.

5. Click the Insert Clip button.

6. Close the Insert Sound dialog box by clicking on the Close button in the upper-right corner.

7. PowerPoint will ask whether you want the sound to play automatically in the slide show. This means that when this particular slide displays, the sound will automatically play. If this is what you want, click Yes. Otherwise, the sound will play only if you click the sound icon that is inserted onto your slide.

After the sound clip has been inserted into a slide, you will see a small speaker icon that represents the sound. You can double-click the icon to play the sound anytime you desire. You can also move or resize the icon just as you would a clip art image, if desired.

Inserting Other Sound Files

PowerPoint also enables you to insert Sound Files that are not in the Clip Gallery, but that you might have on disk or downloaded (see the later section on downloading clips from Microsoft). You probably have many sound files that are available on your computer of which you are unaware. Many of these may have been installed with other software. If you do not know whether you have other sounds, or if you do not know the correct location, PowerPoint comes to your aid once again.

To insert sound files you might have on disk, use the following steps:

1. Select Insert, Movies and Sounds, Sound from File from the menu to open the Insert Sound dialog box.

2. Specify the correct folder location in the Look In box.

3. Click the file you want to insert to select it.

4. Click the OK button to insert the file into your presentation slide.

5. PowerPoint will ask whether you want the sound to play automatically in the slide show. This means that when this particular slide displays, the sound will automatically play. If this is what you want, click Yes. Otherwise, the sound will play only if you click the sound icon.

Playing a CD Track

You can also play music or other sound track from a CD. This does require that you have a CD-ROM drive and a sound card in your computer. Most computers sold now, including many laptop and notebook computers, have these components built in.

To insert an audio track (an icon will be inserted that you can click so the track can be played from the CD), use the following steps:

1. Select Insert, Movies and Sounds, Play CD Audio Track from the menu to open the Movie and Sound Options dialog box, as shown in Figure 29.2.

Use the Movie and Sound Options dialog box to insert a song from a music CD

2. Enter the track number you want to start with and the start time.

3. Enter the track number you want to end with and the end time. The total playing time will be displayed.

4. Click the OK button when finished.

5. PowerPoint will ask whether you want the sound to play automatically in the slide show. This means that when this particular slide displays, the sound will automatically play. If this is what you want, click Yes. Otherwise, the sound will play only if you click the sound icon.

To determine the start and end times of a certain portion of a CD music track, use the Windows CD Player program. Click the Start button and then choose Programs, Accessories, Multimedia, CD Player. The CD Player shows you the running time of a music track. Under the View menu, make sure Track Time Elapsed is checked so you can time the track from beginning to end.

Recording Narration

To record narration for your PowerPoint presentation, you need a sound card with a microphone plugged in. You should also have a script prepared for whatever you want to say.

The sound quality of your narration is directly linked to the quality of your microphone and the amount of ambient noise. Ambient noise can be minimized by closing the door or windows to the room you're in, turning off the radio or TV, waiting for that noisy jet airplane to pass overhead, and so forth. An inexpensive microphone will probably do for the occasional narrative. However, you might want to consider purchasing a good-quality microphone if you plan on creating many high-quality, professional presentations. We do not suggest using built-in microphones as the quality can be extremely poor.

To record narration for a single slide, use the following steps:

1. Choose Insert, Movies and Sound, Record Sound from the menu to open the Record Sound dialog box. (See Figure 29.3.)

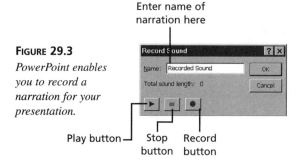

FIGURE 29.3

PowerPoint enables you to record a narration for your presentation.

2. Enter the name of your narration in the Name field.

3. To start recording your narration, click the Record button and start talking into the microphone.

4. When you have finished your narration, click the Stop button. To check your recording, you can play it by clicking the Play button.

5. When you're finished recording, click the OK button. As with other sounds, a speaker icon will appear in the middle of your slide. If you want to play the narration, double-click the speaker icon.

Another option available to you is to record your narration while viewing the slides for your presentation.

To record a narration for the entire show, use the following steps:

1. Select Slide Show, Record Narration from the menu to open the Record Narration dialog box shown in Figure 29.4.

FIGURE 29.4

Record your narration while you view the slides for your presentation.

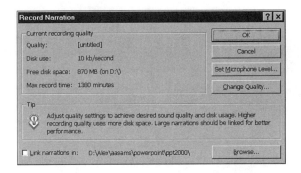

2. Click the Change Quality button to set the recording's sound quality in the Sound Selection dialog box. This enables you to have higher-quality recordings, such as CD quality. After you have set the sound quality, click the OK button.

3. Click the OK button to start the narration.

4. Click the First Slide button to start the narration at the first slide.

5. Record your narration, clicking the mouse to advance to each new slide.

6. When you are finished, you're asked whether you want the save the new timings (because of your added narration) and review them in Slide Sorter View. Click Yes.

You may want to preview your presentation again to see how the narration sounds and then rerecord if necessary.

Adding Video

Video is perhaps the ultimate multimedia object you can add to your PowerPoint presentation. You have a moving picture, as well as sound in a video clip. A video clip, even a short one, can help you make a point in your presentation. Just as with sound clips and photo files, you can get video clips by using either the PowerPoint Clip Gallery or other video files.

Inserting Video Files from the Clip Gallery

As with clip art, pictures, and sound clips, you can also use PowerPoint's built-in Clip Gallery to browse through a selection of video clips.

To use PowerPoint's built-in Clip Gallery to browse through a selection of video clips, use the following steps:

1. Choose Insert, Movies and Sounds, Movie from Gallery to open the Videos tab of the familiar Clip Gallery.

2. Click a Category button (such as Downloaded Clips) to display a list of the video clips available for that category.

3. Use the Back and Forward navigation buttons to help in the viewing of the gallery categories.

4. Click the video clip you want to insert.

 Before you insert a video clip, you·can preview it, just as with a sound clip. To preview a video clip, simply click the clip and then click the Play Clip button.

5. Click the Insert Clip button.

6. Close the Insert Movie dialog box by clicking on the Close button in the upper-right corner.

Inserting Other Video Files

If you have video clips that didn't come with PowerPoint, you can incorporate them, too, just as you can use picture and sound files from other folders on your hard drive. The most common video file formats that work with PowerPoint are AVI, MPG, FLC, and FLI files. AVI and MPG files produce movie-like and television-like video clips. Just as with sound files, you might not even be aware of video files you already have available. You can also download files from the Web or purchase video files if you desire.

To add one of these files to your PowerPoint presentation, use the following steps (they are exactly the same as when you inserted a sound file):

1. Choose Insert, Movies and Sounds, Movie from File to open the Insert Movie dialog box.

2. Specify the correct folder location in the Look in box.

3. Click the file you want to insert to select it.

4. Click the OK button to insert the file into your presentation slide.

5. If you want the video to play automatically in the slide show, click Yes; otherwise, click No.

As with pictures and sound clips, you can resize the video clip and move it to anywhere on the slide. To play the video clip, double-click its icon on the slide (in Slide Show view, just single-click).

You can also search for video files, as you have done for sound files. To search for video files, use the same steps you performed for sound files; simply substitute Movies from File in step 1.

Summary

You now know how to add multimedia object files to your PowerPoint presentation. You now know that in addition to adding clip art to your PowerPoint presentation, you can insert sound and video from the Clip Gallery or from files outside PowerPoint. You also know how to create a narration for your presentation. Your presentations are going to come alive when you insert multimedia into them.

CHAPTER 30

Combining PowerPoint and the Internet

PowerPoint enables you to save presentations in the HTML World Wide Web format so that you can post them on a Web site. This allows people from all over the globe to see your presentation. Although PowerPoint makes converting a presentation into the standard Internet file format very easy, it is not the best tool to use to create an entire Web site. Use PowerPoint's Web publishing option to make your presentation available to others.

Publishing Considerations

There are many benefits available to you when you publish your presentation online. Your presentation can contain hyperlinks to appropriate Web sites anywhere on the Internet. In addition, your audience is not limited to viewing your presentation in a linear format—from slide one, to slide two, to slide three, and so on. Individuals can quickly jump to only the topics in which they are interested, if you have provided the appropriate links. An added bonus is that your audience can view your presentation at any time, from any location, without your assistance.

 A *hyperlink* is text or some other PowerPoint object that has been formatted so that the user can click on it and go to the designated destination. For example, you can click on the words `corvette fever`, in Figure 30.1, and go to the *Corvette Fever* online magazine.

FIGURE 30.1

Click the words `Corvette Fever Magazine` *to link to the online magazine* Corvette Fever.

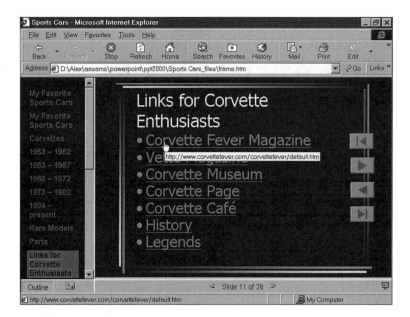

Although you can save any PowerPoint presentation file as a Web page, taking advantage of already completed work, some of the more advanced PowerPoint features, such as animation and sound, may not perform as desired for all your viewers. You need to carefully consider incorporating these features before adding them to an Internet presentation. You should know your target audience's limitations for viewing special effects, large multimedia clips, and complex graphics. For optimum results on the Web, you should design the presentation specifically for the Internet medium.

The Internet offers unique benefits and limitations for a presentation. For the best results, you should keep a few guidelines in mind when you're creating a presentation that will be viewed on the Internet. The next two sections outline the limitations and benefits you need to remember.

Internet Limitations

Unlike standard presentations that rely on a projection screen or printout, the Internet doesn't provide a consistent canvas for your presentation. You must pay attention to the typical hardware and connection limitations of your target audience, as well as the software the viewers will be using. Does your average viewer have a 56K modem and 16-color screen display or a T1 communication line and a true-color screen display? The impact of your presentation depends on how well you target the capabilities of your viewers' machines.

30

You should estimate the page download times and what presentation hardware is likely to be needed. In general, the fancier the presentation, the longer it will take to view it. Using animation, for example, means that the people in your audience must install a special PowerPoint viewer to work with their Web browsers. Most of the time, audience participants don't want to go to the trouble. Therefore, for most projects, you should stay away from animation and large multimedia files. The use of sound, another effective presentation component, depends on an active sound card. Sound cards are not always available in the corporate world and are rare in the educational arena (although it does seem that sooner or later everyone will have these capabilities).

Keep Your Target Audience in Mind

Multimedia items make computer files larger, and the more multimedia, the larger the file. The larger the file, the longer the download time. Therefore, when creating Web pages, you should try to have some idea of who your target audience is and how users will be accessing your Web page(s).

Are you targeting the computer-savvy folks who create games or graphics and have the most up-to-date equipment, including a fast modem or Internet connection? If so, go ahead and throw in some really cool multimedia stuff to attract their attention. They probably wouldn't give your page a second look without it.

If, on the other hand, your target audience is Joe and Jane America, who might be connecting with a much slower modem, keep the graphics and other multimedia stuff to a minimum. If the page takes too long to download, Joe and Jane will usually not stick around long enough to see what you've done.

Internet Benefits

The most compelling benefit of the Internet is being able to gather knowledge from resources around the world. You can greatly enhance your presentation by supplying links to other relevant Internet resources. For example, a presentation on Corvettes can have links to major magazines, company fact sheets, and where to find those hard-to-find parts, as shown in Figure 30.2.

FIGURE 30.2

A presentation designed for the Web about Corvettes has links to other Web sites that may contain useful information.

Navigation buttons ——

Links to other pages —— in the presentation

Links to other —— Internet sites

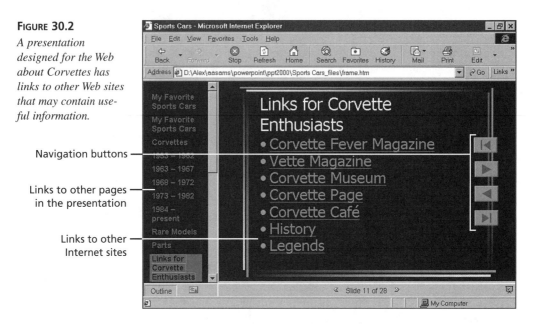

A Web presentation can be more dynamic than an auditorium demonstration because it's not constrained by the one-way dialogue usually associated with standard presentations. On the Internet, the audience is encouraged to interact with the presentation. You can also change the dynamics of the presentation experience; the slide order, for example, could be constructed in a tree hierarchy as opposed to a linear progression.

Publishing a Presentation As a Web Page

If you have already created your presentation in PowerPoint, you can quickly publish it for the Web. Before posting the presentation on the Internet, you must first convert the PowerPoint presentation file into the appropriate format. An Internet presentation is a set of HTML and graphics files that can be viewed by any graphical Web browser. PowerPoint has an option that enables you to easily save and transform a standard presentation into the Internet format.

HTML, which stands for *Hypertext Markup Language*, is the way all documents on the World Wide Web are created. HTML enables every document to be viewed, on the Web, by any type of computer, anywhere in the world. When PowerPoint creates a Web document it uses the standard .HTM extension. All Web pages use this format.

Previewing the Presentation As a Web Page

Before you publish your presentation as an HTML document, you may want to see how it will appear as a Web page. You might be surprised how some things that look just fine in PowerPoint will look a little different on the Web.

To preview your presentation as a Web page (without publishing), use the following steps:

1. If it is not already open, open the presentation by selecting File, Open from the menu. If it is open, save the file by selecting File, Save from the menu.

2. Select File, Web Page Preview from the menu.

PowerPoint will start Internet Explorer and open your presentation file in Internet Explorer, as shown in Figure 30.3. You may want to maximize the Internet Explorer window to better see your presentation.

FIGURE 30.3

You can preview your presentation before you save it as a Web page.

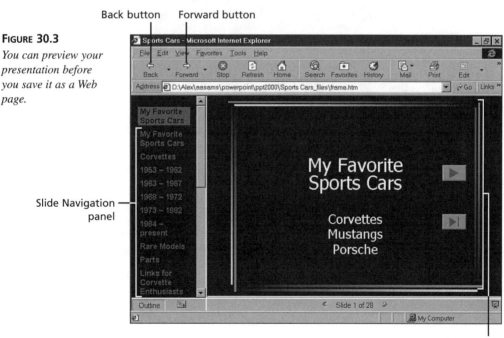

Back button   Forward button

Slide Navigation panel

Slide panel

To view each page in the presentation, click the appropriate title in the Slide Navigation pane. When you are finished, you can exit the Internet Explorer program. If you do not have a Slide Navigation pane in your Web page, this option has not been selected. This option, slide navigation controls, automatically generates the Slide Navigation pane, using the title of each slide as a hyperlink to that slide. This option saves you from hours of work adding links to each slide.

To turn the Automatic Slide Navigation on (or off, if you desire), use the following steps:

1. In PowerPoint, select Tools, Options from the menu to open the Options dialog box.

2. Click the General tab in the Options dialog box, as shown in Figure 30.4.

General tab

FIGURE 30.4

You can change the options of your Web page from the Options dialog box.

Web Options button

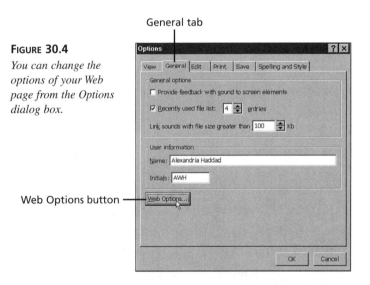

3. Click the Web Options button to open the Web Options dialog box.

4. Click the General tab, if it is not already displayed.

5. Click the Add Slide Navigation Controls check box to turn the feature on, as shown in Figure 30.5. Uncheck this option to turn the feature off.

6. Click the OK button in the Web Options dialog box to close it.

7. Click the OK button in the Options dialog box to close it and accept your changes.

You may find that while viewing your presentation, some items do not look the same on a Web page as they did in a regular presentation. If this is the case, you may need to do a bit of editing to make your presentation Internet-ready. Always keep your pages simple. You do not want your message being overwhelmed by the special effects. Also note that many presentation options do not work well or at all in a Web page, including the following:

- There is no Shadow or Embossed font formatting.
- There are no Spiral, Stretch, Swivel, and Zoom paragraph effects.
- Chart special effects do not work.
- Some animation effects do not work.

FIGURE 30.5

With the Add Slide Navigation Controls check box selected, your presentation will be viewable with a minimum of work.

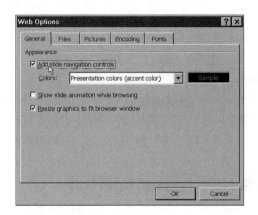

30

For a more complete listing, search the Office Assistant or help files for troubleshooting Web page options.

Publishing the Presentation As a Web Page

After you have your presentation formatted so that it previews nicely, and you have created any navigation buttons necessary, you are ready to publish the presentation as a Web page. When you publish a presentation as a Web page, PowerPoint re-creates the presentation in HTML format. All the graphics that your presentation uses are also saved as separate, supporting files.

Although you can publish a presentation at any time as a Web page on your own computer, it will not be available on the World Wide Web unless you save the file (and all supporting files) to a Web server. Your company may already have access to a Web server; ask your network administrator about the procedures that you need to follow. You can also contact an Internet service provider (ISP) in your area to obtain access to a Web server, to host your Web page, for a small fee. Check with your local library or the Yellow Pages under Internet Services if you do not already have Internet access. There are hundreds of Internet service providers to choose from, so shop around.

When you have access to a Web server, you need to find out where you should save your Web page and supporting files. After you have gotten all this information together, you are ready to go live.

To publish your presentation as a Web page, use the following steps:

1. Save the presentation as you normally would by selecting File, Save from the menu. This step can be skipped if you want to publish your presentation only on the Web and not use it for any other purpose.

2. Select File, Save As Web Page from the menu to open the Save As dialog box.

3. Select the location where you want to save your Web page and supporting files. You should obtain this information from your network administrator or Internet service provider.

4. Enter the filename for your Web page.

5. To change the title that will be displayed in the title bar for all your Web pages, click the Change Title button, enter a new title, and click OK.

6. Click the Save button to save and publish your presentation.

Adding Links in Presentation

With PowerPoint, you can add features quickly to your presentation that are unique to the Internet. Creating a home page, adding hyperlinks to Internet resources, and building action buttons to control the presentation are all tasks you need to learn to build an Internet-ready presentation.

Creating a Home Page

A *home page* is a Web page that acts as an introduction to your presentation. It serves as a type of table of contents for the presentation, providing hyperlinks to the important components. A home page should contain only the main items of interest, so try to keep the home page list of topics as short as possible. Four or five main topic items, at most, are best.

One way to create a home page quickly is to use the summary slide feature of PowerPoint. The summary slide feature enables you to select specific slides, and PowerPoint will create a new slide using each selected slide title as a bullet item on the new slide. Another term for this feature is agenda slide.

To create a summary slide to use for a home page for your Internet presentation, use the following steps:

1. Switch to Slide Sorter view by selecting View, Slide Sorter from the menu or clicking the Slide Sorter button.

2. Select the slides you want to include on the home page (hold down the Ctrl key and click on the slides you're selecting).

3. Click the Summary Slide button on the Slide Sorter toolbar to create the summary slide. (See Figure 30.6.)

Summary Slide button

FIGURE 30.6

Click the Summary Slide button to create a slide with a bullet item by using the title of each selected slide.

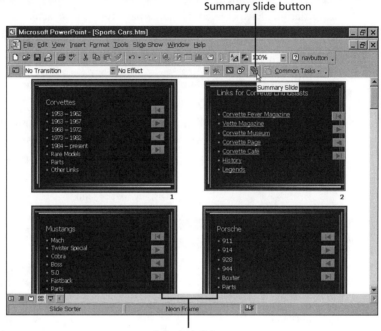

Selected slides

4. After the summary slide has been generated, you may want to move the slide to the beginning of the presentation.

> If you select more than eight slides when creating the home page list, more than one summary slide will be generated. Because Internet browsers enable viewers to scroll the presentation screen, you might want to combine the separate summary screens into one long slide.

After the summary slide has been generated, you should change the generic title Summary Slide to something that is more relevant to your presentation's subject. Simply double-click the summary slide in Slide Sorter view to change to Normal view. You can then edit the title as desired. After you have created a home page, you can format each bullet item with a hyperlink action setting to take your viewers to the appropriate slide, as discussed in the next section.

Hyperlinking to Presentation Resources

A *hyperlink* is a connection between two locations; your presentation viewers can use hyperlinks to guide them to other presentation slides, Internet pages, or even computer files. After you have created the home page for your presentation, you should format each bullet item as a hyperlink to the appropriate page.

Creating a hyperlink is very simple; just follow these steps:

1. Select a presentation item to associate with the hyperlink, such as the first bullet item on your summary slide/home page.

2. Choose Insert, Hyperlink from the menu or click the Insert Hyperlink button on the standard toolbar to open the Insert Hyperlink dialog box.

3. Click the Place in This Document button, as shown in Figure 30.7.

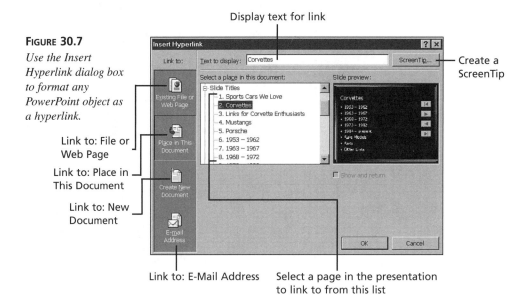

FIGURE 30.7

Use the Insert Hyperlink dialog box to format any PowerPoint object as a hyperlink.

4. Select the page you want to link to from the list of slides.

5. Change the display text, if desired.

6. Create a screen tip, if desired, by clicking the ScreenTip button, entering a tip, and then clicking OK.

7. Click the OK button to complete the hyperlink.

PowerPoint enables you to create hyperlinks that point to many types of resources, including

- Presentation slides
- Internet Web pages or resources
- Email addresses

Slides

A hyperlink can point to any existing presentation slide. In the Insert Hyperlink dialog box, you can select the self-explanatory First Slide, Last Slide, Next Slide, or Previous Slide. These options enable you to provide basic navigation for your viewers. Because most home pages are the first page and "table of contents" of a Web site, you might consider putting a link on each slide that will take your viewer back to the First Slide. Each of your slides should also contain a link to another slide, depending on the course you want your viewers to take while viewing your presentation.

Internet Resources

The most common hyperlink destination added to Internet presentations is the URL hyperlink. A *URL* (uniform resource locator) is the unique address for an Internet resource. When possible, type the full path to the resource so that there are no name conflicts if the presentation is moved to another location. For example, `http://www.sams.com/` is the full path that points to the main index document for the Sams Publishing home page.

To add an Internet resource, use the following steps:

1. Select a presentation item to associate with the hyperlink, such as the first bullet item on your summary slide/home page.
2. Choose Insert, Hyperlink from the menu or click the Insert Hyperlink button on the standard toolbar to open the Insert Hyperlink dialog box.
3. Click the Existing File or Web Page button, as shown in Figure 30.8.
4. Enter the complete Web address in the filename text box or select a Web address from the list of recent files or browsed Pages.
5. Click the OK button when finished.

The URL must be entered as it appears in the address box for the page. URL addresses are also case-sensitive. An easy way to get the address absolutely correct is to copy the address from your Web browser.

Enter the Web address

FIGURE 30.8

The Insert Hyperlink dialog box also enables you to insert a link to any Web page available on the Internet.

Click Recent Files to see files you have recently viewed that are located on your computer

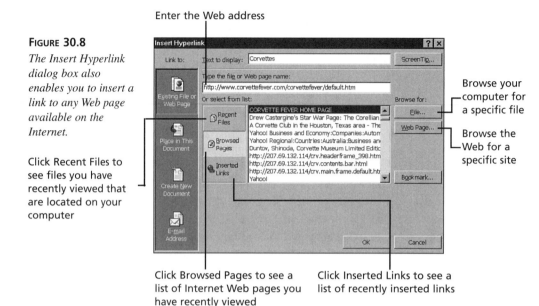

Browse your computer for a specific file

Browse the Web for a specific site

Click Browsed Pages to see a list of Internet Web pages you have recently viewed

Click Inserted Links to see a list of recently inserted links

Using and Adding Action Buttons or Navigation Controls

You can supply action buttons to help your viewers find useful features. When a user clicks an action button, PowerPoint performs a particular action. There are standard icon images that represent common functions or features, or you can create your own custom button image. Here's a list of some common action buttons, although there are several to choose from:

- Home
- Back or Previous
- Forward or Next
- Beginning
- End

Navigation controls can be added to your slide to enable viewers in your audience to view every slide in your presentation without using the Slide Navigation pane. This is necessary, especially for those viewers who do not have browsers that support frames. If you find that you need to add navigation controls to your presentation, it is an easy and painless task. You simply insert a button on each slide that your audience can click to move on to the next slide. Although you need at least one button to go to the Next slide, you are not limited to the number of buttons you can put on your slides.

You can really jazz up your presentation by adding navigation controls. These controls enable the viewer to go to the next slide as well as another section of the presentation.

Use the following steps to add a navigation button to a slide:

1. Display the slide, in PowerPoint, that requires a navigation button.

2. Select AutoShapes, Action buttons from the Drawing toolbar.

3. Click the appropriate button. Figure 30.9 shows the Next button being chosen.

FIGURE 30.9

Select the action button that best represents the type of navigation you want the viewer to perform—for example, move to the next slide.

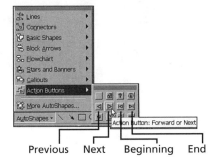

Previous   Next   Beginning   End

4. Drag the mouse on the slide to draw the button, just as if you were drawing any other AutoShape.

5. When you release the mouse button, the Action Settings dialog box will open, as shown in Figure 30.10. If you chose the correct button, you should not need to change any of the settings. Simply click the OK button.

If you have many slides that need the same navigation buttons, you can create all buttons on the first slide, select them all, and then paste them on each slide. For example, suppose you have 50 slides and want each slide to have a Back, Forward, Beginning, and End button. Instead of creating each button one at a time, create all four buttons on slide one. Then select them all (using the lasso method or Shift+Click) and click the Copy button (or select Edit, Copy from the menu). Go to each slide and click the Paste button (or select Edit, Paste from the menu). You will probably want to delete the Back and Beginning buttons from the first slide and the Forward and End buttons from the last slide.

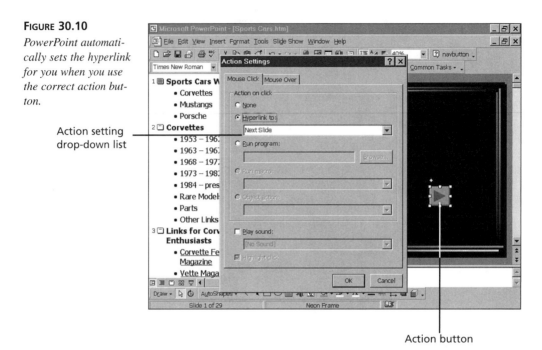

FIGURE **30.10**

PowerPoint automatically sets the hyperlink for you when you use the correct action button.

Action setting drop-down list

Action button

Summary

With PowerPoint, you can display your presentation on the Internet. The presentation is converted into industry-standard HTML pages and graphics files that can be posted on the World Wide Web. Creating an Internet presentation is useful if the audience can't be present in the conference room or auditorium. After reading the material in this chapter, you are now familiar with the steps for creating, saving, and viewing an Internet presentation.

CHAPTER **31**

Automating Presentations with Macros

The true power of computers lies in their capability of automating work that would otherwise have to be done by people. Even though PowerPoint embodies years of user feedback and incorporates many time-saving features, sometimes the developers at Microsoft didn't include a feature or shortcut that you would find useful. What they did include with PowerPoint, however, is a powerful programming language. PowerPoint contains *Visual Basic for Applications* (*VBA*), a subset of the Visual Basic programming language. With VBA, you can create macros that go way beyond mere keystroke recording. In fact, by using the language, macro programmers can now work with many of PowerPoint's internal components. With VBA, you can "teach" PowerPoint to automatically perform many routine tasks at the click of a toolbar button.

Creating and Working with Macros

The Macro dialog box is a centralized location for managing your presentation macros. You can view, run, edit, step into, create, or delete macros. To view all the macros in your presentation, open the Macro dialog box by choosing Tools, Macro, Macros from the menu. Or, you can open the Macro dialog box quickly, shown in Figure 31.1, by pressing Alt+F8 while you're in any presentation view (Slide, Outline, Slide Sorter, or Notes Page).

FIGURE 31.1

The Macro dialog box shows the macros that are available to use in a presentation.

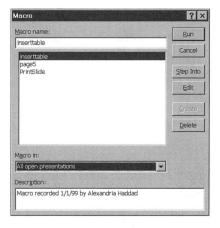

If you have opened a blank presentation without selecting any special templates, the Macro dialog box doesn't list any macros. PowerPoint has three methods you can use to add macros to a presentation file:

- You can record a macro that contains keystrokes, mouse movements, and menu commands.
- You can open a presentation from a macro template.
- You can directly code or copy VB macro subroutines.

Copying existing macros from sample code files is a quick way to become familiar with the power and flexibility of the Visual Basic for Applications language. The section "Finding More Macro Information," later in this chapter, will teach you the steps for finding a wealth of sample code available from the Microsoft Web site.

Creating Macros

The easiest way to create a macro is to record the keystrokes as you replicate the task you want to automate.

To record a new macro, follow these steps:

1. Choose Tools, Macro, Record New Macro from the menu to open the Record Macro dialog box. (See Figure 31.2.)

2. Enter a name in the Store macro in field should indicate which presentation file will contain the macro. You can select the current presentation or select All Open Presentations from the drop-down list to apply the macro to presentations that are currently open.

4. Click OK to start recording.

5. Execute the keystrokes or commands.

6. Click the Stop Recording button when you are finished. (See Figure 31.3.)

FIGURE 31.2

Enter a name for your macro in the Record Macro dialog box.

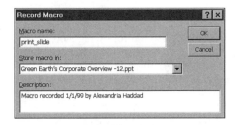

FIGURE 31.3

The Macro toolbar is displayed while you record a macro.

Stop button

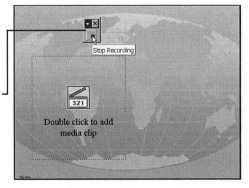

Because PowerPoint doesn't actually record keystrokes in a macro, some actions cannot be used. For example, you can't modify the Tools, Options dialog box using a macro. When you are recording a macro, PowerPoint analyzes your mouse and keyboard actions and converts them into the appropriate VBA text command. If there is no corresponding VBA command for the operation, the macro will not work as intended.

31

Running a Macro

After you have created a macro, you can run it at any time. Running a macro means executing the programming commands within the macro. There are two ways to run a macro: You can use the menu, or add a button to a toolbar that represents the macro.

To run the macro from the menu, use the following steps:

1. Select Tools, Macro, Macros from the menu.
2. Click the macro name you want to run.
3. Click the Run button.

To quickly access and run a PowerPoint macro with a single click, you may want to attach it to a button on either a built-in or custom toolbar. You can then run the macro by clicking the toolbar button.

To add a macro button to a toolbar, use the following steps:

1. Select View, Toolbars to display the toolbar you want to add the macro button to, if it is not already displayed.
2. Choose Tools, Customize to open the Customize dialog box.
3. Click the Commands tab and select Macros from the Categories list, as shown in Figure 31.4.

FIGURE 31.4
Use the Customize dialog box to assign a macro to a toolbar button.

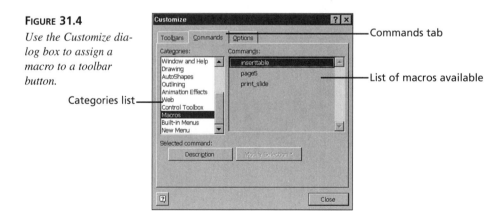

4. Click and drag the macro name onto the appropriate toolbar. A large I-beam will display where the button will appear.
5. Click the Close button.

After you have added a macro button to a toolbar, you may want to customize the button's display attributes so that it is a small icon instead of the macro name.

To add a macro button to a toolbar, use the following steps:

1. Select Tools, Customize from the menu to open the Customize dialog box, if it is not already open.

2. Click once on the macro button you want to customize to select it.

3. Click the Modify Selection button to open the drop-down list shown in Figure 31.5.

FIGURE 31.5

The Modify Selection drop-down list offers many choices.

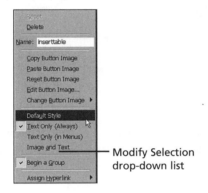

Modify Selection drop-down list

31

4. Select Default Style from the menu. This will change the button to a blank button.

5. Click the Modify Selection button again, select Change Button Image, and click a button image from the choices available.

6. Click the Close button when finished.

To remove a macro button from a toolbar (but not delete the macro), use the following steps:

1. Select Tools, Customize from the menu.

2. Drag the button off the toolbar into the presentation window to remove the button from the toolbar.

Deleting Macros

In PowerPoint, you can also remove unused macros. If you frequently use pre-existing macro templates, you might want to delete the unused macros to conserve memory resources.

Here's how to delete a macro:

1. Choose Tools, Macro, Macros from the menu.

2. Select the macro you want to delete.

3. Click the Delete button.

4. Click the Yes button to verify that you do want to delete the macro.

The macro is then deleted from the presentation file.

Using Pre-existing Template Macros

Macros can be stored in presentation template files and "copied" into your existing presentation. To use template macros in a presentation, you need to create the presentation from the pre-existing template.

Follow these steps to embed template macros in your presentation:

1. Choose File, New from the menu.

2. Select the template containing the macros you want to use.

3. Click OK.

If you have already built slides that you want to include in the new presentation, add them to the newly created presentation by choosing Insert, Slides from Files from the menu.

 When you apply a template to an existing presentation, the macros in the template are not added to the presentation.

Using the VBA Editor

After recording a macro, PowerPoint tries to reduce the sequence of recorded PowerPoint commands to a series of VBA commands that would have the same effect. If you find that you want to record more powerful macros, you may need to use the VB Editor. The VB Editor is a separate program you can use to customize, create, and debug macros using the VB programming language.

Editing a Macro Using the VB Editor

You may find that sometimes a macro is not working the way you had intended. This may be caused by the way your mouse and keystrokes were converted into Visual Basic. For example, if you record a macro and press the Page Down key five times (from slide one), it will be rewritten in Visual Basic as a macro that goes to slide six. To create a macro that would move down five slides, you would have to use the Visual Basic Editor to edit the default macro and make it work the way you intended.

To use the VB Editor and edit a specific macro:

1. Choose Tools, Macro, Macros from the menu.

2. Select the name of the macro to edit.

3. Click Edit. The Visual Basic Editor is then launched, as shown in Figure 31.6, with the edit cursor positioned at the macro you chose. You can now edit the macro commands to modify how it works.

Figure 31.6

The Visual Basic Editor enables you to manually edit a macro.

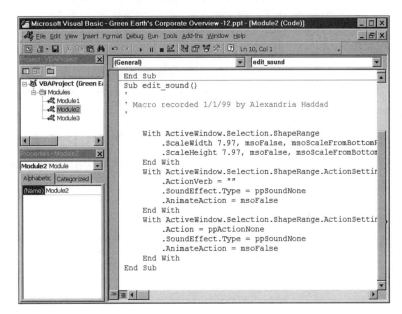

31

4. Edit the macro as desired.

5. Select File, Close and Return to Microsoft PowerPoint from the menu.

 The Visual Basic Editor has a different Help file than PowerPoint does. To view VBE's Help file, choose Help, Contents and Index from the Visual Basic menu.

Using the VB Editor to Create a Macro

By including the Visual Basic Editor (VBE), PowerPoint gives you a built-in programming environment with a wealth of features. The editor is a subset of the popular Visual Basic language. Use the editor to edit, write, debug, and manage macro script code. The editor also has many useful windows that help you explore the VBA language.

You can open the editor in one of two ways:

- Choose Tools, Macro, Visual Basic Editor from the main menu.
- Press Alt+F11 while you're in any view.

There are entire books that focus on Visual Basic's impressive capabilities, but the following sections just highlight the basic features you need to create macros.

You can easily cut and paste or drag and drop sample code into a macro module. Open the Visual Basic Editor and choose View, Code from the menu, or press F7 to display the Visual Basic Editor window. After you copy or add VBA code to the window, the macros are automatically displayed and available in PowerPoint's Macro dialog box.

The Visual Basic Help files and Object Browser are useful reference sources; they can give you insight into the objects with which macro subroutines can work.

Finding More Macro Information

To find the latest information about using Visual Basic for Applications with PowerPoint, check out the Microsoft Support Page on the Web. You can find sample code for common automation tasks and useful tips and tricks that can save you time when programming PowerPoint macros.

To search for PowerPoint macro samples and tips using the Microsoft Support Page, log on to the Internet and point your browser to

http://support.microsoft.com/support/default.asp.

Summary

PowerPoint can be completely customized by adding macros written in the Visual Basic for Application programming language. You can create presentation macros to automate a wide variety of tasks. You might want to invest some time creating macros for tasks you perform often. Macros are also helpful for reducing complex command sequences to a simple button click.

Part X

Designing Web Sites with FrontPage

Chapter

CHAPTER 32

Introducing FrontPage

Although the Web may be old news to you, there's a lot of new news to report about FrontPage. With the release of this software, Microsoft has made Web publishing a core part of its Microsoft Office suite. FrontPage provides advanced generation and editing for Web pages.

Acquaint Yourself with FrontPage

FrontPage comprises all the tools you need to create, publish, and manage a World Wide Web site. Each of these tools is integrated into a single program, which is one of those good news, bad news kind of things.

The bad news is that there are a large number of things to learn about this all-in-one software package. Creating, publishing, and managing a Web site are all substantive tasks that have traditionally been handled by several different types of software: page editors, file transfer programs, hyperlink verifiers, and more.

The good news: You don't have to learn the quirks of several different programs or keep track of which program handles which task. Learning to use FrontPage is like learning to use Microsoft Word; although Word has hundreds of different features, the basic mechanics of creating and editing a document are fairly simple. You type text into a window, click a few buttons or menu options to format the text, and save your work. You can start using Word long before you have mastered its more sophisticated features.

Although most people call a collection of related Web pages a Web site, Microsoft FrontPage refers to them as *Webs*. This term is used throughout the book, because you'll be encountering it often when using the software and its built-in help system.

Discover FrontPage's Features

Like most Microsoft software titles, FrontPage sports dozens of features. Here is a sampling of what you get:

- *Custom themes*—Select one of the 60 existing themes and personalize it by selecting new colors, logos, images, and other page elements.

- *Color tools*—Color selection is enabled throughout the software with a color picker, color wheel, and a dropper that can grab a color from a graphic.

- *Roundtrip HTML*—For the first time, FrontPage can read in an existing Web page and save it without changing any of the existing HTML code or its formatting.

- *Visible HTML tags*—While still viewing a page normally in the editing window, you can make the HTML tags that comprise the page visible.

- *Easy access to Microsoft Access*—Incorporate Access database files into Web pages for viewing and editing. Users can even create Access databases from within a Web page.

- *Web components*—Add sophisticated interactive features to a Web page with FrontPage and Office components such as an Excel Spreadsheet component and a Search component.

- *Automatic page linking*—By using the new AutoLink component, adding a new page to a Web can automatically cause related hyperlinks to appear on other pages.

- *Browser targeting*—If you decide which browsers and features you're creating a Web for, FrontPage will restrict its features to those supported by that target audience.

This list represents only a sample of FrontPage features. Of course, FrontPage shares common user interface elements such as toolbars, shortcuts, and menus with other Office applications.

FrontPage also shares a common file format with the other applications such as Excel and Word: HTML. Each Office program can save its documents as Web pages. These pages can be loaded by FrontPage for editing without losing any of their information. A Word document can go from Word to FrontPage and back to Word, never losing its font selections or paragraph formatting.

Run the Software for the First Time

After you've installed and started FrontPage, you'll see the FrontPage graphical user interface. Figure 32.1 shows the FrontPage screen with a Web page loaded.

FIGURE 32.1

Running FrontPage.

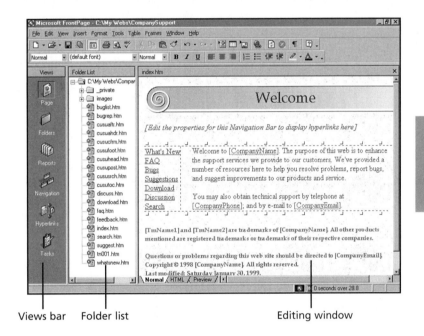

Views bar   Folder list   Editing window

In Figure 32.1, FrontPage is being used to edit a page that's part of a customer support Web. The three main sections of the interface consist of a Views bar, Folder list, and Editing window.

The FrontPage user interface takes on six different appearances depending on the view you've selected. *Views* are different ways that you can explore a Web as you work on it in FrontPage. (You've seen Word, Outlook, and PowerPoint views if you read earlier chapters.)

Views are chosen by using a set of icons inside the Views Bar identified in Figure 32.1. The view you select determines the kind of work you can do to the Web, and the following icons can be selected:

- *Page*—Edit a Web page
- *Folders*—Explore a Web's file folders and files
- *Reports*—View reports related to a Web
- *Navigation*—Navigate a Web's organizational structure
- *Hyperlinks*—View the way a Web's pages have been hyperlinked
- *Tasks*—Plan the upcoming tasks in a Web's development

All work that you do within FrontPage revolves around the Views bar.

The Folder list shown in Figure 32.1 lists all files and folders associated with the current Web. Clicking one of the listed Web pages opens that page in the Editing Window.

> The Views bar and Folder list can be closed to make room for other windows on the FrontPage interface. Use the View, Views Bar and View, Folder List menu options to close these windows. You can use the same options to open these windows if they have been closed.

The Editing window functions like a word processor's editing window. You can add, edit, and delete Web page elements such as text and images.

There are two toolbars running along the top of the FrontPage interface, as shown in Figure 32.2.

FIGURE 32.2
The Standard and Formatting toolbars.

Standard toolbar   Formatting toolbar

The Standard toolbar and Formatting toolbar are used primarily when you're editing a Web page in the Page view. These toolbars are dockable, which means that you can move them around the FrontPage interface if you don't like where they have been placed.

To dock a toolbar, grab it with your mouse and drag it to the left, right, top, or bottom edges of the FrontPage interface. If you place the toolbar on the left or right edge, it will be displayed vertically instead of horizontally. You also can drag a toolbar off the FrontPage interface entirely, which puts it into a new window on your system desktop.

If you can't find a way to grab a dockable toolbar in a Windows program, look for a line that separates two buttons on the toolbar—the Standard toolbar in FrontPage has several of them. Click your mouse on top of one of these lines and hold down your mouse button to drag the toolbar around.

Take Different Views of a Web

Most of the work you do in FrontPage will be accomplished in the Page view. Each of the other five views is more specialized.

The Folders view opens a Windows Explorer-style list of the files and folders that make up a Web. You can use it to do any of the things that Windows Explorer is used for: opening, moving, renaming, and deleting files. You also can see the title, size, and modification date of each page in a Web.

The Tasks view is used to create and manage a to-do list of the tasks associated with your Web. If you're working on a Web alone and want to keep track of your progress, or collaborating with others who need to see what you've been doing, the Tasks view provides a built-in project manager.

View Reports About a Web

The Reports view, shown in Figure 32.3, opens a list of reports that tell you more about your Web.

Each report in this view has a description that explains its purpose. Eight of the reports list files included in the Web based on specific criteria.

The report that lists unlinked files is useful to determine when one or more Web pages are not connected to the rest of your Web. These pages can't be reached by a person who goes to the main page of your Web and uses hyperlinks to visit every page in your site. Unless there's a reason not to make these pages a part of the Web, you can use this report when either deleting the files to save space or adding links on those pages.

Another useful report lists the pages in a Web that would take 30 seconds or more to download using a 28,800-baud Internet connection (also called *28.8*).

One of the things you must keep in mind as a Web developer is the way your audience connects to the Internet. Most people are using a dial-up modem to connect to an Internet service provider, load their Web browser, and start viewing pages, although more people are signing up for DSL and cable modems each month.

32

FIGURE 32.3

The Reports view.

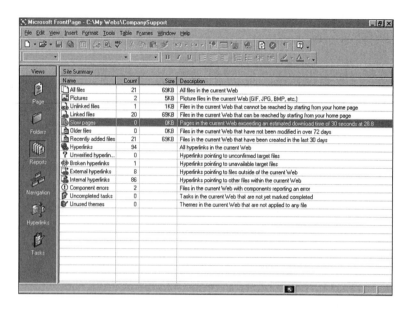

The 30-second report considers all parts of a Web page: text, images, interactive programs like Java applets, and anything else that is downloaded when the page is viewed in a browser. The half-minute wait is a reasonably good benchmark for when you should start worrying if a page contains too much text, graphics, and other elements.

The 28.8 connection and 30 seconds can both be customized. You can set a different speed and different time by selecting the Tools, Options menu item and opening the Reports View tabbed dialog box. Figure 32.4 shows this dialog box and the speeds that can be used: 14.4, 28.8, 56.6, ISDN, T1, and T3.

FIGURE 32.4

Customizing several Web reports.

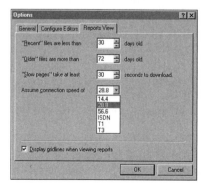

The Reports View dialog box also can be used to change the number of days that constitutes a recently added or older file in a Web—two other reports you can run.

Five reports that you can see in the Reports view concern the hyperlinks used in a Web. These reports enable you to find links that will cause a "file not found" error if they are used. You can report on bad links that are a part of your Web and bad links to other addresses on the World Wide Web.

In order to see a fully up-to-date hyperlinks report, you must click Tools, Recalculate Links before selecting the report. FrontPage will check all links, including external ones to other Web addresses if you're currently connected to the Internet. This can take five minutes or longer, depending on how many other Web addresses are contained in hyperlinks on your Web.

When you find a bad link, you can update it directly from within the Reports view by clicking the line in the report that displays this link. This can be a huge timesaver if your Web contains a large number of hyperlinks, because it's faster than loading each page into the Editing Window and finding the erroneous link.

View the Structure of a Web

The last two views of FrontPage are the Navigation and Hyperlinks views, which provide two different ways to look at your Webs in a visual manner.

The Hyperlinks view displays the relationship between a page and all Web addresses that it hyperlinks to, whether they're part of the same Web or available somewhere else on the World Wide Web. This view is shown in Figure 32.5.

32

FIGURE 32.5

The Hyperlinks view.

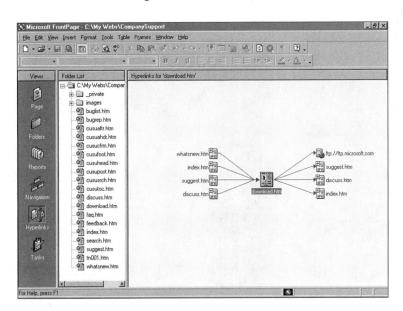

By clicking the + icon on any page in the Hyperlinks view, you can see all of its hyperlinks. You also can move a page to the center of the Hyperlinks view by right-clicking the page's icon and selecting the Move to Center pop-up menu item.

Pages can be opened for editing, deleted, and opened in a Web browser for viewing from the Hyperlinks view.

The Navigation view is used to establish a Web's navigational structure. Figure 32.6 shows the Navigation view for a customer support Web.

Each icon in the Navigation view represents a page in the Web. You might think that this view is redundant, because hyperlinks already establish the way a Web is navigated.

FrontPage supports the use of navigation bars—a group of common hyperlinks that can be placed on all pages of a Web for easy navigation. These bars can be made up of graphics or text.

Almost all large Webs have a common navigational structure. A sports site could have a navigation bar that enables visitors to go to specific hockey-, baseball-, football-, and basketball-related pages. A political news site could have a navigation bar with links to elections, allegations, resignations, condemnations, and legislation.

As shown in Figure 32.6, the customer support Web has several pages that can be immediately loaded using its navigation bar: What's New, FAQ, Bugs, Suggestions, Download, Discussion, and Search.

FIGURE 32.6

The Navigation view.

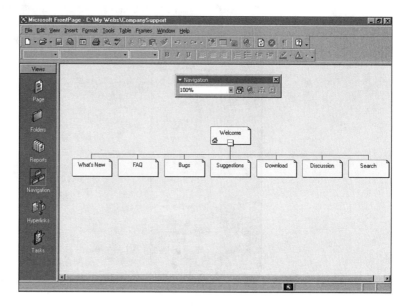

Putting this bar on each page of the Web makes it easier for people to go directly to the information they want from your Web. Navigation bars also can include a link to the Web's home page and establish an order in which pages should be viewed.

Figure 32.7 shows a page of the customer support Web with two navigation bars:

- A vertical bar with home, back, and next graphics
- A horizontal bar with text links for What's New, Bugs, Suggestions, Download, Discussion, and Search (there's no FAQ link because it's the current page)

FIGURE 32.7

A Web page with one graphic and one text navigation bar.

Graphic navigation bar

Text navigation bar

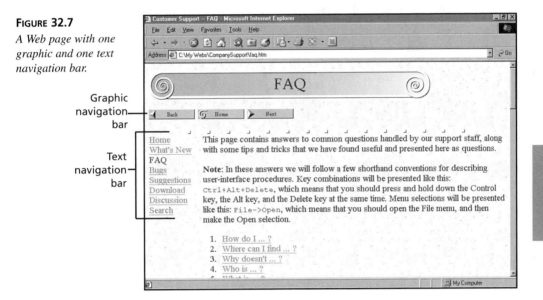

Links added to a page through a navigation bar do not show up in the Hyperlinks view.

Summary

All work you do in FrontPage begins by selecting a view—the six different ways to look at a Web. The Views Bar contains icons for each of these options: Page, Folders, Reports, Hyperlinks, Navigation, and Tasks. Moving from view to view, you can do everything that's needed to create a Web, keep its content up-to-date, and easily fix things such as broken hyperlinks.

CHAPTER 33

Using Templates to Quickly Create a Web

As you get ready to create your first Web in FrontPage, the program may look as imposing as a line of Chinese mountains in need of a wall. Knowing where to start, and what to do, can be a daunting task when you've never used the software. FrontPage makes the task less daunting through the use of templates, built-in Webs that the software knows how to create by itself.

Templates enable you to develop a complete Web in a few minutes, then spend your efforts customizing that Web rather than creating it from scratch. Although they won't work with all Webs, templates are a huge timesaver when they are suitable for your projects. During this chapter, you'll create your first Web in a matter of minutes, an accomplishment made possible through the use of a template.

Discover FrontPage Templates

Templates are standard Webs or Web pages that FrontPage can build upon request. You may have used them earlier if you worked through the Word or

PowerPoint chapters earlier in the book. FrontPage includes 48 different templates, and they match some of the most common ways that publishers use the World Wide Web.

The built-in templates include a personal Web, a corporate Web, customer feedback Web pages, and site search pages.

To create a new Web with a template, use the File, New, Web menu command. To create a new page, use File, New, Page instead. In either case, a dialog box will open listing the templates that are available, along with a list of wizards.

Wizards simplify a task by breaking it down into discrete steps. In FrontPage, wizards can create a Web or Web page based on the answers you provide in a series of dialog boxes.

Figure 33.1 shows a dialog box listing the templates and wizards that you can use to create a new Web.

FIGURE 33.1

Selecting a template for a new Web.

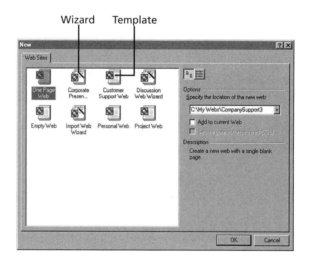

All Webs and Web pages start from templates, even if you don't want FrontPage to do any work for you. If you're creating a Web that should not contain any built-in pages, choose the Empty Web template. If you're creating an empty page, the Normal Page template should be selected.

Select a Web Template

Before you can create a page in FrontPage, you must create a Web that will contain that page. Because all Webs start from a template, you must choose one to start a project.

The following templates can be used to start a Web:

- *Empty Web*—A Web containing no pages
- *One Page Web*—A Web with a single blank page
- *Personal Web*—A Web for personal information
- *Customer Support Web*—A 19-page Web that enables a company to offer customer support for one or more of its products
- *Project Web*—A 23-page Web devoted to a collaborative project, with pages for member information, project status, a schedule, group discussions, and an archive

When choosing a template, you must also choose the location where the Web will be saved. Webs can be saved to disk or to a World Wide Web server.

If you save a Web to disk, you must save it again on a World Wide Web server to make it publicly available. This is also called publishing a Web, because it's analogous to publishing things such as books. A Web must be made available on a Web server before the outside world can visit it.

Before you can save a Web to a Web server, you must have a username and password for that server.

To save a Web to disk, specify a folder where the Web should be stored. This folder should only be used to store files related to your Web. If it doesn't already exist, FrontPage will create it.

Although it adds an extra step, you should save all Webs to disk and publish them on the Web separately. This prevents you from losing any files in the event that the Web server crashes or the server's administrator deletes your site.

33

After a template and location have been selected for a new Web, FrontPage creates all pages contained in the Web, and any subfolders that are needed. Each of the built-in templates includes private and images subfolders.

The images subfolder holds any graphics files that are part of the Web. The private subfolder, which initially contains no files, can be used as a place for files that should be hidden from visitors to your Web. If you create a Web that collects information such as a visitor's name and mailing address, the private subfolder is a good place to keep it away from prying eyes.

Despite its name, the _private folder is actually as public as everything else when your Web is created. You must use FrontPage security features to hide the folder's contents, which is possible only on Web hosts that are equipped with FrontPage Server Extensions. Fortunately, most Web hosts now provide FrontPage Server Extensions so all the FrontPage features should work well for your Webs.

If the template contains any pages, the main page of the Web will be named index.htm.

 The filename index.htm is one of several names that are commonly used for a Web's main page—also called its *home page*. Others are index.html, default.htm, and default.html.

Customize a Template

After a new Web has been created from a template, you can begin making changes to customize the Web.

If you're creating a home page for yourself or someone you're exceptionally familiar with, the Personal Web template is a good starting point.

This five-page template includes the following elements:

- A main page with space for an introduction
- A page to display photos
- A page to describe several hobbies and interests
- A page to list your favorite Web sites

A navigation bar provides links to each of these pages, as shown in Figure 33.2.

By loading each of these pages in the Page view, you can edit several different things: text, hyperlinks, navigation bars, timestamps, and page banners.

Edit text by placing your cursor anywhere within the text and using your keyboard. You also can employ features common to most word processors: text highlighting, cut-and-paste, and the Formatting toolbar.

Some things on a page look like text but are actually something else, such as hyperlinks or timestamps.

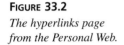

Figure 33.2

The hyperlinks page from the Personal Web.

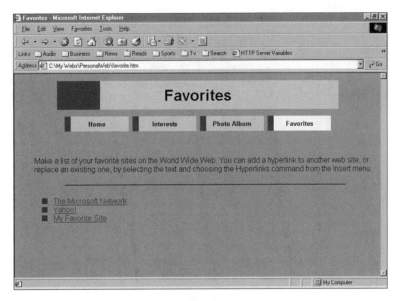

As you move the cursor over different parts of a page, the cursor changes depending on what it's placed on. FrontPage also may display a ToolTip—a small box of informative text—that describes how you can modify that part of the page.

Navigation bars, timestamps, and page banners are all components—special page elements that add functionality to a FrontPage Web.

The main page of this Web, `index.htm`, contains a timestamp component immediately after the text `This page last updated on` and before the period at the end of the sentence. The timestamp displays the date that the page was last edited, and changes automatically each time changes are made to the page.

The timestamp component makes it easy to tell visitors how current the information on a page is. You don't have to enter the date using text and change it manually during each page update.

Placing the cursor above a timestamp causes the cursor to change to a hand-and-page icon. Double-click the timestamp and a dialog box will open enabling you to edit how it is presented. This dialog box is shown in Figure 33.3.

Each FrontPage component is edited using a dialog box like the one shown in Figure 33.3.

The timestamp component can be modified to display a date, a time, or both. You also can choose the format that the time and date are displayed in. After making the change, press the F5 function key, also called the Refresh button.

33

FIGURE 33.3

Editing a timestamp component.

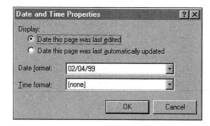

The Refresh button works like the one on a Web browser, which causes a Web page to be completely redrawn. The Refresh button on FrontPage should be pressed after any components on a page are changed.

Another component that you can modify is the page banner, a heading atop a page that can serve as its title.

Each page in the personal Web template has a banner at the top. By default, the banner is graphical—text appears over a simple graphic file.

To change a banner, double-click it to bring up the Page Banner Properties dialog box, as shown in Figure 33.4.

FIGURE 33.4

Editing a page banner component.

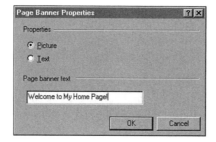

You can change the text of a banner and determine whether it should be displayed as a picture or text.

Any changes to a page's banner will be made to that page's icon in the Navigation view, changing the text of navigation bars that link to the page. A page banner serves as a title for that page.

The Personal Web also includes several different hyperlinks. Some of these are part of the navigation bar, a FrontPage component that uses the Navigation view to determine which links should be displayed.

Other hyperlinks can be edited directly. The favorite.htm page of the Personal template contains three of these hyperlinks. One leads to Yahoo!, another to the Microsoft Network, and a third to something called My Favorite Site.

Each hyperlink consists of two things:

- The Web address that the link leads to
- The part of a page that should be clicked to visit the link

Hyperlinks can be associated with any element of a Web page, including text, graphics, or a combination of both. The Web address is also called a *URL*, an acronym that stands for *Uniform Resource Locator.*

The URL can link to anything on the World Wide Web, such as pages, graphics, and other files. It also can link to something within the current Web.

Text that is being used as a hyperlink can be changed with the keyboard like any other text on a page.

Changing a hyperlink's URL is different than editing a component. Right-click the hyperlink and select the Hyperlink Properties pull-down menu command. The Edit Hyperlink dialog box will open, as shown in Figure 33.5.

FIGURE 33.5

Editing a hyperlink's URL.

33

The Edit Hyperlink dialog box looks like the one that appears whenever you're opening a file in Windows. If you're linking to another page or file in the current Web, you can select it using this dialog box.

If the link is to an address on the World Wide Web such as `http://www.fp2k.com/24`, enter this in the dialog's URL field.

After changing the URL, you can test it in a Web browser by clicking Preview in Browser on the Standard toolbar. If the URL links to an address on the World Wide Web, you need to connect to the Internet before trying it out.

Try It Yourself: Create Your Own Personal Web

You now should be able to create a personalized Personal Web, your first real Web in FrontPage.

Use the Personal Web template to create a person's home page. The person in question can be you, someone you're familiar with, or someone you hope to become familiar with—once they see the Web that has been created in their honor.

This Web should have each of the following:

- An introduction on the main page that describes the person in a few sentences
- An interests page that describes three of the person's interests
- A hyperlinks page that links to three of the person's favorite Web sites

If you have photos of the person, you should use some of them on the photo page that's part of a Personal Web.

Also, change the page banner of the interests page to Hobbies instead of Interests. This change will require some changes to the text of that page, and it also should appear on the navigation bar throughout the Web.

While you're working, you may accidentally delete a component or hyperlink you're working on. You can add a new one to replace it using one of the following menu commands:

- Insert, Date and Time for a timestamp
- Insert, Page Banner
- Insert, Hyperlink

The last thing you should do is personalize the text on each of the pages, removing anything that doesn't make sense. Use interesting, energetic language to describe the subject of this Web, especially if you're developing it in someone's honor.

After making all of these changes, preview the Web in a browser. Before previewing the pages, FrontPage will give you an opportunity to save anything that hasn't been saved yet.

Summary

Templates are a great way to reduce the amount of time it takes to develop a Web. When they are applicable to a project you're working on, they're a great timesaver. Your efforts are spent customizing a template instead of starting from a bunch of empty Web pages.

CHAPTER 34

Applying Themes and Wizards

There was a time when the World Wide Web was almost entirely text. The information contained on a Web was more important than the different ways that browsers displayed it. That time ended a few minutes after a new Web page element was introduced—the image file. Images such as GIF and JPG files could be displayed on the Web as part of pages, creating a new expectation for what sites should look like.

Most Web users expect sites to be easy to use and visually interesting. FrontPage makes this part of Web design easier through the use of themes, packages of coordinated graphics that can be applied to your Webs.

FrontPage automates even more complex tasks through the use of wizards. Wizards, as you encountered in earlier chapters using other Office programs, are programs that ask a series of questions about a project you're trying to complete. Your answers control how the program does its work. Wizards in Microsoft FrontPage can be thought of as templates with brains. They are used to create Webs and Web pages that are too variable to be handled with a template.

Sample the FrontPage Themes

As a Web publisher, one of your most important tasks is to establish the visual appearance of your site. This is determined by each of the following, among other things:

- The color of text and hyperlinks
- The color or image used as a background
- The fonts used
- The images and navigation bars

Another choice you must make is whether these things should vary from page to page or be consistent throughout an entire Web. Using the same visual elements makes it easier for a visitor to know they're still on your Web. It also can make a Web easier to navigate, if you've kept the layout consistent and used navigation bars.

FrontPage enables you to establish the visual identity of a Web by assigning a theme to it.

Themes establish the visual appearance of a Web or a Web page by defining its colors, fonts, text, and images.

Select a Web Theme

There are more than a dozen themes included with FrontPage. Themes are selected by using the Format, Theme menu command. A Themes dialog box opens that enables you to preview each available theme before applying it to any part of your Web, as shown in Figure 34.1.

The themes in FrontPage are given short names that help describe their appearance. Blueprint is a technical-looking theme that resembles draftsman's markings. Citrus Punch features tropical flowers and bright colors. Blank, though not actually blank, is relatively plain.

Select each theme to see a preview of it in the dialog's Sample of Theme window. The Romanesque theme is shown in Figure 34.1.

The first choice you must make is whether to apply your chosen theme to a page or your entire Web. If you choose a single-page theme, it will be applied to the page that's currently open in Page view.

You can remove all themes by choosing (No theme) in the Themes dialog box.

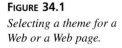

Figure 34.1

Selecting a theme for a Web or a Web page.

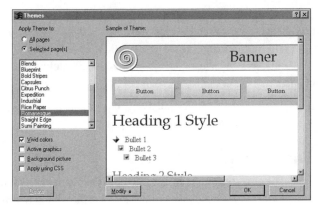

The next decision to make is whether to select any of the following options:

- Vivid colors
- Active graphics
- Background picture
- Apply using CSS

The Vivid colors option determines whether the theme will use a variety of bright colors or a white background and darker colors.

If a theme uses vivid colors, it will have a bright background color such as light green or yellow and other colors that work well on that background.

If a theme does not use vivid colors, the background will be white and all other colors will be darker, making them easier to read.

This color choice will not be as significant if you use the theme's background image. This causes a graphic to be tiled—repeated over and over like tiles on a kitchen floor—underneath the contents of a page. The difference between vivid and darker colors is less noticeable over a background image.

Choosing Active graphics adds some animation effects to the theme. One common feature of an animated theme is a navigation bar with buttons that change in response to mouse movement. These are called *hover buttons*, because the buttons change when a mouse hovers over them.

FrontPage creates this effect through the use of one of the scripting languages that it supports: JavaScript or VBScript. All of the scripting is handled internally by FrontPage, so you don't have to be familiar with these languages to make use of them on your Webs.

34

The last option you can enable with a theme is to apply it using *CSS (Cascading Style Sheets)*. Style sheets are a standard for Web browsers that has been recently implemented in Navigator and Internet Explorer. They enable the basic visual elements of a page—its text, colors, fonts, and formatting—to be defined separately from the information the page contains.

Since a theme is a representation of a Web's visual appearance, it makes sense to define it through the use of Cascading Style Sheets.

Removing Unused Themes

Every theme that you apply to a Web adds more than a dozen graphics files to it. These files are used behind-the-scenes by FrontPage, and they include hover buttons, the background picture, and the graphic behind every page banner.

If you apply a theme to a specific page, the files used by this theme stay around even if that page is later deleted.

You can find and delete these files with the Unused Themes report on the Reports view. This report lists the number of themes that are no longer associated with any part of the current Web.

To remove these files, double-click the line of the Reports view that lists Unused Themes. FrontPage must recalculate the hyperlinks of the Web before it can finish this task, so you need to be connected to the Internet.

Assign a Theme to a Web

During the last chapter, you created a Web using the Personal Web template. Although you might not have realized it at the time, you were using a theme. The Personal Web, like all built-in templates, has a default theme that it applies to all pages in the Web.

Depending on the person for whom you were creating that Web, the theme may not have been quite what you were looking for. A Jimmy Buffett home page is a lot more comfortable in Citrus Punch than Industrial. A Web devoted to the mathematician Martin Gardner probably is more suited to Blueprint than the Artsy theme.

Load the personal Web that you created and apply a new theme to all of its pages.

Because it's so easy to experiment with themes, preview the Web in a browser in three different ways:

- With active graphics
- With non-active graphics and a background image
- With vivid colors and no background image

Figure 34.2 shows a home page with generated with a theme and a background image.

FIGURE 34.2

Trying a theme with a personal Web.

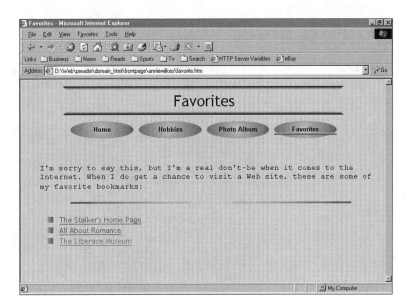

Create Your Own Theme

As you have seen, themes are a quick way to establish the appearance of a Web. Whether your Web contains 5 or 500 pages, the same minimal amount of work is required to apply a theme.

If none of the built-in themes suit the Web you're trying to create, you can develop your own.

To create a new theme, you can begin by modifying an existing one. Start by selecting the existing theme as if you're going to apply it to a Web, and click Modify in the Themes dialog. Three new buttons will appear: Colors, Graphics, and Text. Each of these enables you to change part of the selected theme.

Selecting a Color Scheme

The Colors button is used to pick the five colors that make up the theme's color scheme. These colors can be selected in three different ways:

- Selecting from a list of available schemes
- Using a color wheel
- Manually assigning a color to each Web element that can be placed on a page, including headings, text, and hyperlinks

34

Many of the listed colors correspond with existing themes, so you can borrow them for your new theme.

The color wheel is shown in Figure 34.3.

FIGURE 34.3

*Selecting a theme's
colors from a wheel.*

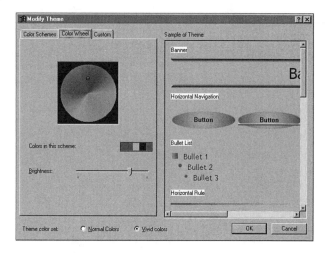

The color wheel is used to pick a set of five related colors. Picking a red area of the wheel creates a color scheme that is predominantly red, for instance.

The scheme changes as you move to different places on the wheel, making it easy to meander around until you find something you like.

Another thing you can do that greatly affects the scheme is to adjust the brightness level of the entire wheel. If you're looking for a gloomy range of colors, you will need to darken the entire color wheel first.

Every change you make while selecting colors is reflected in the Sample of Theme window, as shown in Figure 34.3.

One thing that isn't obvious about selecting a color scheme is what the five colors are used for. The color in the middle is the page's background color. The other colors are used in a variety of different ways, as you'll see in the Sample of Theme window.

The third way to select colors for a theme is to assign them manually. Instead of picking a five-color scheme, you assign specific colors to specific Web elements such as the page background, active hyperlinks, and body text. This is more time-consuming, but it provides total control over the colors employed in the theme.

After you have made changes to an existing theme, you can save them in the Themes dialog box by clicking Save As and giving the theme its own name. This is preferable to clicking Save because it doesn't wipe out the existing theme.

Selecting Text and Graphics

The Text button of the Themes dialog box is used to associate fonts with body text and the six different heading sizes that are used on Web pages. A dialog box opens, enabling you to select any font that's installed on your system, as shown in Figure 34.4.

FIGURE 34.4

Selecting fonts to use in a theme.

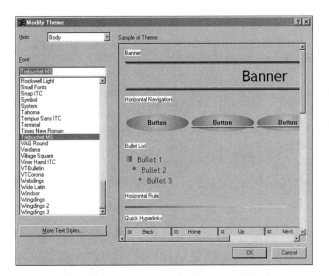

Fonts are a very system-specific element of Web page design. If you use a font on your Web that isn't present on a visitor's system, their browser will default to a standard font such as Arial, Helvetica, or Verdana.

34

If you're developing a Web that only will be seen on a company's intranet, you can use any font that you know will be present on the machines that have access to that Web.

Anything bound for the World Wide Web probably should stick to fonts that are the most widely supported. The built-in themes in FrontPage use the following fonts: Arial, Book Antiqua, Century Gothic, Helvetica, Times, Times New Roman, Trebuchet MS, and Verdana. The safest of these fonts to use are Arial, Helvetica, Times, and Verdana.

If you're concerned that a font won't be present, you can specify one or more alternate fonts when modifying a theme. Instead of picking a single font, enter a list of fonts separated by commas, such as "Verdana, Arial, sans serif" or "Times New Roman, Times, serif." Web browsers will look for each font in the list and use the first one that's present on the system running the browser.

The final way to create a new theme is to modify an existing theme's graphics.

Every theme has graphics files associated with 11 different page elements, including the background image, page banner, and both horizontal and vertical navigation bars. Some of these elements have several different graphics files associated with them—hover buttons have files for each image that appears on the button.

Changing graphics requires strong working knowledge of how the different page elements function.

To change the graphics associated with a theme, click Graphics from the Themes dialog box. A new dialog box opens, enabling you to select graphics and see how they look in a Sample of Theme window, as shown in Figure 34.5.

FIGURE 34.5

Choosing new graphics for a theme.

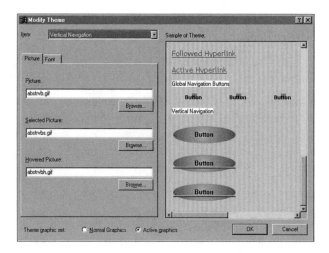

One of the simplest graphics to change is the background picture. This graphic is displayed beneath Web pages when the theme is applied with the Background Picture option selected.

Click Browse to choose a new graphic file. If this file is located anywhere on your system, you can find it using the standard Windows file open dialog box. If it is located on the World Wide Web, you can find it using the image's URL.

Regardless of where you find the file, FrontPage will make a copy of it for use with the theme. FrontPage will use a copy instead of the original whenever the theme is applied to a Web.

Employ a Web Wizard

There are two kinds of wizards in FrontPage: *Web wizards*, which create entire sites, and *single-page wizards*.

As you learned when working with templates, wizards can be selected when you're creating a new Web or adding a new page to an existing Web. Click File, New, Web or File, New, Page and a dialog box will list the templates and wizards you can select.

Figure 34.6 shows the dialog box that appears when you're creating a new Web.

Wizard   Template

FIGURE 34.6

Selecting a wizard or template for a new Web.

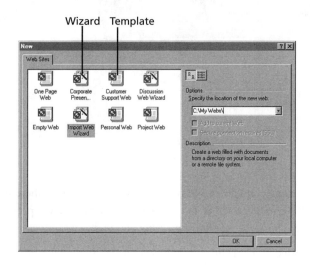

When you select one of the magic-wand wizard icons, a dialog box opens, describing the wizard and its purpose.

Create a Corporate Web

The Corporate Presence Wizard can be used to quickly establish a company's official Web.

If you're developing a site for your own company or for a client that isn't on the Web yet, this wizard guides you through the process of developing a professional Web. You'll be able to choose products or services that should be spotlighted, solicit feedback from customers, incorporate the corporate logo into each page, and other business-related tasks.

The Corporate wizard has numerous features that make it easier to establish a company's Web. One example: The wizard asks for some common information that should be

34

available about any company: its mailing address, phone number, fax number, email address for customer inquiries, and the like. These things can be automatically placed on different pages, and when something changes, FrontPage will update every page where it appears.

For example, if your company has to relocate because no one ever taught your original architect about flood plains, you can change the address by selecting Tools, Web Settings and opening the Parameters tabbed dialog box, as shown in Figure 34.7.

FIGURE 34.7

Changing information used throughout a corporate Web.

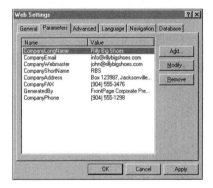

Once this change is made, it will be updated on every page where the parameter appears. You don't have to edit each of the pages individually. The Corporate Presence Wizard offers several shortcuts that make creating and maintaining a company's Web easier.

When you select this wizard, you'll answer a series of questions on 13 different dialog boxes. To make the most effective use of the wizard, you should know each of the following things about the Web:

- The products or services that will be promoted on the Web
- Whether feedback will be solicited from visitors, and how it should be saved
- Whether the Web needs its own search engine
- The company's mission statement, if one should be displayed on the Web
- Other kinds of information, such as catalog requests, that will be collected
- All contact information about the company along with the email address to use for the company and for Web-related inquiries

If you don't know some of these, you can add them later, after the wizard has created the Web. As a general rule, though, you'll be much closer to completing the Web if you gather all the necessary information before calling the wizard.

Figure 34.8 shows the first dialog box that's used to tell the wizard what kind of corporate Web to create.

FIGURE 34.8

Selecting the main pages of a corporate Web.

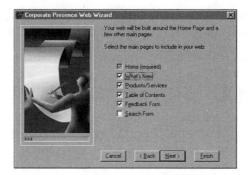

Like all FrontPage wizards, the Corporate Presence Wizard includes a lot of explanatory text that describes what it is capable of creating. If you're still in the wizard and you change your mind about a previous answer, you can use the Back button to return to the dialog box and revise it.

One of the dialog boxes will ask exactly how many products and services you will be describing on the Web. A page will be created for each of these, along with a main page connecting all of them with hyperlinks.

For each product, you can determine whether to display an image or pricing information. Each service can be described along with the relevant capabilities and account information. You'll also be able to associate information request forms for each product and service, so prospective customers can use the Web to ask for more details about the company's offerings.

These aspects of the new Web are determined with the dialog box shown in Figure 34.9.

FIGURE 34.9

Customizing the products and services pages.

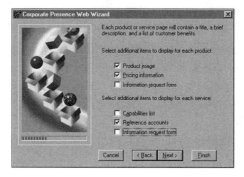

34

After you answer the questions on all 13 dialog boxes, the Corporate Presence Wizard is finally ready to create the actual Web itself.

The wizard creates each of the main pages that you requested—pages for products, services, and other features, and the start of a navigational structure for the Web.

Another thing it will do is add comments to each page offering tips on what you should add to that part of the Web.

These comments will show up in Page view, displayed in a lighter color than the body text of the page and preceded with the word "Comment." Comments are not displayed when the page is loaded by a Web browser, so you can leave them on the page while you're working on the Web.

> To add your own comment to a page, click the menu command Insert, Comment. A dialog box will open, and the comment you enter into it will be added to the page at the current cursor location.

Import an Existing Web

One of the FrontPage wizards will bring an existing Web and all of its files into FrontPage. The Import Web Wizard enables you to take advantage of FrontPage's features on a site that wasn't originally created with the software.

This wizard can import a site from two different places:

- A folder on a hard drive such as your own system or another system on a local network
- The World Wide Web

Local Webs are retrieved using the standard Windows file open dialog box. The Web and all of its pages are copied to a new folder, leaving the original intact.

When you retrieve a site over the World Wide Web, you specify its URL address. FrontPage will download the pages of the site, all of its images, and other files that are part of the same Web. It will even re-create the folder structure of the site—if the site stored all graphics files into an images subfolder that will be maintained when the site is re-created on your system.

FrontPage will also retrieve any other pages that are part of the same Web. If there is a main home page and 20 other pages, each of these will be downloaded along with all of their images and other files.

As you might expect, this can be a time-consuming process. After you specify a site's URL, a dialog box will open that enables you to limit the amount of the Web you retrieve, as shown in Figure 34.10.

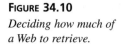

FIGURE 34.10

Deciding how much of a Web to retrieve.

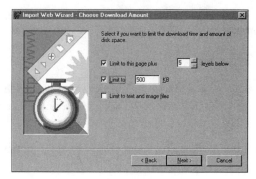

The download can be limited in three ways:

- Reducing the number of levels that are downloaded
- Limiting the Web to a maximum disk size
- Limiting the retrieval to text and image files only

Restricting the number of levels prevents FrontPage from digging any deeper when it visits the pages of a Web. Each level represents a page—if FrontPage goes from the main page to a "What's New?" page and then to a specific news item's page, it has traversed three levels into the site.

Limiting the disk size and the type of files downloaded may cause FrontPage to retrieve only a portion of the Web.

Once you retrieve a Web, you can begin working on it like any other FrontPage site that you create.

As with other retrieval features of FrontPage, the Import Web Wizard makes it easy to incorporate existing Web content into your work. One thing it doesn't do is ask permission before making use of the content of other Web publishers, so you'll have to be careful to secure permissions when using images, pages, and other material downloaded directly from the World Wide Web.

34

Employ a Page Wizard

Most of the wizards you can use in FrontPage are used to create entire Webs. Because pages are generally simple, most can be added to a Web using a template that you customize within the Page view.

An exception to the rule is the Form Page Wizard, which simplifies the process of adding interactivity to your Web.

Add a Form to a Web

One of the new pages you can add to a Web uses a wizard instead of a template. The Form Page Wizard can create a form—a Web page with fields that collect information from a visitor to your site.

Forms can be created in FrontPage by adding the individual elements of a form directly to a page, such as text fields, drop-down menus, and buttons.

The Form Page Wizard can simplify this process for some of the common forms that appear on the World Wide Web:

- A page soliciting feedback from a visitor
- A page for ordering a product
- An entry for a Web guestbook

To use this wizard, you first choose a question or series of related questions that should be on the form. The wizard then will give you a chance to customize this further. Figure 34.11 shows how a set of ordering information questions can be customized.

FIGURE 34.11

Customizing a question on a form.

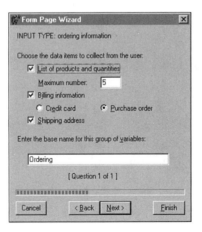

After you tell the wizard about all of the questions that should be on the form, you decide how the information should be saved. FrontPage can save the answers to a hidden data file on the Web, create a Web page that contains the answers, and mail a visitor's responses through email.

The wizard creates the form based on these specifications and adds it to the current Web. You'll be able to make changes to the form in the Page view after that point—working with a form the wizard built is no different than working with one you created by hand.

Summary

During this chapter, you learned how to use FrontPage's built-in themes to establish the graphic appearance of a Web. FrontPage has themes suited to a variety of purposes: corporate sites, personal home pages, hobbies, and more.

If the software's built-in themes did not fit a project, you can create your own theme by customizing an existing one. Themes define several different aspects of a Web, including its background picture, navigation bars, and the color of text, headings, and hyperlinks. They can make use of advanced Web design features like JavaScript to cause buttons to change in response to mouse movements on a page.

Wizards are interactive programs that create templates based on your answers to a series of questions. You can create more complex Webs with wizards than are possible with templates, including a corporate Web, discussion Web, and an interactive form page.

By using these three features, you're able to solve one of the problems any Web designer faces: how to go from an empty file folder to an entire Web, complete with pages, images, hyperlinks, and a navigational structure.

34

CHAPTER 35

Creating Web Pages

During this chapter, you'll face something that has been avoided in the earlier FrontPage chapters:

The blank page.

Filling an empty page is a challenge that the World Wide Web inherited from its ancestors in the written family: books, magazines, and newspapers. You'll be filling blank pages with the basic elements of the Web: text and hyperlinks. You'll work with text in several different ways, changing its font and colors, aligning and formatting paragraphs, and turning text into attention-grabbing headings.

You also will associate text with hyperlinks that connect a page to other documents on your own Web and the World Wide Web.

Create and Title a Page

To edit a page, you first must load it into the Page view of FrontPage.

Every Web page in FrontPage begins as a template. If you want to start from scratch on a new page, the closest you can get is the Normal Page template.

To begin a new page, click File, New Page or the New Page button on the Standard toolbar, which is shown in Figure 35.1.

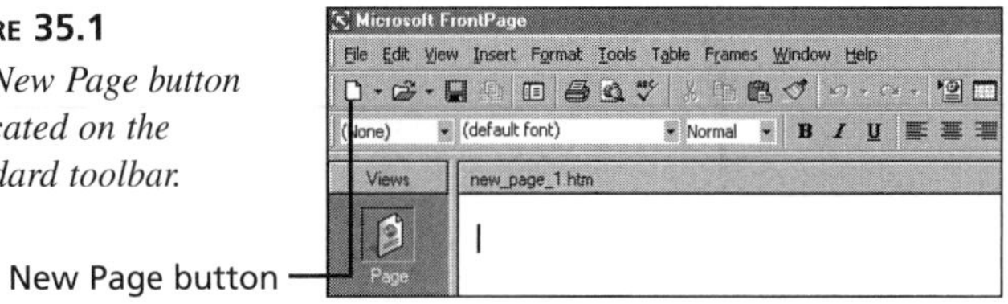

FIGURE 35.1

*The New Page button
is located on the
Standard toolbar.*

New Page button ———

When you select a new page template, the page will appear in the Page view for immediate editing.

If the current Web does not have a theme applied to it, the new page will be completely blank. Otherwise, the theme's background, fonts, colors, and other formatting details will be applied to the page.

The new page will initially be given a unique filename such as *newpage1.htm* or *newpage2.htm*. You can give it a different name by clicking File, Save As, or rename it later in the Folders view. Right-click the file and select Rename from the pop-up menu that appears.

If you close the current Web without making any changes to the new page, FrontPage discards the page. Otherwise, the software will remind you to save it when you close the Web or preview it in a browser.

Add Shared Borders to a Page

Another thing added to a new page upon its creation is any border that it shares with the rest of the current Web.

FrontPage enables you to create border areas that are common to all pages on a Web. Click Format, Shared Borders to see what shared borders are being used. A dialog box will open, indicating which borders are currently shared, as shown in Figure 35.2.

A FrontPage Web can share top, bottom, left, and right borders, though sharing all four doesn't leave a lot of real estate for the rest of each page. They are often used to provide room for things like navigation bars, site logos, and copyright notices.

Many of the built-in FrontPage themes use the left border for a navigation bar that appears on every page of a Web. A do-it-yourself fireworks site should probably consider a shared bottom border with a note disclaiming the publisher from any legal responsibility in the event of unexpected limb loss.

FIGURE 35.2

Adding and removing a Web's shared borders.

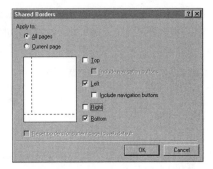

The Shared Borders dialog box can be used to add and remove these borders. Borders are marked in the Page view with dotted lines like those shown in Figure 35.2. Any change made to a border area on one page is instantly reflected on all pages that share the border.

Title a Page

Every Web page is entitled to a title. Although FrontPage will assign a default title, it's usually something along the lines of "New Page 5," which isn't terribly helpful to people navigating your Web.

A page's title appears in the title bar of most Web browsers—the topmost edge of the window containing the browser. (Nonvisual and all-text browsers render it differently.)

To title a page, select File, Properties or right-click the page and select Page Properties from the pop-up menu that appears. A dialog box opens containing six tabbed dialog boxes that can be used to alter the page. Under the General tab, you can enter a new title. The General dialog box is shown in Figure 35.3.

FIGURE 35.3

Setting a new title for a page.

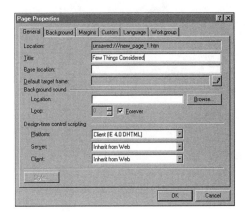

When you title a page, FrontPage uses this text for the page's banner and on navigation bars, if these are used. It also is suggested as a filename for the page when you first save it.

Choosing a succinct, descriptive title is important for two reasons—it helps people use your Web, and it helps others find it.

If you use the Table of Contents template to add that kind of page to your Web, each page's title is used in the resulting table of contents listing.

Also, the title of a page is the most prominent thing shown in a search engine when results are listed. For example, AltaVista lists the title of each page followed by a few lines of text pulled from its contents.

The title may also be used to determine how a Web is ranked during a search, so if you place "Totally Nude Furniture" in a page title, you'll get more visits from people searching for that topic than you might otherwise. (You'll also get more visitors who were expecting something other than unfinished rocking chairs, so keep that in mind when making any easily confused claims involving states of undress.)

Select a Background for Your Page

One of the ways you can dress up a Web is to give a page a background. The background can be either a solid color or a picture that's loaded from an image file.

Select Format, Background to open the Page Properties dialog box that's used to select a background (see Figure 35.4).

FIGURE 35.4

Selecting a page background.

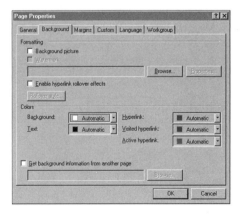

To use a background picture, click the Browse button and a file open dialog box enables you to choose any file on your system. A background picture must be in the GIF, JPG, or PNG format.

You can use a URL to specify the background picture, but this causes FrontPage to use a graphic that isn't part of your Web.

If the graphic is removed from that URL, it will stop appearing on your pages. For that reason, it's better to make a copy of the image on your system—if you have permission to do so—and work directly with that copy.

Background pictures are repeated under the contents of a page. This is called *tiling*, because each copy of the graphic is like an identical tile on a kitchen floor. If you would like the background to be displayed once, select the Watermark option. The background won't scroll along with the rest of the page.

To choose a background color instead of a picture, deselect the Background Picture check box and click the Background Colors pull-down menu. The standard FrontPage color selection dialog box appears with 16 basic colors to choose from. If none of these fit what you're looking for, click the More Colors button and a more advanced color dialog box will appear, as shown in Figure 35.5.

FIGURE 35.5

Choosing a page's background color.

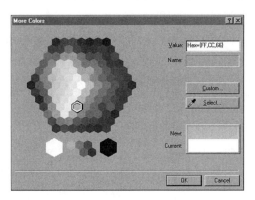

You can select one of the colors shown in the More Colors dialog box or enter a color's hexadecimal value in the Value field. You also can click the Custom button to open a third color selection dialog box with even more options.

Hand Me a Hex Wrench

Knowledge of hexadecimal values is completely unnecessary to using FrontPage because you can pick colors in other ways. For the curious: Hexadecimal values are numbers on a base-16 system, which means there are 16 different single-digit numbers. They're often useful in computer programs because you can represent values up to 255 in only two digits. The first 20 hexadecimal numbers are 0, 1, 2, 3, 4, 5, 6, 7, 8, 9, A, B, C, D, E, F, 10, 11, 12, and 13. Microsoft could have impressed some people in the hexadecimal crowd by naming its software FrontPage 7D0.

35

The color you select is displayed underneath the contents of the page.

When a page has both a background color and a picture selected, the color will be replaced by the picture when the page is fully loaded. To cause only the color to display, deselect the Background Picture check box.

If you want to designate a background for an entire Web, it's much easier to create a new theme with the desired background and apply that theme to the Web. The theme will also be available for use in other projects, unlike a background that is selected manually.

Add Text to a Page

To add text to a Web page, open it in FrontPage's Page view and begin typing. The characters will appear at the currently selected cursor position, whether you are in a shared border or the main part of the page itself.

Shared borders are indicated by dotted lines on the page. These lines won't show up when the page is viewed in a browser.

After you have entered some text on a page, you can highlight a selection of the text and use FrontPage's formatting options on it.

The Formatting toolbar contains the following buttons:

- *Bold*—Makes the text appear in boldface
- *Italic*—Italicizes the text
- *Underline*—Underlines the text
- *Align Left*—Lines up all selected text and other page elements along the left margin of the page
- *Center*—Centers the selected page elements
- *Align Right*—Lines up the selected elements along the right margin
- *Increase Indent*—Indents the selected elements more than they are currently indented
- *Decrease Indent*—Reduces the indentation of the selected elements

Most of these buttons are common to different software, especially the B, I, and U icons used for boldface, italic, and underline as with all the Microsoft Office programs.

When you are working with text on a Web page, you should let text wrap around the right margin at all times and only press the Enter key when you finish a paragraph. On most Web browsers, the text appears in block style, with each paragraph beginning at the left margin and a blank line separating paragraphs.

Pressing the Enter key causes a paragraph break to appear, even when you're arranging images and other page elements along with text.

The main reason you should not worry about the right-hand margin is that it varies depending on the browser and system being used to view a Web page. Someone on an 800×600 resolution monitor is going to see much more text per line than someone on a 640×480 monitor. A person who has enabled large text for easier reading will greatly reduce the number of characters that appear on a line. These are just two examples of the variability of Web presentation.

If you're using FrontPage to publish a Web page for the first time, you must become accustomed to the lack of control you sometimes have over a page's appearance.

Unlike a medium such as print, where a page looks exactly like the designer intended it to look, the Web is a fluid medium where pages can rearrange themselves to fit the space they have available to them.

To see this in action, connect to the Internet, load your favorite Web site, and resize your browser window so that it takes up a portion of your desktop instead of the whole thing. Figure 35.6 shows a page from one of my favorite sites, TeeVee, in two different browser windows.

FIGURE 35.6

How page presentation varies in different browsers.

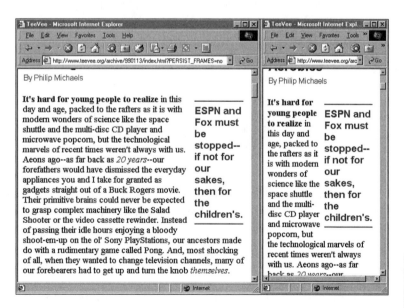

The text of the page wraps differently depending on the space that's available to it.

35

Every paragraph break on a Web page causes a blank line to appear in most browsers, including Netscape Navigator and Microsoft Internet Explorer. To begin text at the left margin without a paragraph break, you can insert a line break by selecting Insert, Break and choosing the Normal Line Break option from the subsequent dialog box.

There's a hidden shortcut for adding a line break without leaving the keyboard—hold down the Shift key while pressing Enter.

Line breaks can be used to ensure that text appears on different lines without a paragraph break separating them. They're also useful when you're aligning images and other page elements.

Turn Text into a Hyperlink

Documents on the World Wide Web are connected to each other through the use of hyperlinks. When you click on a link, your browser opens up the Web page or other type of file that has been associated with the link.

Hyperlinks can be associated with anything you place on a page: text, images, Java applets, QuickTime movies, WAV sound files—you name it.

Text hyperlinks are displayed in a way that sets them apart from other text on a page. In most browsers, they are underlined.

For this reason, underlining other text that isn't a hyperlink is frowned upon. Your users will click the underlined text and wonder why it isn't functioning as a hyperlink.

To create a hyperlink, highlight the part of the page that should be associated with the link and select either Insert, Hyperlink or the Hyperlink button on the Standard toolbar.

Hyperlinks can be associated with files on your system or any URL on the World Wide Web. If the file is another page in your Web, you can select it using a Windows file open dialog box.

A hyperlink to a URL should contain the full URL preceded by protocol information such as http:// or ftp://. Some examples are http://www.sams.com, http://www.fp2k.com/24 and ftp://ftp.netscape.com.

If you're linking to a file on your system, add it to your Web first by using the File, Import menu command. If you don't, the link will not be usable when the page is published to the World Wide Web.

After creating a hyperlink, you can edit it by right-clicking the link and selecting Hyperlink Properties.

Turn Text into a Heading

Text on a Web page can be set apart from other text by turning it into a heading. Headings range in size from 1 (largest) to 6 (smallest), and they can be used for the same purpose as a headline in a newspaper—succinctly describing the text that follows. They also can be used as subheads with a larger article, as enlarged quotations, and for other attention-grabbing purposes.

The easiest way to turn text into a heading is to use the Style pull-down menu on the Formatting toolbar, which is shown in Figure 35.7. This menu has several different options for formatting text, including choices for six heading sizes from 1 through 6.

FIGURE 35.7

The Style pull-down menu.

The actual size of a heading is browser-specific, but as a general rule you can rely on the 1-to-6 ranking system.

Headings can be associated with hyperlinks and used in most other ways as if they are text. One exception is that a heading must occupy its own paragraph.

To see this in action, highlight a single word in a paragraph and turn it into Heading 1 text. Everything else in that paragraph will be turned into that heading also, occupying a very large chunk of the page.

Change the Font and Color of Your Text

When you add text to a page that has a theme applied to it, the text will have the font and color assigned to body text in that theme. If no theme has been applied, the text will be displayed in the default font and color of the Web browser used to load the page— usually a Times Roman, Arial, or Helvetica font.

35

To override the font or color choice for text, highlight the text and click Format, Font to open the Font dialog box (see Figure 35.8). You can use this to select a new font and color for the selected text.

FIGURE 35.8

Selecting a font for text.

You can choose any font that's present on your system, but if it isn't present on the system of the person viewing your Web, a default font will be substituted for it.

As with font selection for themes, you should stick to common fonts such as Arial, Helvetica, Times, and Verdana because they are likely to be present on most systems. FrontPage also relies on Book Antiqua, Century Gothic, Times New Roman, and Trebuchet MS in many of its themes.

You also can specify a font and several alternatives in a list separated with commas, such as "Times Roman, Times, serif" or "Courier New, Courier, monospace".

The size of a font can be designated on a scale from 1 (smallest) to 7 (largest). The point size associated with each of these sizes is a rule of thumb rather than an exact measurement. Though the font will be displayed at that size within FrontPage, it's another thing that differs according to the browsing software being used and how it is configured.

A font's color can be selected with the standard FrontPage color selection dialog boxes. You also can apply several different effects to the text:

- *Strikethrough*—Text will be marked with a line through it, ~~like this~~.
- *Blink*—Text will blink on and off.
- *Superscript and subscript*—Text will be shrunken and appear either above or below other text on the same line.

- *Hidden*—Text will be part of the page but not displayed.
- *Strong*—Text will be displayed with strong emphasis (in most browsers, this causes it to appear in boldface).
- *Emphasis*—Text will be displayed with emphasis (italic in most browsers).

Several of the other text effects are used to define the kind of information the text represents. They are presented differently in different browsers, and are not as commonly used today as effects that describe how text is presented.

The following are descriptive effects you can use:

- *Variable*—A variable name, describing a place used to store information in a computer program
- *Keyboard*—Something that a user should enter with a keyboard
- *Code*—Source code of a computer program
- *Sample*—Sample output from a computer program
- *Citation*—A citation crediting the source of information in an essay or similar paper

Summary

After this chapter, you now have some tools for keeping the blank page at bay. Text, headings, and hyperlinks make up the largest part of the World Wide Web. By combining the three, you can create entire Webs that reach an audience of thousands.

35

CHAPTER 36

Managing Web Sites

In FrontPage, a *Web* is a site that FrontPage knows how to edit, publish, and perform maintenance on. In all other respects, a FrontPage Web is like any other site that you have used, no matter what software created it. All Webs must be FrontPage Webs in order for FrontPage to work on them. This is not to say that you can't edit individual Web pages with FrontPage without it turning them into FrontPage Webs. You can. However, if you use any of the site management features, FrontPage will turn whatever you're are working on into a FrontPage Web.

Create and Explore a Web

A FrontPage Web is created in two ways:

- Creating a new Web using a FrontPage template
- Importing an existing Web using the Import Web Wizard

Once either of these tasks has been completed, you can work with these FrontPage Webs in the same manner.

A Web is begun with the File, New, Web command. A dialog box opens, listing the templates and wizards that can be used to create the new Web. The Import Web Wizard is one of these options.

Two of the Web templates are used to start a new Web from scratch: the Empty Web and One-Page Web. These Webs consist of the standard file folders, no themes, and no other extra features. The only difference between them is that one includes a blank Web page and the other doesn't.

Import Files to a Web

The World Wide Web is a conglomeration of different media. While pages consist of text documents, these pages can include a variety of different file types, including the following:

- GIF, JPG, and PNG graphics files
- WAV and MIDI sound files
- AVI, MOV, and MPG movies
- Java applets
- ActiveX components

To incorporate these media into your FrontPage Web, you should first make them a part of the Web using the File, Import command.

You can import files, entire folders, and World Wide Web sites. Requesting the latter causes the Import Wizard to be called so you can specify the site's URL and how it will be retrieved.

A convention of FrontPage is to create an images subfolder where a Web's images can all be stored. If you're working with other types of media, you might want to create folders for them as well—such as java for Java applets and sounds for any sound files you're using.

Once you have imported a file, it will become part of the Web. Whenever you copy the Web to a new folder or actually publish it to the World Wide Web, that file will be included.

Copy and Delete a Web

You can copy a Web to a new folder on your system by publishing it. In FrontPage, the Publish feature will copy a Web to another location, whether it's on your computer's hard drive or a server that's connected to the World Wide Web.

It's easier to publish a Web to your own system because you don't require a username, password, or other special access.

To copy the current Web to a new folder, select File, Publish Web to open the Publish Web dialog box (see Figure 36.1).

FIGURE 36.1

Choosing how to publish a Web.

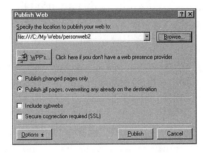

The Browse button on the Publish Web dialog box is used to select the location where the Web should be copied. It opens a Windows file open dialog box with some extra FrontPage-specific features on it.

If there's an empty folder on your system where the Web should be stored, you can use this dialog box to find the folder and open it.

You also can use the file open dialog box's New Folder button to create and name a new folder for the Web.

When you're copying a Web to a new folder, select the option to publish all of its pages so that nothing is omitted. After the Web has been published in full, you'll have two copies of it on your system.

You can delete a FrontPage Web in two different ways:

- Delete only the parts of the Web that control how it is edited in FrontPage
- Delete the Web entirely

To perform either deletion, open the Web and display its folder list (if this list isn't visible, use View, Folder List in the Page or Navigation views). Right-click the name of the Web—the top line in the folder list—and select the Delete command. A dialog box that enables you to delete FrontPage material or the entire Web opens.

Both of these actions are permanent, so you should handle them with due diligence—a phrase I picked up from stock traders that seems to mean "anything bad that happens as a consequence of my advice is entirely your fault."

Deleting an entire Web wipes out the folder containing the Web, all of its subfolders, and all of the pages, images, and other files that comprised the Web.

Deleting the FrontPage material of the Web only makes the site unrecognizable as a FrontPage Web. Everything else—pages, images, and other files—is not removed.

FrontPage places several files in a Web's folders that are used by the software to manage the Web. When you use the Import Web Wizard to bring an existing site into FrontPage for the first time, these behind-the-scenes files are created during the import process.

A Web with none of its FrontPage material can still be viewed normally with a Web browser, but you won't be able to open it for editing in FrontPage.

If you ever change your mind after deleting this part of a Web, you can bring it back into FrontPage as a new Web by using the Import Web Wizard.

Add a Navigation Bar to a Web

It's easy to get lost when you're visiting the pages of a large site on the World Wide Web. One of the ways publishers make these Webs easier to use is through the use of navigation bars—common text or graphic links that are associated with the main pages of the site.

Most commercial news and sports sites have navigation bars that lead to the main topics they cover. A sports site such as ESPN.com has links to its NFL, NBA, NHL, and Baseball pages on a navigation bar that's part of every page. If you dive down several links into ESPN's site while you're reading stories, you can get back to a starting point by using the navigation bar.

Navigation bars can be added to your own FrontPage Webs and placed in shared borders to make them appear on every page. There are four kinds of bars:

- Vertical lists of text links
- Horizontal lists of text links
- Vertical lists of graphic links
- Horizontal lists of graphic links

When you are working with a navigation bar, you don't create any of the hyperlinks that it contains. Instead, these links are determined by the navigational structure you have created for the Web in the Navigation view.

Figure 36.2 shows the Navigation view for a newly created site that used the Personal Web template.

36

FIGURE 36.2

Examining a Web's navigational structure.

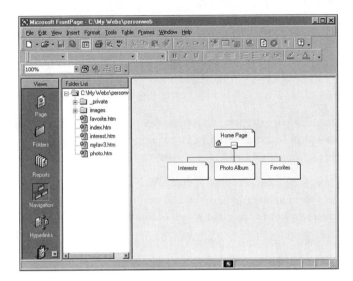

Four of the five pages in the Personal Web are represented in the Navigation view. The fifth, myfav3.htm, is not present because it is not yet part of the Web's navigational structure.

The Navigation view establishes a parent-child relationship between the pages of a Web. In Figure 36.2, the page labeled Home Page is the parent of the other three pages: Interests, Photo Albums, and Favorites.

Pages are added to the Navigation view by dragging them from the Folders list. You can try this out with a new Personal Web by dragging the icon next to myfav3.htm over the Navigation view.

When you drag a page onto the Navigational view, keep hold of it by holding your mouse button down. A dotted outline indicates the relationship that would be established if you dropped the page at that location. The outline changes depending on where you have dragged the page and which page it is closest to.

Figure 36.3 shows an outline around the cursor that shows a parent-child relationship between the Favorites page and a new page that hasn't been dropped. The cursor is closest to the Favorites page.

You can pick up pages in the Navigation view and drag them to new locations. The easiest way to get a feel for this view is to drag a new page around and drop it at several different places to see what relationship is established.

FIGURE 36.3

*Dragging a new page
into the Navigation
view.*

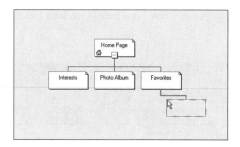

In general, a page dropped above another page becomes its parent. A page dropped below a page becomes its child. A page that's dropped beside a page is its sibling and shares the same parent.

An exception: Pages dropped above a Web's home page will be orphans—no lines will connect them to other pages. You can use this to start new parent-child groups that are completely unrelated to other pages of the Web.

In the Navigation view, a parent can have as many children as desired, but a child has only one parent.

Once you have established the Navigation view for a Web, it will be used to determine which links appear on the Web's navigation bars.

Navigation bars are added to a page with the Insert, Navigation Bar menu command. You also can edit an existing bar by double-clicking it in Page view. Both commands open the Navigation Bar Properties dialog box, shown in Figure 36.4.

FIGURE 36.4

*Working on a naviga-
tion bar.*

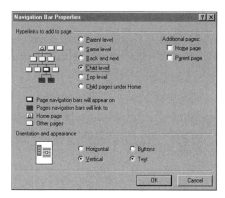

A navigation bar in FrontPage can display six different groups of hyperlinks:

* *Parent level*—Links to the parent of the current page and all of its siblings
* *Same level*—Links to all pages that are siblings of the current page

- *Back and next*—Links to the siblings immediately to the left (back) and right (next) of the current page
- *Child level*—Links to all pages that are children of the current page
- *Top level*—Links to all pages that have no parents
- *Child pages under Home*—Links to all pages that have the Web's home page as a parent

You also have the option of adding extra links for the Web's home page and the current page's parent, if these aren't already in the group.

The Navigation Bar Properties dialog box shown in Figure 36.4 contains a drawing of a Navigational view. As you choose the different hyperlink groups, this drawing will change to show the pages included in that group.

Two more things you can configure are a navigation bar's orientation (horizontal or vertical) and its appearance (buttons or text).

The selection that you make will be immediately reflected in the Web. You can easily experiment with the different styles until you find one that you like.

> If your Web does not have a theme applied to it, you will not see buttons on your navigation bar even if you select that option instead of text. FrontPage relies on themes to provide the buttons that are used on graphic navigation bars.

The Navigation view is used to provide the text that's associated with each hyperlink on a navigation bar. To change this text, right-click a page's icon in the Navigation view and select the Rename menu option.

This text appears on all navigation bars that link to the page, so it should be reasonably short to provide room for other links. It also is used on the page's banner—a FrontPage component displayed in the top shared border of any Web that uses FrontPage's built-in themes.

Figure 36.5 shows the Favorites page from a Personal Web after myfav3.htm has been added to the Web's navigational structure. This page contains two navigational bars—a horizontal one along the top and a vertical one along the left side.

The horizontal bar along the top links to all pages on the same level and the Web's home page. (It also includes a button for the page itself, though FrontPage automatically removes this unnecessary link.)

FIGURE 36.5

A page with two navigational bars.

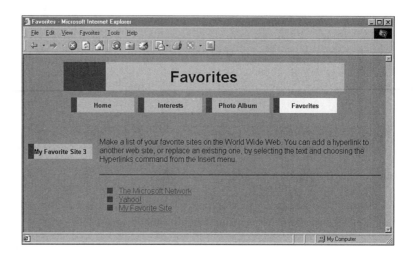

The vertical bar only links to pages that are on a child level from the current page. Because myfav3.htm was established as a child to the Favorites page in the Web's Navigational view, it shows up on this bar.

Summary

In this chapter, you've followed FrontPage Webs from their creation to their relocation to their final deletion. You should be comfortable giving life to new Webs and taking it away when you want to reclaim some disk space.

You also can bring Webs into FrontPage with the Import Web Wizard and take them back out again with the Delete command.

The real family ties in a FrontPage Web occur in the Navigational view, where you take a group of unrelated pages and turn them into a family, complete with parents, children, and siblings.

The navigational structure is one of the things that makes a FrontPage Web different from the other Webs you run across with your browser.

You'll encounter other differences in the coming chapters that make the distinction even more clear.

CHAPTER 37

Dividing Pages into Separate Frames

A few years after the creation of HTML and the World Wide Web, Netscape introduced a new feature for sites called *frames*. In keeping with their name, frames divide windows into smaller sections. They're used to subdivide the browser's window area into two or more areas, each of which holds its own Web page independently of all other frames. The experience is like having two browsers open at the same time. You can load separate pages into the frames and use them as if they were in separate browsers.

During this chapter, you'll learn how to create frames and place pages into them. You'll discover how to resize a frame, take away features like its scrollbar, and convert existing Webs into frames.

Create a Frame

Frames divide a browser window into two or more separate windows. The size of each frame is determined by the page designer, and each frame can have its own scrollbars. You can also resize frames by dragging their borders to new locations. If you don't want a frame to have scrollbars or be resizable, these features can be removed.

The simplest framed page contains two frames—either top and bottom or left and right. Figure 37.1 displays a two-page framed Web page.

FIGURE 37.1

A Web page with left and right frames.

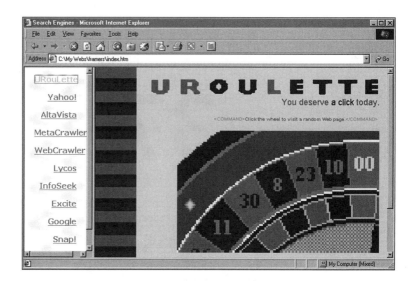

When you're working with frames, a hyperlink in one frame often causes something to be loaded in the other. The frame in which the action happens is called the *target frame*. In Figure 37.1, the frame on the left contains a list of hyperlinks to search engines and other portal sites. When one of these is clicked, the site opens in the right frame.

URouLette, which is located at http://www.uroulette.com, is the namesake of one of the World Wide Web's first random link generators. Clicking a link at URouLette opens a random page on the Web.

You also can cause a hyperlink to open a frame in the page that contains the link. The frame to be opened is determined by additional information in each hyperlink.

Add Framed Pages to a Web

In FrontPage, the first step in creating framed pages is to choose one of the frame templates.

The Frames Pages tab, which you can open when selecting a new page template, contains 10 different combinations of framed pages (see Figure 37.2).

FIGURE 37.2

Selecting a frame template.

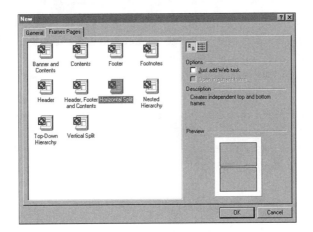

The tab's preview box displays the approximate size and alignment of the different frames. The following frame templates are available:

- *Banner and Contents*—A banner frame on the top, a contents frame on the left, and a main frame. Hyperlinks in the banner frame change the contents frame.
- *Contents*—A contents frame on the left and a main frame. Hyperlinks in the contents frame change the main frame.
- *Footer*—A footer frame on the bottom and a main frame. Hyperlinks in the footer change the main frame.
- *Footnotes*—A footnotes frame on the bottom and a main frame. Hyperlinks in the main frame change the footnotes frame.
- *Header*—A header frame on the top and a main frame underneath. Hyperlinks in the header frame change the main frame.
- *Header, Footer, and Contents*—A header frame on the top, a footer frame on the bottom, and a contents frame. Hyperlinks in the header and footer change the contents frame.
- *Horizontal Split*—Top and bottom frames that are independent of each other.
- *Nested Hierarchy*—A frame on the left that changes a frame on the right, leaving the main frame alone.
- *Top-down Hierarchy*—A frame at the top that changes a frame in the middle, leaving the main frame alone.
- *Vertical Split*—Independent right and left frames.

Selecting a frames template causes each of the frames to be created in the Page view of FrontPage. Unlike with other templates, no new pages are created. Instead, each frame contains three buttons: New Page, Help, and Set Initial.

The New Page button creates a new page and places it in the frame. The Help button opens the frames section of FrontPage's built-in help system. The Set Initial button opens a dialog that enables you to place an existing page in the frame. This page can be an existing part of your Web or an address on the World Wide Web.

Although it isn't readily apparent, every group of framed pages contains one more page than it would appear to need. The extra page holds all of these frames and the information that's needed to determine their size, whether scrollbars are displayed, and similar details. For a two-frame template like Horizontal Split, for example, there's a top page, a bottom page, and the extra page.

When you save a group of pages that are placed within frames, you must save the extra page also or lose all frame information.

In the FrontPage Page view, you work directly on the pages that are contained within frames. A blue border appears around the frame that's currently being edited, and menu commands that apply to pages—such as the Save button—apply to the current frame instead.

Modify a Frame

Because frames are created from standard templates, you will probably need to make adjustments as you're working on a frame-based Web.

To make changes to a frame, right-click anywhere within its boundaries and select Frame Properties from the menu. The Frame Properties dialog box, shown in Figure 37.3, will open.

Every frame is given a name by default, and this name is referred to by hyperlinks that load pages into the frame.

You can adjust a frame's width or row height, but not both. Vertical frames are measured according to their width, and horizontal frames are measured according to their row height.

These measurements can be specified in three ways:

- Pixels
- A percentage
- A relative value

Pixel measurements are the most exact, of course. If you set a frame to 100 pixels in width, it will be displayed at that size whenever possible.

FIGURE 37.3

The Frame Properties dialog box.

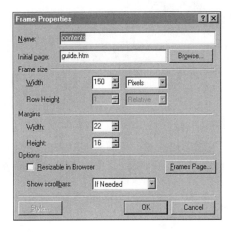

Percentages indicate how much of the browser window will be taken up by the frame.

Relative values are arbitrary numbers that only have meaning when compared to the relative values of other frames. For example, consider a Web page containing two frames, one with a relative value of 2 and the other with a relative value of 8. The first frame will be four times as small as the other frame because its relative value is four times as small.

Create an Alternative to Frames

Although frames were introduced by Netscape in late 1995, people who use text-based browsers and old versions of popular browsers won't be able to use a Web that's reliant on frames. For this reason, many Web developers create an alternative way to view their Webs that doesn't require frames.

In FrontPage, an extra tabbed view called No Frames is available within Page view. This tabbed view displays the alternative page that will appear on non-frame browsing software. The default text for this page states that the Web requires frames in order to use it. No alternative presentation is offered.

You can use the No Frames window to launch a separate navigational route through your Web.

Depending on how a frame page has been designed, you may be able to use it in a Web's nonframe alternative. Its suitability will depend on whether it has hyperlinks of its own rather than relying on another frame page's links.

Open Linked Pages into Frames

When you're using hyperlinks on a framed Web, you must decide which frame will be the target frame. When the hyperlink is selected, the linked page will be opened into this target frame.

Hyperlinks can open a document within its own frame, a different frame, or in a new browser window entirely.

You can designate a target frame whenever you create or edit a hyperlink. The Edit Hyperlink dialog box includes a Change Target Frame button that opens the dialog box shown in Figure 37.4.

You can specify the target frame by name, or you can use one of five alternatives:

- *Page Default*—The frame that all hyperlinks open into when no target frame has been specified
- *Same Frame*—The same frame as the page containing the hyperlink
- *Whole Page*—A new page takes up the entire browser window
- *New Window*—A new page in a new browser window, leaving the existing browser window alone
- *Parent Frame*—The page that contains the hyperlink's frame and any others created at the same time

FIGURE 37.4

Selecting a hyperlink's target frame.

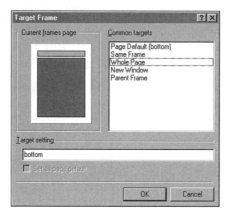

These alternative targets are useful when you want to break out of the currently displayed frames in some way, either to open new frames or to remove frames entirely.

All of the frame templates in FrontPage set a default target for each page contained in a frame. You can change this by editing one of the properties of that framed page—

right-click the frame, choose Page Properties, and modify the Default Target Frame value.

 You can use most of these target frame options with any hyperlink, regardless of whether your Web contains frames. The Whole Page target is useful when you want to make sure a page in your Web is displayed in a full browser window, and the New Window option opens a separate browser window.

37

Summary

Now that you have framed someone that you know, you should be relatively comfortable with the way frames are offered in FrontPage. Frames are a good example of the manner in which software such as FrontPage can simplify Web development by handling things behind the scenes.

During this chapter, you added frames to a Web and explored how they can be used instead of shared borders. You learned how to change a frame's size, yank out its scrollbars, and determine whether people should be able to move its borders around while viewing the page.

Frames take up a lot of real estate on a browser window, so there's definitely a tradeoff when you use them instead of shared borders or tables.

CHAPTER 38

Making a Point with Graphics

One of the easiest things to do in FrontPage is add a picture to a page. This is fortunate because images are an essential part of the World Wide Web experience. Without them, the Web might still be a little-known Internet service, scanners would be far less popular, and eBay items would be harder to sell because you couldn't put up a picture with your rare book collection.

After you add the pictures to a page, arranging them with other parts of the page is a little trickier.

During this chapter, you'll become an image-conscious FrontPage user. You'll lay out large pictures with paragraphs of text, and you'll line up smaller pictures with text and other page elements.

To feed the World Wide Web's enormous appetite for imagery, you'll also explore the FrontPage clip art gallery. This archive includes dozens of icons, buttons, drawings, and photographs you can use on your own FrontPage Webs.

Add a Graphic to a Page

In FrontPage, you can add pictures to a Web page with the Insert, Picture, From File command. The image will be displayed in the Page view, enabling you to see how it looks immediately.

Most pictures that are displayed on the World Wide Web are in the GIF or JPEG formats, because they're supported as a built-in feature of Netscape Navigator and Microsoft Internet Explorer. A newer format, an improvement on GIF called PNG, is becoming the third-most popular choice for Web imagery.

One way to work with picture files is to import them into your Web before you add them to any pages. FrontPage automatically creates an images subfolder with every Web template that can be used to store these files.

You also can add an image that isn't a part of your Web. It can be on any folder on your system or any address on the World Wide Web. Use the FrontPage File Open dialog box to both select local files and specify a file by a URL address.

If you've added images from folders on your system, copies of these images will be made when you either save the Web or preview it with a browser. A dialog box will open that lets you determine where these copies should be saved and what names they should be given. This enables you to create folders on your system that contain commonly used graphics. FrontPage will copy these graphics into Webs when they are used, effectively importing them for you.

> Another good reason to work with copies of common images is that FrontPage can make changes to images. As you'll see later, FrontPage can edit images directly to alter their quality and size. By keeping originals outside of any Webs, you prevent them from being modified.

Align a Picture on a Page

After you add a picture to a page, you can determine how it should be displayed in relation to everything else on the page. This is handled in the Picture Properties dialog box, shown in Figure 38.1.

The Appearance tab enables you to set the alignment of the image. Large pictures are generally aligned in one of three ways:

- The picture appears to the left of the text and other page elements that follow.
- The picture appears to the right of the text and other page elements that follow.
- The picture appears above everything that follows.

FIGURE 38.1

*The Picture Properties
dialog box.*

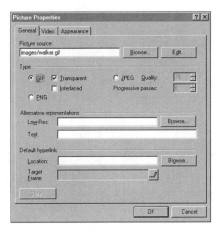

38

The easiest of these three to lay out is the third option: placing the picture above the following part of the page. To do this, the picture is added and a new paragraph or line break is inserted right after it. FrontPage places the Page view cursor at the lower-right corner of a picture after it is added to a page.

Figure 38.2 shows two Web pages. They're identical in every way but one: the picture of a city square has been set to a different alignment.

The pictures are set to either right or left alignment on these pages. This alignment controls where the text that follows is laid out.

As you look at the Web page with the text to the left, you may be confused about how it is that the text follows the picture. Anyone using a language that is written from left-to-right, like English, may think the *picture* follows the *text* because it appears to the right.

On a Web page, text follows a picture if the picture was inserted in one of two places:

- A cursor position closer to the top of the page than the text
- A cursor position to the left of the text on the same line

If you become confused about the cursor position where a picture has been added, the easiest remedy is to move it using cut-and-paste. Press Ctrl+X to delete the picture and add it to the Windows Clipboard, place your cursor in front of the text that should follow the picture, and hit Ctrl+V to paste it back to the page.

The remaining picture alignment options are most useful with small pictures, such as icons and menu buttons. Options such as Top, Middle, Absolute Middle, and Bottom determine how the picture is vertically aligned with the page elements that follow. By default, and when you're using left or right alignment, the top edge of a picture will be lined up with the top edge of whatever follows: text or another picture.

FIGURE **38.2**

*Two versions of the
same Web page.*

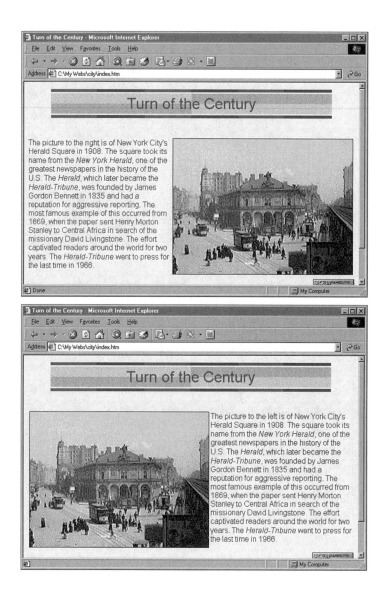

Figure 38.3 shows four "walking man" icons followed by lines of text. A box surrounds each icon to show exactly how big the picture is.

These alignments control layout as follows:

- Top alignment lines up the picture with the top of the following text.
- Bottom alignment lines up the bottom of the picture with the bottom of the text.

- Middle alignment lines up the middle of the picture with the bottom of the text.
- Absolute Middle alignment lines up the middle of the picture with the middle of the text.

FIGURE 38.3

Aligning a picture vertically.

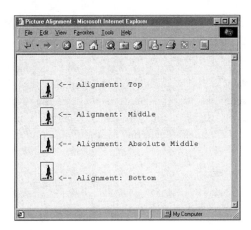

You can use these and other vertical alignment options with text, images, or anything else that is narrow enough to be displayed on a page side-by-side with a picture.

Add Hyperlinks and Descriptions to a Picture

The Picture Properties dialog box can be used to add a hyperlink to a picture and to add alternate text that describes a picture.

Add a Hyperlink

Hyperlinks are added in the same manner that they're associated with elements of a Web page. You can specify the URL of a site on the World Wide Web or pick a file that's on your own system.

You also can associate a hyperlink with a picture in the same manner that you would add a link to any element on a Web page. Select the picture and then either choose Insert, Hyperlink or click the Hyperlink button on the Standard toolbar.

Remember that the linked files on your system should be part of your Web if you're going to publish it.

Add Alternate Text

Providing a text description of each picture is important for making your Webs more usable. When a page is being downloaded, the text description is shown in the area that will be occupied by the picture. If the picture is a menu button or part of a navigation bar, this text enables people to use the picture's function before the picture is downloaded. If you've used a 28.8Kbps or slower Internet connection, you've probably done this many times to get to the page you wanted before the pictures finished loading at glacial speed.

Also, text descriptions are the only way a nonvisual Web browser can make any sense of hyperlinked images. If images are required to navigate your Web, each image should have text that describes its purpose.

Figure 38.4 shows how a Web page looks before the images have been loaded to replace the text descriptions. The text for Interests, Photo Album, and Favorites is shown next to icons with a square, circle, and triangle. These are all part of a navigation bar—FrontPage automatically creates descriptions for them—and they have active hyperlinks associated with them.

You can make all your Web pages look like Figure 38.4 by telling your browser not to display any images. In Internet Explorer, you can do this by clicking Tools, Internet Options and then clicking the Advanced tab. One of the check boxes on this tab controls whether pictures are displayed.

FIGURE 38.4
A Web page with picture descriptions.

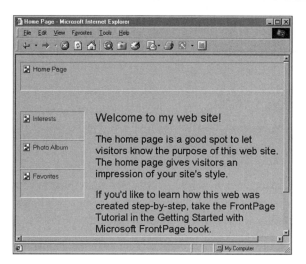

Choose Between GIF, JPEG, and PNG Graphics

Most images on the World Wide Web are in the GIF or JPEG formats, although PNG has become more popular in recent years as a substitute for GIF.

JPEG files, which usually have the .jpg file extension, use a data-compression algorithm that shrinks the file size (and more importantly, the download time) at the expense of image quality. When you save a JPEG file, you must decide how to balance these two factors.

Because of the data compression, JPEG is usually the format chosen to display complex images with a large number of colors. JPEG files are often good for displaying scanned photographs that don't have large areas of solid colors, even when the file sizes of the images have been greatly compressed.

GIF files have the .gif file extension and are often the best choice for simpler images with fewer colors. You can't display more than 256 colors in a GIF picture, so if a photograph is to be displayed as a GIF, it must first be reduced so that no more than 256 different colors appear in the image.

Despite the reduction in colors, GIF pictures often look much better than JPG files for photographs and other images. The problem with displaying a large, multicolor GIF file on the Web is that it takes much longer to download than a corresponding JPEG of the same image. For this reason, GIF files are normally used with small images that don't have a large number of colors, sometimes even eight or fewer.

GIF is much better than JPEG at handling images with large areas of a single color. Because of the way the JPEG data-compression algorithm saves file space, wavy lines will appear along the edges of any solid blocks of color, making the image appear more blurry.

The navigation bar buttons in each of FrontPage's themes are GIF files. Many of them use solid colors and do not take up a lot of room on a page, so GIF is the better choice.

The Reports view will keep track of the download time required for the pages on your Web. You can use this to see when a page might need some JPEGs instead of GIF files to speed things up.

A third format that's often been used on the World Wide Web is *PNG*, which stands for *Portable Network Graphics*. PNG was introduced as an enhanced alternative to the GIF format.

The PNG format was created in response to a 1994 announcement by CompuServe that it would begin charging royalties for some uses of the GIF format. Unisys claimed that the GIF format violated a file compression patent it owned, so PNG was created to be a legally secure public standard for image files.

PNG images have the .png filename extension. They're often used in the same way as GIF files, but PNG also can support thousands of colors and can be used as an alternative to the JPEG format.

Past versions of PNG were supported by Web browser plug-ins—programs that are downloaded and installed separately from a browser and that enhance its functionality. Versions 4.0 and later of Netscape Navigator and Microsoft Internet Explorer can display PNG files without a plug-in.

Another way to enhance the display of pictures on your Webs is to offer low-resolution versions of the pictures. These versions should be extremely small in file size so they load quickly, and they can be specified in the Picture Properties dialog box.

Add Clip Art to a Page

FrontPage includes a gallery of clip art—images you can freely use on your own Webs. To browse through the gallery, select the Insert, Picture, Clip Art menu command.

Clip art is arranged according to more than a dozen section headings. If you know what you're looking for, you can use the search feature to view only the clip art related to that topic. For example, a search for "letter" would produce the images shown in the Clip Art Gallery dialog box (see Figure 38.5). A thumbnail drawing of each picture is shown. You can view a full-size version of each image and add it to a page as if you loaded the picture from a file.

FIGURE 38.5

Searching the Clip Art Gallery.

Adding a picture from clip art instead of another source requires an extra step: You must select the format in which to save the graphic in your Web. You don't actually work with the graphic contained in the Clip Art Gallery. Instead, you make a copy in one of three formats: GIF, JPEG, or PNG. This choice is made in the Picture Properties dialog box.

When you select a GIF file, you can configure the picture to be displayed in an interlaced pattern. *Interlacing* displays a picture as a series of more focused images. If that definition is itself a little blurry, think of a set of binoculars that are completely out of focus when you first look into them. As you adjust the focus, the thing you're looking at changes from a blur of colors into an increasingly sharp image. Interlacing is similar to this, because it displays an image as if you were bringing it into focus. On the other hand, a *non-interlaced* GIF displays the image in successive horizontal lines as it downloads them, so you'll see the top half of a picture in full before the bottom half arrives.

Clip art that's saved as a JPEG file must have a Quality percentage indicated. The scale ranges from 1 (compressed as much as possible) to 100 (no compression at all). The default is 75%.

38

A JPEG file that is compressed loses quality every time it is compressed again. Whenever you create JPEG graphics, you should keep an original file that isn't compressed at all—as the FrontPage Clip Art Gallery does. This enables you to return to the original and compress it at a different quality.

One thing you'll want to do often with clip art is resize it. All the pictures on a Web page can be displayed at different sizes, whether it's larger, smaller, or even distorted so that the width is at a different scale than the height. You can make these changes on the Appearance tab of the Page Properties dialog box (see Figure 38.6).

You can change the picture's size in pixel increments or as a percentage of the original. This does not alter the actual picture, so an image displayed at 10% of its normal size still takes the same amount of time to download.

If you can't find a suitable picture in the Clip Art Gallery that's included with FrontPage, you can find more pictures, photographs, and movie files in Microsoft's online version of the gallery. After connecting to the Internet, choose the Clips Online button on the Clip Art Gallery dialog box to open Microsoft's Web site of clip art. You'll be able to browse through it and search for specific keywords, and the clip art you select will be imported automatically into FrontPage.

FIGURE 38.6

Altering a picture's display size.

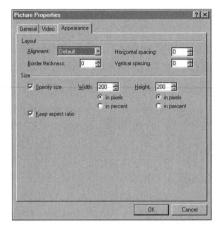

Add Page Banners and Navigation Bars

Page banners and navigation bars are specified with all of FrontPage's themes, so you should already have experience working with them. Page banners look like giant navigation buttons (if they're graphical), and they provide a way to give a page a title. Navigation bars are related groups of hyperlinks that are represented as graphical buttons or text. Both of them are FrontPage components—special interactive elements that can be used on your Webs. They combine editable text and pictures.

You can add these components to pages with the Insert, Navigation Bar and Insert, Page Banner commands.

A page banner contains a single line of text and can have a graphical background. The picture used as the background is defined by the Web's theme—Webs without a theme cannot have graphical page banners.

The text of a page banner will be the same as its title in the Navigation view window. If the page isn't in the navigational structure of the Web yet, it must be added before a banner can be displayed.

When you save or publish a Web, FrontPage creates pictures for each graphical page banner and navigation bar on your Web. The text is displayed over the component's background image.

All of this takes place behind the scenes, so you work with these components differently than you do with pictures.

Summary

This chapter enabled you to set your sights higher on your FrontPage Webs.

By looking into the subject of image handling, you've learned how to make pages and entire Webs more visually compelling. You saw how to add pictures, align them with other parts of a page, and change how they're displayed. You took a gander at the three most common formats for graphics files: GIF, JPEG, and PNG. Finally, you found a sight for sore eyes in the FrontPage Clip Art Gallery, a collection of pictures you can easily add to your own pages.

38

PART XI

Making FrontPage Do More Work

Chapter

CHAPTER 39

Publishing Web Pages

All of the Webs you have seen created so far were viewed locally on your own system. During this chapter, you'll learn how to publish a FrontPage Web on the World Wide Web. The same techniques can be used to put it onto a corporate intranet. You'll be able to publish Webs and partial updates to a server, set up a Personal Web Server on your own system, and save Webs directly to a server.

Publish Your Web to a Server

FrontPage can publish Webs to three different places:

- A hard drive on your system or local area network
- A server on your system such as the Apache Web Server
- A server on the World Wide Web

Saving a Web to your hard drive is a form of publication. You can view each of the pages, test the hyperlinks, and try out many of the features supported by FrontPage.

You won't be able to test some of the features that rely on FrontPage Server Extensions—special programs that run in conjunction with a Web server to offer extra functionality to FrontPage Webs. To test these before you publish on the World Wide Web, you must install a Web server on your system and equip it with FrontPage Server Extensions. Doing this often requires a fairly high knowledge of networking and in-depth operating system commands.

Publishing to a Web Hosting Provider

The only real difference between publishing on your system and to the World Wide Web is in the way you specify the destination. Publishing on your system requires the name of a folder. Publishing to the World Wide Web requires the name of a machine, and possibly the name of a folder where your FrontPage Web can be stored. In both cases, you're copying files from one location to another.

Before you can publish a FrontPage Web to another machine on the Internet, you need a username and password that grant you permission to store files on that machine. You also may need the name of the folder where the Web can be stored, depending on how the Web hosting service is configured.

The location where you can store your Web is indicated by a Web address. Here are some fictitious examples:

- `http://www.fp2k.com/~yourusername`
- `ftp://ftp.fp2k.com/users/yourusername/public_html`

Both of these examples specify a machine name (either `www.fp2k.com` or `ftp.fp2k.com`), followed by a folder name. The folder name tells the Web hosting machine where the files should be stored when they're published by FrontPage. It also can be used after publication to load the site in a Web browser.

Choose Where to Publish a Web

When you're ready to publish a FrontPage Web, select File, Publish. Your first choice will be to publish the Web to the last place a Web was published, which will probably be a folder on your own system. Click the Browse button to use an Open Web dialog, as shown in Figure 39.1.

The Open Web dialog includes a column of icons that resembles the Views bar. Click the Web Folders icon to list shortcuts to Web servers where you have previously published sites.

The Folder name field can be used to enter the full Web address and folder name (if necessary) where the site should be published.

FIGURE 39.1

*Opening a Web folder
for publication.*

GeoCities, a free hosting service that can be used as a place to publish FrontPage Webs, does not require a folder name at this time. To publish a Web to GeoCities, ftp://ftp.geocities.com should be entered in the Folder Name field.

Another free host, Tripod, requires a folder name as part of the Web address. If your username is palmetto, the folder name should be http://members.tripod.com/palmetto.

If you're publishing a Web to the main folder of a Web server on your system, http://localhost should be entered as the folder name (unless your server requires a different location). However, this address publishes the Web in the root folder of a Personal Web Server. Publishing to a subfolder requires a two-step process:

39

- Click the Browse button and open the localhost Web folder.
- Click the New Folder button to give this subfolder a name.

Click the Open button when you've selected the place where your Web should be published.

Publish Your Web to a Server

The last step in the Web publishing process is the moment of truth: Connecting to the server so that files can be published on it.

Figure 39.2 shows the Publish Web dialog box.

You can choose to publish an entire Web or just the files that have changed since it was last published, if this is applicable. If the Web hosting service requires an SSL connection, put a check mark in the Secure connection required (SSL) box.

The Publish button begins the transfer of files. You must be connected to the Internet before you can publish to a server that's on the World Wide Web. If FrontPage can make a connection to the Web server and it requires a login, a dialog box will appear requesting your username and password.

FIGURE 39.2

Publishing a Web.

Barring any login problems, FrontPage will then begin copying files from your system to the Web server. This process can take five minutes or more, depending on the speed of your Internet connection and the number of files in your Web. (Publishing to a Personal Web Server is much quicker, of course.)

Unlike some file transfers, this one doesn't give you an excuse to take care of any tasks you've been neglecting while you learned how to use FrontPage, such as food, drink, taxes, and yelling at the kids who drive past the house too fast. FrontPage may have questions as it transfers files to the server. If it encounters a file on the server that isn't in your Web, it will ask whether to delete it. Also, if a file has been changed on the server since you last published it, FrontPage will warn you about this before overwriting the changed file.

A successful transfer ends with a happy dialog box that invites you to click a hyperlink to the newly published Web.

Solve Any Publishing Problems

When you're just learning how to publish a Web, there are several different problems that can stymie the process. You may begin to suspect that there's no happy dialog box and that Web publishing is a myth, like the 40-hour work week, the Wizard of Oz, and tax refunds.

The following suggestions may help you bring up this wonderful dialog box, and none of them involve clicking your ruby slippers together while wishing you could return to Kansas.

Try the following when good Web transfers go bad:

- If you're publishing to a Personal Web Server, make sure it's running. Click the server's icon on the taskbar to see its current status.

- Double-check your username and password to make sure they're correct.

- If you're specifying a Web address and folder name, such as
  `http://www.fp2k.com/~yourusername/`, load this address in your Web browser. In
  most cases, a test page or file listing should appear because Web hosting services
  often create the folder before you ever publish to it.

- If you're specifying a folder name, try taking it out and specifying only the
  machine name, as in `http://www.fp2k.com`. Some Web hosting services will find the
  right folder for your username automatically.

These examples cover the most commonplace problems that might occur as you're publishing a Web. In some instances, you may encounter problems because the hosting service doesn't offer FrontPage Server Extensions, although this normally doesn't prevent pages and files from being transferred to the Web server.

> One of the buttons on the Publish Web dialog box is labeled WPP's—Web
> presence providers. Click this button to go to Microsoft's list of hosting ser-
> vices that are specifically tailored to FrontPage Webs. Many of these services
> will have guidance and support for your publishing problems.

39

If You Publish Your Web on GeoCities

If you'd like to try to send a Web page to a free host for practice, you can go through the GeoCities sign-up process and choose your own username and the folder where your home page will be located. GeoCities organizes folders as a group of neighborhoods, and each home page has an address number. If you're at address number 1000 in the PicketFence neighborhood, your Web page is located at this address:

`http://www.geocities.com/PicketFence/1000`

Your password will be mailed to the email address you specified during signup. This generally arrives within an hour after you join, but it may take longer.

Once you have the password, you can publish a Web. The folder name you should publish to is simply `ftp://ftp.geocities.com`, with no folder specified. GeoCities will ask for your username and password, and will publish your Web to the folder associated with that account.

One quirk of publishing on GeoCities is that the service only allows approved filename extensions. If you're trying to publish a file with an unapproved extension, you'll get an error message and the Web won't be fully published.

This shouldn't affect any of the files created by FrontPage to support a Web, nor will it prevent Web pages or most file formats, such as GIF, JPEG, or WAV, from being published.

What it will affect are which files you may import into a Web. The most notable example of a forbidden extension is .exe. GeoCities does not allow executable programs to be stored on its Web servers as part of a site.

When you've published a Web and the happy dialog box appears to note this achievement, try it out in your Web browser.

Publishing Your Web to Tripod

As of this writing, Tripod offers support for FrontPage Server Extensions, unlike GeoCities. For this reason, it may be a better free-hosting choice to practice your Web design.

After you go through Tripod's sign-up process for a free home page, Tripod will give your Web an address that's based on your username. If you selected palmetto as your username, for example, your Web's main address would be this:

```
http://members.tripod.com/palmetto
```

If your site requires FrontPage Server Extensions to operate features such as discussion Webs or feedback pages, you must enable these extensions on Tripod before publishing your Web. This can be done from the following Web address:

```
http://homepager.tripod.com/tools/frontpage
```

When you enable the extensions, Tripod will create several new folders in your Web that contain files used by FrontPage. Don't delete these files and folders, or some features of your Web might cease to function.

After your Web is published successfully to Tripod, you'll get a chance to try it out in your browser immediately.

Summary

Throughout this chapter, you learned how to publish on other servers—Web hosting providers on the Internet. Publishing a Web in FrontPage is one of those tasks that's easy once you've done it successfully. It becomes as simple a task as saving files from one folder to another. Getting to that point can be a challenge sometimes, depending on how FrontPage and your Web hosting provider work in conjunction with each other. One advantage to using a Web hosting service that you pay for is that many of them offer free telephone support for newcomers to Web publishing.

CHAPTER 40

Communicating with Web Forms

One of the easiest mistakes to make as a World Wide Web publisher is to treat this medium like its older siblings: television, radio, and print. For the most part, those media are a one-way street because the audience can't immediately respond (with the possible exception of Elvis Presley, who once registered his displeasure with a television by shooting it). Nor can they do anything to change the presentation as it's occurring. At its best, the World Wide Web is a collaboration between the people who publish sites and the people who visit them. As a Web publisher, you can collect information from the visitors to your pages, present it on your site, and use it in other ways to create a more engaging experience. When you collect information on your FrontPage Web, you'll be using a Web page element called a *form*. Forms are made up of text boxes, lists, and other means of gathering information from visitors.

Create a Form with the Form Page Wizard

If you've never created a form before, the easiest way to start is by asking the Form Page Wizard to do it.

Like other wizards in FrontPage, the Form Page Wizard asks a series of questions to determine what you'd like to add to your Web:

- What questions do you want to ask?
- What kind of answers are acceptable?
- How should the questions and answers be formatted on the Web page?
- What should happen to the answers afterward?

When all of this has been determined, the wizard will create a new page in the current Web and add the form to it. You can either use this page or transfer it to another page using copy and paste.

Call on the Wizard

The first step in using the Form Page Wizard is to add a new page to an existing Web by clicking File, New, Page. A list of templates and wizards that can be employed on the new page is shown.

When the Form Page Wizard is selected, you can immediately add questions to the form. You also can either remove or modify existing questions, which makes it easy to change things on-the-fly as you're working with the wizard.

The wizard requires two things in order to add questions to a form: a prompt and an input type. A *prompt* is a succinct line of text that asks a question or describes a group of related questions. The *input type* represents the structure of the information collected in response to the prompt.

Ask a Simple Question

Several of the wizard's input types determine how a single question can be answered. They include the following:

- date—A calendar date
- time—A time
- number—A numeric value
- range—A number from 1 to 5 that's used to rate something

- `string`—A single line of text
- `paragraph`—Text that can be longer than a single line
- `boolean`—A response limited to one of two options, such as yes or no, true or false, and on or off

Figure 40.1 shows the Form Page Wizard being used to add the question "Have you ever been convicted of a crime?" The input type for this question has been set to *boolean*, which limits responses to an either/or proposition such as yes or no. The *string* or *paragraph* input types could have been used instead, giving someone a chance to provide a more unstructured answer such as "Not since I quit using illegal drugs."

FIGURE 40.1

Adding a boolean question to a form.

40

Each of these questions can be customized once the input type and prompt have been defined. You can limit date and time answers to specific formats, restrict a string answer to a specific number of characters, and make other decisions that affect how the form will be used.

One of the things you must customize about a question is the name of its *variable*, which is a place in a computer program where information can be stored for later use. Variables are used in Web forms to keep track of how questions have been answered. Each variable is given a name that can be used to retrieve or modify its value.

A variable's name should describe its purpose. You can use any combination of letters, numbers, and the underscore character (_) when you're naming variables. For example, three appropriate names for the "convicted of a crime" question are *Convictions*, *Any_Convictions*, or *CriminalRecord*.

Choose from a List of Options

There are two input types in the Form Page Wizard that enable answers to be selected from a list of possible choices:

- `one of several options`—A single item can be picked from the list.

- `any of several options`—An unlimited number of items can be picked (including none).

The prompt should identify what the list is being used to answer.

Each choice in a list must be a single line of text. Single-choice lists can be presented in three different ways on a Web page: a drop-down menu, radio buttons, or a list. All of these are shown on the portion of a Web page displayed in Figure 40.2.

FIGURE 40.2

Three ways a list of options can be presented.

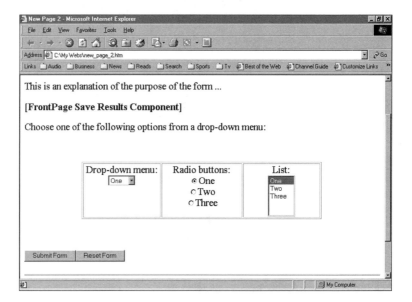

As shown, a drop-down menu shows only one possible answer at a time. If you click the arrow next to the answer, a menu of other answers will appear. Radio buttons and lists show several possible answers.

To make a drop-down menu easier to understand, use the visible answer to provide explanatory text such as "Click to make your selection." This also prevents the visible answer from being picked more often than other answers simply because it is automatically displayed.

A multiple-choice list enables the user to select more than one answer from a list. Each possible answer is shown next to a check box. A single-choice list restricts the answer to a single item in the list. Both types of lists must have a named variable to store answers in.

Multiple-choice lists require a group of variables—one for each possible choice that can be selected. Instead of providing a name for each of these variables, you provide a *base name*. This will be combined with the text of each answer to form variable names.

Figure 40.3 shows the Form Page Wizard being used to create a multiple-choice list. The list is used to answer the question "Which of the following languages do you speak?" One of four answers can be selected: English, Spanish, German, or Esperanto.

FIGURE 40.3

Providing answers and a base variable name for a multiple-choice list.

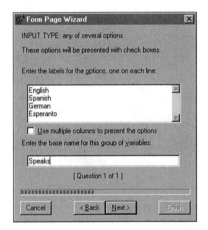

The base variable name is *Speaks*. The answers to this question will be saved in the variables *Speaks_English*, *Speaks_Spanish*, *Speaks_German*, and *Speaks_Esperanto*.

Ask Multiple Questions at Once

The remaining input types in the Form Page Wizard are used to ask several related questions at the same time. They include the following:

- `contact information`—Name, title, address, phone number, and other identification
- `account information`—Username and password
- `product information`—Product name, product version, and serial number
- `ordering information`—Products to order, billing information, and a shipping address
- `personal information`—Name, age, physical characteristics, and related information

40

The Form Page Wizard automatically provides a prompt for each question in the group. If you provide your own prompt, it will be used to introduce the entire group rather than for any specific questions.

These combined input types make it easy to add some of the most common questions to a form. You can customize these questions by removing any questions that you don't want to ask.

In Figure 40.4, the Form Page Wizard is being used to customize a group of questions after the *contact information* input type was selected. The figure shows all of the customization options offered with the `contact information` input type. The Name and E-mail address questions are selected.

FIGURE 40.4

Selecting which contact information questions to use on a form.

For some of these input types, the variable names will be provided by the wizard. Otherwise, a base variable name must be provided for the group of questions. This will be used by the wizard to associate a variable name with each question.

Determine How the Form Will Be Presented

After you've finished adding questions to a form, you can choose how the questions will be presented on a Web page. You can lay out the form as a series of paragraphs or as one of three different lists:

- A numbered list
- A bulleted list, in which each question is indented with a bullet character (like the list you're currently reading)
- A definition list

A definition list is a standard Web page element that's ideal for displaying a group of words and their definitions. The formatting varies depending on the browser being used. Generally, words are presented flush-left, and definitions are indented below the word they define. The following text is presented in the style of a definition list:

```
Do
  A deer; a female deer
Ra
  A drop of golden sun
Mi
  The name I call myself
Fa
  A long, long way to run
```

On a form that's displayed as a definition list, questions are presented flush-left and possible answers are indented.

Another presentation decision you must make is whether to use tables when laying out your form. Tables can be used to arrange elements on a page. If you decide to use a table, the Form Page Wizard will place questions and answers into their own cells on the table, making the form appear more organized. The borders of this table will not be visible when the form is created.

If you decide not to use a table, questions and answers will be arranged more loosely as a series of paragraphs.

Figure 40.5 shows a Web page that contains two versions of the same three-question form—a survey for owners of a company's bread-makers. The upper version of the form is formatted with a table, which lines up the questions and possible answers evenly in two columns. The lower version does not use a table.

40

FIGURE 40.5

Arranging a form with and without a table.

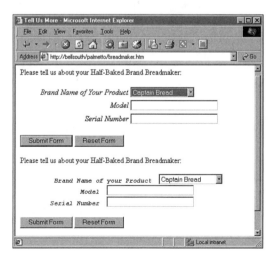

Save the Information Collected on a Form

The last step in creating a form with the Form Page Wizard is to decide how a user's answers will be saved. The following three options are available:

- save results to a web page
- save results to a text file
- use custom CGI script

To save a form's answers to a Web page or text file, you must be publishing your Web on a server that is enabled with FrontPage Server Extensions.

All answers submitted using the form will be saved to the same page. A question is identified on this form using its variable name followed by a semicolon. The answer to that question is presented on the following line. Figure 40.6 shows two sets of form results saved to a Web page.

FIGURE 40.6

Viewing a form's results that have been saved to a Web page.

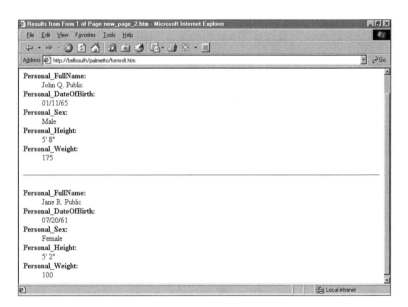

Displaying results as a Web page is useful when you want to view the answers in an easy-to-understand format.

If you're going to use form results with other software (such as Microsoft Access or another database program), they should be saved to a text file. This file can easily be imported into a database program. The first line of the file will identify each of the form's variables, and each subsequent line will contain a set of results.

The following output contains the same form results shown in Figure 40.6, saved to a text file instead:

```
"Personal_FullName"  "Personal_DateOfBirth"  "Personal_Sex"
➥"Personal Height"  "Personal_Weight"
"John Q. Public"  "01/11/65"  "Male"  "5' 8"""  "175"
"Jane R. Public"  "07/20/61"  "Female"  "5' 2"""  "100"
```

This text file uses Tab characters to separate each field: `Personal FullName`, `Personal DateOfBirth`, `Personal Sex`, and `Personal Height`. A format like this is less readable to humans than HTML, but much more readable to database software.

When you save form results, you must name the file that will be used to store them. The Form Page Wizard will provide an `.htm` or `.txt` file extension for you, so all you'll need to choose is the name that precedes the extension. Results are saved in the same folder as the Web page that contains the form, unless you specify a different one along with the filename.

A FrontPage Web's `_private` subfolder is a useful place to save form results that shouldn't be viewed by the people who visit your site. To save results to this folder, precede the filename with the text `_private/`. Also, make sure that access permissions for that folder have been established correctly.

The file that contains form results can be loaded within FrontPage. If you'd like to delete all existing results, delete the file. A new file will be created automatically when new results are submitted using the form.

The final option for saving form results is to use a custom *Common Gateway Interface* (*CGI*) script. CGI refers to the use of special programs—also called *scripts*—that are run in conjunction with Web pages. A Web server that supports FrontPage offers a lot of the same functionality as a CGI program. The main use of CGI on the World Wide Web is to handle the results of Web forms.

CGI programs require special access to the Web server that's hosting your Web. You'll need to know the name of the CGI program to run and its location on the Web site.

40

A Sample Web Form

The form shown in Figure 40.7 was created using the following steps in the Form Page Wizard:

- A question was added with the input type `contact information` and the prompt "Who are you?".

- Only two of the `contact information` questions were selected: Name and E-mail address.

- A question was added with the input type `number` and the prompt "How many times have you been to the park?".

- The question was given the variable name `Visits`.

- A question was added with the input type `one of many options` and the prompt "What is your favorite attraction?".

- Labels were provided for several attractions at the park, and the base variable name was set to `FavoriteAttraction`.

- A question was added with the input type `one of many options` and the prompt "What is your favorite restaurant?".

- Labels were provided for park restaurants, and the base variable name was set to `FavoriteRestaurant`.

- The wizard was told that no more questions would be added.

- The default presentation options were used: normal paragraphs and the use of tables to arrange questions and answers.

- Results were saved to a text file named `parksurvey.txt`, and the wizard created the form on a new page.

FIGURE 40.7

A form that conducts a survey over the World Wide Web.

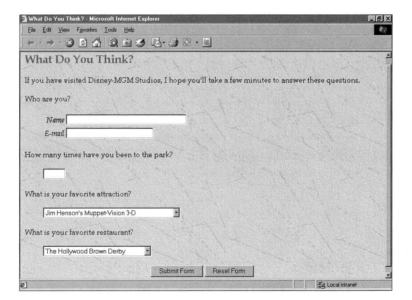

Manually Creating Forms

The Form Page Wizard is well-suited to many of the forms you might want to use on a Web. For the times that it isn't, you can create a form manually by designing it on a Web page.

In the rest of this chapter, you'll learn how to design a form by using text boxes, check boxes, radio buttons, drop-down menus, and more. You'll create these elements, add labels that describe their purposes, and limit the visitor's answers to a range of possible choices.

When the form is completed, you'll determine how to use the information it has collected—saving it to a text file, sending it as email, or calling special Web server programs that can decode the form.

You'll also be able to modify existing forms, which is useful even if they were originally created by a FrontPage wizard.

Creating a Form by Hand

Choose Insert, Form to add a form element to a Web page. Forms are made up of the following elements:

- One-line text boxes
- Scrolling text boxes
- Check boxes
- Radio buttons
- Drop-down menus
- Labels
- Pushbuttons
- Pictures

Figure 40.8 shows all of these elements on a Web page, except for pictures.

Create a new Web page and add any of these form elements to it. When you add your first form element to the page, FrontPage creates a form border and puts the element within this border. It also adds two extra elements:

- A Submit button for transmitting the information collected on the form.
- A Reset button for clearing out all answers on a form and starting over.

These two buttons are placed at the bottom of a form, but you can move them anywhere within the form's border.

All information that is collected on a form must come from elements located within its border in Page view. This border is used only for that purpose, and it does not show up when the page is displayed in a browser.

40

Label   One-line text box

FIGURE **40.8**

Elements of a form.

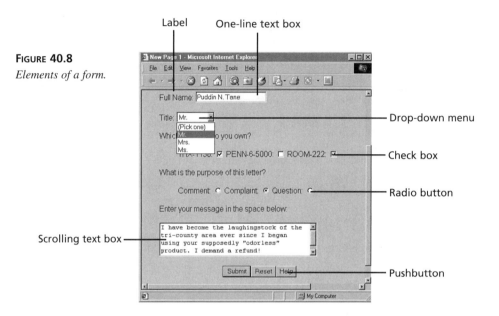

Scrolling text box

Drop-down menu

Check box

Radio button

Pushbutton

Form elements can be arranged within a border, just like anything else on a Web page. You can put them into tables, add pictures, and other things, as long as the form elements stay within the border.

You can add additional forms to a page by dropping form elements outside of a border. FrontPage will automatically border the elements and add Submit and Reset buttons.

Add Text Boxes

Text boxes enable the visitor to enter keyboard input on a Web page—a single line in a one-line box, and an unlimited number of lines in a scrolling box.

Add a text box to a form by choosing Insert, Form, Text Box, and remember to place the text box within the form's border. FrontPage assigns it a default width that approximates the number of characters that can be displayed in the box. More characters can be entered, but they won't all appear within the box. Scrolling text boxes also have a default number of lines that are displayed.

FrontPage also gives each box a default name and value, just as is does with all other form elements. To change these things after the element has been added to a page, double-click it to bring up the Text Box Properties dialog box, shown in Figure 40.9.

Every form element should be given a descriptive name that explains its purpose. This name will be used when the element's information is transmitted, and it also can be used by a scripting language such as *JavaScript* to get the element's value.

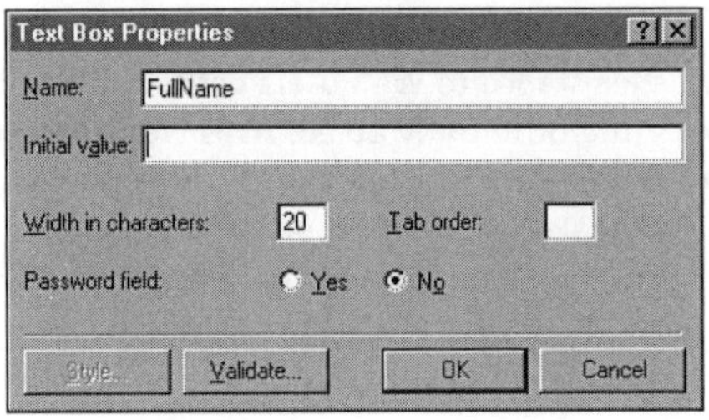

FIGURE **40.9**

Editing a text box.

The name given to a form element should contain only alphanumeric characters and the underscore character (_). If you use anything else, such as spaces, FrontPage will warn you that the form might not work correctly in a browser.

If you give a text box an initial value, it will appear when the form is first loaded or the Reset button is clicked. This can be used to give the text box a default value. For instance, the Internal Revenue Service could put a default value of 100 in the Percentage of Your Income To Pay This Year in Taxes text box. Taxpayers would have to edit this initial value to pay less than 100 percent of their income in federal tax.

Select the password field option to hide all input entered into a one-line text box. Asterisks will appear in place of what's really being typed as a way to protect against snoops.

Add a second one-line text box to a form and select the password field option for that element. Although asterisks appear in that box when you type into it, the real text you're typing will be sent when the form is submitted.

Add Labels

A *label* is text that describes the purpose of another form element. Since elements are often used to answer questions, labels are used to actually ask the questions.

To add a label to a form, begin by typing the text for the label. This text should be on the same line as the form element it's associated with. Enter the text of a label next to a one-line text box, and then highlight both of the text and the form element and choose Insert, Form, Label. A border will appear around the text to indicate that it's now a label.

Turning text into a label makes it easier for people to use a form. In many cases, they can click the label in addition to the form element. Clicking a check box's label is the same as clicking the check box, for instance.

40

Labels provide assistance to Web users with non-visual browsers and other technology for the differently abled. Assistive software can use the label to explain the purpose of a form element. For example, a nonvisual Web browser could speak each label aloud before enabling the user to enter information into the form element that's associated with the label.

Add Radio Buttons and Check Boxes

Radio buttons and *check boxes* are form elements that have only two possible values: selected or not selected. You can set these elements to either value when the page is first loaded.

A check box appears with a check mark if it's selected and appears empty otherwise. Each box is given a name and a value—ON by default—that is sent for each selected check box when the form is transmitted.

One way to use check boxes would be to ask people what political parties they voted for in the past decade. There could be check boxes for the Republican, Democratic, Libertarian, and Reform parties. Between 0 and 4 boxes could be checked, depending on how often the person jumped across party lines at the ballot box. An appropriate value for these boxes would be YES, because it's only transmitted for boxes that are selected.

A radio button is a circle that has a dot in it if it's selected. You group radio buttons together by giving each of them the same name, which should also contain only alphanumeric characters and underscores.

Add a check box and a series of radio buttons to a form by choosing Insert, Form, Check Box and Insert, Form, Radio Button, respectively. Only one radio button can be selected in any group, so if you select one of them, the others will all be deselected. This is where the name *radio buttons* comes from—buttons on a car radio function the same way, limiting you to one station at any time.

The value given to a radio button should describe what selecting the button means. Consider radio buttons with the group name CustomerSatisfaction and the labels Ecstatic, Happy, Undecided, Displeased, and Enraged. These labels could also be used as values for the buttons—so if someone picks the Enraged button, CustomerSatisfaction will be transmitted with a value of Enraged.

Add Drop-Down Menus

Drop-down menus serve a similar purpose to radio buttons: They enable the user to choose from several possible responses. However, instead these possible choices being divided into buttons, they're placed in a menu. Drop-down menus also differ in another way—they can be configured to allow more than one choice to be selected.

When you add a drop-down menu to a form, it doesn't have any possible responses. You add these responses by editing the menu. Double-click it to open the Drop-Down Menu Properties dialog shown in Figure 40.10.

FIGURE 40.10

Editing a drop-down menu.

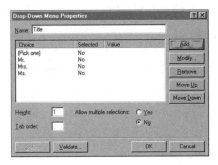

The Add button is used to add new responses to the menu. Each response has a Choice value that will appear on the menu, and the Selected value is transmitted with the form unless you specify an alternative.

The default behavior of a drop-down menu is to allow one choice to be selected and to display the menu on a single-line when it isn't being used. Both of these things can be changed in the Properties dialog box—double-click the form element to make these changes.

After you've added all possible responses to a drop-down menu, you can rearrange them with the Move Up and Move Down buttons.

40

The first choice in a drop-down menu is sometimes used like a label. A value such as "(Pick one)" or "(Click here to select)" is used as the topmost choice. This has the added advantage of preventing the first real choice from being selected simply because it appears when the page is loaded.

Add Pushbuttons and Pictures

Pushbuttons are form elements that look just like the Submit and Reset buttons incorporated into every FrontPage form.

If you delete the Submit or Reset buttons from a form, you can put them back by inserting a pushbutton for each and editing its properties. Otherwise, there isn't a way to use a pushbutton to transmit a value without writing your own interactive programs in a scripting language such as JavaScript.

Pushbuttons can be associated with hyperlinks, so you can add them to a form as links to other pages. One possible use: a Help button that loads a page describing how to use the form.

Pictures on a form, which are added by choosing Insert, Form, Picture, are used for two purposes:

- Replacing the Submit button with a graphical version
- Creating an imagemap that is handled by a Web server

A picture element is placed on a form as a FrontPage imagemap component. This component, unlike other imagemaps, requires a Web server that includes FrontPage Server Extensions.

When the picture is clicked, the form is submitted with some extra information: the exact location on the picture where it was clicked. Neither FrontPage nor its server extensions do anything with this location information. Because of that, the only thing you can do with a picture label is use it as an alternate submit button—if your server has FrontPage extensions.

Receive Information from a Form

The last step in creating a form is deciding where to put all the information you've gathered. Your choices are the following:

- Send it in an email to a specified address
- Store it as a file on your Web
- Store it in a database on your Web
- Send it to a form-handling program on your Web server

The first three options require a Web server that supports FrontPage Server Extensions. Form data that is mailed will arrive like any other email. The name and value of each form element will be displayed in the body of the email, as in the following:

```
FullName: Puddin N. Tane
Title: Mr.
THX-1138: Own
ROOM-222: Own
Purpose: Complaint
```

To save a form to a file, you specify the filename and folder where it should be stored. If this file doesn't exist when someone uses the form, it will be created.

If you don't restrict access to the form results file by using FrontPage's security feature, anyone who visits your Web will be able to read the file by loading its address directly with their browser.

The last way to handle forms is to call up a program on your Web server that can take in form data and do something with it. (Most of these programs simply email the data to a specified address.)

Form-handling programs rely on the Common Gateway Interface (CGI), a protocol that determines how a Web server exchanges information with other programs on the same computer. CGI programs require special access to a Web server, and most Web hosting services don't grant it to their customers for security reasons. Some hosting services install CGI programs that can be shared by all customers.

If you have a CGI program that handles forms, all you need to do in FrontPage is specify the name and location of the program and its delivery method. The method is either POST or GET, and the documentation for the CGI program should specify which one to use.

Figure 40.11 shows how this information is configured in FrontPage.

FIGURE 40.11

Calling a CGI program to handle a form.

40

Figure 40.12 shows a Web form that includes every form element described here except pictures.

Creating this form took the following steps:

- Text was added to a Web page for use as a label.
- A form element was added adjacent to the text.
- The form element was double-clicked and given a name using its Properties dialog box.

An extra step was involved in the creation of the radio buttons—all of these buttons were given the same group name.

After the drop-down menu was placed on the form, items were added to it by double-clicking the menu and using its Properties dialog box.

FIGURE 40.12

An intrusive Web form.

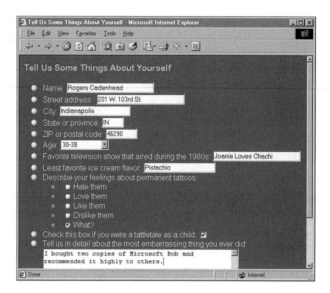

If the form shown in Figure 40.12 was submitted to an email address, it would arrive looking like the following:

```
**************************************************************************
Name:            Rogers Cadenhead
StreetAddress:        201 W. 103rd St.
City:            Indianapolis
StateOrProvince:        IN
ZipOrPostalCode:        46290
Age:            30-39
Favorite80sTVShow:        Joanie Loves Chachi
LeastFavoriteIceCreamFlavor: Pistachio
Tattoo:          What?
Tattletale:          ON
EmailAddress:          frontpage24@prefect.com

MostEmbarrasingThing:

I bought two copies of Microsoft Bob and recommended it
highly to others.
```

Summary

By using the Form Page Wizard, you can easily add interactive features to your FrontPage Web. As you explored the wizard's capabilities and created your own form in this chapter, some ideas on how to use this Web page capability probably sprang to mind.

Forms can be employed to offer user surveys, visitor feedback, polls, questionnaires, tests, and many other interactive features.

Elvis Presley, not having a satisfactory way to communicate with television programmers, shot one of the devices in his home. Forms give visitors to your Webs a satisfactory way to communicate with you that do not involve possible violations of federal, state, or local law.

Forms are an essential feature of the World Wide Web because they immediately connect a publisher with the people who visit a Web. You can create forms quickly with FrontPage's Form Page Wizard. You also can take more control over a form by adding its elements to a Web page directly.

By using text boxes, check boxes, radio buttons, and other parts of a form, you can ask questions in a variety of different ways. A multiple-choice question can be limited to a single answer with radio buttons or multiple answers on a drop-down menu. More open-ended answers can be typed in as one or more lines of text.

40

CHAPTER 41

Seeing What HTML Is All About

All World Wide Web pages are created by using *Hypertext Markup Language* (*HTML*), a set of formatting commands that are added to text documents. These formatting commands, which are called *tags*, turn normal text into headings, hyperlinks, paragraphs, and anything else you can put on a Web page.

When you apply formatting to part of a page, FrontPage marks that section with the corresponding HTML tag. FrontPage acts as an interpreter between what you want to do and how HTML does it. None of this is shown in the Page view, because you work with the page as it's going to look in a browser. For this reason, you can avoid learning HTML entirely.

During this chapter, you'll learn how to edit a Web page using HTML and see the markup tags that make up the document. This skill will come in handy when you're given some HTML-tagged text that should be added to your Webs. It also provides insight into how pages are created in FrontPage and enables you to create and edit Web pages directly with HTML.

Tag a Page with HTML Commands

A Web document is actually an ordinary text file that you can load with an editor, such as Windows Notepad. HTML tags are added to the text to achieve different effects, such as the following:

- Creating a hyperlink
- Turning text into a heading
- Making several lines of text into a list
- Displaying a picture of your 1970 Dodge Dart

All HTML tags begin with the < character. The following tag adds a horizontal line to a Web page:

```
<P>What's with this rule hoo-hah?<HR>
```

"HR" stands for "horizontal rule." You can place an <HR> tag on a Web page anywhere you want a line to appear.

There are two kinds of tags: opening tags and closing tags. An *opening tag* indicates where some kind of formatting should begin. A *closing tag* indicates where it should end.

Consider the following marked-up text from a Web page:

```
<H1>Today's Top Story</H1>
```

This text uses the HTML tag <H1> to turn the text "Today's Top Story" into a size 1 heading. There also are <H2>, <H3>, <H4>, <H5>, and tags for headings with five additional sizes.

There are two HTML tags in this example: the opening tag, <H1>, and its closing tag, </H1>. The names of all closing tags are preceded by the slash character (/).

Most HTML tags require opening and closing tags in order to function correctly. For headings, you must use both tags to show where the heading begins and where it ends.

The <HR> tag is one of several opening tags that do not require a corresponding closing tag. The horizontal line appears on a page exactly where the <HR> opening tag is placed.

> HTML tags aren't case sensitive, so you could place <h1> and <H1> on a Web page and achieve the same effects.

An HTML tag begins with the < character and the name of the tag. It also may contain extra information to control these two characteristics:

- How the tag is displayed on a page
- What the tag can be used to do

All of this extra information is placed before the > character at the end of a tag, as in the following example:

```
<HR WIDTH="60%">
```

This `<HR>` tag has the added text `WIDTH="60%"`. This is an attribute of the tag that causes the horizontal rule to be displayed 60% as wide as it would appear normally. A tag can have more than one attribute as long as they're set apart from each other by blank spaces.

Once you understand the way HTML tags are structured, it becomes easier to understand what they're being used to accomplish. Even if this is your first exposure to HTML, you may be able to figure out what the following does:

```
<A HREF=http://www.sams.com>Visit the Sams Publishing Site</A>
```

This turns the statement "Visit the Sams Publishing Site" into a hyperlink pointing to `http://www.sams.com`, which is the URL for Sams Publishing's site. The `<A>` tag stands for "anchor"—another term for a link—and the `HREF` attribute is named for *Hypertext Reference*.

Work with HTML in Page View

The normal mode in FrontPage is to convert what you do in Page view into HTML. For this reason, if you added the `<HR>` tag to a page, FrontPage would assume you wanted to display these four characters, not a horizontal rule—which you add by choosing Insert, Horizontal Rule.

To work directly with HTML in FrontPage, click the HTML tab at the bottom of the Page view window. There are three tabs for three different editing modes:

- *Normal*—For letting FrontPage write its own HTML behind the scenes
- *HTML*—For writing your own HTML
- *Preview*—For looking at the page as it will function in a Web browser

You can click the HTML tab at any time to see a Web page's HTML formatting. If you're looking at a page that was created in FrontPage, don't expect to make much sense of it unless you're experienced with HTML. The software uses some complex HTML to achieve many of the effects you can use on Web pages.

The easiest way to experiment with HTML in FrontPage is to first create a new Web with no pages and no theme. When you add your first page and view it in the HTML mode of Page view, the document should resemble Figure 41.1.

41

Figure 41.1

Viewing a Web page's HTML formatting.

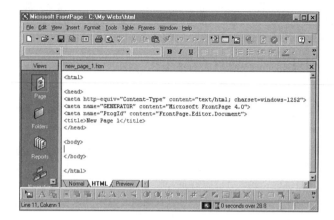

FrontPage starts every Web page with a minimal amount of HTML formatting:

- <HTML> tags to show where the Web page begins and ends (in other words, the entire document).

- <HEAD> tags to indicate the page's header—information about the page that isn't displayed in the main browser window.

- <TITLE> tags to give the page a title in the browser's title bar.

- <BODY> tags to indicate the page's body—the area that will show up in the main browser window.

FrontPage also uses several <META> tags in the header of the page that describe the document and how it was created.

> One of these tags shows that Microsoft FrontPage is the Web editing software being used to work on the page.

You can change the title of a page by editing the text between the opening and closing <TITLE> tags. The text will appear on the title bar of the Web browser when the page is loaded.

Anything you want to display on a Web page should be placed between the existing <BODY> tags.

Paragraphs of text are formatted with the <P> tag in HTML, as in the following:

```
<P>For years, researchers and politicians have been saying
that the amount of violence on television causes children to
behave more violently in real life.</P>
```

```
<P>I've been watching around 7-10 hours of TV every day for
the past 15 years.</P>

<P>When I read things about how TV makes you violent, it
makes me so angry I could hit someone.</P>
```

The `<P>` tags control how this example is formatted when it appears on a page. Adding blank lines after each paragraph and hitting the Enter key at the end of each line does not affect how it is displayed—in an HTML document, tags control all of the formatting.

Figure 41.2 shows how this text appears in a Web browser.

FIGURE 41.2

Paragraphs of text on a Web page.

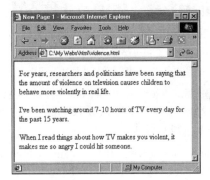

This text behaves like the paragraphs you've been working with in FrontPage. It fills the available space and moves around if you resize the browser window. You can switch back and forth between normal and HTML mode in Page view, editing the page in both views.

A good way to discover things about HTML is to create a simple page using HTML (like the one displayed in Figure 41.2), make a change to it in normal mode, and switch back to HTML mode so you can see what was changed.

The following output shows the TV violence text after a few changes have been made in Page view:

```
<P>For years, researchers and politicians have been saying
that the amount of violence on
<A HREF=http://www.tvultra.com>television</a> causes children
to behave more violently in real life.</p>

<P><i>I've been watching around 7-10 hours of TV every day for
the past 15 years.</i></P>

<P>When I read things about how TV makes you violent, it
makes me so angry <B>I could hit someone</B>.</P>
```

41

Three things are different:

- The word "television" is a hyperlink to TV Ultra, a World Wide Web site recommending the day's best show (whether violent or nonviolent).

- The second paragraph uses the `<i>` tag to italicize the text. (An uppercase `<I>` tag would produce identical results.)

- The words "I could hit someone" are surrounded by the `<B>` tag, which makes them appear in boldface.

Adding a Hit Counter Using HTML

It's possible to use FrontPage entirely as an HTML editor. You can take advantage of its Web management and maintenance features while you mark up pages, as if you were using Windows Notepad or another plain-text word processor.

However, it doesn't take a psychic friend to figure out that most FrontPage users will be content to let the software write its own HTML. If you're one of them, the main reason you'll need HTML mode is to add HTML-tagged text to a page.

The World Wide Web has numerous services that can enhance your Web, including free hit counters, guest books, and banner advertising exchanges. Many of these programs offer their services through HTML tags that you must place on your pages.

One of these services is *FastCounter* from LinkExchange, a company acquired by Microsoft in 1998. FastCounter is a hit counter that you can place on any Web page, or even on each page in a Web. The service is free, in exchange for a hyperlink to FastCounter's Web site.

Full details on how to join FastCounter are at `http://www.fastcounter.com`. When you sign up, you receive HTML-tagged text that must be placed where you want the counter to appear on a page.

The rest of this chapter describes how to add a FastCounter hit counter to one of your FrontPage Webs.

The specific HTML tags for FastCounter will be different depending on the account ID you receive when you sign up. (LinkExchange may also have altered the HTML tags by the time you try the service.) The following is an example of FastCounter HTML for account number 956167:

```
<!-- BEGIN FASTCOUNTER CODE -->
<a href=
```

```
"http://member.linkexchange.com/cgi-bin/fc/fastcounter-login?956167"
target="_top">
<img border="0"
src="http://fastcounter.linkexchange.com/fastcounter?956167+1912341">
</a>
<!-- END FASTCOUNTER CODE -->
<br>
<!-- BEGIN FASTCOUNTER LINK -->
<font face="arial" size="1">
<a href="http://fastcounter.linkexchange.com/fc-join" target="_top">
FastCounter by LinkExchange</a>
</font><br>
<!-- END FASTCOUNTER LINK -->
```

The HTML text for FastCounter is presented in a scrolling text box so you can cut-and-paste it to your Web. This text can be placed anywhere on a Web page. It's often put at the bottom, right above the `</body>` tag that closes out the page's visible contents.

If you have trouble finding the right place within the HTML view, switch to Page view's normal mode before pasting the code. Click your cursor exactly where you want the counter to be placed, and then switch back to HTML mode. Your cursor will be at the same place you clicked.

Figure 41.3 shows a Web page with account number 956167's FastCounter placed at the bottom.

FIGURE 41.3

Counting hits using FastCounter.

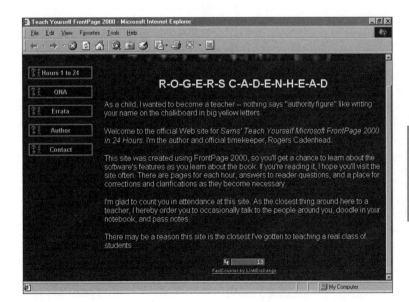

41

Summary

It doesn't take long to become an old fogey, by World Wide Web standards. If FrontPage is your first experience creating Webs, you'll probably hear some "in my day, things were different" stories about HTML.

Before the development of software like FrontPage, all Webs were created by marking up text with HTML tags in text editors like Windows Notepad. Many developers still prefer HTML because of perceived limitations in software that creates these tags for you. They feel that you get more control over the finished product by coding it yourself.

You can be both old-fashioned and newfangled with FrontPage. You can view the HTML when you want to, and hide it when you use the software's graphical user interface to design Webs. You also can use FrontPage to avoid HTML entirely.

No matter how you do it, things are a lot easier than they back in 1995, the Web's early days.

CHAPTER 42

Introducing Cascading Style Sheets

The biggest push in World Wide Web design today is to separate the appearance of a page—its fonts, colors, and alignment—from the information it offers.

This is being done for several reasons. First, it will make a Web publisher's life much easier when the site needs to be redesigned. A site in which specific fonts and font styles are entered one page at a time also must be changed in the same manner.

Second, it makes a Web more adaptable to the diverse audience that will view it. Although Netscape Navigator and Microsoft Internet Explorer users constitute more than 85% of Web surfers today, other types of browsing software may be used to visit a public Web—text-only browsers, nonvisual browsers, screen readers, and lesser-known browsers such as Opera.

Third, it gives a Web publisher much more control over how pages are presented.

Earlier, you learned about themes, which are a way to define a Web's visual appearance in FrontPage. During this chapter, you'll take that principle one step further by using a developing new Web technology called Cascading Style Sheets.

Define Styles on the Web

Most popular word processors today have a feature called *styles*. They enable you to define the kinds of information that will appear in a document—such as headlines, body text, and pictures—and then give each of them its own specific formatting.

For example, you could establish that all body text in your document will be 12-point Courier New text that is indented .25 inches from the left margin. After you have set up this rule for body text, you can apply the style to all paragraphs that are part of the document's main body. They'll show up exactly as if you applied the font and formatting directly. Later, if you decide to pick a different font or font size, you can modify the body text style instead of changing the document itself. All body text will change accordingly.

This idea has been introduced to the World Wide Web through *Cascading Style Sheets (CSS)*, a new language that specifies how a Web page and its elements should look. Cascading Style Sheets are an extension of HTML, rather than a replacement. A Web page incorporates CSS commands as hidden sections of the page, or on separate pages that contain all CSS formatting information.

Currently there are three versions of CSS, which were first supported in version 3.0 of Internet Explorer and version 4.0 of Navigator. CSS 1.0 is most widely supported in current browsers, and it contains commands to set the fonts, colors, and formatting of text, hyperlinks, and other parts of a page.

Use Styles Instead of FrontPage Themes

FrontPage includes a feature that enables you to choose an entire Web's appearance at one time—*themes*. You can modify parts of a theme, like a text font, and all selected Web pages will be updated to reflect the change.

Themes are similar to Cascading Style Sheets, but are much more limited. Everything you use a theme for can be handled manually within Page view. You can set the background, establish all fonts, and create your own navigation bar graphics.

One of the things you can do with CSS is apply a theme. If you choose not to apply a theme using CSS, FrontPage will apply the graphics, fonts, and colors of a theme using standard HTML. CSS can produce the same effects.

CSS can't be used to apply a theme if you're targeting a browser audience with anything below Internet Explorer 3.0 or Navigator 4.0. Style sheets are not supported by WebTV or older browsers.

Unlike themes, Cascading Style Sheets can be used for techniques that are completely impossible in HTML. Take a look at Figure 42.1.

FIGURE 42.1

A Web page that uses Cascading Style Sheets.

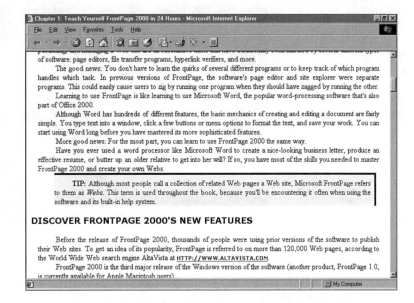

This Web page uses CSS to do several unusual things:

- Remove the blank line between paragraphs of text
- Indent the start of each paragraph
- Justify paragraphs along the right margin
- Give one paragraph its own border edge and background color

Style sheets enable you to take control of formatting decisions that have been automatically handled by the browser until now, such as the blank line between paragraphs that has been standard to most browsers for years. They also give you many more options for determining the appearance of the different page elements.

42

Create a Style Sheet

Style sheets can be implemented as part of a Web page, or on a separate document that's linked to the page. The second method is better because you can attach the same document to other pages, establishing a common style for all of them.

To begin creating a style sheet, choose File, New, Page and then select the Style Sheets tab (Figure 42.2).

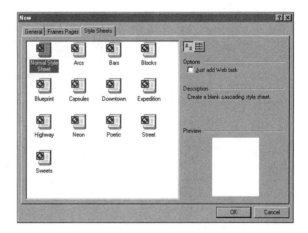

Several of the style sheets from which you can choose have the same names as themes, and they define many of the same fonts, colors, and heading styles. (Cascading Style Sheets don't define navigational buttons or page banners, however.) Choosing a Normal style sheet gives you an empty file to add styles to.

Style sheets should be saved with the .css filename extension. You can place them in the main folder of your Web or any of its subfolders, such as the images subfolder.

Before you make any changes to a new style sheet, save it so you can link it to pages in the current Web. Choose Format, Style Sheet Links to create a link to a style sheet. You can link a page or the entire Web to the .css file that contains the style sheet.

Themes don't mix well with style sheets, especially when you're working on them for the first time. For the Webs you create during this chapter, remove all themes before linking any style sheets.

Once you've established a page's link to a style sheet, the page will automatically display those styles.

Edit a Style

To edit a style sheet, choose Format, Style with either a Web page or a `.css` file open in Page view. The Style dialog box will appear, as shown in Figure 42.3.

FIGURE 42.3

Editing a style sheet.

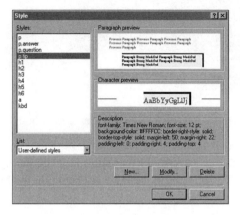

If you edit a style sheet from a Web page, the changes you make will be saved on that page only. Editing styles from a `.css` file enables you to make changes that apply to all pages linked to the style sheet.

Styles are associated with specific HTML tags. You can take an existing tag and establish a new style for how it is displayed on a Web page.

The Style dialog box can be used to display all HTML tags or just the user-defined styles—tags that have new styles applied to them.

To see this in action, display all HTML tags in the Style dialog box and modify the kbd tag. This tag is used to apply the keyboard effect to text, which is one of the options you can select by choosing Format, Font while editing a Web page.

Clicking the Modify button opens the dialog box shown in Figure 42.4.

You can use the Format button on the Modify Style dialog box to make the following changes to how a tag is displayed on a Web page:

- *Font*—The font, size, color, and other attributes of text
- *Paragraph*—The spacing and indentation of paragraphs containing this text
- *Border*—The border and shading that appear
- *Numbering*—The way lists of this text are numbered and indented

42

FIGURE 42.4

Modifying a style.

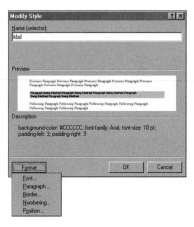

These formatting changes can be applied to any element, although several options are best suited to text.

Choose a new font, color, and size for the kbd tag, and give it background shading. The changes you make will be reflected in the Preview section of the Modify Styles dialog box.

> You also can change the positioning of the tag—a feature called CSS 2.0 in FrontPage that is only supported partially in Internet Explorer 4.0 and higher. The formatting features described during this chapter are much more fully supported in current browsers.

When you modify a style directly from a .css page, FrontPage will display that style using the Cascading Style Sheets language in Page view. Don't edit this document manually unless you're familiar with CSS—if you click Format, Style, you'll be making changes to this file as you work on a style sheet with the Style dialog box.

Apply a Modified Style to a Page

Once you've modified the kbd style, you can try it out in one of two ways:

- If you modified the style on a separate .css file, close and save that file. Open a Web page that has been linked to this style sheet.
- If you modified the style on a Web page, you're ready to apply the style to text.

Highlight text on a Web page and choose Format, Font to open the Font dialog box. Apply the keyboard effect to this text. On most browsers, the keyboard effect causes text to appear in a smaller, monospaced font such as Courier. The new style that was applied to kbd overrides this formatting in browsers that support Cascading Style Sheets. You'll see the text as it was formatted in the Modify Style dialog box.

If you make changes to the kbd style, they will be reflected immediately in all text that has been formatted with the keyboard effect.

Match Tags with FrontPage Features

Style sheets use HTML tags to identify elements of a Web page. If you're not familiar with HTML, you may not know how these tags are used on a Web page.

When you choose Font, Format to add a special effect, the following HTML tags are used:

- blink—Blink effect
- cite—Citation effect
- code—Code effect
- dfn—Definition effect
- em—Emphasis effect
- kbd—Keyboard effect
- samp—Sample effect
- strike—Strikethrough effect
- strong—Strong effect
- sub—Subscript effect
- sup—Superscript effect
- u—Underline effect
- var—Variable effect

Several buttons on the Formatting toolbar can be used to format text. They're associated with the following HTML tags:

- b—The Boldface button
- i—The Italic button
- u—The Underline button
- blockquote—The Increase Indent button

The Formatting toolbar also has a pull-down menu with several formatting options that apply to entire paragraphs. They use the following HTML tags:

42

- p—Normal
- pre—Formatted
- address—Address
- h1 through h6—Heading 1 through Heading 6
- ol—Before and after a numbered list
- ul—Before and after a bulleted list
- dir—Before and after a directory list
- menu—Before and after a menu list
- li—For each item in a numbered, bulleted, directory, or menu list
- dl—Before and after a defined term list
- dt—For each term in a defined term list
- dl—Before and after a definition list
- dd—For each definition in a definition list

There are other HTML tags that FrontPage uses as you create Web pages, including a for hyperlinks, img for pictures, and applet for Java applets.

To determine the tags that are being used by FrontPage, create a new page that contains nothing but a single Web element. Switch to HTML mode for that page and you'll see the tag—or tags—used to create it.

Create a New Style

A style sheet can contain new styles that aren't directly associated with an existing HTML tag. These styles often are used to create styles that have been slightly modified from existing tags, as in the following styles:

- p—A normal paragraph
- p.quote—A paragraph that contains a quotation
- p.author—A paragraph that identifies the author of the text
- p.contact—A paragraph that indicates how to contact the author

You can give each of these styles a different appearance as a way to distinguish them from each other.

In FrontPage, the best way to create a new style is to base it on a paragraph tag that it is similar to, such as p for normal paragraphs or one of the heading tags, such as h3.

To create a new style, choose Format, Style, and then click the New button to give the style a name. The first part of the name should be the tag the style is based on, followed by a period, followed by a unique name that describes what the style is used for. The p.quote, p.author, and p.contact styles are examples of this.

When you name a new style, it will show up on the list of user-defined styles like any other HTML tag you've customized. You can modify how it is formatted, just like any other style.

The best advantage to basing a new style on a paragraph tag is that it shows up in the Formatting toolbar along with the other options to format a paragraph. For example, if you created p.quote, p.author, and p.contact styles, they would show up in the pull-down menu as Normal.quote, Normal.author, and Normal.contact.

Adding a New Paragraph Style

Once you understand the mechanics of how Cascading Style Sheets are employed in FrontPage, working with them is as easy as formatting text in Page view. Most of your time will be spent choosing the right font, and other visual details for each style, and then testing them out on a Web page.

Try for yourself to create a new style called p.smallprint. This is a paragraph style, as the first part of its name indicates. It will be used to format text that's part of a legal disclaimer—the kind of thing you see in the teeny-tiny print of a magazine advertisement.

The p.smallprint style should be formatted as 8-point Verdana text with light gray shading and a thin border around it.

Read the Fine Print

Creating the p.smallprint style involve several options on the Modify Style dialog box.

First, the Format button and the Font option were used to select Verdana as the font and set it to a size of 8 points. Second, the Format button and the Borders option were used to choose a background color for the style. (You might need to experiment with some of the available shades of gray to find one that's light enough to make the small print readable.) Third, the Borders option was used to add a thin line around the text. The width of a line is expressed in pixels, so a value of 1 creates the thinnest possible line.

One thing that you weren't asked to do was to add padding around the border, but this helps to set off the text from the border. You can add padding to the top, bottom, left, and right borders, and a value of 1 also is suitable for each of these.

Figure 42.5 shows an example of p.smallprint on a Web page.

42

FIGURE 42.5

Using styles for special kinds of text.

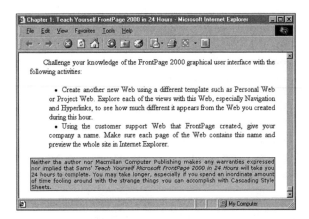

Summary

Cascading Style Sheets provide Web designers with numerous benefits if they're creating a Web for people using current versions of Netscape Navigator and Microsoft Internet Explorer. Style sheets enable you to modify the appearance of a Web in dramatic ways and save all of this information to a single file. Changing the file changes everything in the Web that links to the style sheet.

During this chapter, you learned how to create new styles and modify some existing ones. You can extend the visual appeal of your FrontPage Webs in ways that are not possible through standard HTML.

Another benefit to using CSS is that it provides a way to define the information contained on a page. By creating style sheets with names that describe their purposes, you make the information more coherent and more useful.

For example, a newspaper's Web could define new styles for p.headline, p.author, p.date, p.dateline, and p.lead_paragraph. Even if all of these looked the same on a Web page, software could be written later to search stories based on author or date by the styles present on these pages.

PART XII

Analyzing Numerical Information with Excel

Chapter

CHAPTER 43

Learning About Excel Workbooks

This chapter introduces you to Excel, Microsoft's spreadsheet program. Excel is to numbers what Word is to text; Excel has been called a *word processor for numbers*. With Excel, you can create numerically based proposals, business plans, business forms, accounting worksheets, and virtually any other document that contains calculated numbers.

If you are new to electronic worksheets, you will probably have to take more time to learn Excel's environment than you had to learn Word's. Excel starts with a grid of cells in which you place information. This chapter takes things slowly to acquaint you with Excel and explains the background necessary for understanding how an Excel working area operates. This chapter gives you a broad Excel overview while subsequent chapters return to some of this chapter's features in more depth and cover additional skills you will need to know to use Excel effectively.

Familiarizing Yourself with the Excel Screen

Figure 43.1 shows the opening Excel screen. Your screen might differ slightly depending on the options you have set.

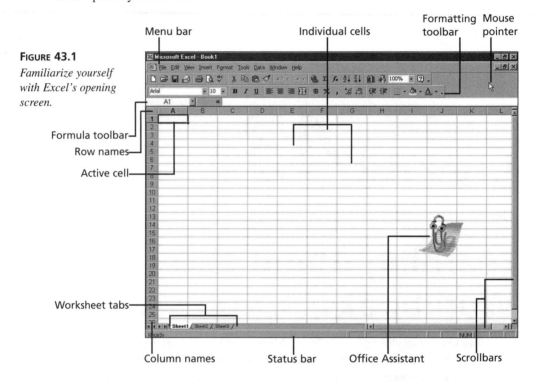

FIGURE 43.1

Familiarize yourself with Excel's opening screen.

Labels around figure: Menu bar, Individual cells, Formatting toolbar, Mouse pointer, Formula toolbar, Row names, Active cell, Worksheet tabs, Column names, Status bar, Office Assistant, Scrollbars

Understanding Workbooks and Worksheets

Excel enables you to create and edit *workbooks*. A workbook holds one or more *worksheets* (sometimes called *spreadsheets* or just *sheets*). A worksheet is a collection of rows and columns that holds text and numbers. Anytime you create, open, or save an Excel file, you are working with a workbook. The workbook approach keeps you from having multiple files that relate to the same project—instead, you can have all worksheets related to the same project in the same workbook (in one *.xls file). Your workbook name is the Excel name you assign when you save a file. You can save Excel worksheets and workbooks in HTML format if you want to maintain file-type consistency and if you ever want to embed your data in a Web page.

As with Word data, Excel often uses the term *document* to refer to a workbook file.

Blank Excel workbooks contain three worksheets named Sheet1, Sheet2, and Sheet3, as shown at the bottom of Figure 43.1. When you click a sheet's tab, Excel brings that sheet into view. If a workbook contains several worksheets, you might have to click one of the sheet-scrolling buttons to view additional worksheet tabs. Each column has a heading; heading names start with A, B, and so on. Each row has a heading, starting with 1, 2, and so on. The intersection of a row and column, called a *cell*, also has a name that comes from combining the row name and column number, such as C4 or A1. A1 is always the top-left cell on any worksheet. The gridlines help you to distinguish between cells, but you can turn off gridlines at any time from the Tools, Options, View page option labeled Gridlines.

No matter how large your monitor is, you will see only a small amount of the worksheet area. Use the scrollbars to see or edit information in the off-screen cells, such as cell *M17*.

Every cell in your workbook contains a unique name or address to which you can refer when you are tabulating data. The cell address of the active cell (the cell that the cursor is in) appears at the left of the Formula bar. In Figure 43.1, the box reads A1 because the cursor is in cell A1.

When you move your mouse pointer across Excel's screen, notice that the pointer becomes a cross when you point it to a cell area. The cross returns to its pointer shape when you point to another part of the Excel work area.

Inserting Worksheets in a Workbook

Just as Word enables you to edit multiple documents in memory at the same time, Excel enables you to edit multiple worksheets simultaneously (but those worksheets must all appear in the same workbook).

To insert a new worksheet into your workbook, right-click the worksheet tab that is to fall *after* the new worksheet. Select Insert from the pop-up menu. Excel displays the Insert dialog box, as shown in Figure 43.2, on which you can double-click the Worksheet icon and press OK. The Insert dialog box contains several kinds of items that you can add to a workbook, but worksheets are the most common items you add. The Insert, Worksheet command also inserts a new worksheet.

FIGURE 43.2

Add a new worksheet to your workbook.

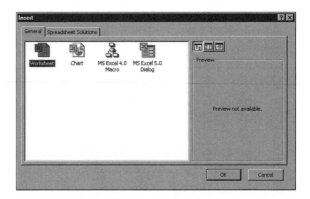

> If you don't like the default worksheet names (Sheet1, Sheet2, and so on), rename them by right-clicking the sheet name and selecting Rename. Type the new name. When you press Enter, the worksheet tab displays the new name.

Deleting Worksheets from a Workbook

Situations arise when you only need a single worksheet in a workbook. You might want to track your monthly household budget, for example; such a budget rarely requires multiple worksheets. For your budget, the workbook is basically the same as the worksheet, but you should pare down excess worksheets instead of wasting memory on them. Excel makes it easy to delete excess sheets. Just right-click the tab of the sheet you want to delete and select Delete from the pop-up menu.

> You can keep multiple workbooks open at once and move between them by pressing Ctrl+F6 (the same keystroke that moves between multiple Word documents in memory). Multiple workbooks are often difficult to keep track of until you become familiar with Excel and its worksheets. Display your Window menu to see a list of open workbooks if you want to review the ones you have opened.

Working with Multiple Worksheets

To specify the maximum number of worksheets that a workbook is to hold, select Tools, Options, click the General tab, and enter a number in the Sheets in New field labeled Sheets in New Workbook. When you create a new workbook, that workbook contains the number of sheets you requested. As you can see from Figure 43.3, Excel's Options dialog box resembles Word's. Many of the options are identical in both products, as well as throughout the Office suite.

Enter the number of sheets here

FIGURE 43.3

The Options dialog box enables you to specify how many worksheets to include in your workbooks.

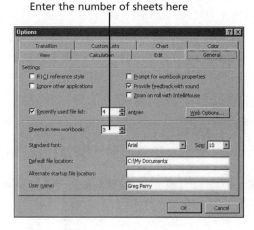

You can refer to a specific cell located within a workbook by prefacing the cell with its workbook name, followed by an exclamation point (!), to refer to a specific worksheet's cell. For example, Sheet3!G7 refers to the seventh row of column G inside the worksheet named Sheet3. Notice that you work from right-to-left when deciphering a reference such as Sheet3!G2.

One interesting workbook feature is the capability to rearrange worksheets within a workbook, and even to move worksheets between two or more workbooks.

If you don't like the current order of the worksheets in your workbook (the worksheet tabs indicate the worksheet ordering), click and drag a worksheet's tag (the mouse cursor changes to let you know you have grabbed the worksheet) to fall before another sheet's tab. If you work with two or three particular worksheets the majority of the time, move those worksheets together so that you can move between them easily.

Make a copy of (instead of moving) a worksheet by pressing Ctrl before you click and drag a worksheet from one location to another. Excel creates a new worksheet and uses the original worksheet for the new worksheet's data. Before you make extensive changes to a worksheet, you might want to copy it so that you can revert to the old version should anything go wrong.

Working with Multiple Workbooks

As your workbook fills up with worksheets, you need a way to manage those worksheets and move from one to another. When you then want to copy or move information from one to another worksheet, you can easily do so.

If you need to move a worksheet from one workbook to another, open both workbooks and select Window, Arrange, Tiled to display both worksheets, as shown in Figure 43.4. Drag one of the worksheet tabs to the other workbook to move the sheet. To copy instead of move, hold Ctrl while you drag the sheet name.

FIGURE 43.4

Display both workbooks if you want to move or copy worksheets or cells between them.

Entering Worksheet Data

Often, entering worksheet data requires nothing more than moving the cell pointer to the correct cell and typing the data. The various kinds of data behave differently when entered, however, so you should understand how Excel accepts assorted data.

Excel can work with the following kinds of data:

- *Labels*—Text values such as names and addresses
- *Numbers*—Numeric values such as 34, –291, 545.67874, and 0
- *Formulas*—Expressions that compute numeric results (some formulas work with text values as well)
- *Special formats*—Date and time values

Excel works well with data from other Office products. Additionally, you can *import* (transfer) data from other non-Microsoft products, such as Lotus 1-2-3.

43

Entering Text

If you want to put text (such as a title or a name) in a cell, just place your cursor in the cell and type the text. Excel left-justifies the text in the cell. As you type, the text appears both in the cell and in the Formula bar. Remember that the *Name box* to the left of the Formula bar displays the name of the cell into which you are entering data. When you press Enter, Excel moves the cell pointer down one row.

Press Tab to move the cell pointer to the right or the arrow keys to move the cell pointer in any direction after you enter data.

If you press Esc at any point during your text entry, Excel erases the text you typed in the cell and restores the original cell contents.

If your text is wider than the cell, Excel does one of two things depending on the contents of the adjacent cell to the right:

- If the adjacent cell is empty, Excel displays the entire contents of the wide cell.
- If the adjacent cell contains data, Excel truncates (cuts off) the wide cell to show only as much text as fits in the cell's width. Excel does not remove the unseen data from the cell; however, the adjacent cell, if that cell contains data, always displays instead.

Figure 43.5 shows two long *labels* (label is another name for text data) in cells C5 and C10. The same label, which is longer than standard cell width, appears in both cells. Because no data resides in D5, Excel displays all the contents of C5. The data in D10, however, overwrites the tail end of C10. C10 still contains the complete label, but only part of it is visible.

You can increase and shrink the width and height of columns and rows by dragging the edge of the column name or row number. If you drag the right edge of column D to the right, for example, the entire column D (all rows in the column) widens.

FIGURE 43.5

Excel may or may not display all of a cell's contents.

Cell D10 contains data that overwrites C10

No data in cell D5 to overwrite C5

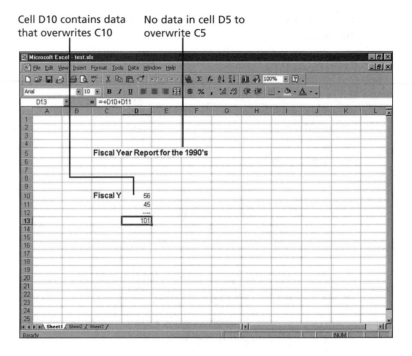

Some text data, such as price codes, telephone numbers, and ZIP codes, fool Excel. As you see in the next section, Excel treats numeric data differently from text data when you type the data into cells. If you want Excel to treat a number (such as a ZIP code) as a text entry (calculations are not performed on the cell), precede the contents with a single apostrophe ('). For example, to type the ZIP code 74137, type '74137; the apostrophe lets Excel know to format the value as text.

Entering Numbers

Excel accepts numeric values of all kinds. You can type positive numbers, negative numbers, numbers with decimal points, zero-leading numbers, numbers with dollar signs, percent signs, and even *scientific notation* (a shortcut for writing extremely large and small numbers). Later in the section "Entering Values," you will learn more about how to put numeric values in worksheet cells.

If you type a number but see something like 3.04959E+16 appear in the cell, Excel converted your number to scientific notation to let you know that the cell is not wide enough to display the entire number in its regular form. Excel does not extend long numbers into adjacent cells.

Excel right-justifies numbers inside cells. You can change the format for a single cell or for the entire worksheet.

Entering Dates and Times

Excel supports almost every national and international date and time format. Excel uses its AutoFormat feature to convert any date or time value that you type to a special internal number that represents the number of days since midnight, January 1, 1900. Excel automatically displays all dates the user enters with four-digit year values by showing the full year. Although this strange internal representation might not make sense now, you use these values a lot to compute time between two or more dates. You can easily determine how many days an account is past due, for example.

 Excel uses a 24-hour clock to represent time values unless you specify a.m. or p.m. To convert p.m. times to 24-hour times, add 12 to all time values after 12:59 p.m. Thus, 7:54 p.m. is 19:54 on a 24-hour clock.

You can type any of the following date and time values to represent 6:15 p.m., July 4, 1976, or a combination of both 6:15 p.m. and July 4, 1976:

```
July 4, 1976
4-Jul-76 6:15 p.m.
6:15 p.m.
18:15
07/04/76 18:15
07-04-76 18:15
```

If you enter any of these date and time values, Excel converts them to a shortened format (such as 7/4/76 18:15). You can enter a date, a time value, or both. As with most Office formats, you can change this default format with the Format menu. The shorter format often helps worksheet columns align better.

Navigating in Excel

Your mouse and arrow keys are the primary navigation keys used to move from cell to cell. Unlike Word, which uses a text cursor, Excel uses a cell pointer to show you the currently *active* cell. The active cell accepts whatever data you enter next. As you press an arrow key, Excel moves the active cell pointer in the direction of the arrow.

Table 43.1 lists the most commonly used navigational keystrokes used within a worksheet. Use your mouse to scroll with the scrollbars. To scroll long distances, press Shift while you scroll with the mouse.

TABLE 43.1   Using the Keyboard to Navigate Excel

This Key...	Moves to Here
Arrow keys	The direction of the arrow one cell at a time
Ctrl+Up arrow, Ctrl+Down arrow	The topmost or bottommost row with data in the worksheet
Ctrl+Left arrow, Ctrl+Right arrow	The leftmost or rightmost column with data in the worksheet
PageUp, PageDown	The previous or next screen of the worksheet
Ctrl+Home	The upper-left corner of the worksheet cell A1
End, Arrow	The last blank cell in the arrow's direction
Ctrl+PageUp, Ctrl+PageDown	Move to next or previous worksheet within current workbook

Automating Your Work

Although the design and set up of an Excel workbook can be exciting, the data entry portion can be dull. Few people like to sit at their computers and type the same information again and again. Fortunately, Excel has some tools to help you automate your data entry.

AutoComplete Speeds the Entry Process

As you create your worksheets, you'll probably find that you enter the same text over and over. Typing repetitive text is boring and, because you might not be paying close attention, increases your chances of making a typing mistake. Fortunately, Excel has a feature called *AutoComplete* to automate the entry of text you type multiple times.

AutoComplete works in two ways. In the first way, Excel completes an entry as you're typing it. (If you've typed URL's using the current versions of Internet Explorer or Netscape Navigator, you may be familiar with how AutoComplete finishes the text you type.) As you type the first few letters of an entry you made previously, AutoComplete assumes that you're typing the previous text and finishes the text for you. If the text AutoComplete fills in is not correct, just keep typing. Whatever you type overwrites the AutoComplete entry.

You can also pick from your AutoComplete entries and insert them only immediately above or below the existing entry (or entries). When you need to repeat a word or phrase you used previously, right-click the cell where you want to place the duplicate text. Remember, the cell must be immediately above or below an existing AutoComplete entry. Choose Pick from List from the shortcut menu that appears. As shown in Figure 43.6, a list of previously typed words and phrases appears underneath the cell. Click the word you want from the list. The list disappears and the word is inserted into the cell.

Selected cell

FIGURE 43.6

AutoComplete makes it easy to type repetitive text.

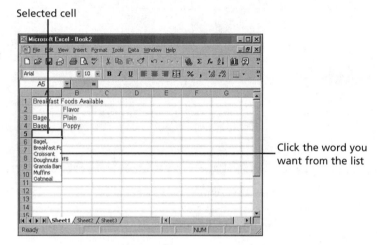

Click the word you want from the list

AutoFill Produces Amazing Results

Excel contains an amazing feature called *AutoFill* to automate your data entry. AutoFill looks at the relationship of a data series that you've already entered into your worksheet and then duplicates its results in an area you select. A data series can be any set of related information, such as the months of the year, the numbers of your personal checks, or incremental interest amounts.

Using AutoFill is a breeze. You select a cell or cells that contain the data and then tell Excel where to fill in the rest. For example, if you have a list that contains Sunday and Monday, AutoFill can enter the remaining weekdays for you.

Fill It in with the Fill Handle

Although Excel gives you several ways to activate AutoFill, the easiest method is to use the *fill handle* on the bottom right-hand corner of the selected cell or cells. When you select one or more cells, the fill handle appears, as shown in Figure 43.7. Drag the handle across the adjacent cells you want to fill. As you drag, the cells appear highlighted. Release the mouse button to fill in the data series.

Fill handle

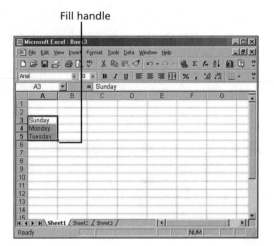

FIGURE 43.7
Select the first few cells of the data series.

Creating a Simple Spreadsheet

Now it's time to put everything you've learned into action as you begin creating a simple worksheet. This section gives you some practice making entries into a cell and using Excel's AutoFit feature. Follow these steps to practice working with Excel:

1. Click into cell A1. A selector appears around the cell. Type My Budget. Notice that the text appears in the cell and the Formula bar. Press Enter when you're done typing.

2. Move down to cell A4 and type Mortgage/Rent. Press the down-arrow key when you're done typing to enter your text and move down to the next cell.

3. Type the following text, making sure to press the down-arrow key after each word: Car, Utilities, Groceries, Entertainment, Other. Be sure not to type a comma after each entry in the cell. When you're done, your screen should look like the one shown in Figure 43.8.

4. Notice that some of the entries in column A are wider than the column and spill over into column B. Select column A by positioning the mouse pointer on the heading for the column (the mouse pointer assumes the shape of an open cross) and clicking one time. The entire column appears highlighted.

5. Click Format, Column and choose AutoFit Selection. The column adjusts to accommodate the longest cell entry. Deselect the column by pressing the right-arrow key.

6. Click into cell B3 and type January. Without pressing any of the arrow keys or Enter, notice that a tiny square called a fill handle appears in the bottom-right corner of the cell.

Entries are wider than the width of the column

43

FIGURE 43.8

Your Budget worksheet
as it's being created.

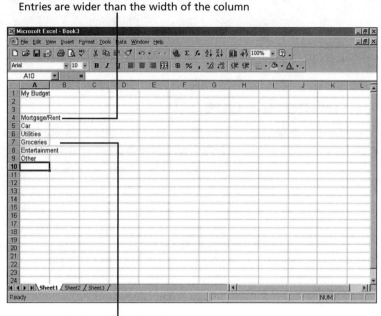

Labels are left-aligned

7. Position your mouse pointer over the fill handle (the pointer assumes the shape of a small cross.) Click the left mouse button and slowly drag to cell M3. As you drag, a ScreenTip displays the value of the cell that the pointer is directly over.

8. Release the mouse button. The other months are filled in and appear highlighted. Notice that some columns are not wide enough for the name of the month to appear correctly.

9. Because all the monthly columns are already selected, you can widen them to the same column width. Click Format, Column and choose Width. When the Column Width dialog box appears, type the number 10 in the Column Width box and click OK. The Column Width dialog box closes and all the columns are the same size.

10. Deselect the columns by pressing the right-arrow key.

Dragging to the right or left of the portion of the worksheet visible on your computer screen can sometimes produce unwanted results. When the mouse crosses the current screen, the dragging process seems to speed up. You might need to practice your drag technique a few times before you get it right. To reverse the result of a fill that has gone too far, click the Undo button on the Standard toolbar. Then try the fill again.

Remember to always select (highlight) the cells, rows, or columns that you want to change. Any change you make from a menu or toolbar affects only the selection.

Entering Values

The procedure for entering values is identical to the procedure for entering labels. After you select the cell in which you want to enter the value, simply begin typing. As with labels, the values you type appear both in the cell and in the Formula bar.

Excel treats numbers and text differently. For one, values are aligned automatically with the right edge of the cell. Values are displayed in Excel's General number format. However, you can always change or customize the alignment appearance and formatting of numbers in the worksheet. If a value is too wide to fit in the current width of a cell, Excel displays a series of # characters, as shown in Figure 43.9, across the width of the cell to let you know that the number cannot be displayed. You need to adjust the width of the cell to display the number properly.

To quickly change the width of a column, select Format, Column, AutoFit. The column width is adjusted.

Values can begin with the following characters:

0 1 2 3 4 5 6 7 8 9 + - . (, $ %

You can also type fractions. However, if the syntax for fractions is not correct, Excel misinterprets what you're trying to enter.

To enter a fraction, type the number, a blank space, and then the fraction, such as 4 1/2. If you want to enter only the fractional portion, type a 0, a blank space, and then the fraction, similar to 0 1/2.

Always check your worksheet after you type in a few fractions. If a fraction is entered incorrectly, Excel may treat it as a label or a date entry, instead of the numeric value you expected.

43

The number appears in the Formula bar

FIGURE 43.9

The number signs indicate that the number is wider than the column.

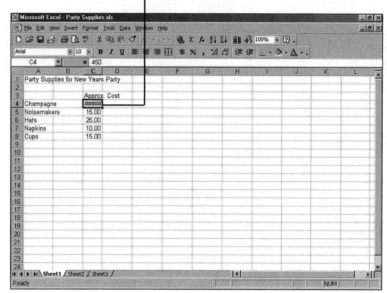

Treating Numbers Like Text

Excel evaluates each of your entries and determines whether the entry is a value or label. A mixed cell entry that contains both values and text is automatically treated like a label. For example, an address like 1750 Clint Moore Road is treated like a label. A mixed cell entry cannot be used as part of a calculation.

You can also enter numbers in a cell and have Excel treat the entry as a label. You might want to consider telephone numbers, ZIP codes, and invoice numbers as labels instead of values. Whenever you want Excel to treat a numeric cell entry as a text, preface the entry with a single quotation mark ('). The quotation mark is not visible in the cell, although you can see it on the Formula bar, as shown in Figure 43.10.

Quotation mark is visible in the Formula bar

FIGURE **43.10**

The single quotation mark tells Excel to treat the entry as a label.

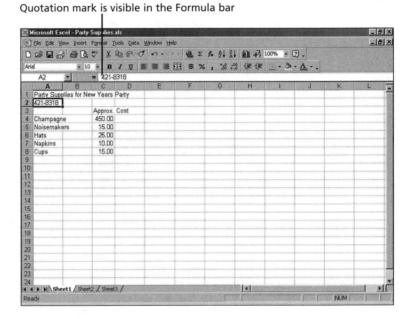

Working with a Worksheet

The next step is to enter some budget numbers into your worksheet. Later you can update the numbers you enter for practice with your own actual amounts. The budget worksheet should be open and visible on the screen from the previous exercise. Follow these steps to improve upon your worksheet:

1. Click in cell B4 and type the value 600. When you're done typing, press the down-arrow key to move down to the next cell.

2. Type 278.30 and press the down-arrow key. Notice that the second number to the right of the decimal point is cut off.

3. Type 160 in cell B6, the cell that displays your Utility expense in January. Press the down-arrow key when you're done typing.

4. Instead of typing a number in the next cell, you're going to let Excel calculate your grocery expense. To let Excel know that you're going to perform a calculation, type an = sign and then type 135, the plus sign (+), and the number 47.82. Your cell entry should look like the following:

    =135+47.82

Take care not to enter any spaces between the numbers and the operators. Press the down arrow when you've checked your typing. The result of the simple calculation appears in the cell.

5. Move down to cell A11 and press Ctrl+:. The current date is displayed. Press Enter to enter the date into the cell.

Copying from Cell to Cell

As with other Windows programs, Excel makes it easy to rearrange the data you enter in your worksheets. You can copy data from one place to another on the same worksheet or to other worksheets in the same workbook. You can even copy data from one workbook to another.

You can copy or cut data in Excel. If you choose to copy, a carbon-copy image of the data you copied is maintained on the Clipboard. If you cut data, the selection is actually removed from your worksheet (as if you'd cut it with sharp scissors).

Copying (and cutting) data is accomplished with the aid of a handy Windows utility called the Clipboard. Whenever you use the Copy or Cut command, the data is placed on the Windows Clipboard. The Clipboard is the intermediary in the copy or cut-and-paste operation. Data can be pasted into an Excel worksheet from the Clipboard one or multiple times. For example, you can copy your company logo, a paragraph, and a graphic to the Windows Clipboard for pasting into your corporate forms.

Selecting the Cells to Copy or Cut

You need to select the cell or cells that you want to copy or cut before you can send them to the Clipboard. Select a single cell by clicking it. If you want to select multiple cells in a rectangular block, click the first cell. Press and hold the Shift key and drag the mouse pointer over the block you want to copy. A black border appears around the block, and the cells inside appear colored, as shown in Figure 43.11. When all the cells that you want to copy are selected, release both the mouse button and the Shift key.

FIGURE 43.11

The cells are selected.

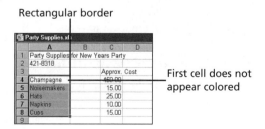

Rectangular border

First cell does not appear colored

The first cell in a block of selected cells might not appear colored or selected. However, if a black border surrounds the block, the first, nonhighlighted cell is included in the selection.

In Excel you can select multiple cells that are not located in a rectangular block. To select nontouching cells, hold down the Ctrl key as you click each cell that you want to copy. Each cell that you click appears highlighted. Release the Ctrl key when the cells you want to copy are selected.

Either way, click the Copy button or the Cut button on the Standard toolbar after the cells are selected. If you can't see the toolbar, or want to access the command from the menu instead, choose Edit, Copy or Edit, Cut. A marquee appears around the copied cells. If you're cutting the cells, they disappear from the worksheet.

Pasting the Copied or Cut Cells

Pasting the cells you copied or cut is a snap. Click the first cell where you want the new cells to appear. If you're pasting a block of cells, you do not have to highlight a rectangular block; Excel assumes that you want the cells to appear in the order and shape in which they were copied. Click the Paste button on the Standard toolbar or chose Edit, Paste. The cells appear in their new location.

Excel pastes data in four ways:

- *One cell to one cell*—A single cell from the Clipboard is pasted to one cell.
- *Multiple cells to one cell*—Multiple cells are pasted into a rectangular block of which only the first cell is selected.
- *One cell to multiple cells*—A single cell from the Clipboard is pasted into a highlighted range of cells.
- *Multiple cells to multiple cells*—The selection of cells from the Clipboard is pasted into a like-sized rectangular block.

If you've copied other data to the Clipboard from Excel or other programs during the current Windows session, the Clipboard toolbar appears.

Working with the Clipboard Toolbar

As you know from earlier chapters on other Office programs, the Office Clipboard toolbar, as shown in Figure 43.12, holds up to 12 of your copied selections. Office XP and later feature the Clipboard Task Pane that holds up to 24 items. The Clipboard toolbar appears and floats across your worksheet whenever you copy or cut more than one selection during your current Windows session.

FIGURE 43.12

The Clipboard toolbar holds your copy selections.

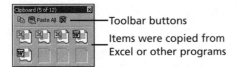

— Toolbar buttons
— Items were copied from Excel or other programs

The Clipboard toolbar provides some wonderful advantages. Instead of having to paste the last data that you copied, you can pick and choose from previously copied data. However, the Clipboard toolbar stores only the last 12 items that you copied or cut doing the current Windows session. When you close Windows, the Clipboard is automatically cleared.

Drag It and Drop It

The drag-and-drop technique is a fast, easy way to copy or move data in the visible viewing area. First, select the cells you want to move or copy. When the cells appear highlighted, move the mouse pointer over the border of the selected cells. The mouse pointer takes the shape of an arrow.

If you want to copy the selected cells, press and hold the Ctrl key. (If you're moving the cells, you don't need to hold down any key.) Now click the mouse button and drag the border. As they're being dragged, an outline of the selected cells appears. When the data is located in the spot in which you want it to appear, release the mouse button. The data appears in the new location as shown in Figure 43.13. You'll see how to copy worksheet entries using the various copy techniques by following these steps:

1. Select cell B4 by clicking it. A border appears around the cell.

2. Hold down the Ctrl key and position the mouse pointer in the border of the cell. A small cross appears.

3. Using the Ctrl key, move the mouse pointer to the cell directly to the right (cell C4). You've just used the drag-and-drop method to copy from one cell to another.

4. With cell C4 selected, press Ctrl+C. This copies the data in cell C4 to the Clipboard.

5. Click cells D4 and E4. Both cells are highlighted, which tells Excel where you want to paste the data.

6. Press Ctrl+V. This pastes the data into the selected cells. You've just used the shortcut keys to copy and paste data from one cell to other cells.

7. Click cell B5 to select it. Point to the small square in the lower-right corner of that cell. Notice the mouse pointer changes to a cross, which is called the fill handle.

8. Drag the fill handle to cells C5, D5, and E5. Now you've used the fill handle method to copy data when cells are adjacent to one another.

9. Select cell B6 (January's Utilities amount) by clicking it and then click the Copy button on the Standard toolbar. A dotted marquee appears around cell B6. The data you selected has been copied to the Clipboard.

10. Click into cell C6 and select cells D6 and E6 by dragging the mouse. The three cells appear highlighted.

11. Click the Paste button on the Standard toolbar. The amount you copied to the Clipboard is copied to the cells you selected.

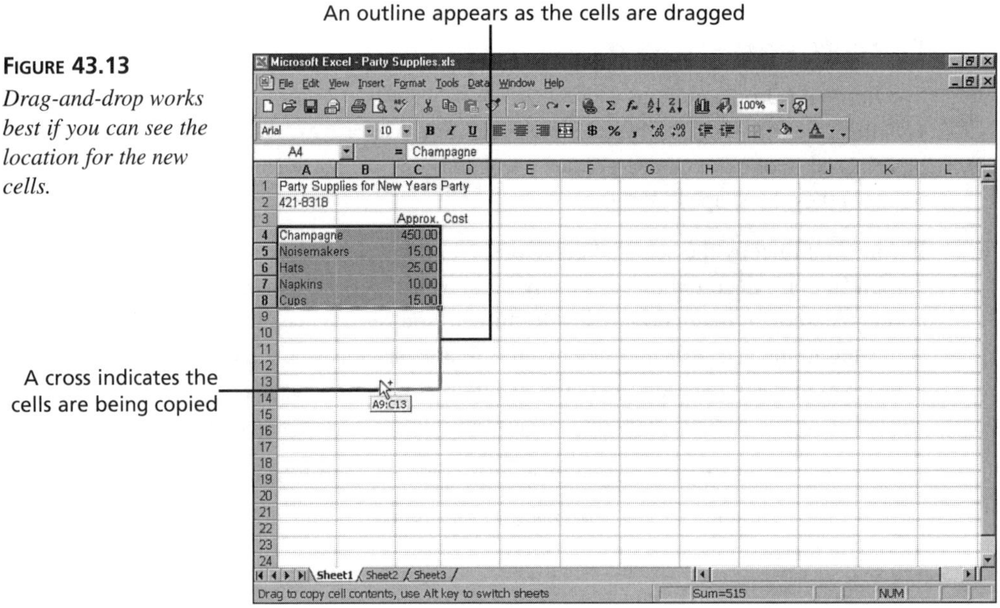

FIGURE 43.13

Drag-and-drop works best if you can see the location for the new cells.

An outline appears as the cells are dragged

A cross indicates the cells are being copied

Making Changes to the Worksheet

In a perfect society, you'd never need to edit your work. However, in the real world, you'll find yourself editing your cell entries time and time again. In addition to editing entries, you can delete an entry you've made. In fact, you can delete an entire row or column. You can also add rows and columns. A worksheet is a work-in-progress and, accordingly, can always be changed or improved.

Editing Cell Contents

Editing cell contents is easy. Double-click the cell that you want to edit and make your changes. You can edit the existing cell contents or replace them. When you're done, press the Enter key or one of the directional arrows, or click the green checkmark on the Formula bar to enter the new data into the cell. Cancel the edit by pressing Esc.

To quickly add to the end of cell contents, select the cell and press F2. The insertion point appears at the end of the existing cell contents. Type the addition to the cell and press Enter.

Clearing Cell Contents

Instead of editing a cell, you can clear the cell's contents. Clearing the contents of a cell is like using an eraser end of a pencil on the cell. Select the cells you want to clear and click the right mouse button. Choose Clear Contents from the shortcut menu, as shown in Figure 43.14. Keep in mind that the Clear Contents command does not place the cell contents on the Clipboard.

FIGURE 43.14

Use the shortcut menu to clear the contents of a cell.

Inserting and Deleting Cells

It's no problem to insert and delete cells in your worksheet. When you insert cells, Excel moves the remaining cells in the column or row in accordance with the direction you specify. Deleting cells is the opposite of inserting cells because the remaining cells are shifted to fill in the deleted cell.

Deleting a cell and clearing a cell are two very different actions. Deleting a cell removes the physical cell from the worksheet and forces the remaining cells to fill in the hole. Clearing a cell erases the contents of the cell, but leaves the cell still in the worksheet.

Working with Rows and Columns

Working with rows and columns is very much like working with cells on a larger scale. When you insert a row, the new row spans all the columns in the worksheets. New columns and rows don't contain data and are unformatted.

Insert a new row or column by clicking the spot where you want the new row or column to appear. If you want to insert more than one row or column, select the number of rows and columns you want. (For example, select three rows if you want to insert three new ones.) Click the Insert menu, as shown in Figure 43.15, and choose either Rows or Columns. Excel inserts new rows above the current row and inserts new columns to the left of the selected columns.

FIGURE 43.15

Add rows and columns from the Insert menu.

The following steps comprise an exercise in which you make some changes to the My Budget worksheet you started earlier, giving you a chance to put some of this knowledge to work. Don't worry if some of the changes don't make much sense; you're fine-tuning your skills right now.

1. Highlight cells B6 through E6 on the My Budget worksheet and click the right mouse button.

2. Choose Clear Contents from the shortcut menu that appears. As you see, you can clear the contents of one cell or a block of cells.

3. Let's add a few rows. From any column, highlight a rectangular block of cells in rows 9, 10, and 11, as shown in Figure 43.16. Because you're going to insert three rows, you do not have to position the mouse pointer in a particular column.

FIGURE 43.16

Your mouse pointer can be located in any column when you're inserting rows.

Row markers of selected rows appear highlighted

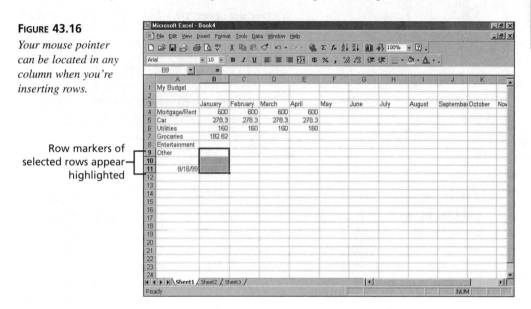

4. When the three rows are highlighted, click the Insert menu and choose Rows. Three blank rows are inserted above the first row you selected.

5. Click in cell A9, type Tuition, and press the down arrow to move down. Enter Insurance and Savings in the cells A10 and A11.

6. Select cell B5, the cell that contains the car expense and click Edit, Delete. The Delete dialog box, shown in Figure 43.17, appears. Make sure the option button next to Shift Cells Up is selected and click OK. Notice that the entry you'd made in the Groceries category for January was shifted upward.

FIGURE 43.17

You need to choose the behavior of the remaining cells whenever you delete a cell.

7. Stop now and save the worksheet so you can work with it later. Click the Save button on the Standard toolbar or click File, Save. When the Save As dialog box appears, type My Budget in the filename box and click Save.

8. If you're planning to go right on to the next hour, click File, Close. If you need a break before you continue, close Excel now by clicking File, Exit.

Summary

This chapter introduced Excel, and covered Excel's screen and the concept of workbooks and worksheets. The workbook documents contain your worksheets, and your worksheets hold data, such as numbers and labels. As you see throughout this part of the book, Excel supports a tremendous number of formatting options so that you can turn your numeric data into eye-catching, appealing output.

Although Excel works best with numeric data, Excel accepts text (called labels), date, and time values as well. Excel is extremely lenient about how you type dates and times but immediately converts such values into a special internal number. This internal number enables you to calculate with dates when you need to determine the number of days between two dates or when you need to add a fixed number of days to a date to arrive at an ending date, such as a due date.

CHAPTER 44

Letting Excel Do the Math

In this chapter, you learn how Excel performs calculations. Excel can do the math for you! You will find out how to work with formulas that take most of the hard work out of the arithmetic portion of your worksheets. When you use Excel, you can put away your calculator, scratch pads, and pencils.

Why Use Formulas?

Formulas are Excel's most powerful aid for getting your work done. Excel formulas handle the mathematical chores in your worksheet. In its simplest form, a formula is a quick calculation, similar to one you'd make on a calculator or adding machine. However, you can also use a formula to make predictions, figure out a car payment, or perform some other complex task.

Formulas speed up the creation of your worksheets. You don't need to worry about whether a calculation is correct, because Excel doesn't make mistakes. Best of all, you can change any value contained in a formula, and Excel will update the results automatically.

How Formulas Work

A formula is a cell entry that calculates values to return a result. Each Excel formula must have three key elements: the equal sign (=) that signifies that the entry is a formula, the values or cell references to be calculated, and the mathematical operators, such as a plus sign (+) for addition or a minus sign (-) for subtraction.

All Excel formulas must begin with the equal sign. The equal sign tells Excel that the entry is a formula. If your formula begins without an equal sign, Excel treats it as a regular cell entry and doesn't perform the calculation.

 If you begin a formula with a plus sign (+), Excel converts it to an equal sign (=). That's because Lotus 1-2-3, another spreadsheet program, uses the plus sign as its opening formula-entry character. Excel makes it easy for Lotus users to switch to Excel.

Mathematical Operators

When you create a formula in Excel, you need to include an operator. All formulas must contain mathematical operators so that Excel knows what calculation to perform. Table 44.1 lists the arithmetic operators used in Excel.

TABLE 44.1   Excel Formula Operators

Operator	What It Does
+	Addition
-	Subtraction
*	Multiplication
/	Division
=	Equal to
>	Greater than
>=	Greater than or equal to
<>	Not equal to
%	Percentage
^	Exponentiation

Figure 44.1 shows a very simple formula. The intent is pretty clear; the formula asks Excel to multiply 8 by 47.

Asterisk indicates multiplication operator

FIGURE 44.1
*The formula in cell A1
contains a mathemati-
cal operator.*

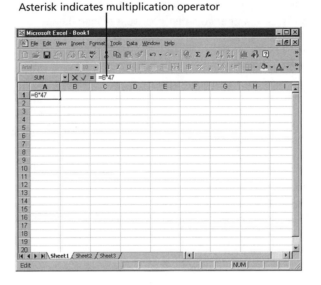

FIGURE 44.1
*The formula in cell A1
contains a mathemati-
cal operator.*

44

Order of Operations

In a simple formula, such as the one shown in Figure 44.1, Excel is asked to perform only one calculation. However, formulas can often contain instructions to perform multiple calculations. If you were to talk out a more complicated formula, you might say something like this: *Add together the price of a toy truck that costs $18.75 and a doll that costs $13.00 and then multiply the combined price by 7.5% sales tax to determine the sales tax due on the combined cost of the toys.*

You might think that you'd enter the value for the formula this way:

```
=18.75+13.00*.075
```

However, if you typed that formula in a cell, Excel would produce the wrong answer. The reason is that Excel uses something called operator precedence to perform calculations. *Operator precedence* determines the order in which calculations are performed. Calculations are performed from left to right in the following order:

1. All operations enclosed in parenthesis
2. All exponential operations
3. All multiplication and division operations
4. All addition and subtraction operations

The best way to force Excel to calculate your formulas correctly is to use parentheses. Group the values and operators that you want to calculate first in parentheses. For example, the formula

`(18.75+13.00)*.075`

tells Excel to first add the numbers within the parentheses and then to calculate the sales tax percentage on the total.

You can even nest parentheses within parentheses to further break down how you want Excel to calculate your formula. Just remember that each opening parenthesis must have a closing parenthesis. If your formula does not contain the required number of parentheses, Excel displays an error message similar to the one in Figure 44.2. Excel even attempts to place the missing parenthesis. If your formula doesn't contain the proper number of parentheses, Excel displays each parentheses set in a different color, to help you track your error.

FIGURE 44.2

Excel tells you when a formula has not been entered correctly.

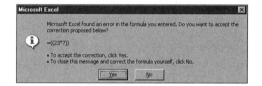

When Excel detects a formula error due to too many or too few parenthesis, it attempts to place the missing characters. If you let Excel correct your formula, check it over carefully. After all, Excel doesn't know what your calculation should accomplish.

Creating a Simple Formula

Simple formulas that work with values are easy to create. In essence, simple formulas use Excel like a calculator. These simple formulas are somewhat limiting because they don't use any values from the other cells in the worksheet. You can enter a formula into a cell, or you can enter it into the Formula bar.

The following steps give you a chance to create and edit some simple formulas. Because the formulas are only for practice, you should be working on a blank worksheet.

1. The first formula adds a series of numbers together. Click into a blank cell on the worksheet and type =35+35+35. When you're done typing, press the Enter key. Notice that the result of the calculation, 105, appears in the cell. The formula is displayed in the Formula bar when the cell is selected.

2. Amend the formula by clicking it and then pressing F2. The formula is displayed in the cell with the cursor flashing at the end of the formula. Type *15 and press Enter.

3. Now edit the formula to add some parentheses. Double-click the cell that contains the formula. The formula appears. Notice that because you're in Edit mode, many toolbar buttons are unavailable. Use the left-arrow keys to move to the first character to the right of the equal sign and then type an opening parenthesis. Use the right-arrow key to move to the last character before the multiplication operator (*) and then type a closing parenthesis. When your formula looks like the one in Figure 44.3, press Enter. Notice how the order of calculations changes the result of the calculation.

44

Excel calculates the equation within the parentheses first

FIGURE 44.3

The parentheses change the order of operation in the formula.

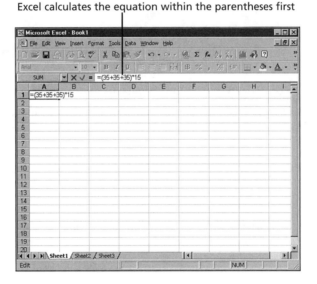

The keystrokes that move you to the beginning and end of a file also work while you're editing a formula. Press Ctrl+Home to quickly move the cursor to the beginning of the formula. Press Ctrl+End to move to the end.

4. Instead of typing formulas directly into a cell, you can enter them into the Formula bar. Select a blank cell and click the Edit Formula button, The Formula palette opens, as shown in Figure 44.4.

Formula result

FIGURE **44.4**

The Formula palette
provides a place to
enter the formula.

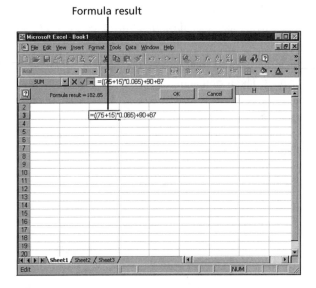

5. As you type, the results of the formula are displayed.

6. Click OK when you're done typing. The Formula palette closes, and the results of the formula are displayed in the cell. The formula itself is visible in the Formula bar.

You can enter a formula into the Formula bar without using the Formula palette by typing an = sign, rather than clicking the Edit Formula button. When you're done typing, you need to click the green checkmark to enter the formula into the cell.

Referencing Cells

In addition to typing values into your worksheets, you can enter references to cells. Using cell references is often more effective than typing actual values when you want to build formulas. If a value in a referenced cell changes, the formula that points to the reference is updated automatically. Best of all, one cell can be referenced in an unlimited number of formulas. A cell reference does not need to contain an operator unless you want to use it to perform a calculation.

For example, if you were calculating the amount of sales tax due on several car purchases, you could reference the cell that held the current sales tax percentage in each formula. If the sales tax percentage changes or you enter it incorrectly, updating the percentage amount also updates each car purchase formula.

As you build a formula, you can point to a cell to include the cell's value in the calculation. For example, if you're building a formula that subtracts cell D16 from D18, begin the formula with an equal sign, click cell D18, type a minus sign, and point to cell D16. Click the Enter button (the green checkmark) when the formula is complete.

44

> Each time you reference a cell while you're building a formula, you need to type an operator. Otherwise, Excel won't store the cell reference, and your formula will be incomplete.

You can reference cells that are not currently visible in the worksheet by scrolling to the cell with the scrollbars. You can even reference a cell in another sheet by clicking the sheet tab and then clicking the cell you want to include.

> Don't press the Enter key while you're still constructing a formula by pointing to cells. Pressing Enter is equal to clicking the green checkmark and tells Excel that the formula is complete.

If you need to edit a formula, press F2 and make your changes. You can type the values and cell references, or you can point to them with the mouse. Click the Enter button when the formula is complete.

Excel uses color coding to assist you when you're editing a cell. Each cell reference and the cell it refers to in the worksheet are displayed in the same color. You can use the color coding to identify which references in the formula match which cells in the worksheet.

Using AutoSum

The AutoSum button on the Standard toolbar is one of the most useful tools in Excel. The *AutoSum* feature automatically totals a range of values. Click into the cell where you want the total to appear and click the AutoSum button. The SUM formula appears in the cell and a marquee surrounds the range of values in the column. Click the AutoSum button again. A total of the range in the column directly appears in the last cell.

AutoSum can total cells in a row, as well as a column. Click the first empty cell in a row that contains values and click AutoSum. The SUM formula appears in the cell and a marquee surrounds the range of values in the row. Click the AutoSum button again. The total of the preceding cells appears in the last cell.

> AutoSum adds ranges that contain values. If an empty cell appears in the column or row, AutoSum does not add cells that appear before the blank one.

Using Ranges

If you know the cell address of the data you need to locate, you'll have no trouble moving to the spot. But unless you have a photographic memory, you probably won't remember the cell locations of all your important data. Even if you can spout cell locations, the cell addresses of your data change as you add and delete cells, rows, and columns.

Ranges provide a better way to organize and describe your data. A *range* is a rectangular block of cells that can be named with a descriptive name. Instead of trying to remember where the Utilities budget is located, you can specify the range name that holds the information to have Excel whisk to the first cell of the range. You can also use ranges for formatting and printing, and you can use range names in formulas.

A range can consist of one cell (after all, one cell is a rectangular block), or it can comprise the entire worksheet. Each range has two anchor points: the top-left and bottom-right cells. You can add or delete cells, rows, or columns within the body of the range, but you cannot make changes at either anchor point of the range.

Assigning Range Names

Instead of calling a range by its coordinates, it makes much more sense to assign it a descriptive name. Follow the rules shown here when you assign names to your ranges:

- Begin each range name with an underscore character or a letter.
- Keep your range names short, descriptive, and to the point.
- You can't use spaces or hyphens in range names so separate words with the underscore character, for example [Jan_Sales].
- You can use upper- and lowercase letters.

In the following steps, you learn to set up and name ranges in the My Budget workbook you created in the previous chapter. The workbook should be open and visible on the screen before you begin.

1. Select cells A4 through A12 on the My Budget workbook. These cells make up the budget categories.

2. When the cells appear highlighted, click the Insert menu, choose Name, and then choose Define. The Define Name dialog box appears, as shown in Figure 44.5. Excel has assigned the range name to the text shown in the first cell.

44

FIGURE 44.5

The name Excel assigns to the range is selected so you can change the range.

3. Because the default name is already highlighted, you don't need to delete it to type a new name. For this example, type `Categories` and click OK. The box closes, and the range name is added to the workbook.

4. Excel provides an alternative way of assigning range names. Highlight the cells that hold the labels January through December (B3:M3). Click inside the Name box and type `Months`. When you're through, your screen should look like the example in Figure 44.6.

5. Deselect the highlighted cells by pressing the right-arrow key.

6. Move to the first range you defined by typing `Categories` in the Name box and pressing Enter. The mouse pointer moves to the first cell in the range, and the cells in the range appear highlighted.

7. Use a keystroke shortcut to view all the range names in the workbook. Press Ctrl+G to open the Go To dialog box, which contains a listing of all the named ranges within your worksheet, both by coordinates and assigned names. Click the range you want to go to and Excel takes you there. By naming appropriate ranges you can quickly navigate throughout a complex worksheet.

Editing Range Names

You're never locked into the ranges you create. You can edit the range coordinates and rename or delete the range. Click the Insert menu, choose Name, and then choose Define to open the Define Name dialog box. When you click a range, the name appears in the Names in Workbook text box. To rename a range, type a new name in the Names in Workbook box. To delete a range, click the Delete button.

Name box   Range is selected

FIGURE 44.6

The Name box holds the range name.

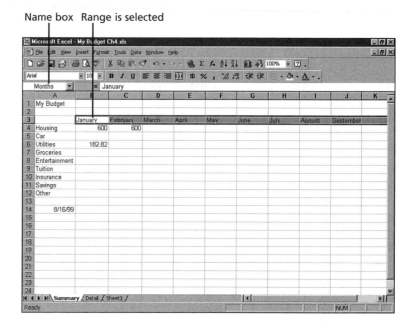

The range coordinates appear in the Refers To text box and are represented by the worksheet and anchor cells of the range. A range name might look something like =Sheet1!$A$4:$A$12. Although it might seem somewhat cryptic, each character has a distinct meaning. The column and row indicators appear after each $ character. If you want to change the range coordinates, replace only the column letters and row letters with the new coordinates for the range. Take care not to delete or change any other characters.

The dollar signs in the range name indicate *absolute cell references.* You'll learn about absolute cell references later in this chapter.

Workbook and Worksheet Navigation Tools

Before continuing learning how to enter numeric values and formulas, it will benefit you to learn to break your workbook into separate worksheets. Individual worksheets make good sense. They allow you to organize your data on separate sheets. The workbook in

Figure 44.7 is a good example; the first worksheet holds the total vacation days and total sick days for each employee, and each monthly worksheet tracks the time by days and hours.

FIGURE 44.7

Multiple worksheets inside a single workbook enable you to organize data better.

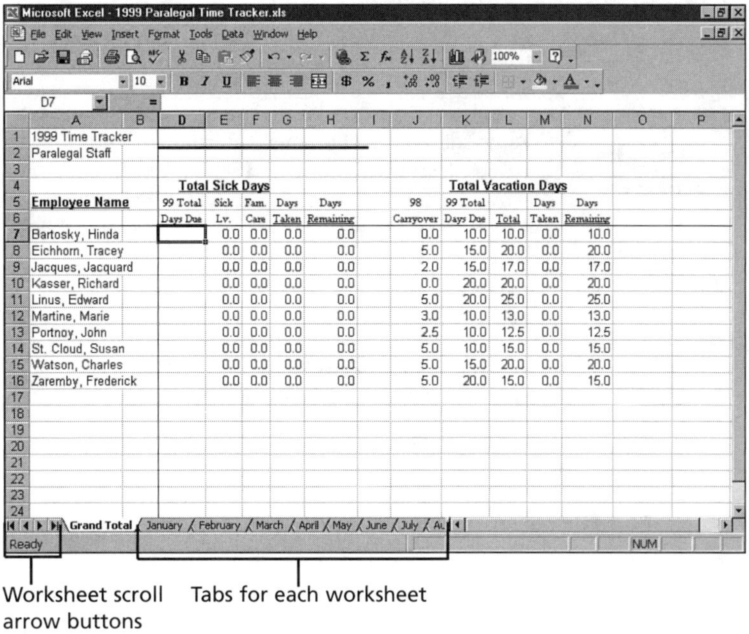

Worksheet scroll   Tabs for each worksheet
arrow buttons

You can add or delete as many worksheets to a workbook file as you want. By default, Excel names the sheets with a number. The name is displayed on the worksheet's tab. Most times, the names Sheet 1, Sheet 2, and so on aren't descriptive of the sheet's purpose; you can easily change the sheet names to be more descriptive.

Moving around a large workbook requires a few simple navigational skills. Clicking a worksheet's tab brings that worksheet to the front of the screen and makes it active. If your workbook contains many sheets or the sheet names are long, it's hard to see all the tabs.

Each workbook file is set up with worksheet scroll arrow buttons, located at the far end of the horizontal scrollbar. The arrow buttons always appear, no matter which worksheet you're working in. Use the arrow buttons to scroll through the individual sheet names. When the sheet name you want appears, click its tab to make the sheet active.

In the following steps, you add worksheets to your My Budget workbook. You also learn how to rename a worksheet. You also copy data from one worksheet to another, using a range name. Make sure the My Budget workbook file is open and visible on the screen before you begin.

1. Double-click the first tab of the My Budget workbook that currently reads Sheet 1. The name is highlighted.

2. Type Summary and press Enter. The new name now appears on the worksheet tab.

> Although worksheet names can contain up to 256 characters, keep the names descriptive, short, and simple. Short names are easier to read as you scroll through the worksheets. Additionally, formulas that reference a cell in a worksheet are easier to construct and edit if the name is short.

> You can rename a worksheet from a shortcut menu. Right-click the tab you want to rename and choose Rename from the shortcut menu. Type the new name and press Enter.

3. Add a new worksheet by clicking the worksheet tab that's before the position in which you want to insert the new sheet. In this case, click the tab that reads Sheet 3.

4. Click the Insert menu and choose Worksheet. Excel inserts a new tab with a default name. Double-click the tab of the new worksheet and type Detail.

5. The second worksheet is not needed in the current workbook. Right-click the tab that reads Sheet 2 and choose Delete. A box appears to ask you to confirm the deletion. Click OK.

6. Click the Summary tab to make that worksheet active. When the Summary worksheet appears on the screen, select the cells that contain the names of the months (cells B3 through M3) by dragging the mouse across them.

7. When the cells appear highlighted, click the Copy button on the Standard toolbar.

8. Click the Details tab and click cell B3 in the Details worksheet.

9. Click the Paste button on the Standard toolbar. The month labels now appear on both the Details worksheet and the Summary Sheet.

10. Save the My Budget worksheet by clicking the Save button on the Standard toolbar.

Using Range Names in Formulas

Using range names can sometimes help you create and troubleshoot formulas. The use of range names is especially important if more than one person is going to be working on the file because names are easier to understand than cell references. For example, a cell named SALES_TAX would make a sales tax calculation easy to understand and locate.

You must name a range before you can use it in a formula. If you remember the range name, you can type it into the formula in place of a cell reference. Remember, though, that you must type the range name perfectly, or Excel won't accept it. If you don't remember the exact name of a range, let Excel provide the name for you.

When you come to the place in the formula where you want to insert a range name, click the Insert menu and choose Name and then Paste. The Paste Name dialog box, as displayed in Figure 44.8, appears. Select the range name you want to include in the formula and click OK. The box closes, and the range name is included in the formula.

The range names have been defined previously

FIGURE 44.8

Choose a range name to include in your formula.

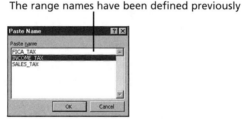

Using Relative and Absolute Addressing

When you enter a formula that contains cell references into a cell, Excel keeps track of it in two ways. The first is to record the value of that cell and use the value in the calculation. The second way is to keep track of the relative position of the cells in the formula to one another.

Here's how relative addressing works if you enter the formula =A1+A2 in cell A3.

If the formula could talk, it would say, "Take the cell two rows above me and add the value of that cell to the cell one row above me and display the results in my cell." If you copied the formula in A3 to C3, the new formula would read =C1+C2. Why? Because the new formula would be looking at the cells one and two rows above it

Relative cell referencing is great if you're adding a number of like columns, such as the ones shown in Figure 44.9. Imagine how tedious it would be to have to create a formula in the total column for each day. With relative cell referencing, you create the formula in the first total column and then copy it to all the other days of the month.

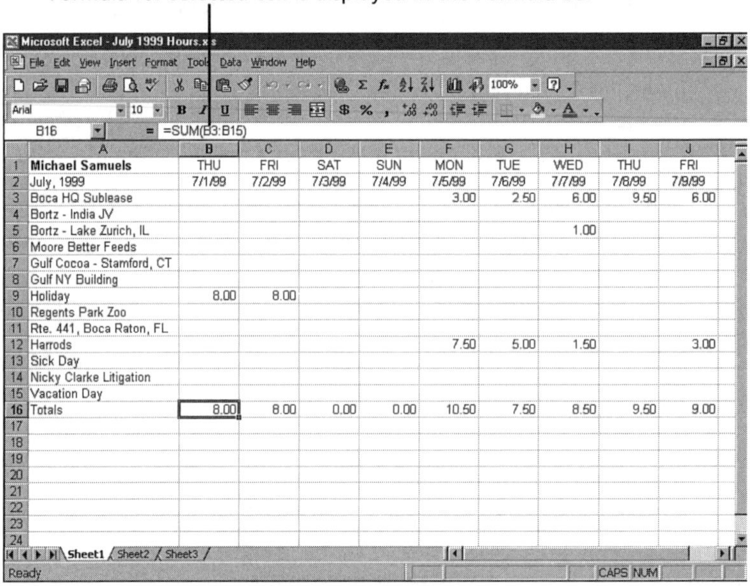

FIGURE 44.9

The formula in each cell in the Totals row adds the hours in the corresponding daily column.

Formula for selected cell is displayed in the Formula bar

Relative cell referencing is Excel's default way of copying formulas. Sometimes, a formula needs to reference a cell location that remains constant. In the illustration in Figure 44.10, an hourly rate has been entered into the worksheet on cell A21. Accordingly, the formula in cell B23 for the daily billable total is =B19*A21. The formula literally translates to "Take the total of the cell three rows above me and multiply by the value located two rows up and one column to my left."

Copying the formula to the other days of the month would produce incorrect amounts. Relative cell referencing dictates that the formula would always multiply the value of the cell three rows up with the cell located two rows up and one column to its left. However, the hourly rate is placed in one specific cell: A21. In this case, the formula would need to absolutely use cell A21. This type of addressing is called absolute addressing. An absolute address remains constant; it doesn't change if the formula is copied or moved to another location in the worksheet. The $ (dollar sign) character indicates absolute addressing; thus a cell reference written as $A$21 would always point to cell A21.

Mixed referencing allows you to keep either a row or column constant. The dollar-sign character placed next to the column indicator, as in $A1, means that the column remains constant, but the row changes as the formula is copied. A $ next to the row indicator, as in A$1, indicates that the column is relative, but the row shown in the cell address is absolute.

FIGURE 44.10

The formula produces the daily billable rate.

	B	C	D	E	F	G	H	I	J
	THU	FRI	SAT	SUN	MON	TUE	WED	THU	FRI
1 Michael Samuels									
2 July, 1999	7/1/99	7/2/99	7/3/99	7/4/99	7/5/99	7/6/99	7/7/99	7/8/99	7/9/99
3 Korean Real Estate									
4 Bortz/Borneim, Brazil									
5 Boca HQ Sublease					3.00	2.50	6.00	9.50	6.00
6 Bortz - India JV									
7 Bortz - Lake Zurich, IL							1.00		
8 Moore Better Feeds									
9 Gulf Cocoa - Stamford, CT									
10 Gulf NY Building									
11 Holiday	8.00	8.00							
12 Regents Park Zoo									
13 Rte. 441, Boca Raton, FL									
14 Harrods					7.50	5.00	1.50		3.00
15 Sick Day									
16 Nicky Clarke Litigation									
17 Vacation Day									
18 Totals	8.00	8.00	0.00	0.00	10.50	7.50	8.50	9.50	9.00
19	*Hourly Rate*								
20	$85.00								
21									
22 Amount due: Billable Hours	$680.00								
23									
24									

B22 = =B18*A20

Cell reference must remain constant

When you're entering a cell reference into a cell, you can type the dollar signs to make the reference absolute. Or if you're using the mouse to point to the cells you want to use in the formula, click the cell and press F4. The dollar sign character appears before both the column and row indicators, meaning the cell reference is absolute.

To make only the column or row portion of a cell address absolute, press F4 again. Each time you press the F4 key, the $ moves to a different coordinate of the cell address. For example, $A$1 becomes A$1, $A1, and so on each time you press the F4 key.

Working with Formulas That Reference Other Workbooks and Worksheets

Because a workbook can contain multiple worksheets, you might need to reference a cell in another worksheet or even another workbook file. As long as you follow the proper syntax, you can type a formula that contains a reference to any file.

If the cell is contained in another worksheet in the current workbook, you need to include the sheet name followed by an exclamation point (!) and then the actual address of the cell. Blank spaces are not allowed. For example, Sheet4!A75, points to cell A75 on Sheet 4 of the current workbook. Anytime you reference another worksheet in the workbook, you must include the exclamation point. If you've renamed a worksheet from its default sheet name, use the sheet name and an exclamation point.

> Although blank spaces are not allowed in cell references, your sheet name might contain one or more blanks, for example, Jan Sales. If your sheet name contains blank spaces, enclose the sheet name in single quotes, such as 'Jan Sales'!A21. The exclamation point character follows the quotes.

Although you can type a cell reference to another worksheet, it's easier to use the mouse. If you need to reference a cell on another sheet as you're building a formula, click the appropriate sheet tab and then point to the cell you want to use. Excel places the sheet name and cell reference, using perfect syntax, into the formula.

You can also reference a cell from another workbook. It's best to point to the cell you want to use, rather than worry about making sure that you've used the correct syntax. Make sure that you open the workbook(s) that contains the cells you want to reference before you begin.

Begin the formula by clicking the Edit Formula button so that the formula appears in the Formula palette. As you construct the formula, switch to the open worksheet by clicking the Window menu, as illustrated in Figure 44.11, and navigating to the worksheet and cell. After you click the cell you want, use the Window menu and click the file that contains the formula you're working on. When you're done building the formula, click the OK button on the Formula palette.

Check mark indicates
the file is active

FIGURE 44.11

*Switch to another
open workbook.*

The next few steps give you some hands-on practice in working with formulas and in entering data. Once again, you're working with the My Budget workbook. If the file isn't open right now, open it before you begin these practice steps.

1. Drag the mouse over the rectangular block of cells that contain data on the Summary tab of the My Budget worksheet. When the cells appear highlighted, click the Edit menu and choose Clear, Contents.

2. Click the Detail tab to make the second worksheet active. When the Detail worksheet appears, click in cell A4 and type =Summary!A4. Click the Enter button. Cell A4 reads Mortgage/Rent, the same text that appears on cell A4 on the Summary sheet.

3. Click the Summary tab to make the Summary worksheet active. Double-click cell A4, highlight the existing text, and type Housing. Press Enter when you're through typing.

4. Switch to the Detail worksheet. Note that the formula in cell A4 references the same cell on the Summary worksheet. Therefore, changes to the cell on the Summary sheet automatically update here.

5. Click into cell A5, type Rent, and press the down-arrow key. Enter Mortgage, Parking, and Condo/Fees into the three cells located below the cell that contains Rent. When you're done, click the A column marker and choose Format, Column, AutoFit Selection to widen the column to the width of the widest entry.

6. Enter values that approximate your real expenses next to Rent, Mortgage, Parking, and Condo/Fees in the January column. (For practice, enter 100 in each cell.)

7. Obtain a total of the amounts you've typed so far with Excel's *QuickSum* feature. Select the range that contains the numbers you entered. The total appears on the Excel status bar, as shown in Figure 44.12.

> QuickSum is a great way to obtain a running total of a range of values. The total is not inserted in the worksheet. It's displayed on the Excel status bar.

8. Click into cell A9 and type Misc to create a new category. If you want, enter a corresponding amount for miscellaneous housing expenses in the January column.

9. Click into cell B10. When a border appears around the cell, click inside the Formula bar, type =SUM(B5:B9), and press Enter. The total for the January housing expense is shown.

44

Selected range

FIGURE **44.12**

*QuickSum adds the
amounts you select.*

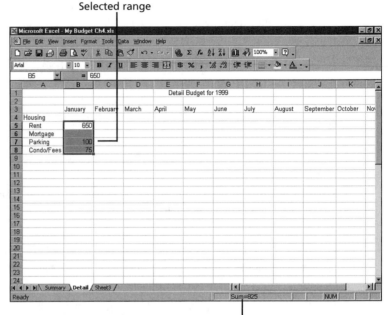

Total appears in the status bar

10. Click the Summary tab to activate the Summary worksheet. You're going to enter the total of housing expenses for January into cell B4. Double-click cell B4 and type = to begin the formula. Next, click the Detail sheet and click cell B10, which contains the sum for the category. Press Enter. The Summary worksheet reappears with the January total amount in the cell and the cell reference displayed in the Formula bar.

11. Click the Save button on the Standard toolbar to save the My Budget workbook. Remember, if you don't save the file, all your hard work will be lost.

12. (Optional) Switch to the Detail sheet and repeat steps 2–10 of this exercise to create details for your car expense. Create subcategories like Insurance, Fuel, and Maintenance. Reference the total amount on the Summary worksheet sheet. Substitute the cells for the new range in your calculation and cell referencing. Save the file when you're done.

Working with Simple Functions

Excel contains a range of *functions* designed to help you enter formulas easily. Excel functions run the gamut of simple calculations to complex, multitiered equations. You can use an Excel function to total a range of numbers or calculate a car payment. Excel contains more than 100 functions for your use.

This section examines a few of Excel's simpler functions. Table 44.2 shows some simple, commonly used functions.

TABLE 44.2 Common Excel Functions

Function	What It Does
SUM	Adds a range
AVERAGE	Determines the average of a range
NOW	Inserts the date based on the system clock; updates the date whenever the worksheet is opened or saved
PMT	Computes a monthly loan payment
HYPERLINK	Sets a hyperlink

Excel functions are handled like formulas. Each function begins with an =. Next enter the function name, which is usually a one-word description of what the function does. Following the function name is an opening parenthesis. Arguments follow. The function is concluded with a closing parenthesis.

The function

`=SUM(A1:A5)`

returns the sum of the cells from A1 through A5. (The colon character indicates *through*.) The function could also be written as `=SUM(A1+A2+A3+A4+A5)`. Although writing it with all the cells is technically correct, it makes more sense (and conserves space) to use range coordinates. If a function has more than one argument, commas separate the arguments.

A few functions don't use arguments. For example, `=NOW()` enters the serial number for the current date in the cell.

Copying Formulas

Instead of creating a formula each time you need one, Excel allows you to copy exiting formulas from cell to cell. Just like text and values, formulas that you copy are sent to the Windows Clipboard. You can paste the formula to one cell or to many.

When you copy a formula, relative addressing will change the cells that are referenced by the formula. If you need any of the cells to remain constant, make sure that absolute addressing has been added to the original formula before you copy it.

44

In this chapter's final exercise, you work with a few simple functions and copy some formulas. The My Budget workbook should be open and visible on the screen before you begin. Follow these steps to practice working with functions:

1. Click the Summary tab on the My Budget workbook to make the Summary sheet active.

2. Click into cell B13. A border appears around the cell. In this cell, you're going to use the SUM function to create a formula that totals all the expenses listed in the column.

3. Click into the Formula bar and click the Edit Formula button. An = sign appears in the Formula palette, signifying the start of a formula. In the Name box to the left of the buttons on the Formula bar, click the drop-down arrow and choose SUM from the list of available functions. The SUM function appears, as shown in Figure 44.13, with the suggested range of cells to be added.

4. Click OK to enter the SUM formula into the cell.

5. The completed formula can be copied to the total columns for the other 11 months. Click the fill handle located at the bottom right corner of the cell and drag it across the row to cell M13. When you release the mouse button, the totals appear in the monthly columns.

6. Use the horizontal scrollbar at the bottom of the worksheet to scroll to the left edge of the screen, and right-click cell A14. Choose Clear Contents from the shortcut menu.

Suggested range of cells to be added

FIGURE 44.13

The SUM function does the hard work for you.

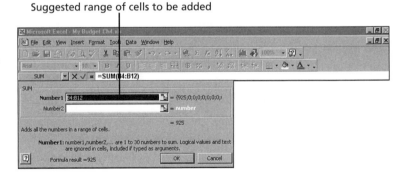

A formula can be placed in advance of values entered into the columns. For example, the February through December columns in the My Budget workbook don't contain entries, so the formulas equate to zero. As values are entered into the columns, the formulas automatically update the correct column totals.

44

7. Click into the Formula bar and type =NOW(). Press Enter when you're done. The current date appears inside the cell. Now whenever you open or save the MY BUDGET file, the correct date appears.

8. Save the file by clicking the Save button on the Standard toolbar. Unless you're planning to make additional changes, close the file by clicking the Close button or by opening the File menu and choosing Close.

Troubleshooting Formula Errors

When you enter a formula incorrectly into a cell, Excel displays an error message. Formulas can be entered incorrectly for a variety of reasons. Typing mistakes are usually the biggest cause of formula errors. If you mistype an operator or function name, Excel returns an error instead of the desired result.

The next biggest reason that formulas return error values is improper syntax. Syntax is everything when you're entering formulas; your formula must conform exactly to Excel's format. For example, if your formula contains a blank space, the formula errors out.

Excel often provides information about the errors it finds in formulas. With Excel's help, you can usually fix the problem. If the formula looks okay but still isn't producing the results you expect, check it over. If you inadvertently reference the wrong cell or use the wrong function, such as SUM instead of AVERAGE, your answer will not be correct.

Summary

In this chapter, you advanced by leaps and bounds as you moved into the world of working with numbers. Mathematics is the heart and soul of Excel, and you practiced constructing formulas and copying them. In the next chapter, "Using Excel Templates," you'll have learn how to leverage your skills by starting with Excel templates.

CHAPTER 45

Using Excel Templates

Excel offers a collection of templates to use in creating a workbook. Templates enable you to create a workbook based on the special text and formatting elements the templates provide. You could create these elements yourself, but the job would take some time.

During this chapter, you discover that creating a workbook, using an Excel built-in template, is easier than you think. Using a ready-made design gives you a running start on creating a professional-looking workbook. You also learn how to change the template, create your own template, and save an existing worksheet as a template.

What Is a Template?

Templates provide a pattern and tools for creating a variety of workbooks. If you read about the Word or FrontPage templates in Chapters 7 and 35, you already know how simple templates enable you to generate attention-getting and helpful documents and Webs. Not only do templates provide an initial design for the worksheets inside your Excel workbooks, templates also help you create workbooks that are consistent and you can do so quicker than creating them from scratch. If you create a weekly expense report and you don't want to re-create the entire report each week, you can save one of your reports as a customized template and then insert new numbers in the basic format each week.

Each newly created workbook must be based on a template. When you create a new workbook, Excel bases it on the default template called WORKBOOK.XLT.

Exploring Excel Templates

An Excel built-in template can contain boilerplate text, graphics, styles, macros, and custom toolbars. Several templates can assist you in planning your finances and running your business: Expense Statement, Invoice, Purchase Order, and Village Software. The Village Software template allows you to order customized spreadsheets from a software company. You can use or modify the general-purpose templates supplied by Excel.

Opening a Template

When you open a template in Excel, you should see several elements such as boilerplate text, comments, a Template toolbar, a Customize button, and two sheet tabs; the first sheet tab is for customizing your template and the second tab, which contains only the template name, is for viewing the template. Boilerplate text is standard text that you can keep or change.

Figure 45.1 shows the Invoice template that contains a placeholder for your company logo, placeholder text for invoice information, and columns where you can enter your invoice data. The template also contains a Template toolbar for working with various elements in the Invoice template.

The following steps walk you through the opening of a predefined Excel template called Invoice.

1. To open the Invoice template, click the File menu and then click New. The New dialog box appears. You should see two tabs: General and Spreadsheet Solutions.

2. Click the Spreadsheet Solutions tab. This tab contains four templates: Expense Statement, Invoice, Purchase Order, and Village Software, as shown in Figure 45.2.

If you don't see all the template icons on the Spreadsheet Solutions tab in the New dialog box, you need to install the templates using your Microsoft Office or Microsoft Excel software CD-ROM.

Placeholder for your logo   Boilerplate text   Invoice Template toolbar

FIGURE 45.1

The Invoice template.

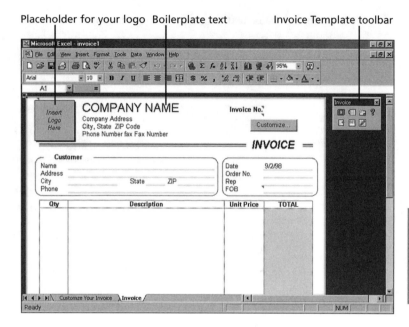

Templates   Preview box

FIGURE 45.2

The Spreadsheet Solutions tab in the New dialog box.

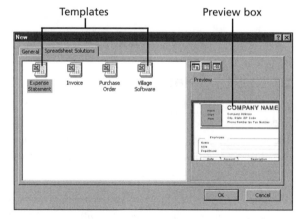

3. Click the Invoice Template icon. Notice how a portion of the Invoice template pops up in the Preview area on the right side of the dialog box. Click OK.

4. Excel then asks you to disable or enable macros associated with the template. You want to enable the macros, so click Enable Macros. Excel copies the template into a new workbook, ready for you to add information or change the template.

5. Save the template in a workbook named My Invoice. Click the File menu and then click Save As. The Save As dialog box appears.

6. In the Filename text box, type My Invoice to name the workbook.

7. Click Save. Excel saves the workbook. You should see the name My Invoice in the title bar. Figure 45.3 shows the Invoice template in the workbook called My Invoice.

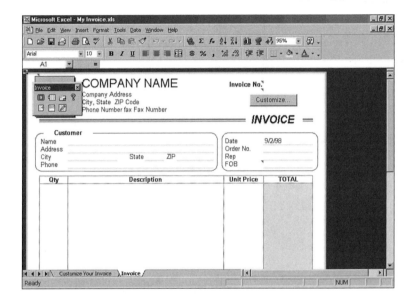

Changing the Template

After you open a template, you can use it right away by entering data, but most likely you'll want to customize the template to meet your needs. You can change a template at any time. Some of the things you can do include adding a comment to a cell, hiding the comments, changing the template options, or adding your company information to the template.

You can add comments to a cell to further explain the data that can be entered in that cell. A red triangle in the upper-right corner of a cell indicates that the cell contains a comment. When you move the mouse pointer over a red triangle on the template, Excel displays a box containing a helpful comment. You can opt to either display or hide comments entered in cells.

Every built-in template contains a floating Template toolbar that you can position anywhere on the template. This toolbar is available only when you open a template file. A Template toolbar takes on the name of the template currently open. The Template toolbar in Figure 45.4 has the name Invoice.

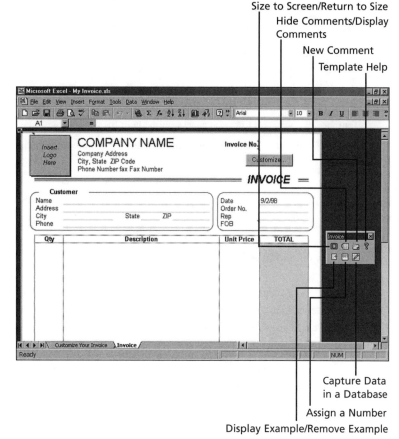

FIGURE 45.4

A Template toolbar.

Size to Screen/Return to Size

Hide Comments/Display Comments

New Comment

Template Help

Capture Data in a Database

Assign a Number

Display Example/Remove Example

The Template toolbar helps you work with the template; Table 45.1 describes the Template toolbar tools.

TABLE 45.1   Template Toolbar Tools

Tool	What It Does
Size to Screen/ Return to Size	Displays the template zoomed in at a percentage that depends on the size of your monitor and the resolution. As an example, on a 14" monitor at 800×600 resolution, you should see the template at 70% magnification; when you click the Size to Screen/Return to Size button, Excel displays the template at 43%. On a 17" monitor at 800×600 resolution, the template is at 85% magnification and 60% when you size the template to the screen.

TABLE 45.1   continued

Tool	What It Does
Hide Comments/ Display Comments	Hides and displays comments entered in cells.
New Comment	Enables you to add a comment to a cell to further explain the data that can be entered in that cell.
Template Help	Lets you access online help for working with the template.
Display Example/ Remove Example	Displays and hides sample data in the cells on the template.
Assign a Number	Assigns a unique number to the template form.
Capture Data in a Database	Transfers data from the template form to a database, which you can specify.

If you want to customize your template, you can use the Customize button on the template form or the Customize Your Invoice sheet tab. The next few steps demonstrate how to make some changes to the Invoice template. You can try out a few tools on the Template toolbar to change the template. The My Invoice workbook that contains the Invoice template should already be open.

1. First, tell Excel that you want to customize the Invoice template. Click the Customize button at the top of the template. If needed, scroll right to see the Customize button. You should see a new worksheet before the template worksheet. In this practice exercise, the Customize Your Invoice worksheet appears before the Invoice worksheet.

2. You can use your company's information to customize the invoice. In the Company Name box, type your company's name. Enter the address, city, state, and ZIP code in the appropriate boxes. In the Phone Number box, type your company's phone number. The information you enter for an item is temporarily no longer displayed. As soon as you enter the new information and press the down arrow, Excel displays the previous information once again.

3. To display some sample data in the invoice, click the Invoice sheet tab. Then, click the Display Example/Remove Example button on the Invoice toolbar. Excel displays sample data in the invoice (see Figure 45.5), which gives you an idea of what kind of data you could enter in the invoice form.

4. To remove that sample data, click the Display Example/Remove Example button on the Invoice toolbar. The sample data disappears.

FIGURE 45.5

Sample data in the invoice template.

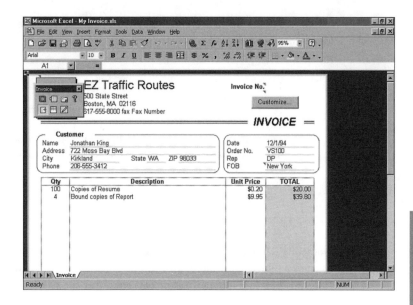

5. To look at a comment, move the mouse pointer over the Invoice No. comment (red triangle) in the upper-right corner of the template. The comment box contains helpful information about entering data in this cell.

6. If you don't want to display the comments on the invoice, you can hide the comments. Just click the Hide Comments/Display Comments button on the Invoice toolbar. Excel hides the comment indicators (red triangles) for the comments in the invoice.

7. Because the comments are helpful, you may decide to leave them on. Click the Hide Comments/Display Comments button on the Invoice toolbar to restore the comment indicators (red triangles).

8. To save the changes you made to your template, click the Customize button on the template. Click the Lock/Save Sheet button at the top of the template. The Lock/Save Sheet dialog box opens, as illustrated in Figure 45.6. The locking options let you lock the changes you made to the template. *Locking the template means that you cannot edit or delete the template.*

FIGURE 45.6

The Lock/Save Sheet dialog box.

9. Choose the Lock and Save Template option. Click OK. Excel displays the Save Template dialog box. This is where you enter a name for the customized version of the invoice template.

 It's best to lock the template to prevent yourself and others from accidentally changing or deleting the template. If you choose the Lock but Don't Save option, you are returned to the customized version of the template. You can't make changes to the template unless you click the Unlock This Sheet button at the top of the customized version of the template. In the Unlock This Sheet dialog box, click OK. Then you can make changes to the template.

10. Name the template, using your company's name. In the File Name text box, type the name followed by the word Invoice. Click Save. Excel locks and saves the customized version of the template. You should see the customized version of the template on your screen.

11. You're finished using the template. Click the Close Window (X) button to close the workbook.

12. To look at the template icon in the New dialog box, click File, New. Click the General tab if necessary. You should see the template icon you created. Click Cancel to close the dialog box.

Creating Your Own Template

You can save yourself lots of time by saving your favorite workbook as a template. Simply take an existing Excel workbook, get it to look the way you want for a template form, and then create a template from it.

For example, suppose you have a budget that you update monthly. You can delete all the numbers that change in the worksheet, leaving the column and row headings intact. Then save the budget worksheet as a template. The next time you want to use the budget worksheet, open the budget template worksheet and just fill in the numbers. It's as easy as pie!

If you follow the next few steps, you prepare the Summary worksheet in the My Budget workbook (the workbook you have been working on the past 2 chapters) for a template form. You need to delete the numbers and keep the column and row headings.

1. To open the My Budget workbook, which contains the Summary worksheet, click the Open button on the Standard toolbar. The Open dialog box appears.

2. To select the file, double-click on My Budget.xls. The My Budget workbook appears in the Excel window. Notice that the worksheet contains column and row headings and data.

3. Select the range that contains the data you want to delete; in this case, select the range B4:B5.

4. Press Delete. Now press the right-arrow key to deselect the range. The data disappears. You want to keep the title, column headings, and row headings, and date (see Figure 45.7). Now the worksheet is ready to be saved as a template (as explained in the next section).

FIGURE 45.7

The worksheet without numbers, with the title, column headings, and row headings, ready for the template form.

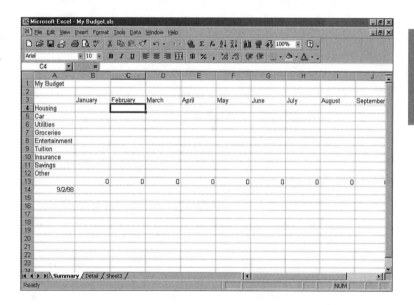

45

Saving a Worksheet As a Template

After you prepare your worksheet for the template form, the next step is to save the worksheet as a template file. A template file has the file extension .XLT. You need to use the Save As command to save the workbook file and change it into a template file format.

You can save your template file into three locations:

- The Templates folder or a subfolder of the Templates folder in the Microsoft Office or Microsoft Excel folder.

- The XLStart folder in the Microsoft Excel folder.

- The location you specified as an alternate startup file location: Click the Tools menu, choose Options, click the General tab, and enter the location (folder) in the Alternate Startup File Location text box.

The following steps show you how to save the My Budget workbook as a template with the name Budget Form.

1. To save the My Budget workbook as a template, click the File menu and click Save As. The Save As dialog box opens.

2. Tell Excel the file type in which you want to save the file. Click the Save as Type drop-down arrow. You should see a list of file types. The Template (`*.xlt`) type is the one you want. Click on it. Now Template (`My Budget.xlt`) appears in the Save as Type box.

3. In the File Name text box, highlight the default filename, and type `Budget Form` over the existing name.

4. The template should be stored in the Templates folder. In the Save In box, you should see Templates. If not, click the down arrow in the Save In box and choose the C: drive, Program Files, Microsoft Office, and Templates. Your Save As dialog box should look like the one in Figure 45.8.

5. Click Save. Excel creates and saves the template. In the Title bar, you should see the name `Budget Form.xlt`. When you want to use this template, you can find it on the General tab in the New dialog box.

6. You're done using this workbook, so click the Close Window (X) button to close the workbook.

7. To try out that new template, click File in the menu bar and choose New. The New dialog box opens. Click the General tab if necessary. You should see the Budget Form Template icon, as shown in Figure 45.9. Click on it. Then click OK.

8. There it is—the Budget Form template, ready and waiting for your data.

9. Now that you've seen your template masterpiece, you can close the workbook. Click the Close Window (X) button.

Template (*.xlt) file type   Templates folder

FIGURE 45.8

Saving a worksheet as a template in the Save As dialog box.

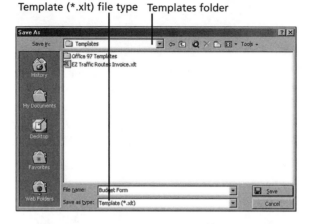

45

FIGURE 45.9

Your template icon on the General tab in the New dialog box.

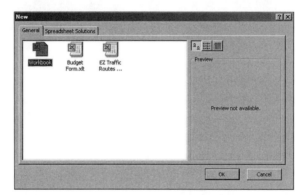

Summary

Templates are valuable timesavers in Excel, and in this chapter you did a nice job with opening, changing, and creating them.

CHAPTER 46

Printing and Formatting Your Workbook

This chapter introduces you to the basics of printing and formatting worksheets. Formatting enables you to change the appearance of text in your worksheets. Fortunately, Excel uses many of the same formatting techniques that Word, PowerPoint, and FrontPage use so you will quickly learn to make worksheets that are attention-getting and that provide their information effectively to their audience.

Checking Your Spelling Before You Print

Excel's spelling checker works similarly to spelling checkers in Word. If the spell-checker finds a word in your worksheet that isn't in its dictionary, it alerts you. If a similar word is in the dictionary, Excel's spelling checker suggests that you might have wanted to use that word instead.

The following are three ways to check spelling:

- Click the Spelling button on the Standard toolbar.
- Click the Tools menu and click Spelling.
- Press F7.

If you use Office XP or later, Excel provides a spell-checker Task Pane (as well as one for the grammar-checker and thesaurus).

Working with AutoCorrect

By default, Excel's AutoCorrect feature automatically corrects common typing errors as you type. For instance, if you type two capital letters at the beginning of a word, AutoCorrect changes the second capital letter to a lowercase letter. If you type a lower-case letter at the beginning of a sentence, Excel capitalizes the first letter of the first word in the sentence. If you type a lowercase letter at the beginning of the name of a day, Excel capitalizes the first letter for you. Finally, if the Caps Lock key is accidentally turned on, in the case of words that should be capitalized, Word reverses the case of those letters and then turns off the Caps Lock key for you.

You can change the AutoCorrect settings at any time. To do so, select Tools, AutoCorrect. The AutoCorrect dialog box appears with the AutoCorrect tab, as shown in Figure 46.1.

FIGURE 46.1

The AutoCorrect dialog box.

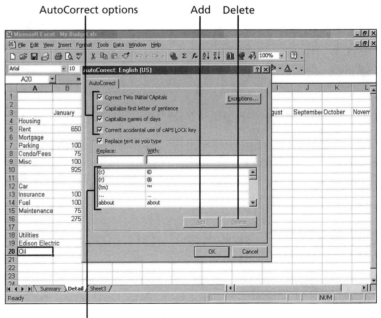

AutoCorrect options   Add   Delete

Replace text as you type list

All the AutoCorrect options are turned on, but you can turn any of them off. At the bottom of the dialog box is the Replace Text as You Type list. This list contains commonly misspelled words and their correct replacement words. For example, if you always type *chnage* instead of *change,* Excel corrects the word automatically because it is in the Replace Text as You Type list. You can add words to or delete words from the list. When you're finished with the AutoCorrect settings, click OK.

Setting Up Your Page

In Excel you can print your worksheets just the way they look after you enter the data, or you can enhance the printout using several page layout options. When you select Excel's Page Setup command, the Page Setup dialog box offers four tabs: Page, Margins, Header/Footer, and Sheet. In this section, you learn how to change the orientation and paper size on the Page tab; change the page margins on the Margins tab; work with headers and footers using the Header/Footer tab; and use the Gridlines option on the Sheet tab.

By default, Excel worksheets print without gridlines, which separate the cells. Your worksheets often look cleaner without the grids. However, you can change the overall appearance of your worksheet by printing the gridlines.

Choosing What to Print

In some cases you may want to choose what to print—only a portion of the worksheet and not the whole worksheet or workbook. Excel's Print Area feature lets you single out an area on the worksheet that you want to print. The Print Titles feature lets you repeat the title, subtitle, column headings, and row headings on every page.

If you have a sizable worksheet that is broken into several pages, you may want to fit those pages on one page. Excel's *Fit To* option lets you shrink the pages to fit on one page, which is another way of choosing exactly what you want to print.

Selecting a Print Area

To print specific portions of a worksheet, such as a range of cells, you can single out an area as a separate page and then print that page.

Before you select a print area, you need to think about which area you want to single out, excluding any column and row headings that are going to print at the top edge and left side of every page. To select the print area, highlight the cells that contain the data. Don't highlight the column and row headings.

Next, click File, Print Area, Set Print Area. Excel inserts automatic page breaks to the left and right and the top and bottom of the range you selected, as shown in Figure 46.2. You should see a dashed line border around the print area.

Automatic page breaks, singling out a print area

FIGURE 46.2

The selected print area.

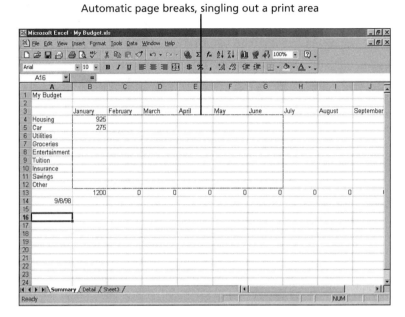

To remove the print area, click File, Print Area, and Clear Print Area. The automatic page breaks should disappear in the worksheet.

Printing the Column and Row Headings

You can select titles that are located on the top edge (column headings) and left side (row headings) of your worksheet and print them on every page of the printout.

Fitting Your Worksheet to a Number of Pages

If you have a large worksheet that is divided into several pages, you can shrink the pages to fit on one page by using the Fit To option. For instance, if the worksheet is two pages wide by three pages tall, you can reduce the worksheet to fit on one page by selecting the Fit To option. Because the default setting for this option is one page wide by one page tall, Excel prints your worksheet on one page. You can compare the Fit To option to the reduction feature on a copier machine.

The Fit To option works this way: Click the File menu and choose Page Setup. When the Page Setup dialog box opens, click the Page tab. In the Scaling section, choose the Fit To option. Specify the number of pages wide by the number of pages tall, as shown in Figure 46.3.

Number of   Number of
Fit to   pages wide   pages tall

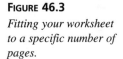

FIGURE 46.3

Fitting your worksheet to a specific number of pages.

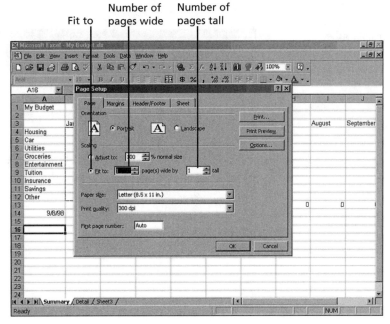

Controlling Where Pages Break

If your worksheet is too large to fit onto one page Excel splits the work onto two or more pages. Excel makes the split based on your current page dimensions, margins, and cell widths and heights. Excel always splits the worksheet at the beginning of a column (vertically) and/or row (horizontally), so the information in a cell is never split between two pages.

An automatic page break appears as a dashed line with short dashes in your worksheet. These dashed lines run down the right edge of a column, as shown in Figure 46.4.

If the automatic page breaks are not right for your worksheet, one of the many ways to make adjustments is to override Excel's defaults. The worksheet still prints on two or more pages, but you can control where each new page begins.

Setting a Manual Page Break

As long as each page fits into the prescribed page size and margin setting, you can set a manual page break anywhere on the worksheet. Manual page breaks remain active until you remove them. Establishing new page breaks does not alter existing breaks; it simply adds to them.

Automatic page break in a column

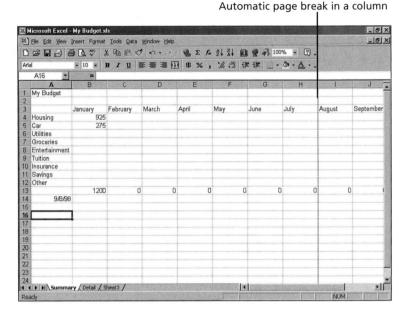

To set a page break, click in any cell, row, or column where you want the break to appear. Click the Insert menu and choose Page Break. Excel inserts a manual page break, which is indicated by the page break dashed line. Onscreen, manual page breaks have longer, thicker dashed lines than automatic page breaks do.

To remove a manual page break, just select the cell, row, or column that was used to create the break and choose Insert, Remove Page Break.

Formatting Your Text

The best way to produce a good-looking worksheet is to worry about the text first and the formatting second. Type in your text and then make the changes in the appearance. Bold, italic, and other formatting changes are easy to accomplish from the Formatting toolbar.

All the buttons on the Formatting toolbar are shortcuts to items that appear in the Format menu. The menu, however, offers a great many formatting options in addition to those on the toolbar. You can use the dialog boxes available through the menu items to fine-tune some of the special formatting effects.

Formatting Characters

In the Normal template, which is the one applied when you create a new workbook, the default font is Arial and the font size is 10 points.

Just like Word, PowerPoint, and FrontPage, Excel displays various fonts on the Formatting toolbar and provides a fast way to change the font. You can select a font from the Font box on the Formatting toolbar. Change the style (bold, italic, and underline), and font size from the Formatting toolbar. For example, when typing the contents of a cell, if you click the Formatting toolbar's Bold button (press Ctrl+B), the rest of what you type in the cell will appear in bold.

> To make better use of your time, this chapter does not go into great character-formatting detail. In case you jumped to this part of the book that covers Excel without reading earlier chapters, you should review Chapter 6, "Formatting Characters, Paragraphs, and Pages," to see how to apply formatting to cell contents. The same character formats apply to your cells as text in Word documents.

46

In the following steps, you change the font, font style, and font size for the title in the My Budget workbook that you've created over the past few chapters. You'll also change the font style for the column headings. If the My Budget file isn't open right now, open it before you begin the exercise.

1. Select cell A1.
2. Click the Font down arrow on the Formatting toolbar.
3. Scroll down the list until you see Courier New and then click it.
4. Click the Font Size down arrow on the Formatting toolbar.
5. Scroll down the list until you see 16. Click it.
6. Click the Bold button on the Formatting toolbar.
7. Select cells B3:M3.
8. Click the Bold button on the Formatting toolbar.
9. Click the Italic button on the Formatting toolbar.
10. Click any cell to deselect the range. Figure 46.5 shows what your formatted text should look like.

FIGURE 46.5

Font, font size, and font style changes.

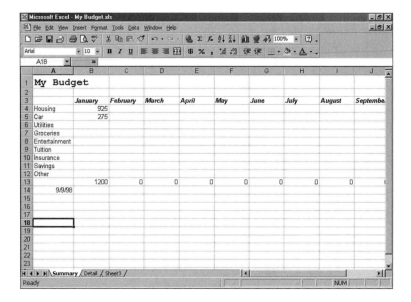

Changing Cell Alignment

The default alignment for data is *General*. When you enter data into a cell, numbers, dates, and times automatically align with the right side of the cell. Text aligns with the left side of the cell. You can change the alignment of information at any time. For instance, you may want to fine-tune the appearance of column headings across columns, or you can right-align column headings across the columns to line up with the numbers that are right-aligned.

In the next few steps, you right-align the column headings in the My Budget workbook.

1. Select cells B3:M3.

2. Choose Format, Cells. Excel opens the Format Cells dialog box.

3. Click the Alignment tab, as shown in Figure 46.6.

4. Click the Horizontal down arrow and choose Right.

5. Click OK to confirm your choice.

6. Click any cell to deselect the range. Excel adjusts the text according to the alignment option you have chosen. In this case, the column headings are aligned right, as shown in Figure 46.7.

FIGURE 46.6

The Alignment tab in the Format Cells dialog box.

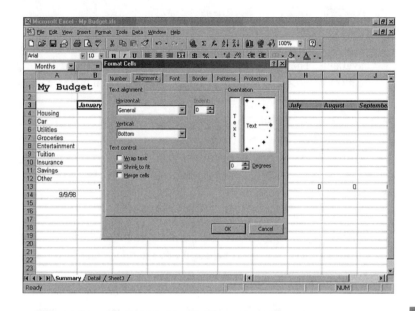

FIGURE 46.7

Column headings aligned right.

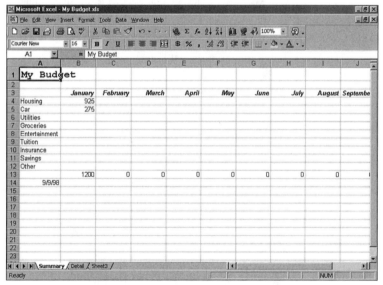

46

To repeat the alignment format command in another cell, use the Repeat Format Cells command from the Edit menu or press the F4 (Repeat) key. Actually, you can repeat any format command in another cell by using the F4 key.

Types of Alignments

The Alignment tab in the Format Cells dialog box makes several types of alignments available. The Horizontal alignment options let you specify left/right alignment in the cell(s). Table 46.1 lists and describes the Horizontal alignment options.

TABLE 46.1   Excel Horizontal Alignment Options

Alignment	What It Does
General	Aligns numbers and dates with the right side of the cell and text with the left side.
Left (Indent)	Aligns selected data with the left side of the cell.
Center	Centers data within the cell.
Right	Aligns selected data with the right side of the cell.
Fill	Repeats the data to fill the entire width of the cell.
Justify	Aligns text with the right and left side of the cell. Use with the Wrap Text option in the Text Control section on the Alignment tab.
Center Across Selection	Centers a title or other text inside a range of cells, such as over columns.

The Vertical alignment options let you specify how you want the text aligned in relation to the top and bottom of the cell(s).

Text orientation, located on the right side of the Alignment tab, is explained in the next section. The Text control options are discussed later in this chapter.

Rotating Cell Entries

One of Excel's most exciting alignment feature lets you change the orientation of text in the cell. You can rotate the text vertically, arranging the text so that you can read it from top to bottom within the cell. Flipping the text sideways lets you print it from top to bottom rather than left to right.

If you don't want to flip the text horizontally or vertically, you can angle the text by specifying the number of degrees of an angle you want to rotate. Rotated text appears slanted and looks fancier than ordinary text.

The following steps show you how to rotate text at an angle.

1. Select the range that contains the text you want to rotate; in this case, select cell A14.

2. Choose Format, Cells. The Format Cells dialog box appears.

3. Click the Alignment tab if necessary.

4. In the Orientation section, type 45 in the Degrees box. This entry specifies the number of degrees you want the text to rotate.

5. Click OK.

6. Click any cell to deselect the range. The text you selected should appear slanted. See Figure 46.8.

FIGURE 46.8

Rotated text.

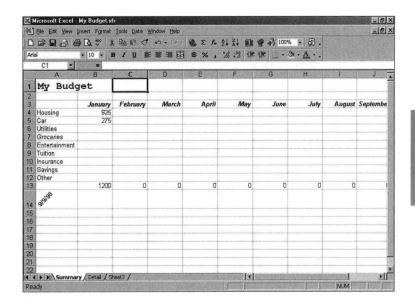

46

Centering a Heading

In Excel, you can use another type of alignment command called Merge and Center. The Merge and Center button (its icon has a page with the letter *a* and two arrows) on the Formatting toolbar lets you quickly center text in the left-most cell across the entire range of cells you select. This feature is good for centering a title and subtitle at the top of a worksheet. Figure 46.9 shows a title centered across the table in cell F1.

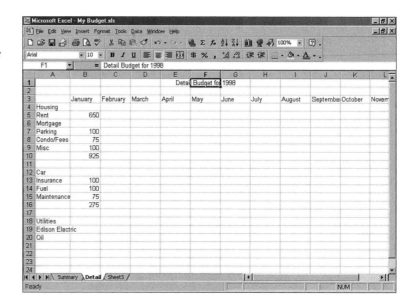

FIGURE **46.9**

A title centered across a table with the Merge and Center button.

Controlling the Flow of Text

Excel offers several ways to control the flow of text within cells. Here are two of the most common text control features:

- Indent text from the left border of the cell
- Wrap text to break the text into multiple lines

Using Indents

You might want to indent your text to make it stand out in a column of text or numbers. Using the Detail worksheet in the My Budget workbook as an example, you can indent the Rent, Mortgage, Parking, Condo/Fees, and Misc row headings beneath the row heading Housing. That way, the items under Housing stand out and are easier to depict in the column.

In the next few steps, you indent data using the Format Cells dialog box and the Increase Indent button on the Formatting toolbar.

1. Click the Detail sheet tab. Select cells A5:A9.

2. Choose Format, Cells. Excel opens the Format Cells dialog box.

3. Click the Alignment tab. You should see Text Alignment options at the top of the tab.

4. Click the Horizontal down arrow and choose Left (Indent).

5. In the Indent box, click the up arrow once. The Indent number changes from 0 to 1, indicating the indentation will be one character width.

6. Click OK. Excel adjusts the text according to the Indent option you chose.

7. Select cells A13:A15.

8. Click the Increase Indent button on the Formatting toolbar.

9. Select cells A19:A20.

10. Click the Increase Indent button on the Formatting toolbar.

11. Click any cell to deselect the range. Figure 46.10 shows the indented text in column A.

FIGURE 46.10

Indented text in a column.

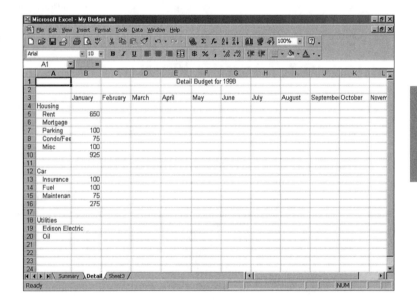

46

Copying Formatting with the Format Painter

The Format Painter is like a miniformatting copier that is available on the Standard toolbar (its tool looks like a paintbrush). To use the Format Painter, select the text you want to use as a model, click the Format Painter tool, and then click the target cell or range of cells to "paint" it with the same formatting. The mouse pointer changes to a paintbrush during this process.

Removing Formatting

To turn off bold, italic, or underline, select the cells that contain the font style you want to remove and click the buttons (Bold, Italic, Underline) again on the Formatting toolbar.

You can remove the alignment you've added to a cell or range of cells by changing it back to the General alignment setting. To do so, select the cells that have the alignment you want to change, choose Format Cells, click the Alignment tab, and choose General in the Horizontal drop-down list.

Another way to remove the alignment you've attached to a cell or range is to use the Edit, Clear command and choose the Formats option from the Clear menu. Be sure to first select the cells that contain the formatting you want to clear. Then click the Format menu, choose Clear, and choose Formats. This action clears not only the alignment but also the fonts and other formatting you added to cells.

Adjusting Column Width

Adjusting column width makes the best use of the worksheet space. You can set the column width manually or let Excel make the adjustments for you with its AutoFit feature. By default, column width is set to 8.43 characters, based on the default font and font size, 10-point Arial.

In the next few steps, you adjust column width with a mouse.

1. Move the mouse pointer to the right column header border at the top of column A. You should see a double-headed arrow, as shown in Figure 46.11. Use the right border of the column header to adjust column width.

2. Hold down the mouse button and drag the border. As you are dragging the border, Excel shows you the column width in a ScreenTip (a buff-color box).

3. When you see a width of 14.00, release the mouse button. The column width is adjusted. Notice that Entertainment no longer spills into column B.

To change the column width for two or more columns, click and drag over the column headers with the mouse pointer. Then release the mouse button. Move the mouse pointer to one of the column header borders. Use the right border of the column header to adjust the column width. Hold down the mouse button and drag the border. Release the mouse button, and the column width is adjusted for all the columns you selected.

The double-headed arrow mouse pointer when
you move it over a column header border   The column width ScreenTip

FIGURE 46.11

*Dragging the right
border of a column
changes its width.*

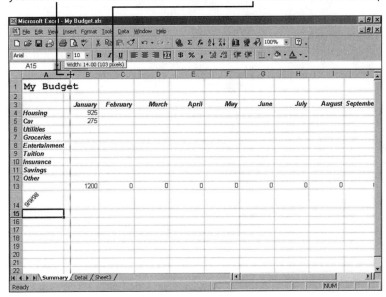

Altering Row Height

Altering row height makes the best use of the worksheet space, just like adjusting column width does. You can set the row height manually or let Excel make the adjustments for you with its AutoFit feature.

By default, Excel makes a row a bit taller than the tallest text in the row. For instance, if the tallest text is 10 points tall, Excel makes the row 13.5 points tall. The default row height is set to 13.5 points, based on the default font size, 10 points.

In the following steps, you will alter row height with a mouse. But first you move the date to another cell.

1. Click cell A14, which contains the date. Point to the cell's border, click, and drag the date to cell C1. This action moves the date next to the title. Notice that the year within the date is hidden. To show the entire date, just make the row taller.

2. Move the mouse pointer to the bottom row header borders, row 1. You should see a double-headed arrow, as shown in Figure 46.12. Use the bottom border of the row header to adjust row height.

46

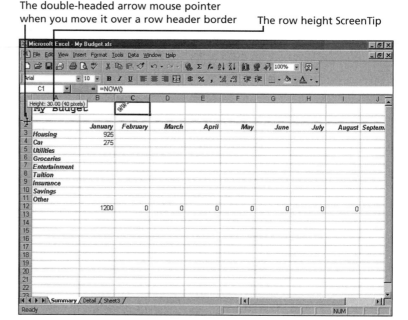

The double-headed arrow mouse pointer
when you move it over a row header border   The row height ScreenTip

FIGURE 46.12

*Dragging the bottom
border of a row
changes its height.*

3. Hold down the mouse button and drag the border. As you are dragging the border, Excel shows you the row height in a ScreenTip (a buff-color box).

4. When you see a height of 30.00 in the ScreenTip, release the mouse button. Excel makes the row taller, and the entire date appears.

To change the row height for two or more rows, click and drag over the row headers with the mouse pointer. Then release the mouse button. Move the mouse pointer to one of the row header borders. Use the bottom border of the row header to alter row height. Hold down the mouse button and drag the border. Release the mouse button, and the row height is adjusted for all the rows you selected.

What Formats Are Available?

Numeric values are usually more than just numbers. They often represent dollar values, dates, percentages, or some other value. You can select the format type that appears as a real value in the Format Cells dialog box. To narrow the list of formats, first select a category in the Category list. Then specify the number of decimal places. The default number of decimal places is two.

Excel lets you display numeric values in many ways. Formatting a number means changing the way it is displayed. You can format the number 500 to look like currency, in which case it's displayed as $500.00. You can even specify as many decimal places as you want to display.

You can choose from four currency styles:

- Currency with negative numbers preceded by a minus sign
- Currency with red negative numbers
- Currency with negative numbers enclosed in parentheses
- Currency with red negative numbers enclosed in parentheses

Excel's preformatted number formats are listed in Table 46.2.

TABLE 46.2 Excel Number Formats

Number Format	Sample Number	What It Does
General	$4,500.50	Default number format. Has no specific number format. With General format, you can type a number with a decimal point, dollar sign, comma, percent sign, date, time, or fraction in a cell. Excel automatically displays the value with the format you entered.
Number	4,500.50	Use for general display of numbers. The default Number format is two decimal places and negative numbers are black preceded by a minus sign. You can display the number of decimal places, whether or not you want a comma for a thousand separator, and negative numbers in red or black, preceded by a minus sign or enclosed in parentheses.
Currency	$4,500.50	Use for general monetary values. The default Currency format is two decimal places, a dollar sign, and negative numbers are black preceded by a minus sign. You can display the number of decimal places, whether or not you want a dollar sign, and negative numbers in red or black, preceded by a minus sign or enclosed in parentheses.
Accounting	$ 4,500.00	Use for aligning dollar signs and decimal points in a column. The default Accounting format is two decimal places and a dollar sign. You specify the number of decimal places and whether or not you want a dollar sign.

46

TABLE 46.2   continued

Number Format	Sample Number	What It Does
Percentage	85.6%	The default Percentage format is two decimal places and a percent sign. Multiplies the value in a cell by 100 and displays the result with a percent sign.
Fraction	1/4	The default Fraction format is up to one digit on either side of the slash. Use to display the number of digits you want on either side of the slash and the fraction type such as halves, quarters, eighths, and so on.
Scientific	4.50E+03	The default Scientific format is two decimal places. Use to display numbers in scientific notation.
Text	278MC99	Use to display both text and numbers in a cell as text. Excel displays the entry exactly as typed.

Choosing a Number Style

After you decide on a suitable number format, you can choose a number style using either of two methods:

- Click the number style buttons on the Formatting toolbar.
- Choose Format, Cells and select a number style from the Format Cells dialog box.

Using the Toolbar to Change Number Formats

The Formatting toolbar a offers several tools for changing number formats that are not available in Word due to the toolbar buttons' numeric purposes.

The following steps show you how to use the Formatting toolbar to change number formats in the My Budget workbook Summary sheet. Your job is to add a column of numbers to the worksheet so that you'll have some numbers to format. If the workbook isn't open now, open it before you start the exercise.

1. Click cell B6, type 75 and press Enter. Type the following numbers to enter the rest of the data in column B: 300, 200, 1000, 1000, 1200, 150.

2. Select the a cells in which you want to display commas; in this case, select cells B4:B12.

3. Click the Comma Style button on the Formatting toolbar. Excel applies the Comma Style, displaying commas and two decimal places.

4. Select cell B13.

5. Click the Currency Style button on the Formatting toolbar. You should see the dollar sign, a comma, and two decimal places in the selected cell.

Using the Format Cells Dialog Box

Instead of using the number style tools on the Formatting toolbar, you can select a value's format type in the Format Cells dialog box. That way, you can get a number format to look exactly the way you want it.

You can see how the Format Cells dialog box works by following along with these steps. You start by entering a column of numbers, so that you can format them, in the My Budget workbook.

1. Click cell C4, type 925, and press Enter. Type the following numbers starting in cell C5 and ending in cell C12: 275, 80, 315, 225, 500, 1000, 1200, 175.

2. Select the cells in which you want to display commas; in this case, select cells C4:C12.

3. Click the Format menu and choose Cells. The Format Cells dialog box opens.

4. Click the Number tab. On the left is a list of number format categories. On the top right is a Sample box, where Excel shows you what a sample number would look like formatted with that type. Also, you should see a description of the selected number category at the bottom of the dialog box.

5. Click Number in the a Category list. On the right, you see a number in the Sample box, the Decimal Places box, the Use 1000 Separator (,) check box, and a list of negative number formats. You need a 1000 separator, which is the comma.

6. Click the Use 1000 Separator (,) check box. A checkmark appears in the box, indicating you want to format your numbers with commas.

7. Click OK. You should see commas and two decimal places in the selected cells.

8. Select the cell in which you want to display a dollar sign; in this case, select cell C13.

9. Press Ctrl+1 to open the Format Cells dialog box.

10. On the Number tab, click Currency in the Category list. On the right, you see a number in the Sample box, the Decimal Places box, a Symbol drop-down list, and a list of negative number formats. The default Currency options is suited to what you want.

11. Click OK. You should a see dollar signs, commas, and two decimal places in the selected cell. Click any cell to deselect the range.

46

Working with Decimal Places

All of Excel's number formats use either two or zero decimal places. The exception is General format, which uses as many places as needed for a value. You can establish a fixed number of decimal places or let Excel automatically round numbers for you. The following sections examine both ways to work with decimal places.

Establishing a Fixed Number of Decimal Places

To establish a fixed number of decimal places, use a numeric format other than General format. Two tools on the Formatting toolbar enable you to change the number of decimal places for numbers. The tools are Increase Decimal (its icon contains .0 and .00 with a left arrow) and Decrease Decimal (its icon contains .0 and .00 with a right arrow). Here's how these tools work:

- Click the Increase Decimal button each time you want to move the decimal point one place to the left.

- Click the Decrease Decimal button each time you want to move the decimal point one place to the right.

Open you're My Budget worksheet and change the number of decimal places from two to zero for the numeric values. Doing so shows you how simple Excel makes such formatting.

Hiding Zeros

Worksheets are often cluttered with zeros as a result of calculations or information that hasn't been entered. Formulas frequently display a zero when referenced cells are blank. These zeros can make a worksheet look confusing.

The Summary sheet in the My Budget workbook provides a good example of formulas that produce unwanted values of zero. This worksheet shows several columns where data has not been entered. Therefore, the cells with the formulas that total the empty columns produce zeros. In this case, you might want to suppress the zeros.

There are a couple of ways to hide zeros in a worksheet:

- Use the Tools, Options command to hide all values of zero in the worksheet. In the Options dialog box, click the View tab. In the Window Options section, click the Zero Values check box to remove the checkmark, which hides all zeros on the worksheet.

- Create a custom number format in the Format Cells dialog box to hide zeros in a range of cells.

Working with Dates

Dates and times are actually numeric values that have been formatted to appear as dates and time. You can change the way Excel displays the date and time if you want.

The Date and Time categories are in the Category list on the Number tab in the Format Cells dialog box. You can use the Date format to display date and time serial numbers as date values with slashes or hyphens. The default Date format is the month and day separated by a slash, for example, 7/2. To display only the time portion, use the Time format.

The Time format lets you display date and time serial numbers as time values with hours, minutes, seconds, AM, or PM. The default Time format is the hour and minutes separated by a colon, for example, 11:00. You can perform calculations on the time values. To display only the date portion, use the Date format.

Understanding Date and Time Formats

Excel offers a wide variety of date and time formats, which are listed in Table 46.3.

TABLE 46.3 Excel's Date and Time Formats

Date/Time Format	Sample Date/Time
m/d	7/2
m/d/yy	7/2/04
mm/dd/yy	07/02/04
d-mmm	2-Jul
d-mmm-y	2-Jul-04
dd-mmm-y	02-Jul-04
mmm-yy	Jul-04
mmmm-yy	July-04
mmmm-d,yyyy	July 2, 2004
m/d/yy h:mm	7/2/04 7:30
m/d/yy hh:mm	7/2/04 19:30
hh:mm	13:35
h:mm AM/PM	1:35 PM
h:mm:ss AM/PM	1:35:50 AM

46

Summary

You now have the tools needed to print your documents in a myriad of ways. In addition, you can format your worksheets to make them present their data in a more effective way. You learned how similar Excel formatting techniques are to Word's and PowerPoint's with the additional numeric formatting techniques needed for worksheet data.

CHAPTER 47

Adding Eye-Catching Borders, Colors, Fills, and Graphics

This chapter covers adding borders, colors, fills and graphics to your worksheets. Excel offers many types of borders that can be applied in different thickness and colors to add pizzazz and style. You learn how to change the font color, add shading to cells, and use color fills to put some spice into the background of your worksheet. In addition, you use the AutoFormat command to apply prefab formats to your worksheets in one shot so that you don't have to apply each type of format individually.

With Excel's drawing tools, pictures in worksheets, and the WordArt feature that lets you create logos and fancy-looking words in your worksheets. In addition, you'll master complete instructions for creating Excel charts. Turn your numeric data into a visual representation of that data. Perhaps you want to use Excel information inside a PowerPoint presentation; if so, a chart is a wonderful way to get your point across to your audience.

Have It Your Way

You can embellish your worksheets with borders, shading, and colors that can be cool, elegant, or professional. Your choice of formatting depends on your mood and the data inside the border. Sometimes a worksheet needs to be decorated to grab the reader's attention.

Always keep your audience in mind when you design a worksheet. If you're giving the worksheet to the comptroller of your company, then you might want to make it more reserved and subtle. You could add thick line borders to point out the bottom-line figures at a glance. Or you could add gray shading to the important numbers on the worksheet. Keep it simple, and you can't go wrong.

Changing the Color of Cell Entries

You already know how to change the font, font style, and font size. This section shows you how to change the font color. By default, the font color is Automatic, which is black. The Font Color command lets you change font color in two ways:

- Choose a color on the Font tab in the Format Cells dialog box.
- Click a color in the Font Color palette on the Formatting toolbar.

A good example of when you would want to change font color is when you add dark cell shading that causes the text disappear. Consider using the Font Color command to select a light color for the text. Another example is when you are using one font color for one set of numbers such as the first-quarter figures and want to use a different font color for numbers in the second quarter.

If you have a color printer, you can get some beautiful and professional-looking results by changing the font colors to draw attention to important data.

To change the color of any selected text, select Format, Cells to open the Format Cells dialog box. Click the Font tab and then click the Color arrow to display the Font Color palette and select the color you want to apply to the selected text.

The toolbar makes it a snap to change the color of cell entries. The Font Color button tool on the Formatting toolbar provides a medley of color choices.

Adding Borders to Cells and Ranges

One way to improve the appearance of a worksheet is to add borders to the data on the worksheet. You can add boxes around cells and ranges, add emphasis lines anywhere on the worksheet, and change the thickness and color of the border lines.

As you work with your worksheet onscreen, each cell is identified by a gridline that surrounds the cell. In print these gridlines may appear washed out. To have better defined lines appear on the printout, you can add borders to selected cells or cell ranges.

You can frame selected cells with a border to make your data stand out. Highlight parts of a table to emphasize the content by placing a thick border around the specific cells you want to attract attention to. Select the cells you want to use and then apply the border.

Adding a border to a title, title and subtitle, total row, and total column are just some ways you can use borders. More specifically, you can have a single, thick, outline border that creates a box around a title for the worksheet. Or you can add a double underline on the bottom of cells to call attention to the totals.

Applying a Border

The Borders feature lets you manipulate the placement of the borders, the thickness of the lines, and color for any border lines. You can make borders a little more interesting by changing the thickness and color of specific border lines. You can have a different thickness and a different color for each border, or any combination of thickness and color.

By combining border options, you get various results. Try combining border options with row-height and column-width options to get different effects. Experiment on your worksheets for best results.

Applying a border is a cinch; it's making the decisions about the elements of the border that's difficult. The standard borders that Excel offers work just fine, but if you want to get creative, just click away on the Borders tab in the Format Cells dialog box until you get the border you want.

47

In the following steps, you add a single-line top border and double-line bottom border to the totals in row 13 in the Summary sheet in the My Budget workbook.

1. Select the cells that will be surrounded by a border; in this case, select B13:M13.
2. Click the Format menu and choose Cells. The Format Cells dialog box opens.
3. Click the Border tab. The Border options jump up front, as shown in Figure 47.1.
4. Click the top of the Border preview diagram to add a top single-line border.
5. Click the double-underline line style.
6. Click the bottom of the Border preview diagram to add a bottom double-line border.

Presets

FIGURE 47.1

*Border options in the
Format Cells dialog
box.*

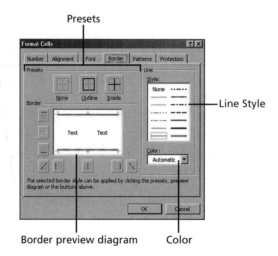

Line Style

Border preview diagram   Color

7. Click OK. Excel should apply a single-line top border and double-line bottom border to the selected cells.

8. Click any cell to deselect the range. Figure 47.2 shows the border on the Summary
   sheet.

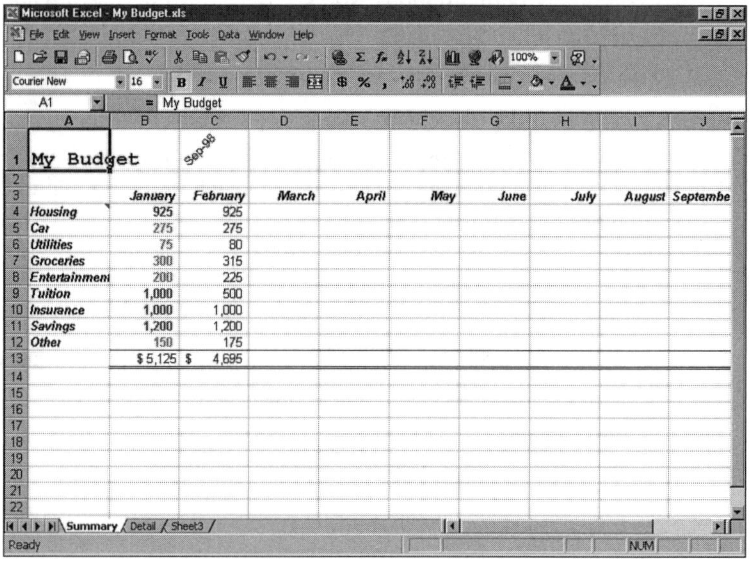

FIGURE 47.2

*A border applied to a
range of cells.*

To remove a border, select the cells that contain the border, click the Borders down
arrow on the Formatting toolbar, and choose No Border.

Working with Fills, Shading, and Color

For a simple but dramatic effect, try adding fills, shading, and color to the cells in your worksheets. Add some zest to the appearance of your worksheets by using splashes of color to illuminate some of your data. Excel provides a way to fill cells with colors and color patterns.

Adding Background Patterns and Colors with the Format Cells Dialog Box

One way to add background colors and patterns is via the Format Cells dialog box. Color adds plain color and overall shading to cells.

A pattern is a black-and-white or colored pattern that lies on top of the overall shading. Patterns put texture into color, creating a more interesting eye-catcher than a plain color. Keep in mind that a pattern is busier than a plain color, so you don't want to use a pattern on a busy worksheet.

The following steps walk you through adding background colors and patterns to selected cells in the Summary sheet.

1. Select the cells you want to shade; in this case, select cells A4:A12.
2. Click the Format menu and choose Cells. The Format Cells dialog box opens.
3. Click the Patterns tab. The shading options jump to the front, as shown in Figure 47.3. The Color options let you choose a color for the overall shading. The Pattern options let you select a black-and-white or colored pattern that lies on top of the overall shading. The Sample box displays a preview of the result.

47

FIGURE 47.3

Shading options in the Format Cells dialog box.

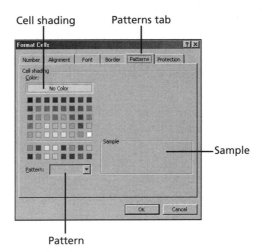

4. In the top Color palette, in the last row, sixth column, click the pale blue color patch.

5. Click the down arrow next to Pattern. You should see a grid that contains all the colors from the color palette, as well as patterns

6. In the first row, last column, click the 6.25% gray pattern. This subtle pattern suits the data on the worksheet.

7. Click OK. You should see shading with a pattern in the selected cells.

8. Click any cell to deselect the range. Figure 47.4 shows the shaded pattern on the Summary sheet.

FIGURE 47.4

Shaded pattern in a range of cells.

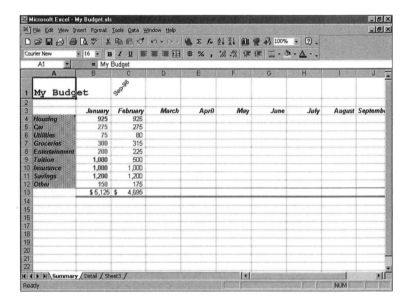

Formatting with AutoFormat

Excel's AutoFormat feature takes away some of the hard work involved in formatting a worksheet. AutoFormat provides you with 16 predesigned table formats that you can apply to a selected range of cells on a worksheet.

Instead of applying each format to your data, one at a time, you can apply a group of formats in one shot with one of Excel's predesigned formats. The AutoFormat command lets you select a format and transform your table with a couple of mouse clicks.

In the following steps, you get to try a predesigned format using the AutoFormat command.

1. Select the cells that contain the data you want to format; in this case, select cells A3:M13.

2. Choose Format, AutoFormat. The AutoFormat dialog box pops open, as shown in Figure 47.5. You see a palette of predesigned table format samples, each with a name.

FIGURE 47.5

Predesigned table formats in the AutoFormat dialog box.

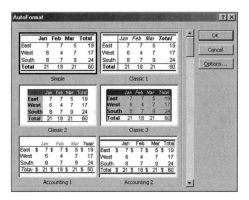

3. Scroll through the table format samples. Stop at the List 2 sample.

4. Click the List 2 sample table format.

5. Click OK. Excel formats your table to make it look like the one in the sample you selected. It looks great!

6. Click any cell to deselect the range. Figure 47.6 shows the table formatted with the List 2 AutoFormat. The green bars make the worksheet more attractive and readable.

47

FIGURE 47.6

The worksheet formatted with the List 2 AutoFormat.

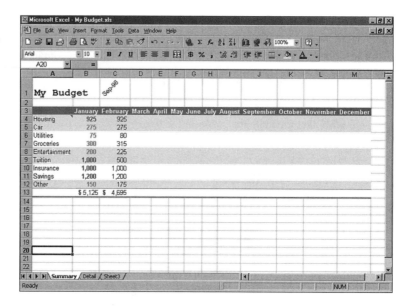

Understanding Graphics Objects

Clip art, word art, pictures, photographs, or any shape you draw is called a graphics object. After you add a graphics object to your worksheet, you can select it and perform actions such as copying, moving, sizing, and applying attributes. The possibilities are endless.

With Excel's powerful drawing tools, you can create a simple illustration with rectangles, squares, ovals, circles, straight lines, curved lines, and freeform lines; and then you can embellish your drawing with the editing tools on the Drawing toolbar.

Why Use Graphics?

Despite the huge variety of wonderful clip art that's available, you still might not be able to find that perfect image. Or perhaps you'd just prefer to create your own art. In either case, you don't have to be a talented artist to create vibrant, eye-catching graphics.

Excel gives you a such a wealth of artwork and effects to add to your worksheets that you might not know where to begin. But, nevertheless, graphics can make your worksheets explode with life and energy.

Using the Drawing Toolbar

Like drawing on paper, using Excel's Draw feature takes patience and practice. The Drawing toolbar offers many drawing tools for drawing and modifying lines and shapes, including 3D shapes. The drawing tools also come in handy for annotating your worksheet data and charts.

To display the Drawing toolbar, you click the Drawing button on the Standard toolbar. Figure 47.7 depicts the tools on the Drawing toolbar. To hide the Drawing toolbar, click the Drawing button on the Standard toolbar again.

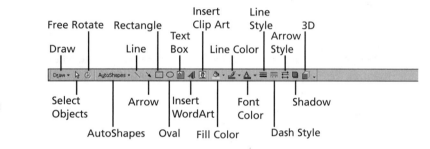

FIGURE 47.7

The tools on the Drawing toolbar.

Table 47.1 lists the drawing tools on the Drawing toolbar and describes what they do.

TABLE 47.1   Excel's Drawing Tools

Tool	What It Does
Draw	Displays a Draw menu that contains commands for rotating, flipping, nudging, and positioning objects.
Select Objects	Selects objects so that you can move or edit them.
Free Rotate	Rotates an object left or right.
AutoShapes	Adds predesigned shapes to your drawing.
Line	Adds solid, dotted, and dashed lines to your drawing.
Arrow	Adds arrows to your drawing.
Rectangle	Adds a rectangle or square to your drawing.
Oval	Adds an oval or a circle to your drawing.
Text Box	Adds a box into which you can type text.
Insert WordArt	Lets you insert WordArt into your worksheet.
Insert Clip Art	Lets you insert clip art into your worksheet.
Fill Color	Adds, removes, and changes the fill color in an object.

47

TABLE 47.1 continued

Tool	What It Does
Line Color	Adds and removes lines and changes the line color in an object.
Font Color	Changes the color of the font.
Line Style	Changes the line style for lines in objects. Choose any line style from thick to thin from the Line Style palette.
Dash Style	Changes the line style from dots to dashes.
Arrow Style	Changes the arrowhead type for a line, an arc, or a polygon.
Shadow	Adds and removes a drop shadow from the border of selected objects.
3D	Adds and formats 3D objects.

After you draw an object, small squares, called selection handles, surround the object's border. The selection handles indicate the object is selected and let you modify the object. Before you can move, resize, or edit an object, you must select it. To select an object, just click anywhere on it. When the selection handles appear, you can then use the handles to move and resize the object.

Other alterations you can make to an object you have created include changing the color, border, and fill. Filling an object places a pattern or color inside the object to make the shape more interesting. You can also delete objects when you no longer need them.

Drawing a Shape

With Excel's drawing tools, you can create an almost endless variety of shapes. You can start with a simple drawing and then build on it. When you want to draw a shape, you click a shape tool on the Drawing toolbar, drag the crosshair pointer straight in a particular direction or diagonally to draw the shape you want, and then release the mouse button. A nice feature about drawing shapes in an Excel worksheet is that you have the gridlines on the worksheet to use as guides for starting and ending an object.

Are you ready to draw some shapes? You don't have to be a talented artist to create vibrant, eye-catching graphics. Try out the Line and Rectangle tools to draw a line and a rectangle in the next few steps for practice. Again, you need to use the My Budget workbook, so be sure to have it open before you begin the exercise. You'll be drawing shapes in the Sheet3 sheet.

1. Click the Sheet3 tab. This sheet is where you'll draw your shapes.

2. Click the Drawing button on the Standard toolbar. The Drawing toolbar appears at the bottom of the Excel window.

3. Click the Line button on the Drawing toolbar. The mouse pointer changes to a crosshair when you move it over the worksheet.

4. Move the crosshair over cell B4. This cell is where you want the object to begin.

5. Click and drag your crosshair from the left edge of cell B4 to the right edge of D4. This cell is where the object ends. Release the mouse button. Notice the selection handle on each end of the object. These handles indicate the object is selected. You can drag the handles to resize the line object.

6. Click outside of the line object to make the selection handles disappear.

7. To draw a rectangle, click the Rectangle button on the Drawing toolbar. The crosshair pointer appears on the worksheet.

8. Move the crosshair over cell F8. This cell is where you want the rectangle to begin.

9. Click and drag diagonally from the top-left corner of cell F8 to the bottom-right corner of cell I12. This cell is where the object ends. Release the mouse button. Now you should see a rectangle on your worksheet.

10. Click outside of the rectangle object to make the selection handles disappear.

Adding an AutoShape

The standard shapes available are a line, rectangle, square, oval, and circle. For a greater variety, use those available via the AutoShapes menu on the Drawing toolbar, as shown in Figure 47.8.

FIGURE 47.8

The AutoShapes menu on the Drawing toolbar.

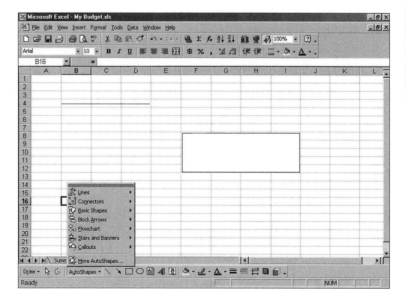

47

To add an AutoShape to your worksheet, click the AutoShapes button on the Drawing toolbar and choose an AutoShape type from the menu. Then click the shape that you like. On your worksheet, click and drag to create the shape. For example, if you click Basic Shapes on the AutoShapes menu, choose the Diamond, and hold down the Shift key while dragging the crosshair pointer diagonally across the cells, Excel inserts the diamond shape on your worksheet.

The Draw menu on the Drawing toolbar contains a command intended for use with AutoShapes. The Change AutoShape command is a special command for converting one AutoShape to another.

To change an AutoShape, click the Draw button on the Drawing toolbar and choose Change AutoShape. You should see a menu of shape types. Click a shape type, and a palette of shapes appears. Click any AutoShape you like. Excel inserts the shape into your worksheet.

Rather than change the AutoShape, you can delete the AutoShape and start over. Be sure to select the AutoShape you want to remove and then press the Delete key. Repeat the steps mentioned earlier to insert a different AutoShape.

Adding Clip Art

Instead of drawing your own pictures in your worksheet, you can use ready-made clip art and photographs to spruce up your data. Plenty of pictures come with Excel, so all you have to do is insert a picture wherever you want it to appear in a worksheet. Excel's clip art collection contains a myriad of professionally prepared pictures that can enhance a wide range of topics.

Clip art is organized into 58 categories that include almost any popular art—from academic to Web site. These categories are arranged in alphabetical order on icons in the Insert Clip Art dialog box.

You can get clip art from the following places:

- Excel's clip art gallery organized by category
- Clip art on the Web
- Clip art software packages

Getting Clip Art from the Gallery

Excel lets you insert clip art pictures in your worksheet with the Insert, Picture, Clip Art command. For example, you could insert a graphic in a sales report to spice it up. In the following steps, you insert clip art in Sheet3.

1. Select cell B8. This cell is where you want to insert the clip art.

2. Click the Insert menu and choose Picture, Clip Art. The Insert Clip Art dialog box opens.

3. Click the Pictures tab, if necessary. You should see categories represented by icons in the Clip Art palette, as shown in Figure 47.9. The Pictures tab contains 57 categories.

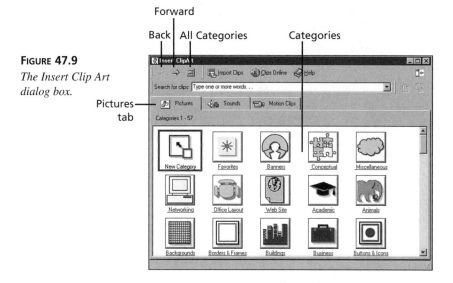

FIGURE 47.9

The Insert Clip Art dialog box.

4. Scroll down through the palette of categories until you see the Nature category.

5. Click the Nature icon. Excel displays a palette of art clips for the category you selected and the number of clips. In this case, 25 (nature) clips are available.

6. Scroll down through the palette of nature clips until you see the clip that shows the sun, clouds, and a tree. When you point to the clip, Excel displays a ScreenTip that contains the clip's name, size (KB), and file type. The clip you selected is called sunshine; its size is 23.0 KB; and it has the WMF file type.

7. Click the Sunshine clip. A menu appears, which contains commands for working with the clip, as shown in Figure 47.10.

8. Choose Insert Clip on the shortcut menu. Excel inserts the clip into your worksheet.

9. Click the Close (X) button in the upper-right corner of the Insert Clip Art dialog box to close the box. You should see the cartoon on your worksheet along with the Picture toolbar, which you don't need now. Selection handles (white squares) surround the picture.

47

FIGURE **47.10**

The Clip Art shortcut menu.

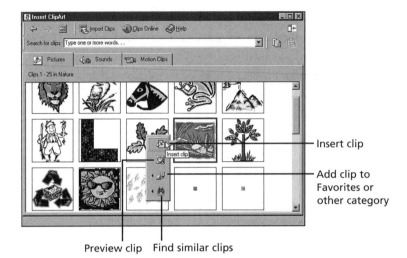

Insert clip

Add clip to
Favorites or
other category

Preview clip   Find similar clips

10. Click the Close (X) button on the Picture toolbar to close the toolbar.

11. Click outside the picture to deselect it. Notice that the picture overlaps the rectangle, but there's no need to worry. We will fix that later by moving objects on the worksheet.

Why Use a Chart?

Rather than using only a worksheet to represent data, you can create a chart to represent the same data. For example, you might want to create a chart and print the chart and worksheet together for a presentation. That way, your audience can easily see trends in a series of values.

Charting is really simple to do. Don't let all the charting commands and options make you think otherwise.

Chart Elements

Before you begin to create charts, you need to be familiar with the chart elements shown in Figure 47.11. Take a few moments to look over the elements of a chart. Figure 47.11 shows a basic column chart with various elements identified.

Table 47.2 lists the chart terms and provides an explanation of each chart element that you need to keep in mind when you're working with charts.

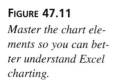

FIGURE 47.11

Master the chart elements so you can better understand Excel charting.

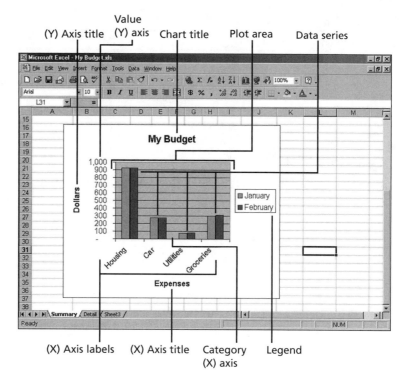

TABLE 47.2   Excel's Chart Elements

Element	What It Is
Data series	The bars, pie wedges, or other elements that represent plotted values in a chart. Often, the data series corresponds to rows of data in your worksheet.
X-axis	The number of elements in a series. For most two-dimensional charts, categories are plotted along the Category (X) axis, which is usually horizontal. Categories generally correspond to the columns that you have in your chart data, with the category labels coming from the column headings.
Y-axis	For most two-dimensional charts, data values are plotted along the Value (Y) axis, which is usually vertical. The y-axis reflects the values of the bars, lines, or plot points. In a two-dimensional bar chart, the axes are reversed, with the values being plotted on the x-axis and the categories on the y-axis. In a 3D chart, the z-axis represents the vertical plane, and the x-axis (distance) and y-axis (width) represent the two sides on the floor of the chart.
Legend	The element that designates the separate categories of a chart. For example, the legend for a column chart shows what each column of the chart represents.

47

TABLE 47.2   continued

Element	What It Is
Gridlines	The lines that depict the x-axis and y-axis scale of the data series. For example, major gridlines for the y-axis help you follow a point from the x- or y-axis to identify a data point's exact value.

Types of Charts

The most common chart types include pie, bar, column (default), line, and area. Table 47.3 lists these chart types, their descriptions, and how you would use them.

TABLE 47.3   Excel's Chart Types

Chart Type	Description/How to Use It
Pie	Plots only one category of data, but each wedge of the pie represents a different data series. Use this chart to show the relationship among parts of a whole.
Bar	Horizontal representations of column charts, often called histograms. Use this chart to compare values at a given point in time, emphasizing the performance of a group of items. Often, different patterns are not required for bar chart data series.
Column	Similar to a bar chart; use this chart to emphasize the difference between items over a period of time. Columns make it easy to compare the values of items in each category. Column charts are best for comparing two or more items.
Line	Use this chart to emphasize trends and the change of values over time, showing how one or more items have changed over time. Lines emphasize the change, not the comparison of one item to another. Also useful for plotting numerous categories of data for multiple data series.
Area	Similar to the line chart and stacked column chart in that an area chart shows how items combine to form a total. Use this chart to emphasize the amount of change in values, providing a more dramatic representation of the change in values over time.

Most of these basic chart types also come in 3D. A standard, flat chart is professional looking, but a 3D chart can help your audience distinguish between different sets of data. When you choose a chart type and a chart subtype, you can display, in a professional manner, interesting and meaningful results based on your worksheet data.

Creating Charts with the Chart Wizard

One of the terrific features in Excel is the Chart Wizard. The easiest way to create a chart in Excel is to use the Chart Wizard. The Chart Wizard leads you step by step through the task of creating a chart. Excel plots the data and creates the chart where you specify on the worksheet.

Creating charts with the Chart Wizard is a snap because you get help every step of the way. You are guided through four dialog boxes from which you create your chart: Chart Type, Chart Source, Chart Options, and Chart Location. You can preview the sample chart in all the steps and make changes to the chart at any time.

A basic concept you should remember when creating a chart in Excel is that you must select data before you can create a chart. You begin with Excel's default (or automatic) chart and then modify it to your liking. With so many chart types and options, you have carte blanche for creating a chart that best suits your needs.

All charts start out basically the same. You have to create a basic chart with Excel's automatic settings before you can create more customized charts. If desired, you can modify the basic chart, using various tools. The first task is to select the data you want to chart. The second task is to bring up the basic chart.

Selecting the Chart Type and Subtype

You can choose a chart type from the Chart Type list and then choose a chart subtype from the Chart Subtype gallery in a Chart Wizard dialog box. A description of the chart type appears in the lower-right side of the Chart Wizard dialog box when you click a chart subtype.

47

Choosing the Data Range and Series

To control the orientation of your chart, you choose the data range and then plot a series in rows or columns. Sometimes when Excel produces a chart from a highlighted range, the chart is backward. The data series appears where categories should be and vice versa. How does Excel know which orientation to use? Well, Excel makes a guess based on your selected data. If you have more columns than rows, then the columns become the categories on the x-axis. If you have more rows than columns, then the rows become categories along the x-axis.

You can always change Excel's orientation for a chart if Excel guesses wrong. Here's how you can change the orientation. Choose to plot your data in rows if you want the rows to be translated into data series and columns into categories. The rows option is best used when the selected data range contains more columns than rows.

In some instances, you might create a chart by plotting your data in columns, which turns your columns into data series and rows into categories. This situation would occur when you have more rows than columns.

The chart's appearance depends on your choice, so make sure you choose a setup that fits your needs best.

Setting Chart Options

All kinds of chart options are available for your chart, including titles, axes, gridlines, legend, data labels, and data table. These are the tabs in the Chart Wizard - Step 3 of 4 - Chart Options dialog box. Here's where you can add descriptive text to the chart if you like. For example, you can add labels to the Category (X) axis along the bottom of the chart and Value (Y) axis labels along the left side of the chart.

Choosing a Location for the Chart

In the final Chart Wizard dialog box, you can specify where you want to place the chart. You have two choices: As New Sheet and As Object In. The As New Sheet option lets you insert the chart on a separate chart sheet. A chart sheet is a separate element from the worksheet and is stored in the current workbook.

The As Object In option enables you to insert the chart as an object in the worksheet that contains the data you're charting. A chart object on a worksheet is useful for showing the actual data and its graphic representation side by side.

The next few steps help you create a default chart (clustered column chart) using the Chart Wizard.

1. Select cells A3:C7 on the Summary sheet of your My Budget workbook to identify the range you want to chart.

2. Click the Chart Wizard button on the Standard toolbar. The Chart Wizard - Step 1 of 4 - Chart Type dialog box opens, displaying the chart types. The Clustered Column chart is the default chart type. You want to use this chart type.

3. Click the Next button to accept the Clustered Column chart type, and the Chart Wizard - Step 2 of 4 - Chart Source Data dialog box should appear with a sample chart, as shown in Figure 47.12.

4. Leave the Columns option selected. Each column or data series represents the values for each budget category by month. January and February are the Category (X) axis labels. The budget category names appear in the legend for the data series.

5. Click the Next button. Excel displays the Chart Wizard - Step 3 of 4 - Chart Options dialog box. The dialog box contains a sample chart and options for adding titles, changing the legend, and formatting other elements in the chart.

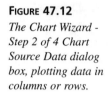

FIGURE 47.12

The Chart Wizard - Step 2 of 4 Chart Source Data dialog box, plotting data in columns or rows.

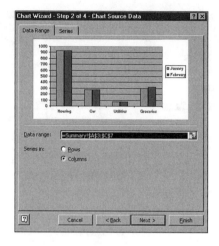

6. On the Titles tab, click the Chart Title text box and type My Budget.

7. Click the Next button. You should see the Chart Wizard - Step 4 of 4 - Chart Location dialog box. You can place the chart on a separate chart sheet or as an object in an existing worksheet. A chart sheet is a separate element from the worksheet and is stored in the current workbook. Keep the As Object In option and Summary sheet selected.

8. Click the Finish button. The chart appears near the top of the worksheet. The chart has a plot area with data series columns, and a legend on the right. Selection handles surround the border of the chart. You also should see the Chart toolbar. Sometimes the Chart toolbar does not always automatically appear when the chart is displayed. Figure 47.13 shows the clustered column chart and the Chart toolbar.

A chart is handled as an object in an Excel worksheet, and so you can move and resize the chart, just as you would any object in Excel.

To move a chart on a worksheet, click anywhere in the chart to select it and then hold down the left mouse button. When the mouse pointer changes to a four-headed arrow, drag the chart to a new place.

To change the size of a chart, select the chart and then drag one of its handles (the black squares that border the chart). Drag a corner handle to change the height and width or drag a side handle to change only the width.

When you save the worksheet, Excel saves the chart along with it. Unless you remove it, this chart appears on the worksheet. You can remove a chart by clicking it and then pressing the Delete key.

47

FIGURE **47.13**

*The clustered column
chart and Chart tool-
bar.*

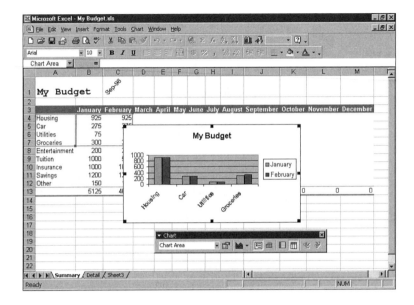

Working with Charts

Now that you know how to create a chart in Excel, you're ready to discover how you can
customize and modify your charts. Excel lets you control most of the chart's elements,
including the axes, chart text, and series patterns and colors.

The Chart toolbar is very useful for making changes to charts. When working with
charts, you frequently add data labels to a chart to further describe the data in each data
series. You decide on the elements of your chart, such as whether to show or hide a legend and gridlines, select a different chart type to fit your needs, and re-order a chart's
data series.

Before you can change anything on a chart, you must select the chart. Click anywhere on
the chart. You should see selection handles (black squares) surrounding the chart, which
indicate that the chart is selected.

In addition, Excel's chart commands require that you select the element on the chart that
you want to change before making any changes. An element can be the entire chart, the
plot area, a data series, or an axis. The command you select then applies to only the
selected elements on the chart.

You can select an element by simply clicking the element in the chart or by choosing a
chart element from the Chart Objects list on the Chart toolbar. Excel then displays selection boxes around the element. At this point, you can customize the chart with the chart
tools on the Chart toolbar or with the commands in the menu bar.

Working with the Chart Toolbar

After you create a chart, you can use various chart tools to edit and format the chart. You can use the Chart toolbar to change legends, gridlines, the x-axis, the y-axis, background, colors, fonts, titles, labels, and much more. Figure 47.14 shows the tools on the Chart toolbar.

FIGURE 47.14

The Chart toolbar.

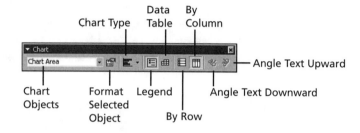

Table 47.4 lists the tools on the Chart toolbar and describes what they do.

TABLE 47.4   Chart Toolbar Tools

Chart Tool	What It Does
Chart Objects	Lets you select a chart object that you want to change
Format Selected Object	Lets you format the selected object
Chart Type	Changes the chart type
Legend	Adds or removes a legend
Data Table	Inserts a data table on the chart
By Row	Plots the data by rows
By Column	Plots the data by columns
Angle Text Downward	Changes the text so that it slants downward
Angle Text Upward	Changes the text so that it slants upward

Adding Data to a Chart

You can add data labels above data series and data points on your chart. To do so, simply select the data series on the chart or in the Chart Objects list on the Chart toolbar. For example, you would choose Series "January" in the Chart Objects list.

Next click the Format Data Series button on the Chart toolbar. Excel opens the Format Data Series dialog box. Click the Data Labels tab. This tab offers data label options that include None, Show value, and Show label. The options that are grayed out are not available for this chart type.

47

Choose the Data Label type, such as Show Value, and then click OK. Excel adds the data labels to your chart. Each data series bar for January should show a value above it, as shown in Figure 47.15.

FIGURE 47.15

Showing data labels as values above a data series.

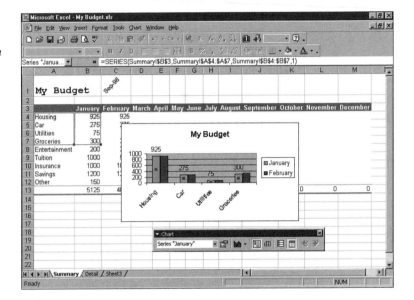

Deciding on the Elements of Your Chart

A chart legend describes the data series and data points; it provides a "key" to the chart. By default, Excel adds a legend to the chart, and it already knows which chart labels make up the legend, that is, the data series labels in the first column of the chart range. Keep in mind that a pie chart does not need a legend, but by default Excel inserts one anyway.

You can hide the legend, if you so desire. To do so, click the Legend button on the Chart toolbar. Excel makes the legend disappear from the chart. To display the legend, simply click the Legend button on the Chart toolbar again.

The default location for a legend is on the right side of the chart. But you can change the placement of the legend by clicking on it and dragging it. Among the standard locations for the legend are the bottom, corner, top, right, and left side of the chart. Experiment to get the results you want. Figure 47.16 shows the legend in the upper-right corner of the chart.

Gridlines are another chart element. A grid appears in the plot area of the chart and is useful for emphasizing the vertical scale of the data series. You can remove the gridlines by clicking on a gridline on the chart and then pressing the Delete key. Excel removes the gridlines from the chart. You can display them again by clicking the Undo button on the Standard toolbar.

FIGURE 47.16

A legend in the upper-right corner of the chart.

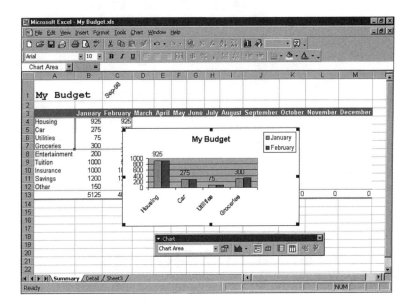

Selecting a Different Chart Type

Excel offers a myriad of chart types for presenting your data. You'll find that certain chart types are best for certain situations. To change to a different chart type, select your chart and click the Chart Type down arrow on the Chart toolbar. A palette of chart types appears, as shown in Figure 47.17. Click any chart type. Excel transforms your chart into that chart type. Experiment with chart types until you get the chart that best suits your needs.

47

Re-ordering Chart Series

You can change the order of the chart series. To do so, click a data series on the chart. Click the Format Data Series button on the Chart toolbar. The Format Data Series dialog box appears. Click the Series Order tab. Choose the data series in the Series order list that you want to move and click the Move Up or Move Down button to move the series in the list. Click OK. Excel places the data series on the chart in the order you specified.

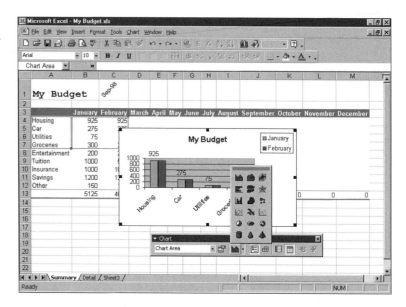

FIGURE 47.17

The Chart Type palette on the Chart toolbar.

Chart Formatting Techniques

Many people like to change the chart colors, lines, patterns, and styles of the data series for special effects. Although Excel's default colors and patterns help to distinguish one data series from another, you might find some colors and patterns more attractive than others. For example, you might want to remove all patterns and use only color.

The vertical axis in a chart is referred to as the Value axis. Excel automatically scales the value axis for your charts to best fit the minimum and maximum values being charted. The values along the vertical (Y) or horizontal (X) axis are set with minimum and maximum values, as well as a number of intermediate points along the axis. These intermediate points are called major units and minor units. You can choose from a number of axis and tick-mark formats to change the appearance of an axis.

You can change the view of a 3D chart by using the Chart, 3-D View command. The view options let you adjust the elevation and rotation of the chart.

Excel places category labels next to the horizontal axis along the bottom of the chart. If you're not satisfied with the category labels that go with your chart, you can change them. You can angle the text upward or downward.

Changing Chart Colors, Lines, Patterns, and Styles

Most of the color, line, pattern, and style options in the Format Axis dialog box are self-explanatory. But here are some highlights if you want the real lowdown on the options.

If you have a color printer, keep in mind that the patterns have two parts: the foreground and the background. Each part can be a different color. The foreground is the pattern itself, and the background is the color on which the pattern is drawn. Experiment with the foreground and background colors to see how these work. Note that the solid pattern (the first pattern in the list) provides the solid version of whichever foreground color you choose.

The Patterns tab is divided into two groups for data series—Border options and Area options—which may require some explanation. The Border options affect the perimeter of the selected element, including the style, color, and thickness of the border line. The Area options control the inside of the element, such as its color and pattern.

The Automatic option tells Excel to take care of choosing the colors and patterns.

Summary

In this chapter, you learned about formatting your Excel data with each individual type of format (borders, shading, colors, and patterns), as well as formatting in one fell swoop with AutoFormat. In addition, you learned how to draw shapes and insert ready-made art objects to spice up your worksheets.

You also now understand Excel's powerful charting capabilities. You can generate charts to import them into PowerPoint presentations and even into Word documents if you want to publish your data.

47

PART XIII

Integrating Excel into Your Work

Chapter

CHAPTER 48

Integrating Excel and Other Office Products

After you learn how to use Excel, and if you already know how to use Word and Outlook, you can use Microsoft Office to share information between applications.

This chapter introduces you to linking and embedding objects, inserting objects that you create in other applications, creating hyperlinks between Office applications, and how to send Excel documents via email using Microsoft Outlook. When your through with this chapter, you'll know how to integrate Excel with other Office applications, making it easy to share data between word processing, spreadsheet, and personal information manager programs.

Using Objects in Excel

Sharing data between applications is called *Object Linking and Embedding*, more commonly known as *OLE*. This may sound complicated but it isn't. It means there's an object in a document in one Windows application that is

linked to or embedded from a document in another Windows application. Many
Windows applications let you link and embed information in any of these applications.
For example, you can copy a Microsoft Excel chart and put it into a Microsoft Word doc-
ument.

If the object is linked, it appears in your Office document but it is stored outside of your
document. Your document holds the link, which is like an address, and when you want to
view or print your document, Excel reads the address, fetches the object, and provides it.
If the original object is changed, the next time you link to it, you see the changes.

When you take an existing Excel worksheet or chart in a Word document and copy and
paste the information or import it into another Word document, you can embed the worksheet rather than linking it. If the object is embedded, it is moved into your document
after it's created and becomes a part of your document, just like the text, numbers, and
clip art you create while you work in Excel.

By embedding the worksheet as an object, you can double-click the worksheet in Word,
and the Word menus and toolbars are temporarily replaced by the Excel menus and toolbars. It's like working in a "super application," in which one window can perform many
different types of applications' tasks—word processor to spreadsheet program and back.
The advantage is that you can quickly and easily make changes to objects from different
applications in the same window. This process is referred to as OLE. Any changes you
make to the worksheet are automatically reflected in the worksheet in Word.

Object Linking

Object linking enables you to share data between programs with OLE. You can link
Office documents. For example, you can take an existing Excel worksheet and copy and
paste its contents or import it into a Word document. Then you can create a link between
the Excel worksheet and the Word document so that each time the worksheet is updated
in Excel, the worksheet data in Word is automatically updated to reflect any changes.

When you link Office documents, one document is called the source document and the
other is called the target document. The *source document* contains the information you
want to link; the *target document* receives the linked information. For example, if you
want to link an Excel worksheet to a Word document, the worksheet file is the source
document and the Word file is the target document.

When you link documents, the source document appears in the target document, but it is
not physically there. For instance, you can see an Excel worksheet in a Word document,
but the worksheet still resides in Excel.

Follow the next steps to link an Excel worksheet to a Word document. You'll be using the My Budget workbook and a blank Word document.

1. First open the My Budget workbook. Be sure to update the links when you open the workbook. Then, click the Summary sheet.

2. Now it's time to start Word. Click the Start button on the Windows taskbar, and choose Programs, Microsoft Word. You should see the Word window with a blank document on your screen.

3. With both applications open, let's switch to Excel by clicking the Microsoft Excel button on the Windows taskbar.

4. Select the data in cells A1:D13 in the Summary sheet. This is the source data for linking the worksheet object to the Word document.

5. Click the Copy button on the Standard toolbar.

6. Click the Microsoft Word button on the Windows taskbar to switch to Word.

7. Choose Edit, Paste Special. The Paste Special dialog box appears. The selected range appears at the top of the dialog box in the Source area.

8. In the As list, choose Microsoft Excel Worksheet Object. This tells Word which object you want to place in the Word document.

9. Click the Paste Link option. This tells Excel that you want to create a link between the source data and the Word document. Figure 48.1 shows the Paste Special dialog box with all the selections you should have made.

FIGURE 48.1

The Paste Special dialog box.

48

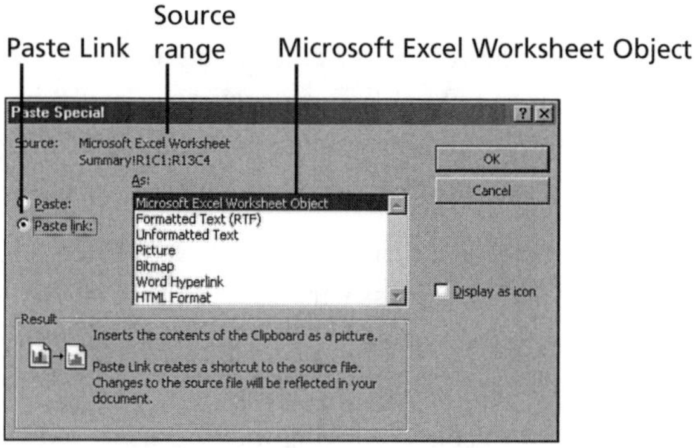

10. Click OK. The Excel worksheet should appear in the Word document as an object with selection handles (white squares) surrounding the worksheet's border. These handles indicate that the object is selected (see Figure 48.2).

11. Save the Word document by clicking the Save button on the Standard toolbar. Name the file My Integration, and click the Save button.

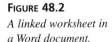

FIGURE 48.2

A linked worksheet in a Word document.

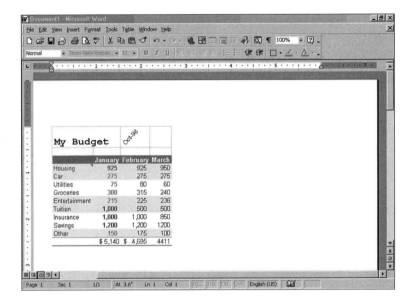

Object Embedding

Just like linking documents, you have a source document and a target document when you embed an object in a document. Embedding a document as an object physically places a document within another document. For example, if you embed an Excel worksheet or chart in a Word document, the worksheet or chart physically resides in Word as well as Excel.

In the upcoming exercise you'll see how embedding an Excel worksheet as an object in a Word document is similar to linking Office documents. You'll be using the My Budget workbook and the My Integration document again. Follow these steps to begin embedding an object:

1. In the Word document, press Enter a few times to insert some space beneath the worksheet object, and then press Ctrl+End to move to the bottom of the document. Press Ctrl+Enter to insert a page break. The insertion point should be at the top of page 2 now.

2. Now we'll switch to Excel by clicking the Microsoft Excel button on the Windows taskbar.

3. Press the Esc key to clear the flashing marquee border.

4. Select the data in cells A1:C13 in the My Budget workbook. This is the data that we'll embed in the Word document as an object.

5. Click the Copy button on the Standard toolbar.

6. Click the Microsoft Word button on the Windows taskbar to switch to Word.

7. Choose Edit, Paste Special. The Paste Special dialog box appears. The selected range appears at the top of the dialog box. Leave the Paste option selected.

8. In the As list, choose Microsoft Excel Worksheet Object. This tells Word which object you want to place in the Word document. Figure 48.3 shows the Paste Special dialog box with the selection you should have made.

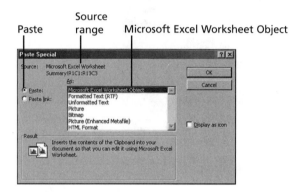

FIGURE 48.3

The Paste Special dialog box.

9. Click OK. The Excel worksheet is now an embedded object in the Word document. Now let's change a couple of numbers in the Excel worksheet and see how Excel treats an embedded object.

10. Double-click the worksheet object. Notice the Word window takes on the appearance of an Excel window, displaying Excel's menus, toolbars, and the formula bar (see Figure 48.4).

11. Click cell C6, type 100, and press Enter. Next, click cell C8, type 200, and press Enter. This changes two numbers in the Excel worksheet. Notice that the value in the Total row has been updated to reflect the new numbers.

12. Click outside the worksheet. The Word menu and toolbars appear. Notice the worksheet now contains the new numbers and the formulas have been recalculated automatically to reflect the changes you made. It's like magic!

13. Close the Word document and save the changes. Then, close Word by double-clicking the Word Control icon in the upper-left corner of the Word window. You should see only the Excel window on your screen.

48

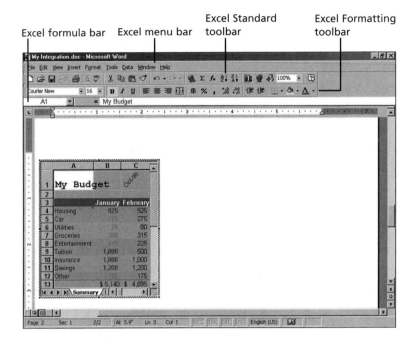

Excel formula bar · Excel menu bar · Excel Standard toolbar · Excel Formatting toolbar

FIGURE 48.4

*An embedded work-
sheet in a Word docu-
ment.*

Inserting Objects

In addition to pictures, you can insert objects created in other applications.

When you choose to insert an object, Excel runs the required application and lets you create the object. When you quit the other application, the object is inserted on the current worksheet or chart.

Inserting an Object from the Menu

The following steps show you how to insert an object from another application using the Insert, Object command. Use the My Budget workbook for this exercise. You're going to create a simple freehand drawing in the Microsoft Paintbrush application and insert the drawing as an object in the Summary sheet.

1. In the Summary sheet, press Esc to remove the marquee. Select the cell on the sheet where you want the upper-left corner of the object placed. In this case, scroll down to row 35, and click cell C35.

2. Choose Insert, Object. The Object dialog box pops opens, as shown in Figure 48.5. There are two tabs: Create New and Create from File. The Create New tab lets you run another application and create the object. The Create from File tab allows you to insert an object that you have already created and saved.

FIGURE 48.5

The Object dialog box.

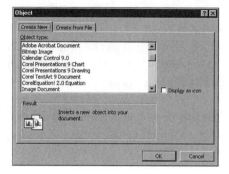

3. Make sure the Create New tab is up front. From the Object Type list, select the program you need to run to create the object. In this case, click Paintbrush Picture.

4. Click OK. Excel runs the selected application. Now you should see the application window on your screen. The Paintbrush Bitmap Image window appears (see Figure 48.6).

FIGURE 48.6

The Paintbrush Bitmap Image window.

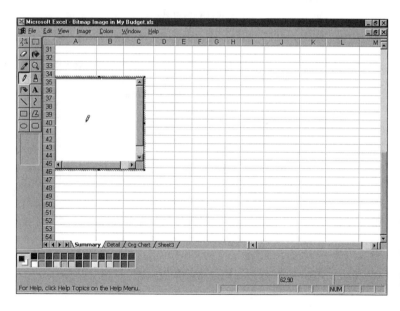

If you want the object to appear as an icon in your worksheet or chart, click the Display as Icon check box. Otherwise the object itself will appear in the worksheet or chart.

48

5. Use the application as you normally would to create the object. In our case, click the Rounded Rectangle tool (second column, last row) on the Paintbrush toolbar. Point to the upper-left corner of the object box (near row 36), and click and drag diagonally down to about cell C43 to draw a rounded rectangle. When you're finished, click any cell in the Excel worksheet to save the object, and exit the application. Excel places the object on your worksheet. You should see a rounded rectangle object. When you click the object, Excel displays the Picture toolbar, so that you can make changes to the object. If you double-click the object, you are returned to Paintbrush.

Using the Clipboard Toolbar

If you want to insert an object using the Clipboard toolbar instead of the Insert, Object command, it's easy to do. Create the object in the application and use the Copy command to copy the object to the Clipboard. In Excel, click the worksheet where you want the object to appear. Right-click any toolbar, and choose Clipboard to display the Clipboard toolbar. (Office XP and later will show these items on the Office Clipboard Task Pane.) Notice the selection on the Clipboard, ready for you to insert as an object in your worksheet (see Figure 48.7).

FIGURE **48.7**

The Clipboard toolbar.

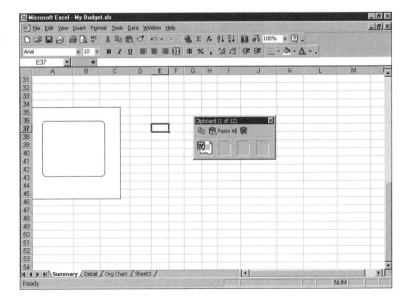

Then click the selection on the Clipboard toolbar to paste the object into the worksheet. Excel shows the object in your worksheet.

Using Hyperlinks with Other Office Documents

What is a hyperlink? A hyperlink is a '90s term that refers to a piece of text or graphic in a document that links to other documents. You can create your own hyperlinks to move to a Word, Excel, PowerPoint, or Access file. You can even link to a specific location in a document. When you point to a hyperlink, Word displays the document path (for example, `c:\excel\mydocuments\mybudget.xls`) to which the link points. When you click a hyperlink, Excel moves to the location to which the link points. A hyperlink appears in blue (default color) text in the worksheet.

Hyperlinks are useful when you're distributing your document electronically and expect people to read it onscreen. Make sure that your readers will be able to access the documents to which you link. As an example, if you link a workbook on your local hard drive (C:) instead of a network drive, other people on your network won't be able to jump to the workbook, unless you make the entire contents of your machine available to other users on the network.

You can browse through files on your computer or on a network drive that contain hyperlinks.

Creating the Hyperlink

You need to use the Insert Hyperlink command to create a hyperlink so that you can move among Office documents. Perform the following steps to create a hyperlink to move from an Excel worksheet to the Word document. Once again, you'll be using the My Budget workbook and the Word document you created earlier called My Integration.

1. Click cell B75 on the Summary sheet. This cell will contain the hyperlink that brings you to the Word document.

2. Select Insert, Hyperlink (or press Ctrl+K). Excel opens the Insert Hyperlink dialog box, as shown in Figure 48.8.

3. Click the Browse for File button. Choose the folder, select the file named My Integration, and choose OK.

4. Click OK in the Insert Hyperlink dialog box. The document name is now a hyperlink and appears as blue, underlined text in cell B75.

5. Point to the hyperlink. Notice how the mouse pointer becomes a hand. A ScreenTip containing the filename and path appears below the hyperlink (see Figure 48.9).

6. Click the hyperlink. Microsoft Word opens and you see the My Integration document.

48

FIGURE **48.8**

The Insert Hyperlink dialog box.

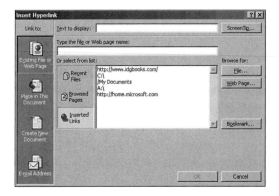

FIGURE **48.9**

The hyperlink and ScreenTip with the pathname.

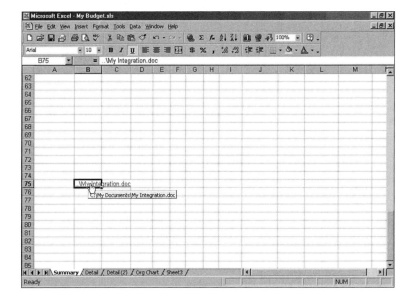

7. In Word, select File, Exit. This closes the document and Word, and then returns you to the Excel worksheet.

8. Click the Microsoft Excel button on the Windows taskbar. You see the My Budget workbook again. Notice the hyperlink text appears in purple, indicating that the hyperlink is selected.

Sending Your Document Via Email with Outlook

You can send your Excel workbooks via email with Outlook directly from Excel. You have a choice to send to either one recipient or to a distribution list of multiple recipients. The nice part is that you don't have to leave Excel to send your documents to others.

Sending to One Recipient

To send an Excel workbook to one recipient, open the workbook you want to send. Choose File, Send To, and select Mail Recipient (as Attachment) or click the Email button on the Standard toolbar. Excel's Office Assistant asks if you want to send the entire workbook as an attachment or send the current sheet as the message body. Choose the option you want. If you choose the workbook attachment option, you should see the Outlook message window, illustrated in Figure 48.10.

FIGURE 48.10

Send someone an attached spreadsheet.

Set up the Outlook information requested in the message window, and type your email mail message. Notice that Excel automatically attached the workbook to your email message. Click the Send button to send your message with the attached workbook via Outlook.

If you choose to insert the current sheet in the message body, you will see the Outlook message window, shown in Figure 48.11.

Complete the address information at the top of the message window. Notice that Excel automatically inserted the current sheet into the email message box. Click the Send This Sheet button to send your message with the worksheet as the message body via Outlook.

48

FIGURE **48.11**

*Send a spreadsheet
from within Excel.*

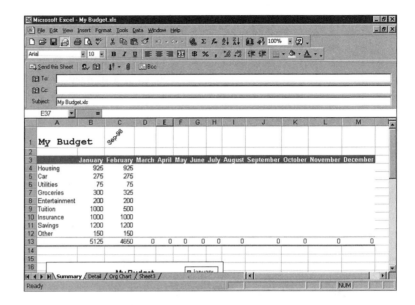

Summary

You've now seen how to integrate Excel with other Office applications. One of the primary reasons to own the Microsoft Office suite is to share data between the programs so you don't have redundant information in several locations. Excel works well with the other programs and is able to transfer information to and from them.

CHAPTER 49

Introducing Macros

During this chapter, you will learn how to use macros to simplify your work in Excel, making you more efficient and leaving you time for other things you need to do on the job. Macros are not difficult to create and use. They are special instructions that control how Excel functions. This chapter will hone your skills and teach you the Excel-specific advantages and problems you'll encounter with macros.

What Is a Macro?

As you work with Excel, you might discover yourself repeating many actions and commands. For example, every time you create a new worksheet, you might immediately enter a series of titles (such as months) across one row or format a set of numbers using the currency style.

Although you can make some repetitive work more efficient by using the toolbar or templates, you might find it easier to create a macro to repeat a sequence of actions and commands.

You store macros in a macro sheet, a special type of Excel worksheet that is very similar to a regular worksheet. You must have a macro sheet open to be able to use the macros written in that file.

Each macro has three parts:

- Macro name
- Macro shortcut key
- Macro steps

The macro name is a description you use to manage and run the macro. For example, a macro you create to change the font for data on the worksheet can be called Font_change.

The macro shortcut key is an optional key combination you can use to run the macro. For example, you can assign the shortcut key Ctrl+Shift+F to run the Font_change macro.

The macro steps are simply the commands expressed in the Visual Basic language that execute when you run the macro. These steps are a list of instructions that Excel executes in sequence, starting from the first line and moving down to the last line. Note that each instruction in the macro must start with a period (.). An equal sign (=) follows the instruction. If you omit the period at the beginning of the line or the equal sign following the instruction, Excel ignores that step in the macro.

The first command should be Sub, a special command that tells Excel the macro has begun its operation. The last command should be End Sub, a special command that tells Excel the macro has finished its operation. For example, examine the macro in Figure 49.1. Notice the three parts to the macro.

Macros are useful for automating repetitive or complex tasks. Although a macro is a series of programming instructions, you do not need to know anything about programming to create one. Excel offers a macro-recording feature that translates your actions into macro instructions.

Macro name Macro shortcut key

FIGURE 49.1

*Macro instructions for
changing the font.*

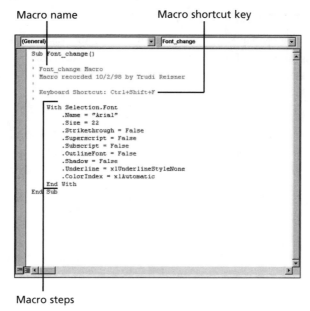

```
(General)                        ▼  Font_change                    ▼
Sub Font_change()
'
' Font_change Macro
' Macro recorded 10/2/98 by Trudi Reisner
'
' Keyboard Shortcut: Ctrl+Shift+F
'
    With Selection.Font
        .Name = "Arial"
        .Size = 22
        .Strikethrough = False
        .Superscript = False
        .Subscript = False
        .OutlineFont = False
        .Shadow = False
        .Underline = xlUnderlineStyleNone
        .ColorIndex = xlAutomatic
    End With
End Sub
```

Macro steps

Creating a Macro

By recording a series of macro instructions into a macro module or macro sheet in a
workbook, you can tell Excel to perform any series of commands or actions for you. A
macro can take the place of any mouse or keyboard action that you can perform in Excel.
That is, a macro can cause Excel to accomplish a task by itself. You simply record a
macro that shows Excel what you want to accomplish. Then Excel can repeat the task at
any time.

You can create a macro by manually typing the instructions in a macro sheet or by
choosing Tools, Macro, Record. Manually creating a macro requires you to carefully
write down each step of the macro in the macro sheet. A single misspelling can affect the
operation of the macro. Choosing Tools, Macro, Record, on the other hand, simply
records each movement and action you take while using Excel. When you have completed the action, you stop recording by choosing the Stop Recording button on the Stop
Recording toolbar. If you make a mistake while recording your macro, you can edit the
macro later.

For most purposes, then, you should use Tools, Macro, Record to create macros. This
method ensures that your macro will work when you use it.

49

Naming the Macro

A macro name can have up to 256 characters with no spaces. It's best to make your macro names meaningful and short so that you and others can quickly discern which macro to use. You name the macro right after you select Tools, Macro, Record New Macro.

The default macro name that Excel assigns to a macro is the word *Macro* followed by a number that looks like this: Macro1, Macro2, and so on. The name appears highlighted in the Macro Name box when the Record Macro dialog box first appears. That way, you can easily type right over the default name with any name you want. Remember, a name cannot contain spaces. If you enter a space anywhere in the name, Excel will not accept the macro name.

Selecting a Keyboard Shortcut

All macro shortcut keys must include the Ctrl key in combination with one other keyboard key. You can also use the Shift key in combination with the Ctrl key when assigning the shortcut key. For instance, you might assign the key combination Ctrl+Shift+F to run the Font_change macro.

Excel reserves many Ctrl shortcut key assignments for its own use. Excel will tell you when a combination key is already assigned and won't let you use an existing shortcut key. To avoid conflicts with these existing key assignments, you should use the Ctrl+Shift key combination for your shortcut keys.

Describing the Macro

An optional step is to enter a description of your macro to explain its function. A description can be helpful for you and others who use the macro. The default description contains the date you created or last modified the macro and your user name. In the example of the Font_change macro, you might want to explain that the macro changes the font and font size for data.

Recording the Macro

A macro is recorded on a macro sheet in a workbook. When you record a macro, Excel displays the Stop Recording toolbar that contains two buttons: Stop Recording and Relative Reference. The Stop Recording button does just what it says—it stops the recording of a macro. The Relative Reference button allows you to switch between relative and absolute references. By default, Excel records absolute cell references unless you click the Relative Reference button on the Stop Recording toolbar to specify that a cell or range of cells should be a relative reference. When you choose relative reference, the Relative Reference button appears depressed on the toolbar. Click the Relative Reference button again to switch back to absolute reference. The button no longer appears depressed.

The following steps guide you through creating a macro called Font_change that changes the font and font size for data on your worksheet. You should be using the My Budget workbook you've worked with before.

1. Open the My Budget workbook. This workbook will contain the macro. Click cell B80 so that when you perform actions to record the macro, it will not change anything you didn't intend to change.

2. Choose Tools, Macro and click Record New Macro. The Record Macro dialog box pops up, as shown in Figure 49.2. You should see the default macro name Macro1 in the Macro Name box. You want to change that name to Font_change.

Macro Name

FIGURE 49.2

The Record Macro dialog box.

Description   Shortcut Key

3. In the Macro Name box, type Font_change. This step names the macro.

4. Press Tab. In the Shortcut Key box, hold down Shift and type F. This step assigns the shortcut key Ctrl+Shift+F to the macro.

When you run the macro, press the appropriate letter key along with the Ctrl key, without pressing the Shift key, unless the Shift key is part of the shortcut key sequence. For example, Ctrl+Shift+F.

5. Click OK. The Record Macro dialog box disappears. Notice the recording indicator in black letters at the left end of the status bar at the bottom of the Excel window. From this point on, until you choose Stop Recorder, Excel stores every action and command on a macro sheet. Also note the Stop Recording toolbar that contains two buttons: Stop Recording and Relative Reference. Figure 49.3 shows you what your worksheet looks like just before you begin to record a macro.

49

FIGURE 49.3

Recording a macro.

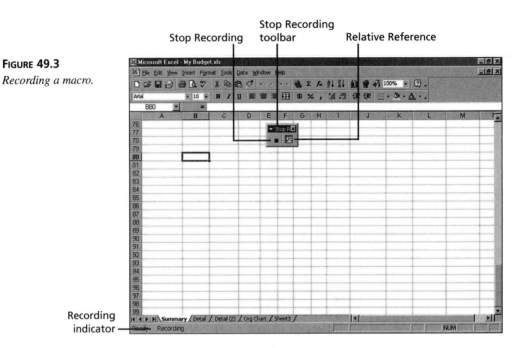

6. Click the Font drop-down arrow on the Formatting toolbar and choose Arial.

7. Click the Font Size drop-down arrow on the Formatting toolbar and choose 22. Now you're finished recording the macro, so stop the recorder.

8. Click the Stop Recording button on the Stop Recording toolbar. Excel hides the toolbar and stops recording the macro. You can tell because the Recording indicator in the status bar disappears. You have now recorded a macro that changes the font and font size for data on the worksheet.

9. Save the workbook. This step saves your macro, too.

Saving the Macro

When you save your workbook, Excel saves your macro on the macro sheet with the workbook. You don't have to do anything else to save the macro. If you accidentally close the workbook without saving changes, Excel doesn't save the macro. You have to start all over and re-create the macro.

Running the Macro

After you create a macro, you can use it to repeat its commands. Excel offers many ways to run a macro. Here are the two most common methods for running a macro:

- Select Tools, Macro, Macros, Run.

- Use the macro shortcut key (if you defined one).

The quickest way to run the macro is to use the macro shortcut key. If the macro doesn't have a shortcut key assigned to it, then you must use Tools, Macro, Macros, Run.

In the following steps, you run the macro you just created by using the macro name, Font_change.

1. First select cell A1 in the Summary sheet. This data in this cell needs a font change.

2. Choose Tools, Macro, Macros. The Macro dialog box appears, as shown in Figure 49.4.

FIGURE 49.4

The Macro dialog box.

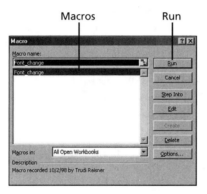

3. In the Macro dialog box, select Font_change.

4. Click Run. Excel runs the Font_change macro by changing the title in the worksheet to a 22-point Arial font. You'll have to make column A a little wider to accommodate the long entry in cell A1.

If you want to run the macro using a shortcut key, just press the shortcut key you assigned to the macro. Before testing the Font_change macro, select cell J16. Then, to run the Font_change macro, press Ctrl+Shift+F. Excel should format the data in cell J16 with the 22-point Arial font. Macros are powerful, aren't they?

You can stop a macro while it's running by simply pressing the Esc key. Excel stops the macro before it completes its actions.

49

Fixing Macro Errors

Macros don't always work perfectly. That is, you might make a mistake while recording the macro, or you might leave out a step. You don't need to worry about a macro that displays an error message because you can always fix those macro errors in Excel by editing, adding, and removing commands from the macro instructions.

A macro might need additional commands or actions, or you might want to delete some command or action from the macro. What if you want to make changes to existing macro commands and actions or correct errors in a macro that doesn't run properly? No problem. You can make any of these changes to a macro by editing the macro.

Looking at Macro Code

Macro instructions are written in Visual Basic, a fairly easy-to-use programming language. With the macro sheet in view onscreen, you can use Excel's editing commands to make changes to the Visual Basic instructions. You can remove macro commands, edit the specific contents of a cell in the macro worksheet, or even insert new commands into the middle of a macro. Of course, some changes require knowledge of Visual Basic. Specific commands that relate to actions that you want are described in the Microsoft Excel manual that comes with the software.

You can view macro code in the macro sheet by switching to that sheet. To open the macro sheet, choose Tools, Macro, Macros. In the Macro dialog box, select the Font_change macro. Click the Edit button.

 Another way to look at macro code is to choose Tools, Macro, Visual Basic Editor, or press Alt+F11.

The Microsoft Visual Basic window appears, as shown in Figure 49.5. You should see the Visual Basic toolbar and three window panes:

- Project – VBA Project
- Properties – Module1
- Visual Basic Instructions

At the far right end of the Visual Basic toolbar, notice the line and column indicator: Ln X, Col X. These indicators tell you the line and column where the insertion point is located in the active pane. To activate a pane, simply click the pane.

FIGURE 49.5

The Microsoft Visual Basic window.

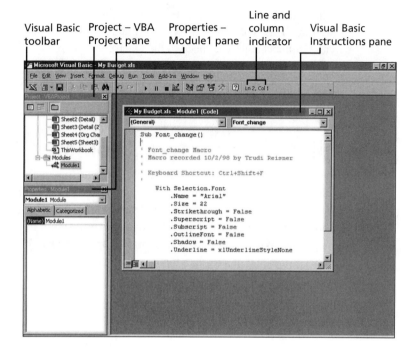

Editing the Macro

You can insert a command manually, remove a command, or edit a macro command on the macro sheet to make changes to the macro. You'll work with the Visual Basic Instructions pane on the right to make your changes. To get a better view of what you're doing in the Visual Basic Instructions pane, click the Maximize button in the upper-right corner of the pane. Excel enlarges the pane so that you see more macro instructions.

The following steps teach you how to edit the macro. You change the macro's font size from 22 point to 28 point.

1. Click anywhere in line 10 in the Visual Basic Instructions pane, where it states Size = 22. This step activates the pane and positions the insertion point where you want to make a change.

2. Click and drag over the number 22 to select it.

3. Type 28.

4. Click the Save button on the Visual Basic toolbar. This step saves the changes you made to the macro.

49

5. Click the Close (X) button in the upper-right corner of the Microsoft Visual Basic window. This step closes the window and returns you to the workbook. Now you can test the change you made to the macro.

6. Click the Detail sheet tab and click cell F1, which contains the title. Press Ctrl+Shift+F. The macro applies the 28-point Arial font to the text in the selected cell. Your macro works perfectly!

Attaching a Macro to a Toolbar

As you build macros, you might not remember the macro names or even their shortcut names. You can use Tools, Macro, Run to choose the macros, but this method requires you to continually pull down the menu and scroll through the list of names in the Macro dialog box. A more efficient way to run a macro is to assign it to a button on a toolbar. Assigning a macro to a button makes the macro run whenever you click the button with your mouse. Attaching macros to a toolbar is a quick way to organize your macros so that any user can easily run them.

The following steps show you how to attach a macro to the Standard toolbar for the Detail sheet.

1. In the Detail sheet, choose Tools, Customize. The Customize dialog box appears.

2. Click the Toolbars tab. The Standard toolbar check box should have a checkmark in it. The checkmark means that the Standard toolbar is currently displayed, and you can make changes to it. You're going to attach the macro to this toolbar.

3. If the button you want to run the macro from is not on a toolbar, click the Commands tab and then click Macros in the Categories list.

4. In the Commands list, you should see the Custom Button with a smiley face next to it, as shown in Figure 49.6. Drag the Custom button onto the Standard toolbar, placing the button between the Zoom box and the Help button at the far right end of the toolbar. You should see a thick border surrounding the Custom button with the yellow smiley face on it.

5. Right-click the Custom toolbar button and choose Assign Macro. The Assign Macro dialog box opens, as shown in Figure 49.7.

6. Click the Font_change macro name. This step enters the name of the macro in the Macro Name box.

7. Click OK. Excel attaches the macro to the Custom button on the Standard toolbar. Click the Close button to close the Customize dialog box. Now you want to test the new macro button on the toolbar.

FIGURE 49.6

The Macros category and Custom Button command.

FIGURE 49.7

The Assign Macro dialog box.

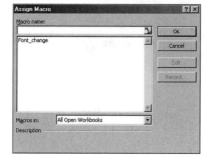

8. Select cell A4. Click the Custom Button button on the Standard toolbar. Bingo! Excel changes the font and font size for the data you selected on the worksheet. You should see the 28-point Arial font.

Using a Macro in Other Workbooks

It's important to know what goes on behind the scenes when you create a macro. When you create a macro, Excel stores your keystrokes and mouse actions as a set of instruction on a macro sheet. You can tell Excel to store the instructions in one of the following places:

- The active workbook
- A new workbook
- The Personal Macro workbook

Excel stores your macro in the active workbook by default. If your macro works only on the current workbook, then store the macro in the active workbook. If your macro works in a new workbook, then create a new workbook and store your macros there. If your macro works on any workbook in Excel, then store that macro in the Personal Macro

49

workbook. The macros in a Personal Macro workbook are available every time you start Excel. You can open the Personal Macro workbook at any time to display the macro sheet.

When you record a macro and choose Tools, Macro, Record New Macro, Excel opens the Record Macro dialog box. This dialog box is where you can specify where you want to store your macros. Click the Store Macro In drop-down arrow to look at the choices, as shown in Figure 49.8.

FIGURE 49.8

Choices for where to store your macros.

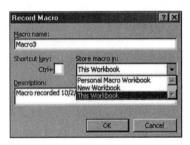

Select an item in the list and continue creating the macro. Excel stores your macros in the place you specify.

Understanding Macro Viruses

You've probably heard a lot of talk about viruses that your computer can catch from other computers on a network, the Internet, or disks. But what if your macros contain viruses? Viruses can contaminate your macros if the workbook is from an unsecure network or Internet site.

To prevent your computer from becoming contaminated with macro viruses, you can display a warning message whenever you try to open a workbook that contains a macro. This warning message always appears whether or not the macro actually has a virus. When the message displays, try to make sure that you know and trust the source of the workbook before you continue.

To check workbooks for macro viruses and display that warning message, choose Tools, Macro and then select Security. The Security dialog box opens. The Security Level tab should be up front. If it isn't, click the tab.

The High option lets you run signed macros from trusted sources. Unsigned macros are automatically disabled when you choose the High option. Choose the Medium option and click OK. Medium security displays the virus warning message. The Low option does not check workbooks for macros that may contain a virus. Therefore, the low security does not display the warning message. Now, click OK.

When you open a workbook that contains macros and the security level is medium, Excel displays the warning message that's in Figure 49.9. If you click Disable Macros, Excel ignores the macros in the workbook. If you click Enable Macros, Excel lets you use the macros in the workbook.

Figure 49.9

The macro virus warning message.

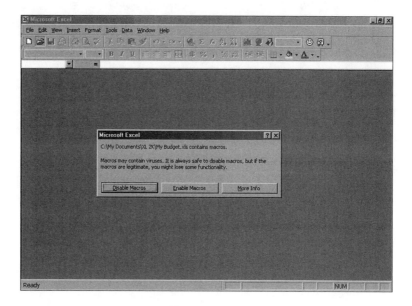

Summary

This chapter covered the basics for building and working with macros. Now you can create your own simple macros. You must have some idea now of which macros you need to automate the repetitive tasks you perform. When you're ready, you can graduate to building complex macros with advanced macro instruction. Who knows? Maybe this chapter motivated you to learn Visual Basic; if so, you'll be automating a lot more Excel tasks than you ever dreamed of.

49

CHAPTER 50

Using an Excel Database

This chapters introduces you to Excel databases. You learn about database concepts and how to plan and build a database. You also learn how to enter and add data in a database, search for specific data, and save the database.

Basic Database Concepts

In your earlier work with Excel, you created worksheets to store and summarize information or data. Often you organize this information so that you can easily find the entries for a series of values, or calculate the totals for a group of numbers.

In Excel, a *database* is simply a more organized set of data. By organizing the data into a database, you can use the built-in database commands to find, edit, and delete selected data without manually scrolling through the information.

Suppose you want to save the names and addresses of all the people on your holiday card list. You can create a database for storing the following information for each person: first name, last name, address, and so on. Each piece of information is entered into a separate field (cell) in the list. All the fields for one person in the list make a record. In Excel, a cell is a field, and a row of field entries makes a record. The column headings in the list are called field names in the database.

Figure 50.1 shows the organization of an Excel database.

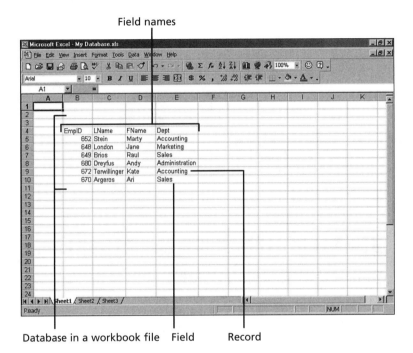

FIGURE 50.1

Sample database.

Database in a workbook file   Field   Record

Before you work with a database, you should know these database terms:

- *File*—A collection of related data.
- *Field*—A column in the database.
- *Field name*—A column heading in a database. Excel uses the term *column label*.
- *Record*—A row in the database.

After you learn the database terms, here are two more things to think about when creating a database:

- Designing the database on paper
- Building the database with the field names and records

Starting with a Plan

Before you consider building a database in Excel, you need to plan how you want to structure the database. Whether you just think about the plan or write it down on paper, it's advisable to have a plan. That way, you'll save yourself a lot of time and effort because you are less likely to build a database that doesn't work for you.

Structuring Your Database

Consider these helpful questions and answers before structuring your database:

What is the size of the database going to be when I'm finished with it? Well, Excel gives you plenty of room on a worksheet. The size of the database can be as large as your worksheet, 256 columns by 65,536 rows.

What should I know about field names in relation to structuring my database? The field names must be placed in the first row of the database and must contain text. You cannot use values as field names. You can use a field name with a maximum of 255 characters; however, you should try to use shorter names because you can manage the database columns more easily.

How should I handle the records in my database? Each record must have the same number of fields. But you don't have to fill in each field of the record.

How does Excel handle spaces in data that I enter in the database? Excel doesn't deal with spaces at all. First of all, you cannot use spaces in a field name, and you shouldn't use extra spaces in a record entry. That is, don't "pad" an entry with extra spaces at the beginning or end of an entry.

Do I need to be concerned with upper- and lowercase letters? Excel's answer to this question is No. You can use any combination of uppercase and lowercase letters in your field names and records. Excel ignores capitalization when sorting or searching a database.

Can you plan on using formulas to calculate data in my database? Sure you can. You can create computed fields that evaluate other fields in the database, such as a `Total` field that would be equal to the `Cost` field times the `Quantity` field.

Creating a Database

You build your database by entering the information into your worksheet. Enter the field names into the first row and then enter the information under the row of field names, which are your records. Now you have yourself a database.

The following steps enable you to create a database from scratch. Use a new workbook for your database. Before you start the exercise, create a new workbook and name it My Database.

1. The first step toward building a database is to enter the field names. In the My Database workbook on Sheet1, select cells B4:E4. This range is where you will enter the field names for your database.

2. Type EmpID and press Enter.

3. Type LName and press Enter.

4. Type FName and press Enter.

5. Type Dept and press Enter.

6. Save the workbook.

7. Click any cell to deselect the range. Your field names should look like the ones in Figure 50.2.

FIGURE 50.2

Field names.

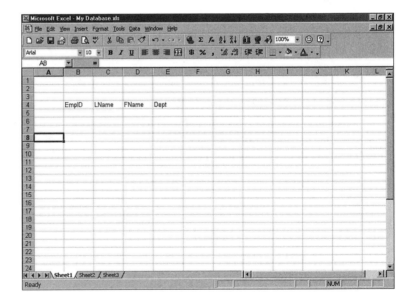

Entering and Adding Data

After you create your database, you can enter your records and add more records to it any time. You append these records at the end of the current database. To make adding these records easier, you can do one of the following:

- Use a data form
- Enter the data directly in the cells on the worksheet

Working with a Data Form

The data form is a dialog box that you use to review, add, edit, and delete records in a database. This dialog box shows one record at a time, starting with the first record. Each field name has a text box that you use to enter a new word or value.

The data form also has several buttons on it that you can use to move through the database, add or delete a record, or find a particular set of records.

Here's how you create a data form. Click any cell in the database. In the My Database file, click any cell in row 4, which contains the field names. Choose Data, Form. Excel displays a message (see Figure 50.3) asking you where your column labels (field names) are in the worksheet.

FIGURE 50.3

The column labels message.

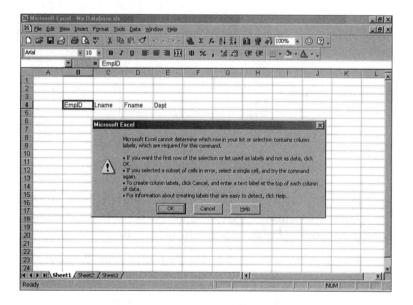

Click OK. This step tells Excel that you want to use the first row of the selection or list as labels and not as data. Excel displays the data form in a dialog box, as shown in Figure 50.4. The dialog box's title bar contains the name of the database sheet, in this case, Sheet1. You should see field names, field text boxes, a scrollbar, the record number indicator, data form buttons, and navigation buttons.

Using the Form

The New button in the data form lets you add new records to your database. Each time you click New or press Enter, Excel adds a new, blank record to the database.

FIGURE 50.4

The data form.

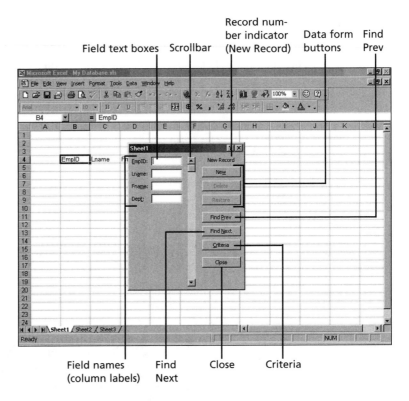

In the data form, you should see a new record with blank boxes next to the field names. Type the data in the boxes, using the Tab key to move to each box. You can use the data that appears in Figure 50.5 to enter the data for one record.

When you're finished typing the information in the boxes, click the New button or press Enter. Excel adds the new record to the database and presents a blank data form.

Excel adds the new records at the end of your database, starting with the first blank row beneath the last row in the database. You should see the first record in row 5, right below the field names in your database.

Navigating Through Records in the Form

To move around in the data form, you can use either the scrolbar in the middle of the dialog box or the navigation buttons on the right side of the data form. Here are the navigation possibilities:

- *Scrollbar*—Displays the first record in the database when you drag the scroll box to the top and displays the last record when you drag the scroll box to the bottom; displays each record as you click the up or down scroll arrow.

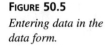

FIGURE 50.5

Entering data in the data form.

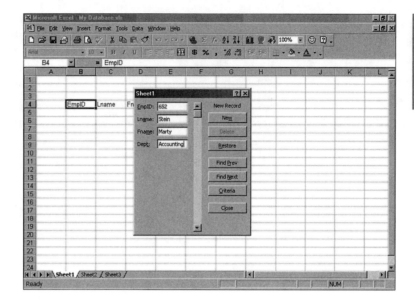

- *Find Next*—Displays the next record in the database.
- *Find Prev*—Displays the previous record in the database.

When you have a substantial number of records in your database, use the navigational tools in the data form to move around your database. But try using the navigational tools now so you'll see how they work.

Drag the scroll box to the top of the scrollbar or click the up scroll arrow. The boxes contain information for the first record. You can tell that you are viewing record 1 because the record indicator in the upper-right corner of the data form reads 1 of 1. The indicator always shows you the current record you are viewing and the total number of records.

To get back to the new, blank record, drag the scroll box to the bottom of the scrollbar or click the down scroll arrow. The record indicator shows New Record now.

When you're through with the form, click the Close button in the data form. The data form disappears.

Adding Data Directly to the Worksheet

The second method for adding data is very simple. Just type the data directly into your worksheet. Enter the necessary information to create the database entries.

Use the data in Figure 50.6 to add records to your database directly to the worksheet.

FIGURE 50.6

Entering data directly to the worksheet.

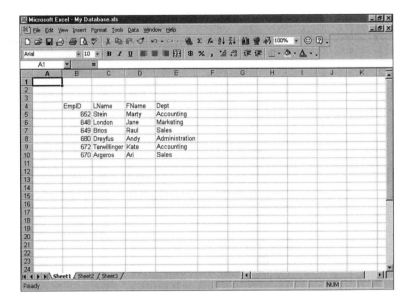

The records appear in the rows beneath the field names. Rows 5 through 10 contain data, and now you should have six records in your database. Widen any columns if necessary. You could widen columns C and E to make the data easier to read.

Searching for Data

After you enter data into the database, you can use the criteria form or Excel's AutoFilter feature to search for data. The criteria form lets you use comparison criteria in two ways to find records:

- Enter matching data

or

- Use comparison operators

Entering Matching Data Criteria

You can find specific records using a criteria form, which is a subset of the data form, to create a special criteria record. You enter a word, phrase, or value into the criteria record. This type of criteria is a comparison criteria.

You can also use the following wildcards, which are characters that represent information you don't know or information that is common to many records, when specifying criteria:

- A question mark (?) represents a single character.
- An asterisk (*) represents multiple characters.

For example, you can use the ? wildcard to find everyone whose three-digit department code has 30 as the last two digits by typing ?30. Or you can use the * wildcard to find everyone whose last name begins with a B by typing B* in the LNAME field.

After you create the criteria record, the Find Prev and Find Next buttons in the data form jump only to the record that matches the criteria.

The following steps help you set up a criteria record that uses the criteria form to search for specific data. You'll search for all last names that begin with a D.

1. Select any cell in your database. This step selects a cell within the list you want to search.

2. Choose Data, Form. Click the Criteria button. The criteria form pops up, which looks similar to the data form, as shown in Figure 50.7. You should see field names, field text boxes, the Criteria indicator in the upper-right corner, criteria form buttons, and navigation buttons.

FIGURE 50.7

The criteria form.

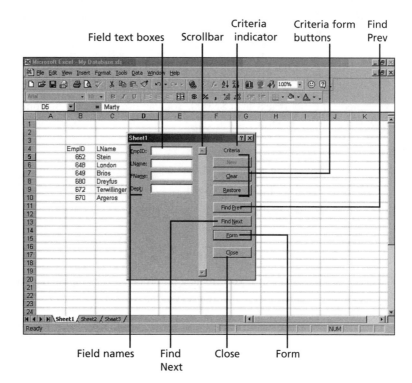

3. You want to use the * wildcard to search for all last names that begin with the letter D. Click the LName box and type D*. Entering * with the letter D tells Excel to find any entry whose last name starts with a D.

4. To use the data form criteria record, click the Find Next button. The fourth record displays in the data form because the last name is Dreyfus.

5. Click the Find Next button again. You hear a beep because no more records match the criteria.

Clearing Criteria

It's a good idea to clear the information from the criteria record when you're done finding the matching records. Otherwise, as you continue to use the data form, Excel uses the same criteria when you click the Find Prev and Find Next buttons.

To remove the criteria, click the Criteria button in the data form. You should see the criteria form. Click the Clear button. Excel removes all the information from the criteria record. If you want to restore the criteria, you can click the Restore button. Click the Close button to close the data form.

Using Comparison Operators

You can also search for a condition that must be evaluated, such as all records containing medical benefits less than $5,000. You can use the following comparison operators in Excel search criteria:

- = (equal to)
- > (greater than)
- >= (greater than or equal to)
- <> (not equal to)

To use a comparison operator to search for records containing medical benefits greater than $5,000, you would enter >5000 in the MedBene field in the criteria form.

In the following steps, you create a criteria record using the data form to search for all employee ID numbers that are greater than 670.

1. Select any cell in your database. This step selects a cell within the list you want to search.

2. Choose Data, Form. Click the Criteria button. The criteria form appears.

3. In the EmpID box, type >670 (see Figure 50.8). Entering the greater than symbol and 670 tells Excel to find any entry whose employee ID number is greater than 670.

FIGURE 50.8

Entering a comparison operator in the criteria form.

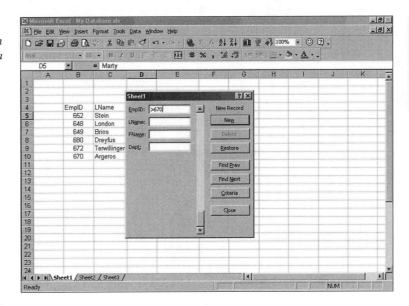

50

4. To use the criteria record, click the Find Next button. The fourth record displays in the data form, showing the employee ID number 680.

> When you choose Data, Filter and a checkmark appears next to AutoFilter, select AutoFilter to turn it off before selecting another Excel database.

5. Click the Find Next button again. The next record matching the criteria, record 5, displays. You should see the employee ID number 672.

6. Click the Find Next button again. You hear a beep because no more records match the criteria. You are done searching for data.

7. Click the Clear button to clear the criteria in the form.

8. Click the Close button to close the criteria form.

Using AutoFilter

Another way to search for data in a database is to use AutoFilter. This feature displays a subset of data without moving or sorting the data. Filtering data inserts drop-down arrows next to column headings in an Excel database. Selecting an item from a drop-down list hides all rows except rows that contain the selected value. You can edit and format the cells that are visible.

At certain times, you might want to work with a subset of data. For example, you might want to extract a partial list of data to give to someone who doesn't need the entire database list. Or maybe you want to use a filtered view of the data to create a report uncluttered by extraneous information. You can filter your data and move it somewhere else, such as to another worksheet, workbook, or application. At some point, you might want to delete unwanted records from the data. You can do so by filtering or extracting data from your list.

Filters enable you to display five types of criteria:

- *All*—Displays all records in the field.
- *Custom*—Opens the Custom AutoFilter dialog box so that you can create AND or OR criteria.
- *Exact Values*—Shows only records with this exact value in the field.
- *Blanks*—Shows all records with blanks in the field.
- *Nonblanks*—Displays all records with values that are not blanks in the field.

Perform the following steps to filter data and display specific data in your My Database file. First, you add a field name and field to the database, adding a column for the number of years an employee is with the company.

1. Click cell F4 and type EmpPeriod. This entry is a field name for an employee's employment period with the company.

2. Select cells F5:F10 and type 20, 12, 5, 8, 10, 15. Remember to use the Enter key to move to the next cell. Now, in column F, you have the length of employment for each employee.

3. Click the Save button on the Standard toolbar to save the new data in your file.

4. Select any cell in the list. This step selects a cell within the list you want to filter.

5. Choose Data, Filter, AutoFilter. Excel displays drop-down arrow buttons next to each column heading in the database, as shown in Figure 50.9.

6. Click the drop-down arrow for the Dept column. The drop-down list shows the unique values for the column.

7. Select Sales. You should see two records, and the rest of the records are hidden. The blue arrow on the filter button indicates the filtered data is based on criteria you selected in the Dept column. The row header numbers for the filtered records also appear in blue.

FIGURE 50.9

AutoFilter arrow buttons next to the column headings.

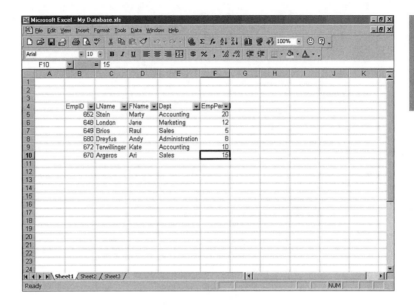

8. To show all the records again, choose Data, Filter, Show All. Now you should see all six records so that Excel can filter records based on all the records in the entire database.

9. Now that you're finished filtering, shut off AutoFilter. Choose Data, Filter, AutoFilter. This step removes the drop-down arrow buttons from the column headings in the database, redisplays the hidden rows, and turns off the AutoFilter feature for this database.

Saving the Database

You save a database the same way you save a worksheet. Just click the Save button on the Standard toolbar. Excel saves your database that contains all the field names and records you entered on the worksheet.

Summary

During this chapter, you learned database terminology, how to build a database, search for data in the database, and filter records. Now you should have a basic understanding of how databases can be created in Excel.

CHAPTER 51

Combining Excel and the Web

By the end of this chapter, you'll be creating Web pages from your Excel worksheets, spending time on the Web, and getting there directly from Excel.

Using the Web Toolbar

To work with the Web inside Excel, it helps to display the Web toolbar. To display the Web toolbar in Excel, right-click any toolbar and choose Web from the shortcut menu. Excel docks the Web toolbar above the Formula bar.

Figure 51.1 shows the tools on the Web toolbar that are for browsing pages backward and forward, refreshing the current page, searching the Web, storing Web pages in the Favorites folder, and entering a URL.

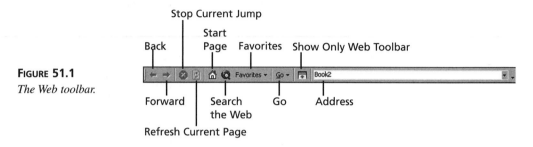

FIGURE 51.1
The Web toolbar.

Table 51.1 lists the Web tools on the Web toolbar and what they do.

TABLE 51.1   Web Toolbar Tools

Tool	What It Does
Back	Displays the previous Web page
Forward	Displays the next Web page
Stop Current Jump	Stops the browser from searching for a Web page
Refresh Current Page	Reloads the current Web page and updates it with the latest information
Start Page	Displays the home page for a Web site
Search the Web	Displays the Web site you requested in the Address box
Favorites	Stores your favorite Web site addresses
Go	Displays the Go menu that contains commands for navigating through Web pages
Show Only Web Toolbar	Hides all other Excel toolbars and displays only the Web toolbar
Address	Lets you enter a Web address

Opening a Web Page in Excel

When you find the Web page you want to read, you can open that page directly in Excel. To do so, make sure you are connected and online. With the Web toolbar displayed in Excel, type the URL into the Address box on the Web toolbar. When the browser finds the Web site you requested, the Web page displays in your Excel window.

Adding a Hyperlink to a Worksheet

In Chapter 48, "Integrating Excel and Other Office Products," you learned how to create a hyperlink that links to other Office documents. Now, you'll add a hyperlink to a worksheet that links to Web pages on the Internet.

When you point to a hyperlink, Excel displays the document path (for example, http://www.sams.com) to which the link points. When you click a hyperlink, Excel moves to the location to which the link points. A hyperlink appears in blue (default color) text in the worksheet.

Hyperlinks are useful when you want to browse through files on the Internet. The Web toolbar displays a list of the last 10 documents you jumped to by using the Web toolbar or a hyperlink. This feature makes it easy for you to return to these documents.

The Insert, Hyperlink option lets you create a hyperlink so that you can move to a Web page from a worksheet. In the following steps, you create a hyperlink to move from an Excel worksheet to a Web document. Once again, you should be using the My Budget workbook.

1. Click cell D4 on the Detail sheet. This cell will contain the hyperlink that brings you to the Web document.

2. Choose Insert, Hyperlink. Excel opens the Insert Hyperlink dialog box, as shown in Figure 51.2.

FIGURE 51.2

The Insert Hyperlink dialog box.

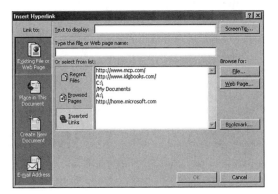

A quick way to create a hyperlink is to press Ctrl+K or click the Insert Hyperlink button on the Standard toolbar. Excel displays the Insert Hyperlink dialog box.

3. Click the (Browse for) Web Page button. The Microsoft Internet Explorer window appears.

4. Search for the Web page you want to include in the hyperlink. Once you have found the page you want to insert, return to Excel. The URL to the page that you

browsed to is now displayed in the Insert Hyperlink dialog box. Click OK in the Insert Hyperlink dialog box. The Web page name is now a hyperlink and appears as underlined blue text in cell D4.

5. Point to the hyperlink. Notice how the mouse pointer becomes a hand. A ScreenTip containing the Web page address appears above the hyperlink (see Figure 51.3).

FIGURE 51.3

The hyperlink and ScreenTip with the Web page address.

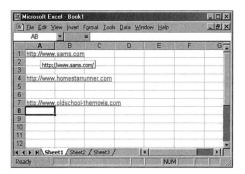

6. Click the hyperlink. Internet Explorer opens, and you see the Sams Publishing home page.

7. Click the Close (X) button in the upper-right corner of Internet Explorer. This step closes the Internet Explorer document and then returns you to the Excel worksheet. Notice the hyperlink text appears in purple, indicating that you have visited that site.

Saving Excel Documents to the Web

You can publish an Excel document to the World Wide Web so that other people on the Web can see your work. To place Web pages on the Web, you need to have an ISP that provides you with space for Web pages, or you need access to a Web service established at your company. You can ask the Webmaster (or whoever manages the Web servers) at your company where to place your Web pages.

You can use an existing Excel document for a Web page by saving it as a Web page. Excel closes the document and reopens it in Hypertext Markup Language (HTML) format. The alternative is to create your own Web page in Excel from scratch and then format it the way you want. No matter which method you use, you can publish many types of Excel documents on the Internet, for example, an annual report or a database.

You can even add audio and video to your Web page in Excel. That way, the reader of your Web page can play a sound file or view a video while visiting the Web site. You can use the Insert, Object command to insert sound and video clips into your Web page.

Understanding HTML Formatting

Every Web page is basically a plain text file with additional formatting instructions for the text, graphics, and links. This file is called the HTML source because the instructions are written in HTML format. The way a Web page looks on the Web is similar to the way it looks in Excel's Web Page Preview.

When you save a document in HTML format, Excel saves any graphics and other objects in separate files.

51

Saving As a Web Document

You can convert an Excel document into a Web page by selecting File, Save as Web Page. In the following steps, you convert the My Database workbook into a Web page. Be sure to open the My Database workbook before you start the exercise.

1. Choose File, Save as Web Page. The Save as Web Page dialog box pops up (see Figure 51.4). It looks the same as a Save As dialog box except for the HTML document choice in the Save as Type list.

FIGURE 51.4
The Save As dialog box for saving an Excel document as a Web document.

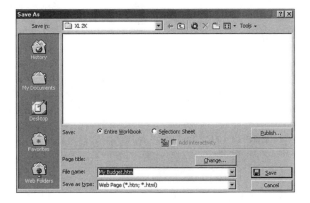

2. Type My Web Database in the File Name text box.
3. Click the Save button. If you are advised that the Custom Views feature will not be saved in the HTML file, then click Yes to continue saving. Excel converts the document to HTML format so it can be published on the Web. The document appears with the name My Web Database.htm in the title bar.

Previewing Your Document in Web Page Preview

The Web Page Preview in Excel enables you to see your document as it will look in a Web browser. A browser is a program with which you can read information on the

Internet. This preview makes the data (text and numbers) easy to read because it wraps to fit the window. You cannot edit and format data in Web Page Preview.

Your Web page might look different in a browser such as Netscape Communicator or Internet Explorer than it does in Excel, depending on how your browser interprets HTML codes.

To look at your document in Web Page Preview, choose File, Web Page Preview. Excel shows the document in the Web Page Preview window (see Figure 51.5). By default, Excel shows you the Web page the way it would look in the Microsoft Internet Explorer window even if you use a different browser.

FIGURE 51.5

The Web Page Preview window.

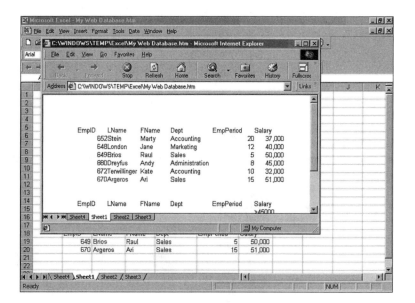

You can use the scroll bar to see the rest of the document. To close Web Page Preview, click the Close (X) button in the upper-right corner of the Microsoft Internet Explorer window.

Summary

This chapter presented a brief overview of the features built into Excel for creating and working with Web pages. Now you have an idea of how to use Excel to create a Web page. After you're comfortable with the tools and features you practiced here, you'll be able to experiment with Excel and learn the advanced concepts.

INDEX

A

Lock/Save Sheet dialog box (Excel), **623**
locking templates (worksheets), **623-624**

M

Macro dialog box
  Excel, 697
  PowerPoint, 440-441
Macro, Macros command (Tools menu) (Excel), 697
Macro, Macros, Run command (Tools menu) (Excel), 697
Macro, Record command (Tools menu) (Excel), 693
Macro, Record New Macro command (Tools menu)
  Excel, 694-695
  PowerPoint, 441
Macro, Security command (Tools menu) (Excel), 702
macros
  presentations, 440-446
  worksheets
    attaching to a toolbar, 700-701
    creating, 693
    descriptions, 694
    editing, 699-700
    fixing macro errors, 698
    keyboard shortcuts, 694
    naming, 694

    recording, 693-696
    running, 695-697
    saving, 696
    stopping, 697
    storing, 692, 701-702
    using, 692
    viruses, 702-703
    Visual Basic, 698
magnifying documents, 20, 83-85
Mail Delivery Options dialog box (Outlook), 244-245
Mail Format Options dialog box (Outlook), 245-246
mail merge
  data source, 172-175, 180-181
  envelopes, 181-184
  labels, 181-182
  main document, 171-172, 176-177
  running, 177-180
Mail Merge command (Tools menu) (Word), 172
Mail Merge Helper dialog box (Word), 172-173
Mail Merge toolbar, 176
main document (mail merge), 171-172, 176-177
margins
  documents, 108-109
  Web pages, 488-489
marking tasks as completed, 301
mass mailings, 171
Master Category dialog box (Outlook), 259

maximizing windows, 39
Meeting Minder (PowerPoint), 321
Meeting Minder command (Tools menu) (PowerPoint), 321
Meeting Minder dialog box (Outlook), 321
Memo Wizard (Word), 65-66
memos, 65-66
menu bar, 29
menus, 29-30
merging cells in document tables, 150-151
Message Options dialog box (Word), 318-319
microphones, 420
Microsoft Office
  accessibility features, 20
  capabilities, 8
  commonalties among programs, 10
  customizing, 10
  sharing data between programs, 10
  versions, 8-9
minimizing windows, 39
Modify Style dialog box
  FrontPage, 563-564
  Word, 123-124
modifying
  columns in documents, 143-144
  document templates, 126-129
  frames (Web pages), 506-507

Your Guide to Computer Technology

www.informit.com

Sams has partnered with **InformIT.com** to bring technical information to your desktop. Drawing on Sams authors and reviewers to provide additional information on topics you're interested in, **InformIT.com** has free, in-depth information you won't find anywhere else.

ARTICLES

Keep your edge with thousands of free articles, in-depth features, interviews, and information technology reference recommendations—all written by experts you know and trust.

POWERED BY
Safari

ONLINE BOOKS

Answers in an instant from **InformIT Online Books'** 600+ fully searchable online books. Sign up now and get your first 14 days **free**.

CATALOG

Review online sample chapters and author biographies to choose exactly the right book from a selection of more than 5,000 titles.